# FISHING CALIFORNIA

## A Travel Guide to Proven Spots & Proven Methods

by

David Colby

Mission Viejo / California

NOTICE

The information contained in this document is subject to change without notice.

**SABERTOOTH PUBLISHING COMPANY MAKES NO WARRANTY OF ANY KIND WITH REGARD TO THIS MATERIAL. SABERTOOTH PUBLISHING COMPANY SHALL NOT BE LIABLE FOR TECHNICAL OR EDITORIAL ERRORS, OR OMISSIONS CONTAINED HEREIN; NOR FOR INCIDENTAL OR CONSEQUENTIAL DAMAGES RESULTING FROM THE FURNISHING, PERFORMANCE, OR USE OF THIS MATERIAL.**

This document contains proprietary information protected by copyright. All rights are reserved. No part of this document may be photocopied or reproduced in any form without prior written consent from the author, except for the inclusion of brief quotations in a review.

Copyright © 1991 by Sabertooth Publishing Company

Sabertooth is a Registered Trademark of Sabertooth Publishing Company

First Printing - 1991
Printed in the United States of America

Cover Art by Tom Waters

Library of Congress Catalog Card Number: 91-60254

Publisher's Cataloging in Publication Data
Colby, David P.
Fishing California: A Travel Guide to Proven Spots & Proven Methods
Includes Index.
ISBN 0-9628688-1-7: $19.95 Softcover

# TABLE OF CONTENTS

                                                        Page Number

Fishing Opportunities Index ....................... 1
Fishing Calendars:
   Northern California ......................... 2
   Southern California ......................... 4

The Basics ........................................ 6

Alphabetic Listing by Fish Name:

     Key.................................................... 10
     ALBACORE .............................................. 12
     BARRACUDA ............................................. 15
     BASS:
         CALICO (Kelp) ................................. 20
         LARGEMOUTH (& Smallmouth, Spotted) .... 24
         SAND .......................................... 66
         SPOTTED BAY ................................... 69
         STRIPED ....................................... 71
         WHITE ......................................... 96
     BONITO ................................................ 99
     CATFISH:
         CHANNEL & BLUE ............................... 101
         FLATHEAD ..................................... 104
     CORVINA, Salton Sea Fishing ............... 106
     CRAPPIE .............................................. 115
     HALIBUT .............................................. 121
     LINGCOD .............................................. 128
     MARLIN, STRIPED ..................................... 137
     PERCH, SACRAMENTO (Crowley Lake) .......... 151
     ROCKCOD, COWCOD ..................................... 154
     ROCKFISH ............................................. 160
     SALMON, CHINOOK (KING) ............................. 162
     SALMON, KOKANEE ..................................... 193
     SEABASS, WHITE ...................................... 200
     SHAD ................................................. 205
     SHARK:
         General ...................................... 213
         BLUE & MAKO ................................. 216
         THRESHER ..................................... 229
         SEVENGILL, SOUPFIN, LEOPARD .......... 232
     SHEEPHEAD ............................................ 235
     STEELHEAD ............................................ 236
     STURGEON ............................................. 254
     TROUT:
         BROOK ........................................ 261
         BROWN ........................................ 262
         CUTTHROAT .................................... 267
         GOLDEN ....................................... 269
         MAKINAW ...................................... 273
         RAINBOW:
           Organization and General Info ...... 279
           Lakes .............................. 281
           Streams ............................ 289

# TABLE OF CONTENTS

Alphabetic Listing continued:

Page Number

    TUNA:
- BIGEYE .................................. 306
- BLUEFIN ................................. 312
- YELLOWTAIL .................................... 314

Bay / Harbor Fishing:
- General Information ....................... 321
- San Francisco Bay ......................... 323
  - Shore Fishing Areas ................. 324
- Long Beach Harbor ......................... 325
- Newport Bay ............................... 327
- Mission Bay ............................... 329
- San Diego Bay ............................. 329

Baja Fishing:
- Baja Long Range Trips ..................... 332
- Baja Sea of Cortez Fishing ................ 366
  - Travel Planning Map ................. 373
  - Access Map .......................... 374
  - MARLIN, BLUE & BLACK ................ 376
  - DORADO .............................. 376
  - ROOSTERFISH ......................... 377
  - YELLOWFIN TUNA ...................... 378
  - WAHOO ............................... 378
  - PARGO ............................... 380

APPENDIX A: Salt Water Launching Sites ......... 381
APPENDIX B: Sportfishing Landings / Partyboats . 393
APPENDIX C: Sources of More Information ........ 395
APPENDIX D: Hook Size Chart .................... 396
APPENDIX E: Standard Fishing Rigs .............. 397
Glossary ....................................... 398
Index

OPPORTUNITY INDEX 1

# INDEX TO FISHING OPPORTUNITIES

Use this map to determine regional fishing opportunities. Example: If you are planning a business trip to Sacramento, check to see what sportsfish are caught in the Sacramento River Region. Get futher information on best times by checking the Fishing Calendar and by looking up the specific fish type.

**Northwest Rivers and Coast**
Salmon
Steelhead
Trout
Rockcod/Lingcod
Bass
Shad

**Northeast Area**
Trout

**Reno / Lake Tahoe Area**
Trout
Makinaw Trout
Kokanee Salmon

**Sacramento River Area**
Salmon
Striped Bass
Sturgeon
Trout
Shad
Steelhead
Bass
Crappie
Catfish

**San Francisco Ocean & Bay**
Salmon
Striped Bass
Sturgeon
Halibut
Shark
Trout
Bass
Steelhead
Rockcod/Lingcod
Albacore

**Eastern Sierra**
Trout
Kokanee

**Stockton - Modesto - Fresno**
Trout
Bass
Crappie
Kokanee Salmon
Catfish

**Santa Barbara / Ventura Area**
Halibut
Rockcod/Lingcod
Salmon
Albacore
Calico Bass
Sand Bass
Bass

**Colorado River**
Striped Bass
Bass
Trout
Catfish

**Los Angeles Area**
Sand Bass
Calico Bass
Bonito
Barracuda
Trout
Yellowtail
Bass
Shark
Striped Marlin
Rockcod/Lingcod
Striped Bass

**San Diego Area**
Bass
Yellowtail
Albacore
Sand Bass
Calico Bass
Bonito
Barracuda
Striped Marlin
Shark
Halibut
Bigeye Tuna
Rockcod/Lingcod
Salton Sea Fish

**Baja, Mexico**

Pacific Side
Long Range
Yellowtail
Yellowfin
Wahoo
Bluefin
Bigeye
Calico Bass
Pargo
Black Sea Bass
Dorado
Etc.

Sea of Cortez Side
Yellowtail
Dorado
Marlin
Roostertail
Pargo
Wahoo
Yellowfin
Grouper
Cabrillo
Sailfish
Etc.

Bass = Largemouth or
   Smallmouth or
   Spotted

Trout = Rainbow or
   Brown or
   Brook

FISHING CALENDAR 2

Northern California:

**JANUARY:**
| | | |
|---|---|---|
| Sturgeon | - | San Francisco Bay |
| Steelhead | - | Coastal rivers north of San Francisco |
| Sevengill Shark | - | San Francisco Bay |
| Lingcod, Rockcod | - | Farallon Is., Cordell Bank, Soap Bank |
| Rockcod | - | All along the coast |

**FEBRUARY:**
| | | |
|---|---|---|
| Steelhead | - | Coastal rivers north of San Francisco |
| Salmon | - | Ocean Fishing starts |
| Sturgeon | - | San Francisco Bay |
| Sevengill Shark | - | San Francisco Bay |
| Rockcod | | All along the coast |

**MARCH:**
| | | |
|---|---|---|
| Largemouth Bass | - | Spawn - Clear Lake, Berryessa, etc. |
| Striped Bass | - | Sacramento Delta |
| Salmon | - | Monterey Bay |
| Makinaw Trout | - | Lake Tahoe |

**APRIL:**
| | | |
|---|---|---|
| Largemouth Bass | - | Spawn - Clear Lake, Berryessa, etc. |
| Striped Bass | - | Sacramento Delta |
| | - | Sacramento River, Colusa to Grimes |

**MAY:**
| | | |
|---|---|---|
| Shad | - | Sacramento River System |
| Brown Trout | - | Eastern Sierra Lakes |
| Striped Bass | - | Sacramento River, Colusa to Grimes; San Luis Reservoir |

**JUNE:**
| | | |
|---|---|---|
| Halibut | - | San Francisco Bay |
| Shad | - | Upper Sacramento River System |
| Trout | - | Upper Sacramento, McCloud, Pit, Hat, Fall Rivers |
| Striped Bass | - | San Luis Reservoir |

**JULY:**
| | | |
|---|---|---|
| Striped Bass | - | San Francisco Peninsula Coastline, South Tower - Golden Gate |
| Catfish | - | Amador, Clear, Folsom, etc. |
| Salmon | - | San Francisco Peninsula Coastline |
| Trout | - | Upper Sacramento, McCloud, Pit, Hat, Fall Rivers |

Northern California:

**AUGUST:**
| | | |
|---|---|---|
| Catfish | - | Amador, Clear, Folsom, etc. |
| Striped Bass | - | San Francisco Peninsula Coastline, South Tower - Golden Gate |
| Halibut | - | San Francisco Bay |
| Kokanee Salmon | - | Lake Tahoe |
| Salmon | - | San Francisco Peninsula Coastline |

**SEPTEMBER:**
| | | |
|---|---|---|
| Albacore | - | Monterey |
| Striped Bass | - | Sacramento Delta, San Antonio Reservoir |
| Catfish | - | Amador, Clear, Folsom, etc. |
| Lingcod, Rockcod | - | Farallon Is., Cordell Bank |
| Salmon | - | North Coast Rivers, Sacramento River System |
| Kokanee Salmon | - | Lake Tahoe |

**OCTOBER:**
| | | |
|---|---|---|
| Striped Bass | - | Sacramento Delta, San Antonio Reservoir |
| Lingcod, Rockcod | - | Farallon Is., Cordell Bank |
| Salmon | - | North Coast Rivers Sacramento River System |
| Trout | - | Butt Lake, Eastern Sierra, Twin Lakes |
| Brown Trout | | Eastern Sierra Lakes |

**NOVEMBER:**
| | | |
|---|---|---|
| Striped Bass | - | San Francisco Bay, Delta |
| Steelhead | - | No. California Rivers |
| Salmon | - | Sacramento River |
| Lingcod, Rockcod | - | Farallon Is., Cordell Bank |

**DECEMBER:**
| | | |
|---|---|---|
| Sturgeon | - | San Francisco Bay |
| Soupfin Shark | - | San Francisco Bay |
| Steelhead | - | No. California Rivers |
| Lingcod, Rockcod | - | Farallon Is., Cordell Bank |

FISHING CALENDAR 4

Southern California:

| | | | |
|---|---|---|---|
| **JANUARY:** | Rockcod | – | All along the coast |
| **FEBRUARY:** | Rockcod | – | All along the coast |
| | Halibut | – | Southern California |
| **MARCH:** | Largemouth Bass | – | So. California Lakes |
| | White Bass | – | Nacimiento |
| | Halibut | – | So. California |
| **APRIL:** | Largemouth Bass | – | So. California Lakes |
| | White Bass | – | Nacimiento |
| | Crappie | – | Late at Silverwood, Henshaw, etc. |
| | Calico Bass | – | Catalina, Kelp beds |
| | Halibut | – | So. California |
| **MAY:** | Sand Bass | – | So. California |
| | Striped Bass | – | Havasu, Mead |
| | Corvina | – | Salton Sea |
| | Crappie | – | Early at Silverwood, Henshaw, etc. |
| | Calico Bass | – | So. California |
| | Halibut | – | So. California |
| **JUNE:** | Albacore | – | San Diego - late |
| | Catfish | – | Irvine Lake |
| | Sand Bass | – | So. California |
| | Corvina | – | Salton Sea |
| **JULY:** | Albacore | – | San Diego |
| | Mako Shark | – | Los Angeles & pts. south |
| | Yellowtail | – | Coronados |
| **AUGUST:** | Albacore | – | San Diego to Morro Bay |
| | Catfish | – | So. California Lakes |
| | Mako Shark | – | Los Angeles & pts. south |
| | Yellowtail | – | Coronados, Catalina, Horseshoe Kelp |
| **SEPTEMBER:** | Albacore | – | Monterey |
| | Striped Bass | – | Lake Mead, Mohave, Havasu - surface |
| | Striped Marlin | – | Outer Banks, Catalina from mid-Sept. |
| | Mako Shark | – | Los Angeles & pts. south |
| | Yellowtail | – | See August |
| **OCTOBER:** | Striped Bass | – | Lake Mead, Mohave, Lake San Antonio |
| | Striped Marlin | – | Catalina |
| | Bluefin Tuna | – | Tanner & Cortes Banks |
| | Lingcod | – | Bodega Bay |
| | Rockcod | – | All along the coast |
| | Tuna | – | San Diego banks |

Southern California:

| | | | |
|---|---|---|---|
| **NOVEMBER:** | Striped Marlin | – | Catalina – early November |
| | Rockcod, Lingcod | – | All along the coast |
| | Bluefin Tuna | – | Tanner & Cortes Banks – early November |
| **DECEMBER:** | Calico Bass | – | Clemente Is. (Corresponds with squid season) |
| | Rockcod | – | All along the coast |

For Baja California Fishing Calendar – See Baja Sea of Cortez Fishing

# THE BASICS

As in sports, if the team doesn't thoroughly know the basics, it's in trouble from the start. The following are the basics you must follow for every fishing trip. Although all the following are important, they are in priority order - the most important listed first.

1. **FISH IN THE RIGHT SPOT & DEPTH:**

    90% of the fish are concentrated in less than 10% of the water. Unless you are fishing in that 10%, you are wasting time.

    a. Look in this book for known hot spots in your area.

    b. Fish Finder - if you own a boat, invest in a good fish finder and use it. Do not waste time fishing blind.

    c. A matter of feet can spell success or failure. If you are fishing 5 feet away from a suspended school of Calicos and your buddy is dropping his lure straight through the school, you'll be the spectator, he'll catch the fish.

    d. If you fish saltwater a lot, buy a Loran. Its use will allow you to quickly locate honeyholes over offshore structure. Buy Frank Grabenstatter's book "Fishing Spot Locator" covering fishing holes from Morro bay to Mexico. Write to: Perfect 10, 1048 Eilinita Ave., Glendale, Calif. 91208, $22.50 (1991).

2. **FISH AT THE RIGHT TIME:**

    a. Tides and Currents:

    Peak fishing for many fish species often coincides with maximum tidal movements. This applies to northern California Salmon runs, to Stripers and Sturgeon in San Francisco Bay, to Surf fishing all along the coast, and to most Bay fishing. Get a tide table and use it.

    b. Moon Phases:

    Fish during new moon (no moon) phases. Bright evening moons allow fish to feed at night leaving them less hungry at daybreak.

    c. Fish Seasons:

    Different fish species have different active seasons. Look under individual species for specifics. Also see the Fishing Calendar.

    Warm water years can cause significant changes in the "best seasons" listed for saltwater sportfish. For most

# THE BASICS 7

summer season fish, i.e. Yellowtail and Barracuda, the effect is to extend the good fishing to start earlier and end later in the year. Other sportfish that are cool water seekers, Albacore & Salmon, may have their "season" shortened or eliminated entirely in some areas. Warm water or "El Nino" years may also bring "exotics" such as Yellowfin Tuna, Dorado, Triggerfish, or even Sailfish into the So. Calif. waters. 1990 was a warm water year and there are signs that 1991 will also bring warmer than usual water.

d. Get Current Information:

Southern California & Baja: Call fishing info service - (213) or (818) 976-TUNA

Northern & Southern California & Baja: Call fishing info service - (900) USA-FISH

See also specific fish sections and Sportfishing landings areas for more info sources.

3. **USE THE FRESHEST, LIVIEST BAIT POSSIBLE:**

On a partyboat, be selective in getting bait from the bait well. Typically, the harder it is to catch, the better it is. Avoid bait with bloody noses, missing scales.

Private boaters should be very selective in purchasing a live bait tank. Quality and effectiveness varies widely. Quality tanks are designed to minimize bait damage and provide ideal water flow.

Superior quality tanks are made by,

Pacific Edge Inc., 5842-Q McFadden Ave., Huntington Beach, CA 92649, 714-895-1159

4. **FISH YOUR LURE OR BAIT WITH THE RIGHT ACTION:**

Pay special attention to lure action and bait movement. The right action will generate a strike. This is a tough skill to teach in a book. Watch the good fishermen and imitate. Specific sections will describe the correct action in more detail. Here are a few examples;

a. Every lure has a best speed where it generates the best action. Test a lure alongside the boat at different speeds before letting it out to troll. Often lures are trolled too fast.

b. When retrieving a cast lure, often a small change in speed can spell success. Another trick is to stop reeling, let the lure fall as if wounded, and than start reeling again fast to provoke a strike. For Yellowtail

THE BASICS  8

**FISH YOUR LURE OR BAIT WITH THE RIGHT ACTION** continued:

   and for Salmon Grouper a good technique is to let the jig fall straight down to the bottom, sit there motionless for a couple seconds, then retrieve quickly.

  c. The rate of fall, jig weight used, can spell success or failure when fishing for Calicos with a leadhead jig.

5. **USE THE RIGHT LINE:**

  a. Use the lightest line possible:

  This varies considerably by the type of fish and the fishing conditions - but, if the bite is slow, go to lighter line. On the other hand don't waste time with too light line or old line on bruiser fish like Tuna or Yellowtail. Respool with new line before the trip.

  b. Use high quality line:

  The following brands have limp, flexible line that has the maximum strength for the minimum line diameter - Ande, Maxima, Stren, Trilene.

  c. Check your line:

  After every fish caught, run the last 3 feet of line between your index finger and thumb. If you feel any abrasions or kinks, cut off the length and retie the hook. Test the hook/lure knot by pulling stiffly on the line while holding the hook stationary.

6. **USE SHARP HOOKS:**

There are very few packaged hooks that don't need to be sharpened - Sheffield and Gamakatsu are examples. Also sharpen your lure hooks. This is critically important. The simple and inexpensive sharpening tool below can do the job. Form a sharp diamond cross-section point by first forming the sides of the diamond by running the hook point down the file groove. Eliminate the burr and form the base of the triangle by filing the bottom of the point with the flat side of the tool. A properly sharpened hook should cut a groove in your fingernail when lightly pulled across it. Ideally, the point should catch as it digs in.

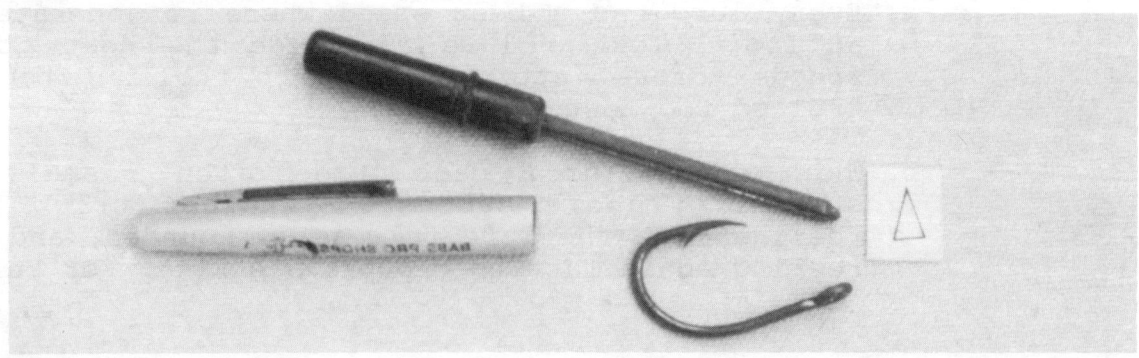

7. **CHUMMING:**

   Whenever and wherever legal, chum.

8. **MAKE A PLAN:**

   Develop a plan that concentrates on the fish you are targeting, but also covers the "what if" situations. The plan should consider other kinds of fish in the area should your target species not be active, such as a White Seabass on a Yellowtail trip. It should include the tackle and rigging for the chance meeting with a large fish, a Bigeye tuna on an Albacore trip, etc. Remember, "Luck is where preparation meets opportunity".

9. **PAY ATTENTION TO DETAILS:**

   This is all important. A very minor detail often can make the difference between catching a limit or being skunked. If someone is catching a lot of fish, find out exactly what they are doing and start doing it!

10. **NOISE:**

    Avoid making noise while actively fishing. Talking is OK, but any noise in contact with the water should be minimized such as banging things on the bottom of the boat, stomping along a stream bank, etc.

    In a boat either use a quiet electric motor to approach target areas or position the boat upwind/current of the kelp paddy, etc. and drift toward the fishing area.

11. **VARY YOUR TECHNIQUE AND LOCATION:**

    There are no sure fire techniques or spots. There are techniques that work most of the time and spots that often hold fish. If you aren't catching fish - CHANGE.

12. **BIG FISH:**

    Often you must change your techniques to catch big fish. What works for the average sized fish of a species stands little chance of catching a jackpot fish. For example, when Rockcod fishing, the person jigging will most likely win the jackpot. When fishing for big trout, the person trolling the #18 Rapala or the person using large nightcrawlers will catch the big fish, the person using a salmon egg wont.

## Key to Alphabetic Sportfish Listings

All Sportfish listings have the following standard format

**FISH VARIETY (Alternate name or Mexican name):**

**Where:** Often **Where** and **When** are interdependent and are detailed under the combined title of **Where/When**.

Hot Spots: This will contain a listing of specific California spots that have consistently produced good catches of this variety of fish in recent years. The listing is in priority order. Most hot spots are provided in a comprehensive, detailed map format.

Structure: This area indicates environmental factors that create preferred fish holding areas for this fish species. It will indicate such things as preferred water temperature, water depths, cover.

On Maps: ✱ = launching ramps, ⓧ = bait receivers, ☁ = Sportfishing landings, ▨ = prime fish areas, ⌒ = best trolling route

**When:** Only the good fishing periods are listed. Fish usually can be caught at other times & seasons but the success rate is much lower. Most of the times given in this book are very reliable, however they can vary significantly from year to year. Albacore, for example, did not even show in significant numbers from 1986 to 1988.

When planning a trip, you should monitor info sources for current conditions.

**Bait/Lures:** Baits and lures are again listed generally in order of effectiveness/popularity. If one bait/lure isn't working, try a different color or try a different bait/lure. In general "match the hatch" by choosing a lure that mimics the water's prevalent forage both in size and color. The lures listed and pictured are ideal choices but sometimes difficult to find. If using a substitute, try hard to match action, size and color. Note that all lure and bait pictures are actual life size unless the illustration includes a tape measure for sizing.

**Rig:** General rig recommendations are made indicating rod & reel class and reel capacities. Specific examples are given. Note that the examples given are based on the authors experience and are NOT the only reliable, quality brands available on the market. Terminal rigging is usually diagrammed on a separate page.

See Appendix E for suggested standard fishing rigs.

**Key to Alphabetic Sportfish Listings** continued:

**Technique:** Often more than one technique will be listed. These are in order of proven effectiveness. If one technique doesn't work try one of the others.

**The Law:** California fishing regulations are revised annually and are effective from March 1 to the end of February in the following year.

Only general regulations information will be given here. There are many special Department of Fish & Game regulations that change each season. You must consult a current DFG regulations booklet.

**Records:** All-tackle State and IGFA records are here

**Info:** Reliable, current information sources are listed here. Sportfishing landings can also be a good source of current information and fish counts. Also the fishing information numbers listed in Appendix C can be helpful.

References for more detailed reading may also be included here.

**Access:** This area gives address and phone numbers for Guides, and rental boats. Saltwater partyboat symbols and reference numbers are on the maps. The reference number refers to a detailed listing of Partyboats in Appendix B. Launch ramps are indicated on the maps by stars. Detailed maps of saltwater launch ramps can be found in Appendix A.

**See Also:** This area lists other sport fish that are generally found in the same area/time. The interested angler should carry recommended bait/lures/rigs/and tackle so that luck will be with them if those fish show up (Luck = where preparation meets opportunity).

**ALBACORE:** (Albacora)

**Where:** Southern California north to Morro Bay
25 to 100 miles out
In clear blue, 62° to 66° water.

**When:** Mid-June and August - San Diego.
August - Sept., early Oct.; from San Clemente Is. to Morro Bay, San Luis Obispo.
Late September - Oct, from Monterey to San Francisco.

Infrequently a second run occurs in September, October between San Clemente Is. and Morro Bay. Late runs bring larger fish.

Moon Phases:

Worst - from 2 days past first quarter through the full moon, about 10 days.

Best - from new moon (no moon) through first quarter.

**Bait/Lures:** Always use the largest, liveliest bait. Some claim that "green" anchovies are best. Change bait often, every 3 to 5 minutes.

For Trolling - use "Feathered" Jigs (i.e. Zukers or Sevenstrand Clones). Best colors are green; green/yellow; red, white/blue; purple; Zucchini pattern; Mexican flag. Metal jigs such as the Salas YoYo 4 and the Tady AA Heavy in blue/white color are effective for jigging.

**Rig:** **TROLLING RIG:** Consisting of 4/0 (Penn 113H) or 6/0 (114H) size reels with stiff action 5 1/2 to 6 1/2 foot pole. With 50-80# monofilament line. Also Daiwa Sealine 450H or 600H; or Shimano TTS 30, TTS50, or TTS 50W.

**BAIT RIG:** A typical rig is a Penn Jigmaster 500 or 500H reel loaded with 200 to 300 yards of 15# to 40# monofilament line.

Hook size is limited to the size of the bait. For pinhead anchovies, use No. 6 or No. 8 Normally use No. 2 to No. 4. In a light bite use a smaller size. In a heavy bite, use up to a size 1.

Also usable are large ocean spinning outfits with a 5 1/2 to 6 1/2 foot medium action rod. Examples are Daiwa 7000 or Shimano Baitrunner. Spinning rods should be loaded with a lighter test of monofilament such as 15# to 25# because they usually have a smaller capacity than a casting reel.

**Technique:** Get on the top of the trolling list

Troll early with dark colors especially if overcast. Use green and purple jigs.

Troll mid-day with bright colors - especially green/yellow.

Troll 60 to 100 feet behind the boat in the trough of a boat wake.

**Trolling Reel:** If someone else gets a hookup, wait a couple of seconds, take off the freespool and drag a few seconds, reel in fast keeping the rod tip low to the water.

**Jigmaster Reel:** Leave on jig (Sea Strike, Salas). Cast and jig with lure when bite is off, let lure sink deep, jig by sweeping your rod up several times, and reel up fast. Try this at different depths. Watch the line carefully on the drop for any hesitations.

**Spinning Reel:** Use for casting over back of stern. Cast to windward side of stern the boat will drift away from chum line. While trolling keep the hook in the bait well with a live anchovy.

When working "the slide", when the boat slows down after a hook-up, chrome-plated rubber-core sinkers work best.

**The Law:** No size or bag limit. (1990)

**Records:** State: 79 lbs., Santa Barbara Is., Oct. 1985
IGFA: 88 lbs., Canary Is., 1977

**Info:** See San Diego Landings numbers 36 through 39. They have daily fish count phone numbers.

Yesterday's fish counts are also listed in the Orange County Register and the Los Angeles Times daily sports sections in the "Sports Summary" area.

**See Also:** Bigeye Tuna, Yellowfin tuna are occasionally caught along with Albacore. Skipjack are regularly caught with Albacore, especially during the later part of the season. Skipjack, not listed in this book, require the same tackle as Albacore.

ALBACORE 14

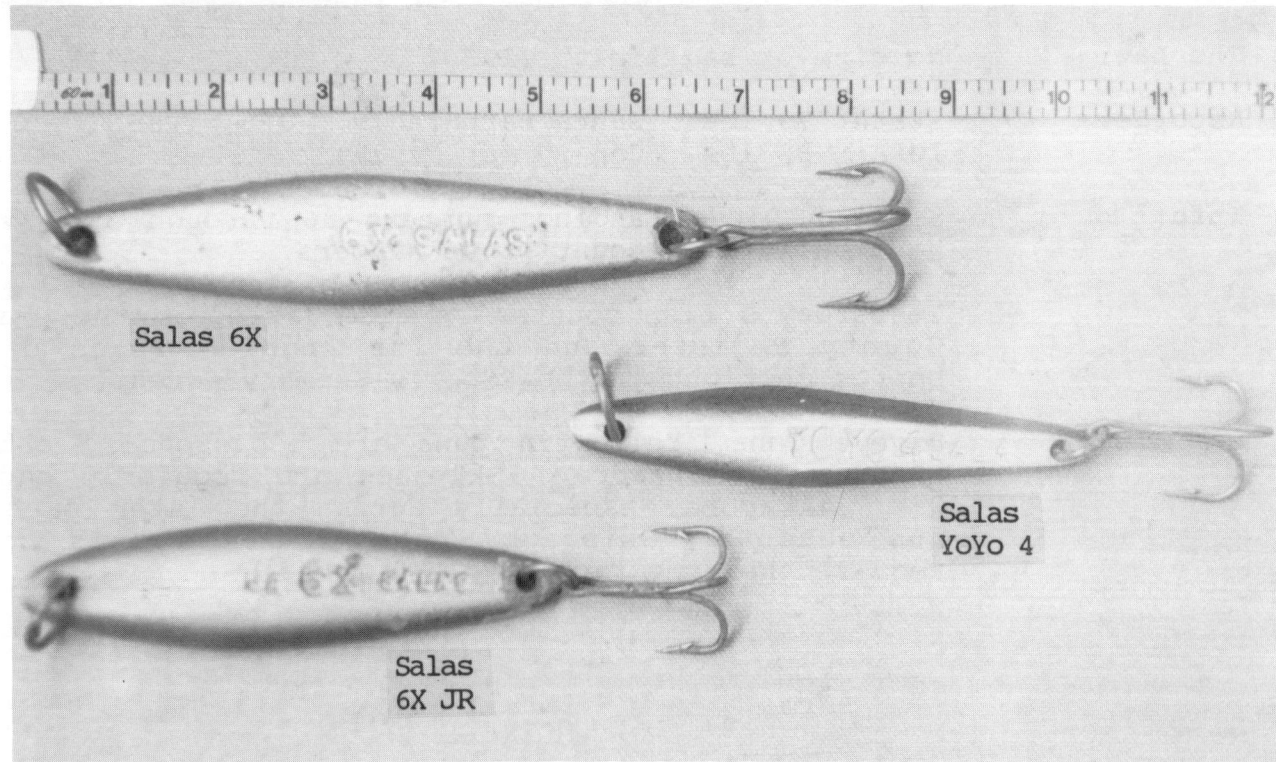

Salas 6X

Salas YoYo 4

Salas 6X JR

**BARRACUDA:** (Picuda)

**Where/When:** Barracuda are generally surface fish although they may suspend at intermediate depths, especially in early spring.

In general, a string of 3 to 4 relatively calm, warm days will trigger the first good bite in the following areas;

April - Pt. Loma kelp, San Diego
Late April - Off LAX, Santa Monica Bay
Late April through July - Horseshoe Kelp
Late May through mid-July - Catalina, Coronados
Early August - 150 Spot (double oil rigs between Long Beach and Catalina)

**Bait/Lures:** Live Anchovies

Chrome, blue/white jigs - Sea Strike #21 (light weight and heavy versions)
Tady AA & A1 jigs
Silver Scrounger - 4 to 6"
Krocodile

**Rig:** For fishing anchovies: A light to light-medium weight rod and reel with 10 to 25# mono. A 6 to 7 foot rod with a flexible tip for lobbing anchovies.

For tossing jigs: A light-medium to medium weight rod and reel with 10 to 30# mono. A 6 to 8 foot rod for tossing jigs - example Fenwick 1870.

**Technique:** Chumming can be very important in fishing for barracuda. Light but steady chumming with live anchovies can bring the barracuda schools to the boat and continued steady chumming can keep them there for sustained periods. Without chumming, the schools will randomly arrive and quickly depart.

Early in the year, barracuda are deeper and often won't rise to a chum line. Locate the fish with your fish finder, drop a jig to the right depth and yo-yo. Or, if fishing anchovies, try "pumping". Drop the bait to the bottom, slowly lift the rod tip, drop the rod tip and reel in the slack, repeat.

When flylining anchovies, on the pickup, set the hook quickly. This will help prevent deep hooking and resultant cut lines - barracuda have sharp teeth. To minimize cut lines, retrieve the fish with a steady pull - don't pump.

On Jigs - Find the right depth by, on consecutive casts, allowing the jig to sink 5, 10, 15, 20, and 25 seconds or more before retrieving the lure to the

BARRACUDA 16

**Technique** continued:

>boat. If hit, note the depth and repeat. On the retrieve, point the rod tip down the line. Use a slow to medium speed retrieve. For lightweight jigs, use lighter line for easier casting, line in the 10# to 20# class.

**The Law::** Size: 28"; Limit: 10. (1990)
See DFG regs. for ocean bag limits.

**Records:** State: 15 lb. 15 oz., San Onofre, August 1957
IGFA: "Slender" barracuda - 17 lbs. 4 oz.
"Mexican" barracuda - 21 lbs.

**See Also:** Bonito are surface fish generally found with Barracuda. Yellowtail may also be around. Bottom or near bottom fish include Sand Bass, Calico Bass, Halibut, White Seabass.

# SOUTHERN CALIFORNIA – PRIME OCEAN FISHING AREAS

CAUTION: Not to be used for Navigation. See NOS maps

BARRACUDA 18

# SOUTHERN CALIFORNIA - PRIME OCEAN FISHING AREAS

| | Latitude/Longitude | Course/Distance |
|---|---|---|
| 1. 60 Mile Bank | 32° 04.0'/118° 13.0' | From Pt. Loma<br>220° / 60.0 NM |
| 2. 150 Kelp<br>Double Oil Platform<br>called "Elly & Ellen" | 33° 07.5'/118° 35.0' | From Alamitos Bay<br>170° / 9.5 NM |
| 3. Anacapa Is. | 34° 02.4'/119° 21.5' | From Oxnard, Pt. Hueneme<br>203° / 10.3 NM<br>From Ventura Marina<br>180° / 13.6 NM |
| 4. Barn Kelp | 33° 18.6'/117° 29.1' | From Oceanside Harbor<br>315° / 9.6 NM |
| 5. Big Kelp Reef (BKR) | 34° 02.0'/118° 45.3' | From Marina del Rey<br>270° / 14.2 NM |
| 6. Catalina Is. | .................... | From Alamitos Bay<br>215° / 23.8 NM to<br>Ship Rock, 2 Harbors |
| 7. Clemente Is. | 33° 2.1'/118° 36.8' | Castle Rock - NW end |
| 8. Coronado Is. | 32° 26.5'/117° 25.0' | From Pt. Loma<br>170° / 12.5 NM |
| 9. Cortes Bank | 32° 26.5'/119° 07.5' | From Marina del Rey<br>186° / 97 NM<br>From Pt. Loma<br>250° / 95 NM |
| 10. Deep Hole | 34° 01.5'/118° 57.5' | From Marina del Rey<br>277° / 24.2 NM |
| 11. Horseshoe Kelp | 33° 40.0'/118° 13.5' | From Alamitos Bay, out<br>from Federal Breakwater<br>212° / 4.8 NM |
| 12. La Jolla Kelp | 32° 50.0'/117° 17.5' | From Mission Bay<br>310° / about 3 NM |
| 13. Point Dume | 33° 49.0'/119° 00.0' | From Marina del Rey<br>262° / 17.0 NM |
| 14. Pt. Loma Kelp | 32° 42.5'/118° 16.3' | From Mission Bay<br>just south of entrance<br>to Pt. Loma |
| 15. Pt. Vicente | 33° 45.2'/118° 24.6' | From Marina del Rey<br>155° / 13.2 NM |
| 16. Rincon Reef | 34° 19.4'/119° 27.0' | From Santa Barbara<br>170° / 10 NM |
| 17. Rocky Point | 33° 47.8'/118° 24.4' | From Marina del Rey<br>151° / 10.3 NM |
| 18. Santa Barbara Is. | 33° 29.2'/119° 01.8' | From Marina del Rey<br>211° / 41.0 NM<br>From Newport<br>250° / 41.0 NM |
| 19. Santa Cruz Is.<br>West Point | 34° 04.6'/119° 55.1' | From Santa Barbara<br>198° / 24.2 NM |
| San Pedro Pt. | 34° 02.0'/119° 31.2' | From Oxnard, Pt. Hueneme<br>235° / 17.4 NM |
| 20. Tanner Bank | 32° 42.0'/119° 08.0' | From Marina del Rey<br>190° / 83.1 NM |
| 21. Topanga Bubbles | 34° 01.5'/118° 34.2' | From Marina del Rey |

BARRACUDA 19

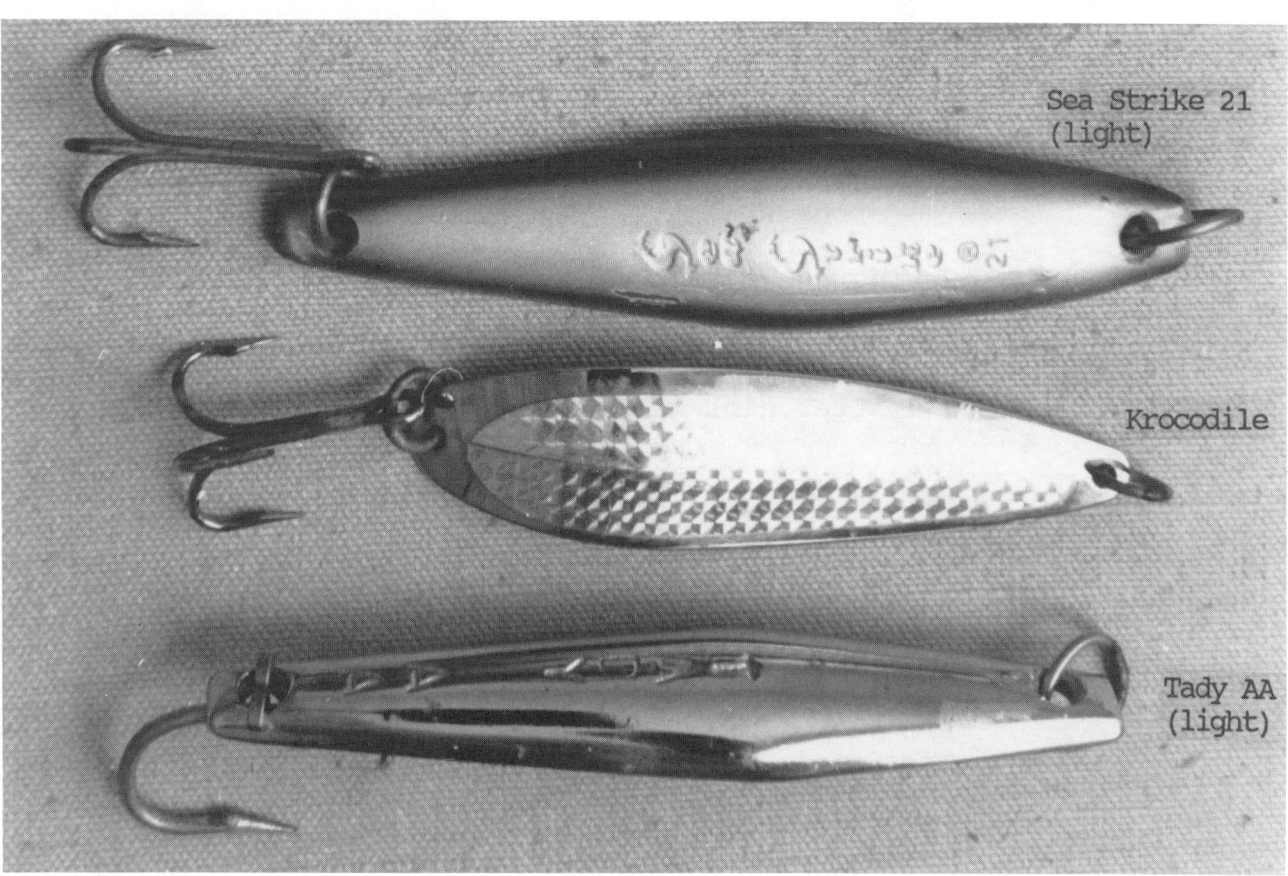

Sea Strike 21 (light)

Krocodile

Tady AA (light)

## CALICO BASS (KELP BASS):

**Where:** Southern California shallow ocean around kelp beds. Lee side of Catalina Island; lee side of San Clemente Island - especially the northwest end; Kelp beds off Malibu; Naples reef; Deep Hole.

See also 2-5 day Baja long range trips to great Calico Bass spots like San Martin Is. to as far as Guadalupe Is.

Structure:

Calicos stay around rocks and kelp and suspended close to small hills or humps over a relatively flat bottom, preferring 60-63 degree waters. In winter look for warmer water areas, especially near the 60 degree level. Isolated offshore rocky bottom structure can be found in the winter months by locating concentrations of lobster pots.

Also look for hard bottom areas in water 25-60 feet deep.

In kelp beds, they tend to be at the surface in the early morning and move toward the bottom at mid-day.

Breakwaters:

San Diego Harbor
Dana Point Harbor
Long Beach Federal Breakwater

**When:** During squid season, normally November to April.

Success can be had around the breakwaters of So. California harbors. Fish these a little before, to, and after high tides, at night.

The rising waters wash crabs from the rocks. Use a lead head jig, with pork rind, and bounce it where the waves break white on the rocks.

**Bait/Lures:** Live squid, cut squid strips, brown baits. Small twin T-tails with skirt - red or brown, on a No. 2 long shank hook with a leadhead.

1/2 to 1 oz. leadhead plastics preferably with Aberdeen style hooks (fine wire hook penetrates easier on strike).

Scampi

**Bait/Lures continued:**

    Scroungers
    Worm King or Shakin Shad - Brown Bait pattern
    Colors: rootbeer, smoke, red flake, chartreuse

**Rig:**

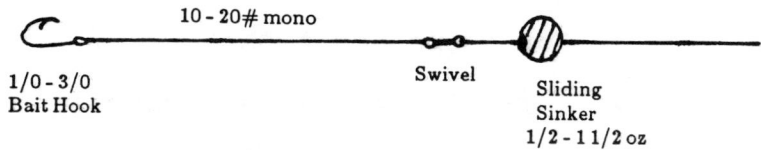

**Brown Bait or Squid Rig**

- 10-20# mono
- 1/0 - 3/0 Bait Hook
- Swivel
- Sliding Sinker 1/2 - 1 1/2 oz

**Technique:**

**General Tactics:**

- Troll with Rapala, Krocodiles, Scrounger, until you locate fish.

- Move up current of the kelp or hard bottom structure and drift toward it while jigging spoons or leadhead jigs

    OR

- Anchor up current and chum kelp bed or hard bottom structure with cut anchovies, squid, mackerel for 15 minutes.

**Fishing Off Breakwaters:**

- Use a dark colored Scampi (rootbeer, blue, red) with squid strip.
- Cast parallel to the rocks
- Retrieve slowly - bouncing along the bottom
- The inside breakwater is calmer, although it generally has smaller fish.
- A trolling motor is almost a necessity.

**Using Squid:**

- Cast out
- Put reel in gear
- Let sink to bottom
- If the squid reaches the bottom without being touched, take the reel out of gear and wait for a hit.

**Using Leadhead Plastic Lures:**

1. On the bottom:

BASS, CALICO

**Technique continued:**

- Keep the rod tip high and lower it as the fish starts to take the bait, then set the hook.
- If close to a kelp bed, cast as close as possible. Be prepared for a strike on the drop.
- In shallow, rocky water, bounce the bait off the rocks into the breaking foam. Retrieve slowly to avoid hang-ups.

2. For suspended fish:

- Troll until locate school
- Throw marker
- Use trolling motor to maintain boat directly above fish
- Free-spool, dull or painted head football head plastic lure straight down through fish.

Leadhead Weight versus Fishing Depth:

A fast current will require a step up in weight from the following chart.

| Depth (ft) | 1-10 | 5-15 | 10-20 | 20-30 | 30-40 | 40-50 |
|---|---|---|---|---|---|---|
| Ounces | 1/8 | 1/4 | 3/8 | 1/2 | 3/4 | 1 |

Lures: Scampi, Scrounger, Worm King, Shakin Shad
Colors: Root Beer, Chartreuse, Silver Flake, Smoke, Motor Oil

**Using Brown Baits:**

- Let rig sink to the bottom with the reel in free spool.
- Move bait occasionally with a rod lift.
- When hit, let the fish run.

**The Law:** Limit: 10 alone or in any combination with Sand or Spotted Bay Bass.
Sizes: 12"
See also DFG ocean bag limits.

**Records:** State: 28.5", 14.5 lbs.

**Info:** Call landings noted on map or general info number.

**Access:** Guide: Kit McNear, "El Bajo" Charters, Marina del Rey, 818-762-5873

**See Also:** Sand Bass, Halibut, Sheephead, possibly Yellowtail and White Seabass.

**Guide Kit McNear holds a Sand Bass & Calico Bass caught by angler Ryan McNear**

BASS, LARGEMOUTH   24

**LARGEMOUTH BASS** (Also Smallmouth, Spotted):

General Organization of Largemouth Bass Section:

This section is organized in the following major subsections:

1. General information in standard format with extensive structure description in the Where/When section ............... Pgs. 24-28

2. Detailed description of Seasons and techniques ...................... Pgs. 29-38

3. Detailed techniques for using major bass baits and lures ................. Pgs. 39-57

4. Maps of major bass lakes ......... Pgs. 58-64

There are two strains of Largemouth bass in California. The Northern strain and the Southern strain. The Northern strain is commonly found in lakes north of Lake Isabella (Bakersfield). The Southern strain (Florida strain) is a larger bass of the So. California area.

Smallmouth Bass are found especially in lakes of northern California. Smallmouth fishing techniques are similar to Largemouth. Notable Smallmouth lakes: Trinity, Clear, Shasta, Millerton (near Fresno), Almanor, and Pine Flat.

There also is a Spotted Bass which is considered a separate species. Spotted Bass are also prevalent at Pine Flat Reservoir, Millerton Lake, and Lake Perris.

**Where/When:**       **Hot Spots - Largemouth Bass:**

**SEE MAPS**

Lakes of Southern California. Big bass lakes: Casitas, Hodges, Isabella, Sutherland, Otay, El Capitan, San Vicente, Morena

Lakes of Northern California. Clear Lake, Berryessa, Lake Amador.

**Horizontal Location - Structure:**

Horizontal location depends largely on the season, water temperature, and available structure. See section organized by the

**Where/When continued:**

following "seasons":

| | |
|---|---|
| Pre-Spawn: | January to early March |
| Spawn: | March, April, early May |
| Post-Spawn/ Pre-Summer: | Late May |
| Summer: | June to September |
| Fall: | September and early October |
| Winter: | November through early Feb. |

There is definite overlap of these "seasons". For example during late Pre-spawn significant numbers of fish will still be schooled deep in a winter pattern, others will be in the spawning pattern.

**Vertical, Depth Location:**

Factors moving bass shallower:

1. Food/bait normally is in the shallows.
2. When shallow water temperature is close to ideal - low 70 degrees.
3. Structure is in the shallows.
4. A wind blown, choppy water surface provides protection from above.
5. Stained, muddy water
6. Spawning drive in spring.

Factors moving bass deeper:

1. Temperature:
   Summertime - mid-day heat forces bass deeper.
   Winter, Spring - changing weather conditions, storm fronts drive fish deeper.
2. Lack of shallow water cover.
3. Fishing pressure, water skiers, jet skiers, etc.
4. Clear water and a calm surface.

**Structure - other bass species:**

Smallmouth: Differ from Largemouth in the following ways:

- prefer colder water.
- seldom found below 20'
- will spawn in deeper water
- eat mostly crayfish, but drifted minnows can be effective
- prefer shady areas of rocky ledges and points

BASS, LARGEMOUTH 26

**Where/When continued:**

>Spotted (Alabama) Bass: Differ from Largemouth in the following ways:
>
>- spawn earlier, especially good mid-December to mid-to-late January at Lake Perris
>- must be fishing on bottom to be effective
>- prefer rocky structure
>- in summer, best at night using small plastic worm or single spin small spinnerbait.
>- grub jigging is effective in deeper water structure. Color: green, watermelon. Haddock split-tail, Super Float worm.
>- live crawdads are effective.

**When:** Best in Spring, late March through early May, and fall before turnover - see Early Fall, Late Fall. Most fish are caught in the early morning. For specifics see detailed "seasons" section.

**Bait/Lures:** Note that some baits, notably crawdads and shiners are illegal to use at some lakes.

Crawdads (also called Crayfish & Crawfish) - use small 2" crawfish, preferably ones that have just molted, having a soft shell and a greenish color instead of a reddish-brown color. Nose hooking is most effective but requires a gentle cast to avoid tearing loose. Can also be hooked through tail.

Nightcrawler Worms - use a worm inflator to inject air into worm - this makes the worm float off the bottom. Add #5 or smaller split shot for better control especially at greater depths. Run hook through collar and re-embed in body to make weedless.

Shiners - minnows.

>Techniques:
>
>>a. Cast lip-hooked shiners to shallow water structures. Keep minnow in bait well between casts. Minnow will only stay lively 5 to 6 casts.
>>
>>b. Fish below bobber near tules, lily pads, etc. Hook lightly above the spine, behind the dorsal fin.
>>
>>c. Flyline near shallow structure.
>
>Lures - depends on season and technique, see Technique and special section describing lures.

**Rig:** Basically 2 rigs will suffice.

1. A conventional freshwater casting reel combined with a 5 1/2 to 6 foot medium action graphite rod.

2. A medium weight spinning reel with a 5 1/2 medium-to-stiff action rod.

**Tools:** Fish Finders - LCR (Liquid Crystal Recorders), Paper Graphs, and Flashers:

These devices are essential for finding the 10% payoff water. They are needed to locate structure, bait, and the targeted fish and some of the more sensitive instruments can also detect the thermocline.

Color-C-Collector:

This device is the result of intensive and prolonged scientific testing of Bass color preferences. The best colors can vary with depth, water clarity, etc. Since the ideal color or color combination changes with depth it is important to know at what depth your crankbait will run. Note that the baits running depth will vary somewhat with cranking speed. This device can take the guess-work out of lure color selection.

PH-Meter:

Changes in water PH (acidity) can dramatically affect Bass behavior. The PH of a lake can be affected by runoff waters, lake vegetation, etc. Since the deeper California lakes experience limited runoff and typically have a low concentration of vegetation, PH-meters are not widely used. However, in lakes affected by PH variation; a. Search for areas within or closest to the ideal PH range of 7.5 to 8.5, b. When checking PH at different depths, check for PH changes of greater than .02 within 1 foot and fish structure at depths above this PH break.

Water Temperature Gauge:

Water temperature gauges again are not widely used by California Bass anglers. However they can be useful in locating warmer, Bass holding areas in the Pre-Spawn season, and the cooler holding areas or thermoclines in the Summer and Early Fall seasons.

BASS, LARGEMOUTH 28

**Rig continued:**  Markers:

Markers can greatly facilitate working invisible underwater structure, whether it is a submerged mound, rockpile, breakline, or deep weedline. By metering the structure and then marking it with one or more floating markers, you can then concentrate on using your electric trolling meter to maneuver the boat and effectively and accurately work the area.

**Technique:** The Largemouth bass is the most sought after sportfish in America. Bass fishing is close to a religion to some fishermen and this fervor has led to a myriad of techniques. What follows is my attempt to put order into this chaos. Generalized technique recommendations are listed in the "Seasons" section. Specific lure handling techniques are in the "Lures" section.

**The Law:** Generally the limit is 5 fish 12" or longer, however several exceptions occur. Check current DFG regulations for "Black Bass" which includes Largemouth, Smallmouth, and Spotted Bass.

**Records:** State Record: 21.74 lbs.; Lake Castaic, 1991
World Record: 22 lbs. 4 oz.; Georgia; 1932
Smallmouth:   9 lbs. 1 oz., Trinity Lake, 1976
Spotted:      9 lbs. 4.5 oz., Lake Perris

**Info:** See maps for information phone numbers.

**Access:** See maps for launch ramps and boat rentals.

Guide: Northern Calif - Clear Lake, Berryessa, etc.
Terry Knight
707-263-1699

Los Angeles Area Lakes
Don Iovino's Guide Service
818-848-6180

For San Diego Bass Lakes
Jim Murphy
619-566-0868

Boat Reservations for all San Diego Lakes:
619-390-0222

**See Also:** Rainbow Trout, Striped Bass, Crappie, Catfish.

BASS, LARGEMOUTH 29
Pre-Spawn

**When:** **Pre-Spawn**

Surface Water Temperature = 50 - 60 degrees

Generally from January to early March.
Varies somewhat on the specific lake as some lakes are known to be earlier then others.
Especially during a trend of warm, calm days.
Best time of day: 10 AM to 4 PM.

**Where:** Protected northern bays, coves, inlets - especially over dark (heat holding) bottoms.

In deeper water areas (10'- 25') adjacent to spawning areas.

In structure in the above areas such as:
- creek channel ledges and bends
- stumps & stickups
- Especially vertical cover leading from deeper water to spawning shallows

The tightly schooled bass will move along paths defined by structure. The structure will include anything that affords protection in moving from the deeper water 15 to 30+ feet, toward the spawning flats - river channels, raised roadbeds, tree lines, or combinations of such structure especially in the north end of the lake. When searching for the bass follow the structure paths, fishing at the changing depths until you find the school.

They will move to the shallow water flats with warmer weather. They will retreat to the deeper water if a storm comes through.

**Lures/Techniques:**

Work all baits and lures very slowly in these cold water conditions.

Crawdads (2-4"), Shiners, and Fat Gitzit lures are effective in the above structure areas during pre-spawn. Crawdads are especially effective for lunker bass during this time of the year.

A. In 3' - 9' deep, stained water in northern coves, especially over creek channels, ledges, and rocky, rip-rap areas;

Use a Crankbait (especially crawdad colors) like a Poe 1100, Bagley Fat Rap #7 or CD (countdown) sinking Rapala #9 or #11 slow ripped with a stop-and-go retrieve, or jerk a floating Rapala.

BASS, LARGEMOUTH 30
Pre-Spawn

**Lures/Techniques continued:**

    In rip-rap areas, hold the boat in 10' deep water and cast diagonally across rip-rap. This will allow keeping the crankbait hitting bottom almost up to the boat.

    Also effective is a slow fished Spinnerbait. Note that spinners with Colorado and/or tandem blades can be fished slower.

B.    On bottom structure 10' - 25' deep, especially over rocky bottoms.

    Use a 1/2 to 3/8 oz. Jig N' Pig, with 2" Uncle Josh pork rind. Hop it along the bottom and across the structure. Let it fall off of submerged ledges. The Jig N' Pig is effective on big fish during this period.

    Split shot worms or grubs. Shake or doodle a worm. Use a 4" worm or reaper.

C.    On deeper metered fish, 25+ feet.

    Try vertical jigging with a spoon, i.e. a Hopkins 3/4 oz. "shorty", Haddock Jig'N Spoon, or Kastmaster.

**When:**    **Spawn**

Surface Water Temperature = 60 - 70 degrees.
Largemouth spawn at 62 degrees, during full moon periods.
Smallmouth spawn at 59 degrees.

March, April, early May.
Best time of day: Daybreak to 10 AM, Twilight hours.

During spawn the smaller male fish will hit your lure first, keep casting or come back for the big female.

**Where:**    Usually on north end of lake in protected coves.
In 3' to 8' deep water, especially on the flats close to a channel or other structure leading to deep water.
Hard mud or mud/fine gravel bottoms.
They will NOT be in areas of moving water currents such as the back of coves with running streams.

Within the above areas, specifically;

A.    Shallow Structure and Spawning Areas:

    1. In spawning beds and shallow cover,

Spawn

**Lures/Techniques continued:**

 Use a split-shot plastic worm, 4", black, purple, or brown. Cast past the nest and move it into the nest and wait for the bass to pick it up. Use a stiff 5 1/2' graphite rod with 14# - 20# mono.

 2. In spawning beds, if no wind, early mornings and late evenings;

- use a #11 Floating Rapala
- cast 2-3 feet past the spawning bed
- let plug sit motionless for 10-25 seconds
- twitch it once or twice
- run it under the water 2 - 3 feet toward the bed.
- let float to surface.
- repeat.

 Rig should be a 6 1/2' spinning outfit with 8-12# mono

 3. In spawning areas, in tules, over grass, in the trees during early mornings and late evenings;

 Use Flipping technique, especially if wind is breaking up the surface and allowing a close enough approach to the shallows. Flip with Jig N' Pig or Spinnerbait.

B. Points,

 1. In shallow, 1 1/2 - 3', heavily stained or muddy water;

 Use Spinnerbaits with a trailer hook.
 1/4 oz. with #5 to #6 blade

 2. In stained water, 3 - 8 feet deep;

 Use a Spinnerbait with a trailer hook. Size: 1/4 oz. with a #5 or #6 blade.

 3. In clear water, 3 - 8 feet deep;

 Use Buzzbaits. Retrieve it just below the surface. White with nickel blades works well.

 4. In clear water, less than 15 feet deep;

 Use a Crankbait.

BASS, LARGEMOUTH
Spawn

**Lures/Techniques continued:**

    Crank down until the lure scrapes the bottom, stop and let rise, crank down again.

5. In water over 15 feet deep;

    Use a #7 Countdown Rapala
    There is a learning curve with this plug. You need to learn how quickly this plug sinks on a particular test line. Go to an area where you know the depth, cast out, count until the plug hits the bottom. Determine rate of drop, i.e. 1 foot/sec., and use this to get the plug to the fish depth.

**When:**    **Post-Spawn / Pre-Summer:**

Note that there is a Post-Spawn season where the spawning bass move out of the shallows and are very reluctant to feed. This short season comes between Spawning and Pre-Summer. In northern lakes, the Pre-Summer season is quite short and can produce excellent fishing. In southern reservoirs this season is less noticeable.

Surface Water Temperature = 70 - 75 degrees.

Late May, early June

Best time of day:

    Early morning until sunlight hits the water and sundown to early darkness.

**Where:**    **In Weedy Lakes:**

Fish move out of the spawning areas and into the newly developing weed beds on gradually or gently sloping banks and points.

The fish are spread out in the lake. If you are unfamiliar with the lake, using a fast fish-locator technique is imperative.

**In Reservoirs with minimal weed/reed cover:**

The bass will move along structure from shallow areas off of spawning flats down to structure in 15 to 20 feet of water. Typically this means movement along secondary creek channels toward junctions with the main lake channel. They will tend to cluster at brush or tree covered areas along the creek channel.

BASS, LARGEMOUTH 33
Post-Spawn

**Lures/Techniques:**

    A. In the mornings and late evenings;

       Use a top water lure - Zara Spook, Chugger Spook, Jitterbug. This is the best season for top water fishing.

    B. Along isolated weedbeds, or weed line structure - points or coves;

       Use a Crankbait, and work parallel with the weed line

       Use a #7 Countdown Rapala, especially if the fish are holding deeper than can be reached easily with a crankbait.

    C. Once any fish are located try subtle baits such as p-heads or darter heads on small plastic worms.

**When:** **Summer:**

Surface Water Temperature = 75+ degrees.

Generally June to September

Best time of day:

    If water is 75 - 80 degrees, early morning.
    If water 80 + degrees, fish at night.

**Where:** In the early morning and evening hours, the bass can be found in shallow water, but as the sun comes up they will move to deeper, outside structure or near structure.

Bass depth is typically limited by the thermocline that develops in deeper lakes from early summer to early fall. By turning up the sensitivity on fish finders you can usually detect a lightly shaded, uniform depth area located between the surface and the bottom. This band is wider in mid-summer and narrow in early summer and into fall before turnover. Bass will generally stay just above the thermocline. Look for lake areas where good fish holding structure is at a depth just above the thermocline.

**In Weedy Lakes:**

    On lakes with weed banks, summer bass are in the weeds. They will be within 2 feet of the outside (deep side) of weed banks.

BASS, LARGEMOUTH    34
Summer

**Where continued:**

In heavy reed areas, the bass are concentrated on the inside (shallow) structure areas. Reed structure areas include points, sharp inlets in the reeds, or channels cutting through the reeds. The best reed areas are located over a slight dropout - even as small as 1 foot in 3 feet of water. Note that the bass will definitely move out of the reeds on windy days.

**In reservoirs without extensive weed/reed cover:**

As the water warms with summer, the bass daytime holding area will shift from structure near the spawning beds to structure near the main lake channel. The bass route will follow the most available structure leading to the deeper water.

**In reservoirs without extensive weed/reed cover:**

Often they will be moving down the secondary creek channels to the junction with the main channel. Often they will hold at concentrations of submerged brush or trees situated along this route. In the summer the bass are on the bottom - they will not be suspended. The following structures in less than 30 feet of water are prime summer spots:

Creek channel junctions with the main channel.
Roadbed/creek junctions
Outside bends in the main river channel.
Sharp bends in the main channel.
Timbered points near channels.
Sunken mounds.

Fish will generally be up-current, up-wind of such structures. They will be closer to the surface and shallows in the early morning and late evening.

There can also be mid-day, surface action caused by bass chasing shad schools to the surface. Be on the lookout for this action and have a setup pre-rigged.

**Lures/Technique:**

A.  In the early morning, inside tules/reeds/lily pads/weeds:

The best lures are:

Plastic worms with 1/4 oz. bullet sliding sinkers.

BASS, LARGEMOUTH 35
Summer

**Lures/Technique continued:**

    Buzzbaits, 1/4 to 3/8 oz.
    Weedless spoons like the 3/8 oz. Johnson Silver Minnow.

    These lures should be fished on 12 - 20# mono.

    Where the weeds are below the surface, a buzzbait works well. Early mornings are best for these locations especially over a choppy surface.

B. In the early morning and twilight hours, work shorelines over rock bottoms or combination rock and brush, especially over dropoffs from a shallow 3 to 7 feet to a deeper 15+ feet area;

    Use Spinnerbaits, worked on the shorelines, just below the surface. If the shore features steep banks without any major points or if gradual sloping with a weedline, brush and /or submerged bank that parallels the shoreline, first move close to the bank and cast & retrieve parallel to the bank. Then move out and work the area by casting to shallow water and working down the bank and break.

C. Like the post-spawn, the fish are more spread out than during other times of the year. A fast locator technique is imperative.

    1. To locate fish;

        Troll with a Crankbait, Rapala, Spoon, or Worm.

        Troll at different depths over the above mentioned structure.

    2. After locating fish by trolling;

        Shake, doodle or drag dart-head worms or grubs on 1/4 oz. leadhead. Grubs hangup easily, thus work better in open, clear water areas, especially over gravel and rocky bottoms. Work the grub like a crawfish swimming quickly off the bottom. Use 6-8# mono on a 5 1/2' to 6' stiff action graphite rod. For fishing brush covered channels use a plastic worm with a pegged 3/16 oz. (heavier for deep water) sliding bullet sinker. The sinker is "pegged" by forcing a toothpick between the line and the sinker and breaking

BASS, LARGEMOUTH 36
Summer

**Lures/Technique continued:**

off the toothpick. This fixes the sinker in front of the worm. To be effective, you MUST keep the worm on the bottom. In heavy brush, it may be necessary to vertical jig the worm to get it to the bottom where the fish are.

D.  In some lakes, notably some of the San Diego Lakes like Hodges, there can be significant surface boiling as schooled bass chase shad to the surface.

Fish these actions by cautiously approaching to within casting distance and casting to the action with small, 1/4 oz. Kastmasters, Scroungers, or Haddock Jig'N spoons.

**When:**     **Early Fall:**

Surface Water Temperature = 65 - 75 degrees.

September

This is a time when the lake shallows are generally still too warm to be ideal for bass activity, BUT, fishing action picks up when the water cools.

Therefore, fish:

In the morning hours while the shallows are still cool.

Fish after cool windy days, or one or two days after a cooling storm.

**Where:**    The shallows - in the back end of coves and secondary channels and bank areas with cover near these channels.

Points - that are slow tapering on the main lake near dropoffs or remaining weeds.

In deep water, off points with cover near channels.

If there is little lake cover,
try creek channel intersections with the main channel, or
sharp, outside bends in main channels in water 5 to 15 feet deep.

**BASS, LARGEMOUTH** 37
Early Fall

**Lures/Technique:**

1. The bass are still scattered. Use a fast working lure to cover area quickly and locate fish. Use a deep running crankbait or a small blade spinnerbait.

2. In the early AM, in the shallows, use buzzbaits, spinnerbaits, and crankbaits like the Fat Rap, and Rapala. Try jerking the Rapala.

3. Later in the morning, work deeper with reapers and larger 6 to 8" worms especially on the breaks where 5 foot deep shelves drop to around 15 feet.

**When:** **Late Fall**

Water temperatures are still stratified before turnover:

Surface Water Temperature = 55 - 65 degrees

Generally early October

This is a time when the lake shallows have now cooled below the ideal for bass activity, BUT, after warm weather periods shallows do become ideal.

Therefore, fish:

During the mid-day hours, from 10 AM to 2 PM.

Fish after a trend of warm, calm days.

**Where:** Bass will move deeper with the cooling weather. They will school in 10 - 30 ft. deep water.

Look,

- on the steep side of points
- in deeper water channel intersections
- off rocky bluffs near channels

As the water cools, crawfish will move out of the dying weed areas to rocky bottoms, ripraps. If Shad are present, they will become the main forage.

1. Therefore, use shad colored, smaller lures and retrieve at a slower speed. For example, Bill Norman crankbaits, Fat Raps, and Bomber lures.

2. Large blade or double spinnerbaits worked just below the surface are effective now.

## BASS, LARGEMOUTH
### Winter

**When:** **Winter**

Surface Water Temperature less than 50 degrees.

Generally late November, December, January & early February

**Where:** Fish school in deeper water from 25 - 45+ feet. Fish are usually close to the bottom.

Around January, fish are still in deep water, but become more concentrated outside spawning areas adjacent to deep water. The schools will gradually move along the easiest paths of structure toward shallower waters as the waters warm.

Warmer days, esp. a series of clear, calm, warm days can move fish to 10 feet deep or less.

In general, all bait/lure presentations must be very slow in this cold water. This translates to short lift jigging when using spoons off the bottom. During this slow movement season, a big bass might watch 25+ strokes before being provoked into striking - be patient.

1. In deeper water, 25 to 40+ feet, use spoons jigged off the bottom in graphed fish concentrations. Hits will be subtle, often just changes of pressure, often on the fall.

2. In more moderate depths, 10 to 30+ feet, either shake a split-shot worm, reaper, or grub or

3. Doodle off 2nd or 3rd breaks off points in 12 to 18+ feet of water.

4. Try spinnerbaits in darker colors, tipped with #9 pork rind and worked slowly like a jig over dropoffs in 10 to 15 feet of water.

**BASS - Shallow Water techniques (3 - 15'):**

**When:**   Pre-spawning period ... about Jan - Feb
Spring spawning period ... about Mar - April
Summer - early morning, evening; from May on


The following techniques are listed in approximate order of most successful/most popular technique:

1. Plastic Worms, Grubs, Reapers
2. Spinnerbaits / Buzz baits
3. Crankbaits
4. Jig N' Pig
5. Tube baits, P-heads, Darter heads
6. Zara Spook
7. Surface Plugs, Poppers, Chuggers
8. Flipping

BASS, LARGEMOUTH 40
Shallow Techniques

**Plastic Worms, Grubs, Reapers:**

**When:** Plastic worms are very versatile. They can be used effectively all seasons and in shallow water to deep water structure. Worms colors, sizes, and rigs can be modified to imitate the current bait forage. Split-shot worms, worked downwind in the summer will be more horizontal, imitating the dominant shad forage. Slip, bullet sinker rigged worms worked off the bottom will have a more vertical orientation imitating a crawdad - the dominant spring forage.

In general, a longer worm is used when the bass are actively feeding; a shorter worm is used when fish are inactive. The next thing to be determined is the position of the fish. If they are shallow or near the surface of the water, they usually are feeding actively and a slow dropping worm (with a light weight) gives them more time to look over the lure. A fast dropping worm (with a heavier weight) is more effective for the line control and feel necessary to fish for bass that are near the bottom.

**Rig:** Worms: 4 - 6", Examples: Super Float, Fluttercraft, Don Iovino worms, reapers, grubs, etc.
Worm Colors: Black, purple, brown, cinnamon, and cinnamon combinations

Grubs: Yamamoto, Kalin
Grub Colors: Salt and Pepper, Salt and Pepper/Chartreuse, also worm colors above

Hooks: 4" Worms: Use a 2/0 hook, 3/0 for larger worms. Grubs: Use a 2X or 3X long-shank sproat hook with baitholder barbs on the shank. Quality brands are Grey Shadow (fine wire), Black Weapon, Gamakatsu.

Bullet Weights: Non-lead, environmentally safe weights are new. Iovino markets a brass weight that is claimed to make fish attracting noise when used with a faceted glass bead. 3/16 oz is standard. Use heavier for deeper.

To keep the worm from slipping down the hook shank, insert a piece of 70-80# mono through the head of the worm and the eye of the hook. Cut off any excess.

If a seam is visible, embed the hook and penetrate along the seam. If the worm has a flat side, re-insert the hook through the middle of that side. It is important that the worm is straight on the hook. This will minimize unnatural spin on the retrieve. This is especially true when using curly-tailed, action type worms when they are drifted or reeled in for action.

**Plastic Worms Technique continued:**

**Technique:** There are many techniques for working a worm. Probably the most common technique used with split-shot, Carolina & Texas rigged worms is;

- Cast out and let the rig sink to the bottom. Keep undue slack out of the line on the line during the drop and watch the line for indications of a pickup, hesitations in the drop, sudden slack in the line, etc. IMPORTANT: 95% of the pickups CAN'T BE FELT, you must constantly watch the line for unexplained movements. When in doubt, strike!

- Once the lure has reached the bottom, retrieve moving the rod tip SLOWLY and erratically,

- Using only the wrists, move slowly from almost a horizontal position to short of vertical. If you are working slowly enough, the lure should be maintaining contact with the bottom.

- Lower the rod tip again to almost horizontal while reeling in the slack line and repeat.

- If you either know or can feel that the lure has dropped over a break or ledge, then try to let the lure fall naturally by releasing tension on the line. Many hits will come on such a drop.

- If you get a pickup, set the hook by swinging back up sharply with both hands. By working the rod only between 9 and 11 o'clock, you will have room to strike on any hit.

Doodling requires a rod with a flexible, sensitive rod tip but stiff back and a medium weight conventional reel such as an Ambassadeur 2500 or 3500L reel. As soon as the sinking worm is in the fish holding area, start shaking the rod tip with light, short, rapid movements. Make the worm wiggle. Take up line to keep the worm off the bottom. Experiment with different depths. Watch the bouncing rod tip carefully. A hit will be just a slight pull on the rod tip. A specialized Doodling worm and rig may be used with this technique.

Dragging a worm very slowly across the bottom can also be effective. The special Do-Nothin rig can be combined with this technique.

Swimming a worm is done by slowly drifting a worm or by casting and reeling in. This technique is especially effective with curly-tailed, action type worms, grubs, or reapers.

BASS, LARGEMOUTH 42
Shallow Techniques

# PLASTIC WORM, GRUB, AND REAPER RIGS

Note: All worms, reapers, and grubs should be carefully rigged with the hook on the center line or seam of the bait to eliminate unnatural spinning, twisting of the lure on retreives.

### Texas Rig

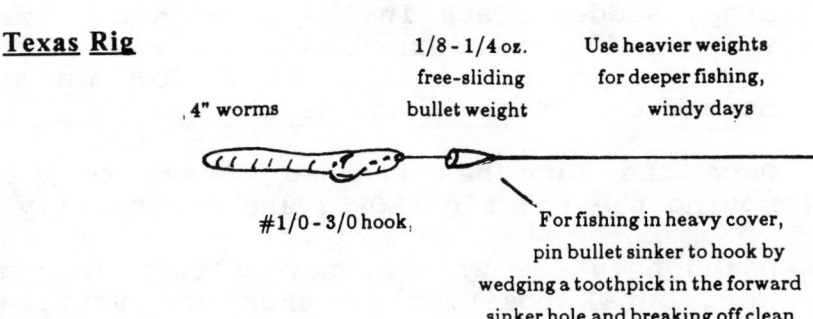

4" worms | 1/8 - 1/4 oz. free-sliding bullet weight | Use heavier weights for deeper fishing, windy days

#1/0 - 3/0 hook

For fishing in heavy cover, pin bullet sinker to hook by wedging a toothpick in the forward sinker hole and breaking off clean

### Splitshot Rig

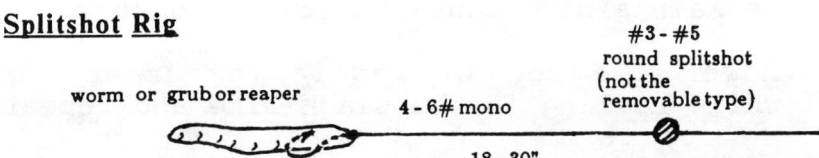

worm or grub or reaper | 4 - 6# mono | #3 - #5 round splitshot (not the removable type)

18 - 30"

Works best with a curly-tailed, action type worm either slowly bounced along the bottom, dragged, shaked, or drifted/reeled through cover areas

### Carolina Rig

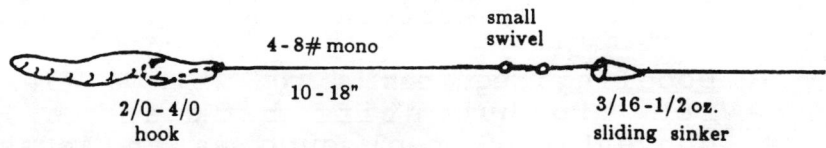

4 - 8# mono | small swivel

2/0 - 4/0 hook | 10 - 18" | 3/16 - 1/2 oz. sliding sinker

### Doodling Rig

Toothpick inserted through head of worm and eye of hook and broken off. This holds the worm on the hook.

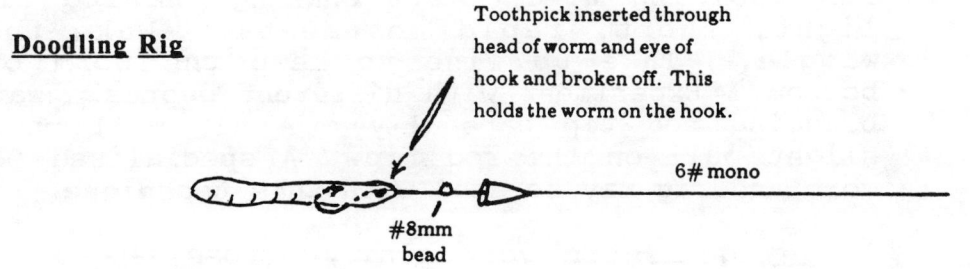

#8mm bead | 6# mono

### Do-Nothin Rig

Small exposed hooks

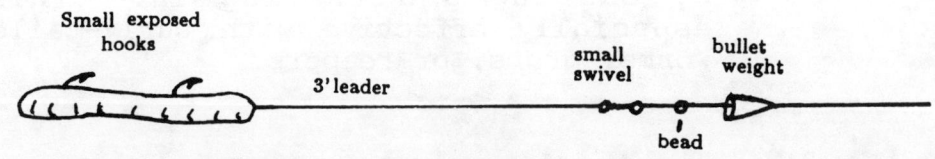

3' leader | small swivel | bullet weight

bead

## BASS, LARGEMOUTH
Shallow Techniques

**Spinnerbaits & Buzz Baits:**

**When/Where**  Generally a shallow water technique for spring through fall seasons. However Spinnerbaits can be effective at deeper depths worked like Jig N' Pigs.

**Rig:**  Spinnerbaits:

Rubber skirts are best.
Blade Size: Normally #4 or #5
Brands: Turnabout, Haddock, Eagle, Strike King.

Use tandem leafs and/or Colorado blades for slower retrieves in cloudy, muddy water or in cooler water. In cloudy water, use copper or gold blades. Use tandem blades in shallower waters, 5 to 8 feet deep or over weed beds.

Use single leaf, willow shaped for clear, warmer water conditions. In clear water, use nickel or silver blades. Use single blade, 1/2 to 1 oz. spinners for deeper water fishing working the lure like a Jig N' Pig.

Colors: White, Chartreuse & White, Chartreuse

Add a pork rind trailer to get a slower lure or an action-tailed plastic worm for bigger fish.

Buzz Baits: 1/4 to 3/8 oz.
Good for windy conditions
Color: White, Chartreuse

**Technique - Spinnerbaits:**

1. Since this can be a fast working bait, it is effective for locating fish concentrations.

2. Spinners are also good "weedless" lures for working fairly heavy cover, i.e. stickups, etc. Work the lure to bump cover than give it a short fall. Many hits come on the fall.

3. Spinnerbaits can be effective in muddy, shallow water. Work past points, structure junctions, along fallen tree trunks.

4. Spinnerbaits can also be very effective worked like a Jig N' Pig in deeper waters.

Buzz Bait:

After casting, this lure must be retrieved immediately to keep it at the surface. Try to keep you line on or near the surface. The Buzz bait blade(s) should be breaking the surface.

BASS, LARGEMOUTH 45
Shallow Techniques

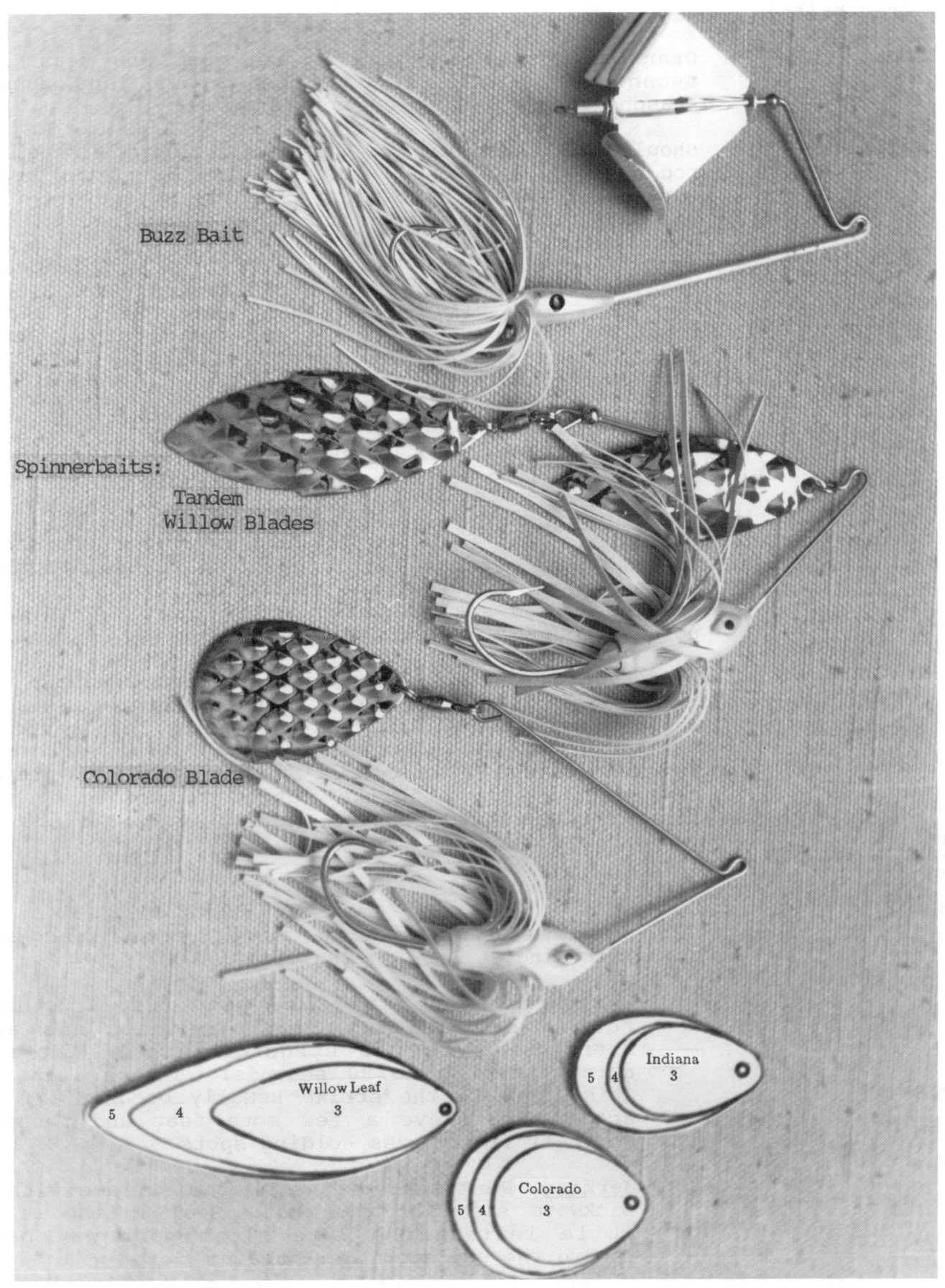

BASS, LARGEMOUTH 46
Shallow Techniques

**Crankbaits:**

**When:** Crankbaits are fast working and good for searching techniques, especially in post spawn, and summer seasons when the bass are scattered.

**Rig:** Should be fished with a semi-soft tipped fibreglass rod using 12-15# mono. Make sure the lure runs true, straight. Adjust by bending the lure attachment ring opposite to the direction the lure is running.

Examples: Floating Rapalas, #7 & #11, Countdown Rapalas (CD) #7 & #11, Rapala Fat Rap #5, Rapala Shad Rap #5 & #7, Bill Norman Baby N/Little N, Bomber Model A, Bagley DB2 or DB3 - deep diving lures, Rebel Fastrac Shad, Storm Wiggle Wart, Bagley Balsa B, Rattle Trap, Rattle Spot.

Colors: Match size and color to available bait, i.e. spring crayfish, spring smaller shad, summer larger shad. Crayfish color, Chrome, Tennessee Shad.

**Technique:** Crankbaits are fast working and good for searching techniques, especially in post spawn, and summer seasons when the bass are scattered. Crankbaits are effective from shallow water to 15+ feet. Cast past points, retrieve over holding area.

Different lures work best at different speeds. If unfamiliar with the lure, test retrieve it within sight to see the retrieve that gives the best action.

Never retrieve a crankbait with a regular, steady retrieve. Give lifelike action to the lure with irregular retrieves, pauses, jerks, brief periods of rapid retrieves, etc.

Floating Lure Techniques:

Successful floating lure techniques are Twitching, & Jerking (Pulling).

<u>Twitching</u>: Cast the lure past the structure. Let it sit quietly for a few seconds and retrieve up to the structure area. Let sit quietly for up to 30 seconds. Twitch lightly. This is where the strike usually occurs. If no action, retrieve a few more feet and repeat. Work all likely bass holding spots.

<u>Jerking</u>: Jerk the lure below the surface with a backward sweep of the rod. Reel in the slack while letting the lure float part way back toward the surface. Jerk again.

BASS, LARGEMOUTH 47
Shallow Techniques

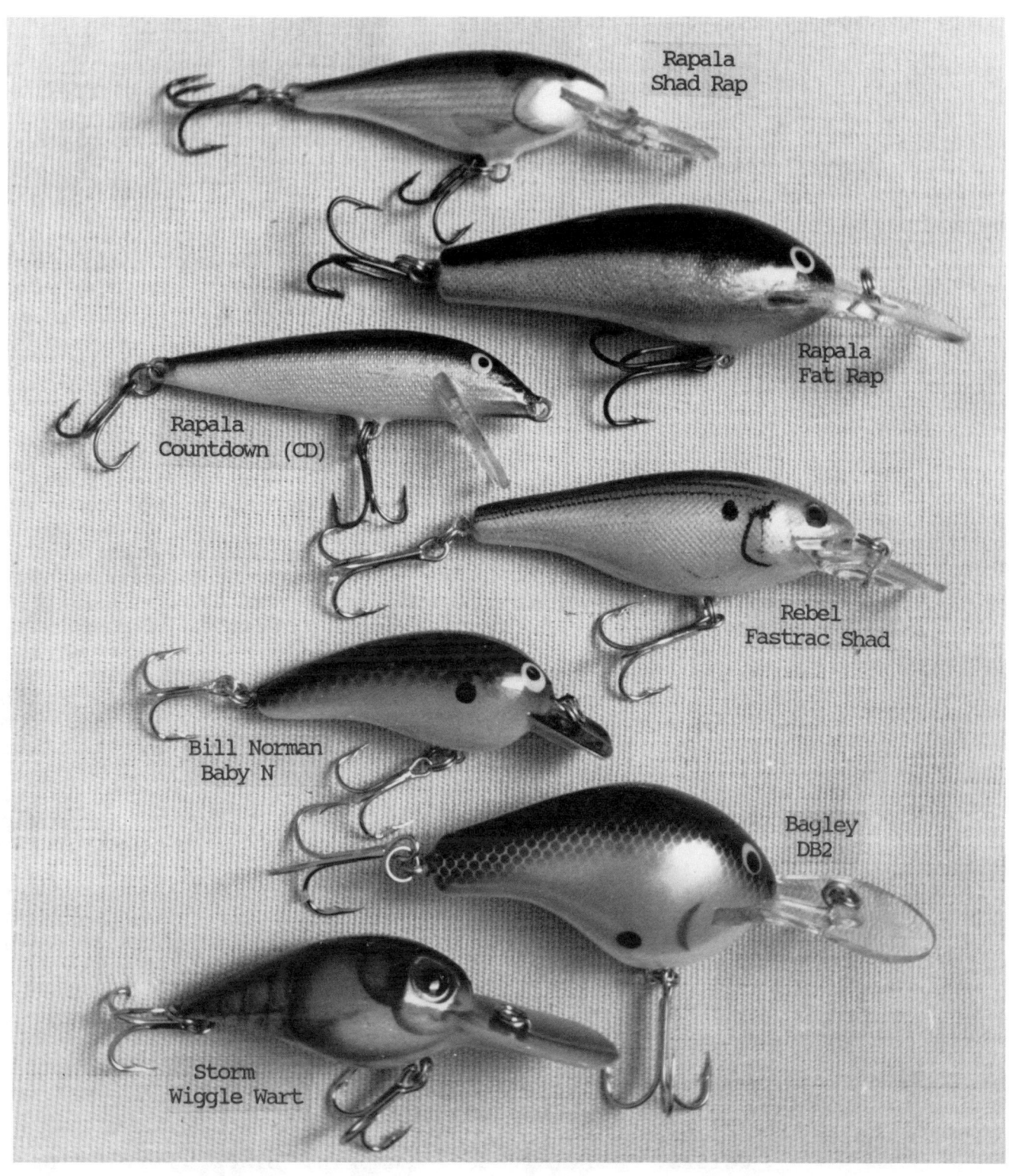

## BASS, LARGEMOUTH
### Shallow Techniques

**Jig N' Pig:** A pork rind trailer on a skirted, leadhead jig.

**When:** This versatile lure is effective in intermediate and deeper waters. Jig N' Pigs are especially effective during Pre-Spawn season and during winter months. Because of their weight they are easier to work in water 20+ feet deep.

**Rig:** Use a heavy action casting rod with 12# mono

Banana heads and Football heads are relatively snagless for hopping off the bottom since they land hook up.

- Leadhead: Banana heads are the most popular jig shape and are good for sinking techniques such as flipping.

  Football heads are good for working on the bottom. It sinks fast and wont turnover on the sink or when it hits the bottom. Use lighter weights (3/16, 1/4, 5/16, & 3/8 oz.) for shallower depths. Use heavier weights up to 5/8 oz. for penetrating heavy surface weed cover or for sinking to deeper winter depths of 40 to 60 feet.

  Arrow shaped or Power head jigs sink slower and drift on the drop giving more action but causing more hangups. This jig type will usually land properly - with the hook up.

- Skirt: Live rubber skirts tend to give more action than plastic skirts.

- Trailer: Pork trailers are best in cooler water. The standard trailer is a Uncle Josh #11 Bait Frog. Use crayfish colors in early season. Hook the trailer "meat down".

  Use Plastic trailers in warm water over 65 degrees or in depths greater than 20 feet.

- Brands: Stanley Jigs, Bobby Garland Spider Jig, Haddock Kreepy Krawl'r.

- Colors: Clear Water: Pumpkin, Black, Purple, Brown or combinations of these colors.
  Stained or Muddy Water: Brown & Orange, Black & Chartreuse.

**Technique:** How to "Swim" a jig:

- cast beyond the target

## Shallow Techniques

**Jig N' Pigs Technique:**

- count down to the desired depth or drop to the bottom
- crank up with several rapid turns
- stop
- repeat

Hits occur on the crank or the fall after the stop.

Other methods with Pig N' Jig:

    Flipping
    Vertical jigging
    Bouncing along the bottom

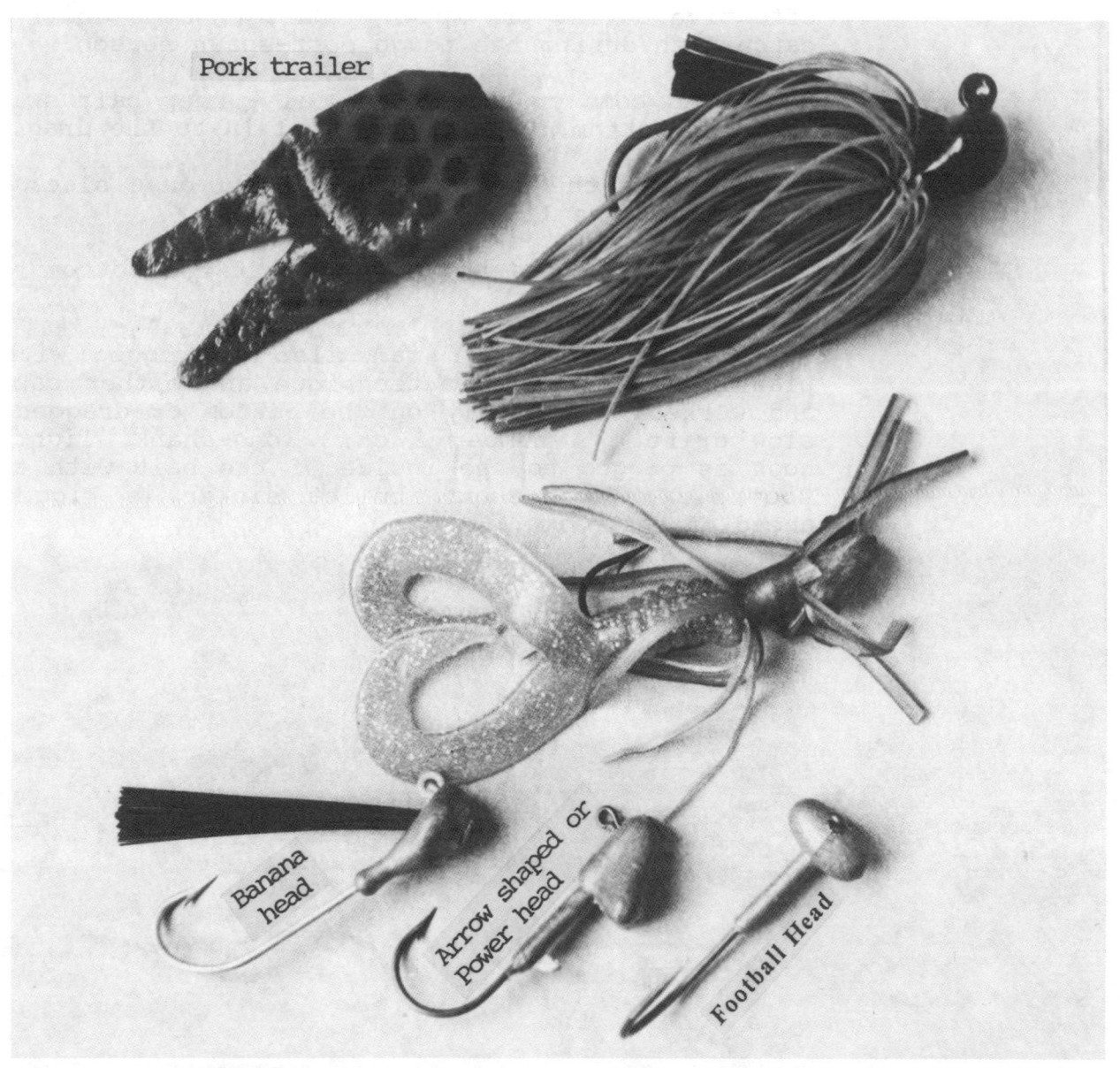

BASS, LARGEMOUTH 50
Shallow Techniques

## Tube Baits (Gitzits), Darter Heads, P-Heads:

**When:** Best especially pre-spawn and early spawn periods, also post-spawn period.

**Rig:** Medium Weight Spinning on a 6 to 7 foot rod.
Fish these lures on 4# to 6# line.
1/16 oz. in water around 5' to 6' deep
1/8 to 1/4 oz. in water > 6' deep
Colors: Shad Colors: Smoke, Smoke Sparkle, Clear
Crawfish Colors: Pumpkin, Motor Oil, Smoke & Red Flake, Green & Orange Flake.

**Technique:** These are subtle lures for fishing medium depths during tough fishing conditions requiring smaller baits & lighter lines. Tube Baits are especially effective during pre-spawn, Darter Heads and P-Heads catch fish during the tough post-spawn season.

Most hits come on the fall. Goal - keep bait swimming just off bottom. On pickups, reel in to the drag.

1. Cast into the wind, let lure fall on a slack line, reel in some line, let fall again

2. Let fall to the bottom, pop off the bottom making the lure jump.

Tube Baits (Gitzits) can also be rigged with the plastic worm splitshot technique and either cast out and worked back slowly on the bottom or dragged on a slow drift. A number 2 or 3 long-shank, light wire hook is pegged to the inside of the bait with a flat toothpick. A 1/8 oz. bullet sinker is rigged 18" ahead of the bait.

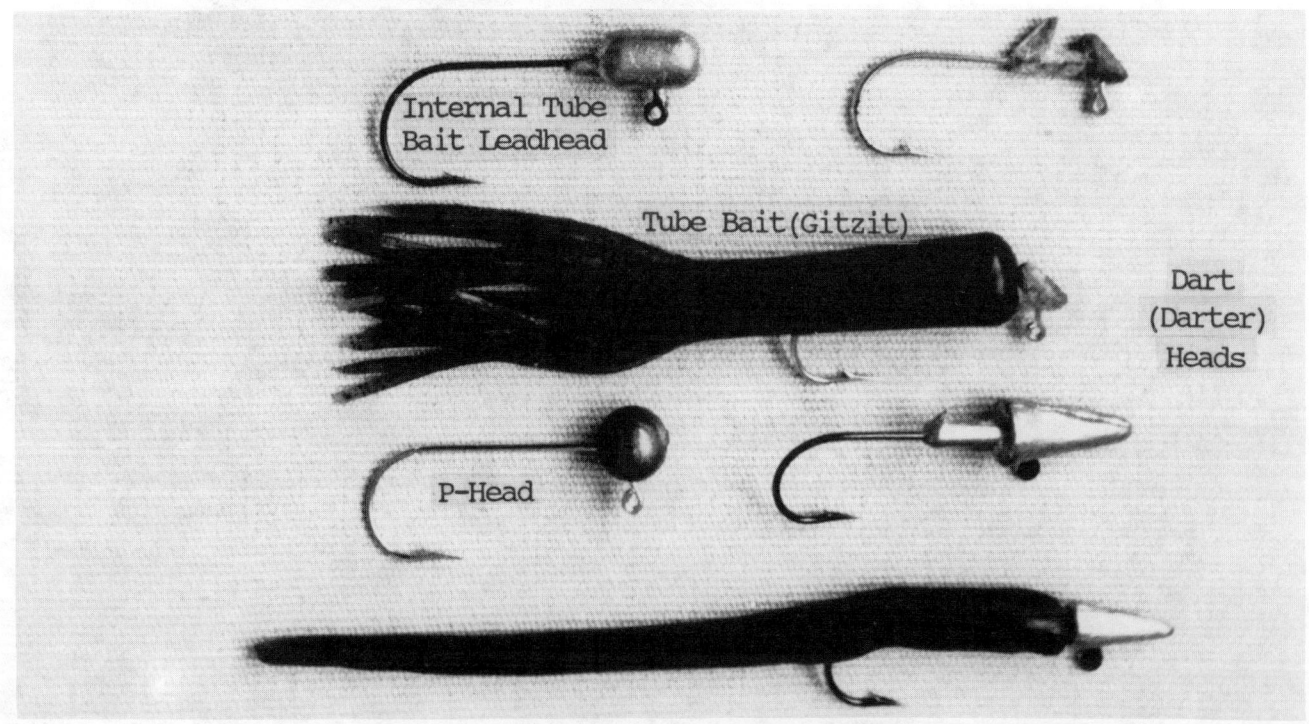

## "Zara Spook"

**When:** Surface technique - calm surface, effective all hours but especially early morning, evening.

**Rig:** Long handled Triggerstick, a flexible light 6 1/2 to 7' casting rod, 10-12 lb. line.
Lure Colors: Striper, Shad, clear patterns

Add a split ring to the nose eye. This maximizes lure action. If the lure does not properly move from left to right on alternate jerks, it may need to be tuned.

**Technique:** Spooks are worked with a technique called the "Dog Walk", that results in alternate left and right, side-to-side slides, not splashes. This action is accomplished by casting out, turning 90 degrees to the direction of the cast, placing rod butt end against the inside wrist and pointing the rod tip down. Retrieve the lure with sharp wrist action jerks.

On a hit, let the lure go under before setting the hook. After a missed strike, slow down the retrieve, using short small sideward moves.

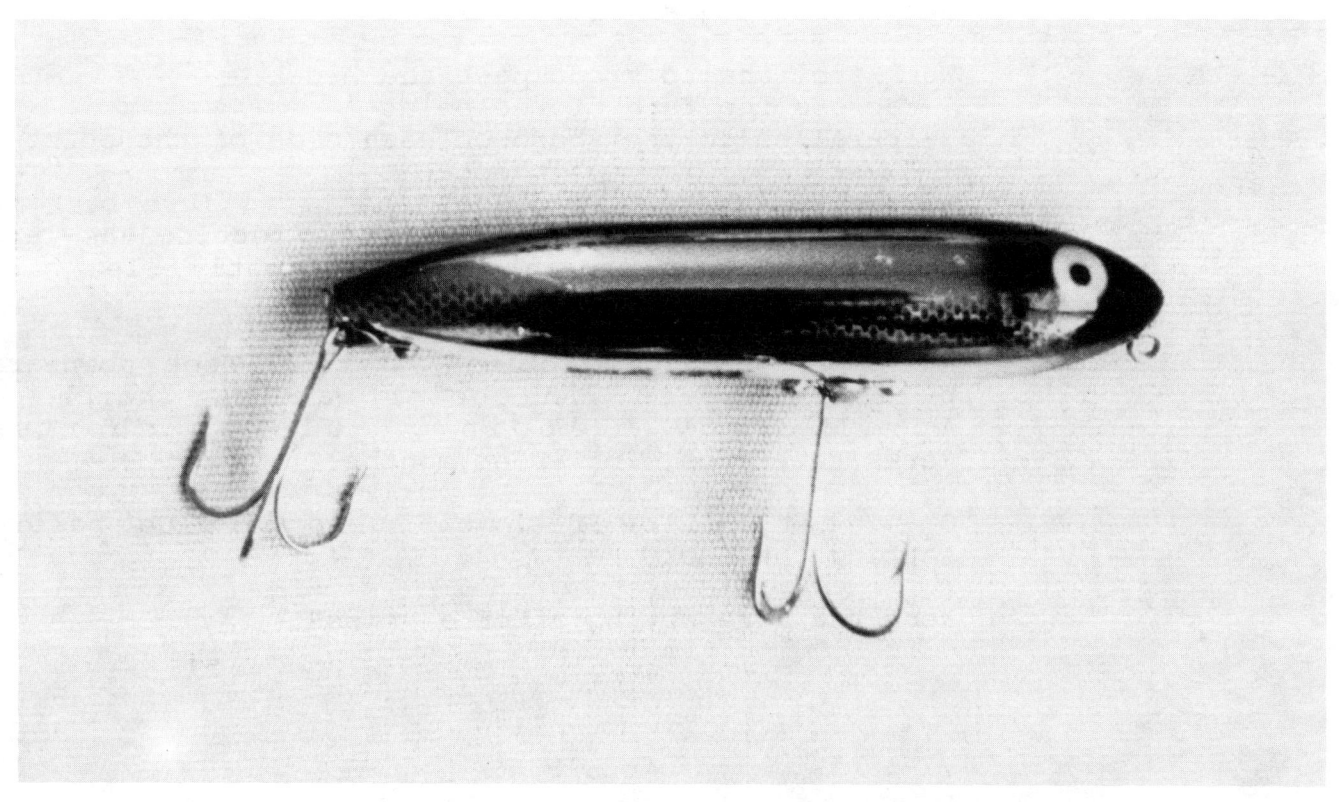

# BASS, LARGEMOUTH 52
## Shallow Techniques

**Surface Plugs, Poppers, Chuggers:**

**When:** Warm water, summer months, especially early morning and evening hours with relatively calm surface conditions. User louder lures such as the Woodchopper or Devil's Hourse during windier, choppier conditions.

**Rig:** Surface Plugs: Examples: Floating Rapala (#7 or #11, silver foil with black back); Bagley Bang-O-Lure; Rebel Floating Minnow.

Poppers: have a cup shaped head that caused a "pop" when jerked on the surface. Examples: Rebel Pop-R, Arbogast Hula Popper.

Chuggers: have less prominent cupped head than poppers and makes less noise when pulled over the surface. Examples: Storm Chug Bug, Bagley's Chug-O-Lure, Heddon Chugger Spook.

Use 15 to 20# mono.

**Technique:** Fish points where water depth drops off (break) to deeper holding areas.

Work from shallows out past the break
  - across the face of the point
  - parallel to the shore on each side of the point

Always cast past the target and bring lure back to the prime spot. Twitching involves letting the lure sit still after landing, twitch lightly, let sit, twitch, retrieve.

Also try using "Stroking", 2 to 3 foot downward pulls/retrieves, in cooler waters - March or April. Try "Rippin", quicker shorter jerks/retrieves, in warmer months.

On a hit, allow fish to submerge plug before setting the hook.

Keep the lure moving after a "miss".

BASS, LARGEMOUTH 53
Shallow Techniques

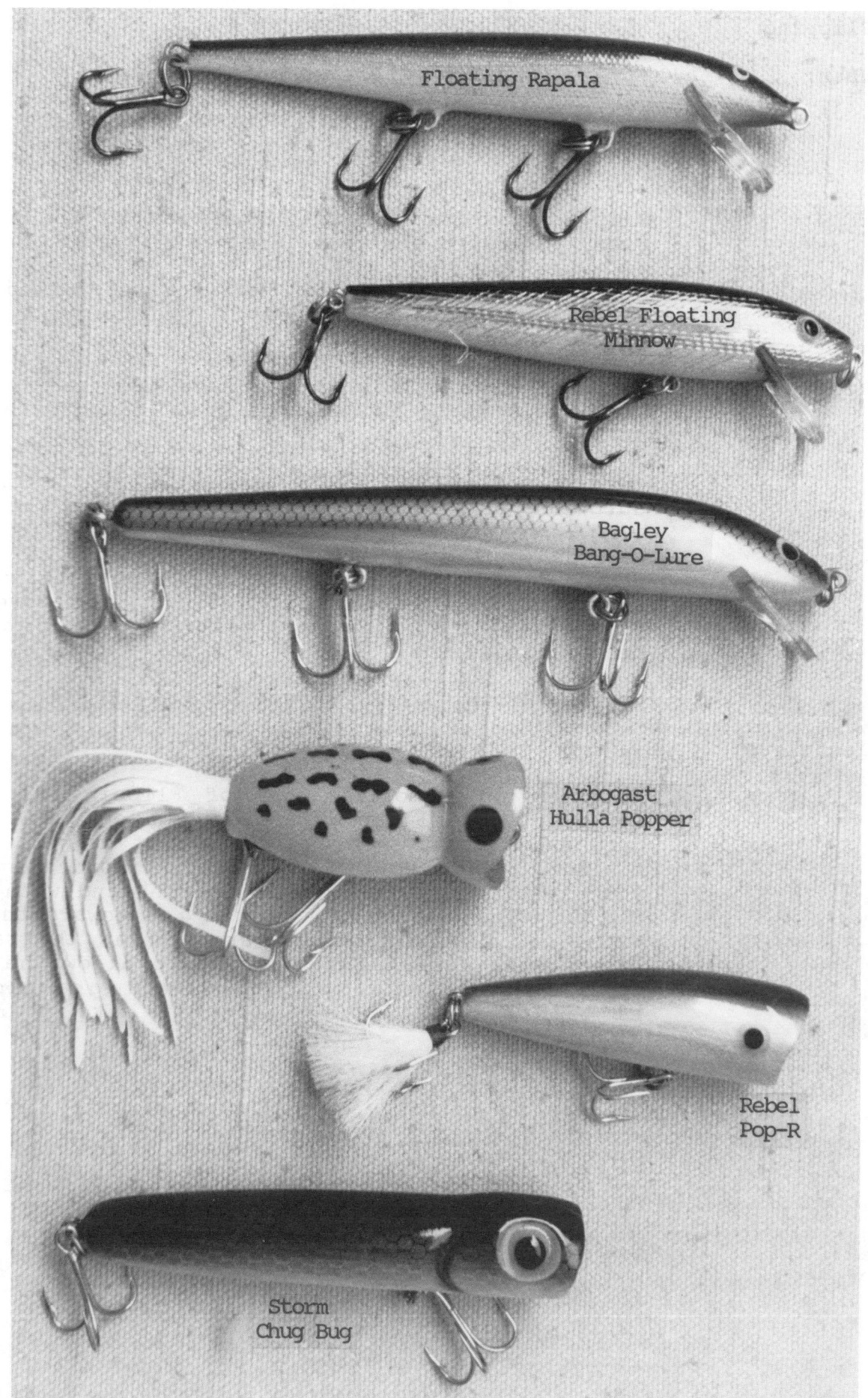

BASS, LARGEMOUTH 54
Shallow Techniques

## Flipping

**When:** Spring, shallow water, spawning season.

Works best when wind is breaking up the surface, reducing visibility, thus shallow fish are not spooked.

Flip if you can see only half way to the bottom or less, you can't see your lure past 5' deep.

Also use to fish areas of heavy grass, cattail cover, etc. where jig is flipped to small open areas and allowed to fall.

**Rig:** Flipping rods are long and have very stiff actions with reels that can lock the drag loaded with 17, 20, or 25# mono.

Special Flipping Reels have release buttons which automatically engage without cranking the handle, i.e. - Shimano "Brush Buster".

Banana head shaped jigs are best for fishing on the sink. Lighter weights fall slower for more subtle presentation. Heavier weights are better for penetrating weeds.

Colors: Brown, Black, Blue & Black

**Technique:** See Diagram

Pitching is a modification of Flippin for reaching targets beyond Flippin range. Let out line so that lure hangs about 6" above reel. Set magnetic drag to minimum. Put reel in freespool. Hold the lure in your left hand (watch those hooks!) and with the rod tip pointing downward, flip the rod toward the target with your right wrist and arm and at the same time release the lure. Don't engage to allow the lure to free fall to the bottom. With practice this technique can be very accurate at intermediate distances.

With both pitching and flippin, allow the lure to drop to the bottom, let sit, move slightly, repeat.

# LARGEMOUTH BASS - SHALLOW WATER TECHNIQUES

## FLIPPING

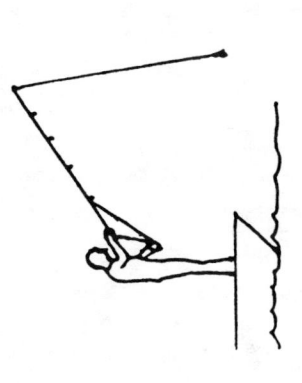

1. Let out enough line so that the lure is hanging just below knee level,
   a. With the rod tip held high and
   b. A length of line being held out, down, and to the side with your left hand.

2. Swing the lure backward than forward by lowering the rod and than lifting the rod, extending the arms, and finally flipping the wrist. Your left hand should simultaneously move forward toward the right hand extending the length of line.

3. While the lure flies toward the target let line freespool through the left hand. Just before the lure hits the water, grip the line and lift the rod tip slightly. This action stops the lure in mid-air and minimizes the splash.

BASS, LARGEMOUTH 56
Deep Techniques

**Winter, Vertical Methods:**

1. Jig N' Pig - see Shallow Water Techniques, Jig N' Pig.
2. Doodling / Split-shotting - see Shallow Water Techniques, plastic worms.
3. Jigging Spoons
4. Do-nothing Worms - see Shallow Water Techniques, plastic worms.

**General Technique:**

Use a Jig N' Pig to locate the fish - it can be worked fast. Add a pork rind to the Jig N' Pig.

Work sharp breaks next to deep water. Bass will usually hold on the edge of a break. 20 to 40 foot depths are easiest to work. Use marker buoys.

Move your boat directly over the fish, winter bass won't move very far.

Work lures straight up and down, vertically.

Spoons: Use Hopkins, Kastmaster, or Haddock spoons for more aggressive fish.

# BASS, LARGEMOUTH
## Deep Techniques

**Jigging Spoons**

**When:** A winter technique used for metered deep water fish. However, spoons can also be effective for summer, surface shad boils.

**Rig:** Spoons: Hopkins #075 "Shorty (3/4 oz.)
Kastmaster, 1/2 oz.
Haddock Jig'N Spoon, 3/8 oz.
Mann-O-Lure
Chrome color
10 - 12# mono
Add an "O" ring to the lure
Optional: Add chartreuse florescent tape to the spoon.
Optional: Replace factory hook with larger hook for better results, i.e. a 2/0 treble.

**Technique:** Work vertically over graphed fish, especially fish suspended near breaks or around suspended shad schools. For shad schools work the lure just below the shad. For bottom graphed bass, let the spoon drop to the bottom. Jig the spoon vertically so that at bottom of jig, the spoon is laying on the lake bottom. Use short, about 1 foot, slow jigs. On the fall, don't allow slack in the line. Strikes usually come on the fall. Watch for any hesitation in the line. Be patient, it often takes 25+ jigs in one spot to get a strike.

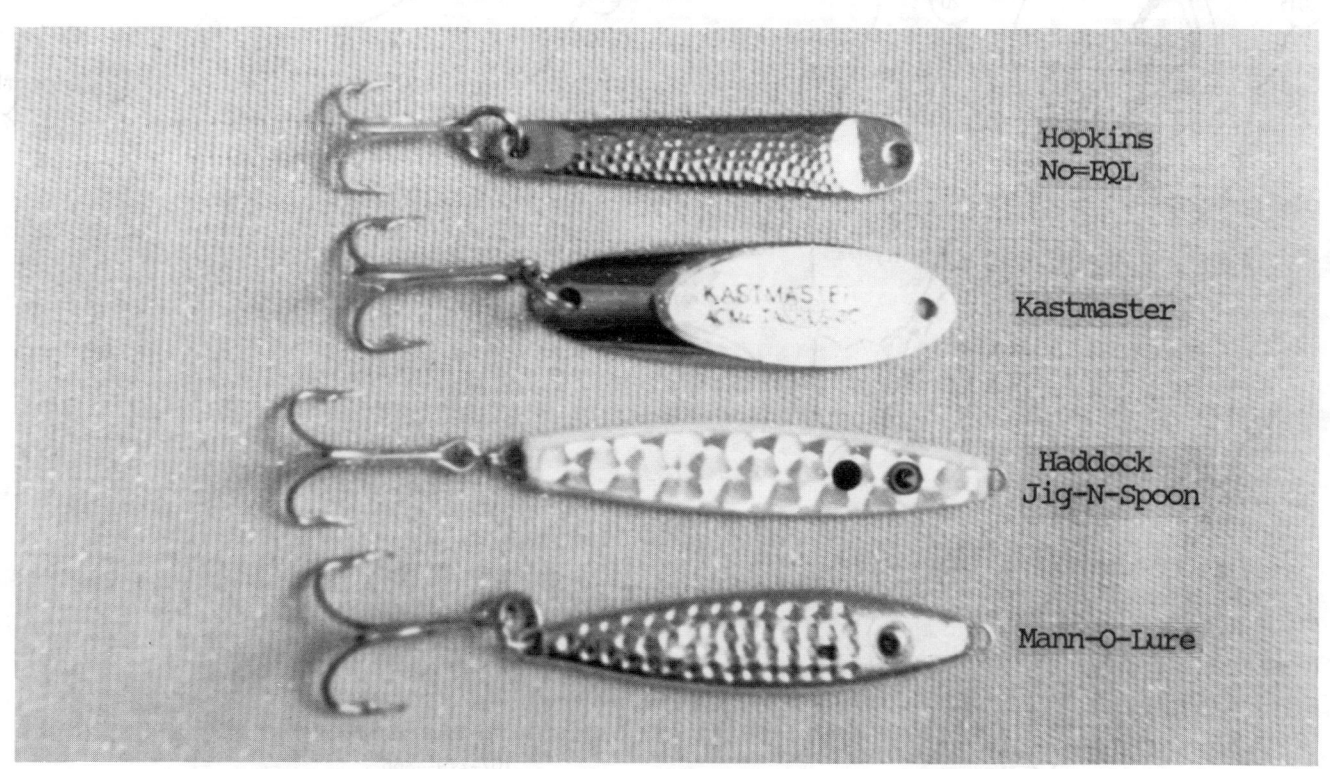

BASS, LARGEMOUTH 58

# NORTHERN CALIFORNIA BASS LAKES

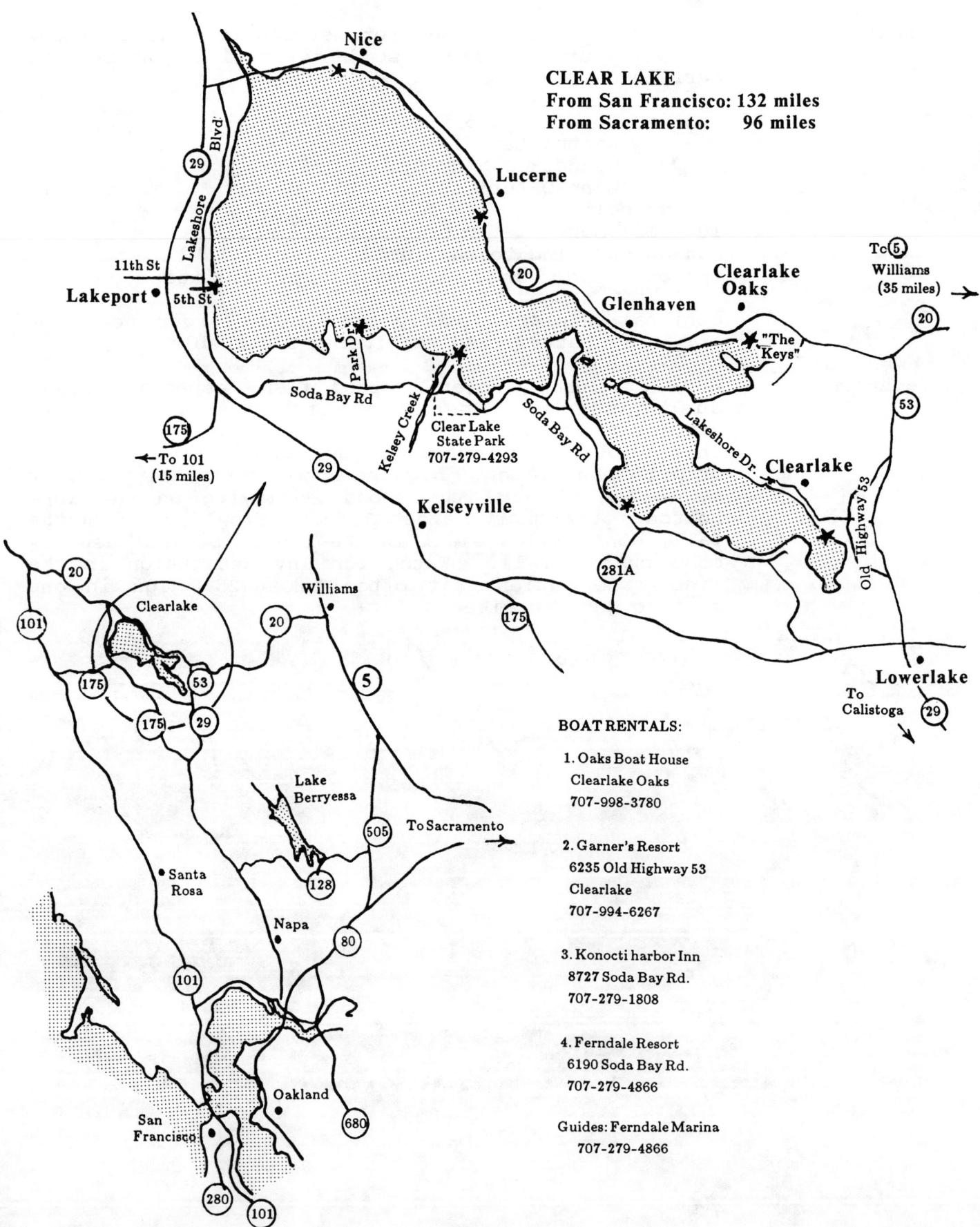

**CLEAR LAKE**
From San Francisco: 132 miles
From Sacramento: 96 miles

**BOAT RENTALS:**

1. Oaks Boat House
   Clearlake Oaks
   707-998-3780

2. Garner's Resort
   6235 Old Highway 53
   Clearlake
   707-994-6267

3. Konocti harbor Inn
   8727 Soda Bay Rd.
   707-279-1808

4. Ferndale Resort
   6190 Soda Bay Rd.
   707-279-4866

Guides: Ferndale Marina
707-279-4866

BASS, LARGEMOUTH 59

# NORTHERN CALIFORNIA BASS LAKES

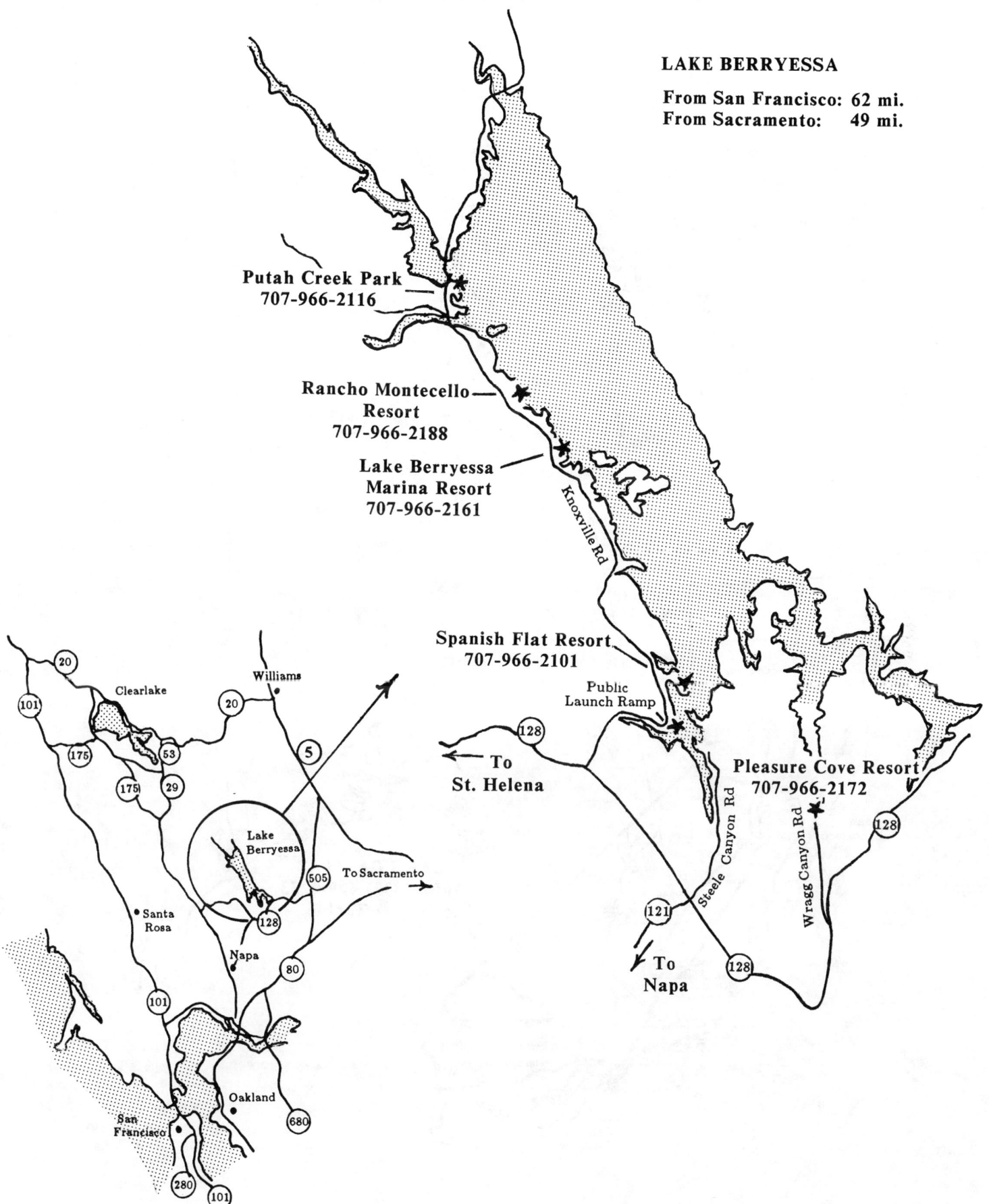

BASS, LARGEMOUTH 60

# SOUTHERN CALIFORNIA – BIG BASS LAKES, MAP 1
## Call about private boat type and size restrictions

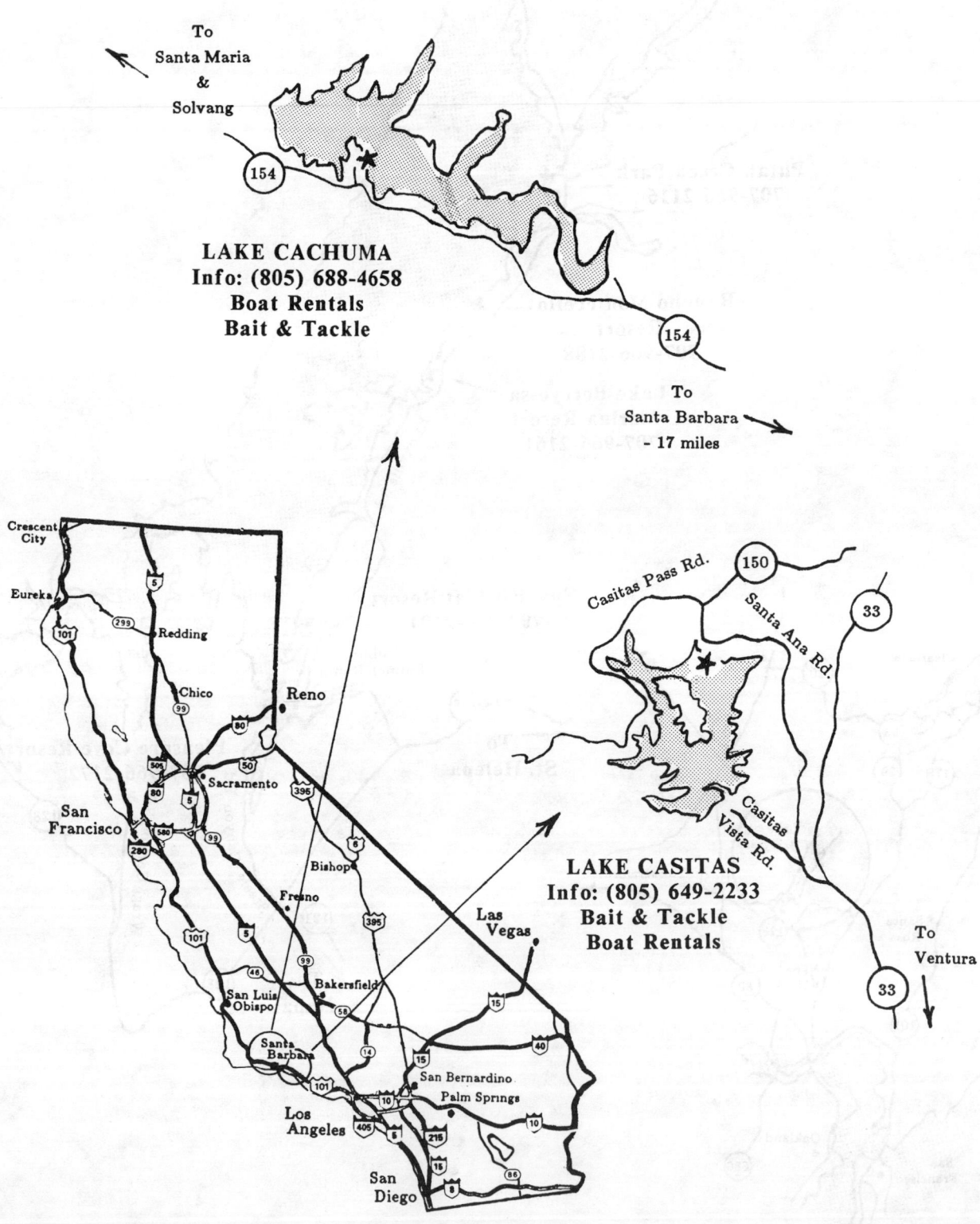

BASS, LARGEMOUTH 61

# SOUTHERN CALIFORNIA – BIG BASS LAKES, MAP 2
## Call about private boat type and size restrictions

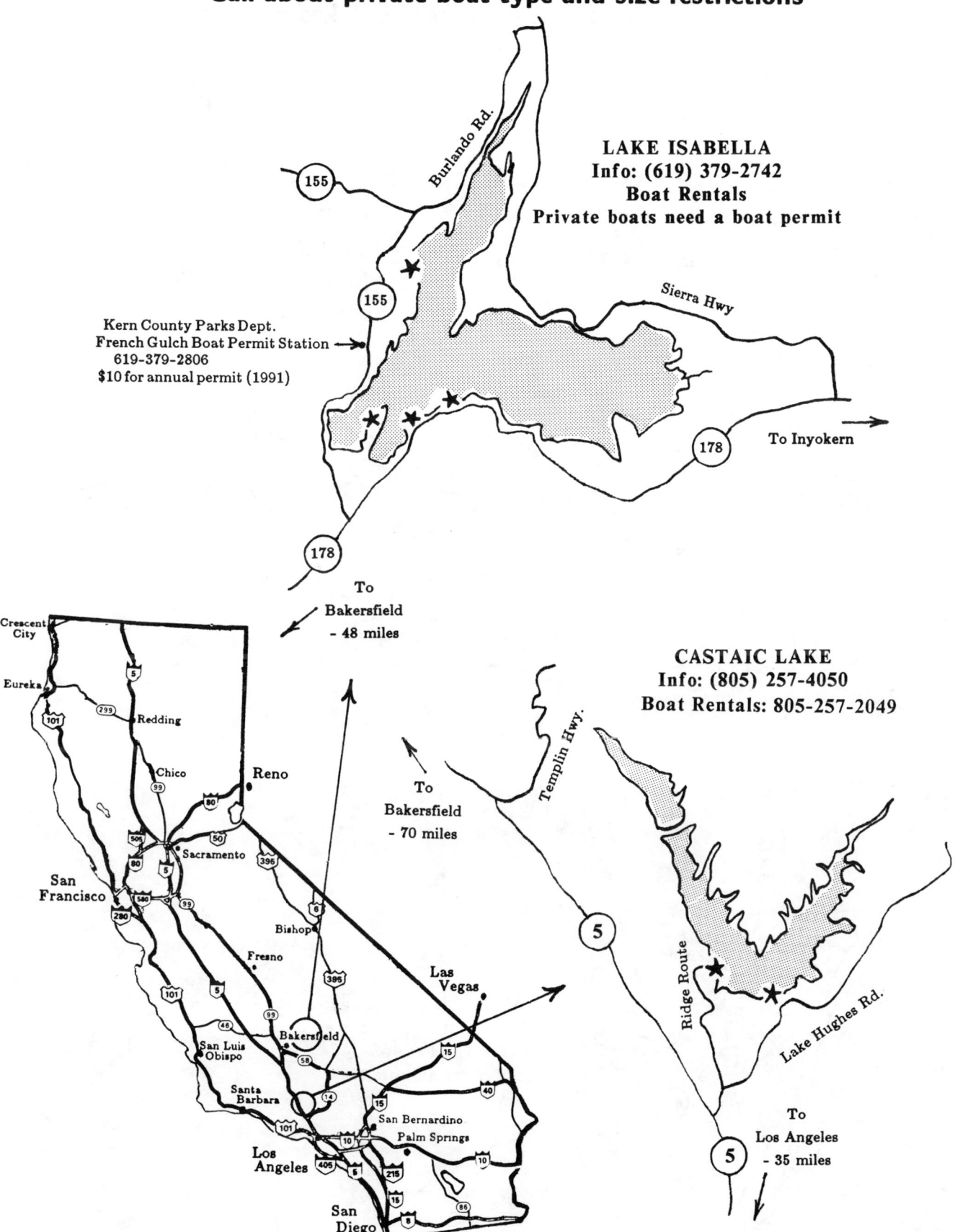

BASS, LARGEMOUTH 62

# SAN DIEGO AREA – BIG BASS LAKES, MAP 1

**Call about private boat type and size restrictions**
**Call about days/season lakes are open**
Boat Rentals, all Lakes: 619-390-0222

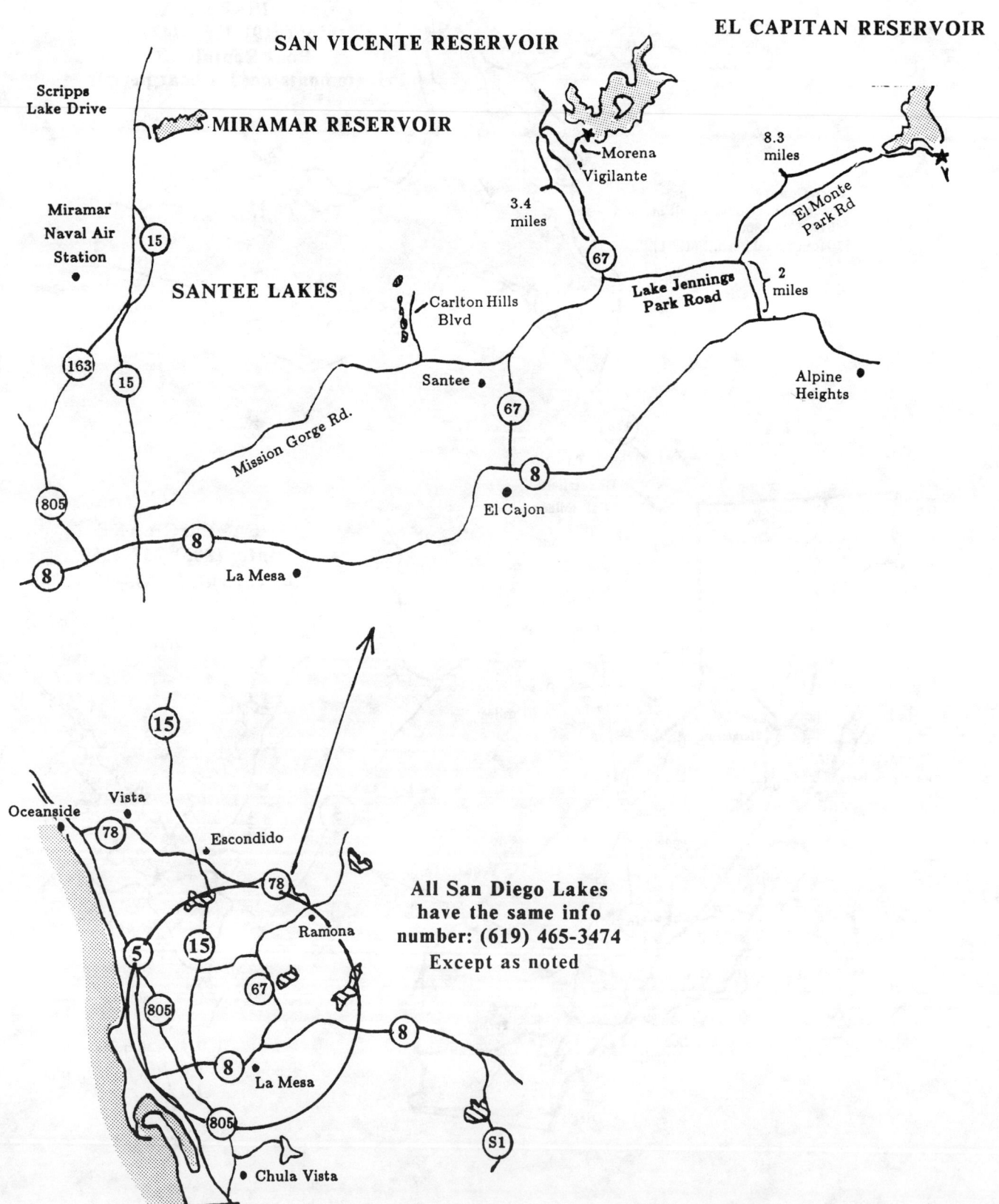

All San Diego Lakes have the same info number: (619) 465-3474 Except as noted

BASS, LARGEMOUTH 63

# SAN DIEGO AREA - BIG BASS LAKES, MAP 2

## Call about private boat type and size restrictions
## Call about days/season lakes are open

Boat Rentals, all Lakes: 619-390-0222

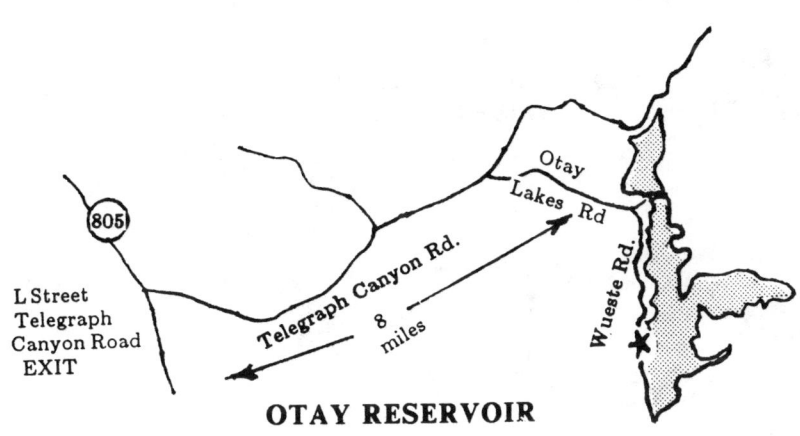

**OTAY RESERVOIR**

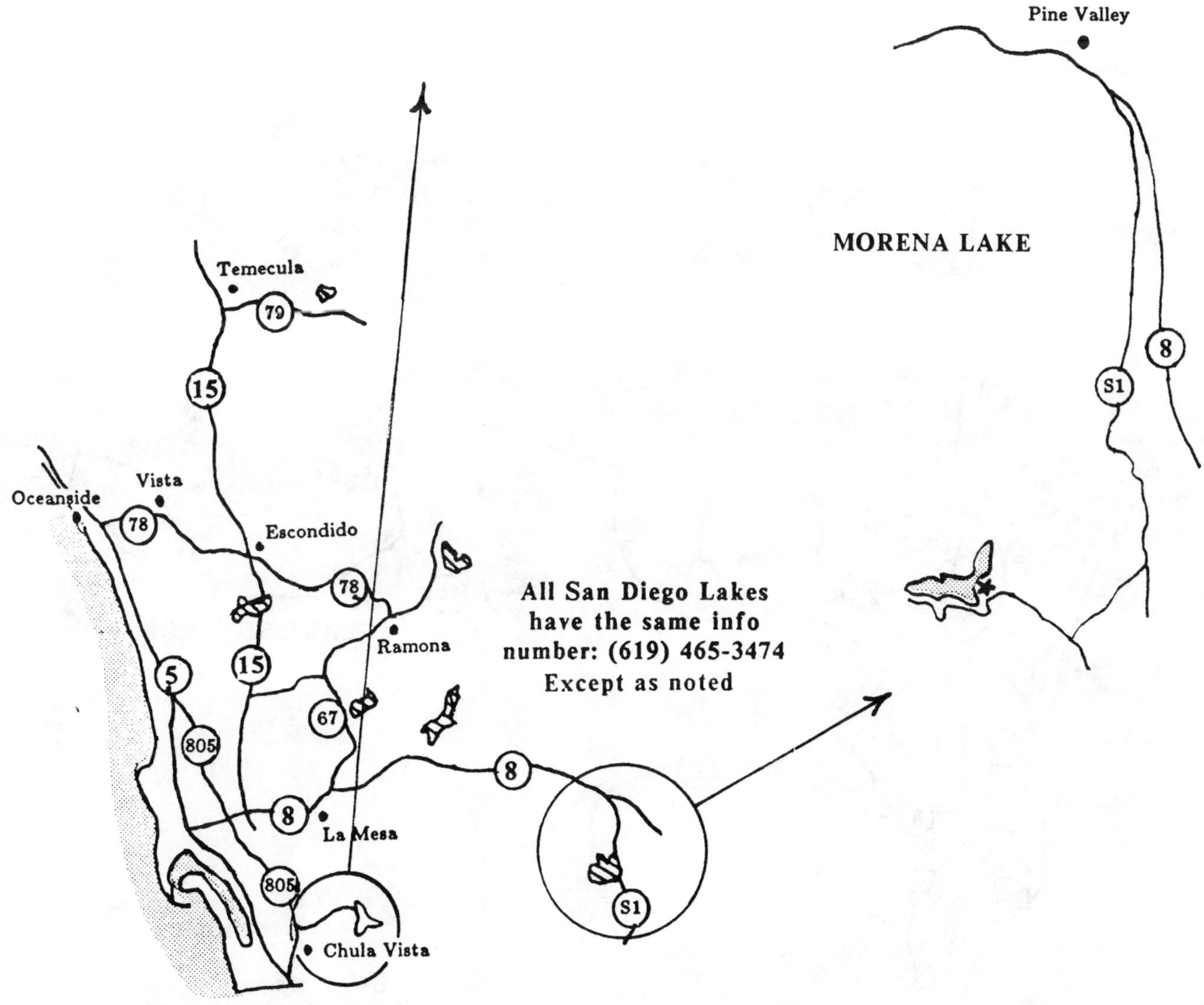

**MORENA LAKE**

All San Diego Lakes have the same info number: (619) 465-3474 Except as noted

BASS, LARGEMOUTH 64

# SAN DIEGO AREA – BIG BASS LAKES, MAP 3

**Call about private boat type and size restrictions**
**Call about days/season lakes are open**

General Info Number: (619) 465-3474
Boat Reservations: (619) 390-0222

**LAKE WOHLFORD**
Open: January to early Sept.
(619) 749-2661

**LAKE HODGES**

**LAKE HENSHAW**
Info: Lake Henshaw Resort
(619) 782-3501

**LAKE SUTHERLAND**

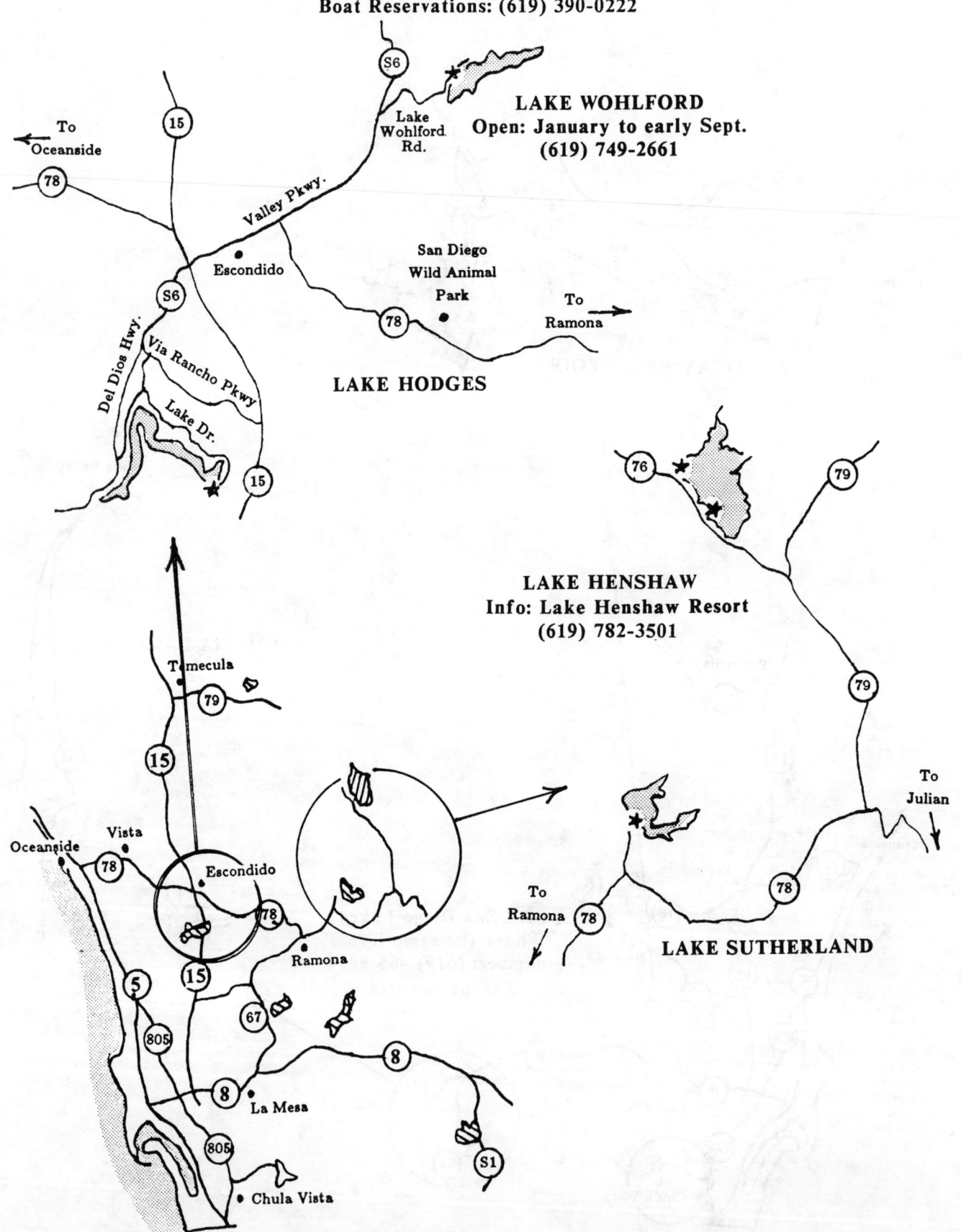

# BASS, LARGEMOUTH 65

San Diego Guide Jim Murphy

Don Iovino's Guide Service services the Los Angeles area Bass Lakes

## SAND BASS

**Where:** Hot Spots: Huntington Flats
Barn Kelp - off Oceanside
The Flats - off San Diego

**See Map**

Structure:

Southern California shallow ocean. Bass move from kelp beds to sandy bottom areas around May or June. Although most often found on the bottom, schools will suspend between the surface and the bottom. Finding the right depth is important. Note also that good Sand Bass fishing can be found in major So. Calif. harbors during the winter months.

**When:** May or June, through summer. Best: Mid-June through July. Fishing at night, off "twilight" party boats, is often productive.

**Bait/Lures:** Shiny or painted 1/2 to 3 oz. leadhead hook with plastic lure. Scampi, Scrounger, Worm King with cut squid sweetener. Good Colors: Light Green, Shrimp-colored Pink, Chartreuse, Rootbeer, Smoky, Motor Oil (See Calico Bass lure picture).

Live squid
Multiple dead squid, frozen squid on jig
Live anchovy
Brown bait

**Rig:** Light rig, less than 15# mono. Conventional free-spool reels work best for working suspended schools on the drop.

**Technique:** Before putting the plastic tail on the lead jig head, slide a small piece of squid up the hook, then put on the tail.

Schools of Sand Bass will suspend off the bottom. This is usually closer to the bottom than the surface. However, after an extended period of chumming, a school will often move closer to the surface and suspend under the boat.

For suspended fish, drop the lure/bait straight down to the right depth by freespooling. As the lure nears the fish-holding depth, use your thumb on the spool to slow the drop. The key to success is working the lure in the limited range of the suspended schools.

**The Law:** 12", 10 fish alone or in any combination with Calico (Kelp) Bass, or Spotted Bay Bass, (1990)
See also DFG ocean bag limits.

BASS, SAND 67

**Records:** State: 11 lbs. 4 oz., Imperial Beach, August 1986
IGFA: 8 lbs. 4 oz., Dana Point, Calif;1981

**Access:** See Map for landings and launch ramps.

Guide: Kit McNear, "El Bajo" Charters, Marina del Rey, 818-762-4806

Jim Murphy, San Diego - See Bay / Harbor Fishing Section.

**See Also:** Calico Bass, Halibut, Sheephead

**San Diego Guide Jim Murphy with a Sand Bass (left) and a Spotted Bay Bass (right)**

# SAND BASS - SOUTHERN CALIFORNIA

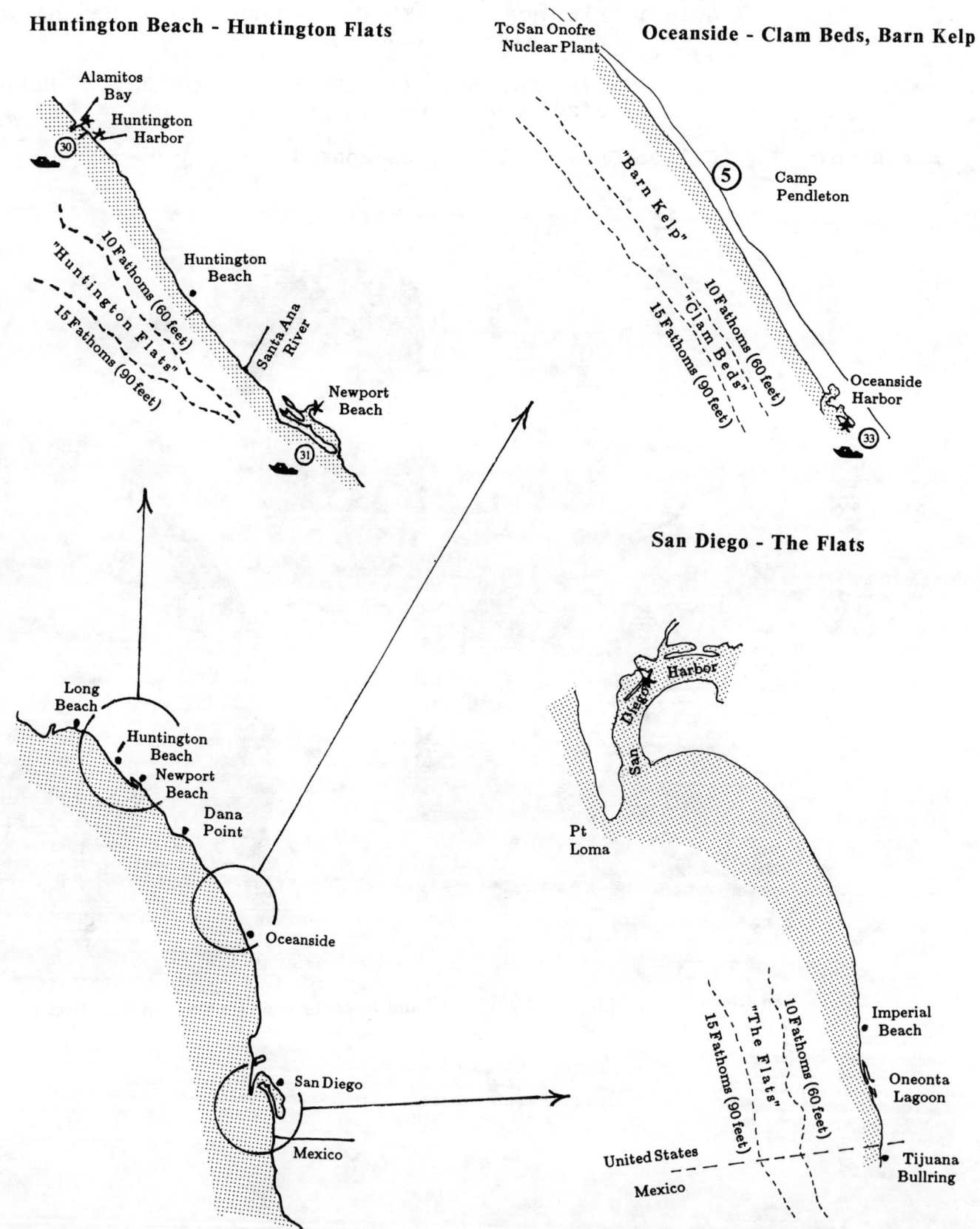

## SPOTTED BAY BASS:

**Where:**  Structure:
- Bays of Southern California
- Always on the bottom; near dock pilings, underneath and between narrowly spaced docks.
- In the shade.
- Isolated rocky areas near the above structure.
- Near jetties, dropoffs, over clam beds

Hot Spots: (**See Bay / Harbor Section** for detailed maps)

- Alamitos Bay
- Newport Bay
- Anaheim Bay / Huntington Harbor
- San Diego Bay

Note also that very good Spotted Bay Bass fishing can be had in Baja along the northern inshore reaches of the Sea of Cortez.

**When:** During large water movement between large high and low tides.
Best during spawn in May and June.

**Bait/Lures:** Small leadheads with plastic tail, small feather.
Colors: Light Green, Shrimp, Chartreuse, etc.
Small Worm King or Shakin Shad on 3/8 oz. leadhead.
Small Crankbaits: Hellbender, Bomber Model A.
Colors: All Chrome, Chrome with black back

See Bay / Harbor Fishing section for more detail and pictures.

**Rig:** Light bass casting rig - 5 1/2 foot graphite rod, light-weight casting reel, 4 - 6# mono.

**Technique:** Bounce the jig off the bottom while drifting slowly using the rod tip for action. Work the lure with the current if possible - cast upcurrent and work slowly back to boat. Watch the line for slight pickups. Feel the line for a slight increase in weight. Set the hook when in doubt. ALWAYS fish right on the bottom.

These are slow-growing fish in a limited fishery. Please practice catch and release using barbless hooks.

**The Law:** 12"; Limit: 10 alone or in combination with Calico (Kelp) Bass or Sand Bass (1990). See also DFG ocean bag limits.

BASS, SPOTTED BAY 70

**Access:** Launch Ramps & Boat Rentals:

Guide: Mike Gardner
714-993-2328

See Bay / Harbor Section for detailed maps of Hotspots listed above and available boat rentals.

**See Also:** Bay/Harbor Fishing for Croaker, Halibut, Calico Bass, Sand Bass, Halibut, Jack Smelt

**Guide Mike Gardner holding two Spotted Bay Bass**

## STRIPED BASS:

**General:** Striper populations have been severely reduced in many areas due to pressures on water quality and quantity. The California Striped Bass Association is fighting to preserve this excellent game fish and the fishing fun it can provide. Join this beneficial organization.

    San Francisco Bay Area:    Stockton Area:
    3537 Hoover St.                    P.O. Box 7922
    Redwood City, CA 94063     Stockton, CA 95207

**Where:** See below, Striper Cycle diagram and Fishing Calendar

Structure:

Stripers lie in wait to ambush bait fish at points and in corners of small inlets and bays.
They congregate near dam spillways. They wait at trout stocking areas
In the late summer, they surface feed in the early morning, especially on the Colorado river system.

Hot Spots: See following pages & Calendar:

Striper Calendar................ page 73
California Lakes ............... page 79
San Francisco/Sacramento River .. page 83
Colorado River System .......... page 90

**When:** Stripers are nocturnal feeders. The best bite is in the early morning and dusk hours. Generally the bite is off when the sun hits the water. The fish move deeper during the day or congregate at spillways on the edge of the white water. Top-water, boil boiling is limited to late summer, early fall, morning hours.

**Bait/Lures:** Depends on season and area. See below.

**Rig:** Depends on the season and area. See below.

**Technique:** Techniques are organized by;

Short Distance Casting .. pg. 75
Long Distance Casting ... pg. 76
Trolling ................ pg. 76
Bait Fishing ............ pg. 77

**The Law:** Limit is generally 2 fish with a minimum length of 18" but regulations vary widely by area. A Striped Bass stamp/fee is required. Also another stamp/fee is required for fishing the Colorado River and its reservoirs. The Colorado River has a 10 fish limit and no minimum size (1990). Silverwood, Pyramid, San Luis Forebay and O'Neill Forebays have a 5 fish limit and no minimum size (1990). See current regulations.

BASS, STRIPED   72
**Records:**    State: 65 lbs., San Joaquin River, May 1951
                IGFA: 78 lbs. 8 oz., New Jersey, 1982

**See Also:**   Other sport fish vary widely depending on location - see Hot Spots section.

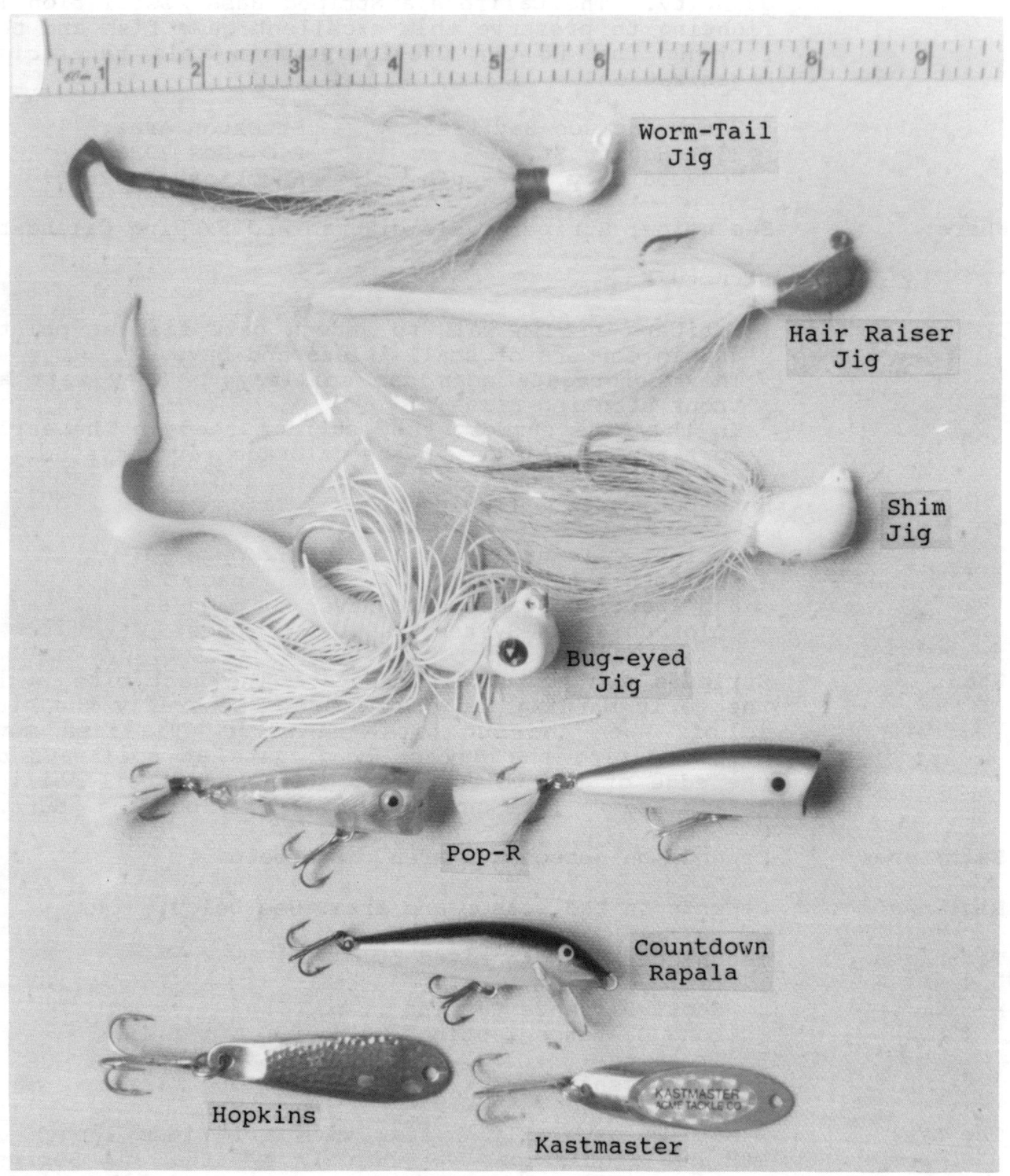

BASS, STRIPED 73

## STRIPER FISHING CALENDAR

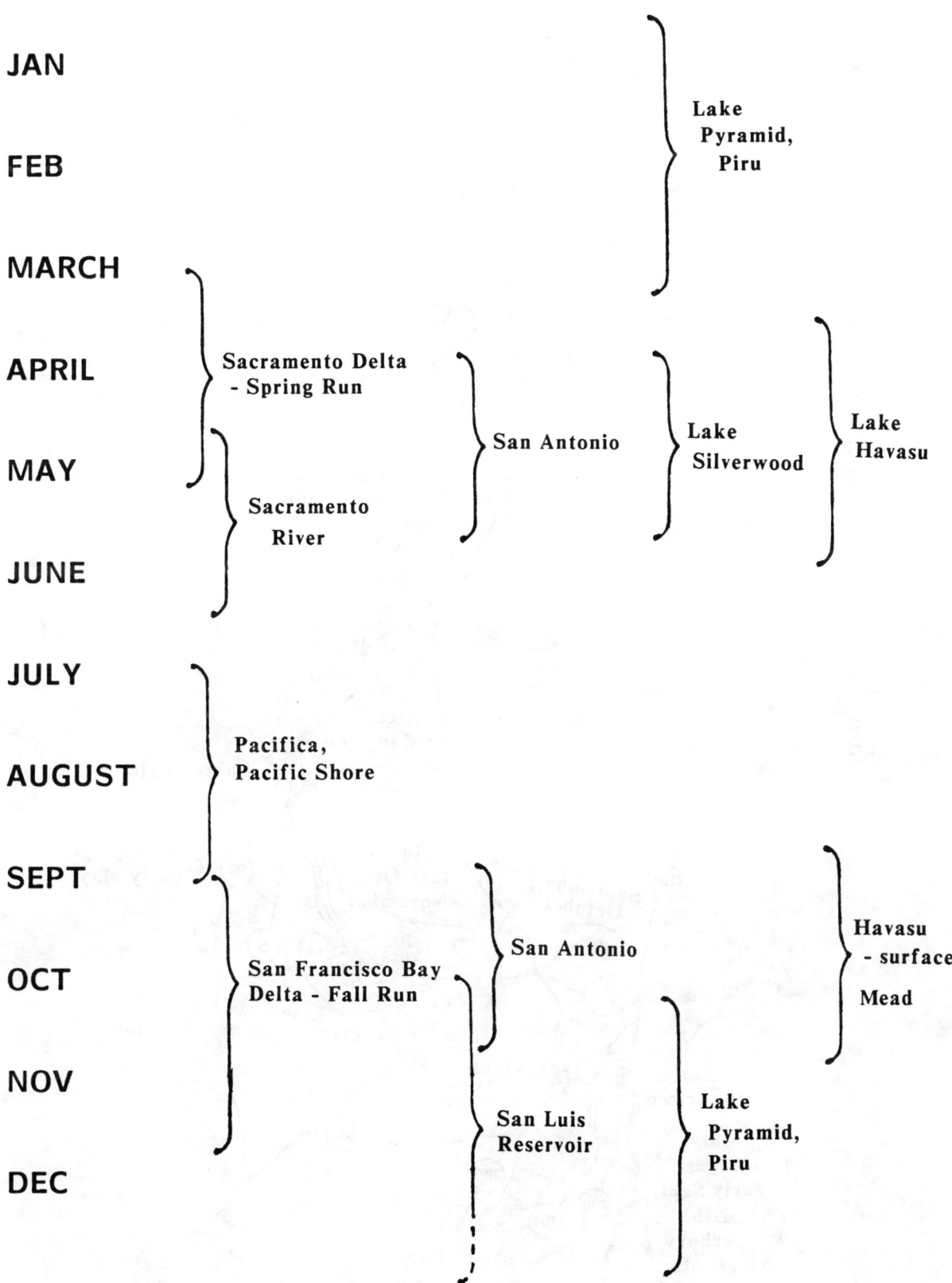

# STRIPER CYCLE
## San Francisco Bay / Sacramento River Systems

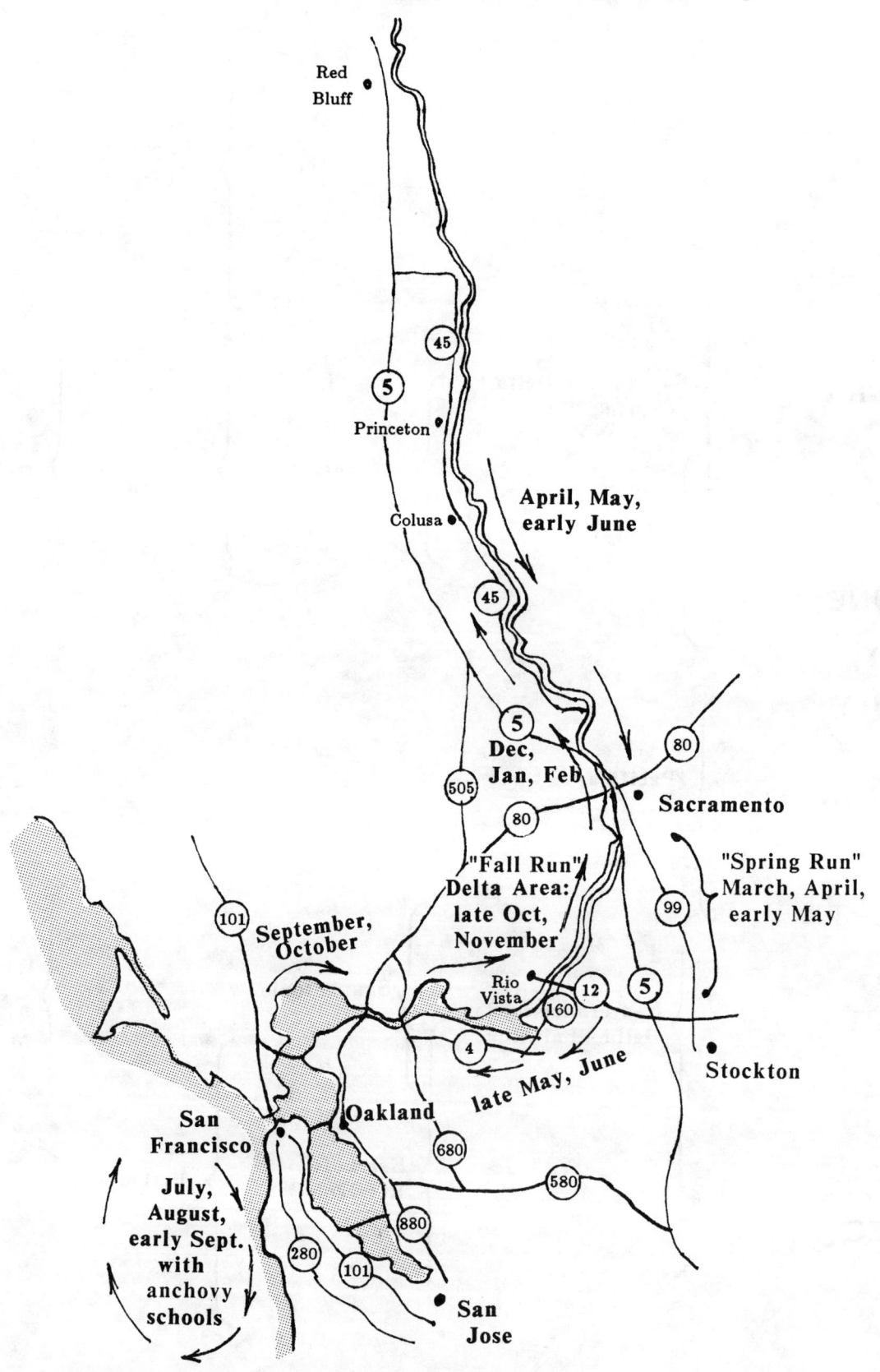

**STRIPED BASS - RIG:**

---
SHORT DISTANCE CASTING
---

**Spinning Tackle:**

Rod: 6 - 7 1/2' for 3/8 - 1/2 lures

Reel: Daiwa RS1300
Daiwa RS1600

or

Comparable model - reel that can hold 200 yards of 6# mono.

**Casting Tackle** (especially for jigs and spoons)

Rod: Fenwick Triggerstik (HTC 695, for 12# - 17# mono) or comparable

Reel: Ambassadeur 5500C or comparable

Lures:

Surface conditions - fish boiling

When approaching boils, cut the motor at least 50 yards away from the fish. Position boat upwind of the fish and drift to the side of the fish.

NOTE: For surface lures, i.e. Zara Spooks, use a buffer knot or similar knot or split ring which allows unrestricted side-to-side motion.

Pop R's
Bomber Long "A"
Cotton Cordell "Spot" Shad
Cotton Cordell Red Fin naturalized rainbow
Pencil Poppers, Rainbow trout, colored, red and white,
Zara Spook, Sassy Shad.
Large jointed Rapalas

Below surface conditions - shallow

Shallow running Rebel minnows, 4 1/2" - 7"

Cordell Spots, Kastmaster jigs (1/4 - 1/2 oz.), Hair Raisers (3/8 - 1/2 oz.), Pet Spoons, Hopkins Spoons, Shad Rap, Rapala - Silver & Black

**Techniques - SHORT DISTANCE CASTING** continued:

>Later in the day, fish are deeper;
>
>>Lunker Lures
>>deep spoons
>>1/2 - 5/8 oz. jigs or Rubber Trout
>>Leadhead jigs - with bucktails and/or long plastic tails. White and red, yellow and red, black

---
**LONG-DISTANCE CASTING**

---

Dam spillways. Spillways are off-limits, so you need to cast 100 - 125+ yards to reach fish holding areas.

Example: Davis Dam

Also distance casting is required for ocean surf fishing, i.e. San Francisco, Pacifica Shore starting mid-July through August, and also in the evening.

**Rig:** SEE DIAGRAM, STRIPER-1

>Ocean surf fishing rig - 8-10' rod
>15 - 25# mono
>Spoons are 3 - 4 1/2 oz.

**Lures:** See Picture

>Colors: In general shad colors, black & blue-backed with chrome or silver bodies. Use Rainbow Trout colors in trout lakes, especially during stocking activities.

**Techniques:** (long-distance casting)

>Fish are usually on the bottom. After cast, retrieve slowly until lure sinks to bottom. If fishing from shore, reel fast near shore to avoid rocks. If you are not snagging rocks occasionally you are not deep enough.

---
**TROLLING**

---

Trolling is often used to locate Striper schools followed by casting lures or jigs or bait fishing.

**Techniques - TROLLING** continued:

Trolling techniques are more effective when fish are near the surface - in the dark early morning or late afternoon hours. Stripers will move deeper, and into holes as the day gets brighter.

In areas affected by tidal action, Stripers tend to be closer to the surface during slow tidal movement (peak and bottom of tides), moving deeper, toward the bottom at peak tidal movements (mid-points between high and low tides).

Troll lure 40 to 50 feet behind boat.

**Bait/Lures:**

   Bomber Long "A", 16A, 25A
   Blue-backed Rebel, single hook
   Broken-backed Rebel
   Bucktail jig and spreader
   Leadhead jigs with bucktails and/or
      plastic tails
   White bucktails trolled fast with an
      intermittent side pull.
   Rebel on wire spreader with Bug-eyed jig
   Rebel on spreader with Hair Raiser jig

------------------
**BAIT FISHING**
------------------

**Rig:** SEE DIAGRAM

**Bait/Lures:**

   Anchovies, mudsuckers, gobeys, bullheads - Staghorn Sculpin. With bullheads, you should cut off the sharp spines on the gill covers to make it more edible to the Striper.

   Fresh water - anchovies, shad, sardines, gobeys on the Sacramento river.

   Also, mudsuckers, pile worms, mackerel, bloodworms, and grass shrimp.

On Lakes, locate shad schools and jig fish with a leadhead (Hair Raiser) or Hopkins spoon bounced along the bottom or fish bait 3 turns off the bottom with a sliding sinker rig.

**Techniques - BAIT FISHING** continued:

Bait fishing is especially effective for reaching the bottom of holes where stripers hold out during bright, daylight hours.

In areas affected by tidal forces, bottom bait techniques work better during the strong water movements that cause the fish to hunker down near the bottom.

Still Fishing "Balance Bar" Technique:

A Striped Bass will quickly drop a bait if it feels any resistance or drag. The balanced bar technique is used to balance the rod and reel so that when the fish picks up the bait, the balanced rod tips forward easily, releasing the tension on the bait. The angler must then quickly and carefully pick up the rod while lowering the rod tip, put the reel in freespool, and very gently thumb the outgoing line until the fish has moved 10 to 20 feet and has taken the bait. Finally, the reel is engaged and the line allowed to straighten out and tighten before setting the hook.

BASS, STRIPED 79
Lakes

**WHERE - CALIFORNIA LAKES:**

| | |
|---|---|
| **Where/When:** | Lake Silverwood - **See Map**<br>San Bernardino County<br>(near Highway I15) |
| | April to June: |
| | a. At the spillway - the aqueduct inlet. Long distance casting from boats with homemade lures made from 3 oz. torpedo sinkers painted white, with split rings at both ends and a 4/0 hook on one split ring. Note that currently a double boom line makes casting to the spillway infeasible.<br>b. The rock quarry<br>c. Casting from shore at corners of the dam |
| | October/November - surface action, Cleghorn Canyon and Miller Canyon near outlet towers. Short-distance casting. |
| | During winter trout plants, Cleghorn Canyon or around marina. Short-distance casting lures such as Silverwood Special - leadhead, rubber trout. |
| **Bait/Lures:** | Anchovies work best fished on the bottom during the day. Lures are more effective during first hours of dawn or last hours of dusk. |
| **Rig:** | See "long-distance casting" in previous section.<br>For surface, boiling action see "short-distance" section.<br>Bait fishing with anchovies |
| **Info:** | Marina - 619-389-2320 |
| **Access:** | Guide: Max's Guide Service, 619-247-8492 |

---

| | |
|---|---|
| **Where:** | Lake Piru -**See Map**<br>Los Angeles County<br>(Near Highway I5) |
| **When:** | December, January during trout plants |
| **Info:** | Marina - 805-521-1231 |

BASS, STRIPED   80
Lakes

**Where:**    Pyramid Lake - **See Map**
Los Angeles County
(near Highway I5)

a. Near marina - especially during trout stocking
b. The dam area
c. Spanish point - channel between the pumping station and the marina

**When:**    October, November through May
Day use only - opens at 6 am. daily

---

**Where:**    Lake San Antonio - **See Map**

a. North marina
b. South marina
c. Off land points

**When:**    May - June
Surface action late September to early October

---

**Where:**    San Luis Reservoir - **See Map**

a. Highway 152 causeway near rocky area
b. Below dam at O'Neill forebay under highway 152 bridge at deep channel. You can fish from shore here.
c. Boaters - troll at inlet on forebay's back side.

Bigger fish are typically deeper, 25 - 60 feet deep.

**When:**    March to May, Late September - November

**Technique:**    Bait fishing with minnows.

**Bait/Lures:**    Minnows

**Info:**    The Worm Hole, Morgan Hill, 408-779-2407
Pete's Sport Shop, Madera, 209-673-5951

# STRIPER LAKES - MAP 1

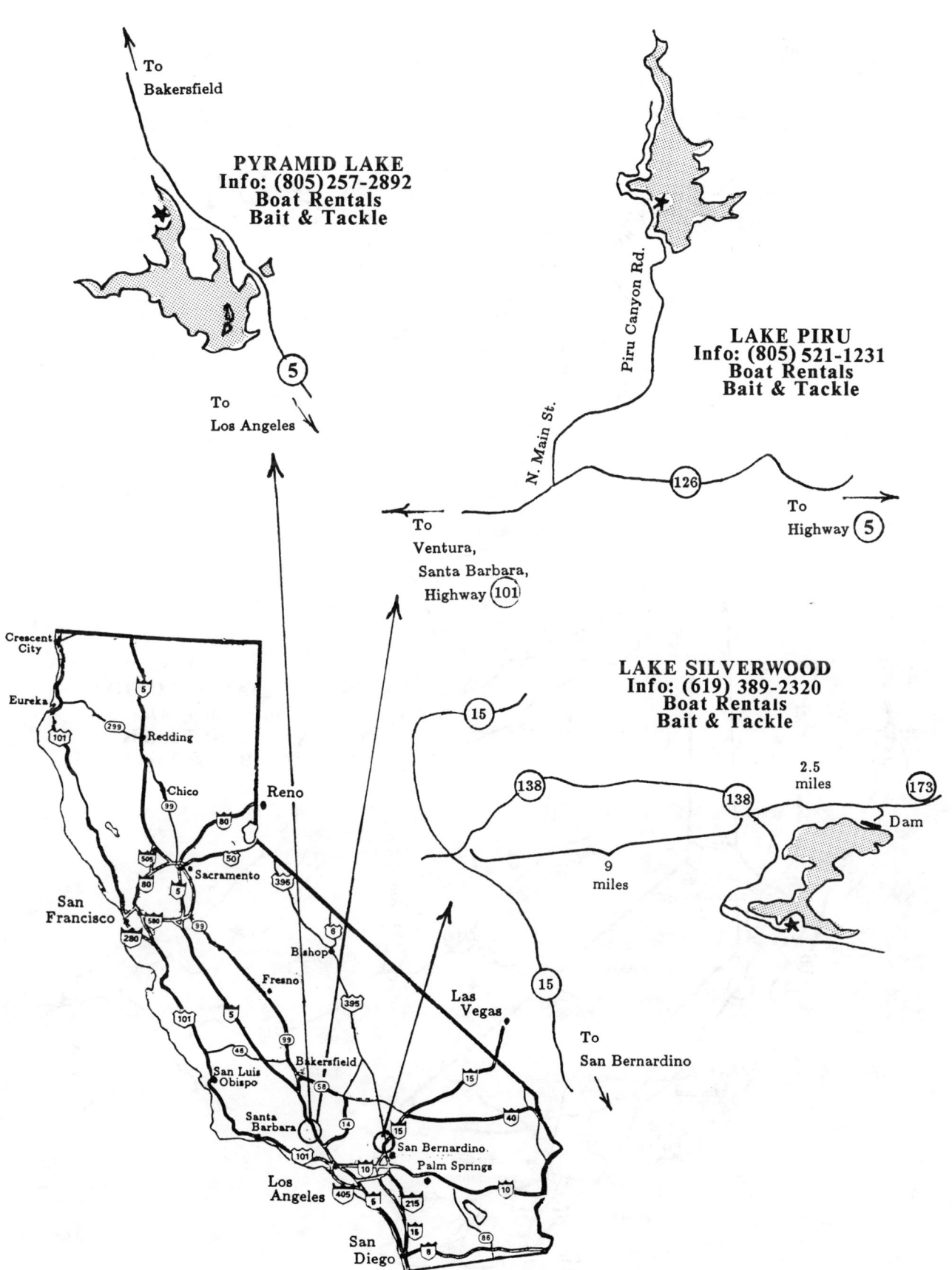

BASS, STRIPED
Lakes

# STRIPER LAKES - MAP 2

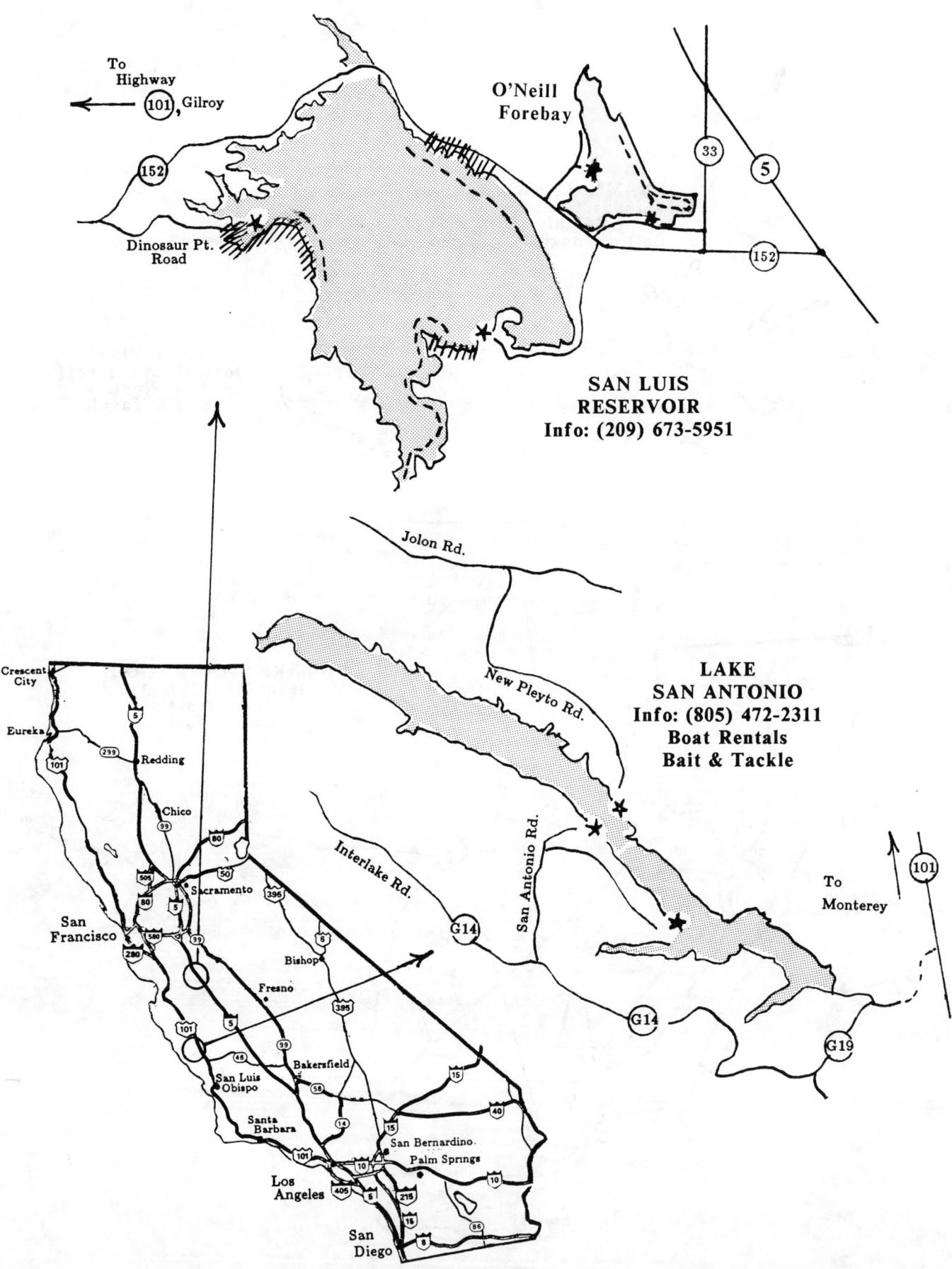

## STRIPED BASS - SAN FRANCISCO PENINSULA COASTLINE

**Where:** Golden Gate Bridge south to Half Moon Bay. Best from Thornton Beach to Montara (see map). Fish land points and corners of coves. The Golden Gate south tower, Seal Rocks, Bonito Cove during quarter moon phases - minimal tides but during the tidal movement.

Boat fishing is generally best but occasionally Stripers will be close enough to the shore, especially in the evening, for surf casters. Best surf fishing areas are located at the south end of Pacifica at Mussel Rock, Sharp Beach, off Sharp Park Golf Course, Rockaway Beach and off Linda Mar.

**When:** July, August, early September
- with influx of anchovy schools.

**Bait/Lures:** Surface Conditions:

Pencil Poppers

Near Surface:

Rebel Minnow, 5 1/2" to 7"
  Colors: Black & Silver
          Blue & Silver
Krocodile Spoons, 1 - 5 oz.
Hair Raiser Jigs & Shim Jigs

**Rig:** Fenwick 7' 1270S rod
Spinning Reel
3 feet of 80# shock leader

**Technique:** Watch for purple masses of anchovies on the surface. If they are balled up tightly, it's likely that feeding Stripers are nearby.

Work land points and corners of inlets using surface and subsurface lures.

When moving from place to place, slow troll a lure about 60' back of the boat.

With surface plugs DON'T strike as soon as the fish hits the lure. Wait briefly until you feel the weight on the line, then strike.

For schools suspended off the bottom, trying the following pumping chrome technique.

BASS, STRIPED 84
Ocean

## STRIPED BASS - SAN FRANCISCO PENINSULA COASTLINE

**Technique continued:**

    **See Striped Bass Rigs diagram.**

    Fish on the drift. Cast close to the structure and let rig sink to below level of suspended school. Start a slow, rhythmic pump-and-retrieve. Try faster retrieve for a faster current. Watch others who are catching fish and imitate action and speed. A slight difference in action can have a big effect on results.

**Info:**     Call landings shown on map.

    Surf Fishing Info:

        Coastside No. 2, Pacifica, 415-359-9790

**See Also:**     Salmon

---

## STRIPED BASS - SAN FRANCISCO BAY

**Where:**     San Francisco Bay - **See Map**

    Structure:

        On flats - 3 to 10 ft. deep that are close to rocky areas/shorelines.
        Isolated offshore rocks
        Grass beds
        Dock pilings
        Coves, points swept by currents.

    Hot Spots:

        The Pumphouse to Buoy 9
        The flats off McNears Point
        San Quentin flats
        The Berkeley / Emeryville area

## BASS, STRIPED
### San Francisco Bay

Richmond-San Rafael bridge from west end at Pt. San Quentin to where bridge splits into 2 levels.
Berkeley Pier
Around pilings on east side of Treasure Is.
Alameda Rockwall
San Francisco Airport pilings.

For Launching Sites - see Sturgeon maps.

**When:** September, October, November

Quarter moon phases, minimal tides.

Fishing is usually better in clearer water conditions that precede winter storms and a few days after storm runoffs when waters clear.

**Rig:** Trolling rig, casting rig with,
- Rebel Fastrac or
- Bomber Long "A" or
- Cordell Spot
- Rat-L-Trap

or

Leadhead jigs with bucktails and/or long plastic tails or worm-tail jigs. Colors: white/red, black, yellow, yellow/red

**Technique:** Jigs - toss upcurrent from rocks or pilings. Let sink to bottom on a tight line. Retrieve at medium speed with current with slight pumping action of rod.

**Info:** Call landings shown on map. Sun Valley Bait, San Mateo, 415-343-4690 (recording)

**See Also:** Halibut, Sturgeon on the bottom.

## STRIPER FISHING - SAN FRANCISCO BAY & COAST

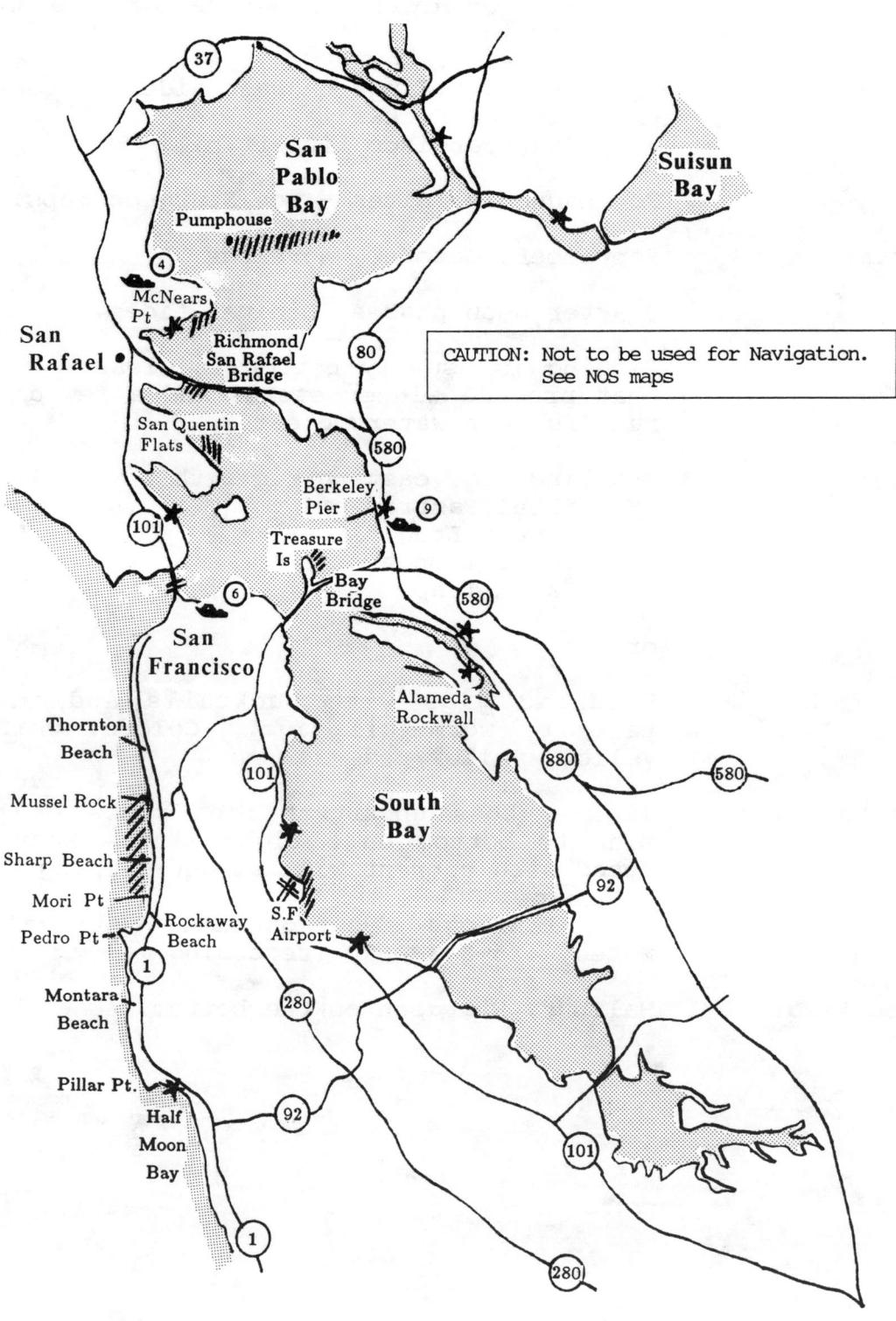

## STRIPED BASS - SACRAMENTO DELTA & RIVER

**Where:** Sacramento River Delta - from Collinsville to Freeport and Sacramento
Decker Island - where slough feeds into the river
Rio Vista bridge
Franks Tract
Mouth of Mokelumne River

For Freeport area map - see Shad section

**When:** Fall Run - mid-September to mid-November
Spring Run - April and May

**Technique:** Trolling or bait - Gobeys & Shad

**Info:** The Trap - 707-374-5554
Haps Bait - 707-374-2372

**Access:** Guides: Jay Sorensen, 209-478-6645
Jack Findleton, 916-487-3392
The Trap can also recommend local guides

Boat Rentals:

Korths Pirate's Lair
Mokelumne mouth
916-777-6464

Delta Bay Club
near Mokelumne
916-777-5588

Sherman Lake Marina
Sherman Is.
415-860-5104

Lloyd's Holiday Harbor
near Antioch Bridge
757-2346

Carol's Marina, near Bethel Is.
415-684-2803

**See Also:** Sturgeon.

---

**Where:** Sacramento River
- between Grimes and Colusa
Trolled lures on the bottom, near rocky, vertical shorelines.

**When:** April - May
Early mornings and at night - trolled lures
During the day - drifted bait on the bottom, especially at the mouths of creeks and agricultural inlets.

**Technique:** Troll 5 - 6", Rebels with long plastic lips
Colors: Black, Blue-backed with silver bodies
Cordell Redfin or Bomber Long "A"

Bait: Filleted Anchovies, Sardines

**Info:** Bert's Steelhead Marina, 916-458-2944

## STRIPER FISHING – SACRAMENTO DELTA

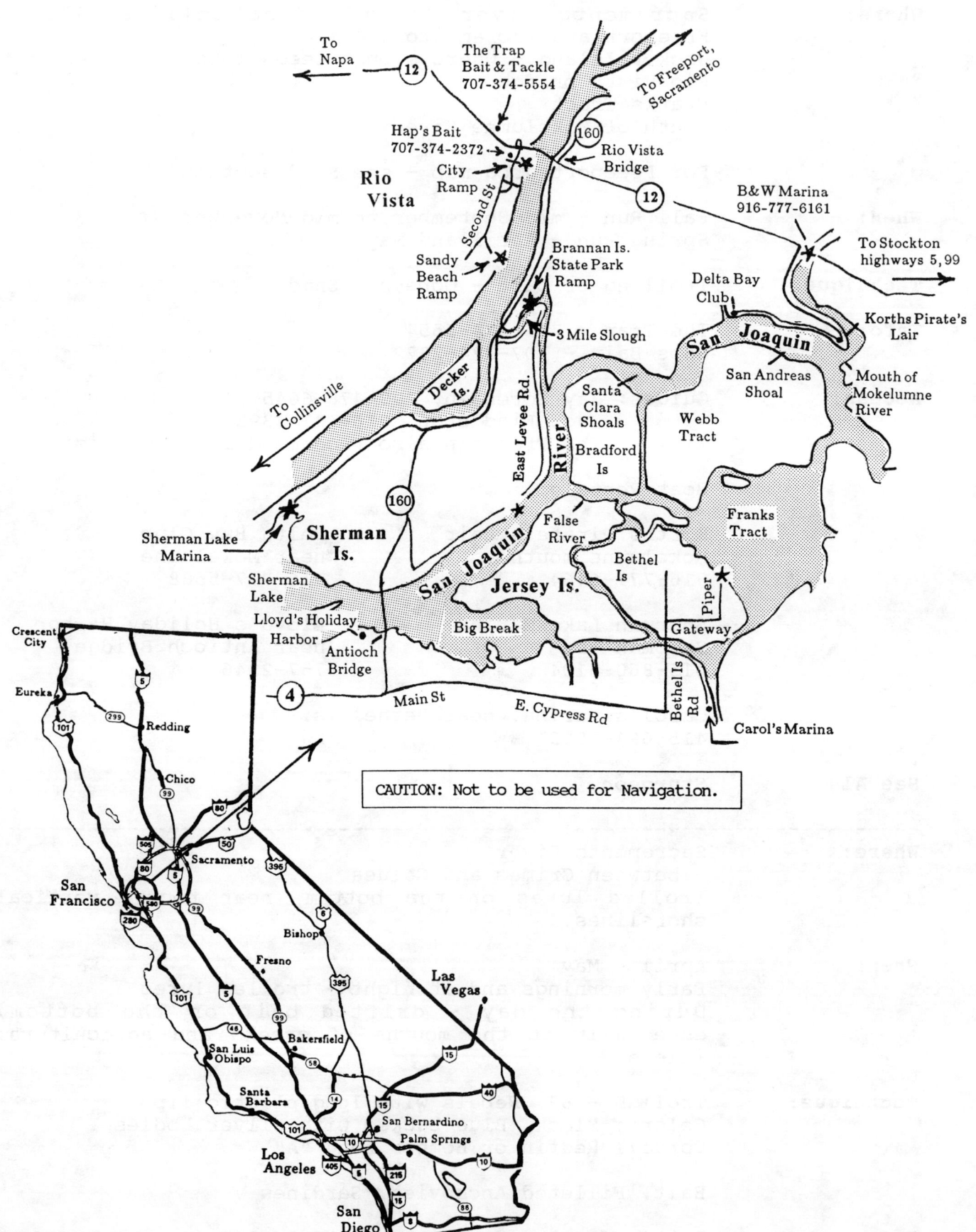

# STRIPER FISHING - SACRAMENTO RIVER

BASS, STRIPED
Colorado River

**Where:** All of the following areas are within 1 1/2 hours drive of Las Vegas, Nevada and Needles, California:

Lake Mead - Las Vegas Bay area, between Vegas Wash and Saddle Island, Crawdad Cove, Boxcar Cove, etc.
Lake Mohave - Cottonwood Cove area
- Willow Beach area

**When:** March - June
Late September, October, early November

**Technique:** Trolling and Bait
Lures: Bomber Long "A"

**Info:** Las Vegas Boat Harbor, Nevada (Mead), 702-565-9111
Willow Beach, Arizona (Mohave), 602-767-3311
Cottonwood Cove, Nevada (Mohave), 702-297-1464

**Access:** Guide: Karen Jones, 702-361-1972
Boat Rentals: Available at Las Vegas Boat Harbor and at Cottonwood Cove
All above resorts/marinas have launching facilities.

**See Also:** Largemouth Bass, Rainbow Trout

---

**Where:** Lake Havasu
Surface schooling from 6 am - 9 am
If the water temperature is greater than $65°$ - look for a surface bite; try drifting anchovies,
If the water temperature is less than $65°$ - try cut anchovies near the bottom.

**SEE MAP**

a. Behind pilot rock
b. Pittsburgh point
c. Around sand bar (caution - shallow!)
d. Mouth of river at Blankenship
e. In shallows, near Lake Havasu state park

**When:** May - June; October

**Technique:** Surface Action: Surface lures such as Pop R's, Zara Spook or Baby Spook; near surface, shad-colored crankbaits, or small spoons (i.e. Kastmasters, Hopkins).

Constantly scan the lake for feeding birds or splashes of white water caused by shad-busting Stripers. Take care in approaching surface boils not to scare the action away.

BASS, STRIPED 91
Colorado River

**Access:** Guides: Bob Lee, Lake Havasu City, 602-855-6744 or Parker, 602-669-8484; Bob Foell, Sandpoint Marina Tackle Shop (602) 855-0549

Lake Havasu boat campsites, Cattail Cove near Sandpoint. Look for picnic tables.

Boat Rentals:

Havasu Springs
  near Parker Dam
  602-667-3361

Havasu Marine Service
  Havasu Landing Resort,
  on Calif. side of lake
  619-858-4392

Fisherman's Bait & Tackle
  1509 El Camino Way
  Lake Havasu City
  602-855-3474

Lake Havasu Marina
  Lake Havasu City
  602-855-2159

Sandpoint Marina
  Hwy 95, 7 miles north of
  Parker Dam
  602-855-0549

**See Also:** Largemouth Bass, Channel Catfish

# BASS, STRIPED 92
## Colorado River

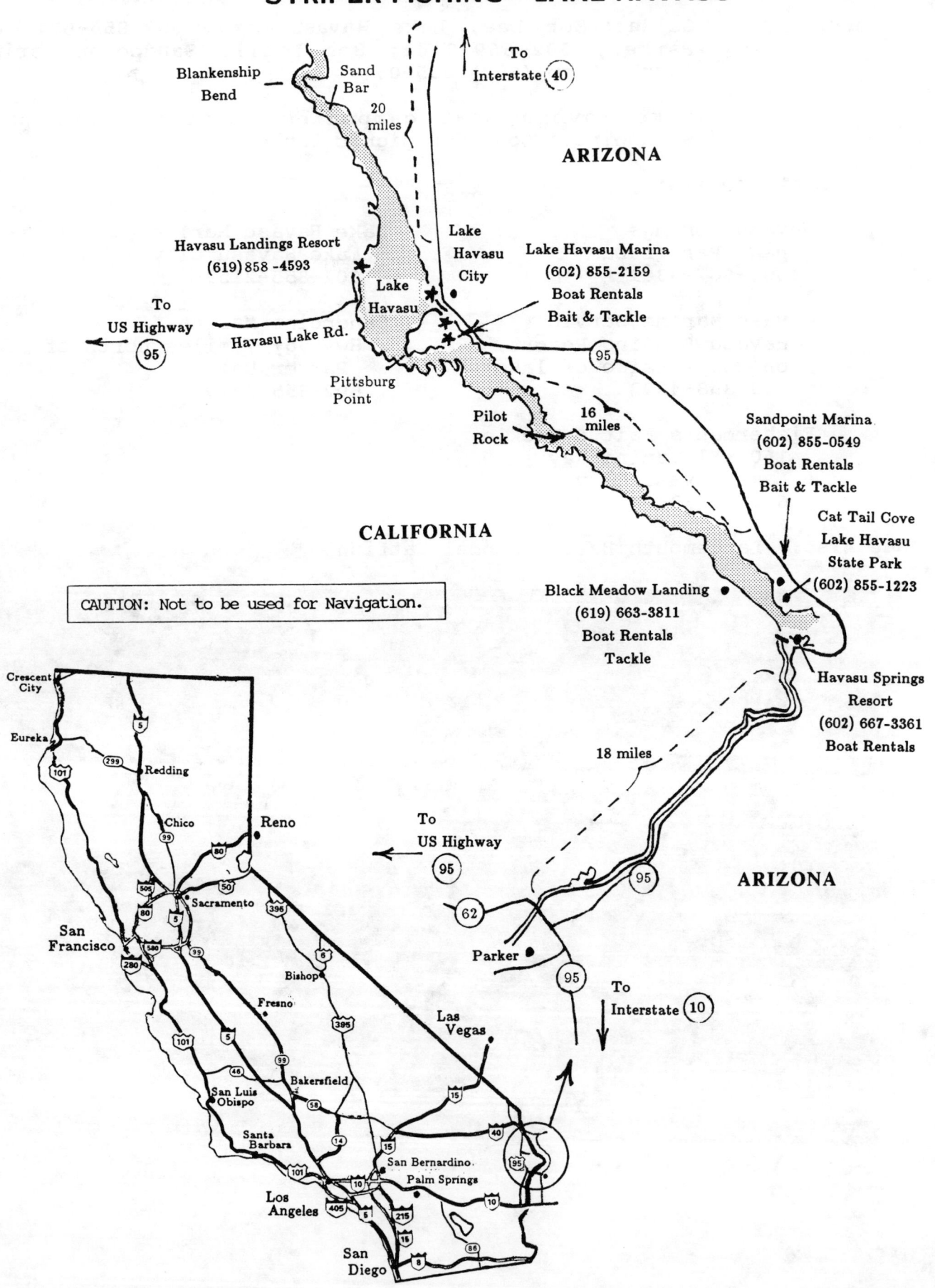

BASS, STRIPED 93

# STRIPED BASS RIGS

### Bait Rigs:
#### Bottom Fishing:

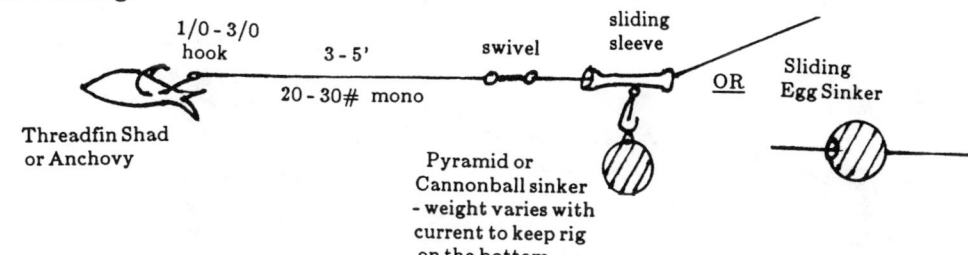

#### Special Bullhead Rigs:

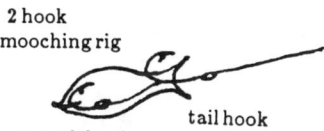 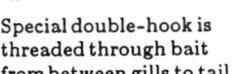

#### Drift Fishing (also for Halibut):

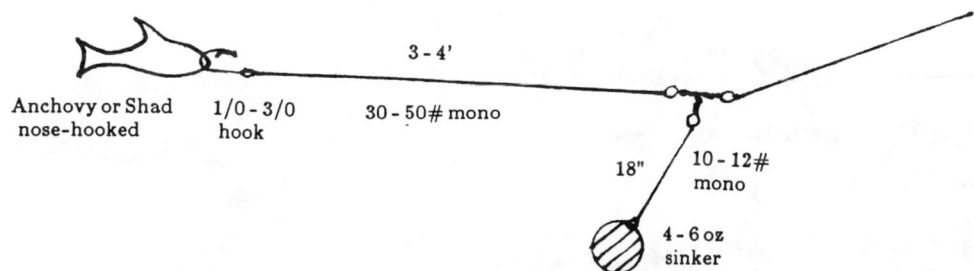

#### Pump & Retrieve:

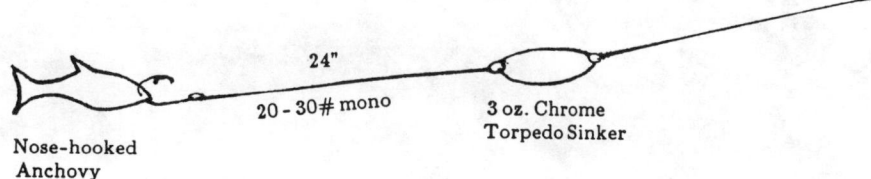

### Trolling / Casting

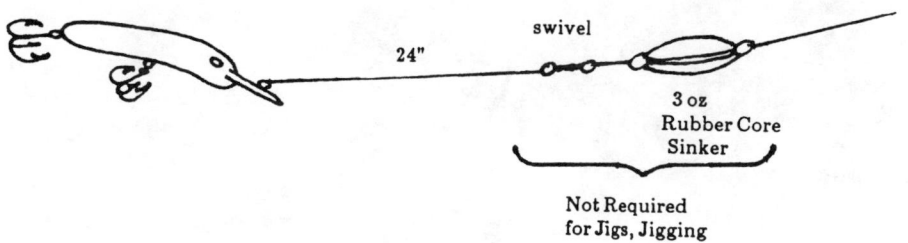

BASS, STRIPED 94

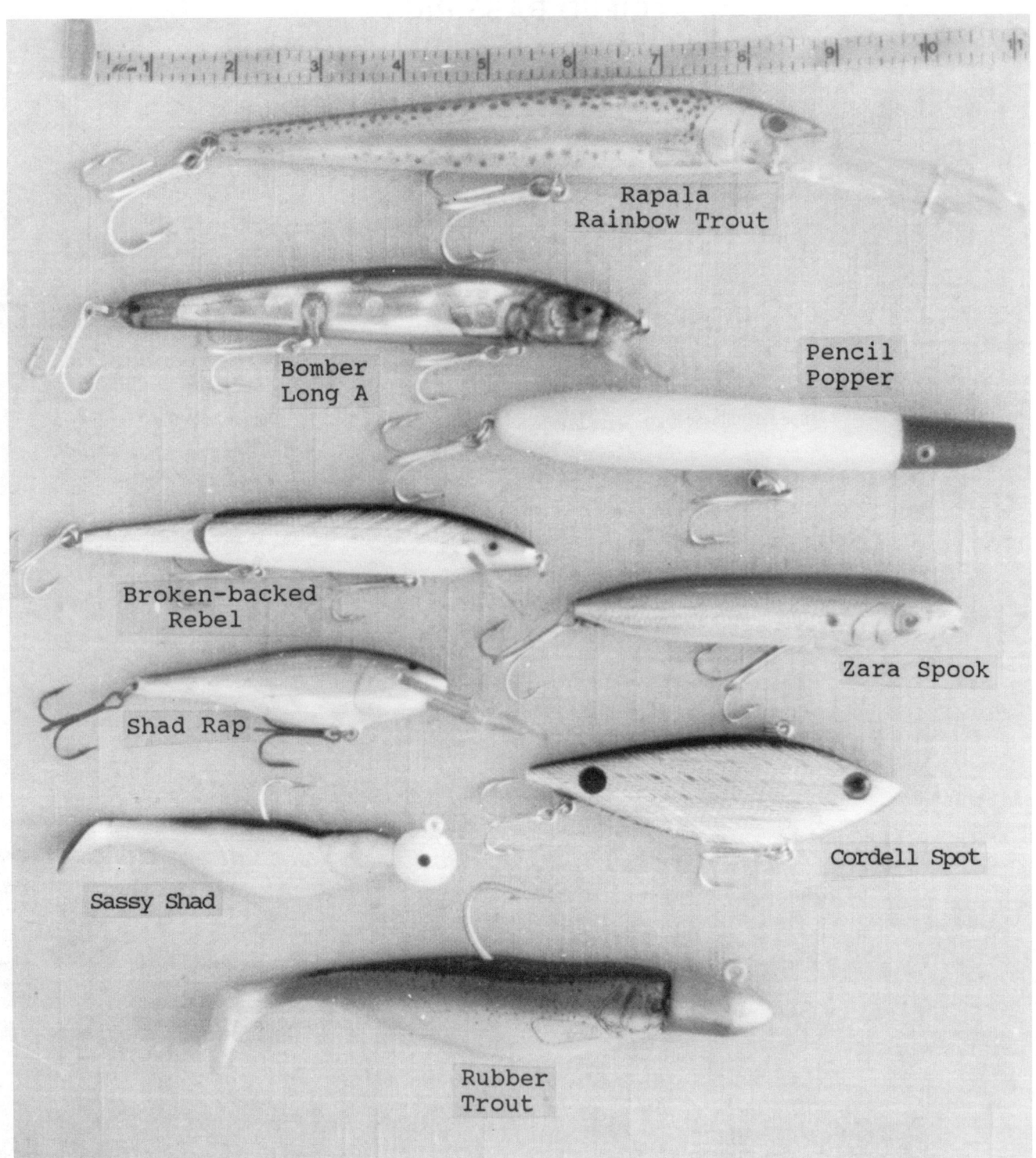

BASS, STRIPED 95

Max Moore of Max's Guide Service — Silverwood Lake

Delta Guide Jay Sorensen with his 52 lb. Striper

BASS, WHITE 96

**WHITE BASS:**

**Where:** Lake Nacimiento
The fish are with the shad schools, watch for bird feeding activity

**When/Where:** NOTE: CURRENT DROUGHT CONDITIONS (JAN. 91) MAKE ACCESS DIFFICULT.

SPAWN: March - early May
   Clear, warming water periods
   Warm days in the Narrows
   Where Las Tables narrows into Franklin
      Creek
   Spawning in the narrows at night

POST SPAWN: late May - early June
   Las Tables basin
   Shoreline across from Oak Shores
   Southwest shore of Snake Creek

Late September - early November
   From the gravel pits to mouth of Las Tables.

Early November - morning and evening
   Near the dam
   Off the peninsula from Snake & Dip creeks.
   Las Tables areas

**Rig:** Light to ultra-light spinning or casting.

**Bait/Lures:** Live shad, cut anchovies
To net your own shad, you must be on the water by the break of dawn.
Kastmaster, Roostertail, Feather jigs, Small Surface plugs, Crappie jigs, Sassy Shad
Colors: White, silver, chartreuse, yellow

**Technique:** Cast to surface feeding schools
Troll slowly with the lure well back from the boat.
Use light line, 2# - 4#, especially for surface bite.
Similar size fish school together.

**The Law:** No limit, size or number.
No live White Bass may be possessed or transported. These fish are aggressive and would endanger other fisheries if released in other lakes or streams.

**Records:** IGFA: 5 lbs. 14 oz., N. Carolina, 1986

**Info/Access:** Lake Nacimiento Resort, 805-238-3256
Has Rental Boats

Guide: Dan Frazier, 805-481-7539

**See Also:** Largemouth Bass

# WHITE BASS - LAKE NACIMIENTO

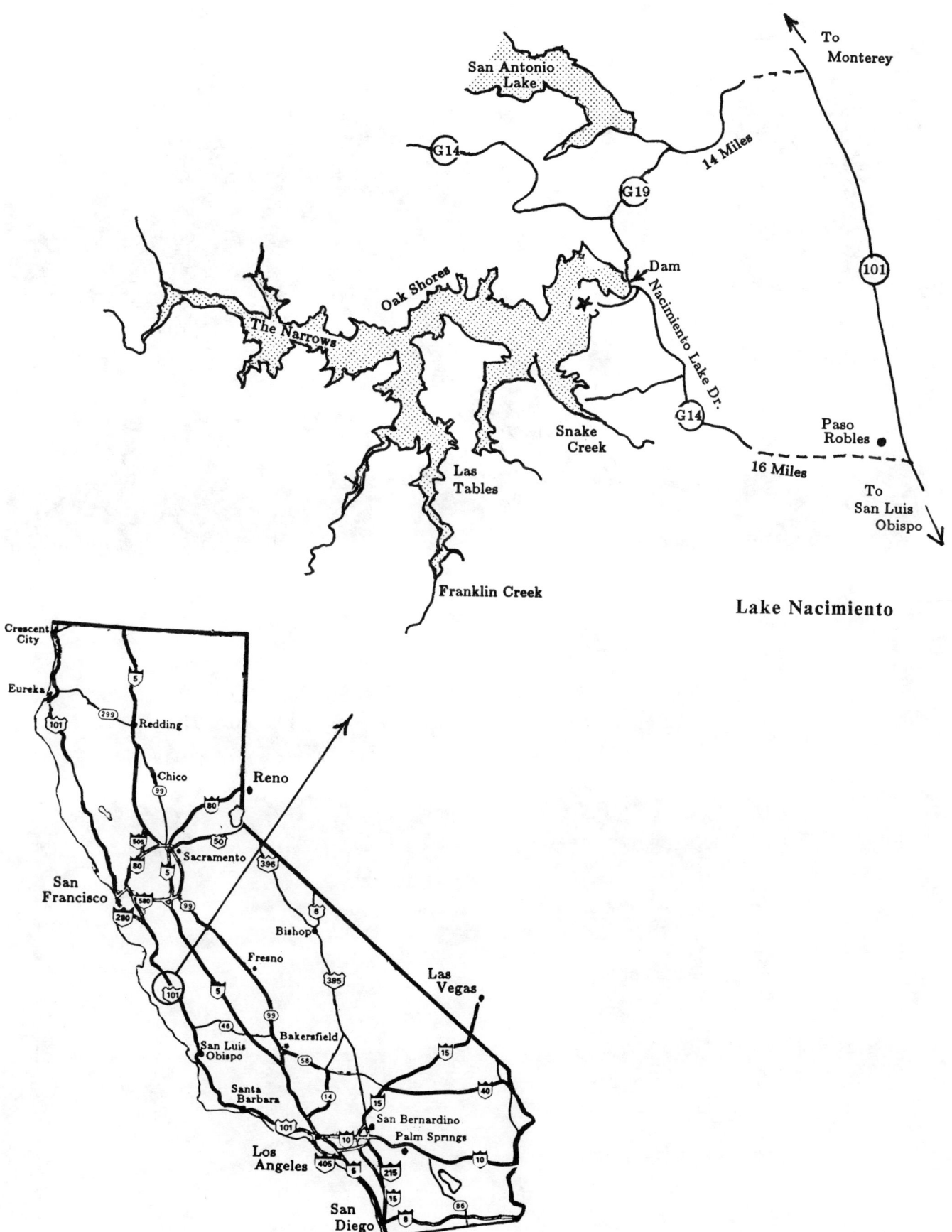

Lake Nacimiento

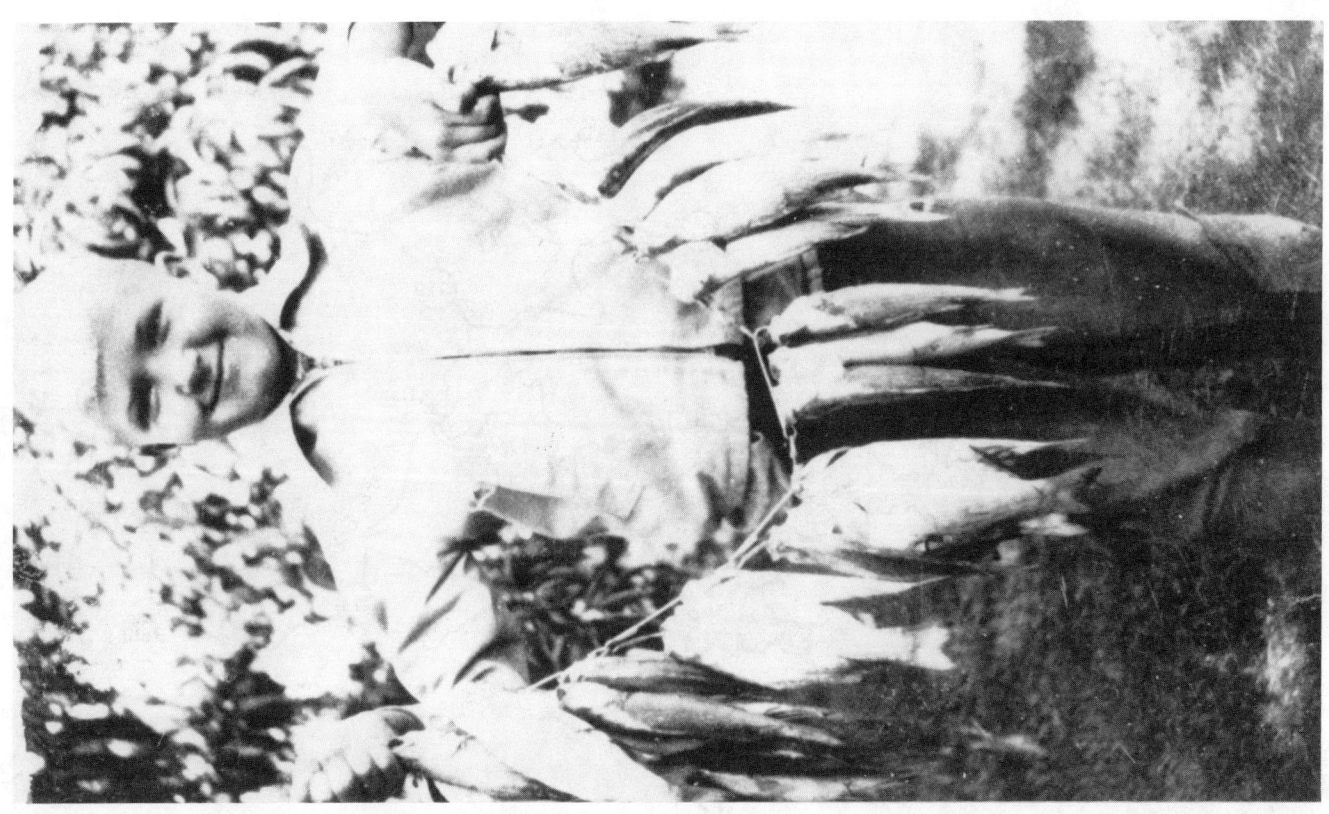

## BONITO, PACIFIC:

**Where:** Generally, wherever you can find schools of anchovies, Bonito will congregate. Specifically areas identified on the Prime Ocean Fishing Areas map are good spots for Bonito (See Barracuda section). Usually Bonito are not the targeted species but are caught while fishing for other game fish however Kings Harbor in Redondo Beach is known for its excellent Bonito fishing.

In the fall months, schools of large Bonito can be found generally within 3 miles off the coastline. These schools hold at greater depths than during the summer months. Thus some kind of device is necessary to get the lure down.

**When:** Almost anytime of the year, winter months are generally slower.
Big fish runs occur in the fall months, especially September and October.

**Bait/Lures:** Anchovies
Chrome spoons - Krocodiles
                - Hopkins
Feathers - long shank Malibu fly lure

**Rig:** Medium to light spinning or casting.

Bonito Jig or Feather on a 18" to 24" leader above a plastic "splasher" float. The plastic float when retrieved over the surface causes a splashing disturbance which attracts the Bonito.

**Technique:** In general, Bonito are quite easy to catch with a simple cast and retrieve rig using any number of lures.

**Misc.:** Bonito have a tendency to go soft quickly, so ice them down as soon as possible. Much of the bonito's dark meat can be eliminated by bleeding the fish immediately. Do this by cutting the fleshy portion under the head near where the gill covers come together while it is still alive. Remove all of the dark lateral meat and the skin when preparing the fillets.

**The Law:** Limit: 10, five can be under 24" length to the fork of the tail. Five must be longer than 24" See DFG regs. for more details.

**Records:** IGFA: 23 lbs. 8 oz., Seychelles Is., 1975

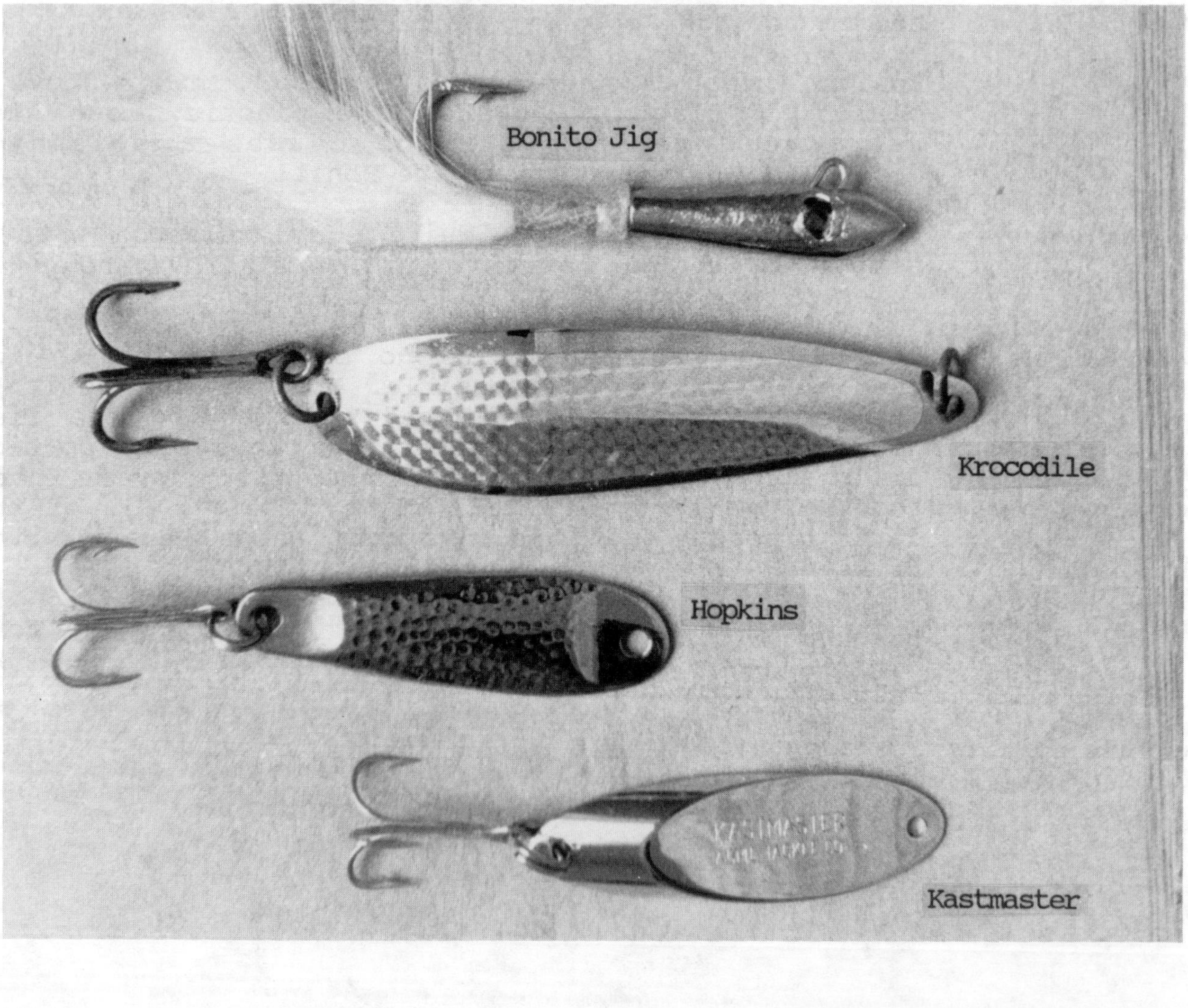
Bonito Jig
Krocodile
Hopkins
Kastmaster

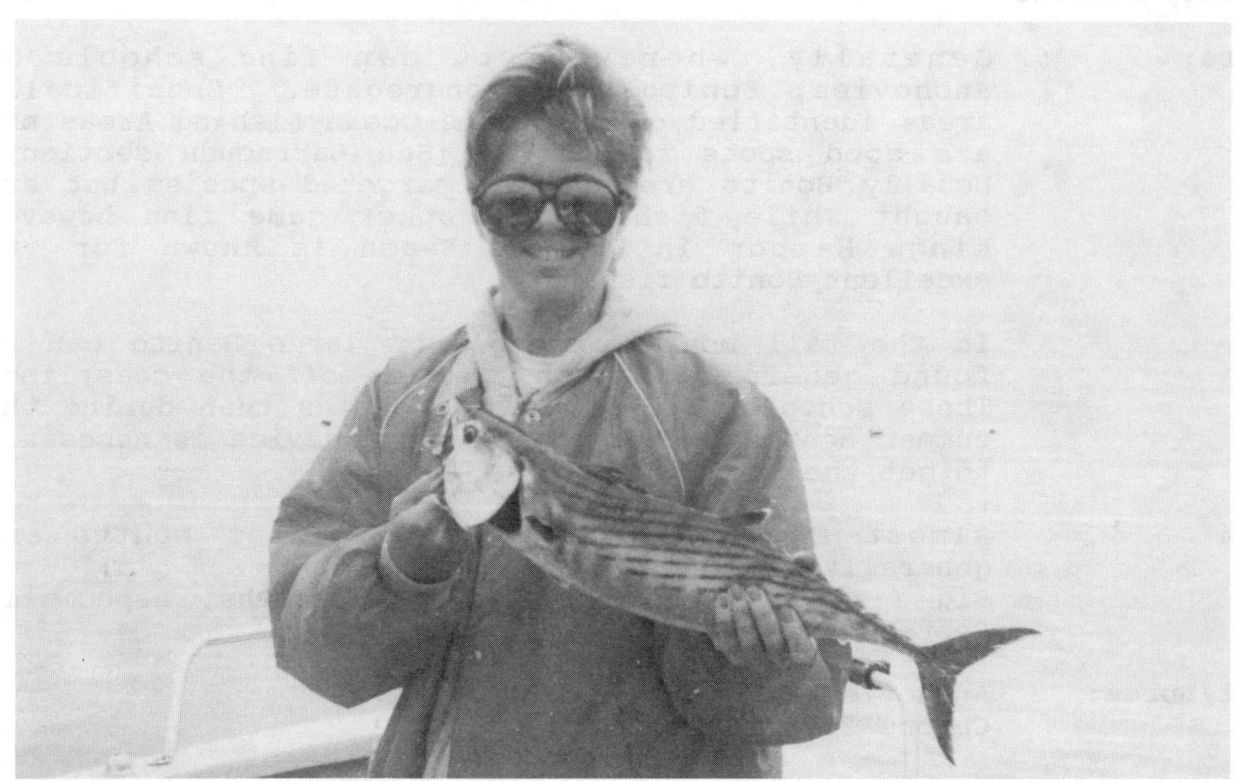

**CHANNEL CATFISH, BLUE CATFISH, WHITE CATFISH:**

**Where/When:** Catfish can be found in plentiful supplies at many California lakes and rivers. Amador, Clear, and Folsom lakes in northern California provide good fishing. The Feather, Sacramento River, Sacramento Delta and Colorado River are loaded with catfish. The smaller White Catfish is quite common in the Sacramento. In southern California, some of the more notable lakes are Lake Perris, Casitas Lake, Cachuma, Otay, San Vicente Reservoir, Corona, Santa Ana River Lakes, Irvine Lake. The map following shows only 3 top southern California catfishing lakes.

In lakes, catfishing is best at night during the warmer weather months, from June through early November. During the winter months, catfish hold in deep water - 50 to 80 feet deep and can be caught.

In Rivers, winter fishing for river catfish is best during the day in waters muddied by recent rains.

Structure:

During daylight hours, catfish hole up in holes or beneath structure such as fallen trees on the bottom of lakes and streams. In rivers, these honey holes are often at bends in the river.

At dusk, they become active and wander into the shallower waters to feed.

In Lakes, November through December the fish are deep during the day, 40 - 55'.

**Bait/Lures:** Cut mackerel, stinkbait, worms, chicken livers, fresh water clams (especially for White Catfish), live & dead minnows, Threadfin Shad, etc.

**Rig:** Sliding Sinker Rig

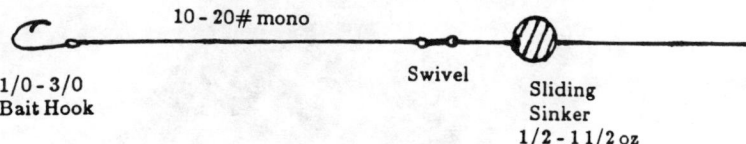

**Technique:** Lake fishing is normally best at night in the warmer late spring and summer months. Best technique is to fish the shallow water flats with cut bait on the bottom with a slip sinker rig.

Daytime: Fish hold in lake bottom depressions in the daytime sun.
Cast directly toward the sun.
Let rig settle to the bottom.
Retrieve very slowly - 1/2 foot per minute.

In late summer and early winter, at Lake Irvine,

CATFISH 102

**Technique continued:**

catfish will often boil on topwater shad, at night near the dam. These fish will hit flylined chunks of mackeral.

If fishing rivers, put the bait upstream of holding structure like stream holes, or fallen timber.

When a fish picks up the bait, immediately release any tension on the line until the fish starts moving steadily away. Then set the hook.

**The Law:** No limit or size restrictions for the Catfish lakes on the map, however see regulations for other areas.

**Records:** Channel Catfish; 48 lbs. 8 oz., Irvine Lake, 1984
IGFA: 58 lbs., S. Carolina, 1964
Blue Catfish; 59 lbs. 4 oz., Irvine Lake, 1987
IGFA: 97 lbs., S. Dakota, 1959

**Irvine Lake Manager Bennett Davison and his giant catfish**

# CATFISH HOTSPOTS
## 3 Southern California Lake Areas

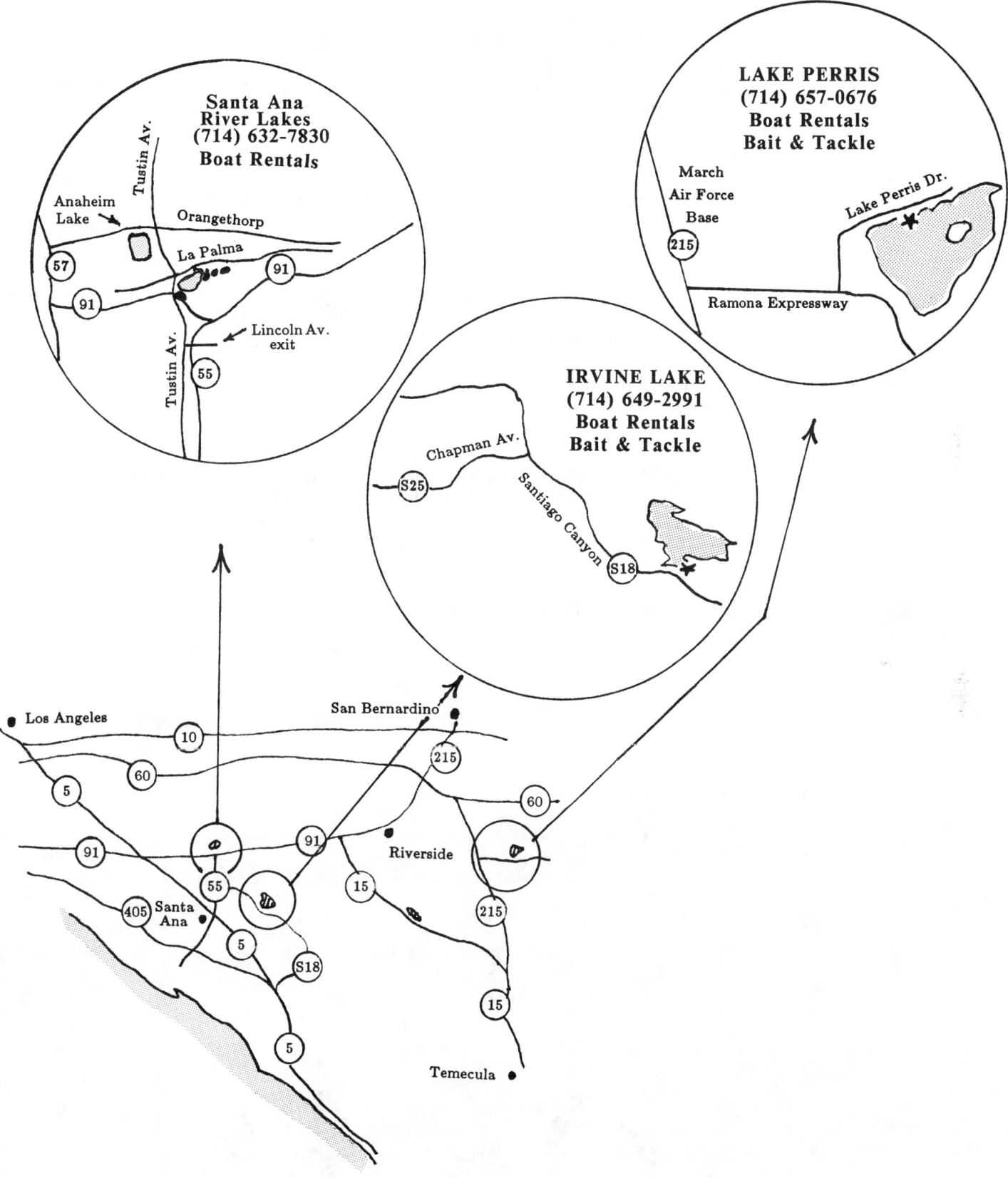

**CATFISH, FLATHEAD:**

| | |
|---|---|
| **Where:** | Lower Colorado River, Laguna Dam south to the Mexican border, including Mittry, Martinez lakes.<br>Around Yuma, Blythe, above Palo Verde diversion dam<br>Wister Ponds, Ramer & Finney lakes south of the Salton Sea |

**SEE MAP**

Structure: Slow current areas -holes below eddies, alongside the main river flow, around outside bends.

| | |
|---|---|
| **When:** | Summer months at night |
| **Bait/Lures:** | 4 - 6" goldfish, threadfin shad<br>Also bite on waterdogs, nightcrawlers, crawfish |
| **Technique:** | Let the fish run with the bait before setting the hook. |
| **The Law:** | 10 fish limit, no size restrictions. No closures in Colorado River (1990-91). Need a California or Arizona license with a Colorado river stamp. |
| **Records:** | State: 55#, Colorado River, April 1980<br>IGFA: 98 lbs., Texas, 1986 |
| **Access:** | See launch sites on map |

# FLATHEAD CATFISH – LOWER COLORADO RIVER

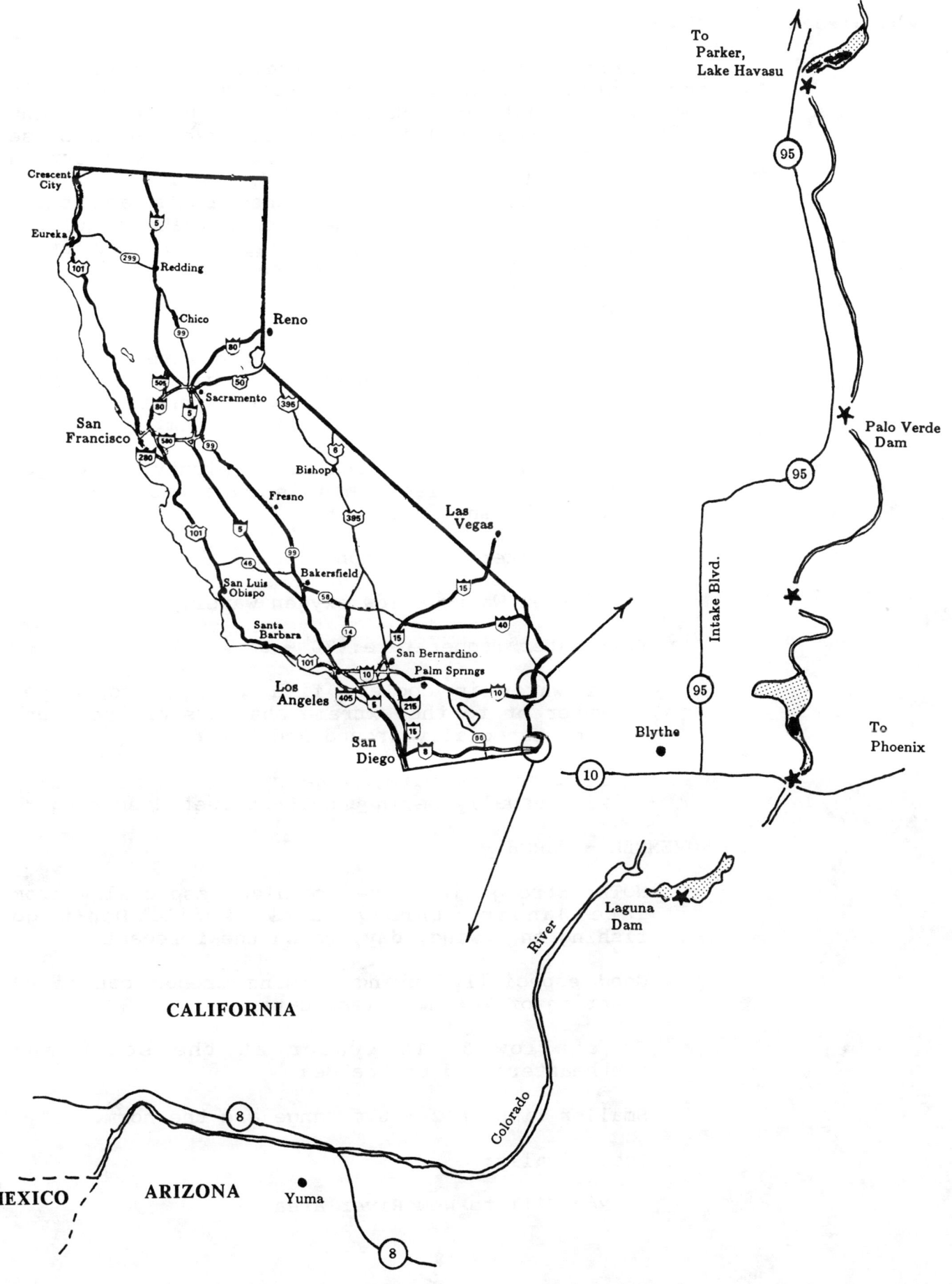

CORVINA / SALTON SEA

**CORVINA:**

**Where/When:**   SEE MAP

The Salton Sea is very large. Corvina move considerably from day to day. Therefore it is recommended that you ask where the fish are from any of the sources listed in the "Info" section as close as possible to your planned fishing day. Once out on the water watch for action on other boats. Also watch for concentrations of other boats and their movements - the Salton guides communicate regularly on marine channels and generally keep each other informed of what is working and where.

STRUCTURE:

Closely observe the color of the water. Almost all of the water is brownish, however this brown takes on different shadings depending on the oxygen content and any plankton bloom.

BEST: Brown Water - indicates plenty of oxygen and plenty of fish. This is pure brown with no sign of the shadings below.

OK: Red Water - plankton bloom

BAD: Green Water - low oxygen water.

Best Water Temperature: 70 - 85

If water is cooler, fish will go to deeper water or to the extreme shallows of the south end, especially around Red Hill.

If water is warm, late spring to fall, fish will usually be in the 10-25 feet deep range.

NOVEMBER - MARCH

NOTE: Strong winds are prevalent especially from late January through early April. Don't go fishing on a windy day, watch the forecast.

Good especially during warming trends caused by a series of 70+, windless days.

In shallow 3'-10' water at the south and southeastern end of the sea.

Smaller fish in 2 - 6 # range are the norm.

Specifically:

Red Hill to New River area

**Where/When continued:**

>Area from Black Rock (Obsidian Butte) to the Steam Plant around submerged trees.
>Mullet Island

NOT near cooler water areas of river mouths, i.e. New River and Alamo River.

APRIL THROUGH MAY:

Larger fish, 10 - 15#, appear in the shallows as the water temperature rises above 70 degrees.

Live bait becomes more effective during this period - especially Tilapia

Best action is often between 10 AM and early afternoon.

Specifically:

>The "Hog Pens"
>Between Mullet Island and the "Basketball Court" near the "Mud Pots". The Basketball court is a partially submerged pole with a sheet of plywood nailed to it. The Mud Pots are geothermal bubbling holes barely visible through the muddy waters.
>Red Hill area, off the jetty and back in the Refuge. The Refuge opens April 1.
>Around the Alamo River
>Late in this season, larger fish can be found below Sandy Point, off the Navy Base.

LATE MAY THROUGH JULY - THE BEST TIME FOR BIG FISH

This is the best period for the larger fish. Fish up to 15# are common in May. Fish over 20# are common in June and July.

Fishing is best in the morning hours in May.
Fishing is best in the VERY early morning hours in June and July. The best times are typically from 4:30 to approximately 7:30 AM. The bite typically turns off completely around 9 AM when an East wind starts blowing.

In early May, the fish can be found in waters less than 10 feet. In June they are usually around 10 to 15 feet deep. In late June to July they will be in water from 15 to 25 feet deep.

At the southwest end of the sea, specifically:

>Sandy Point

CORVINA / SALTON SEA

**Where/When continued:**

>  The Keys
>  Navy Pier Area
>  Mesquite Beach

**Bait/Lures:**  Small Croaker, less than 6", which can sometimes be caught on jigged Hopkins "Shorty" spoons.
Small Tilapia or Sargo, 2 - 3 inches.
Mudsuckers.
Minnows.

ThinFin lures, 3 1/2", sinking (S) model
   Colors: Silver Shad, Orange, Red, Green.

   If Fish are:
      3 - 6 feet deep, use T series
      8 - 12 feet deep, use AT series
      10 - 15 feet deep, use BT series

Hopkins "shorty" spoon - 1/2 to 3/4 oz.

Lunker Lure, 3/8 or 1/2 oz.
   Colors: Pink, Orange Sparkle, Chartreuse, Gold & Green Speckled, Chartreuse with Black Back, Orange & Black.

**Rig:**  Medium weight spinning rig or bass rig strung with 150-200 yards of 10 to 15# mono.

**See Diagram**

**Techniques:**  Note: All trolling and drifting is at a very slow speed. You may have to control the drift with a Sea-anchor or with a trolling motor. While drifting, monitor the fish finder to determine how far fish are suspended off the bottom and adjust your bait to that depth. If fishing mudsuckers, keep the bait moving with an occasional flick of the rod. If hit on bait, lower the rod tip to give slack. When you feel weight on the line set the hook firmly. Corvina have soft mouths which tear easily.

In Shallow water - 3 to 8 feet:

>  If fish are near surface, cast Lunker lures at right angles to the boat heading and let the lure sink and drift back to the boat's wake and retrieve slowly. Troll Lunker Lures at very slow speeds in shallows along the shore. Use your electric motor at the lowest speed. Cast out at right angles from the boat direction and let the lure sink and drift back to the boat's wake. AVOID MAKING NOISE.

**Techniques continued:**

In Water 8 to 15 feet deep:

Motor around the general area until you locate a school of fish on your fish finder.

If light winds and fish are on the bottom, set the boat up to drift with live bait or Lunker Lures bouncing off the bottom through the area of the located school. With bait fishing, if the fish are suspended off the bottom, use less weight so the bait is pulled up to the fish by the drift. A sea anchor or large bucket may have to be dragged to slow the drift.

If fish are suspended, especially in winter & spring and in water 4 to 25 feet deep,
slow troll Thin Fins and about 75 to 85 yards behind the boat at different depths - see Bait/Lures section. When hit, note plug type and depth.

Deep Water - 15 to 25 feet:

If fish are on the bottom, jig with a Hopkins spoon. Drop the lure to the bottom, sweep the rod tip up, let lure flutter back to the bottom, repeat.

**The Law:** Limit: 5 (1990-91)
No size limit

**Records:** State: Corvina, 36 1/2 lbs.
IGFA: 23 lbs. 4 oz., Calif., 1986

**Info:** Chamber of Commerce
State Rec. Area, 619-393-3052

Call bait stores listed on map.

**Access:** Guide: "Lucky" Pugh, (619) 395-5558

Rental Boats: Bob's Playa Riviera - (619) 354-1835
Bombay Marina - (619) 354-4049

## TILAPIA:

**When/Where:** Best in early Summertime - in the shallows
Dec. to May - from Desert Shores to 81st Av.

**Bait/Lures:** Cut Nightcrawlers
Redworms

**Rig/Technique:** For Bait: Use a light to medium weight spinning outfit with 4# to 10# mono. Terminal Rig - **See Diagram**

Jigging: In 10 to 20' deep water.

**Misc:** Avoid cutting into the bad smelling stomach contents while cleaning your catch.

**The Law:** No limit, no closures.

**Records:** Average size fish is between 1/2 to 2 lbs.

---

## SARGO:

**When/Where:** BEST in November through April.

The shoreline at Salton Sea State Rec. jetty
Sunken City - 1/4 mile north of Varner Harbor
This area is marked by a partially submerged telephone pole.

Structure: Submerged buildings, submerged trees, piers, jetties.

**Bait/Lures:** Canned sweet corn kernels.

**Rig:** Light to medium weight spinning outfit.
Terminal Rig, **See Diagram.**

**Technique:** Chum generously with canned corn.
Bring about 3 cans per angler.

**The Law:** No limit, no closures.

**Records:** State: 4 lbs. 1 oz.

# SALTON SEA RIGS

### Corvina

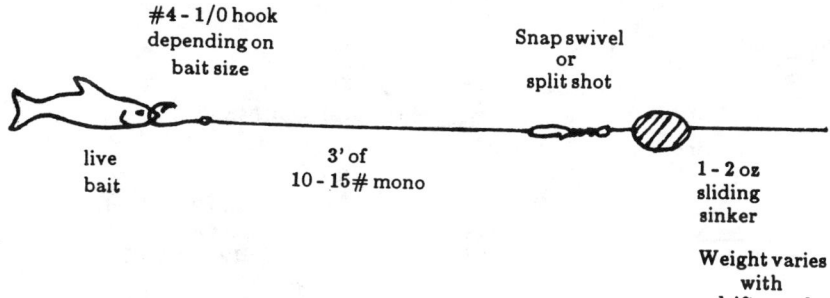

### Tilapia

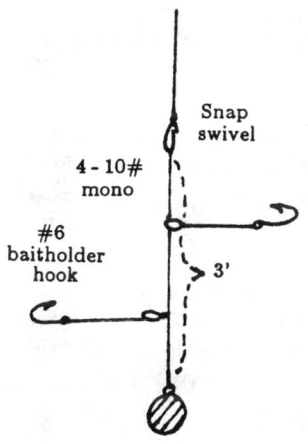

### Sargo

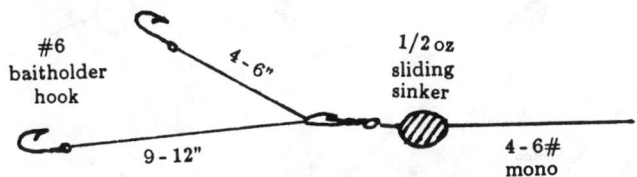

**Load hooks with corn kernels**

# THE SALTON SEA

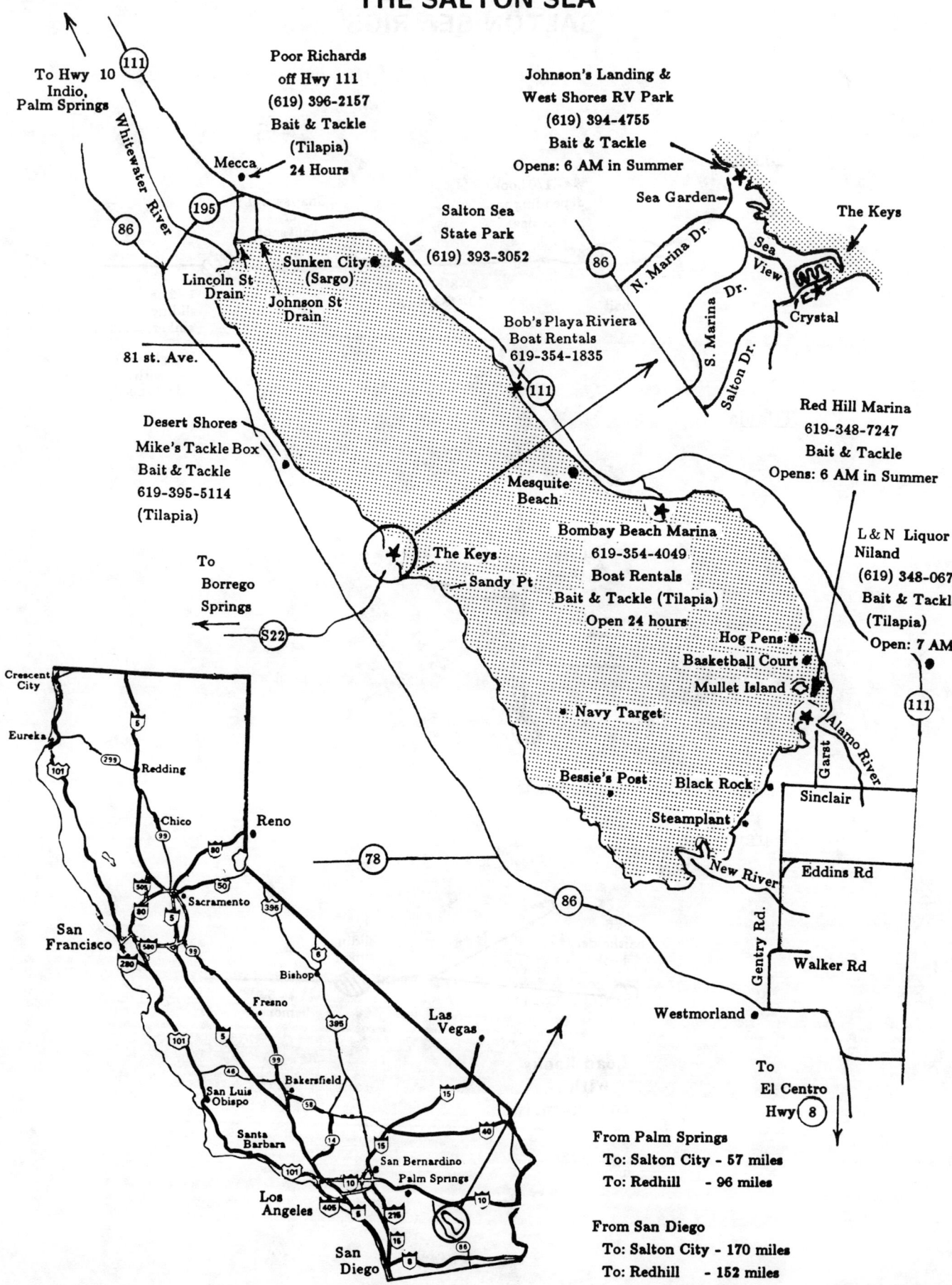

CORVINA / SALTON SEA   113

## SALTON SEA GAMEFISH

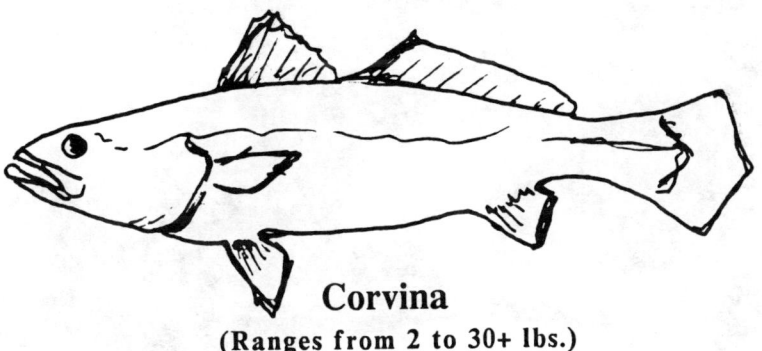
**Corvina**
(Ranges from 2 to 30+ lbs.)

**Tilapia**
(Averages 1/2 to 1 1/2 lbs.)

**Sargo**
(Averages 1/2 lb.)

**Croaker**

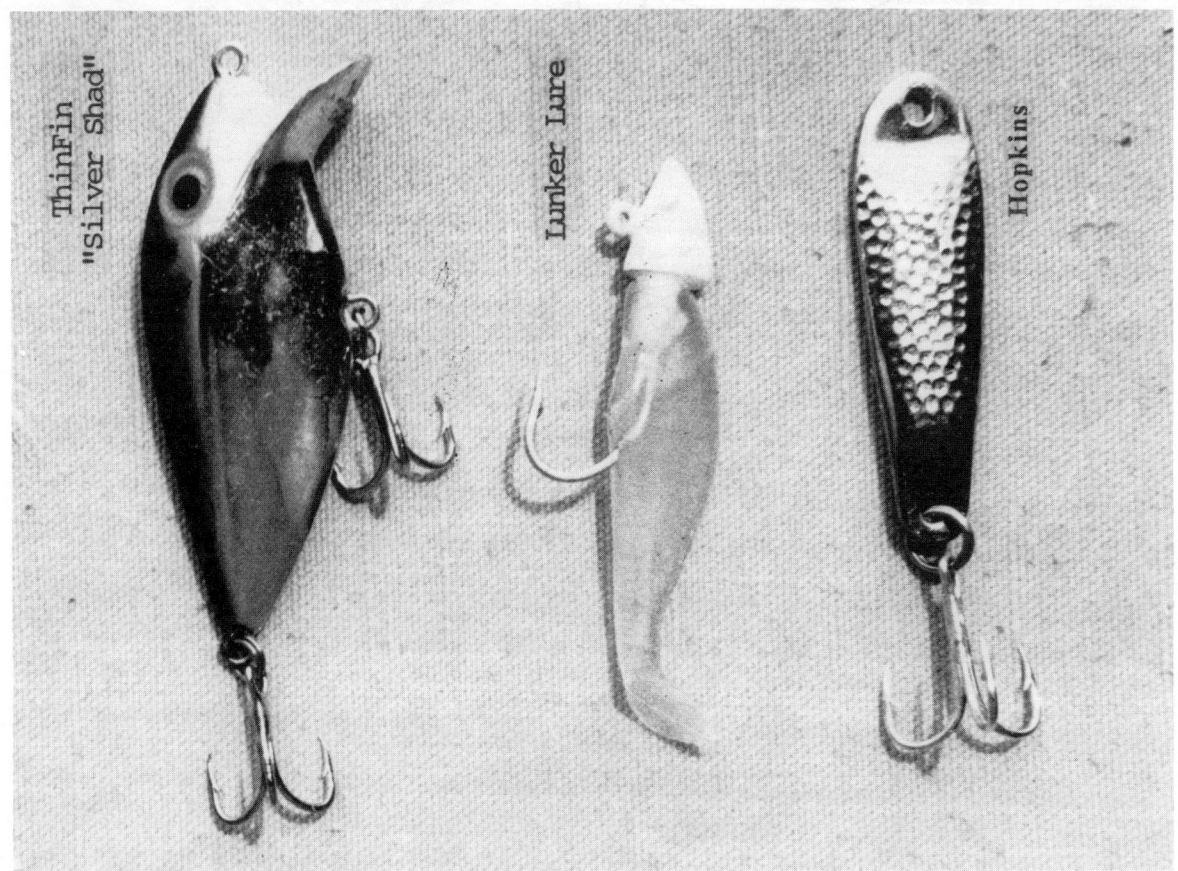

**CRAPPIE:** (pronounced CROP-PEE)

**Where/When:** There are numerous good Crappie lakes. Here are the top lakes in northern, central and southern California.

    Northern California: Clear Lake, Berryessa, Uvas, Black Butte

    Central California: Isabella

    Southern California: Silverwood, Irvine, Henshaw, El Capitan, Wohlford, Hodges

STRUCTURE BY SEASON:

SPRING: Late February through May.

In general, the fish will be inside of or tight to the edge of shallow water cover in 1 to 12 feet deep water.

In early spring, look,
- along channels and steep dropoffs outside of protected coves.
- outside of creek inlets off steeper banks leading to flats with cover.

In mid-spring, spawn occurs in areas close to above areas with the heaviest concentrations of reeds, tules, cattails, submerged trees, or brush,
- in clear lakes, at visible depth plus 4 to 6 feet.
- in stained, muddy lakes, at visible depth + 2 feet
- however, if no acceptable cover at these depths, fish will move to shallower structure.

In late spring - move to deeper water close to;
- outside weedlines,
- steeper dropoffs, and
- deeper, outside limbs of sunken trees.

Note: In deep water California reservoirs, especially if a good population of bass are present,
- Crappie will be forced out of the typical shallow flat spawning areas

CRAPPIE 116

**Where/When continued:**

- Look for any structure, esp. fallen trees, on main lake points nearest submerged channels.

SUMMER: June through mid-September.

In general schools will be suspended from 12 to 20 feet deep in water depths of 15 to 40 feet. Preferred locations will be close to underwater structure - outside weedlines, breaks, submerged trees, underwater rocky mounds.

Fish suspended away from structure are usually on the move and hard to follow. Concentrate on schools suspended off structure.

Around submerged islands or rock piles, fish will frequent the top of these mounds in the early morning and evening hours. They will move to the deeper, shaded side during the mid-day hours. If there is a current, the fish will concentrate on the protected, down-current side of the mound.

FALL: Late September to early November.

Crappie again move tight into the cover and are actively feeding.

WINTER: Cold water conditions.

Fish are usually within 5 to 10 feet of the bottom in wooded channels, off points, tight to the deepest parts of fallen, submerged trees, and on inside shoreline curves in water 15 to 30 feet deep.

**When:** Best in early morning and at dusk. Also can be good at night, especially the first 2 hours of darkness. Cloudy, dark, overcast days can extend the good hours even to the middle of the day.

Spawning Period - best, March through early May
Pre-Spawn and Fall periods - very good, late September through early November.
Summer - good, May through early September
Winter - OK
Turnover - bad

## CRAPPIE

**Bait/Lures:**   Live Shiners or Shad - best at 1 1/2 to 2 1/2 inches.

    Small jigs - 1/16 to 1/8 oz., i.e.;
- Crappie John finger jigs
- Sassy Shad
- Mini Jigs, Micro Jigs
- Finger (tube) Jigs

Colors:

    All day, all conditions - Green & White
    Off-color water - Black
    Use white, yellow & white on cloudy days, early mornings and late evenings.

**Rig/Technique:**   **See Diagram:**

Use very light line - 2#, 4# test leader.
Work the jig very slowly. If casting and retrieving, retrieve slowly. If using vertical method, move slowly, let sit motionless, twitch occasionally.

Crappies like to attack their prey from below. Work the jig just above and slightly into the fish.

FOR SPRING, FALL SHALLOW WATER PERIODS:

If a slight wind or no wind, and open, isolated cover - use a quill bobber and jig and

- cast past structure
- slowly reel up to edge of cover
- wait
- twitch
- wait
- repeat above

If some wind and some cover and
  Crappie are 1 to 5 feet deep,
use an adjust-a-bubble bobber and jig and

- position boat upwind of structure
- cast short of structure
- let wind push the bobber to structure edge
- twitch
- wait

Fish nearby structure by using rod and wind drifts to move bobber rig.

If not getting hit on outside edges, try inside heavy cover, especially during early spring (pre-spawn and spawn periods,

- use lightweight spinning rig and jig.

CRAPPIE 118

**Rig/Technique continued:**

- cast over submerged, weed beds
- retrieve slowly, just above weed tops
- give slight action by slight lift and drop of rod tip, and/or

hold the rod slightly above the spinning reel and extend the index finger of your right hand to intercept the mono as it rolls around the spool on the retrieve. This gives an extra motion to the jig.

OR
- use a long pole, 10 - 14 feet, no bobber.
- slowly lower jig through openings in cover
- stop & twitch
- wait
- drop deeper and repeat

IN EARLY SPRING OR EARLY SUMMER, when fish are out from spawning areas in slightly deeper waters, typically 5 to 10 feet deep,

- use slip bobber and jig/bait.

IN MID-SUMMER when fish are suspended between 12 and 20 feet in water 15 to 40 feet deep,

- use a tight line rig - **See Diagram.**
- locate fish schools with a fish finder
- mark the location with a marker buoy don't drop anchor, it will spook the fish)
- backtroll through the school (a slow wind drift controlled with an electric trolling motor)
- try to keep your jig within a couple feet of the top of the school. If no action, lower the jig into the school depth
- occasionally lift rod 2 to 3 feet, hold, then slowly drop
- rest your index finger on the line, out from the spool, to help detect light pickups

IN WINTER, COLD WATER CONDITIONS, fish will normally be near the bottom. Use same technique as above.

**The Law:** No Limit, no closures (1990-91)

**Records:** Black Crappie - 7 or 8 dorsal spines
State: 5 lbs. 4 oz., Rollins Lake, 1989
IGFA: 4 lbs. 8 oz., Virginia, 1981
White Crappie - six dorsal spines
State: 4 lbs. 8 oz., Clear Lake, 1971
IGFA: 5 lbs. 3 oz., Mississippi, 1957

**See Also:** Largemouth Bass

CRAPPIE 119

# CRAPPIE RIGS

### Shallow Water Rigs: 1 - 10+ feet deep

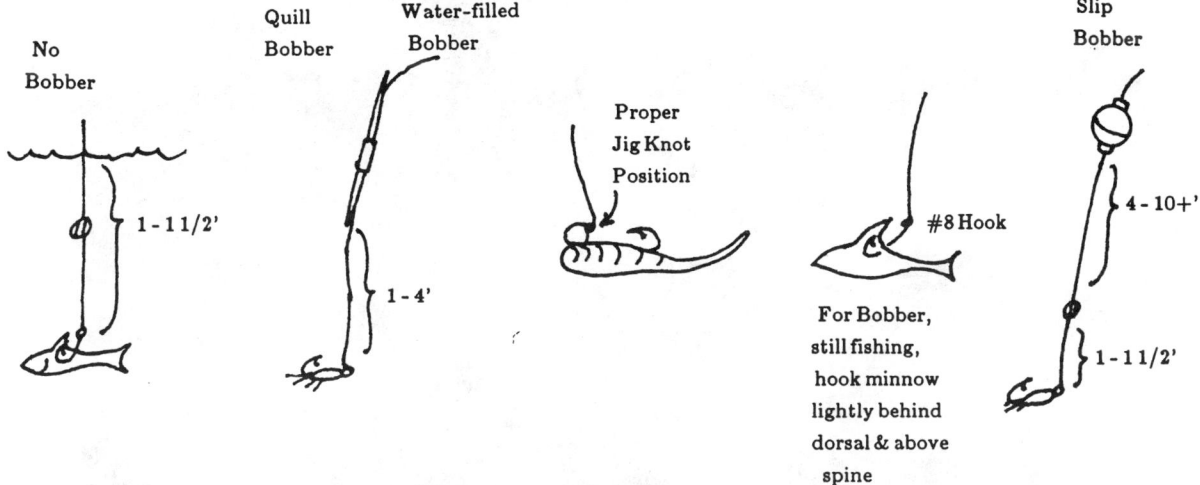

### Deeper Waters: 10 - 22+ Feet Deep

**Tightline Rigs:** **Live Minnow Rig:**

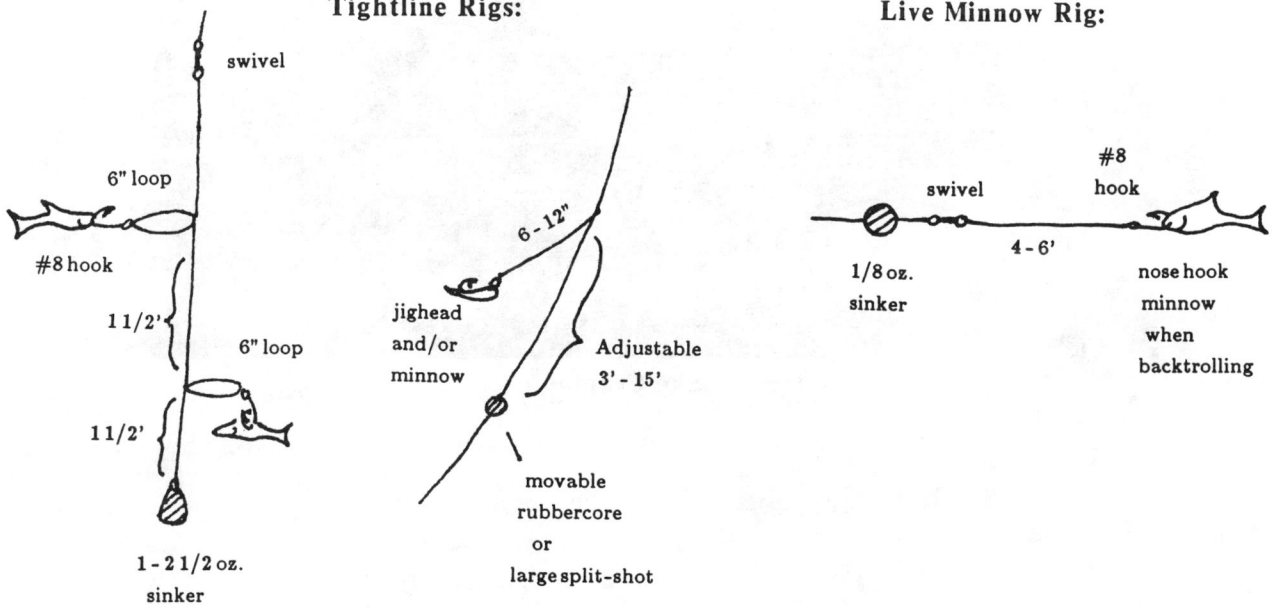

### Casting

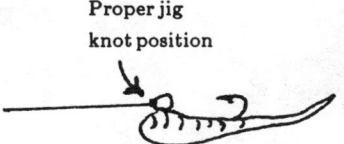

# CRAPPIE 120

**Irvine Lake Crappie**

Micro Jigs

Tube (Finger) Jigs

Crappie Jigs

## CALIFORNIA HALIBUT: (LENGUADO, ALABATO)

**Where/When:** Los Angeles Area and Channel Islands: February and March for the largest on sandy bottoms
Catalina Island sandy bottom areas - Whites Landing, Goat Harbor up to Cabrillo Beach, Farnsworth Bank
San Francisco Bay - June through early August
San Francisco Coastal areas - June through August
Northern Monterey Bay off Santa Cruz and Capitola - May, June
Channel Islands, Santa Rosa, - late June through July
San Diego - late April through early June

**SEE MAPS** for;

San Francisco Bay
Santa Monica Bay area
San Diego / Ensenada area

Structure:

On sandy bottoms adjacent to rocky bottom structure.

Generally shallower waters and surf regions are productive in spring and during grunion runs. Fish can be close to the beach starting at high tide and a few hours after. Bite is often best during the minimal water movement just between the high and low tide shift.

During other times of the year, especially summer months, for the best fishing and larger fish look for 50 to 80 foot deep structure in clean, green-to-blue water.

**Bait/Lures:** Live anchovy - most popular bait, Sardines, small Mackerel, Brown Bait - hook up through the lower and upper jaw to keep mouth closed.

Live squid - but not in Santa Monica Bay.

Typically Halibut are caught on bait but the following lures/techniques can be fruitful;

Bump A Pet Spoon on the bottom while trolling. Should feel the sinker gently slide along the bottom. These fish like sandy bottoms.

Slow troll a floating Rapala off a bottom dropper weight.

**Rig:** **SEE DIAGRAM**

HALIBUT 122

**Rig continued:**

Light Rig for 2 to 6# lines and anchovies:

A soft tip rod, i.e. Sabre 1926, 2 - 6# mono, medium-sized, freshwater-type, conventional reel, i.e. Ambassadeur 5500C.

Medium Rig for 10 to 16# lines:

Sabre 1956, Shimano TLD5

Heavier Rig for 20 to 30# lines for use with Brown baits, Herring or small Mackerel:

**Technique:** Halibut fishing is normally done on the drift. During light breeze conditions, a free drift works well. During moderate wind or dead wind conditions, slow trolling or controlled drifting works well.

Put out many rods so area is covered, halibut doesn't have to move. Put rod in holder. Set the drag just to keep the line from going out as the sinker is drifted along the bottom.

There is a saying "Bow to a Halibut". This simply means when you feel a Halibut bite, lower your rod tip to take the pressure off the line and let the fish take the bait. This rule works well but the following technique can give you an even better hooking percentage.

For hand-held rods, drift with the reel in freespool, controlling the line with your thumb.

- if hit, let the fish run with the bait
- put some thumb pressure on the spool to feel for "taps"
- if taps are weak, let the fish run some more
- if taps are heavy and you feel some weight, set the hook by reeling in to the drag

**The Law:** 5 fish, minimum size 22"
There are exceptions to these regulations in Bodega and Tomales Bays - see regulations.

**Records:** State: 53 1/2 lbs. Santa Rosa Is., May 1975.
IGFA: 45 lbs., Santa Cruz Is., June 1982

HALIBUT 123

# HALIBUT RIGS

**Bait:**

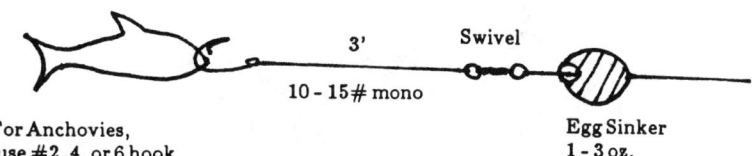

For Anchovies, use #2, 4, or 6 hook

For Brown Bait, use 1/0 to 5/0 single or treble hook

OR

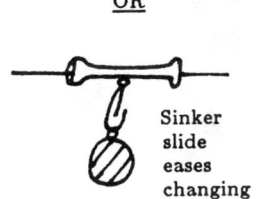

Sinker slide eases changing weights

OR

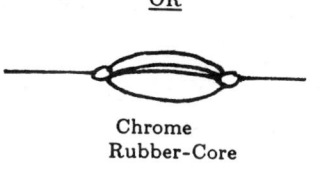

Chrome Rubber-Core

OR

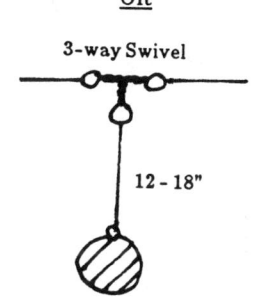

3-way Swivel

12 - 18"

## Slow Trolling, 2-4 MPH:

1. Shallow

   The lure should occasionally hit bottom.

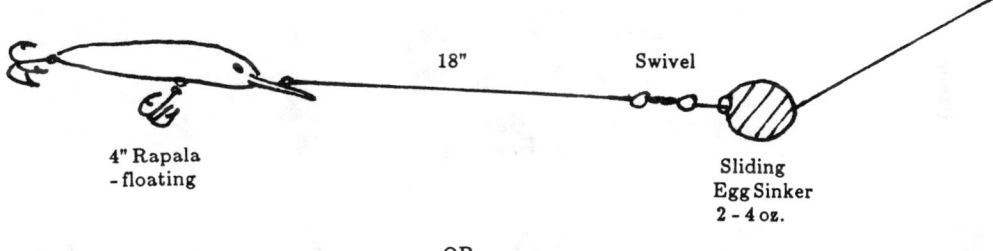

OR

Use deep-running 7 - 9" Rebels or Rapalas in Mackeral or Anchovy patterns <u>without</u> weights

2. Deeper Water, 40 - 60 feet.

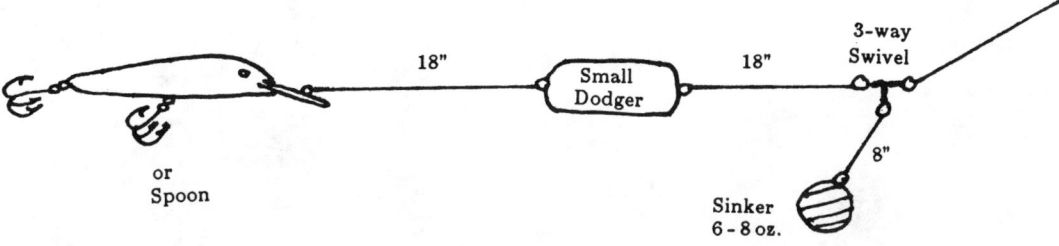

# HALIBUT - SAN FRANCISCO BAY

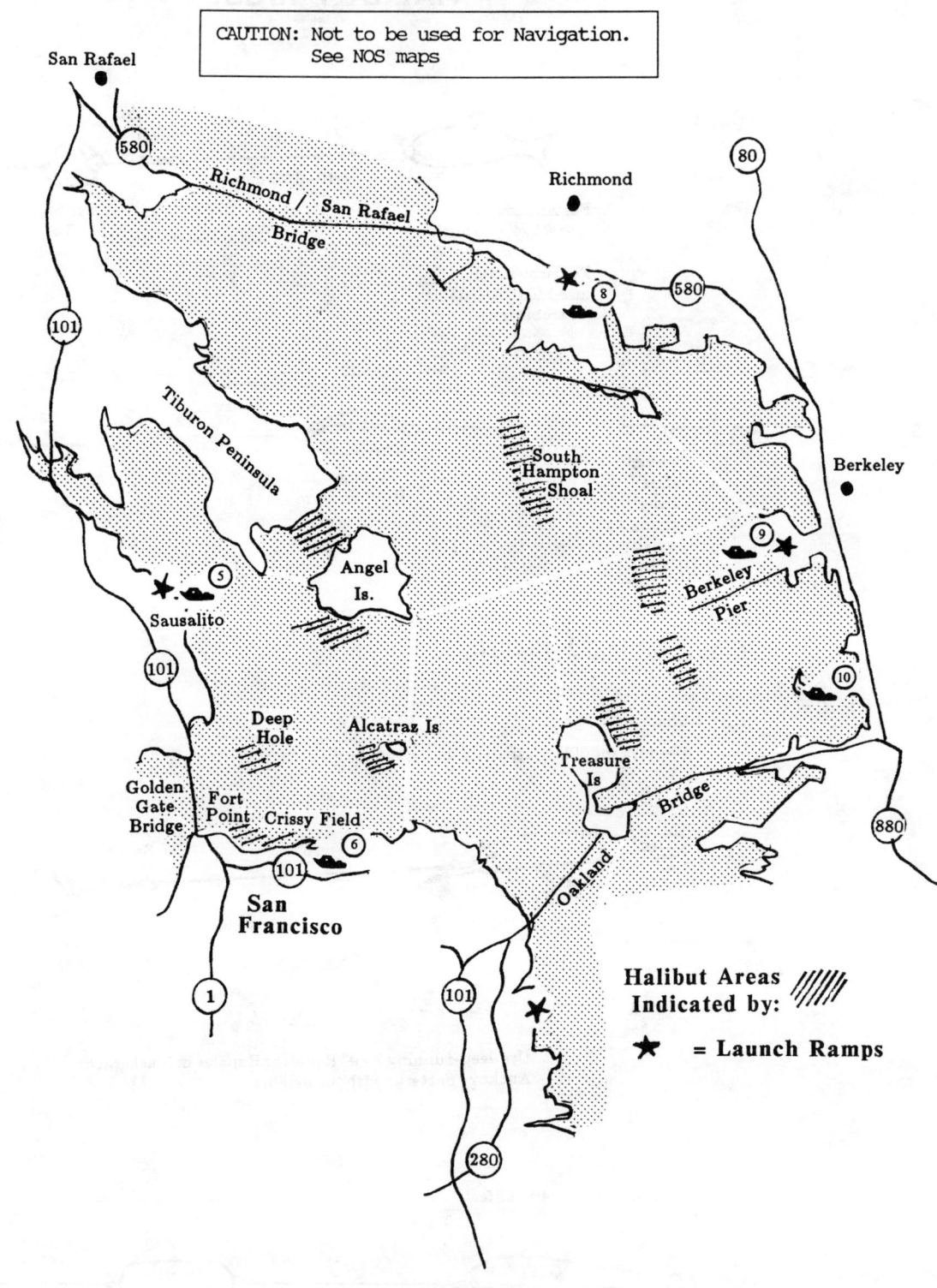

# HALIBUT - SANTA MONICA BAY

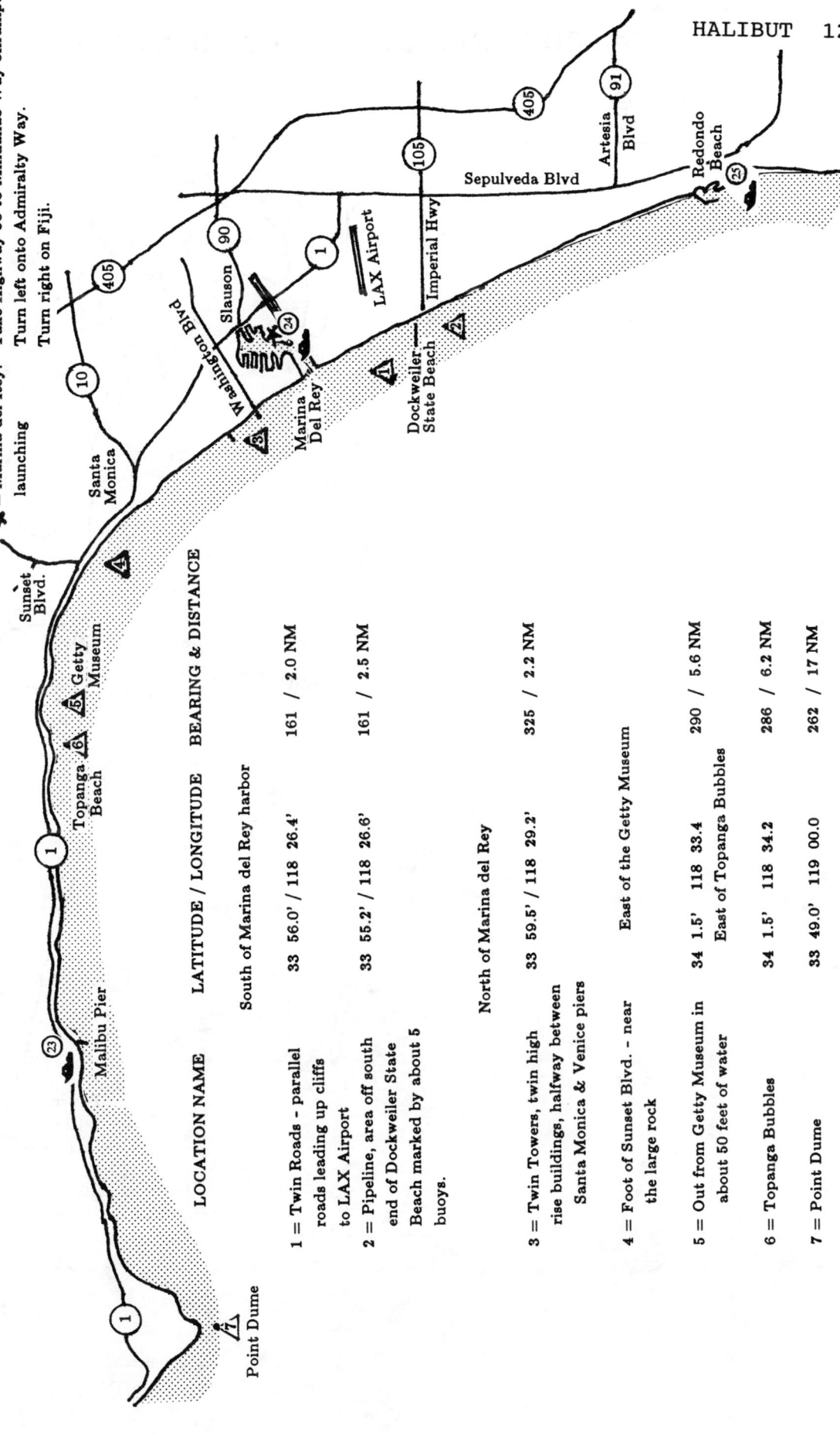

CAUTION: Not to be used for Navigation. See NOS maps

★ = Marina del Rey: Take Highway 90 to Mindanao Way offramp. launching Turn left onto Admiralty Way. Turn right on Fiji.

| LOCATION NAME | LATITUDE / LONGITUDE | BEARING & DISTANCE |
|---|---|---|
| | South of Marina del Rey harbor | |
| 1 = Twin Roads - parallel roads leading up cliffs to LAX Airport | 33 56.0' / 118 26.4' | 161 / 2.0 NM |
| 2 = Pipeline, area off south end of Dockweiler State Beach marked by about 5 buoys. | 33 55.2' / 118 26.6' | 161 / 2.5 NM |
| | North of Marina del Rey | |
| 3 = Twin Towers, twin high rise buildings, halfway between Santa Monica & Venice piers | 33 59.5' / 118 29.2' | 325 / 2.2 NM |
| 4 = Foot of Sunset Blvd. - near the large rock | | East of the Getty Museum |
| 5 = Out from Getty Museum in about 50 feet of water | 34 1.5' 118 33.4 | 290 / 5.6 NM East of Topanga Bubbles |
| 6 = Topanga Bubbles | 34 1.5' 118 34.2 | 286 / 6.2 NM |
| 7 = Point Dume | 33 49.0' 119 00.0 | 262 / 17 NM |

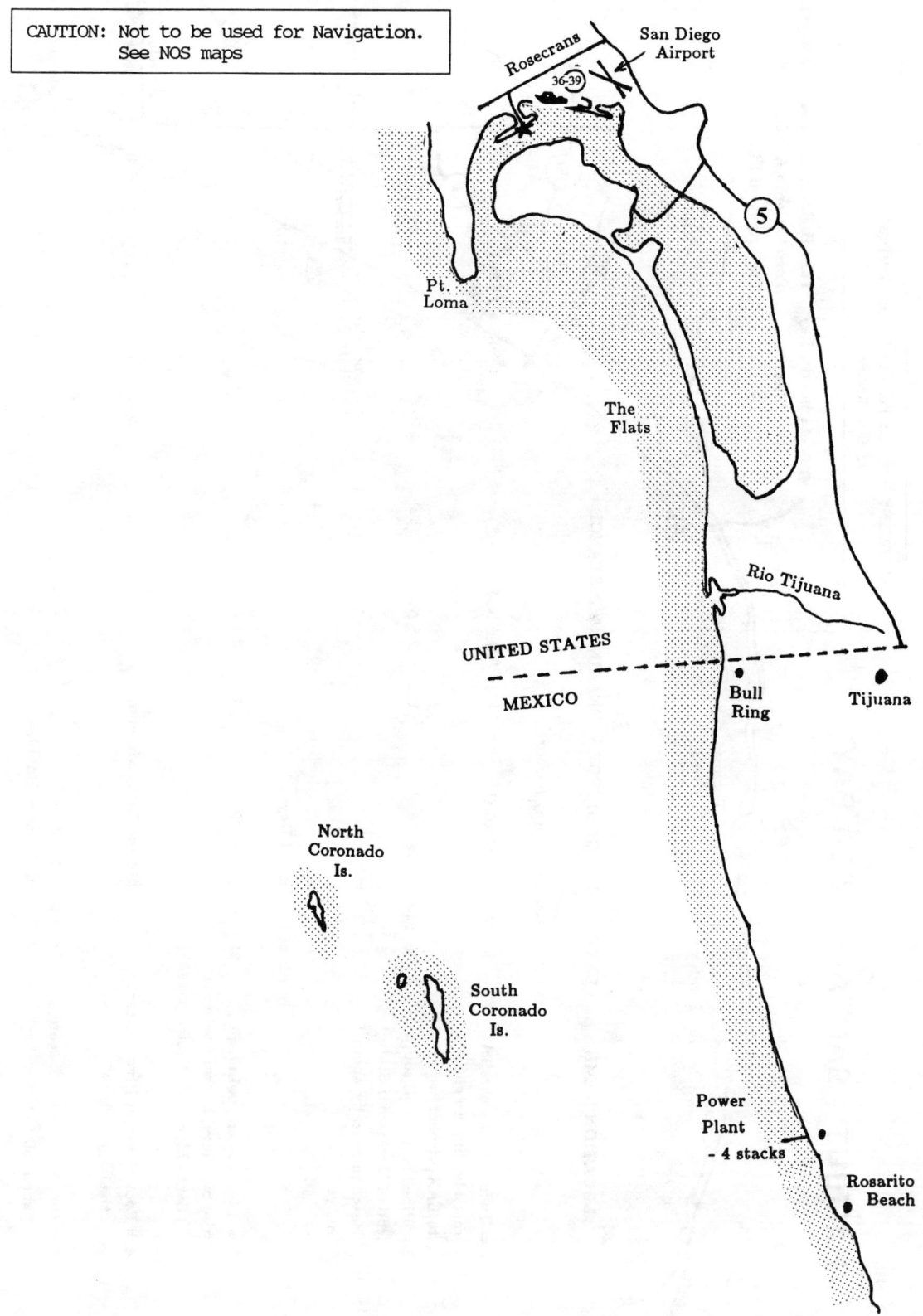

## LINGCOD:

**Where:** Two general areas offer excellent Lingcod fishing,

- Soap Banks, Farallon Islands, Cordell Banks area reached out of the San Francisco, and Bodega Bay landings and

- Morro Bay, San Simeon area.

Also Fair to Good are San Miguel Is, the west end, and Descanso Bay (Mexican Waters). See also other southern California spots indicated on map.

Structure:

Lings favor reef and near island areas with rocky, jagged bottoms. Lings lurk in ambush at the high points of this underwater structure in water up to 300 feet deep. Look for large rocks and position boat to drift over them.

**SEE MAPS**

**When:** There are two good "seasons"

The fall spawning season. This is when the lings move to shallower water to spawn - August through October.

The spring season focuses on the rocky reefs off Morro Bay and San Simeon - from February to June.

Lings actively feed during slack periods at high tides.

**Bait/Lures:** Squid, small mackerel
Small Rockcod or Greenling - a kelp fish, for shallow water drifting.
Slab bait with tail on a 8/0 hook and about an 8 oz. torpedo sinker.

Medium to heavy (12 - 48 oz.) jigs:
Yo Ho Ho, Hex Bar, Diamond, UFO, and large Scampi leadheads - especially in shallower waters.

Colors: White, chrome, orange\yellow\white work well.

**Rig:** A medium-sized, saltwater conventional reel with capacity for about 400 yards of 30 to 40 lb. test mono. A rod stiff enough to cast jigs up to 16 oz. A good jig casting rod works well on the lighter jigs for shallow-water lingcod fishing. Example: Fenwick 1870 or Sabre 870.

**Technique:** Jigging:

Straight heavy leader with several bait loops with shrimp flies. Tie a chrome, hex bar jig on the end which acts as a sinker and attraction.

Mustad's 3551 3/0 or 4/0 bronze treble hook - can pull off a snagged bottom, and 100# test shock leader. Add a whole squid to the jig and the lowest shrimp fly

Deep Water - Drift Fishing:

Search for particularly jagged reef and mark with buoy - 300 - 350' of rope and inexpensive weight. Set boat up for drift over buoy area. A good, steady, fast-walk drift is ideal.

If you are on the bottom and you feel a small fish on the line, leave it on the bottom a while. Often a large Ling will latch on to this bait. If you feel this extra weight come on the line, reel the rig slowly and steadily to the surface. The Ling probably wont be hooked, just hanging on. Do not lift the head out of the water - if legal size get the deckhand to gaff it.

Shallow Water Drifting - 40 to 80':

- use lighter rig for anchovies
- smaller jigs - 2 to 16 oz. with pork rind or a hootchy teaser - bounced along bottom

Jigging - for deep or shallow waters:

- let the jig fall to the bottom
- Let it rest on the bottom for 2 to 3 seconds
- slowly lift it for about 20 cranks of the reel
- let it drop again; repeat from step 2
- most hits occur on the drop. Strike any hesitation in the drop.

How to fight:

- strike quickly and apply steady pressure to lift fish away from the rocky bottom
- once off the bottom, reduce the drag somewhat, as a Lingcod will often make a spirited run about halfway to the surface
- crank in smoothly - there is a chance the Lingcod isn't hooked
- don't lift head out of water until gaffed

LINGCOD   130

**Technique continued:**

    Snagging Rocks:

        Once snagged avoid pulling hard on the line. Release line until there is a slight amount of slack. Violently, repeatedly, swing the rod up and down so that the line is tight and stretched at the top of the swing and slack at the bottom. This causes a line pulse which often frees the jig. Avoid extreme line angles when drifting, as a vertically snagged jig is much easier to free.

**The Law:**    Minimum Length: 22 inches; Limit: 5 (1990)
             See also regulations on ocean bag limits.

**Records:**    State: 53 lbs., Trinidad
            IGFA: 61 lbs., Washington, 1986

**See Also:**    Rockcod, Cowcod

# LINGCOD RIGS

**Shallow Water (50 - 250') Drift Rig**

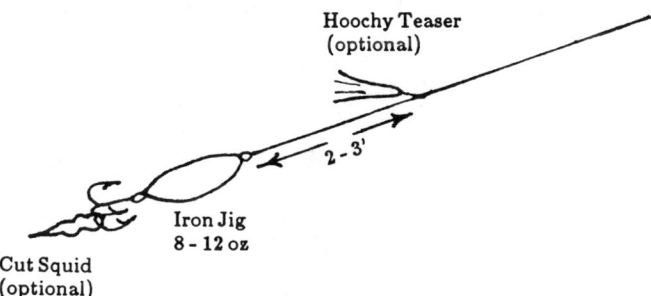

**Whole Bait, Deep Water Rig**

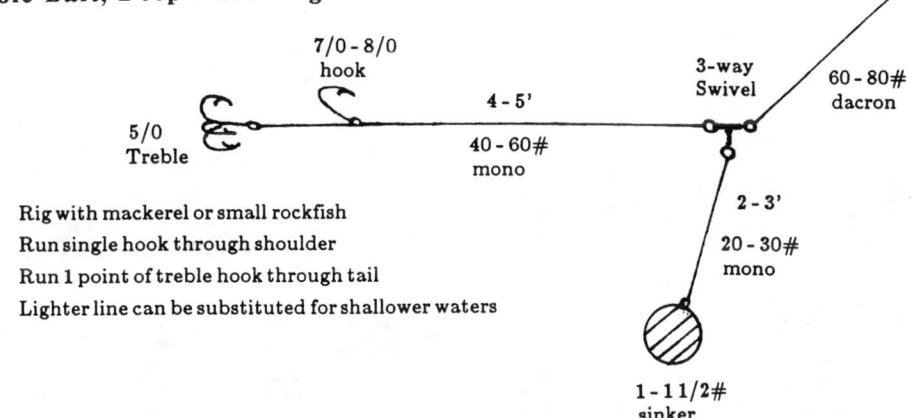

Rig with mackerel or small rockfish
Run single hook through shoulder
Run 1 point of treble hook through tail
Lighter line can be substituted for shallower waters

## LINGCOD - SAN FRANCISCO AREA

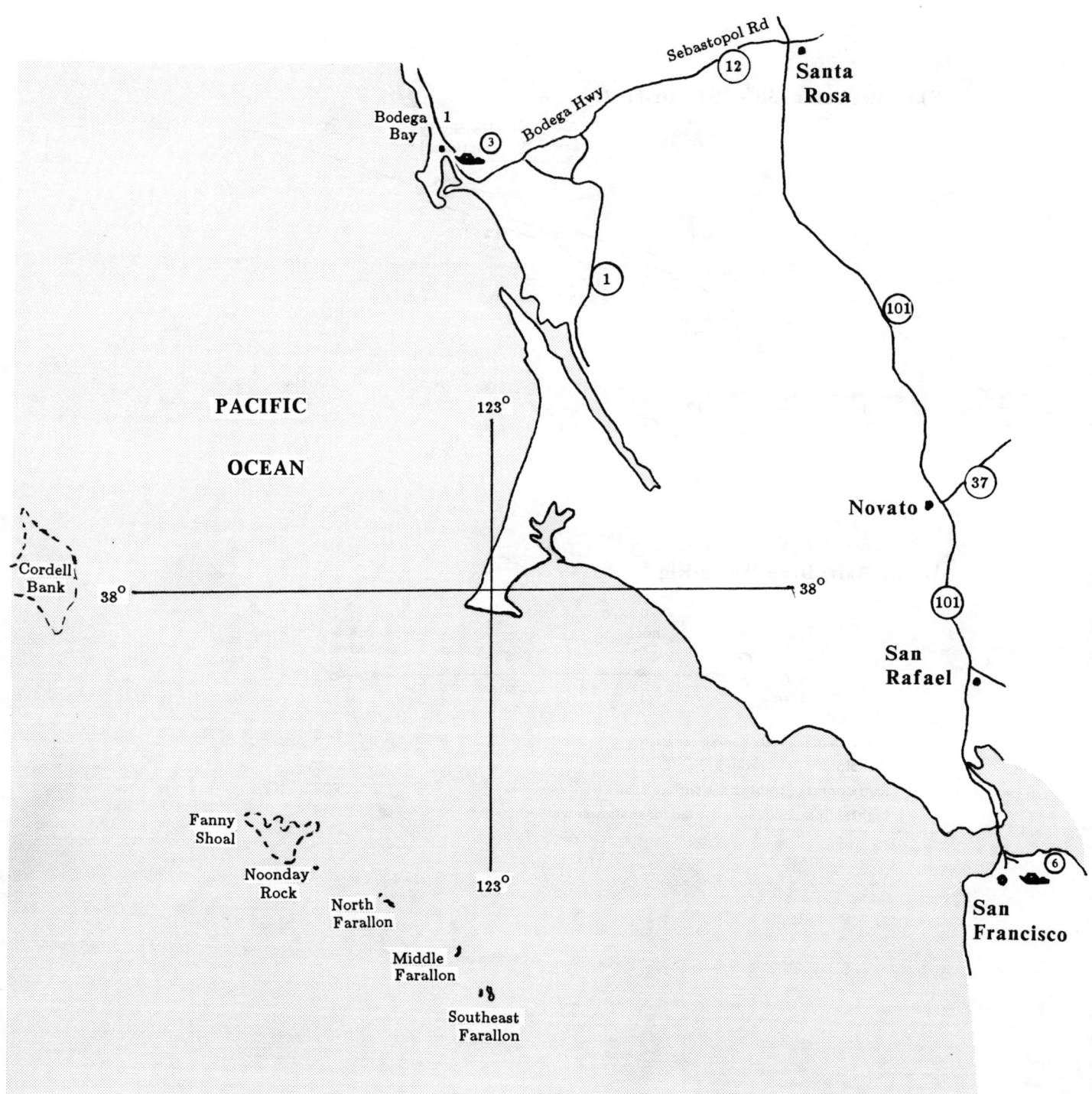

# LINGCOD - MORRO BAY / SAN SIMEON

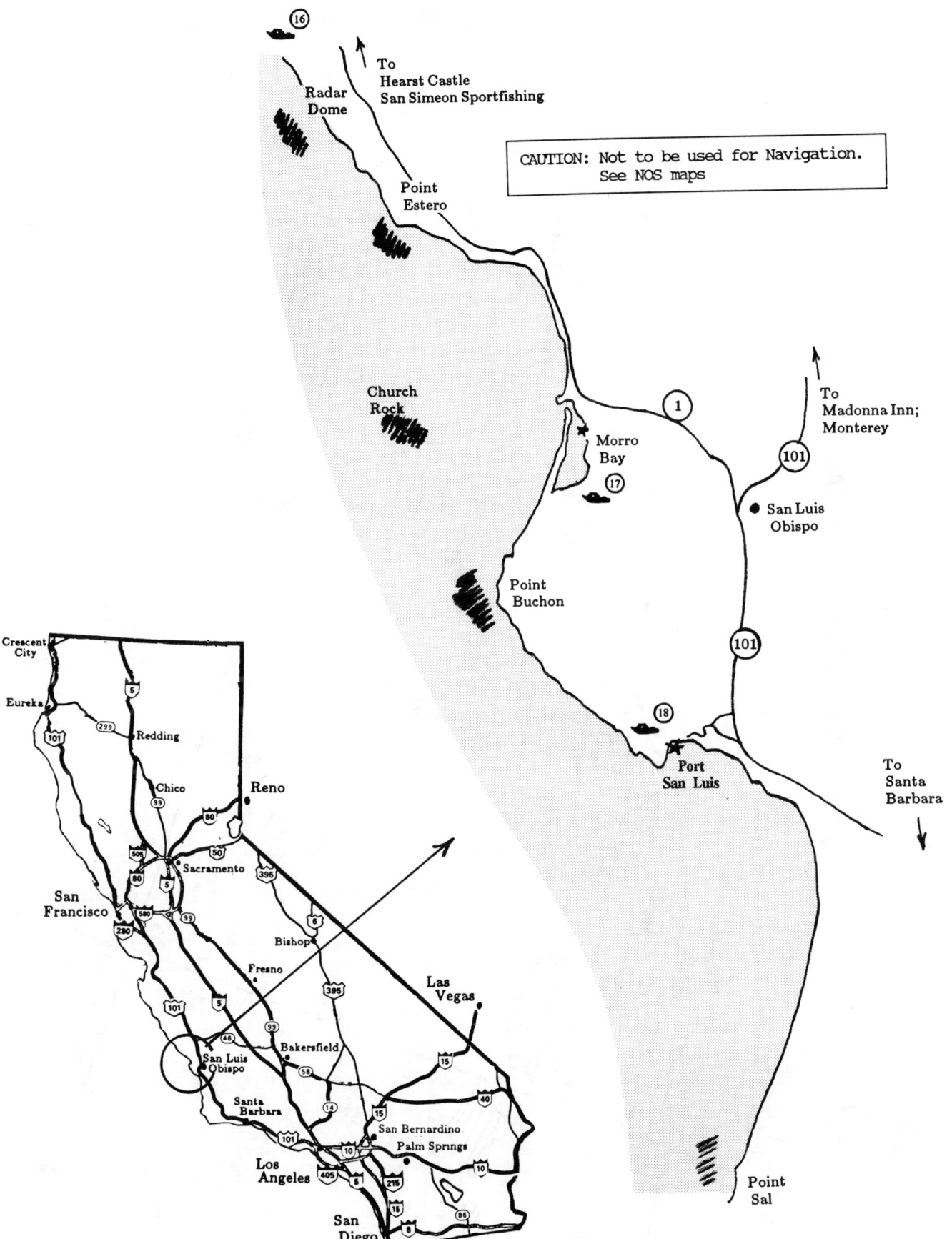

LINGCOD 134

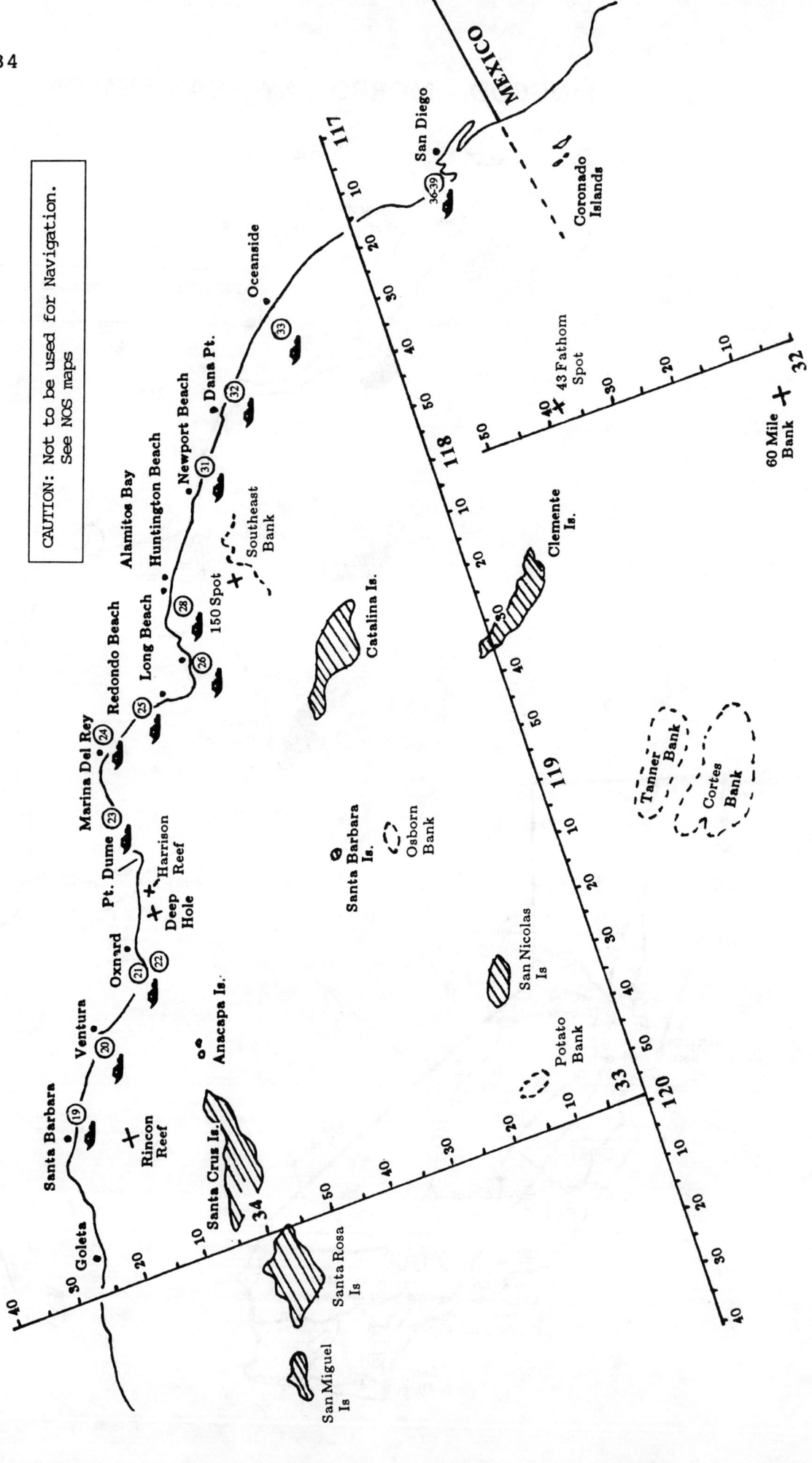

## LINGCOD AREAS - SOUTHERN CALIFORNIA

1. 43 Fathom Spot    32° 39.2'/ 117° 58.3'    From Pt. Loma
                                              262°/ 37 NM
2. 60 Mile Bank      32° 3.7'/ 118° 13.2'     From Pt. Loma
                                              220°/ 60 NM
                                              From Newport
                                              176°/ 77 NM
3. Catalina Is.      ........................ From Alamitos Bay
                                              215°/ 23.8 NM to
                                              Ship Rock, 2 Harbors
4. Clemente Is.      33° 2.1'/ 118° 36.8'     Castle Rock - NW end
5. Cortes Bank       32° 26.5'/ 119° 7.5'     From Marina del Rey
                                              186°/ 97 NM
                                              From Pt. Loma
                                              250°/ 95 NM
6. Harrison Reef     34° 2.6'/ 118° 58.0'     From Marina del Rey
                                              278°/ 24 NM
7. Osborn Bank       33° 21.5'/ 119° 2.5'     From Marina del Rey
                                              205°/ 46.6 NM
8. Rincon Reef       34° 19.4'/ 119° 27.0'    From Santa Barbara
                                              170°/ 10 NM
9. Santa Barbara     33° 29.2'/ 119° 1.8'     From Marina del Rey
   Is.                                        211°/ 41.0 NM
                                              From Newport
                                              250°/ 58.2 NM
10. Southeast Bank   South & East of 150 Kelp - see below
    "150 Kelp"       33° 7.5'/ 118° 35.0'     From Alamitos Bay
    Double Oil Platform                       170°/ 9.5 NM
    called "Elly & Ellen"
11. Tanner Bank      32° 42.0'/ 119° 8.0'     From Marina del Rey
                                              190°/ 83.1 NM

# LINGCOD 136

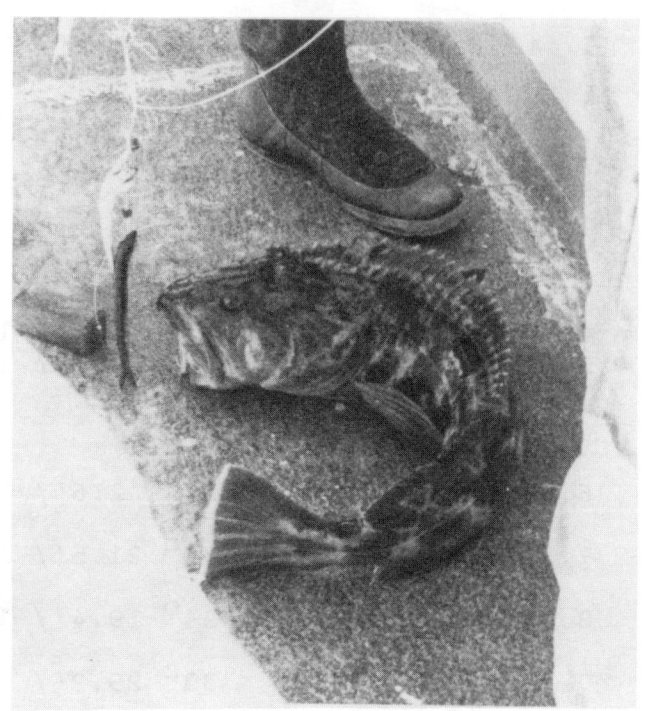
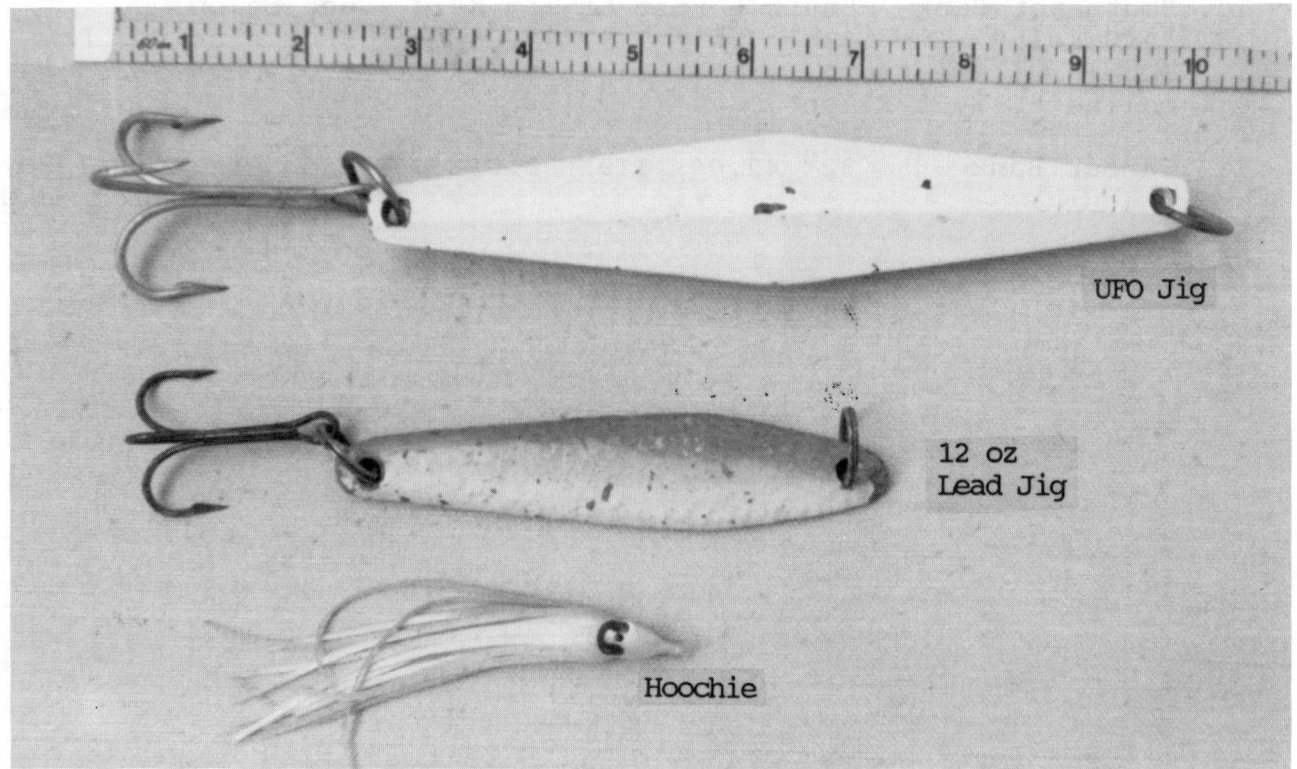

## STRIPED MARLIN:

**Conservation:**

The marlin fishery of Southern California is healthy but very limited. There only hundreds of fish available, not thousands as in Cabo, Baja and other renown billfishing areas. These magnificent fish are not edible and because of their size, cost a small fortune to have mounted. It is imperative that we all consciously participate in sane catch-and-release practices such as the following;

1. Avoid using live bait techniques. If live bait used, set the hook quickly on a pickup. Unlike lures, a marlin will swallow a live bait. A gut hooked fish has little chance of surviving.

2. Do not use stainless hooks - non-stainless hooks will rust out quickly, increasing fish survival rates.

3. Work a fish quickly. Get him to the boat and release him in short order. This can be done if the drag is set correctly, not too light, and the fish is worked skillfully by the angler and through proper boat handling.

**Where:**

Southern California - **SEE MAP**
See also **Baja Sea of Cortez** section

Structure:

Marlin are generally found concentrated in offshore, blue water areas, over underwater seamounts. They prefer water $68°$ to $74°$. They will congregate near bait concentrations, on the warm water side of cool/warm current interfaces, and on the blue water side of blue/green water interfaces. Most of the important equipment needed for successful marlin fishing is used to locate this Marlin holding structure. Predominant current patterns change from year to year. These currents concentrate the bait and the Marlin in certain areas. The first step toward success is to get very current, reliable reports.

Marlin spend most of their time in the top 30 feet of water. Sleepers are resting, inactive fish at the surface. Tailers are active, bait-hunting fish that will virtually surf the downwind sides of waves in search of food.

## MARLIN, STRIPED

**When:** July through early November
Best: late August to early October

1 hour before and after the turn of high & low tides are prime times.
Full moon periods can have a negative effect on daytime fishing.
Early morning calm periods are excellent for spotting and baiting "sleepers". Be on the fishing grounds at first light.

**Bait/Lures:** Baits: Mackerel, Squid

It is important to catch and maintain live mackerel baits.

Lures: In general, flat or cup-head jigs 8-10" long. Sevenstrand Kona-Clone 1220C and Pro Series - Flathead Pushers PR3, PR5 and Swimmers PR6 trolled 4 to 14 knots. Chrome Jethead lures by Mako Products. Also similar lures from Zuker (Mean Joe Green) and Boone.
Also effective are the fast trolled Nobbies or Doornobs from Area Rule.
Colors: Mackerel, Pro Dolphin, Sablefish, Dorado, Bleeding Mackerel, Squirrelfish, etc.

**Rig:** **SEE DIAGRAM**

You MUST have very sharp hooks. A Marlin's mouth is very tough.

Trolling: Use a 30 - 50# outfits with 400 to 500 yards of quality mono. Examples: Penn Senator 114H, Daiwa 600H, Penn International 30, etc.

Live Bait: Use a 20 - 30# rig with 300 to 400 yards of quality mono.

Hooks: For Jigs use size 8/0 for the larger types - Konaclone 1220C. Use 6/0 to 7/0 for the smaller lures - i.e. Nobbies.

**Equipment:** You don't need a 50 foot Bertram with a tuna tower to catch marlin, a 25 foot deep-V hull boat will suffice. However, Marlin fishing, probably more than any other fishing is highly dependent on having and properly using the right equipment.

1. LORAN:

A Loran can get you quickly to the proven marlin spots with reliability and confidence. A few spots in So. Calif. year-in and year-out produce 90%+ of the Marlin. If you are not in these areas you are wasting your time and gas.

**Equipment continued:**

2. BINOCULARS (7 X 50):

    You need to LOOK FOR THE SIGNS. A good pair of binoculars is vitally important for finding the signs. See "LOOK FOR THE SIGNS" under Technique. A tuna tower is a valuable aid in sighting surface fish and bait balls.

3. FISH FINDER:

    A good fish finder is needed to locate bait concentrations. "Zone" and "Fish Alarm" functions are very helpful.

4. WATER TEMPERATURE SENSOR:

    Marlin will search for and remain in warmer water. They tend to congregate with the bait concentrations along lines of water temperature gradient where a warm body or current of water meets a cooler area. Find and fish the warmer side of this junction.

5. A MARINE RADIO:

    Monitor station 72 especially. Also monitor stations 2, 5, 11, 65, and 73. A word of caution - don't completely trust all you hear on these channels.

6. A SPRING SCALE:

    Use a reliable spring scale to properly set the strike drag on your trolling and bait rigs. Without it you can easily set the drag too light resulting in a missed hook set or in a battle that endures for hours. Set drags at 25% of line test, i.e. set the drag at 10 lbs. for 40 lb. line.

7. BAIT TANK:

    A good bait tank of at least 20+ gallons is needed to hold and maintain live mackerel. Allow 2 gallons per mackerel - do not overcrowd with bait.

    Superior quality tanks are made by,

    Pacific Edge Inc., 5842-Q McFadden Ave., Huntington Beach, CA 92649, 714-895-1159

**Technique:**

1. LOOK FOR THE SIGNS:

    Fins.

    Use your binoculars to sight these surface fish. Once sighted approach them with care. See "Techniques - Sighting Tailers & Sleepers".

Hovering or circling birds.

> They are probably over a marlin boil or surface bait ball. Certain birds are associated with marlin and the bait marlin prey upon, especially Jaegers and Terns. Know how to identify and look for Jaegers, Skuas, and Terns. Observe their flying behavior and how it changes when the bird sights bait fish.

Bait Balls:

> These are sighted on the surface as dark, purple colored masses or scoped on the fish finder. Arc around the area so the lure passes around the perimeter and preferably under the massed bait.

Warm Water & Changes in Water Temperature:

> Marlin prefer 68+ water temperatures. Where you find warm water, cooler water boundaries - troll along a 1 mile wide band on the warm water side of junction.

Changes in water color/clarity:

> Fish along the clear water side of the boundary.

Boundaries of different ocean currents:

> These are usually indicated by the presence of long slicks where the two currents meet. They are also indicated by different surface water action at the junction. Troll the boundary by crisscrossing down the length.

2. TROLLING LURES:

**SEE TROLLING DIAGRAMS**

Use trolling as a search technique to locate active fish. For maximum success switch to live bait techniques after strikes or upon sighting fish.

Troll fast, 6 - 10 knots with Marlin Clones, approximately 50 to 75 yards behind the boat.

Adjust the trim tabs to minimize boat white-water turbulence behind the stern. Troll lures in the clean water behind the prop turbulence.

**Technique continued:**

2. TROLLING LURES continued:

    Use a roller troller to create a "drop back" in trolled lines. The drop back is a length of loose line that is released on a lure hit. This loose length of line allows the marlin to naturally roll and turn his head with the bait. This natural rolling action sets the marlin up for a much better hook set.

    Troll on the top, forward face of the boat wakes and troll diagonally down-swell.

    Troll away from sun so fish can see your lures.

    Adjust speed until you get some lure turbulence Keep jigs running 75% under the surface, 25% breaking the surface.

    Use one traveling jig - darts, back and forth.

    Rubber band the centerline to reel handle for a short dropback and to keep jig off the surface.

    When moving from spot-to-spot put jig out at 10 - 15 knots. Nobbies work well at 9 - 15 knots. Nobbies are small Doornobs.

    IF A FISH IS FOLLOWING:

    a. Pull the bait or lure away just as the fish approaches.

    b. Pump the throttle hard forward 2 to 3 times in quick, short bursts.

    c. Hold the throttle down causing the lure to skip 30-40 feet, then slow down.

    d. If the fish strikes the lure with his bill, drop the rod tip toward the fish, releasing line tension and making the lure look like it is stunned.

    e. Drop back a pre-rigged live mackerel from the bait tank. **SEE DIAGRAM**

3. SIGHTING "TAILERS" & "SLEEPERS" AND CASTING LIVE BAIT:

    Tailers are actively feeding marlin on the surface - moving tail fins are visible. Sleepers are resting marlin with dorsal fin evident. They are usually seen in early morning, calm water periods.

## MARLIN, STRIPED

**Technique continued:**

Tailers are less wary, - swim down-swell. Tailers are actively searching for food. They are typically seen in the afternoon when the winds kick up the swells.

Try to approach the fish upwind, with the sun toward your back and up-swell if possible.

Approach so bow-caster can cast at 2 o'clock or 10 o'clock. Pull the boat to within 50 to 60 feet of the Marlin.

- Cast to the outside and at least 10 feet ahead of the fish, away from the boat. This will require a cast of 40 to 50 feet.

- Use a swinging underhand cast to get the mackerel to the right spot with a flat arc and minimal splash.

- Put thumb pressure on the reel to determine if the Marlin has taken the mackerel. Use enough pressure to stop the line if only the mackerel is pulling. When you stop feeling the vibration of the swimming mackerel and the thumbed spool keeps going out - you are on!

- Accomplished Marlin anglers can time the hook set when using live bait to avoid the damage and bleeding caused by a swallowed hook. Occasionally an early set will lose a billfish but that fish will live to fight again.

- Meanwhile have another angler drop a live bait rig off the stern, letting it out 50 - 75 ft. Marlin are usually in schools.

- If the fish goes down, wait 15 to 20 minutes as they will often resurface - especially in the downswell direction. Keep your fresh bait in the water while waiting.

- Slow troll (idle speeds) the area with live bait for up to 30 minutes.

- Before moving on, note the Loran position for a possible return later in the day.

- On a hookup, follow the direction of the line entering the water, not directly after the sighted fish. This will minimize the accumulated effects of line drag.

MARLIN, STRIPED 143

**Technique continued:**

    4.    TROLLING LIVE BAIT (near surface or off downrigger):

    **See Diagrams**

    Troll live mackerel slowly. Troll at idle speeds, 1-2 knots. If the mackerel is surfacing, go slower.

    When using downriggers to fish deeper, set the rig to bait school depths or if there is no metered bait, look for a thermocline at 100 to 150 feet.

**The Law:**    Limit: 1, No Size Limit

**Records:**    State:
IGFA: 494 lbs., New Zealand, 1986

**Info:**    Info:    Orange Cty/Los Angeles Area:
        Balboa Angling Club, 714-673-3520
        John Daugherty, JD's Big Game Tackle,
          Newport Beach, 714-723-0883
    San Diego Area:
        San Diego Marlin Club, 619-222-2502

Monitor VHF channel 72. Also monitor channels 2, 5, 11, 65 and 73.

Detailed Ocean Temperature Charts:
    Ocean Imaging, 1289 1/2 Cave Street, La Jolla, CA 92037, 619-454-1993
This service will provide updated temperature maps twice a week from June 15 to Oct. 15 on Mondays and Thursdays via FAX or mail.

**Access:**    Guides: L.A. County:
        The Chase, Huntington Harbor, 213-596-7151

    San Diego Area:
        Bob Hamm, 619-424-6027
        Ron Costa, "Happy Kanake", 619-225-1770
        Mike Hurt, 619-945-1553
          Mike guides on your boat or a charter

    Orange County:
        Fin Fever, Dana Pt., 714-831-1850
        Bongos, Newport Beach, 714-673-2810

    Catalina, Avalon
        Martin Curtin, "Keeper"
          Catalina Is. Inn, 213-510-1624

**See Also:**    Bigeye Tuna - especially around San Diego Marlin areas, Mako Shark, Blue Shark, Thresher Shark

MARLIN, STRIPED   144

## STRIPED MARLIN AREAS

CAUTION: Not to be used for Navigation. See NOS maps

| Area | Latitude | Longitude | Direction & Distance |
|---|---|---|---|
| 1. Osborne Bank | 33 21.6 | 119 2.5 | from Marina del Rey 205, 46.6 miles |
| 2. 9 Mile Bank | 32 37.1' | 117 24.7' | from Pt. Loma, San Diego 254, 8.5 miles |
| 3. 182 Spot | 32 41.4' | 117 42.4' | from Pt. Loma, San Diego 266, 23.7 miles |
| 4. 43 Fathom Bank | 32 39.3' | 117 58.3' | from Pt. Loma, San Diego 262, 37.0 miles |
| 5. 209 Bank | 33 5.7' | 117 52.5' | from Dana Pt. 180, 20 miles from Newport 165, 29.9 miles |
| 6. 279 Spot | 33 17.5' | 117 49.0' | from Dana Pt. 193, 11.5 miles from Newport 167, 17.9 miles |
| 7. Farnsworth Bank | 33 20.5' | 118 31.5' | west side of Catalina off Ben Weston Pt. |
| 8. 277 Spot | 33 11.9' | 118 4.7' | from Newport 190, 25.5 miles |
| 9. 14 Mile Bank | 33 23.8' | 118 0.2' | from Newport 192, 13 miles |
| 10. Avalon Bank | 33 24.4' | 118 13.2' | from Newport 224, 20.2 miles |
| 11. The Slide | 33 17' | 118 17' | east end of Catalina - off Church Rock |

# MARLIN TROLLING PATTERN
## Troll at 8 - 9 knots

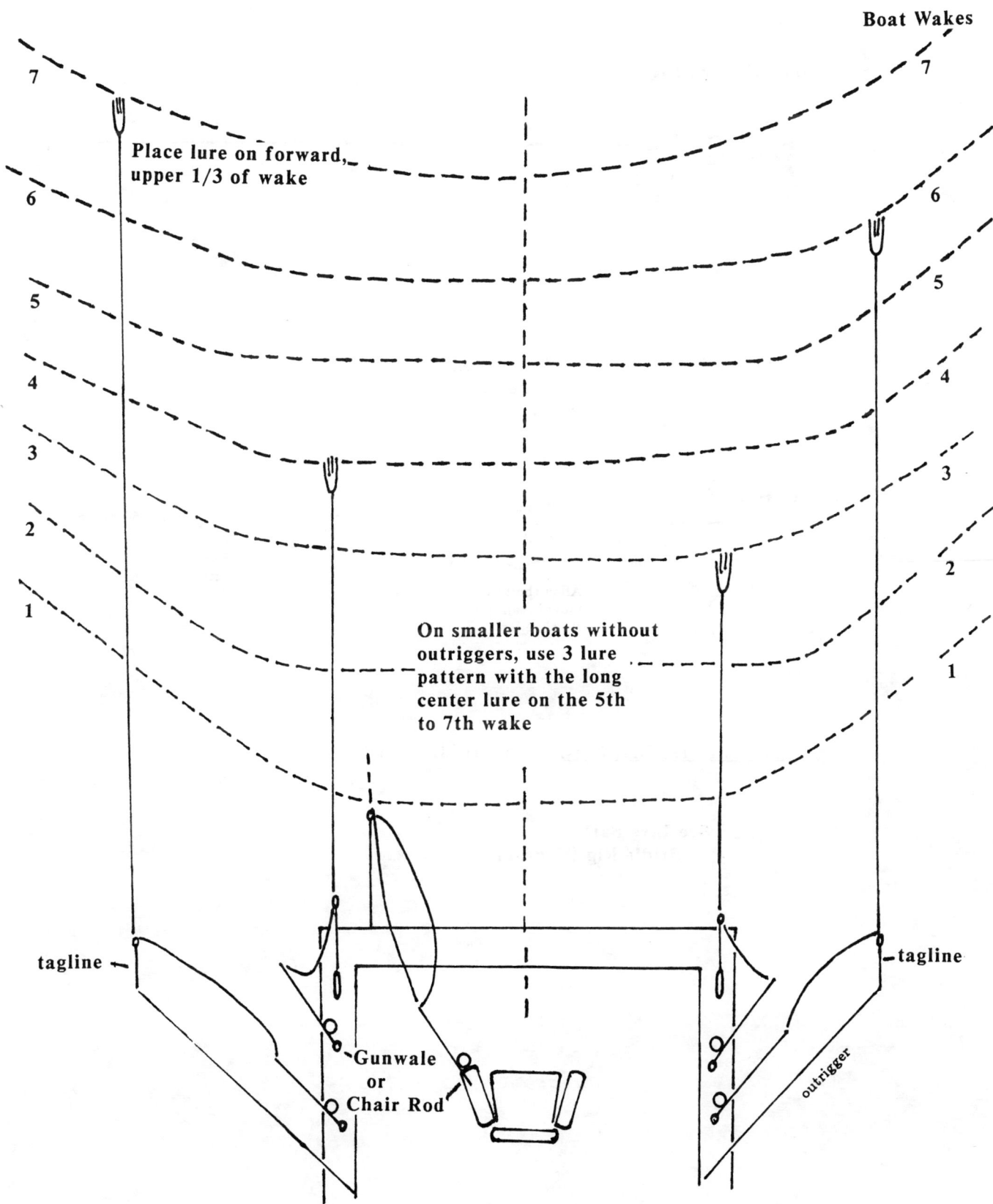

MARLIN, STRIPED  146

# MARLIN LIVE BAIT RIGS

**Bait Casting Rig:**

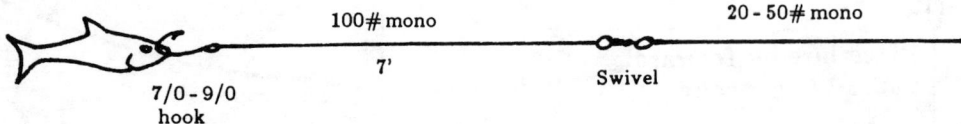

**Drop Back Rig:** Have this rig ready with a nose-hooked mackerel in the stern bait tank

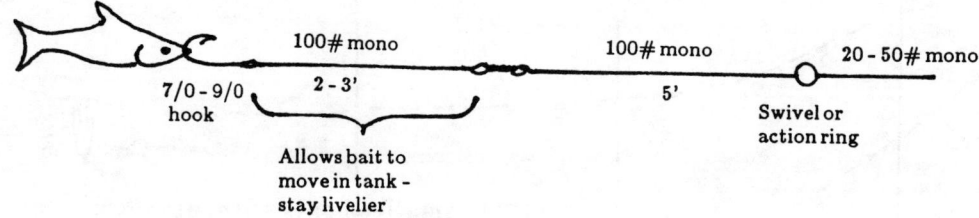

**Trolling Live Bait Rigs:** Troll at idle speeds

    See Live Bait
       Bridle Rig Diagram

MARLIN, STRIPED 147

# TROLLING - LIVE BAIT BRIDLE RIG
## Troll Mackeral or Bonito at slow, idle speeds

① Turn the bait upside down to calm it, and hold in lap with a wet towel.

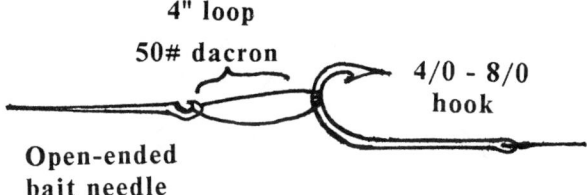

4" loop
50# dacron
4/0 - 8/0 hook
Open-ended bait needle

③ Remove line from bait needle and put loop over hook.

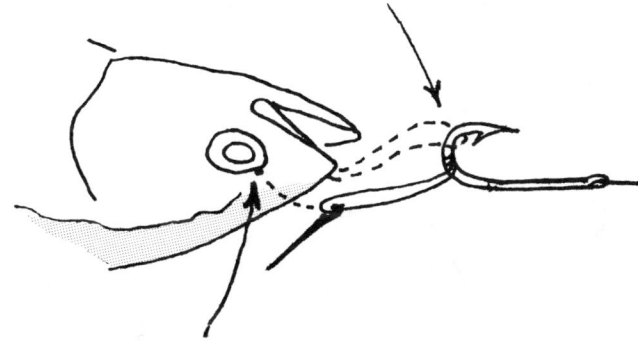

② Push needle through bait at point above and slightly forward of the eye socket. Do not puncture the eyes.

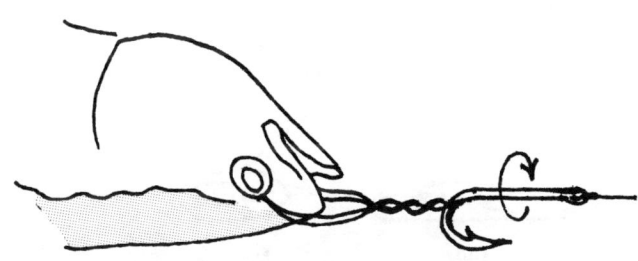

④ Twist hook until line tight.

Alternative double hook rig for tail biters - Mako & Wahoo

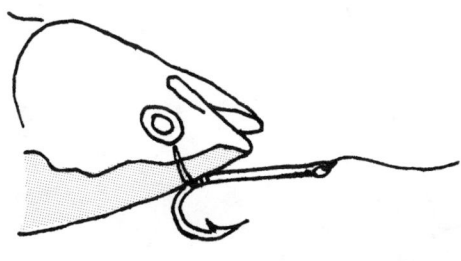

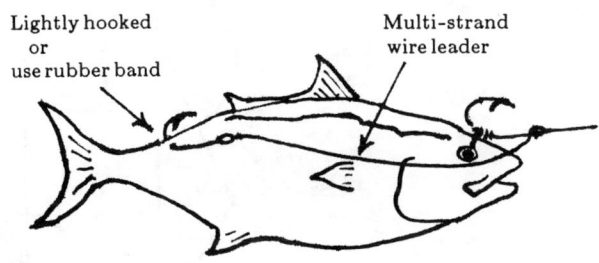

Lightly hooked or use rubber band

Multi-strand wire leader

⑤ Insert hook point under the twisted loop at the bait's head to secure and prevent the bridle from unwinding.

MARLIN, STRIPED  148

# MARLIN TROLLING RIGS - DROPBACKS

A dropback is a length of free line that is released when the Marlin hits the trolled lure. Dropbacks are rigged with taglines and rubber bands or trolling clips.

The dropback allows the Marlin to turn it's head sideways after taking the lure. The hook set occurs with the Marlin's head turned, significantly improving the chances of a solid hookup

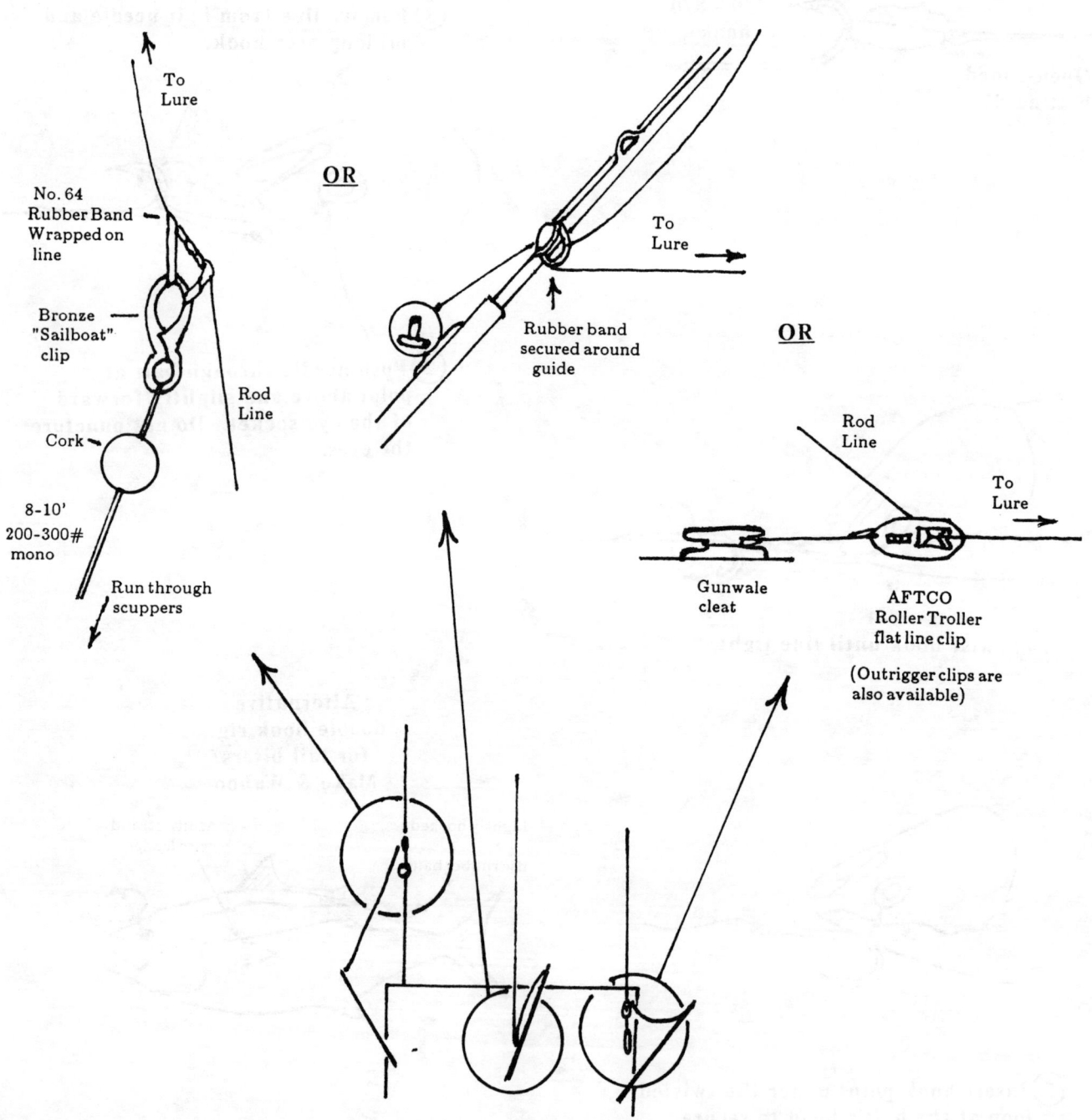

MARLIN, STRIPED 149

San Diego Marlin Guide Ron Costa (right)

Catalina Charter Guide Martin Curtin (right)

MARLIN, STRIPED  150

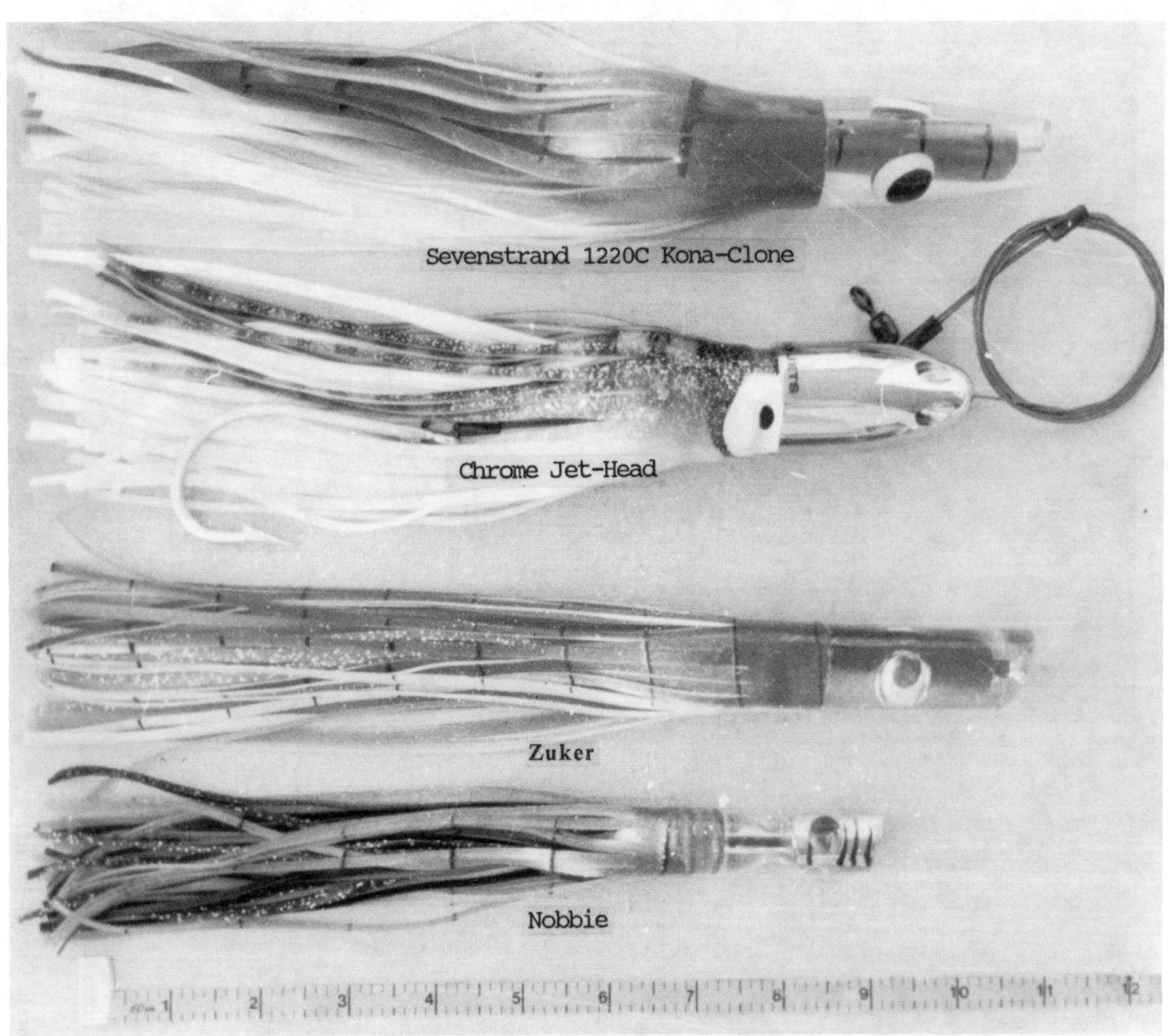

## SACRAMENTO PERCH:

**Where/When:** Lake Crowley - **See Map**
The lake opens at 6 AM.

Be on the water early as strong winds normally pick up quickly about 11 AM to noon. If you are at the far side of the lake, you might want to head back toward the marina before the winds start.

Ask at the lake store where the fish are biting.

Deeper Water - late May to early June

- between Green Banks and The Bluffs across the channel to the east shore.
- the points between Hilton Bay and McGee bay.
- deep water of McGee bay off McGee creek.
- around Alligator point

Shore/Shallow Water - early June to mid-July

- on the east side in 10 to 15 foot deep water out from weedline from Alligator point north towards the Owens river.
- the channel side of Sandy Point.
- the bay area of Crooked Creek.

**Bait/Lures:** Finger/Tube jigs, 1/16 to 1/32 oz or Micro jigs. Purple or yellow Crappie jigs with a piece of worm or slice of squid. See Crappie lure picture.

**Rig:** Ultra-light to light spinning rig.

**Technique:** Fish jigs about 4 feet below a bobber. Give lure occasional action by flicking rod tip.

Action will come in spurts as schools of perch intercept your rig. Keep watch for other anglers success as best area can shift as the day wears.

**The Law:** No Limit

**Records:** State: 3 lbs. 10 oz., Crowley Lake, 1974

**Info:** Culver's Sporting Goods, Bishop
619-934-8474

**Access:** Boat Rentals: 213-485-4853 (That's right, the Los Angeles Dept. of Water & Power controls this!)

**See Also:** Rainbow Trout, Brown Trout

PERCH, SACRAMENTO 152

# CROWLEY LAKE - SACRAMENTO PERCH

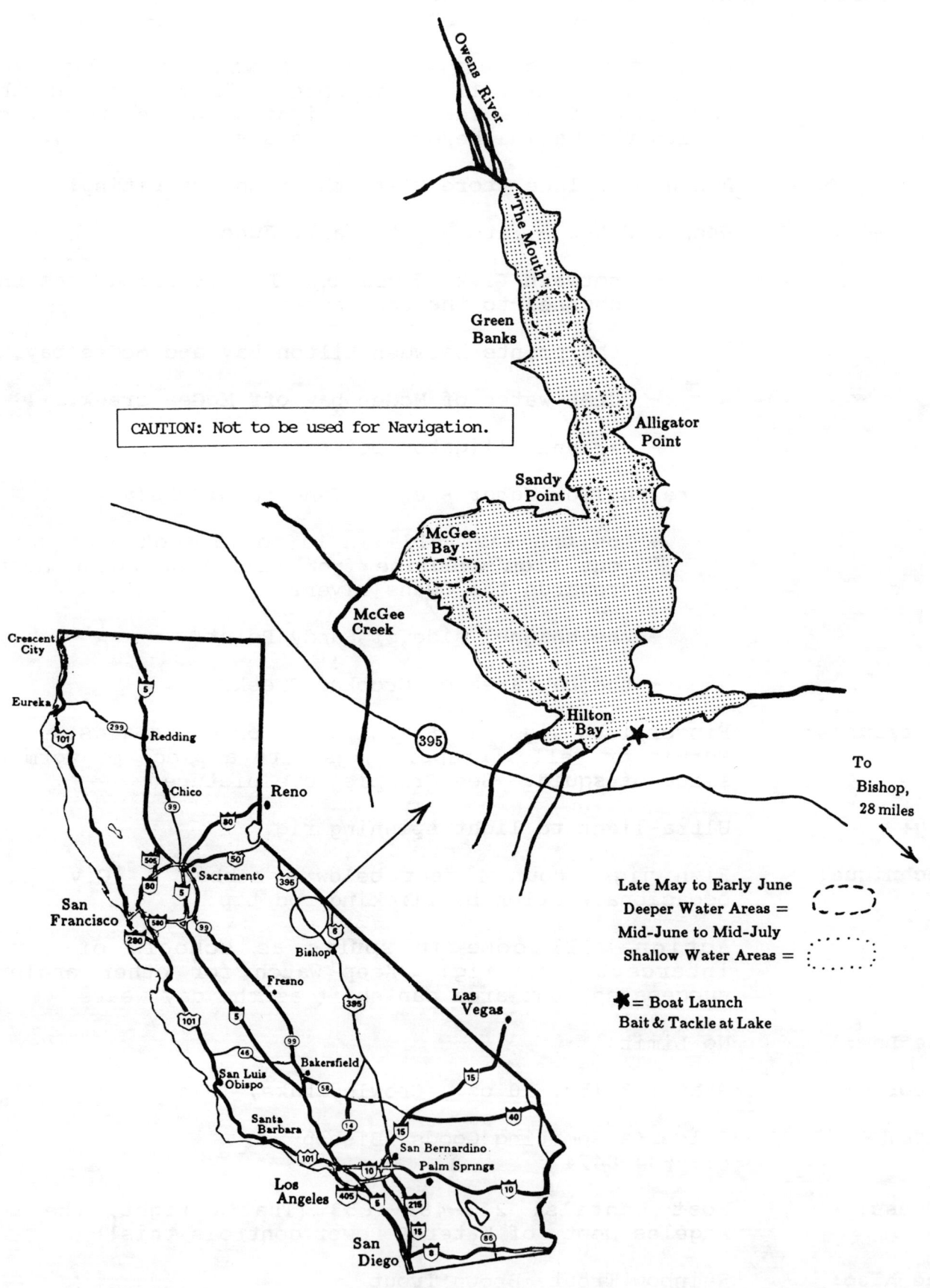

# ROCKCOD / COWCOD:

**Where:** Southern California

**SEE MAP**

**When:** December to April
Cowcod especially from January to mid-April at Tanner Bank, 43 fathom spot, Potato Bank

**Bait/Lures:** Jigs can be "Bounced" off the bottom if attempting to catch larger specimens. These are large jigs typically from 16 to 32 oz such as PDQ, UFO, Hex Bar, and Diamond Jigs. Chrome, white and red, white and orange, or all white are effective colors.

Anchovies or squid either fished on a bare hook or on shrimp fly tied hooks - hooks tied with colored line or tinsel.

**Rig:** **See Picture**

A reel with capacity of 1000 ft. of at least 50# test dacron line (6/0 size or larger).

3 to 5 lb. lead sinkers.

Ganglions with #3/0 to 7/0 hooks spaced at least 9 inches apart. If the hooks are closer than this it will reduce your success. Convenience store gangions usually have hooks spaced too close together. Ganglions with shrimp fly decorations, usually orange, red or yellow will out catch bare hooks.

Railing plate
Long shaft reel handle

Unless you only fish for Rockcod or do a lot of Rockcod fishing, it makes more sense to rent a rig from the landing than to go through the effort/expense of either buying a rig just for Rockcod or changing your big game reel.

**Technique:** Almost all fish are caught just off the bottom or near it. The bottom can range from 200 - 1000 feet so make sure you have enough line or you wont catch a single fish. Double hook the anchovy through the eye and back. It really is unnecessary to try to set the hook on a bite. Leave the bait down for at least 10 series of bites or longer.

USE SHARP HOOKS.

Drop to the bottom. As soon as you hit bottom, reel up 5 turns. Try here first. If no action try different depths from 5 to 20 reels off the bottom.

**Technique continued:**

If the fish are sonared off the bottom, the skipper will let you know about how many reels off the bottom to try. Observe and copy those anglers catching fish as to depth and bait.

After a series of bites, reel the rig up with moderate speed. A rapid retrieve can spin off hooked fish as the line comes toward the surface.

Bring a small bucket to hold anchovies at your fishing station. By putting 10 to 20 anchovies in the bucket at one, you can avoid wasted time and effort in going to the bait tank and fishing out anchovies one at a time.

Put your initials on your weights. If you bring up a tangle with several other fishermen, your initials will help identify which fish are yours. A better way is to be able to identify your own hooks, either by the knot or some other method.

With jigs - drop to bottom, crank up a couple turns off the bottom, drag a while, crank 20-30 times, let fall to bottom, repeat. Try different retrieve and drop speeds. Keep the jig moving. Salmon Grouper will often hit a jig retrieved rapidly off the bottom.

HOW TO MINIMIZE TANGLES:

1. Use only dacron except for terminal rigging.
2. Use a heavy enough weight.
3 Only drop your line when the skipper says "Let em go".
4. Position your rig as far as possible from the other fishermen, or as the last person at the bow.
5. Get next to fishermen that follow rules 1 to 4.

**The Law:** Limit: 15
Also see regulations for ocean bag limits.

**Records:** Bocaccio (Salmon Grouper): 21 lbs. 4 oz.
Cabezon: 15 lbs.
Rockfish, Vermilion: 7 lbs.
Rockfish, Yelloweye: 20 lbs. 12 oz.

**Info:** Call landings indicated on map.

**Access:** Best access is by partyboat, especially in southern California where the best fishing is found considerably offshore and at depths that most private boat sonars aren't designed to reach.

**See Also:** Lingcod

ROCKCOD / COWCOD 156

# ROCKCOD RIGS

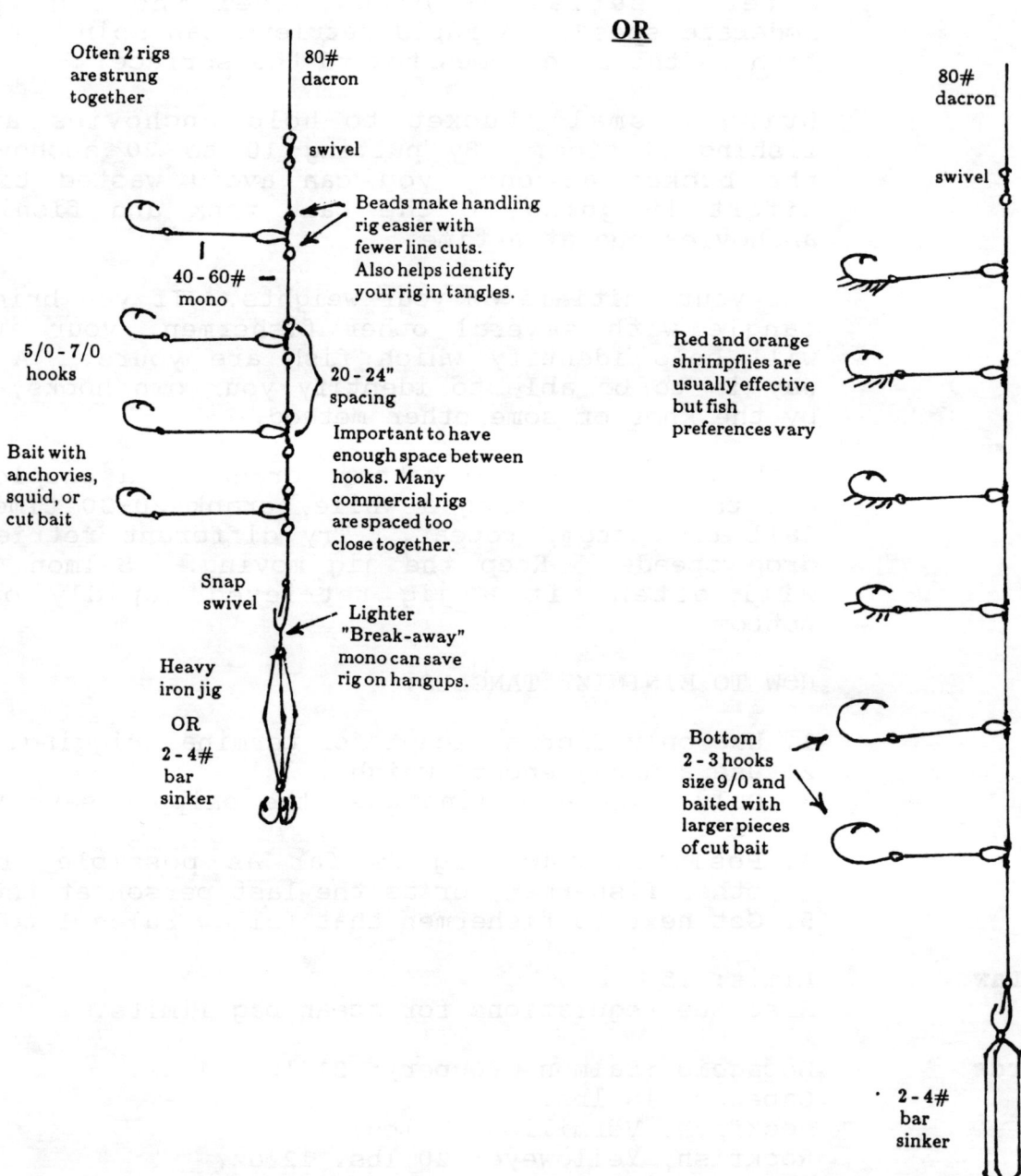

## ROCKCOD AREAS - SOUTHERN CALIFORNIA

1. 43 Fathom Spot     32° 39.2'/ 117° 58.3'     From Pt. Loma 262°/ 37 NM
2. 60 Mile Bank     32° 3.7'/ 118° 13.2'     From Pt. Loma 220°/ 60 NM
   From Newport 176°/ 77 NM
3. Catalina Is.     .......................     From Alamitos Bay 215°/ 23.8 NM to Ship Rock, 2 Harbors
4. Clemente Is.     33° 2.1'/ 118° 36.8'     Castle Rock - NW end
5. Cortes Bank     32° 26.5'/ 119° 7.5'     From Marina del Rey 186°/ 97 NM
   From Pt. Loma 250°/ 95 NM
6. Harrison Reef     34° 2.6'/ 118° 58.0'     From Marina del Rey 278°/ 24 NM
7. Osborn Bank     33° 21.5'/ 119° 2.5'     From Marina del Rey 205°/ 46.6 NM
8. Potato Bank     33° 15.0'/ 119° 49.5'     From Marina del Rey 224°/ 81 NM
9. Rincon Reef     34° 19.4'/ 119° 27.0'     From Santa Barbara 170°/ 10 NM
10. Santa Barbara Is.     33° 29.2'/ 119° 1.8'     From Marina del Rey 211°/ 41.0 NM
    From Newport 250°/ 58.2 NM
11. Southeast Bank "150 Kelp"     South & East of 150 Kelp - see below
    33° 7.5'/ 118° 35.0'
    Double Oil Platform called "Elly & Ellen"     From Alamitos Bay 170°/ 9.5 NM
12. Tanner Bank     32° 42.0'/ 119° 8.0'     From Marina del Rey 190°/ 83.1 NM

# SOUTHERN CALIFORNIA - PRIME OCEAN FISHING AREAS

CAUTION: Not to be used for Navigation. See NOS maps

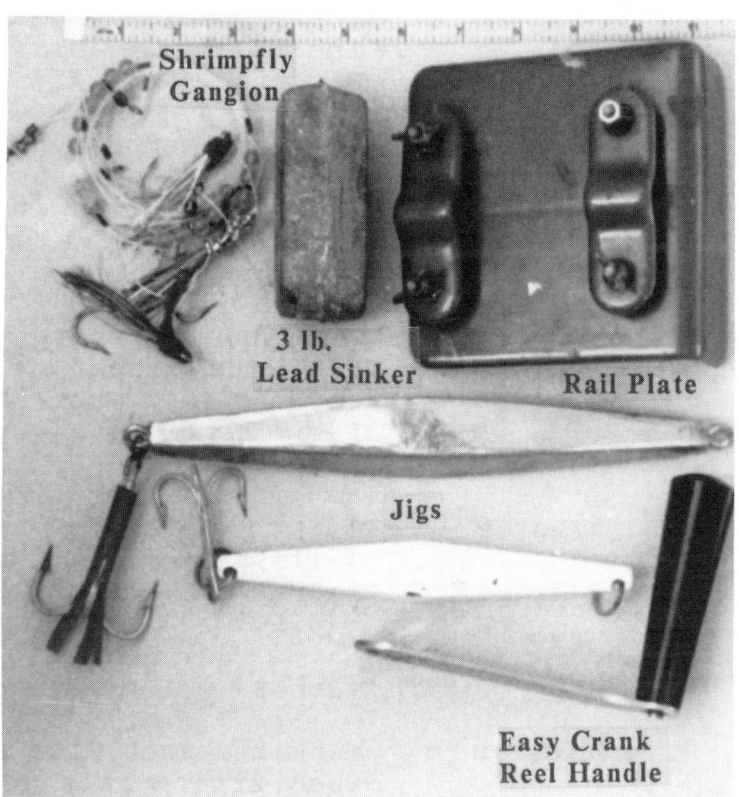

Shrimpfly Gangion
3 lb. Lead Sinker
Rail Plate
Jigs
Easy Crank Reel Handle

A Nice Catch of Salmon Grouper from a Single Drop

| | |
|---|---|
| **ROCKFISH:** | Rockfish refers to the smaller kelp bass and shallow rocky reef fish of the northern California coast. Included are Olive (Johnnie Bass), Blue and Black Rockfish. |
| **Where:** | Northern Monterey Bay Area - **See Diagram**<br>Typically in depths of 40 to 50 feet.<br>Fish for schools in open water over rocky reefs.<br>Fish kelp beds along outer edge and through channels that regularly run between the beds. |
| **When:** | Late spring through early fall - best in August.<br>Fish the neap tides - moderate tide periods between new and full moon phases.<br>Fish tend to be nearer the surface in the early hours. |
| **Bait/Lures:** | 1/4 to 1 oz. leadhead lures. Plastic worms, Twister Tails, (3" - 5") Shabby Shrimp, Scroungers, Scampis - in yellow, green, white. |
| **Rig:** | Use light tackle - spinning or bass plugging tackle with 8# - 12# mono |
| **Technique:** | Mark the area with a buoy. Work area while drifting.<br>Cast artificials (see photo) and let sink on a tight line to depth of school.<br>Use a countdown method to locate school holding depths and repeat.<br>If you don't get a hit on the fall, retrieve slowly with light jigging motion.<br>If action heavy, anchor the boat, else continue to drift, search the marked area. |
| **The Law:** | 15 fish in any combination of species (1990).<br>See regulations for ocean bag limits. |
| **Access:** | Launch Ramps  **See Diagram**<br><br>Boat Rentals: Santa Cruz Boat Rentals<br>Santa Cruz Municipal Wharf<br>408-423-1739<br>Opens at 7 AM<br><br>Capitola Boat & Bait<br>End of Capitola Wharf<br>408-462-2208<br>Opens at 6 AM<br><br>Club Nautique<br>Monterey<br>408-373-4448 |
| **See Also:** | Halibut, Lingcod in Monterey Bay |

Haddock's Split-Tail Worm
Worm King on small leadhead
Curly-tailed Grubs
Kreepy Krawl'r
Worm King

To San Jose
17
San Lorenzo River
9
San Lorenzo River Dr
1
Shadowbrook Restaurant
Soquel Wharf Rd
To Monterey
Soquel Av
Santa Cruz
Capitola
1
Suncliff Beach
Mission St
River St
Ocean St
Small Craft Harbor
7th Ave
41st Av
Capitola Rd
Capitola Reef
Murray
13
Front
Lake
Cabrillo Hwy
1
Black Pt
Ramp
Capitola Wharf - boat rentals
Marine Lab Towers
14
Pt Santa Cruz
Harbor Reef
Soquel Pt
Natural Bridges Beach
Soquel Reef
40'
40'
40'
Park Reef
Santa Cruz Wharf - boat rentals
East Reef
60'
60'
60'
Santa Cruz Reef
Buoy Reef
Adams Reef
Mile Reef
Buoy South Reef
MONTEREY BAY
South Rock
CAUTION: Not to be used for Navigation. See NOS maps

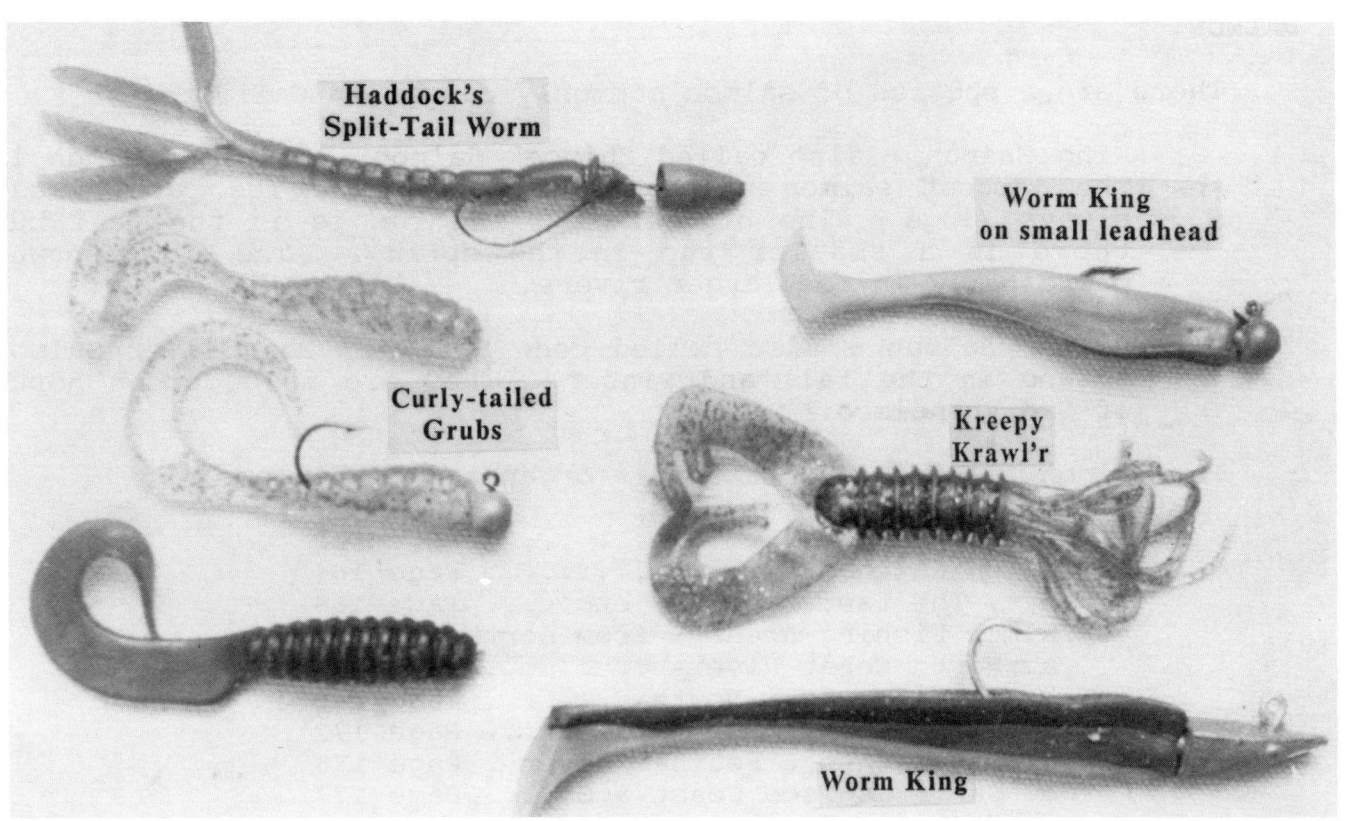

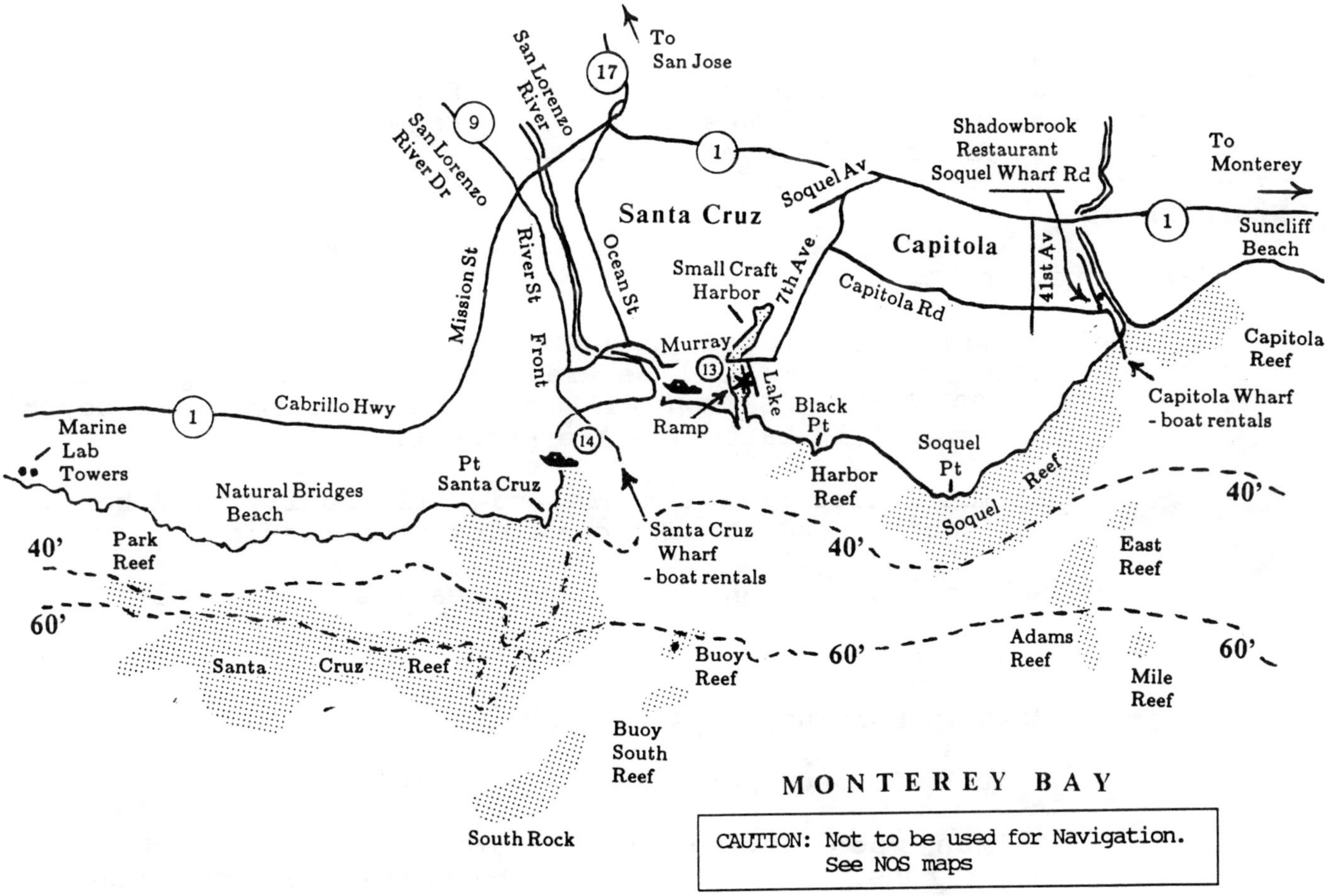

**SALMON:**

There are 2 species of salmon commonly caught in California;

King Salmon - also called Chinook Salmon. The King Salmon is the largest salmon species. Fish over 20 lbs. are almost always Kings. The biggest spawning run is in the fall but there is a smaller run in the spring. The King spawns principally in the larger rivers.

Silver Salmon - also called Coho Salmon. The Silver Salmon spawns in the fall and winter. They are most common north of San Francisco.

The Salmon fishing information is organized as follows;

1. Where / When ................... Page 162
2. Salmon Calendars ............... Page 164
3. Bait, The Law, Records, etc .... Page 168
4. Salmon Fishing Areas - from north to south.
   a. North Coast Rivers ......... Page 169
   b. Klamath River Mouth ........ Page 170
   c. North Coast Ocean .......... Page 172
   d. Sacramento & Feather River . Page 173
   e. San Francisco Coast & Bay .. Page 177
   f. Monterey Bay ............... Page 179
   g. Ventura, Oxnard area ....... Page 179
5. Salmon Fishing Techniques
   a. Techniques Diagram ......... Page 182
   b. Ocean Techniques ........... Page 183
   c. River Techniques ........... Page 188

**Where/When:**

Structure, Ocean:

Salmon seek ideal temperatures of 53 to 55 degrees. This preference will generally put them at depths of 30 to 90 feet. Salmon will tolerate temperatures beyond this ideal if bait fish are present.

Salmon follow bait schools and will usually hold beneath the schools and attack from below when feeding.

Salmon avoid bright light and clear, shallow waters.

Structure, Rivers:

Best in morning, 6 AM to 9 AM

Avoid full moon periods.

Salmon when moving will follow the deeper and slower water runs. They will often be found along the edges of the main current.

**Where/When continued:**

Salmon when resting will hold in the larger holes, especially at the junction of major creeks and rivers. The good holes are well known and all have names, for example: Minnow Hole, Barge Hole, etc.

When fishing near a river's mouth in the area affected by tidal action, the bite often is better at high tide.

SALMON Calendar

# SALMON FISHING CALENDAR

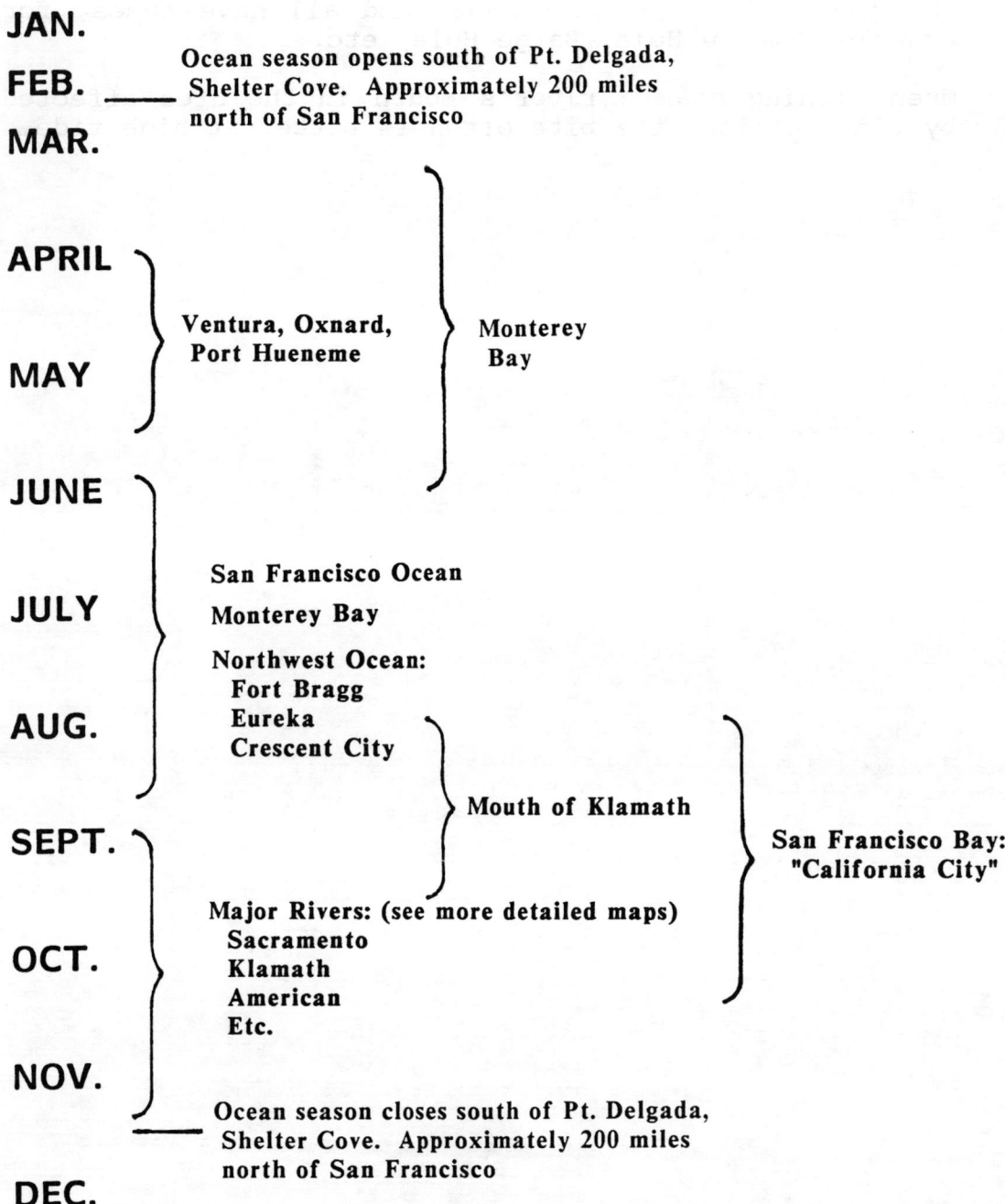

JAN.

FEB. — Ocean season opens south of Pt. Delgada, Shelter Cove. Approximately 200 miles north of San Francisco

MAR.

APRIL ⎫
⎬ Ventura, Oxnard, Port Hueneme ⎫
MAY ⎪ ⎬ Monterey Bay
⎭ ⎪
JUNE ⎫ ⎭
⎪ San Francisco Ocean
JULY ⎬ Monterey Bay
⎪ Northwest Ocean:
⎪   Fort Bragg
AUG. ⎭   Eureka
    Crescent City ⎫
                  ⎬ Mouth of Klamath ⎫
SEPT. ⎫                               ⎬ San Francisco Bay: "California City"
⎪ Major Rivers: (see more detailed maps) ⎪
⎪   Sacramento ⎭
OCT. ⎬   Klamath
⎪   American
⎪   Etc.
NOV. ⎭
— Ocean season closes south of Pt. Delgada, Shelter Cove. Approximately 200 miles north of San Francisco

DEC.

# SALMON FISHING CALENDAR
## Northern California Rivers

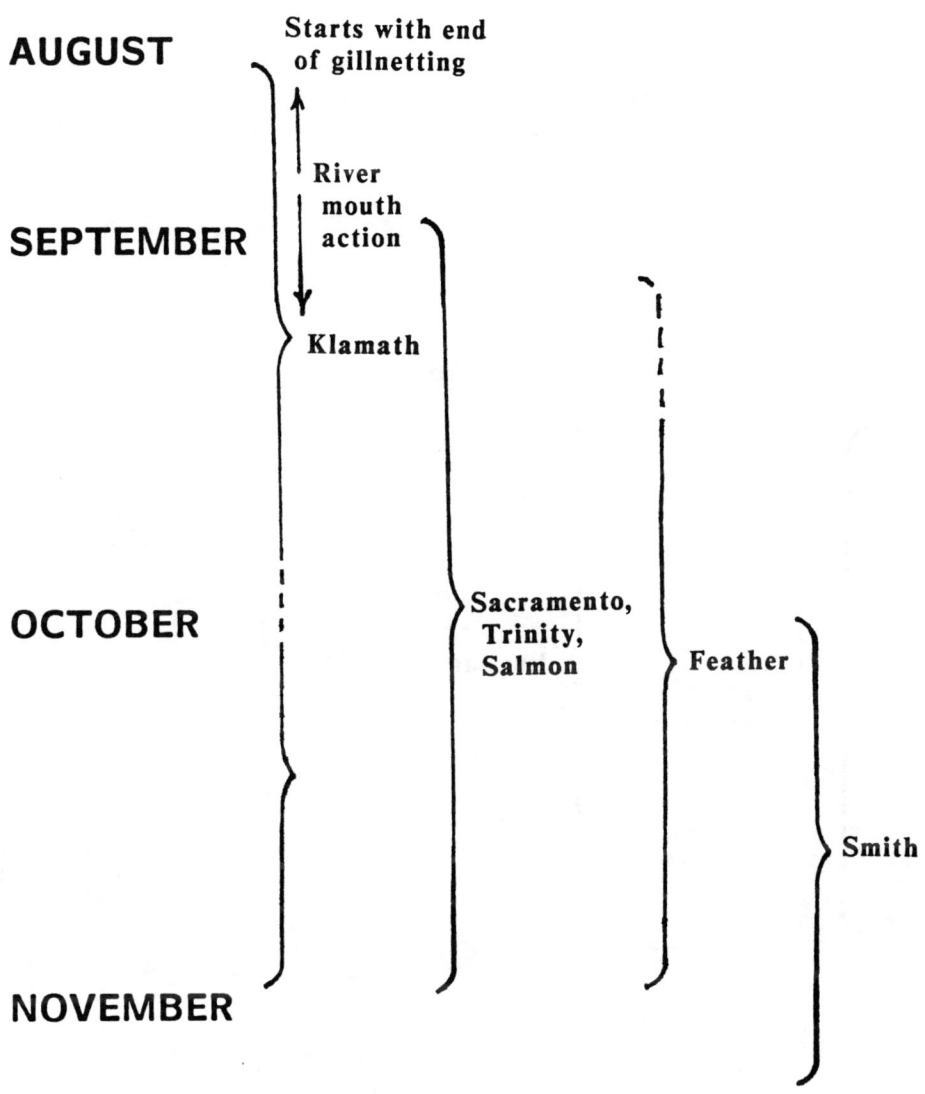

SALMON 166
Calendar

# SALMON FISHING CALENDAR
## Northern California Rivers

**SEPTEMBER**

**OCTOBER**

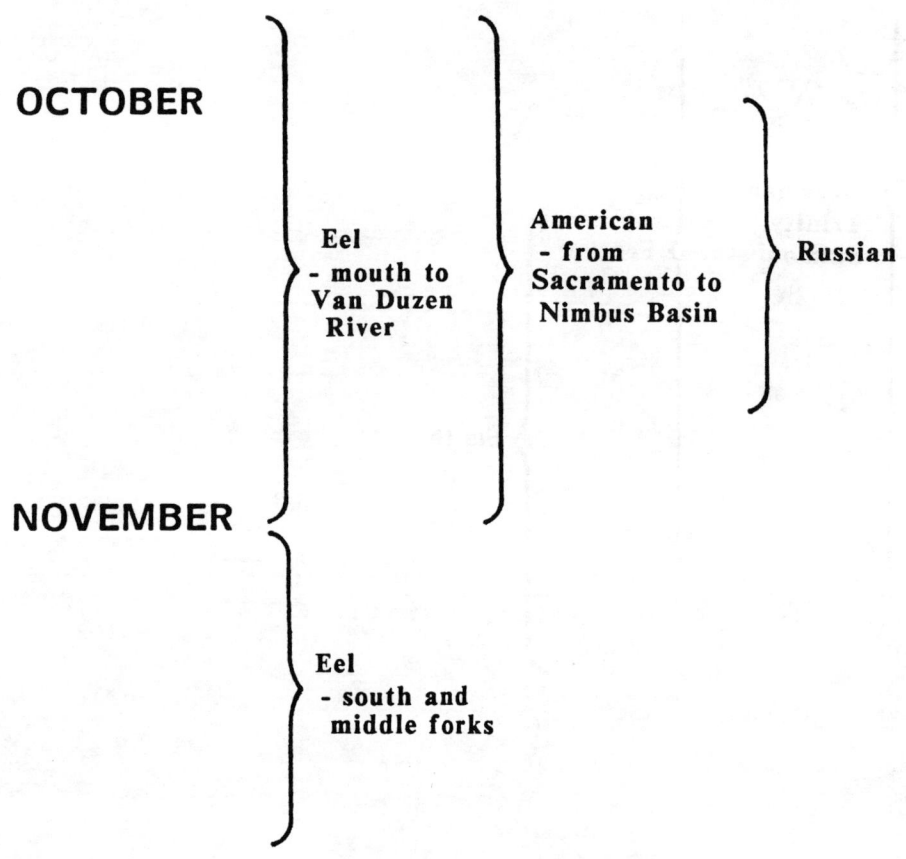

Eel
- mouth to
Van Duzen
River

American
- from
Sacramento to
Nimbus Basin

Russian

**NOVEMBER**

Eel
- south and
middle forks

# SALMON FISHING TECHNIQUES
## When and Where the common techniques are used

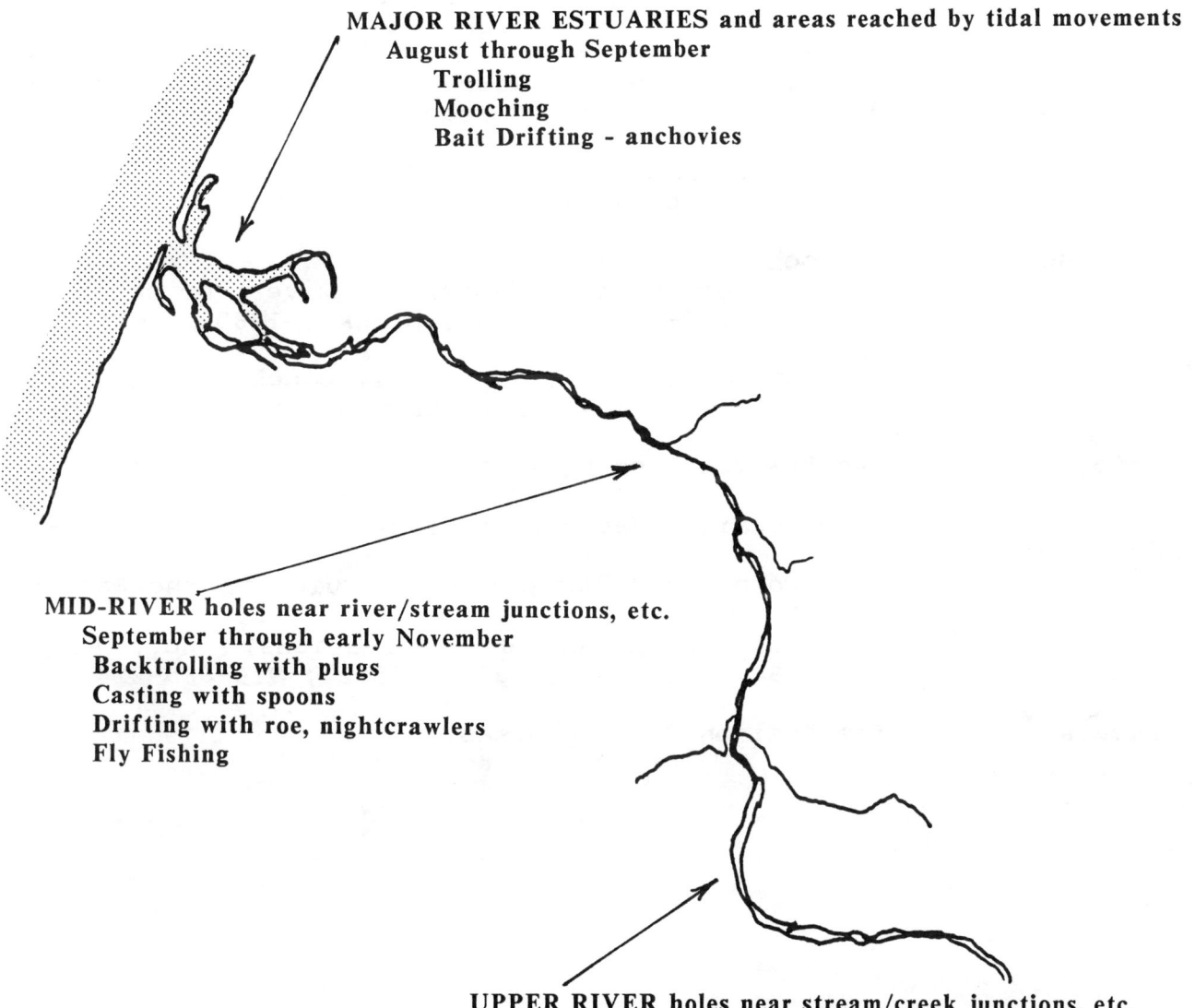

OPEN OCEAN:
    Trolling: Spring through early fall
    Mooching: Summer through early fall
    Jigging: Summer through early fall

MAJOR RIVER ESTUARIES and areas reached by tidal movements
    August through September
      Trolling
      Mooching
      Bait Drifting - anchovies

MID-RIVER holes near river/stream junctions, etc.
    September through early November
      Backtrolling with plugs
      Casting with spoons
      Drifting with roe, nightcrawlers
      Fly Fishing

UPPER RIVER holes near stream/creek junctions, etc.
    September through early November
      Casting with spoons
      Drifting with roe, nightcrawlers
      Fly Fishing

SALMON 168

**Bait/Lures:** Anchovies: Best near river mouths and for ocean fish.
Roe: Best upriver near spawning grounds.
Tuna Balls: Oil packed tuna balls in Maline, a red net material cut to a small square.

Lures: Hoochies are best when prevalent bait is shrimp such as early season fishing near the Farallon Islands. Spoons are better for deep water, low visibility. Also see "Salmon Fishing Techniques" and "Salmon Fishing Areas" sections.

**The Law:** Ocean limits are generally 2 fish per day with a minimum length of 20 inches. Note that single barbless hooks are required north of Point Conception - a point of land just north of Santa Barbara (1990). However regulations vary by area so see current DFG regs. In lakes and streams, salmon are often combined with trout catches to determine daily limits. See DFG regs. for details.

More Info: Dept. of Fish & Game
707-445-6493

**Records:** Chinook
State: 88 lbs., Sacramento River, November 1979
IGFA: 97 lbs. 4 oz., Alaska, 1985
Silver
State: 22 lbs., Paper Mill Creek, January 1959
IGFA: 31 lbs., B.C. Canada, 1947

**Info:** See "Salmon Fishing Areas"

More Detail - Sacramento River:

Complete Atlas & Anglers Guide to the Sacramento River, Shasta Dam to San Pablo Bay; Northern California Angler Publications, Inc.; P.O. Box 994; Elk Grove, Calif. 95624; 916-685-2245

**Access:** See "Salmon Fishing Areas"

## North Coast Rivers

**Where:** North coast rivers:
- Eel
- Russian
- Smith - can handle heavy rains without silting

**When:** October - November

After the first rains; the rain cools and oxygenates the rivers. Subsequent rain raises the water too high and discolors the water.

November - river mouth to Panther Flat using roe, Spin-N-Glos, and Hot Shots.

**Bait/Lures:** Anchovies, roe, nightcrawlers

No. 2 Mepps Spinner
Black Roostertail
Panther Martin

**Technique:** See River Fishing - Floating, Bank Fishing or Wading
See River Fishing - Float Fishing
See River Fishing - Backtrolling

**The Law:** Call the Calif. Dept. of Fish & Game at 707-442-4502 for current restrictions, such as low flow closures.

**Info:** Eel & Smith Rivers:

Grundman's Sporting Goods
707-764-5744

Bucksport Sporting Goods, Eureka
707-442-1832

Russian River:

King's Sport & Tackle, Guerneville
707-869-2156

More Detail: For a complete description of major north coast rivers bank fishing access, see;

California Steelhead
Jim Freeman
Chronicle Books, San Francisco

**See Also:** In Streams: Steelhead, Rainbow Trout, Brown Trout
Off San Francisco: Striped Bass are active around ocean near-shore structure in July and August.

SALMON 170
Klamath River Mouth

**Where:** Mouth of Klamath River; Waukel Riffle by 101 bridge

**SEE MAP**

Also upriver at Weitchpec near mouth of Trinity River and downriver at Pecwan Bar.

**When:** August, September

After indian gillnetting halt allows Salmon into river. The gillnetting is controlled by the DFG who sets a quota every year. The netting starts around labor day and is usually over within 3 weeks or less. The DFG regulations handbook gives a number to call for information, 707-442-4502.

When high tides bring fresh runs into the river mouth.

**Rig/Technique:**

Bank Casting during outgoing tides with large Kastmasters, Panther Martins, or Bear Valley Spinners

Troll at mouth of river with Bear Valley No. 3 spinner. A 2-10 oz. sinker is needed to get lures down near the productive bottom.

See River Fishing - Bank Casting or Float Fishing
See River Fishing - Plunking
Backtrolling anchovies

**Info:** Klamath:

    Del's Camp, 707-482-4922

Trinity:

    Brady's Sporting Goods, 916-623-3121
    Weaverville, 916-623-3121

DFG River Closures: 707-442-4502

**Access:** Guides: Ray Benner, 503-469-5965
        Jack Ellis, 707-526-9077
        Upriver: call Damm Drifter Tackle Shop, Klamath Glen, 707-482-6635
Boat Rentals: Del's Camp, 707-482-4922

**See Also:** Steelhead

**Lodging:** Requa Inn, 707-482-8205
Steelhead Lodge, 707-482-8145
Motel Tree's, 707-482-3152
Camper Corral, 707-482-5741

# SALMON 171
## Klamath River Mouth

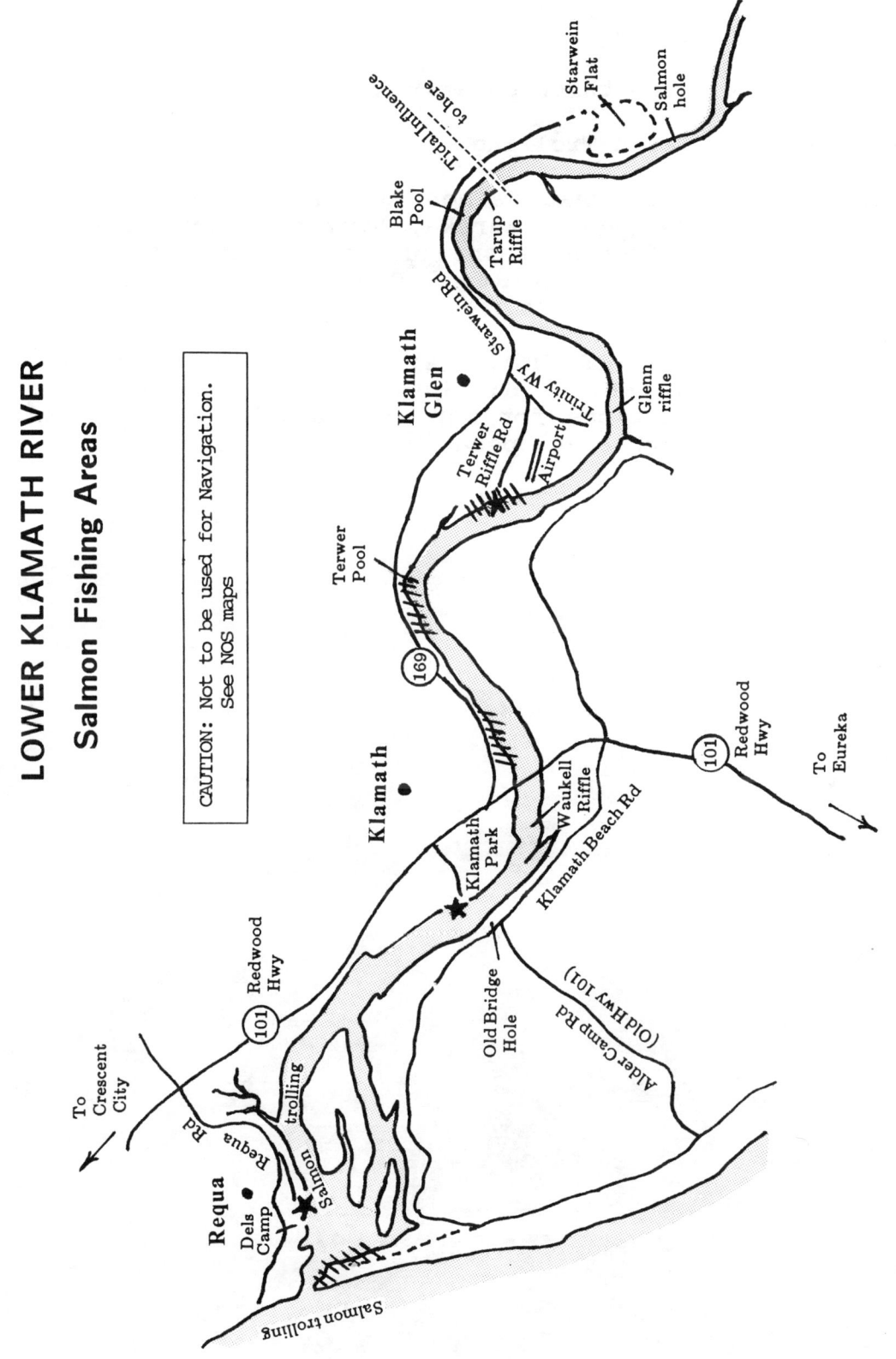

LOWER KLAMATH RIVER
Salmon Fishing Areas

CAUTION: Not to be used for Navigation. See NOS maps

SALMON 172
North Coast Ocean

**Where:** Crescent City
Eureka/Trinidad
Bodega Bay

**When:** June through early August

**Technique:** Ocean Trolling

**The Law:** Note that Salmon Regulations for areas north of Pt. Delgada - Eureka, Trinidad, Crescent City, etc. are different than for areas south of Pt. Delgada - Fort Bragg, Bodega Bay, etc. Check DF&G current regulations.

**Access:** See APPENDIX A: Saltwater Launching Sites and APPENDIX B: Sportfishing Landings / Partyboats sections for maps of launching ramps and location of partyboat operations.

# SALMON 173
## Sacramento & Feather Rivers

**Where:** Sacramento River - Los Molinos to Redding

**SEE MAP for Sacramento River, Los Molinos to Redding**

Also the Feather River, and the American River to Nimbus Basin.

Feather River:

- Upstream of Gridley Bridge
- Mouth of Feather at Verona (need boat)
- Below Star Bend - Star Bend launch ramp
- Downstream of Oroville Afterbay Outlet - highway 162 to Larkin Rd. and 6 miles to the river for bank fishing.
- Shanghai Bend (need boat)

**When:** September through early November - when the river is not muddied from recent rains.

Active bite influenced by volume of water released from Keswick dam. Flows of about 8000 cubic feet/second are about ideal.

Best action usually in the early morning.

**Bait/Lures:** Roe

Flatfish, Models: M2
Kwikfish, Models: T-50, T55
The larger lures are better in slower currents.
Colors: Silver, pearl, red, pink, white

Needlefish: Models: K14 to T60
Use with a #3 or #4 silver or brass spinner.

With both lures, put a slab of sardine fillet between the middle and terminal hook of the lure. See diagram.

**Rig:** 6 - 7 foot rod with a small levelwind reel such as a Penn 930, 940, or 9M loaded with 20# mono.

SEE RIGGING DIAGRAM

**Technique:** See River Fishing - Floating
See River Fishing - Backtrolling

**Info:** Sacramento River:

Shasta Cascade Association provides fishing and recreational information for north central and northeast counties of Siskiyou, Medoc, Trinity, Shasta, Lassen, Tehama, and northern Plumas including Lake Almanor. Call: 916-243-2643

SALMON   174
Sacramento & Feather Rivers

**Info continued:**

        Sacramento River:

            Red Bluff Diversion Dam
              Fish Counts: 916-527-1408

        Feather River:

             Johnson's Bait & Tackle
              Yuba City
              916-674-1912

        American: 916-363-6885

**Access:**        Guides: Sacramento River

            Shasta Cascade Wonderland Assoc.
            P.O. Box 1988
            Redding, CA 96001
            (916) 243-2643

            Bob Wigham, 916-222-8058
            Hank Mautz, 916-365-1447
            Barry Gravier, 916-527-7024
            Jack Findleton, 916-487-3392
            Al Vasconcellos, 916-365-7818
            Balls Ferry Number: 916-365-2224

**More Detail:**    See Sportsman's Maps, Red Bluff

**See Also:**      Steelhead, Sturgeon, Striped Bass, Rainbow Trout

# SALMON CYCLE
## San Francisco Bay / Sacramento River Systems

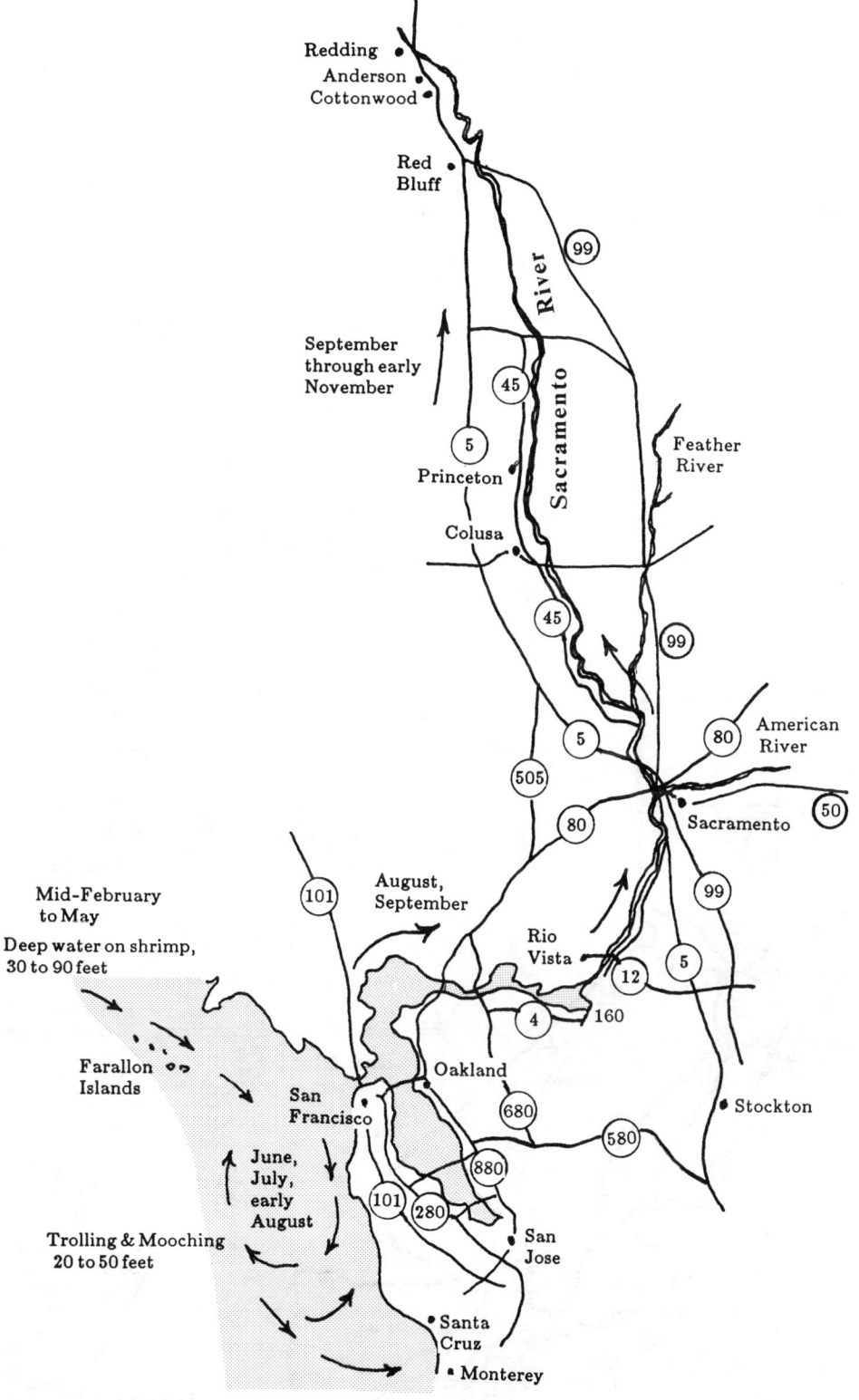

# SACRAMENTO RIVER SALMON
## Fishing Holes, Guides, Information, Launch Ramps

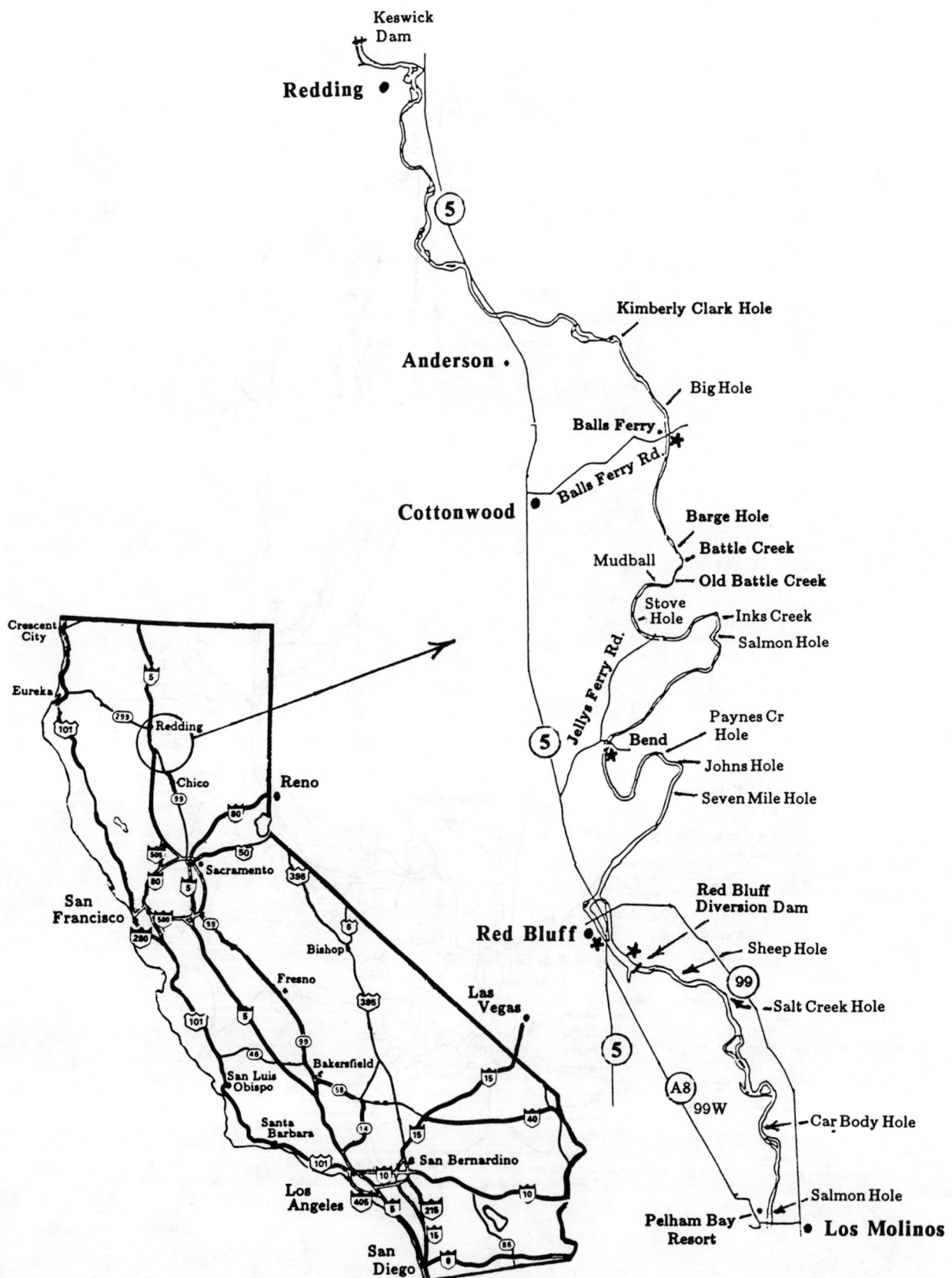

SALMON 177
San Francisco Coastline

**Where:** **SEE MAP**

**When:** June, July, and August

Early morning is the best time.

**Rig/Technique:** See Ocean Fishing - Live Bait
See Ocean Fishing - Trolling
See Ocean Fishing - Mooching

**Access:** Launch Ramps: Pillar Point
Sausalito

Partyboats: See Map

**Info:** Fish Counts
24 hour recording
Emeryville Sportfishing
415-654-6696

**See Also:** Striped Bass

---

**Where:** "California City" refers to San Francisco Bay waters east and north east of Tiburon peninsula. See Map.

**SEE MAP**

**When:** August, September

Approximately 1 hour before and after moderate high tides. Usually not good following negative tide conditions.

**Rig/Technique:** Trolling

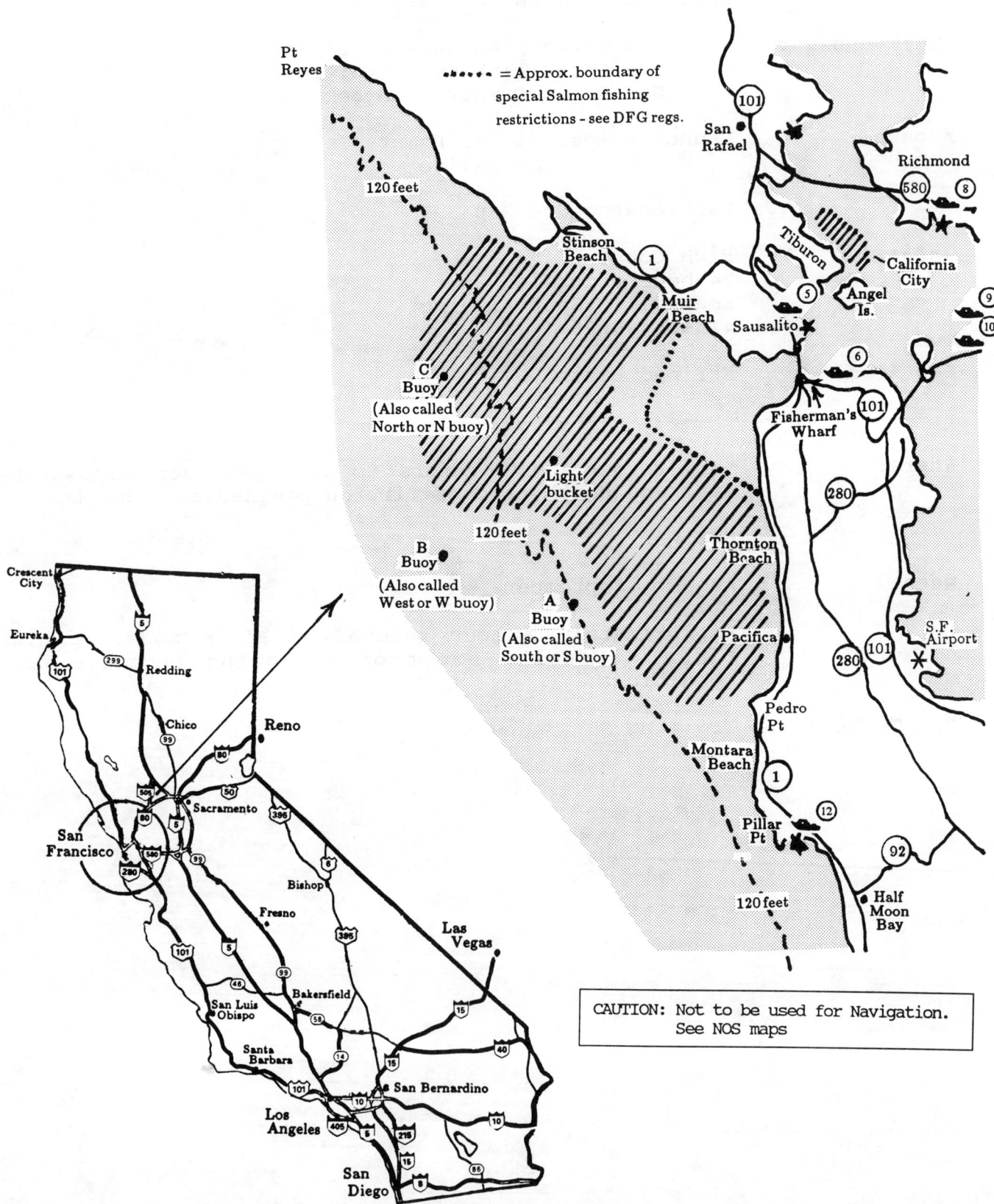

# SALMON FISHING MAP

**San Francisco Coastline, Half Moon Bay, "California City"**

## Monterey Bay, Ventura

**Where:**	Monterey Bay - Moss Landing
Between Fort Ord and Moss Landing

**SEE MAP**

**When:**	April through June
The first 2 hours of daylight are best

July & August, some mooching just out from Moss Landing

**Bait/Lures:**	Live or frozen anchovies

**Rig/Technique:**	See Ocean - Trolling
See Ocean - Mooching

**Access:**	Boat Rental:

Club Nautique
408-373-4448

---

**Where:**	Ventura, Oxnard, Port Hueneme

**SEE MAP**

Top water to 30-40' down
Around anchovy bait balls

**When:**	May to Mid-June

**Bait/Lures:**	Anchovies flylined or fished deep

**Rig/Technique:**	See Ocean Fishing - Trolling

**Access:**	Boat Rentals:

Club Nautique
Ventura
805-642-1722

SALMON 180

# SALMON FISHING MAP
## Monterey Bay

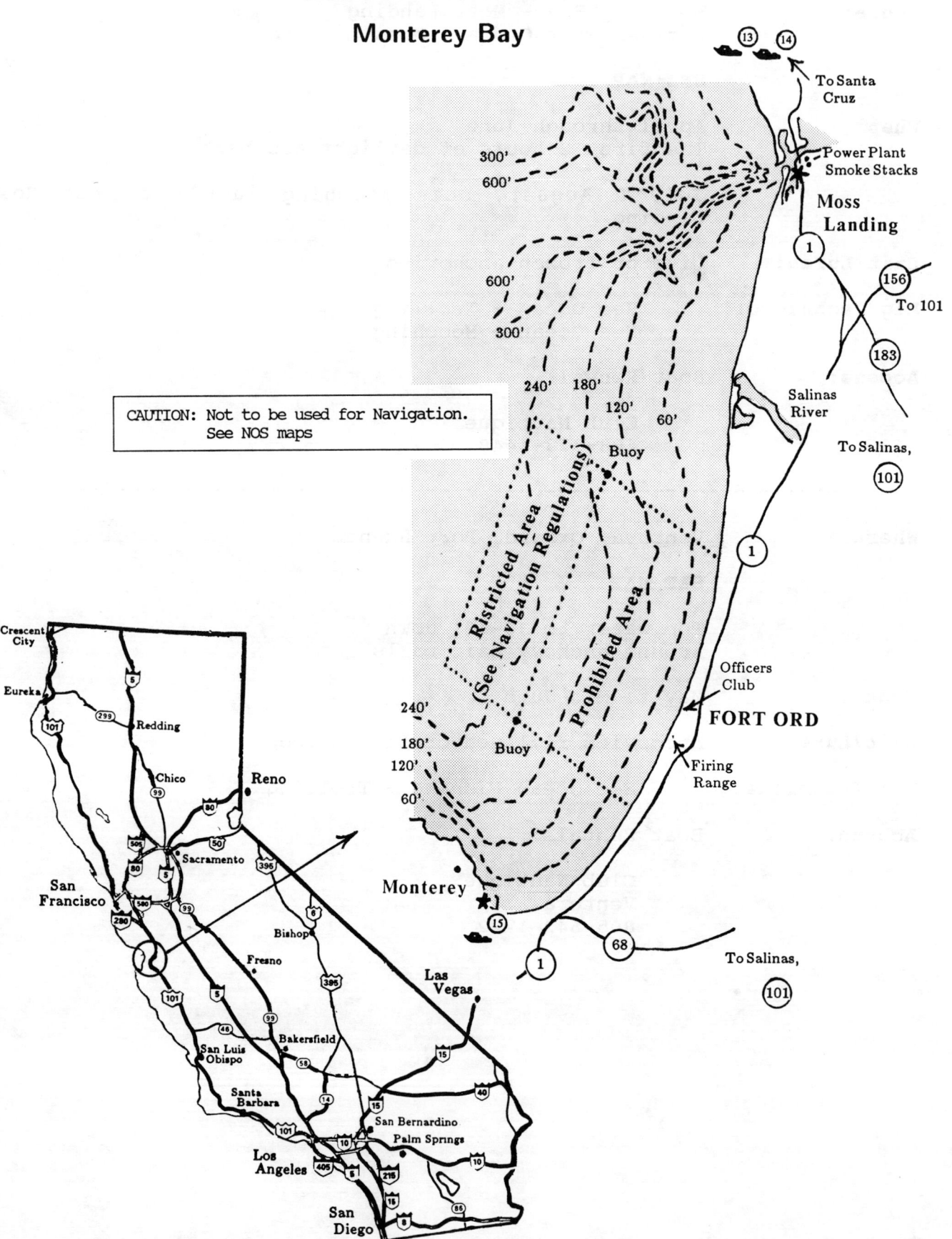

# SALMON FISHING AREAS
## Ventura / Oxnard

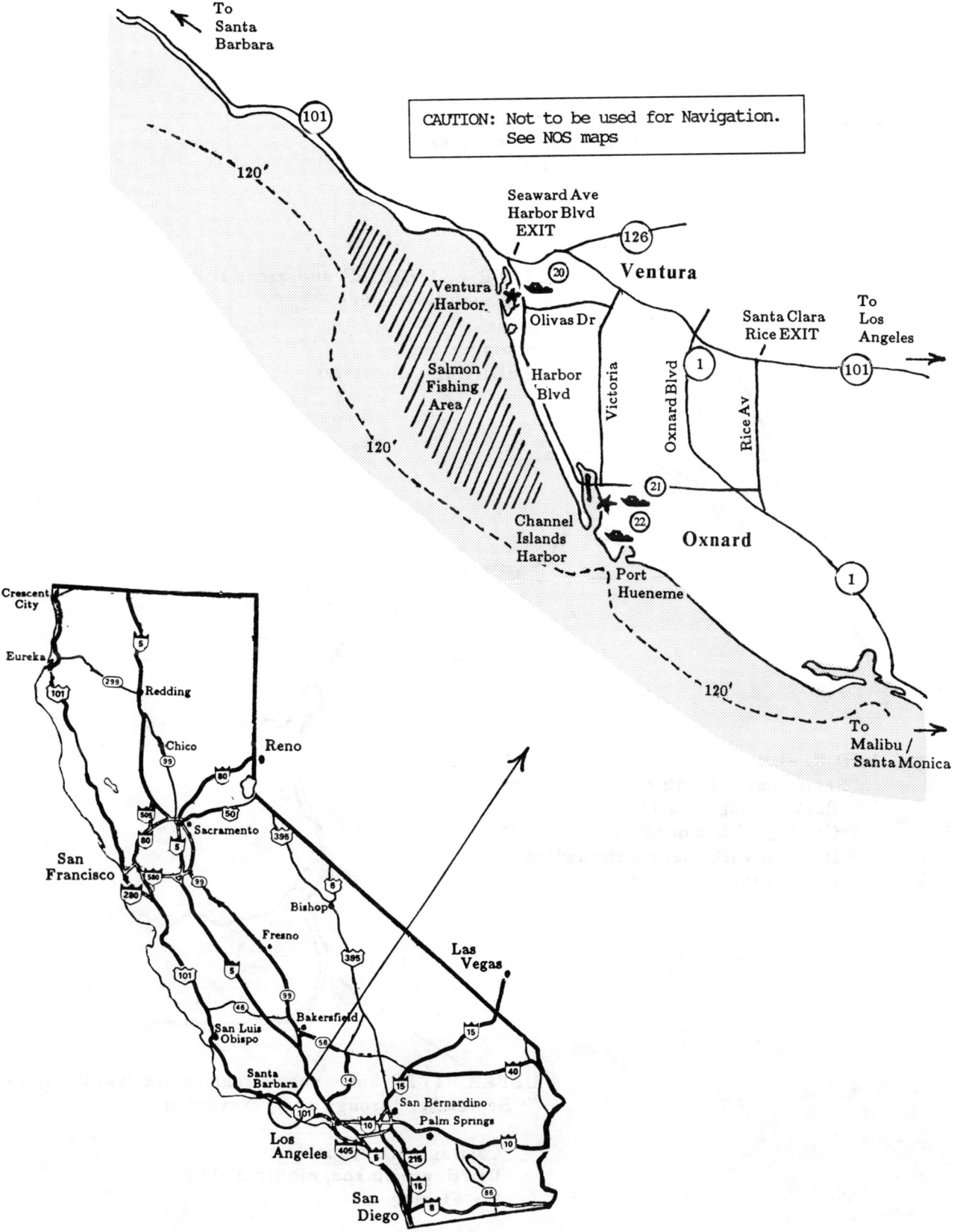

SALMON 182
Techniques

# SALMON FISHING TECHNIQUES
## When and Where the common techniques are used

**OPEN OCEAN:**     Trolling: Spring through early fall
                            Mooching: Summer through early fall
                            Jigging:  Summer through early fall

**MAJOR RIVER ESTUARIES** and areas reached by tidal movements
    August through September
      Trolling
      Mooching
      Bait Drifting - anchovies

**MID-RIVER** holes near river/stream junctions, etc.
    September through early November
      Backtrolling with plugs
      Casting with spoons
      Drifting with roe, nightcrawlers
      Fly Fishing

**UPPER RIVER** holes near stream/creek junctions, etc.
    September through early November

      Casting with spoons
      Drifting with roe, nightcrawlers
      Fly Fishing

# SALMON
## Ocean Techniques

**Rig & Technique:** The proper rig and technique depend on the area fished and the season as follows;

Ocean Fishing - Trolling:

Trolling is most popular and effective in the early season when the salmon are scattered and deep, especially up until late May and June when mooching becomes more effective.

There are 2 common trolling rigs - using large lead or cast iron cannonball sinkers with a strike release device, and using a downrigger. The large sinkers are used on the partyboats, downriggers are used on private boats.

Troll about 3 to 5 miles/hour. This is equivalent to a fast walking pace.

Ocean Fishing - Trolling with Cannonball Sinkers:

**SEE DIAGRAM**

Trolling speeds are 3 - 5 miles/hour, about equal to a fast walking pace.

6 1/2' to 7' stiff action rod to handle up to 3 lb. trolling weights and a medium weight saltwater reel, i.e. Penn 3/0

20 - 30# mono

Fish are typically 30-90' deep in 53-55 degree water although this technique is not effective much beyond 50 feet.

The skipper will let you know how many "pulls" to let out your line. A pull is equal to the length between your reel and the nearest rod guide.

2 - 3 lb. cannonball sinker on sinker release tied 4 feet up the line.

Use a light drag setting - Salmon have soft mouths. Check/replace your bait every 15 - 20 minutes. Also replace the bait if you hook a jellyfish.

The anchovy or herring should have a "wounded fish" action such as spinning or shaking. One way of getting this action is to use a Salmon Rotary Killer. Without a Rotary Killer, rigging the anchovy with a slight bend in the body can produce the desired rolling action.

A Dodger is a reflective, rectangular piece of metal that is rigged between the bait and the weight or downrigger clip. Dodgers can be very effective especially in spring, dirty water conditions where their vibration attracts salmon, but are generally not used on partyboats since they can aggravate line tangles.

The use of stiff-action rods to handle the heavy sinkers and the fact that the boat often will continue trolling when there are hookups, considerably reduces the action of catching and playing a fish. A technique called mooching can add more fun to the catching. Some boats specialize in mooching. The trade-off is that trolling is frequently more effective - especially in the early season when the fish are scattered and deeper. See Mooching.

-OR-

Ocean Fishing - Trolling with a Downrigger:

**SEE DIAGRAM**

Slow troll at about 2 knots.

This technique is especially effective in the early season when the salmon are scattered and deeper.

The downrigger allows effective trolling to depths of 100+ feet using lighter tackle than with the cannonball sinker release technique. A more flexible rod can be used and lighter line.

Salmon have soft mouths - keep the drag light.

Lures: Andy Reeker, Krocodile (3/4 to 1 oz.)
   Colors: Gold, Silver, Hoochies - Red & white

Ocean Fishing - Trolling with a Downrigger:

The Dodger gives flash and action like a school of live bait fish. It is rigged between sinker and bait on lure to produce a darting action to the bait.

A Dodger can be very effective. These are not commonly used on charter boats since their movement can cause tangles.

SALMON 185
Ocean Techniques

# SALMON OCEAN RIGS: TROLLING

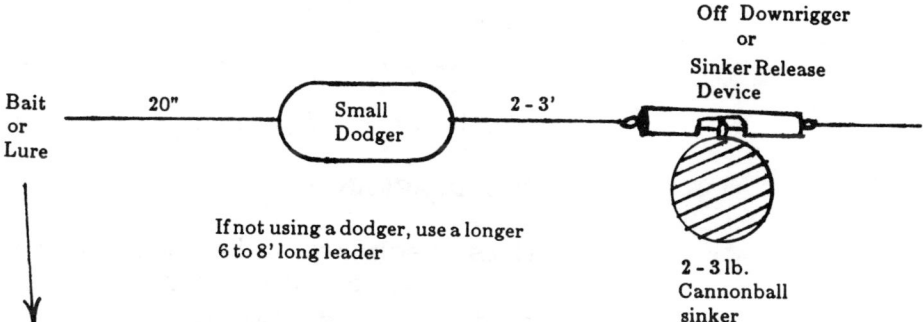

### 1. Bait Harness

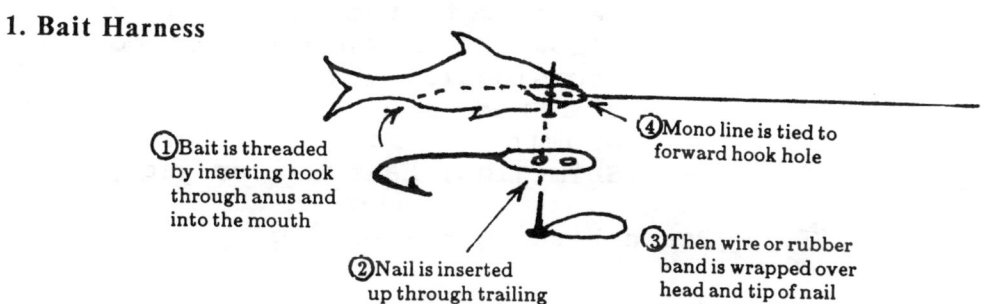

### 2. Salmon Rotary Killer

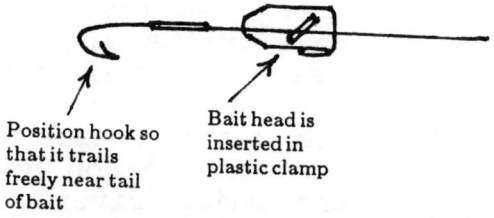

### 1. Double Hook Rig

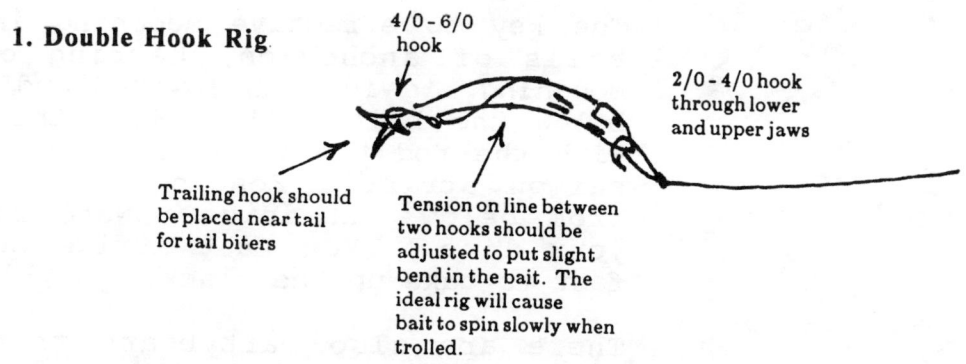

SALMON 186
Ocean Techniques

Ocean Fishing - Live Bait:

Penn 500SL, Daiwa 30 or 50 or equivalent
6 - 6 1/2 foot light-medium to medium weight rod
10-25# Mono
Mustad live bait hooks, size 1 - 1/0

Ocean Fishing - Jigging:

**SEE DIAGRAM**

This technique is most effective during minimal tidal water movement - just before, during and after a tide change.

Cast jig out from the boat.
Let sink to the bottom or to fish holding depth. Allow the ocean surge to move the lure or jig by occasionally lifting the jig off the bottom with the rod tip, letting drop on a slack line, pausing a couple seconds and repeating. Use Shim jigs, Hair Raiser jigs.

Ocean Fishing - Mooching

**SEE DIAGRAM**

Mooching allows for the use of lighter rigs and no heavy weights. This makes fishing a lot more sporting and fun.

Bait, wet fly, or spoon is trolled from a boat that drifts with the current. This technique is used in the middle season when salmon concentrate around anchovy schools and also in the later season for fishing coastal estuaries when the salmon concentrate in the deep holes of the major river estuaries, usually starting in late August, and lasting through early October before the first fall storms.

The key to effective mooching is locating bait balls of anchovies, herring or squid. The mooching rig is then lowered and drifted to just below the bait ball. Move the bait regularly with the rod tip to entice more bait action and salmon strikes. Feeding salmon strike quickly from below and drive upward putting slack in your line. You must strike quickly and reel fast to take up the slack.

There are also partyboats that specialize in mooching for salmon in the open ocean especially during the late summer starting in August.

SALMON 187
Ocean Techniques

## SALMON OCEAN RIGS: JIGGING

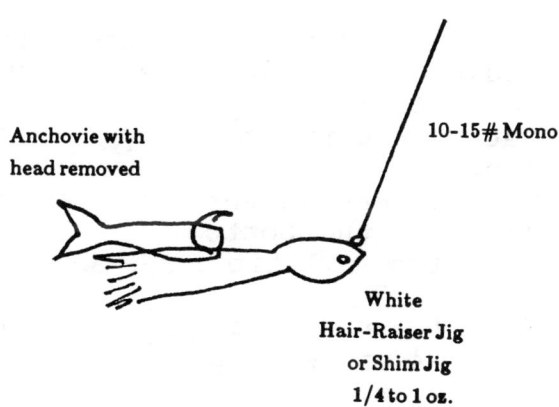

## SALMON OCEAN RIGS: MOOCHING

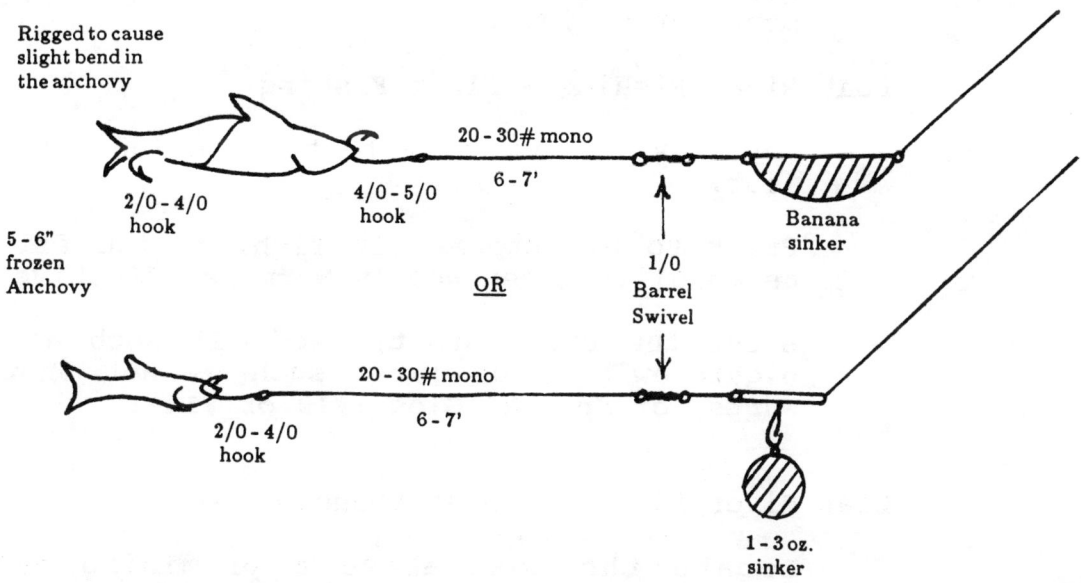

## River Techniques

River Fishing - Drift Fishing, Bank Fishing or River Wading.

Locate a promising deep hole, such as at the mouth of a feeder creek or stream.
Cast upstream.
Let the current carry the bait down the "run" areas.
Use enough weight to keep the bait on or very close to the bottom.
Hold the rod tip high and keep slack out of the line.
For lure fishing, systematically work the channels and pools with short casts and retrieves.

Bait: Anchovies work best close to the river mouth. Salmon roe works better mid-stream and upstream.

Lures: Salmon egg imitations - Corkies, Yarn. Hot Shot, Wee Wart, Krocodile, Little Cleo, Dardevle, Panther Martin, Mepps #4 or #5 Spinner, Gold Kastmaster (3/4 oz.), Bear Valley Spinners.

Boat River Fishing - Plunking

This technique differs from the standard rig with the addition of a heavy sinker to keep the bait from drifting. Used most frequently at the mouth of a river.

Boat River Fishing - Float Fishing

Involves the use of a boat and guide. See Guide list.

Prior to big storms fly fishing with flies such as an olive green Woolly Worm is effective.

After the rains start, use bait such as roe or nightcrawlers, or lures such as Hot Shots, Wee Warts, or Spin N' Glos (#12 or #14).

Boat River Fishing - Back Bouncing Roe

Locate the boat above a promising hole and adjust the motor speed to drift very slowly downstream while doing the following.
Freespool to let rig/roe to bottom.
Pump rod to lift your weight off the bottom and let rig slip downcurrent while letting some line slip off the reel.

Repeat working different downstream lanes.
Strike on any unusual change in action or feel.
You MUST have enough weight to be on the bottom.

River Fishing - Backtrolling

The boat motor is run just fast enough to keep the boat stationary in the river current above a productive hole.

Lures are dropped back 8 - 20 levelwinds.

The motor is eased-off slightly to let the lure slowly move back into the hole.

Work very slowly downstream.

Watch carefully for any change in motion

The objective is to;

- work the lure so that it slowly wobbles downstream toward the salmon's face. Work slowly to give the fish time to get irritated by this thing hanging in their face.

- keep the lure working just off the bottom, and drifting slowly downstream.

This technique is used with large Flatfish (M2, T50 or T55), Kwikfish (K15 or K16), and roe.

SALMON 190
River Techniques

## SALMON RIVER RIGS: DRIFT OR BANK FISHING

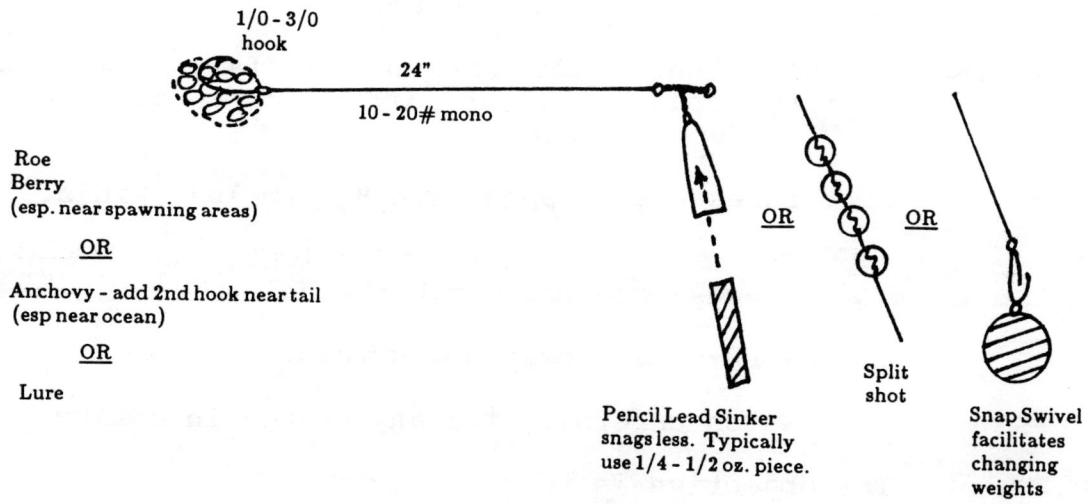

## SALMON RIVER RIGS: BACK-TROLLING

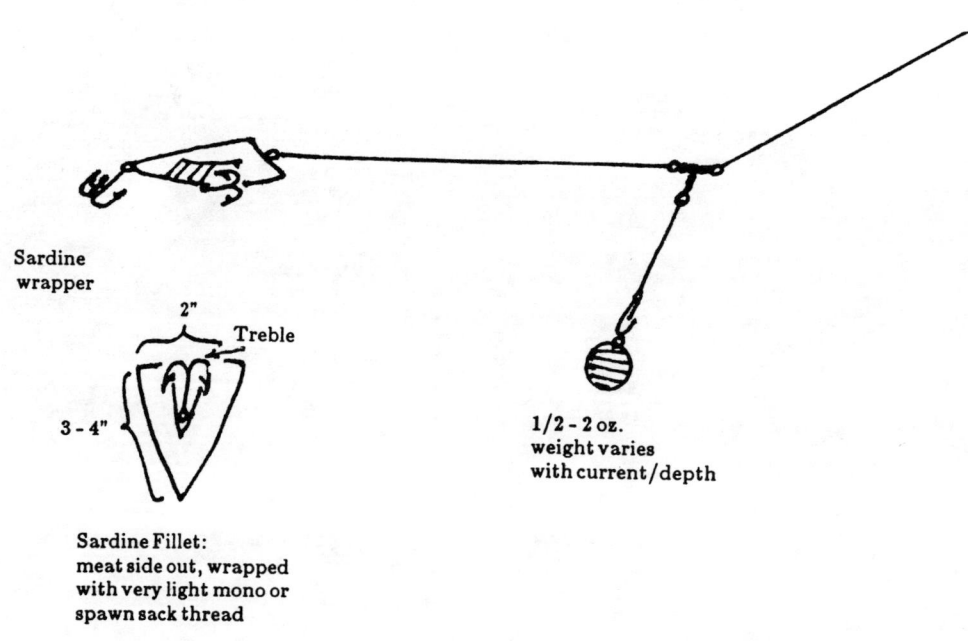

SALMON 192

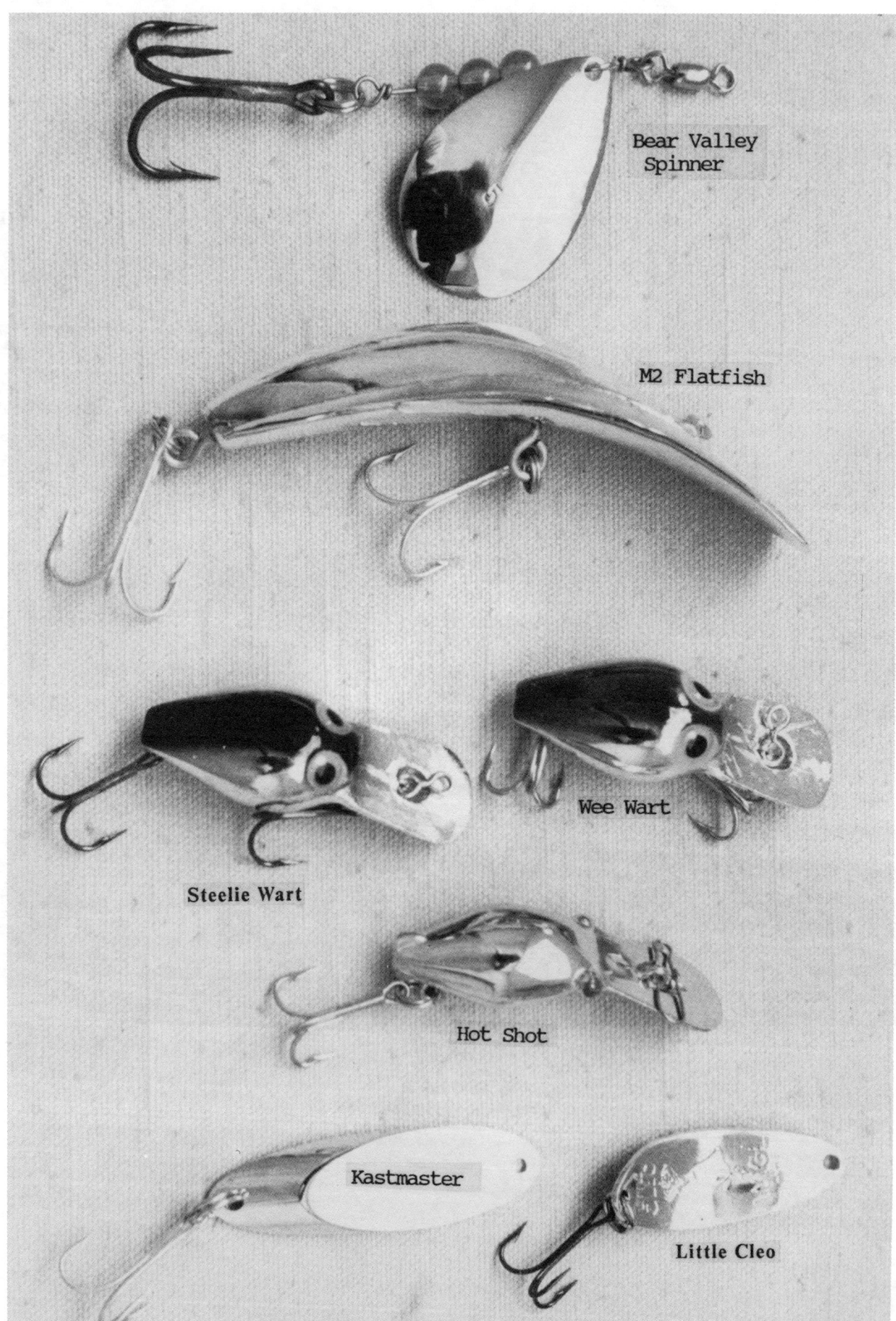

**KOKANEE SALMON (SOCKEYE):**

These lake-bound, small (average 1 lb.) salmon exhibit typical salmon characteristics. They congregate in the southwest corner of Lake Tahoe in the fall and spawn in Taylor Creek in September. As September nears, the Kokanee acquire spawning colors and shapes and their flesh becomes less firm and less palatable.

**Where/When:** Lake Tahoe - **See Map:**

In Lake Tahoe:
June to early September
They concentrate in the southwest corner - **See Map**. Look for other fishing boats. In California, if you are fishing alone, you are most probably in the wrong place.

In other lakes;
Donner Lake, Twin Lakes - Bridgeport, Bullards Bar, Stampede, Shaver, Pardee, Bass.
Best Fishing is in August and September when they concentrate for spawning but they can be caught all year.

Most fish are caught in the early morning hours.
Dusk hours can also be a prime time.
However, they can be caught at mid-day - see Technique.

Structure:

Schools of Kokanee will suspend at depths which vary with the time of day and the season.
In early summer and in the fall they will typically suspend 40 to 70+ feet deep.
In mid-summer, they are deeper, down to 100 - 120 feet.
The fish will be shallower in the morning and move deeper toward mid-day. The fish can be quite shallow in the spring, morning hours.
In Lakes other than Tahoe, during the summer months, the Kokanee will typically be close to the thermocline 40 to 70+ feet deep.

**Bait/Lures:** Red Magic, #2 or #3, Colors: Flame Red
Lucky Knight
Wedding Ring
Kokanee King
Needlefish, #1 or #2, Colors: Pearl, Bikini
Small Buzz Bomb Lures or Luma lures for jigging

Trolling lures are commonly tipped with Green Giant, green-labeled canned white corn.

**Rig:** For Trolling:

A conventional reel and rod with a flexible, sensitive tip.
Trolling Blades: Ford Fenders - Model A, Jim Rice Blades,
For leadcore trolling - 15 colors of 15#-18# leadcore line.

For Jigging:

A faster stiffer tipped rod is useful for feeling pickups and setting the hook.

**SEE DIAGRAM**

**Technique:** Since these fish are not shoreline or structure oriented and essentially wander around the middle parts of the lakes considerably below the surface, a boat with a good fish-finder is essential for locating the suspended schools.

In Lake Tahoe, trolling is the most effective technique when the Kokanee are still scattered in June and July. Jigging becomes effective in August when the schools become more concentrated.

For all techniques, you must first locate the correct trolling or jigging depth. Call the listed info sources. Troll multiple lines at different depths until successful then change other rigs to the right depth and/or use a good fish finder to locate the schools (near thermocline in summer).

Slow trolling with downriggers - **See Diagram**

Slow trolling with leadcore line:

> Note that you will not get a lot of fishing action out of a 1 lb. Kokanee using leadcore line rigged with blades. For more "sport" use a downrigger or try jigging when appropriate.
>
> You need to determine how many colors of lead core to let out. Generally this ranges from 2 colors (early morning, early season) to 8 colors (mid-summer, mid-day). One (1) color will equal about 7 feet of depth.

Jigging with Buzz Bomb or other jig type lures:

> This technique can be effective during mid-day hours.
> Locate suspended school with fish finder.

SALMON, KOKANEE 195

**Technique continued:**

Drop lure (i.e. Buzz Bomb) straight down and work by jigging either slightly above or below the school depth. The larger males are typically deeper.

**The Law:** Kokanee Salmon are included in the "Trout" regulations. Even though the general rule is a 5 trout daily bag limit, many special restrictions apply. See current DFG regulations.

**Records:** Average Size: 1 lb.
IGFA: 6 lbs. 9 oz., Idaho, 1975

**Access:** Guides: Lake Tahoe

Dan Hannum
Tahoe Bait and Tackle, S. Lake Tahoe
916-541-8801

Jack Martin
The Outdoorsman Store, S. Lake Tahoe
916-541-1660

Rick Muller, 916-544-4358

Bruce Hernandez
916-577-2246

Bullards Bar:

Sep Hendrickson
707-449-8413

Boat Rentals (Late Spring to Fall):

Bullards Bar, Emerald Cove Marina, 916-692-2166
Lake Tahoe, Meek's Bay Resort, 916-525-7242
    or 916-525-4403
    Homewood High and Dry Marina,
        916-525-5966
    Tahoe Keys Marina, 916-541-2155
    Ski Run Marina, 916-544-0200

**See Also:** Rainbow Trout, Brown Trout, Makinaw Trout in Lake Tahoe and Donner Lake

SALMON, KOKANEE 196

# KOKANEE SALMON RIGS

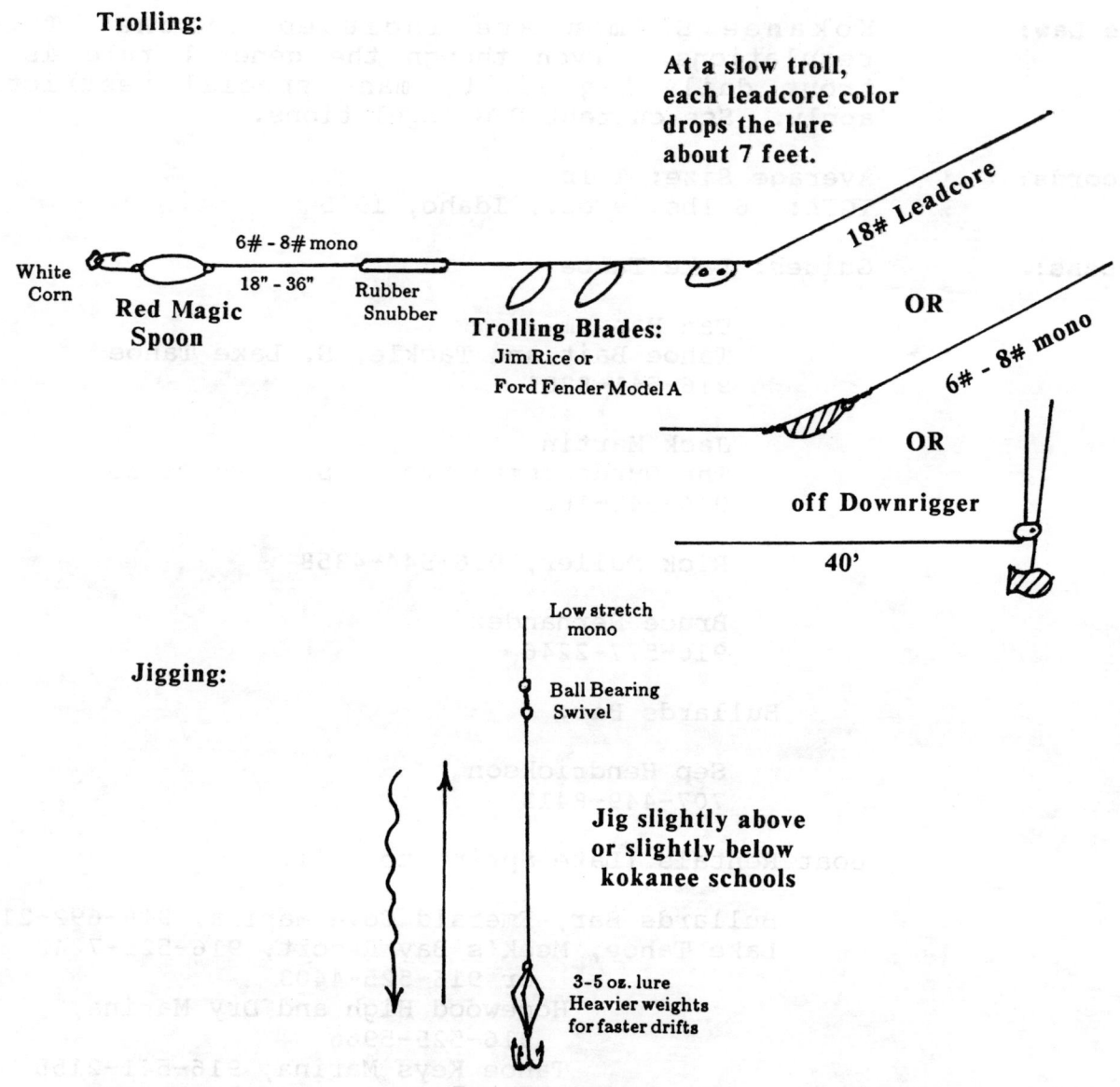

# KOKANEE SALMON
## Lake Tahoe Area

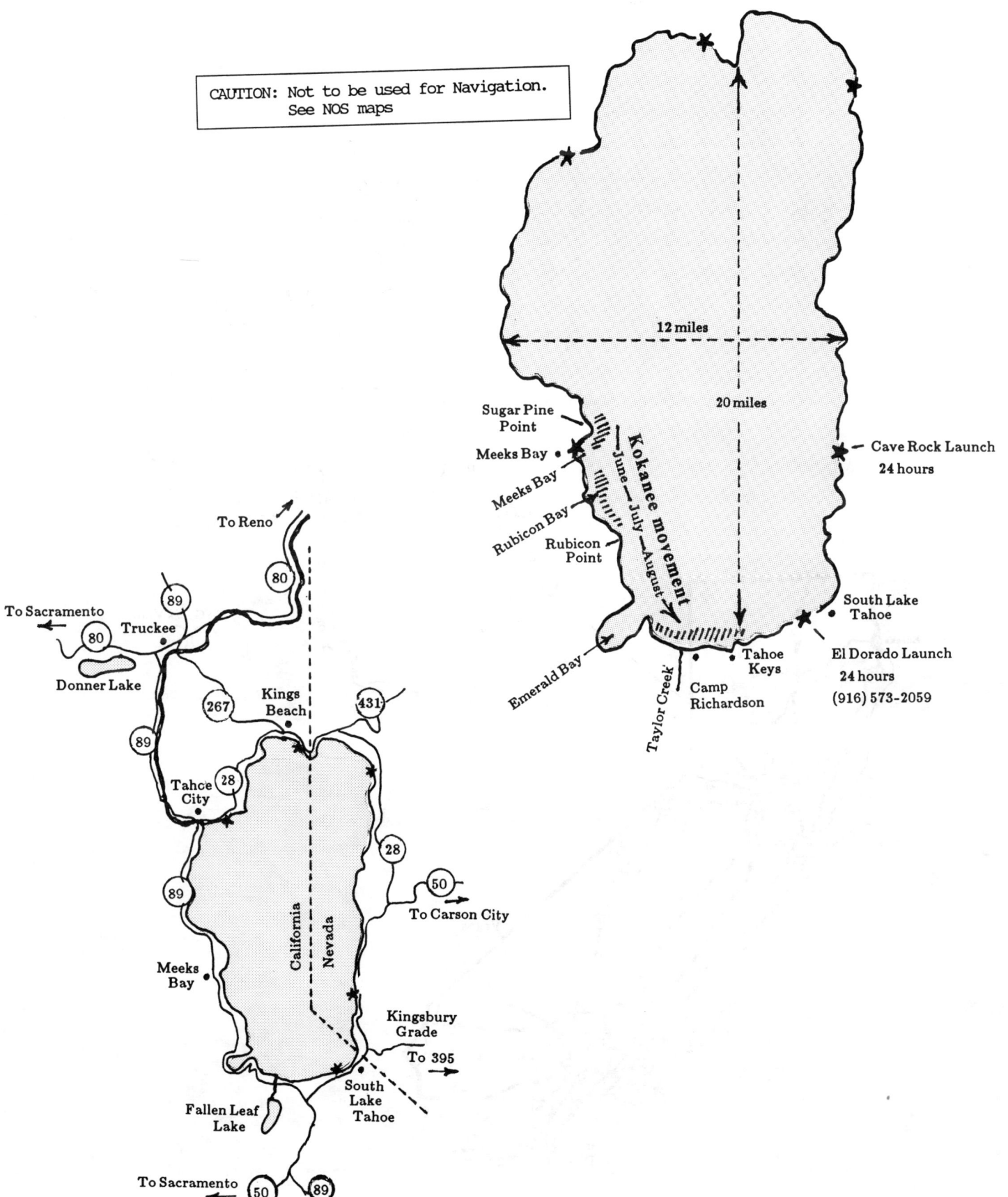

# KOKANEE SALMON
## Bullard's Bar Reservoir

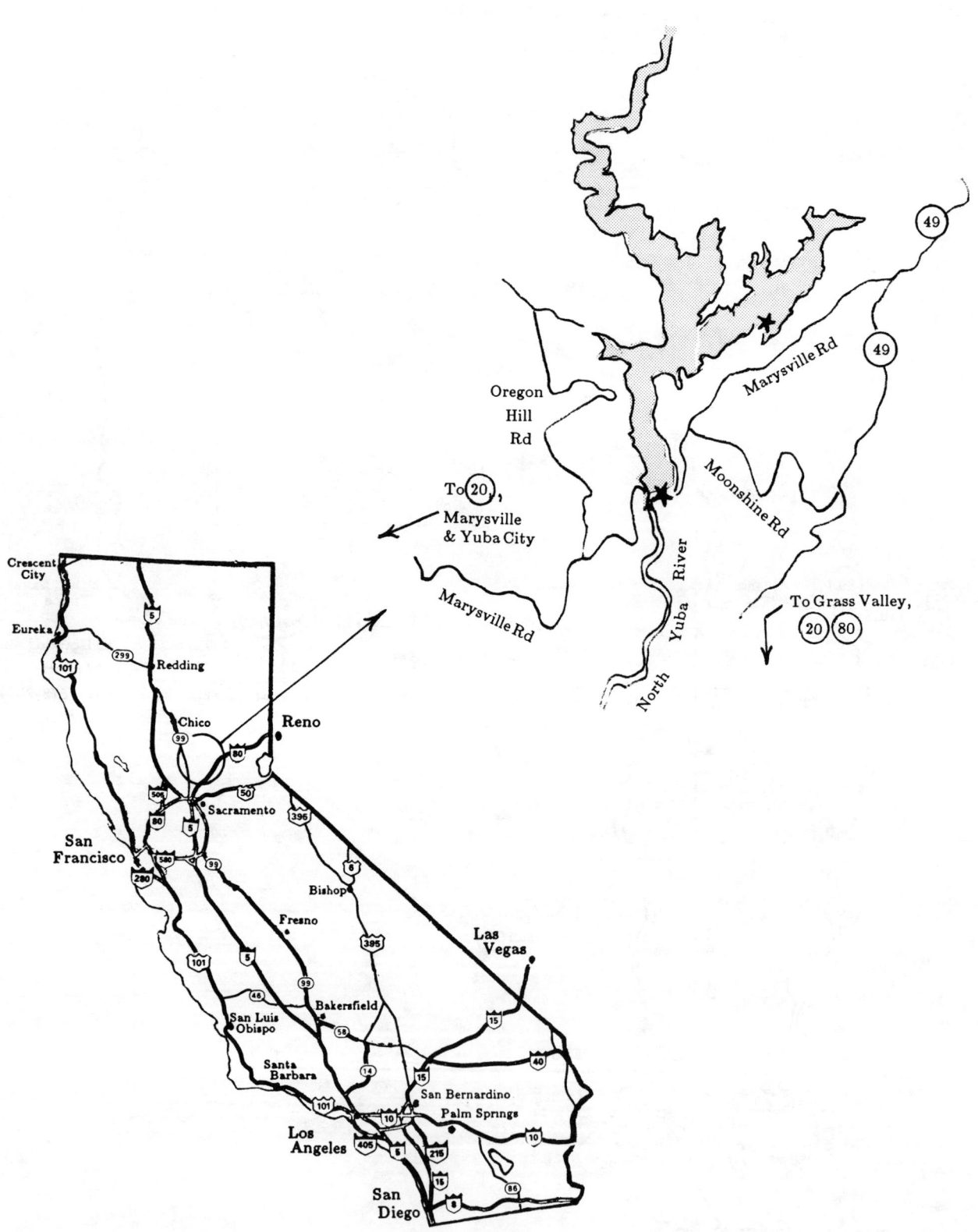

Red Magic
Wedding Ring
Dick Nite
Needlefish

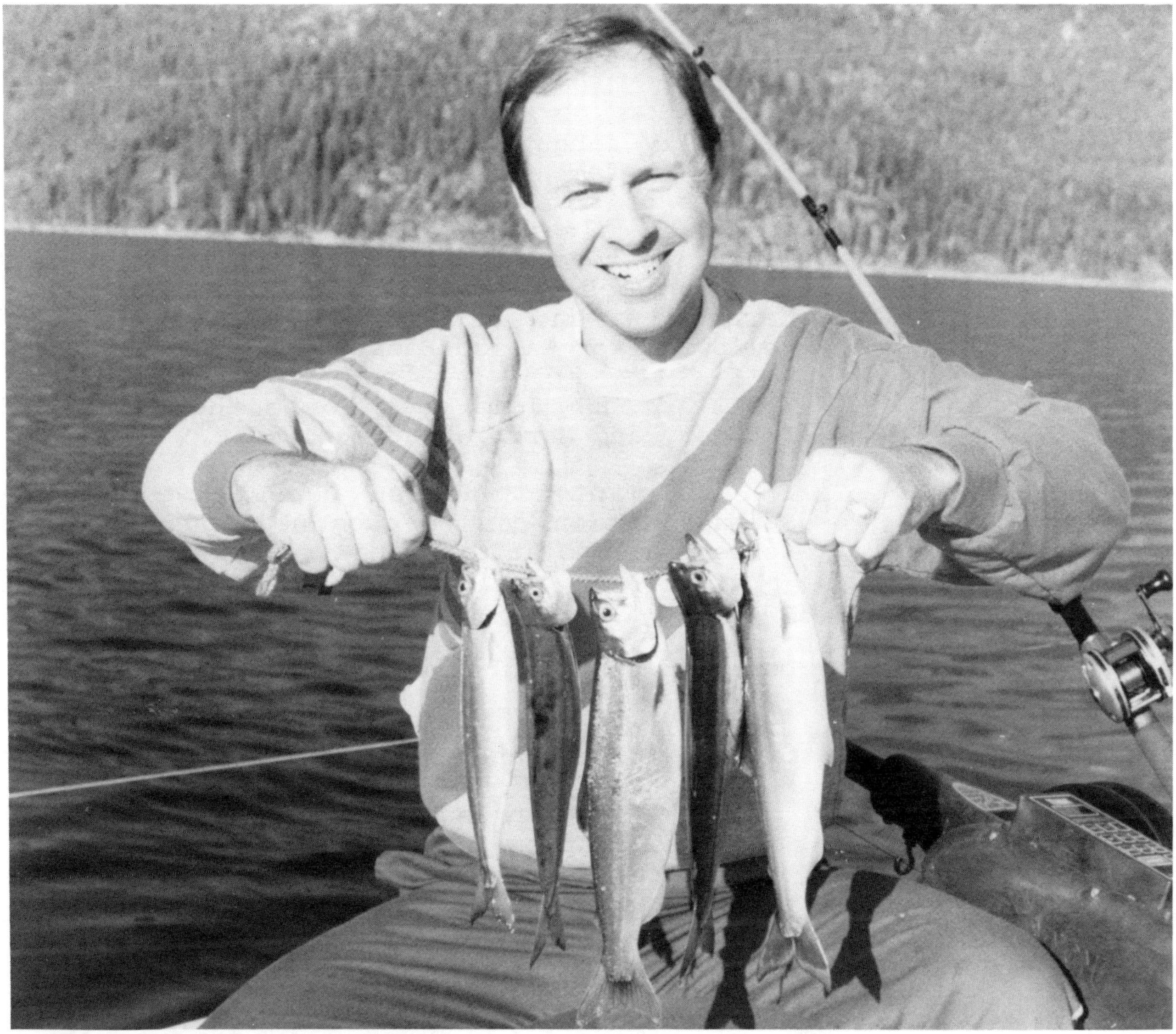

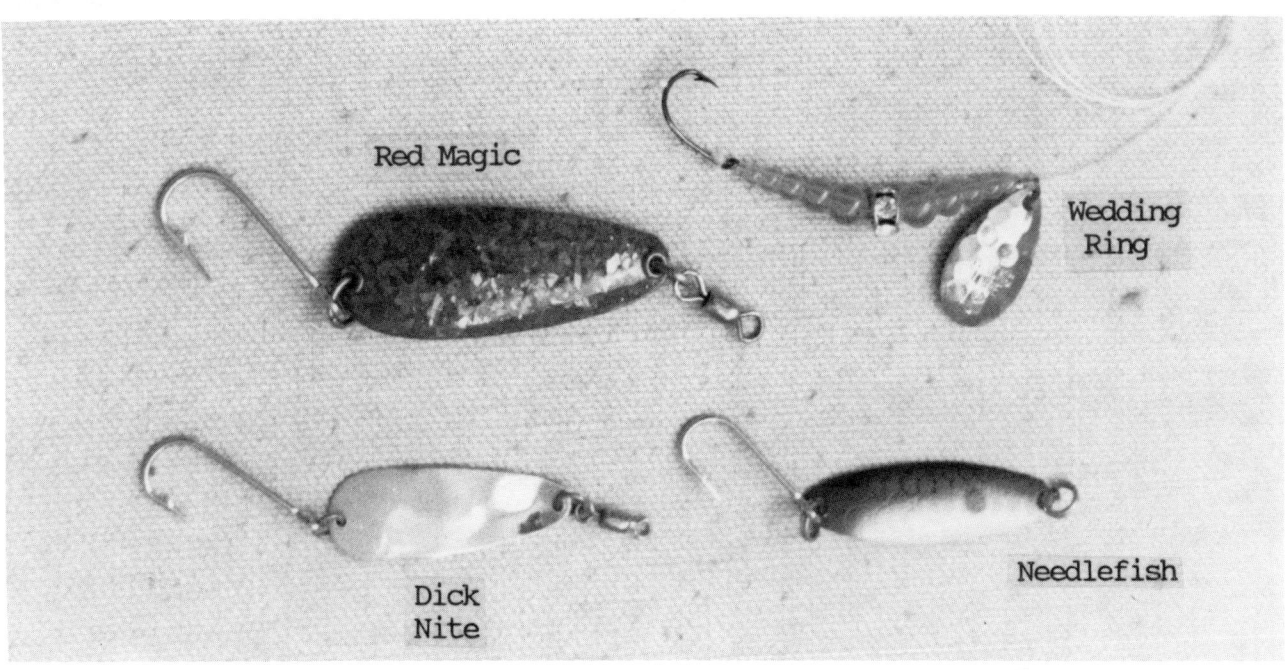

# SEABASS, WHITE

**WHITE SEABASS:** (CORVINA BLANCA)

**Where/When:** Structure:

Generally caught at or near the bottom in water 50 to 80 feet deep, off points of land, or in corners of coves. Look for rocky or hard-bottom areas of clear, clean water outside of kelp beds. Best in early morning but nighttime bites can be good. Generally Seabass are not the targeted fish, but are caught while seeking Yellowtail or Calico Bass.

April through June seem to be the best months, February and March about the worst.

In the winter months, December - February, Seabass action can be good near schooling squid concentrations at Catalina Island.

Hot Spots:

December through January:

    Catalina Is.
    Deep Hole - late fall, night, squid spot
    Rocky Point
    BKR - Big Kelp Reef
    La Jolla Kelp
    Pt. Loma Kelp
    Rincon Pt.
    Santa Barbara Is.


Late March through May:

    Catalina
       - Iron Bound Cove
       - Little Harbor
       - Church Rock
       - China Point
       - Silver Canyon Area
    Clemente Is.
    Horseshoe Kelp
    Rocky Pt.
    Pt. Loma Kelp

June through August:

    Horseshoe Kelp
    Huntington Flats
    Rocky Pt.
    Santa Cruz Is.
    Topanga Bubbles

**Where/When continued:**

    June through August continued:

        BKR - Big Kelp Reef
        Cortes Bank
        Coronado Islands (Mexico), especially during the Yellowtail run

    September through November:

        Horseshoe Kelp
        Deep Hole
        Catalina
        BKR - Big Kelp Reef
        Rocky Point

**Bait/Lures:** Live squid, mackerel, or sardine
Hopkins Jig (5 oz.) or white Salas 6x Jr. sweetened with a live or dead squid. Lures usually only effective on hot bite.

**Rig:** Medium-weight conventional reel with 20 - 30# mono. A 2/0 to 6/0 live bait hook. Depending on the current, a 3/4 oz. or larger sliding egg sinker. However, if the fish are on the surface, flyline your bait.

**Technique:** Anchor up-current of structure, and chum with chopped squid for 15+ minutes.

Yo-Yo off the bottom
or
Bounce down current
or
Leave on Bottom

**The Law:** Season: Three fish, except in waters south of Pt. Conception (a point of land just north of Santa Barbara) one fish between March 15 through June 15.

Minimum Size: 28"

**Records:** IGFA: 83 lbs. 12 oz., San Felipe, 1953

**See Also:** Yellowtail, Calico Bass, Sand Bass

## SOUTHERN CALIFORNIA – PRIME OCEAN FISHING AREAS

|   | Latitude/Longitude | Course/Distance |
|---|---|---|
| 1. 60 Mile Bank | 32° 04.0'/118° 13.0' | From Pt. Loma<br>220° / 60.0 NM |
| 2. 150 Kelp<br>Double Oil Platform<br>called "Elly & Ellen" | 33° 07.5'/118° 35.0' | From Alamitos Bay<br>170° / 9.5 NM |
| 3. Anacapa Is. | 34° 02.4'/119° 21.5' | From Oxnard, Pt. Hueneme<br>203° / 10.3 NM<br>From Ventura Marina<br>180° / 13.6 NM |
| 4. Barn Kelp | 33° 18.6'/117° 29.1' | From Oceanside Harbor<br>315° / 9.6 NM |
| 5. Big Kelp Reef (BKR) | 34° 02.0'/118° 45.3' | From Marina del Rey<br>270° / 14.2 NM |
| 6. Catalina Is. | .................... | From Alamitos Bay<br>215° / 23.8 NM to<br>Ship Rock, 2 Harbors |
| 7. Clemente Is. | 33° 2.1'/118° 36.8' | Castle Rock – NW end |
| 8. Coronado Is. | 32° 26.5'/117° 25.0' | From Pt. Loma<br>170° / 12.5 NM |
| 9. Cortes Bank | 32° 26.5'/119° 07.5' | From Marina del Rey<br>186° / 97 NM<br>From Pt. Loma<br>250° / 95 NM |
| 10. Deep Hole | 34° 01.5'/118° 57.5' | From Marina del Rey<br>277° / 24.2 NM |
| 11. Horseshoe Kelp | 33° 40.0'/118° 13.5' | From Alamitos Bay, out<br>from Federal Breakwater<br>212° / 4.8 NM |
| 12. La Jolla Kelp | 32° 50.0'/117° 17.5' | From Mission Bay<br>310° / about 3 NM |
| 13. Point Dume | 33° 49.0'/119° 00.0' | From Marina del Rey<br>262° / 17.0 NM |
| 14. Pt. Loma Kelp | 32° 42.5'/118° 16.3' | From Mission Bay<br>just south of entrance<br>to Pt. Loma |
| 15. Pt. Vicente | 33° 45.2'/118° 24.6' | From Marina del Rey<br>155° / 13.2 NM |
| 16. Rincon Reef | 34° 19.4'/119° 27.0' | From Santa Barbara<br>170° / 10 NM |
| 17. Rocky Point | 33° 47.8'/118° 24.4' | From Marina del Rey<br>151° / 10.3 NM |
| 18. Santa Barbara Is. | 33° 29.2'/119° 01.8' | From Marina del Rey<br>211° / 41.0 NM<br>From Newport<br>250° / 41.0 NM |
| 19. Santa Cruz Is.<br>West Point | 34° 04.6'/119° 55.1' | From Santa Barbara<br>198° / 24.2 NM |
| San Pedro Pt. | 34° 02.0'/119° 31.2' | From Oxnard, Pt. Hueneme<br>235° / 17.4 NM |
| 20. Tanner Bank | 32° 42.0'/119° 08.0' | From Marina del Rey<br>190° / 83.1 NM |
| 21. Topanga Bubbles | 34° 01.5'/118° 34.2' | From Marina del Rey |

# SOUTHERN CALIFORNIA - PRIME OCEAN FISHING AREAS

CAUTION: Not to be used for Navigation. See NOS maps

 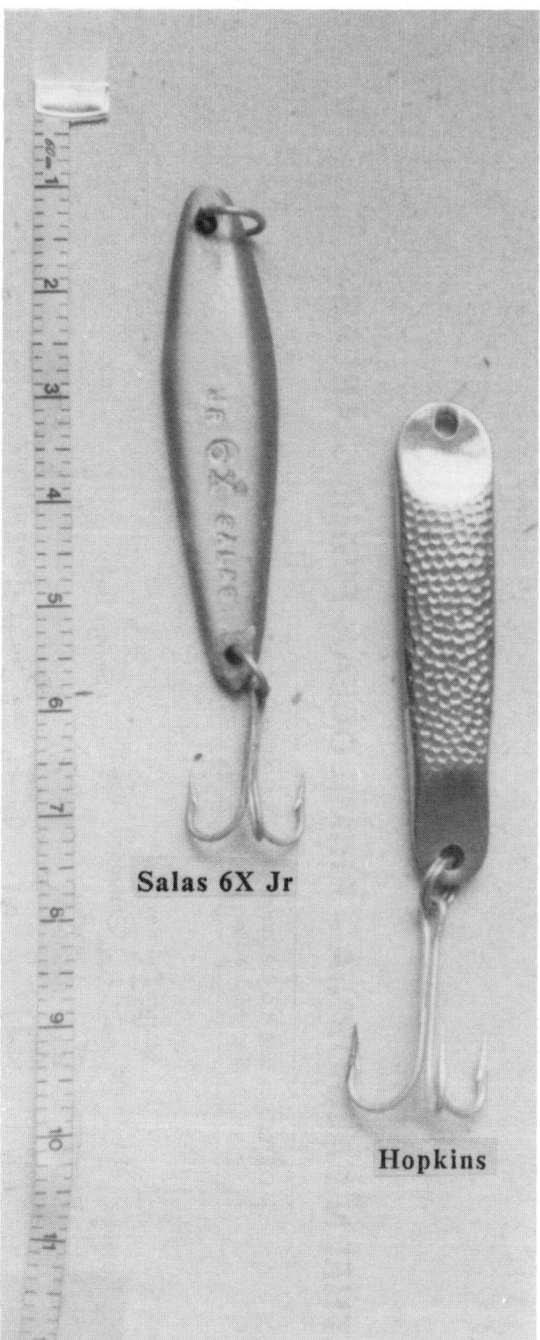

**SHAD:** Shad are generally not considered to be good eating, although they can be pickled or smoked. Males are smaller and average 2 to 3 pounds. Females average 3 to 5 pounds. Females run later, following males by 2 to 3 weeks.

**Where/When:** Sacramento River drainage system including the American, Feather, and Yuba rivers.

May to July; **SEE MAP & CALENDAR**

Shad runs also occur in the Klamath River and the Trinity, and in the Russian River.

> Russian River - mouth of Dry Creek and below Rock Dam in Healdsburg. Mid-April to mid-June.
> Trinity River - Willow Creek near Hoopa
> Klamath River - Somes Bar and downriver, esp. from Somes to Orleans around mid-June.

In clear water river areas (American River, etc., shad activity is best early morning and early evening hours. In muddy river waters,(the Sacramento near Freeport, Verona, etc.) daytime fishing can continue to be good.

Structure:

> Shad typically hold in medium current to semi-fast current areas that vary from 2 to 10 feet deep. Fish prefer the juncture (seam) of the medium current with adjoining slow currents. Shad hold next to the bottom
> Shad will align themselves in long lines oriented upstream/downstream. Therefore it is very important to fish the right upstream/downstream line to put the lure in their faces.
> Shad congregate and hold below the junction of major rivers and creeks.
> Shad congregate and hold below dams (Red Bluff Diversion Dam, Nimbus Dam)

**Bait/Lures:** Leadheads, Darts, Weighted Flies, Chartreuse Tiny Rounder. Colors: Yellow, chartreuse, red & white, orange

**Rig:** Lightweight Spinning outfits with 6# mono.
8 to 9 foot, #6 to #7 Fly Fishing outfit

**Technique:** If wading or bank fishing;

> Cast upstream of fish holding area.
> Let lure drift through prime area.

**Technique continued:**

> Lure should move with the current occasionally bumping the bottom. The lure must be hitting off the bottom to be effective.
>
> Shad don't strike, they inhale the lure. Watch carefully for any hesitation in the line movement.

> In a boat;
>
>> Let the lure swing with the current directly behind the boat.
>>
>> Work the lure by occasional jigging or by jigging and retrieving.
>>
>> Try different "lines". Remember that shad hold in long upstream/downstream lines. These lines are not stationary but will shift somewhat. If you are catching fish, stick with your "line". If the action slows try other lines by reaching out one side or the other with your rod and work a different line. If your boat has bow cleats on both the starboard and port sides, simply shifting the anchor line can swing your boat in the current and give you a different, perhaps better line to work. Since the shad lines are long, if you see another boat catching shad, moving a respectable distance directly upstream or downstream from that boat can be successful.

> Fishing near restricted dam areas, may require a surf casting rig or plastic bubble to reach the productive white water.

**The Law:** Limit, 25; No minimum size. (1990-91)

**Records:** State: 7 lbs. 5 oz.; Feather River
IGFA: 11 lbs. 4 oz., Massachusetts, May 1986

**Info:** Sacramento River  - Los Molinos

> Pelham's Bay Resort
> 916-384-1919.

Sacramento River - Chico area:

> Powell's Fly Shop
> 916-345-3393

Sacramento River/Feather River at Verona:

> Verona Marina
> 916-927-8387

**Info continued:**

    Feather River:

        Johnson's Bait & Tackle, Yuba City
        916-674-1912

    American River:

        Wilderness Exchange, Fair Oaks
        916-965-3355

**Access:**    Guides:

        Bill Adelman
        415-232-9991

        Barry Gravier's Guide Service
        916-527-7024

        Bob Wigham
        916-222-8058

**See Also:**    Sturgeon, Striped Bass, Rainbow Trout

# SHAD RIGS

For heavier lures (i.e. 1/8 - 1/4 oz.) a straight rig (no weight) can be used, although lighter lures, 1/16 to 1/32 oz., work best.

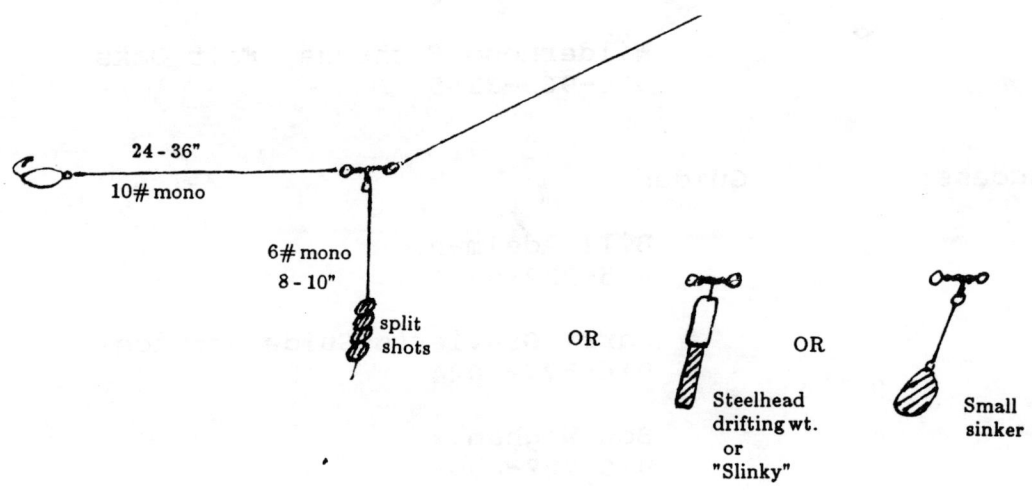

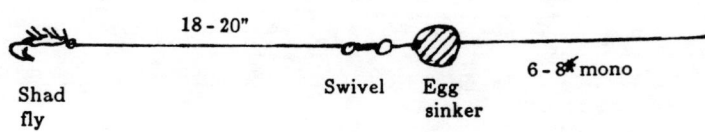

**Fly Fishing Rig**

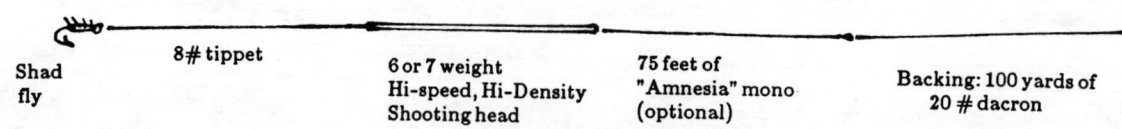

Let out about 60 to 80 feet behind anchored boat.

# SHAD FISHING MAP/CALENDAR

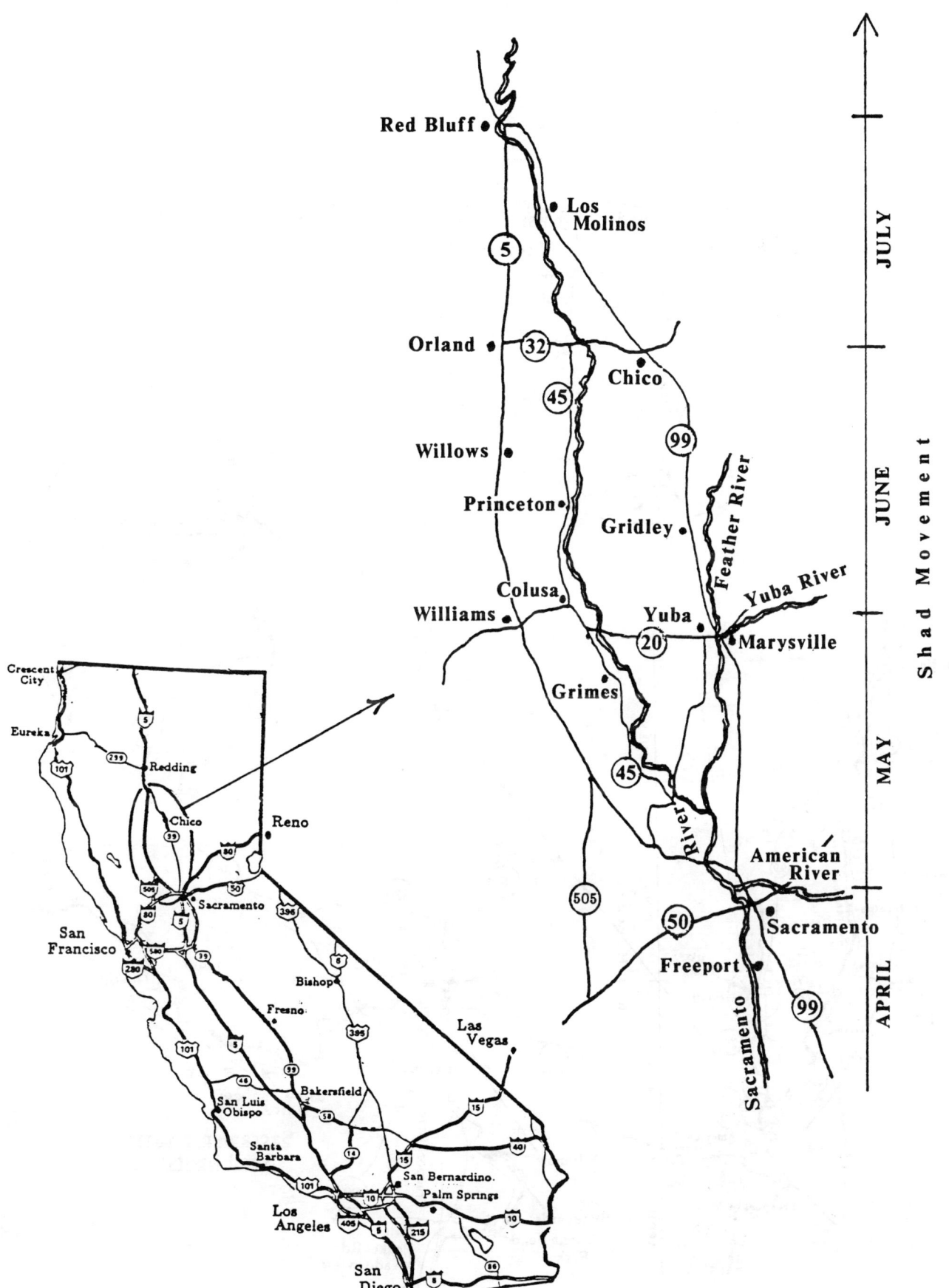

# SHAD SPOTS
## April through May

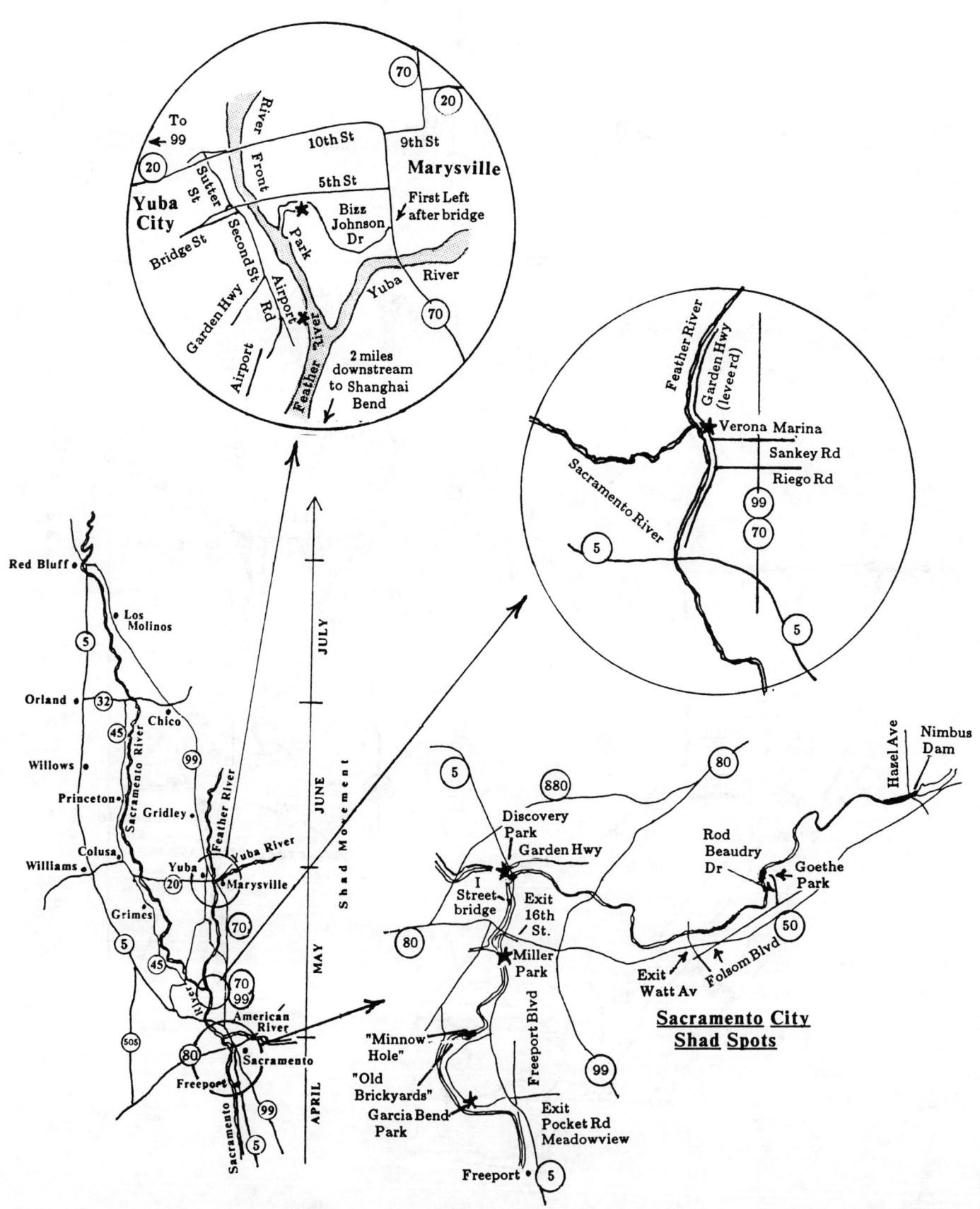

# SHAD SPOTS
## June through July

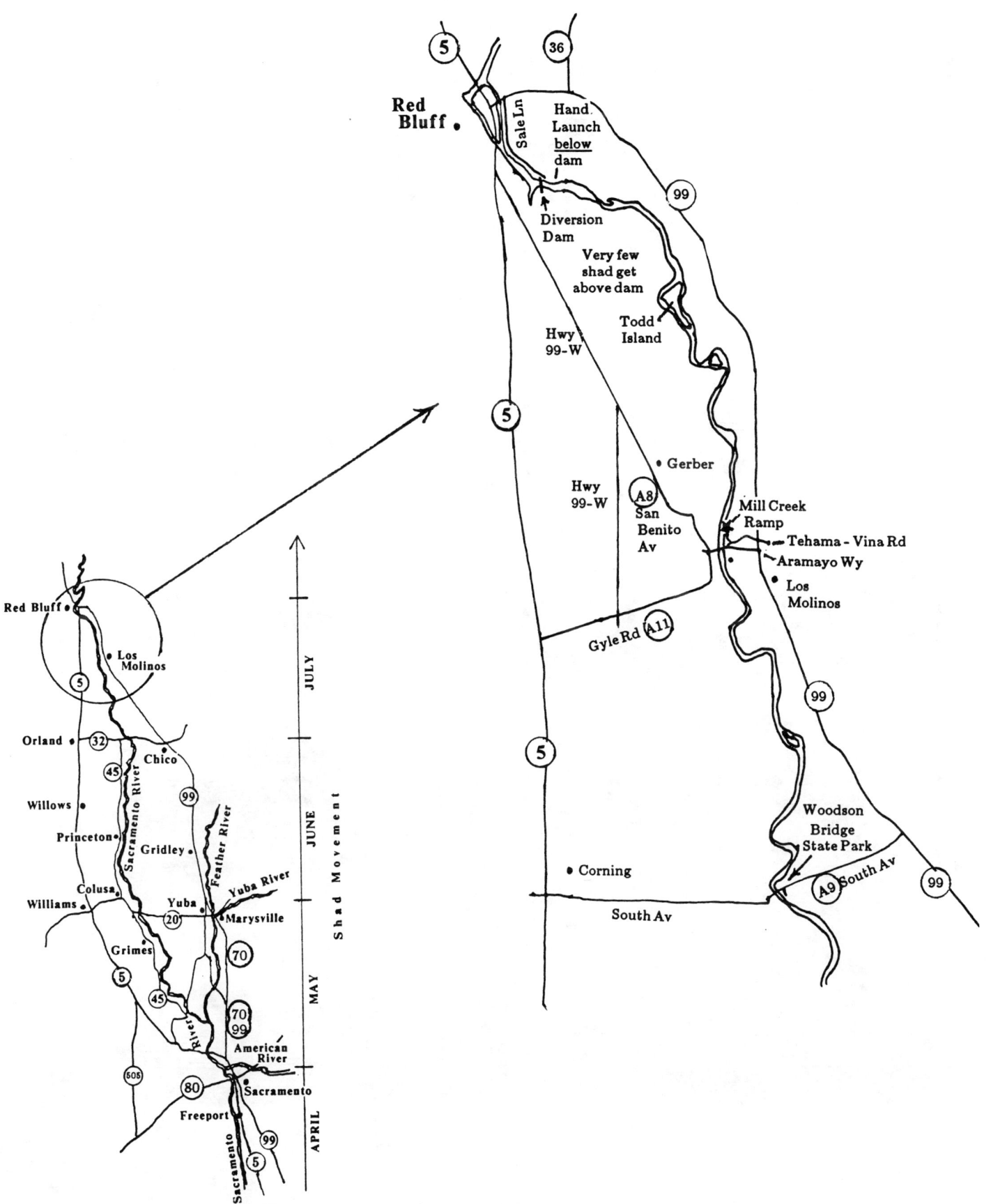

**Guide Bill Adelman on Sacramento River near Verona**

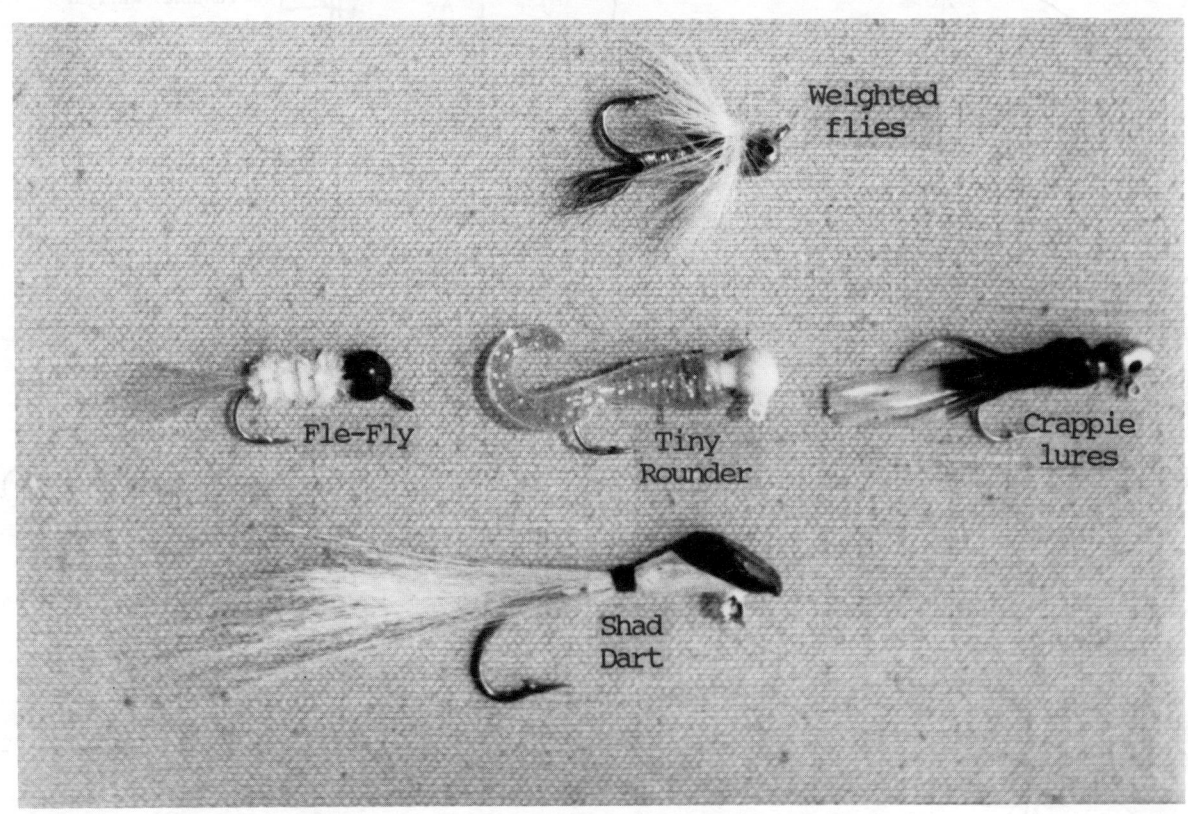

**SHARK:** (Tiburon)

General Information

All sharks are slow growing fish with very limited numbers of offspring. This makes them very vulnerable to overfishing. Severely limit your take of these fish.

**Rig:** The leader should be longer than the fish you expect to hook - a shark's skin is very abrasive.

Single strand wire tends to kink and break but is light and strong. The Haywire Twist is used to make leaders from single strand.

Multi-strand wire requires crimping tools and sleeves.

**SEE DIAGRAM**

**Chum Making:**

Equipment: Meat grinder, either manual or electric. Empty 1 gallon ice cream containers thoroughly washed out or plastic (paint) buckets with lids.

Procedure: Use only freshly caught or freshly frozen mackerel or bonito. It's easier to grind the fish while they are still partially frozen. Chum must be uniformly finely ground with no chunks. Pack the ground fish into the empty ice cream containers or paint buckets and keep frozen solid until your trip. Do NOT fill the containers to the top as the chum will expand on freezing causing a messy, smelly spillage. Once at the fishing site the chum lid is removed and the container inverted over a suspended milk carton to start the chum line - see diagram in the Mako Shark section.

SHARK 214

# OFFSHORE, BLUE WATER SHARKS
## Near Surface Feeders

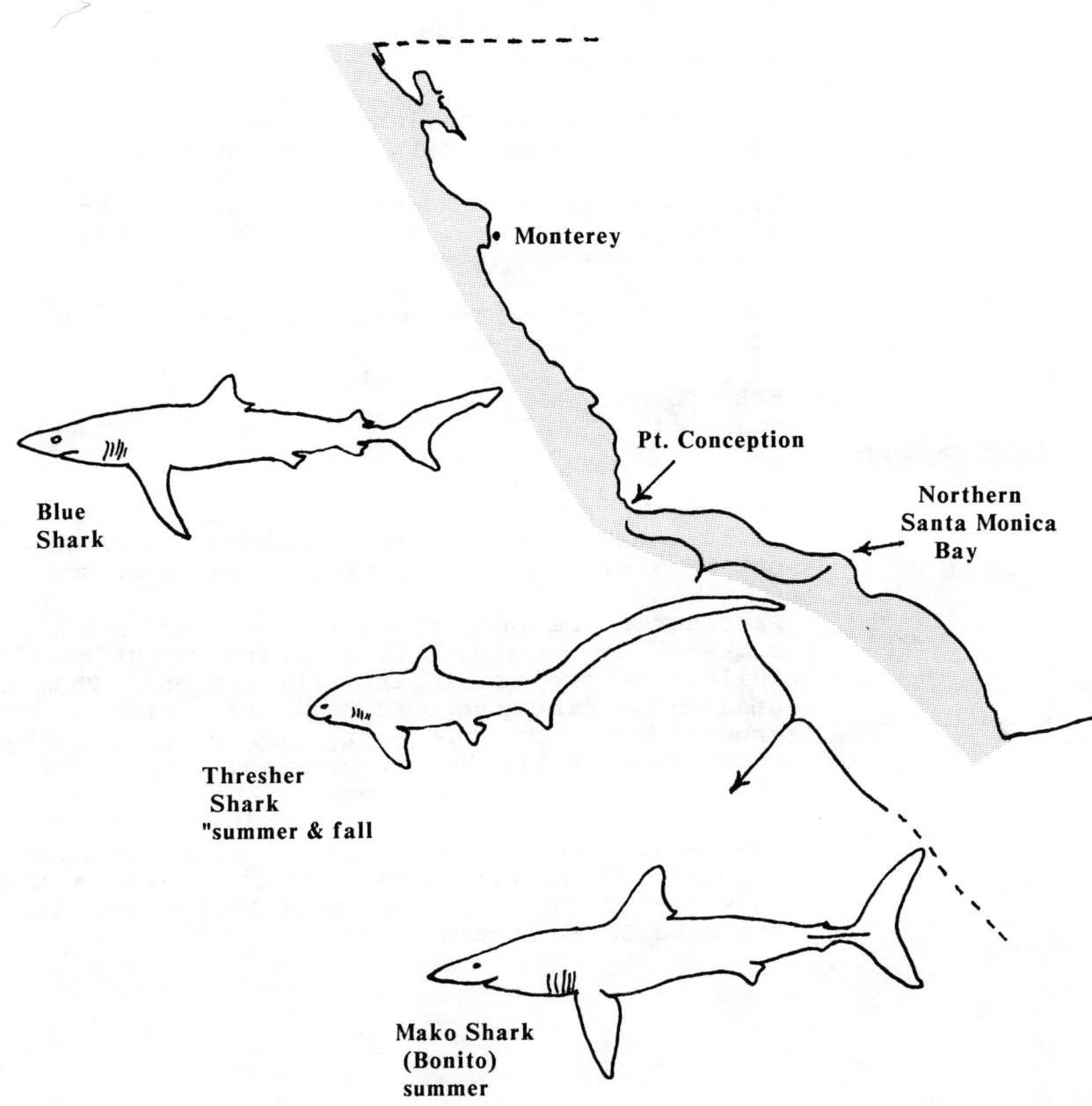

# CALIFORNIA INSHORE AND BAY SHARKS
## Bottom Feeders

All Sharks listed below considered good eating except Grey Smoothhounds

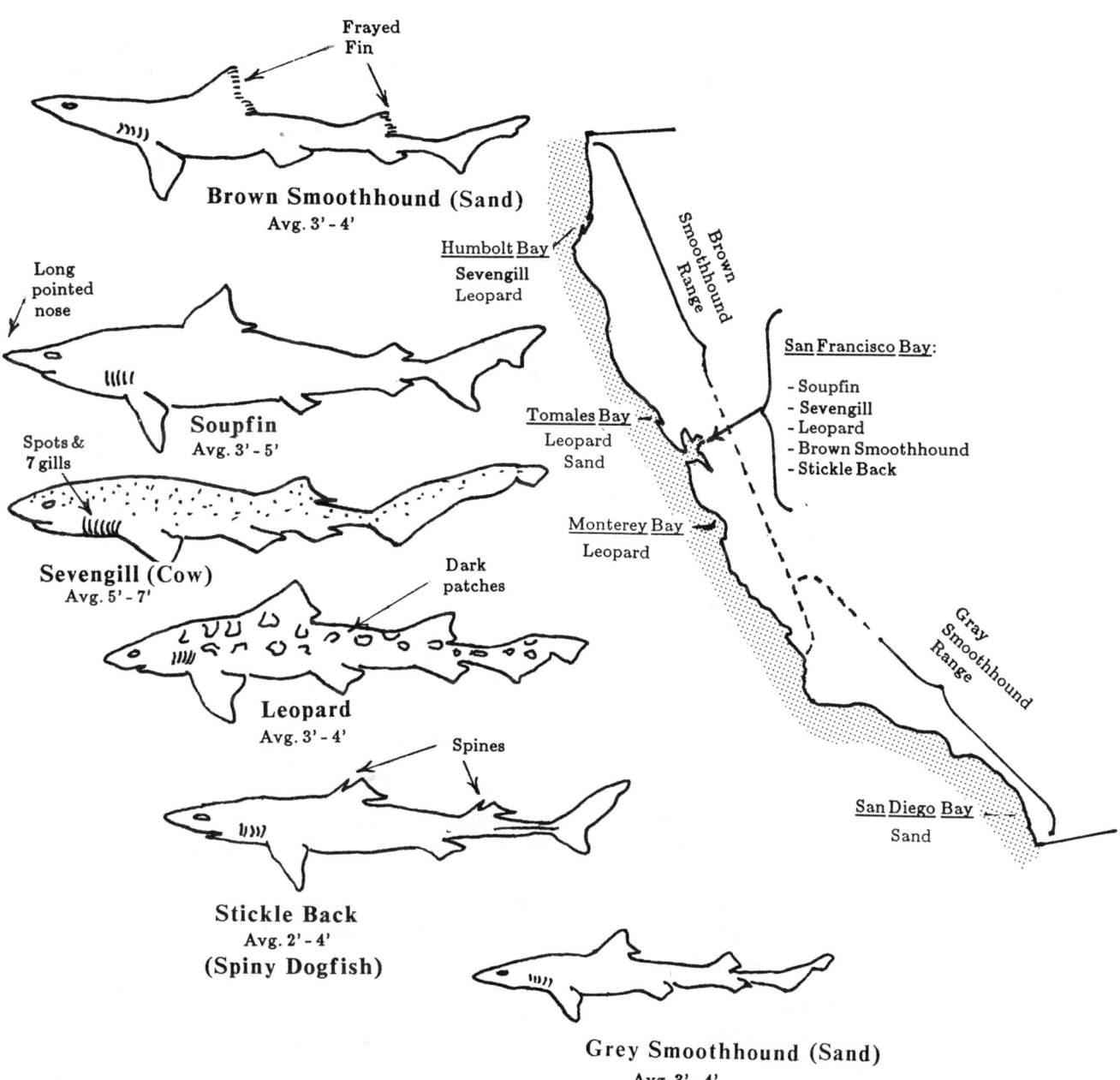

**BLUE & MAKO SHARKS** (Makos are also called Bonito sharks):

**Where:** In general, the popular offshore banks that are prime spots for marlin and tuna (14 mile bank, 277 spot, 279 spot, Avalon bank, etc.), are also prime shark spots. See Marlin Map.

Blue Sharks are also off Moss Landing, Monterey Bay - southwest of the harbor in 150+ foot deep water, off the Monterey Dunes condos. September is the best month for this area.

However, it isn't really necessary to burn so much fuel to get to productive areas. Simply finding the deeper, clearer, blue waters, typically 3 to 5+ miles directly offshore, will do the trick.

Structure:

1. Blue water over structure.

    "Blue water" refers to the cleaner, blue tinted waters that are generally found 3+ miles offshore. More inshore waters are greener, less clear.

    Structure means sharp bottom dropoffs, underwater canyons, offshore banks, etc. In general, perennial marlin and tuna hotspots are also prime shark areas. **See Marlin map.**

2. Look for life - bird concentrations, bait, porpoises.

3. Warmer waters and breaklines.

    Makos prefer water from 64 - 70 degrees. If there is a warmer/cooler water breakline caused by surface currents, the Mako will generally cruise near the break on the warm water side (this is also true of marlin).

**When:** Spring & Summer months when offshore surface temperatures reach 64+ degrees.
June through October
Sharks are caught at all times of the day and night. There is some evidence that Makos can be found closer to the surface during nighttime and early morning hours.

**Bait/Lures:** Mackerel/Bonito - live, fresh dead, fillet/cut bait
Braid Granade, Braid Flashdancer, Jap Head jigs, Magnum Rapalas (#26) replace trailing treble with a single hook, Marlin jigs - purple & black.

# IDENTIFICATION & CONSERVATION

Blue sharks and Mako (bonito) sharks are the two most common offshore sharks. Here is how to distinguish between them.

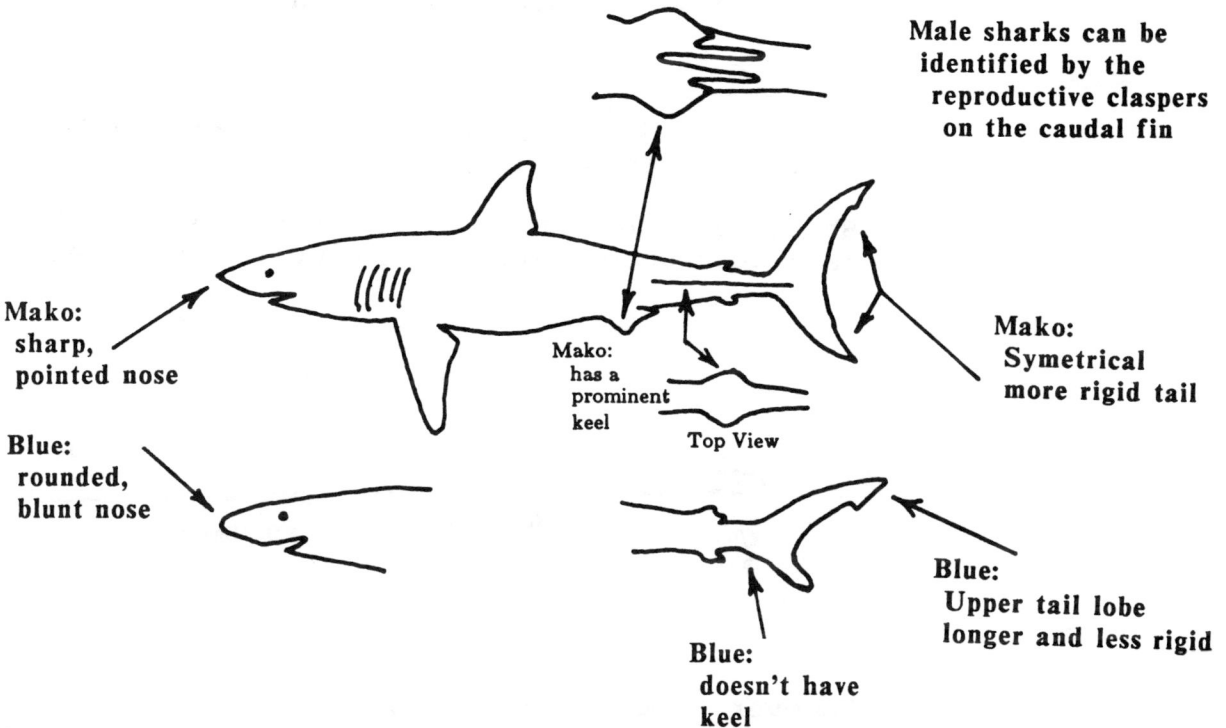

Also:

1. Makos are darker colored.
2. Makos typically swim faster than blues.
3. Makos are usually smaller. Typical weight is between 30 and 80 lbs.
4. Makos will jump when hooked.

Conservation:

IMPORTANT, very limited takes are possible with this fishery. Males are only sexually mature at 3+ years and around 6 feet long, females at 8+ years and 9 feet long. Then the females only give birth every other year to an average litter of 6 pups.

We strongly recommend only taking an occasional male over 40 lbs, larger than 4 feet long.

Also, do NOT use stainless hooks, and do NOT let the fish swallow the bait. Even though these techniques may loose an occasional fish, they will greatly increase the survival rate of released fish.

# SHARK, BLUE & MAKO

**Rig/Technique:**

The great majority of Mako and blue sharks can be handled with gear as light as a good, heavy duty, saltwater spinning reel loaded with 150 yards of 30# mono.

Trolling rigs should be sturdier, conventional reel models.

For those anglers wanting to be properly rigged for Moby Dick, heavy duty rods and reels up to large big game, 2-speed models are used.

Shark fishing can be quite easy. Really all you need is a good chum slick and a simple rig as below.

### Simple Shark Rig

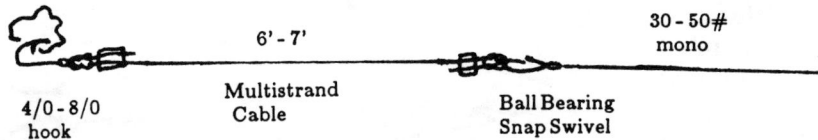

However, increased success on larger fish can be had with the more complicated rigs and techniques as follows:

Advantages/Disadvantages of More Complicated Rigs

1. Single strand wire can be cut easily to release unwanted fish. Disadvantage - single strand will kink easier and kinked wire will break.

2. Longer wire leaders lessen the chance of the sharks rough skin cutting the mono line. Disadvantage - a longer leader necessitates a knowledgeable wire man to grab the leader and pull the shark in close for either cutting loose, tagging, or gaffing. Therefore, 3 people are required - the angler, a wire man, and someone to tag, cut loose, or gaff the fish.

3. Double hook setups increase the chance of a solid hookup.

4. Rerigging after cutting off a fish can be quick and easy by snapping a new pre-tied single strand wire leader on the snap swivel.

**Rig/Technique** continued:

### See Following Rigging Diagrams

1. Identification & Conservation
2. Drift Fishing: Chumming
3. Trolling Bait
4. Big Game Wire Connections
5. Big Game Mono Connections
6. Gaffing & Securing

CHUMMING:

Chumming is the easiest, most effective method of catching sharks. There are two negatives associated with chumming,

1. If commercially sold chum is not locally available, you will have to make your own - a smelly, messy, disgusting job. Note that there is currently a source for chum at several southern California fuel docks. Call Bongos Sportfishing Products, Newport Beach, (714) 673-2810.

2. Chumming typically attracts many Blue sharks (inedible and tired fighters) and few Makos (excellent eating and sometimes outstanding fighters).

The chumming technique is quite simple. Find a likely shark area, stop the boat, start the chum line and drift until the sharks show up.

It is very important to have an unbroken chum line that **doesn't** contain even small chunks of bait. The chum line is like an underwater fence. When a wandering shark intercepts that fence, it will follow it up to your boat. If there are holes in the fence, the shark will lose the trail and wander away. If there are bait chunks in the slick, the shark will soon be satisfied and will wander away.

TROLLING:

Trolling eliminates catching Blue sharks.

I only recommend trolling when you locate an area of clear, blue water, there are clear signs of life, and you have marked significant concentrations of bait fish on your fish finder. Otherwise, chumming is much easier and more effective. Troll 1-2 knots with live bait, up to 4 knots with dead bait rigs. Drift or Troll mackerel or a mackerel fillet. Change bait every 30 minutes.

On a pickup, let the shark run and stop. Set the hook on the second run.

**Wiring and the Wire Man:**

If a long wire leader (anything over 6 - 7') rig is used, a wire man is needed, in addition to the angler and someone to tag, release, or gaff the fish.

The purpose of the wire man is to bring the shark in close to the boat for tagging or gaffing and if the shark is NOT large, to hold it there for securing. The following procedure will maximize safety and success.

Pre-assign a wire man. The wire man should be know how to perform the following procedure:

1. When the desired shark is hooked, the wire man puts on canvas work cloves.

2. Once the wire leader is within reach, at the same time,

   a. The wire man grasps the leader and

   b. The angler loosens the drag and concentrates on keeping any loose line/wire untangled and away from the wire man

3. To prevent injury, the wire man should;

   a. Extend his arm with the palm facing out and the fingers pointing up.

   b. Grasp the wire at the base of the fingers and,

   c. Take a wrap by rotating his hand in toward his body so that his fist moves in toward his chest and the wire wraps across his knuckles. Do this with alternate hands until the shark is to the boat. Try to keep a steady pull on the wire to minimize spooking the shark. If a large shark bolts, release the wire by extending and releasing the grip with arms out and hands extended.

The above safe technique is not a natural action and really should be practiced before the real thing.

# DRIFT FISHING: Chumming

The goal is to have a continuous oily chum slick, with no chunks, that will last a maximum length of time.

If there are bait chunks in the chum, the shark will fill up on these and swim away. The chum MUST BE FROZEN. Only if frozen will the slow melting of the bait create a proper slick that will last a reasonable length of time.

At this writing, there is a commercial source of good chum from;

> Bongos Sportfishing Products
> Newport Beach
> (714) 673-2810

The chum comes in various sizes up to about 5 gallons. This size will last 5 hours is rigged properly. These buckets can be rigged as below since the lid is on securely and the handle is strong.

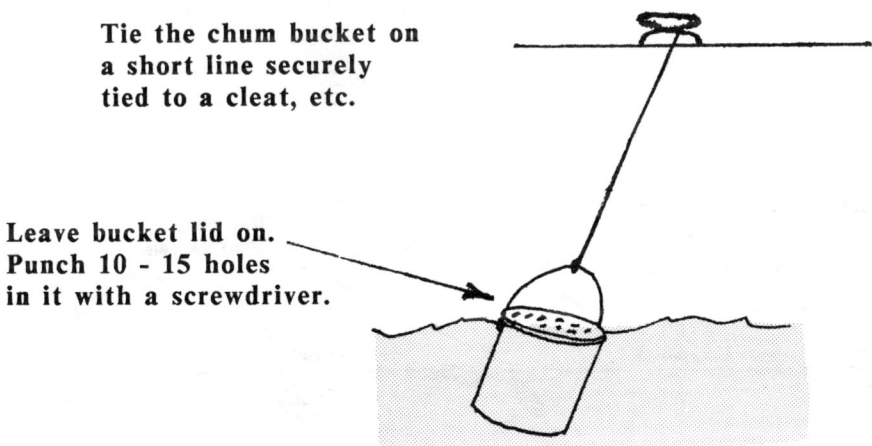

Tie the chum bucket on a short line securely tied to a cleat, etc.

Leave bucket lid on. Punch 10 - 15 holes in it with a screwdriver.

OR

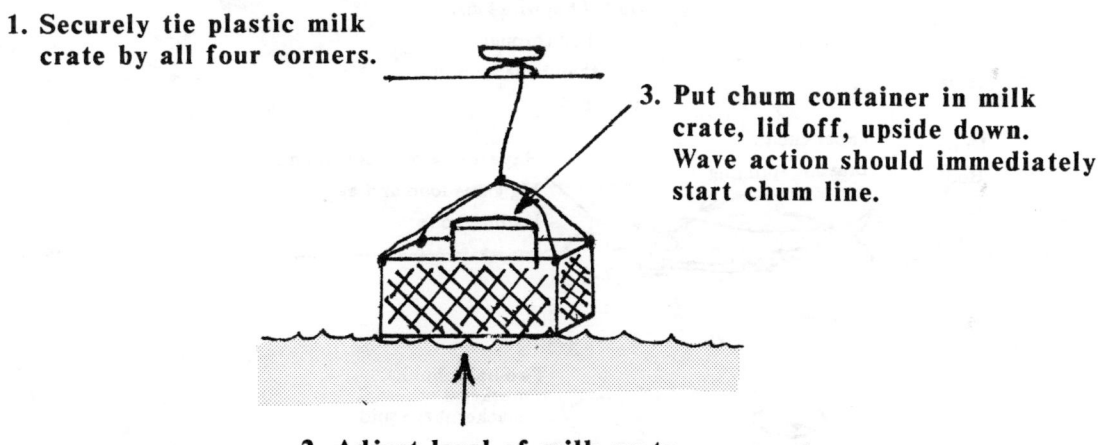

1. Securely tie plastic milk crate by all four corners.

2. Adjust level of milk crate until bottom is regularly lapped by water.

3. Put chum container in milk crate, lid off, upside down. Wave action should immediately start chum line.

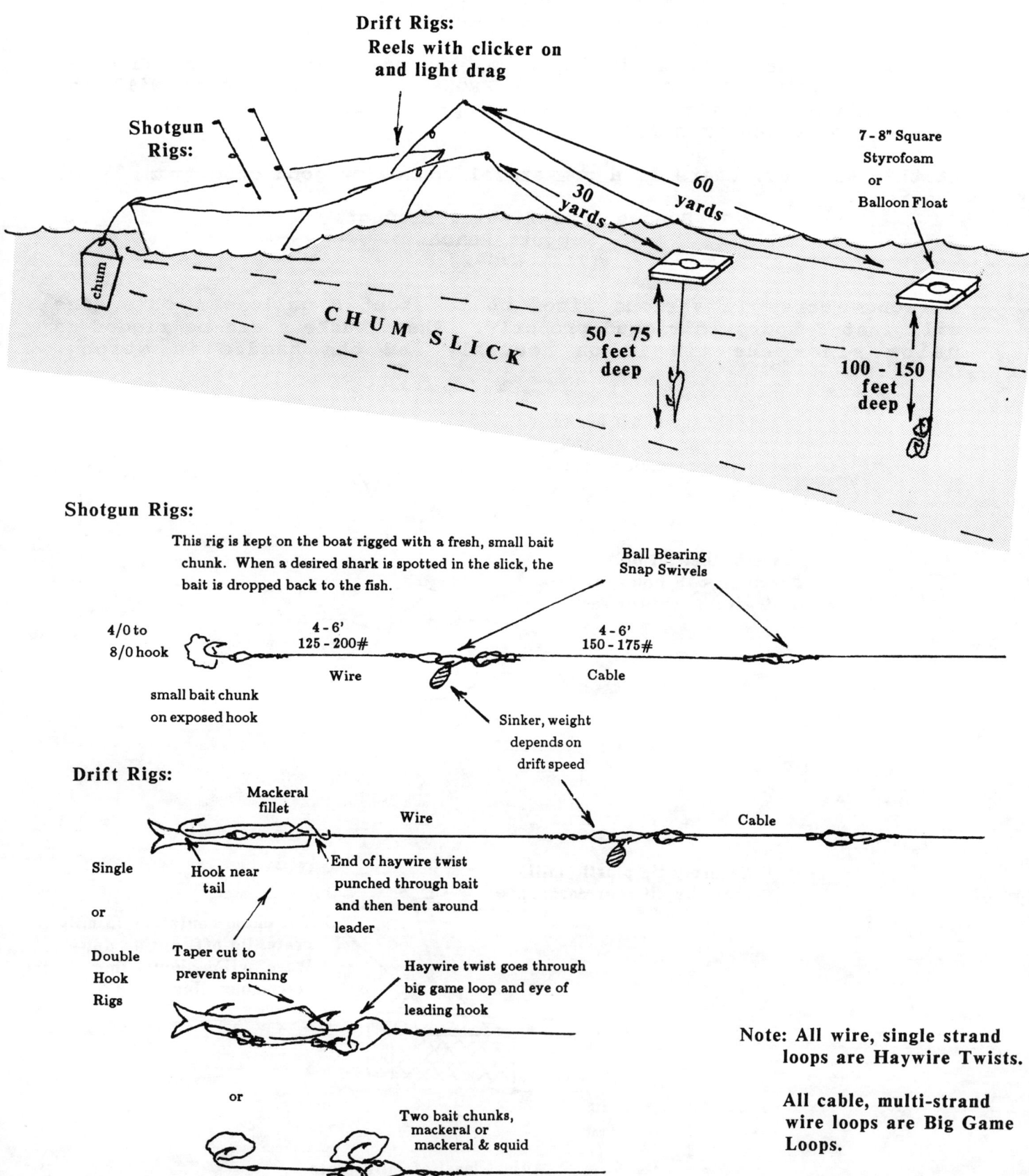

# TROLLING BAIT

### 1 - 4 knots
### Whole Mackeral or Fillet

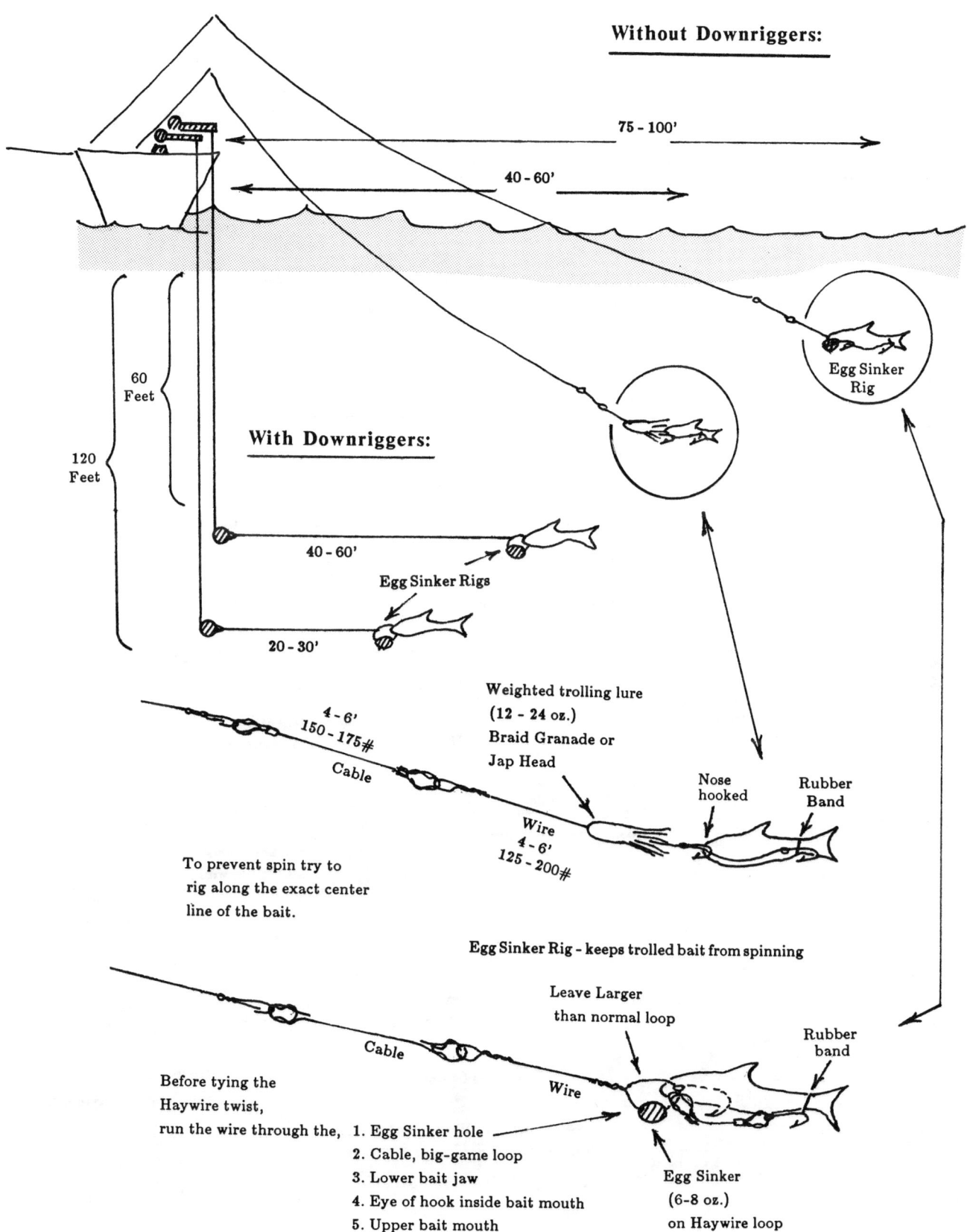

## TROLLING LIVE BAIT
### Idle Speeds: 1 - 2 knots

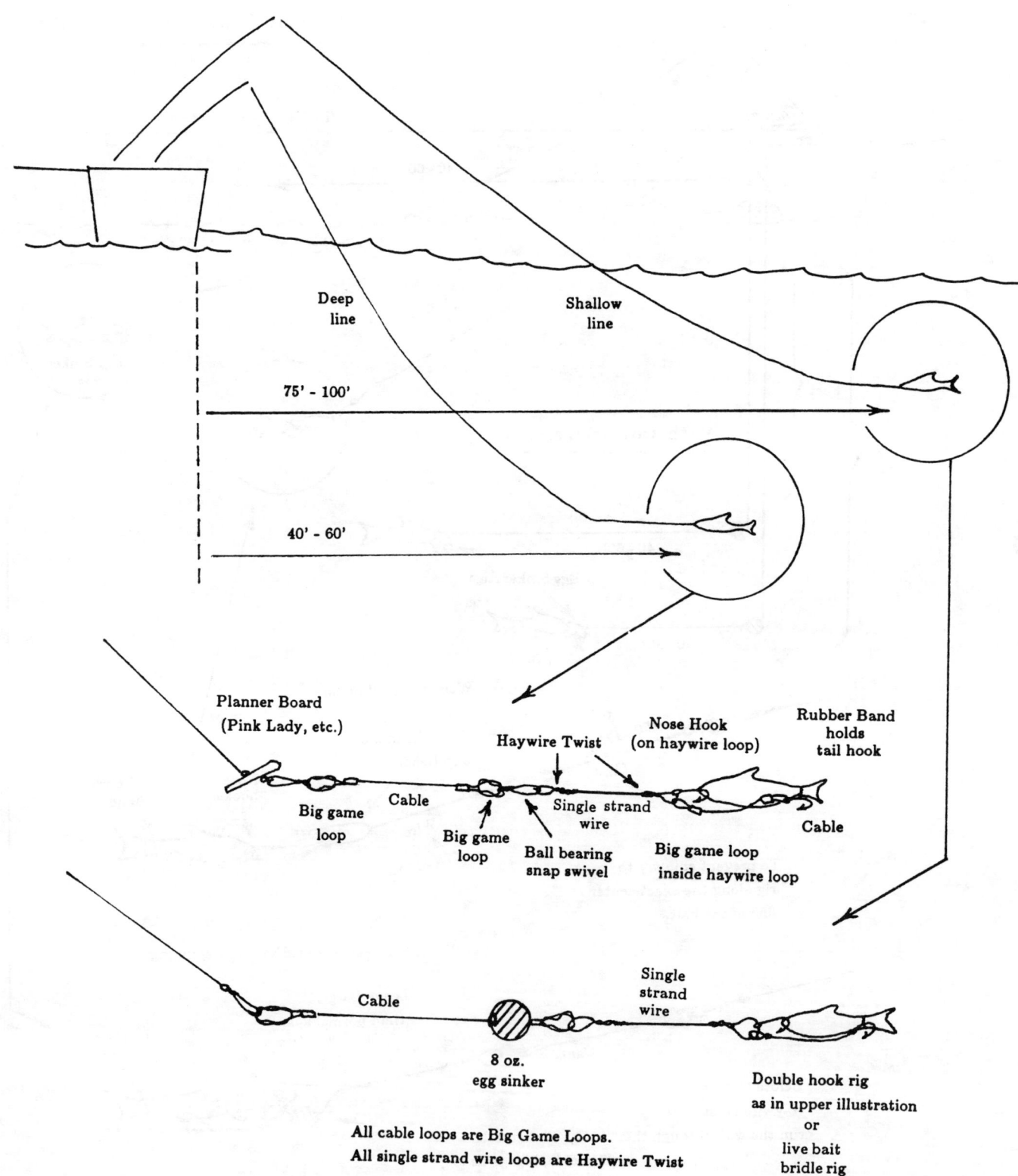

All cable loops are Big Game Loops.
All single strand wire loops are Haywire Twist

## TROLLING - LIVE BAIT BRIDLE RIG
### Troll Mackeral or Bonito at slow, idle speeds

① Turn the bait upside down to calm it, and hold in lap with a wet towel.

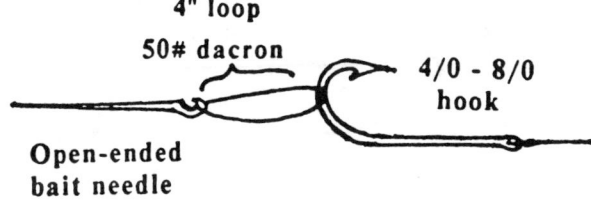

4" loop
50# dacron
4/0 - 8/0 hook
Open-ended bait needle

③ Remove line from bait needle and put loop over hook.

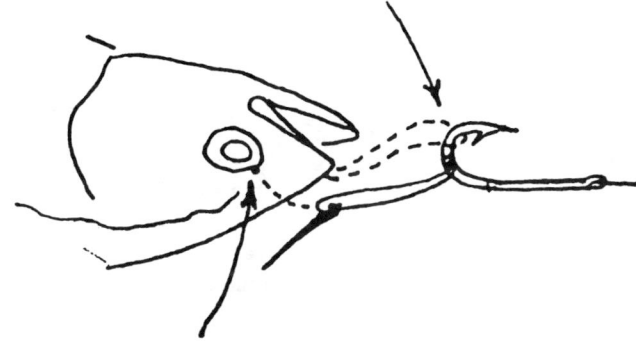

② Push needle through bait at point above and slightly forward of the eye socket. Do not puncture the eyes.

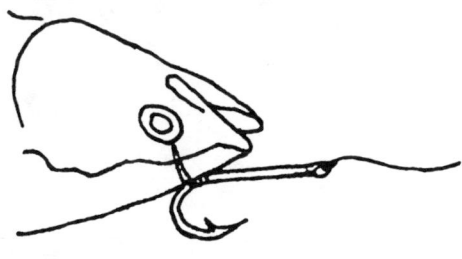

④ Twist hook until line tight.

Alternative double hook rig for tail biters - Mako & Wahoo

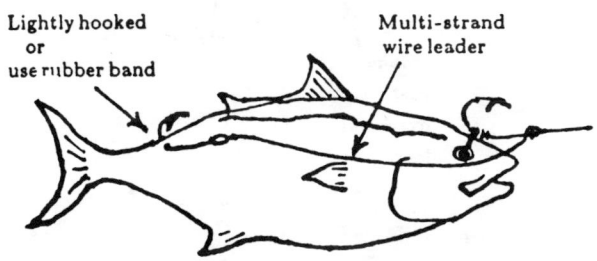

Lightly hooked or use rubber band

Multi-strand wire leader

⑤ Insert hook point under the twisted loop at the bait's head to secure and prevent the bridle from unwinding.

# BIG GAME WIRE CONNECTIONS

## HAYWIRE TWIST

### Single strand wire

1. Thread on sleeve and hook, if needed.

about 45°

2. Make 4 turns by twisting both wires at same time. Do not twist one strand around a straight second strand.

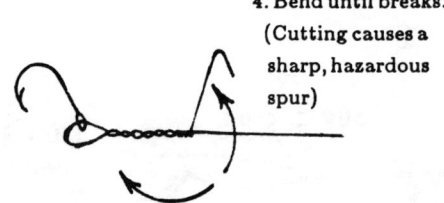

4. Bend until breaks. (Cutting causes a sharp, hazardous spur)

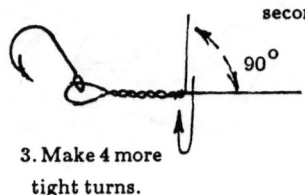

90°

3. Make 4 more tight turns.

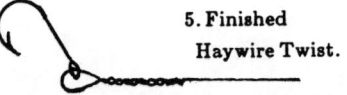

5. Finished Haywire Twist.

## BIG GAME LOOP

### Multi-strand wire

1. Thread on sleeve, and hook or swivel if needed.

2. Make first overhand loop

sleeve

3. Thread wire through hook or swivel 2nd time.

4. Second overhand loop.

5. Pull tight and crimp sleeve.

## GAFFING & SECURING

**Be Carefull!**
 a. Stay away from the shark's mouth
 b. Dont be in a hurry
 c. Dont bring the fish into the boat

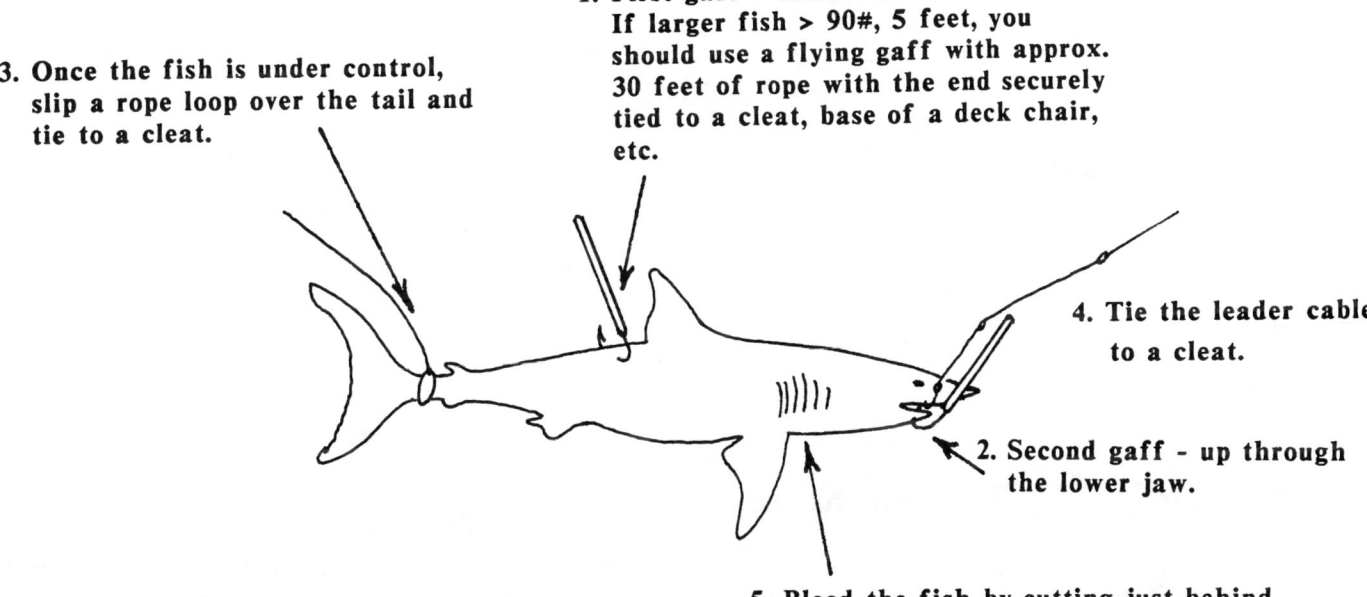

1. First gaff - behind the dorsal fin. If larger fish > 90#, 5 feet, you should use a flying gaff with approx. 30 feet of rope with the end securely tied to a cleat, base of a deck chair, etc.

3. Once the fish is under control, slip a rope loop over the tail and tie to a cleat.

4. Tie the leader cable to a cleat.

2. Second gaff - up through the lower jaw.

5. Bleed the fish by cutting just behind the anal fin and/or by cutting into the gills.

6. Let the fish sit for a considerable length of time before attempting to gut it, etc.

SHARK, BLUE & MAKO

| | |
|---|---|
| **The Law:** | Unfortunately, no size or possession limits (1990-91) |
| **Records:** | Mako Shark: State - 687 lbs. 1989<br>　　　　　　　IGFA - 1080 lbs.; Montauk, New York<br>Blue Shark: State - 231 lbs.; Santa Cruz Is., Aug 1974<br>　　　　　　　IGFA - 437 lbs.; Australia |
| **Info:** | See partyboat numbers below |
| **Access:** | Partyboats:<br><br>Davey's Locker in Newport Beach, So. Calif, has summertime shark-only open-party boats.<br>714-673-1434<br><br>Helgrens Sportfishing, Oceanside<br>Night shark fishing<br>714-722-2133<br><br>Pt. Loma Sportfishing<br>Has all night trips<br>San Diego<br>619-223-1627<br><br>Guides:<br><br>Bongos<br>Newport Beach<br>714-673-2810<br><br>Widowmaker,<br>Miguel Martinez<br>213-827-3359<br>Marina del Rey |
| **See Also:** | During the early spring and summer months, offshore kelp pads encountered while Shark fishing, can be home to Yellowtail, Bonito, Bluefin Tuna, or Yellowfin Tuna. |

SHARK, BLUE & MAKO 229

**THRESHER SHARK:**

These fish have already been overfished in the southern California area and are not usually the target fish when caught.

**Where:** Generally, the coastal waters between Point Conception and Port Hueneme.
Bubble Hole off Topanga Canyon, Santa Monica Bay
Northern, inside edge of Santa Monica Bay
Santa Monica Bay - between Topanga & Big Rock Beach, 1/2 - 3/4 miles off the "slide" area.
Santa Monica Bay - Between Topanga Bubbles & Point Dume.
Santa Monica Bay off Malibu and Paradise Cove
Steamer lanes outside of Rocky Point

Structure: Offshore blue waters but younger threshers can be found in nearshore green waters in the summer.

**When:** Summer and Fall
4 AM to about 8 AM when the sun first hits the water.

**Bait/Lures:** Live mackerel

**Rig:** **SEE DIAGRAMS in - SHARK, BLUE & MAKO**

**Technique:** Chum on top with oily fish - mackerel, etc.

Troll or drift live mackerel weighted to get down approx. 100 feet.

**See - SHARK, BLUE & MAKO technique**

**The Law:** Unfortunately, no size or possession limits

**Records:** State: 527 lbs.
IGFA: 802 lbs., New Zealand

SHARK, SEVENGILL, SOUPFIN, LEOPARD

SEVENGILL (COW), SOUPFIN, AND LEOPARD SHARKS:

**Where:** San Francisco Bay - **See Map**;
Sevengill shark are also caught in Humbolt Bay.

For Soupfin - to 100 lbs.
20-80 feet deep
Paradise Cove, Alameda Rockwall, Treasure Is., south bay shipping channels esp near Cow Palace.

For Sevengill - to 300 lbs.
80-150 feet deep
Off Golden Gate north tower, Sausalito, Belvedere, Treasure Is.
Just off Alcatraz shore, on the bottom.
Near Harding Rock.
Central and South Bay ship channels
  a. Between Angel & Alcatraz Islands
  b. South and east sides of Angel Is.
  c. Off Hunter's Point
  d. Out from San Francisco airport

For Leopards - to 40 lbs.:

Main channel, South Bay - Dumbarton Bridge
Harding Rock Buoy
San Mateo Bridge
Ship channel out from Cow Palace
Alameda Rockwall
Angel Is.

**When:** Sevengill - best season February through April
Soupfin - best in June and July
Leopards - best from April through August

In slow moving tide periods at the top of high tides and at the bottom of low tides.

**Bait/Lures:** 1 - 1 1/2 foot Stickleback Sharks (dogfish) and other small sharks. Midshipmen - a small fish native to the bay. Mudsuckers - a bottom sculpin.
Whole or cut squid, especially for Leopard sharks

**Rig:** Penn Jigmaster, 4/0 or 6/0 Senators, Daiwa 400H
100 - 150 lb. wire leaders and 9/0 - 12/0 hooks
Lead weights up to 3 lbs.

**Info:** General Bait & Tackle, 415-422-6731

**Access:** All Year: The "Fury" shark fishing in San Francisco
    Bay out of Point San Pedro, 415-357-4390
Summer Months: The Fish Hookers out of Richmond -
    Marina Bay: 916-777-6498 (Isleton),
Mid-Feb through May: "Nobilis", Vallejo, 415-757-2946

SHARK, SEVENGILL, SOUPFIN, LEOPARD 233

# SHARK FISHING SPOTS
## San Francisco Bay

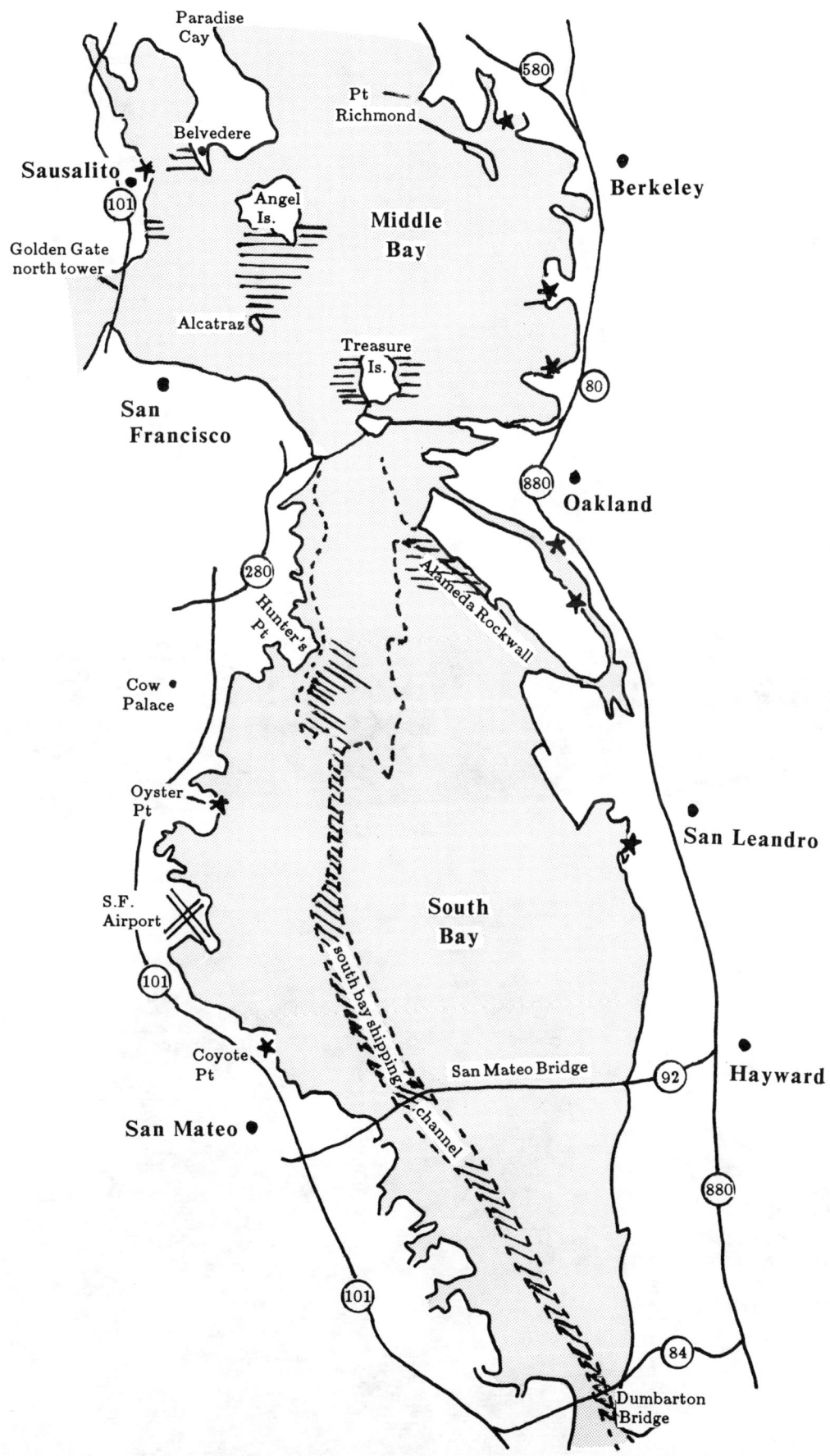

SHARK, SEVENGILL, SOUPFIN, LEOPARD 234

**286 lb. Sevengill caught on the "FURY"**

**59 lb. Soupfin caught on the "FURY"**

**"FURY" Captain Ernie Trito (left) with a big Leopard Shark**

**SHEEPHEAD:**

**Where:** Structure: Kelp beds, especially near rocky terrain
On the bottom

Hot Spots: Horseshoe Kelp
Catalina & Clemente Islands
Anacapa Island
La Jolla & Del Mar Kelp

Note also that excellent Sheephead fishing can be had on long range, 5 to 10 day, Baja trips.

**When:** Winter and spring months
Best months probably January & February

**Bait/Lures:** Live & dead Squid, Live Mackerel, Mussels, Ghost Scrimp, Razor Clams

**Rig:** Medium weight ocean rig.

**The Law:** Limit: 15
Also see regulations for ocean bag limits.

**Records:** Largest Recorded: 36 lbs.

**Access:** Horseshoe, Catalina and Clemente Is. are accessible through the partyboats of Long Beach & Redondo, etc.

La Jolla and Del Mar Kelps are fished by
Islandia Sportfishing, 619-222-1164
Seaforth Landing, 619-224-3383

**See Also:** Calico Bass, Sand Bass, Lingcod

A big Sheephead can swallow a live mackerel, fight like a yellowtail, and is great eating.

**STEELHEAD:**

**Where:**     **SEE MAPS**

The major Steelhead rivers are:

1. Klamath and Trinity
2. Smith
3. Eel
4. Russian

These rivers support sustained runs and can be relied upon to hold Steelhead during the season.

The smaller Steelhead streams have much shorter runs, and their fishing status can change so quickly that only local anglers can effectively fish them.

As of this writing, the Steelhead fishery of the Yuba and American are in bad shape and the Feather and Sacramento are fading fast. Since these areas are close to the major Sacramento populations, some details are provided on these rivers.

Average Steelhead size varies considerably between major rivers. A trophy Steelhead on the Klamath is 10+ pounds. A trophy Steelhead on the Smith is 20+ pounds.

**IN GENERAL:**

Smith: Between 101 and junction of South and middle river forks.

Klamath: From Somes Bar to Iron Gate dam.

Trinity: Early Season - Hoopa Valley to Willow Creek, Cedar Flat.
Late Season - Cedar Flat to Lewiston, Douglas City.

Mad: At Blue Lake below fish hatchery.

Eel: From High Rock, below the forks, to Miranda on the south fork.

Russian: Cloverdale upstream to Squaw Rock.

Feather: North of Yuba City/Marysville, between Live Oak and 162 bridge.

Sacramento: Los Molinos upstream to Red Bluff Diversion Dam.

# SALMON / STEELHEAD RIVERS

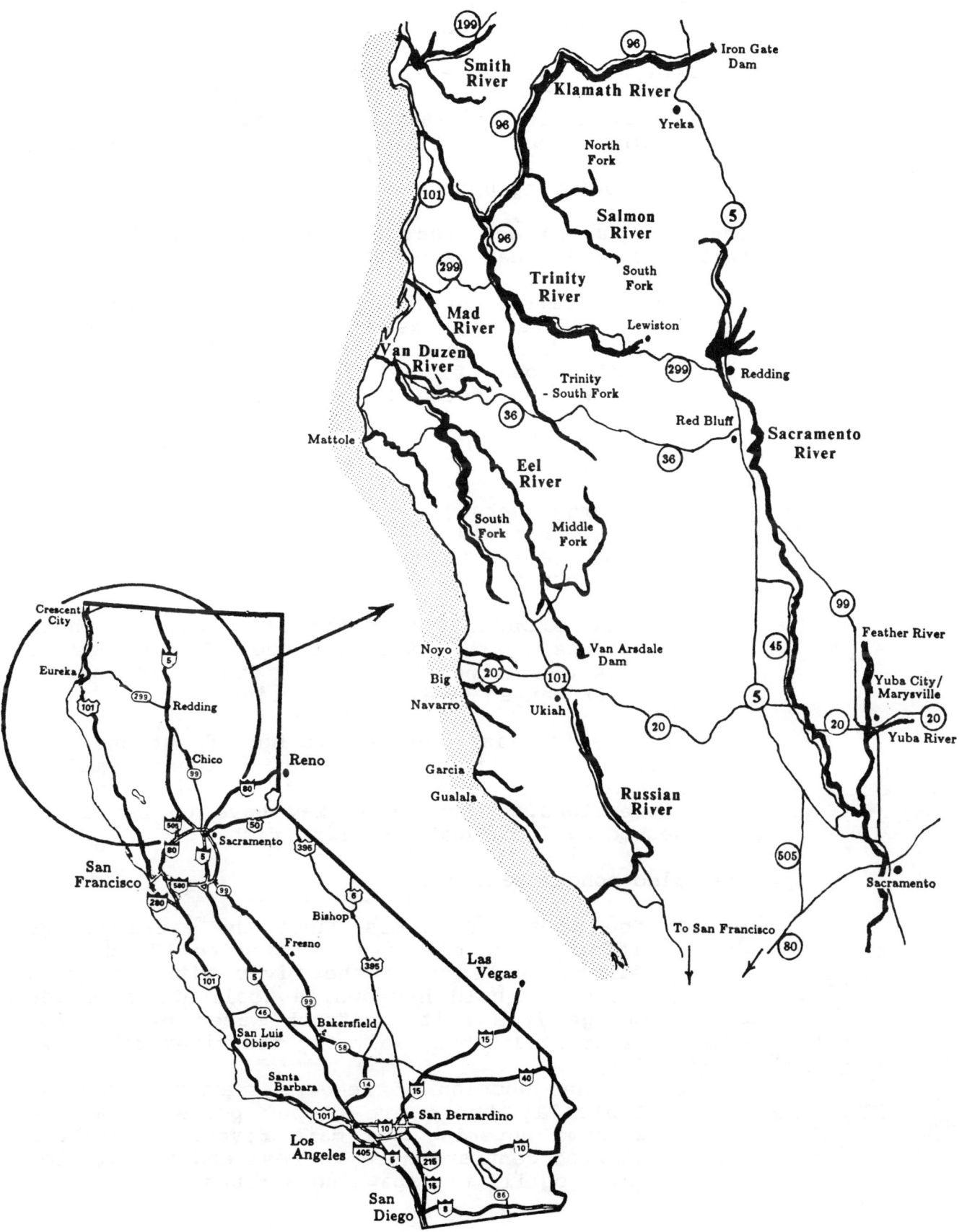

# STEELHEAD
## Structure

**Where:** STRUCTURE:

Steelhead Holding Areas, Winter Season:

**See Steelhead Structure Diagram**

Steelhead hold in water that is quieter than surrounding waters. These holding areas are usually adjacent to their runs, or preferred paths of least effort in swimming upstream.

**Look for Steelhead just off the bottom in water that is 3 to 10 feet deep,**

In tailouts, the downstream end of pools or runs, before the faster moving, more turbulent riffle. Look especially above and to the sides of "V" shaped, flatter slicks where the riffle meets the end of the deeper pool or run.

Fish behind larger objects that slow the current in runs;

- Large Rocks
- Fallen Trees
- Bridge Abutments
- Points of land, etc.

Specifically, not directly behind these objects in the turbulent eddies, but 3+ feet back and along the seam of faster and slower water caused by the obstruction.

In runs the fish can be more spread out and will hold in less obvious structure - behind smaller submerged rocks and in stream bottom depressions. These runs may have to be fished methodically in order to find fish.

Fish also concentrate at:

1. The mouth of rivers where the tidal swings affect the river level. Steelhead (and Salmon) will enter the river with the high tides and hold here while acclimating to the change from salt to fresh water or, in low water conditions, wait for the river to rise.

2. At the junction of feeder, spawning streams. Typically there are deeper pools formed by streams entering the main river. Steelhead will concentrate here to rest and to wait for rain to fill the spawning streams.

**Steelhead Holding Areas, Winter Season continued:**

Note that because of the vulnerability of fish holding at these junctions, there are some restrictions at the major spawning streams. See current DFG regulations for details.

3. Fish will stack in areas below dams that prevent or significantly hinder their upstream progress. Also the water conditions are consistently good in these areas because of the controlled releases of water.

    Examples are;

    a. Below Iron Gate dam on the Klamath River off highway 5 north of Redding.

    b. Below Van Arsdale dam on the Eel river, off highway 20, north of Ukiah.

    c. Near Lewiston and Douglas City on the Trinity River off highway 36.

**Steelhead Holding Areas, Fall Season:**

Steelhead are feeding, are more active, and require more oxygenated water in the fall. They will hold more in typical Rainbow Trout structure. They will be at the head of pools and at the downstream end of the deeper riffles.

**See Steelhead Structure diagram.**

STEELHEAD 240    **STEELHEAD STRUCTURE**

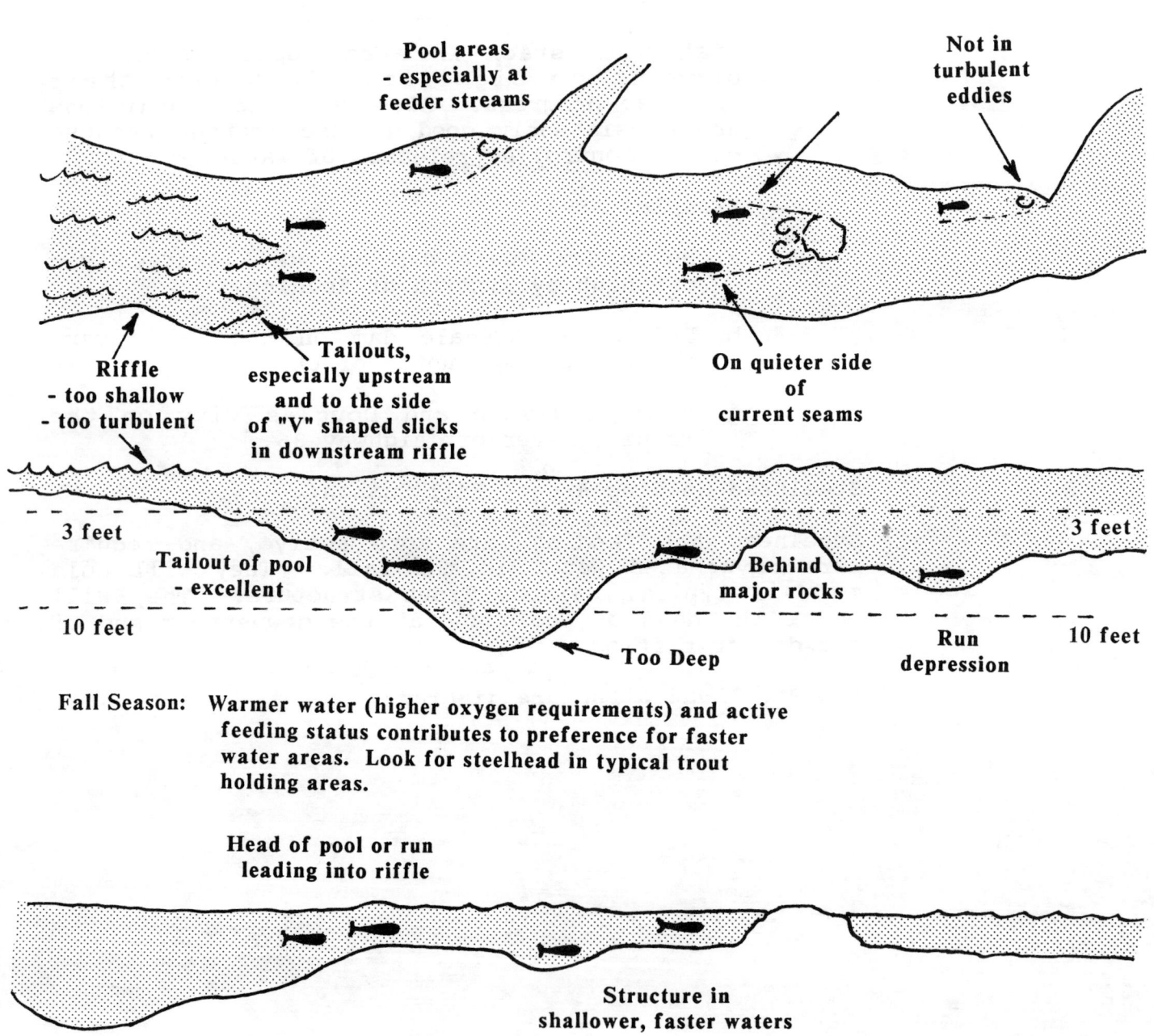

Winter Season: Colder water (lower oxygen requirements) and non-feeding status contribute to preference for quieter water areas.

Fall Season: Warmer water (higher oxygen requirements) and active feeding status contributes to preference for faster water areas. Look for steelhead in typical trout holding areas.

Steelhead prefer holding at the tail end of gravel bottom Salmon spawning riffles. Here they intercept roe as it floats downstream. Fish with roe or Glo Bugs.

# STEELHEAD FISHING CALENDAR

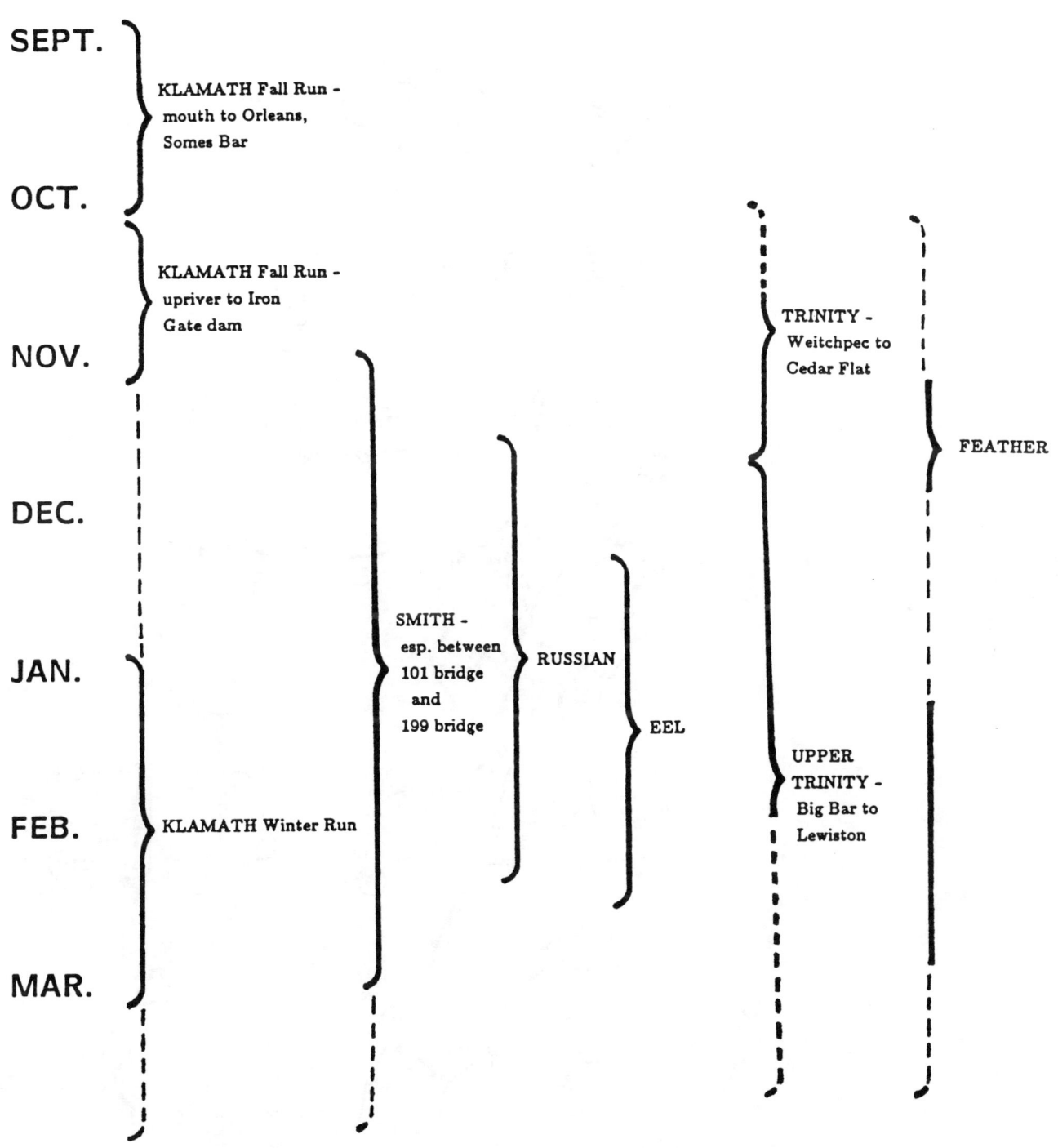

STEELHEAD 242
When

# STEELHEAD RIVERS - Clearing Speeds
### The first heavy rain is usually in late September

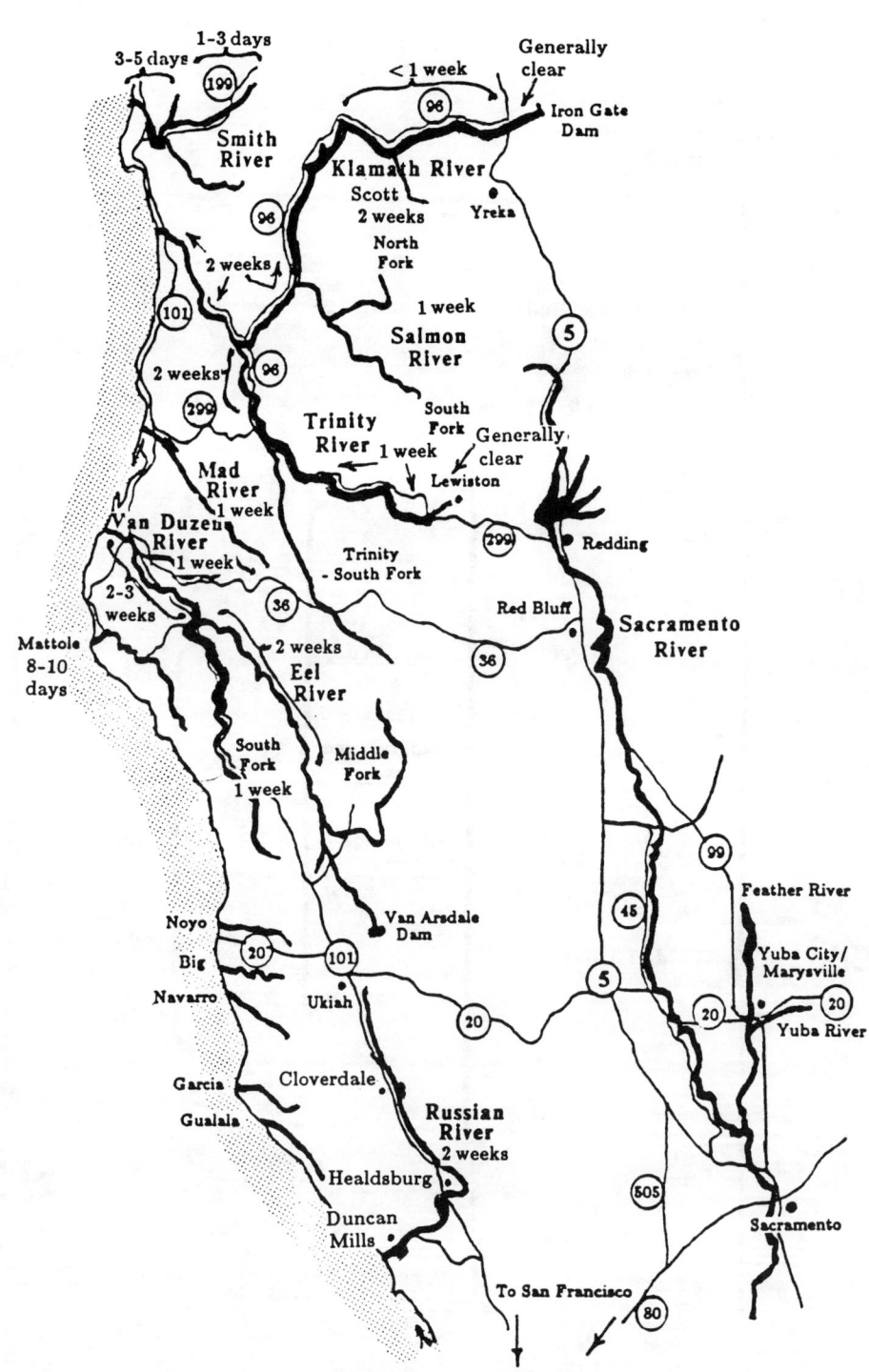

**When:**

Dry (Fall) Season: September until first rains, normally late October or November.

The Klamath has a fall run of "half-pounders", smaller fish from 1/2 to 3 pounds. These fish are active, feeding fish and are easier to catch and provide more action than the larger sized winter run fish. Fly fishing for the smaller fish is popular.

Wet (Winter) Season: October to February. January and February are typically the best months

Winter fish are considerably larger but are not actively feeding.

When you can see your lure in 2 to 3 feet of water, start fishing.

**Bait/Lures:**

Bait: Roe, Nightcrawler, Tuna Ball, Crayfish tail. In tidal areas: Cut Mackerel, anchovy.

Back Trolling - boat drift fishing:
Hot Shot, No. 30 to 50; Wee Warts; Colors: Silver & Black, Silver & Green, Gold.

Drift Fishing - floating lures:
Glo Bug - pink or red, Spin-N-Glo, Okie Drifters, Lil Corkies, Glo Go.

Casting & Spinning - sinking lures:
Bear Valley spinner, Wob-L-Rite (3/4 oz.)

Spinners - small Panther Martin, Roostertail

Winter Season: especially in dirty water and/or low light, shady conditions - use size #5 or #4 lures with bright, shiny French style blades. Colors: Florescent orange, red, yellow, chartreuse.

Fall Season: especially in clear water, bright light conditions use smaller #2 to #3 lures still with dull, dark French style blades. Colors: Florescent Kelly green, darker reds, yellow, black.

Fly Fishing: Black Skunk, Estuary Shrimp - tidal areas, Black Comet, Silver Hilton, Brindle Bug, Burlap. Sizes: #2 to #6 weighted

**Rig:** See Diagrams

# STEELHEAD RIGS

A. Bait Drift Rig: Roe, Nightcrawler, etc.

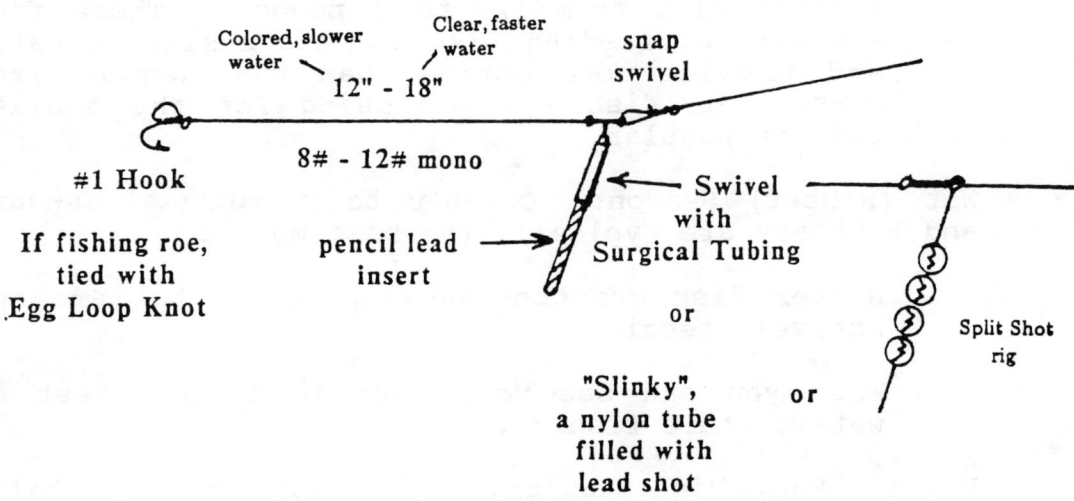

Egg Loop Knot - start with 24" of 8# to 12# mono.

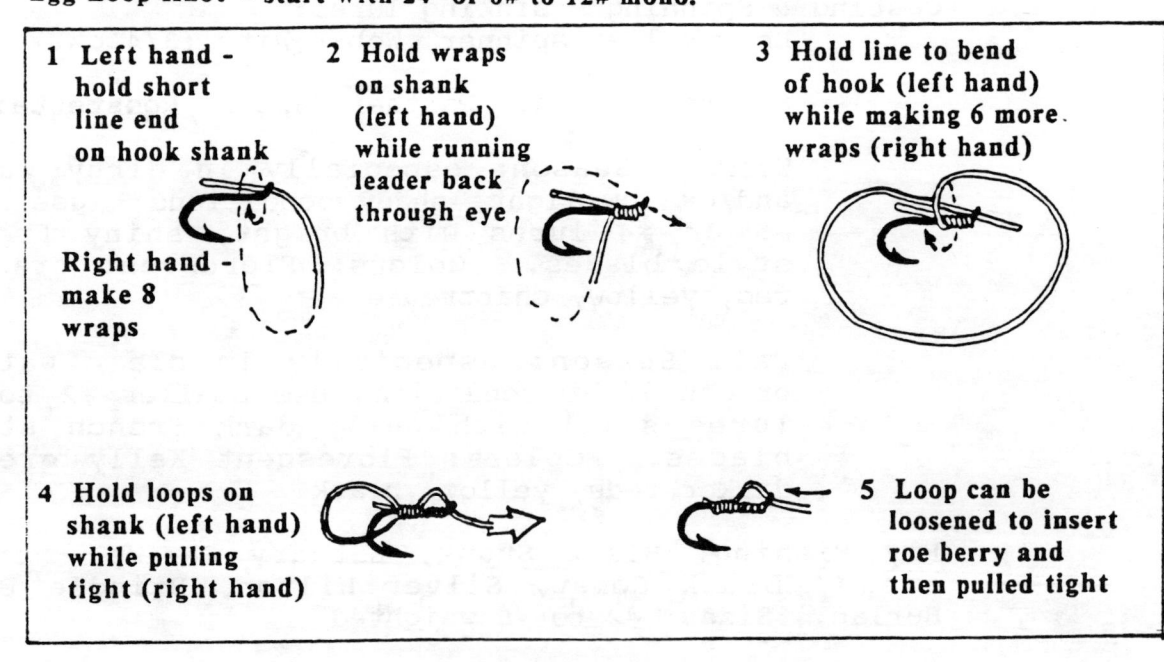

# STEELHEAD RIGS

STEELHEAD 245

**B.** Floating Lure Rig: Often fished with roe using an Egg Loop Knot

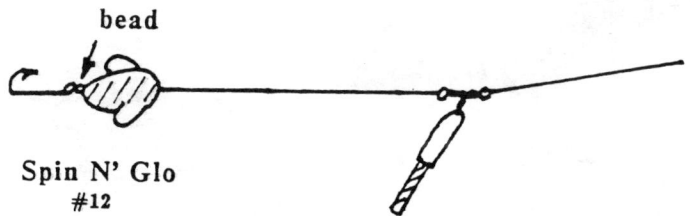

Spin N' Glo #12

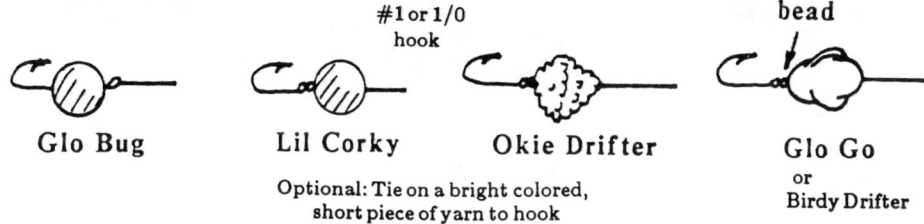

#1 or 1/0 hook

Glo Bug     Lil Corky     Okie Drifter     Glo Go or Birdy Drifter

The bead facilitates rotation of the lure

Optional: Tie on a bright colored, short piece of yarn to hook

**C.** Casting/Spinning Sinking Lures:

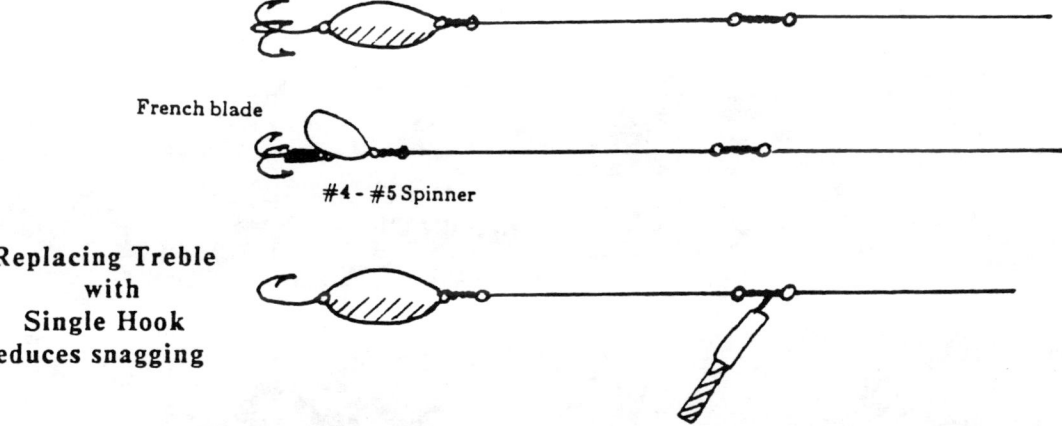

French blade

#4 - #5 Spinner

Replacing Treble with Single Hook reduces snagging

**D.** Fly Fishing Rig:

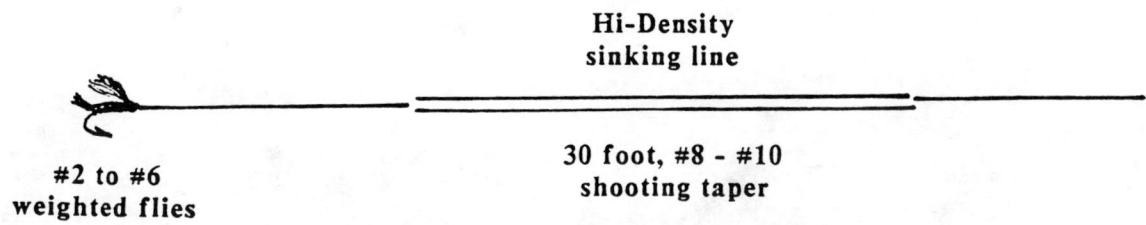

Hi-Density sinking line

#2 to #6 weighted flies

30 foot, #8 - #10 shooting taper

STEELHEAD 246

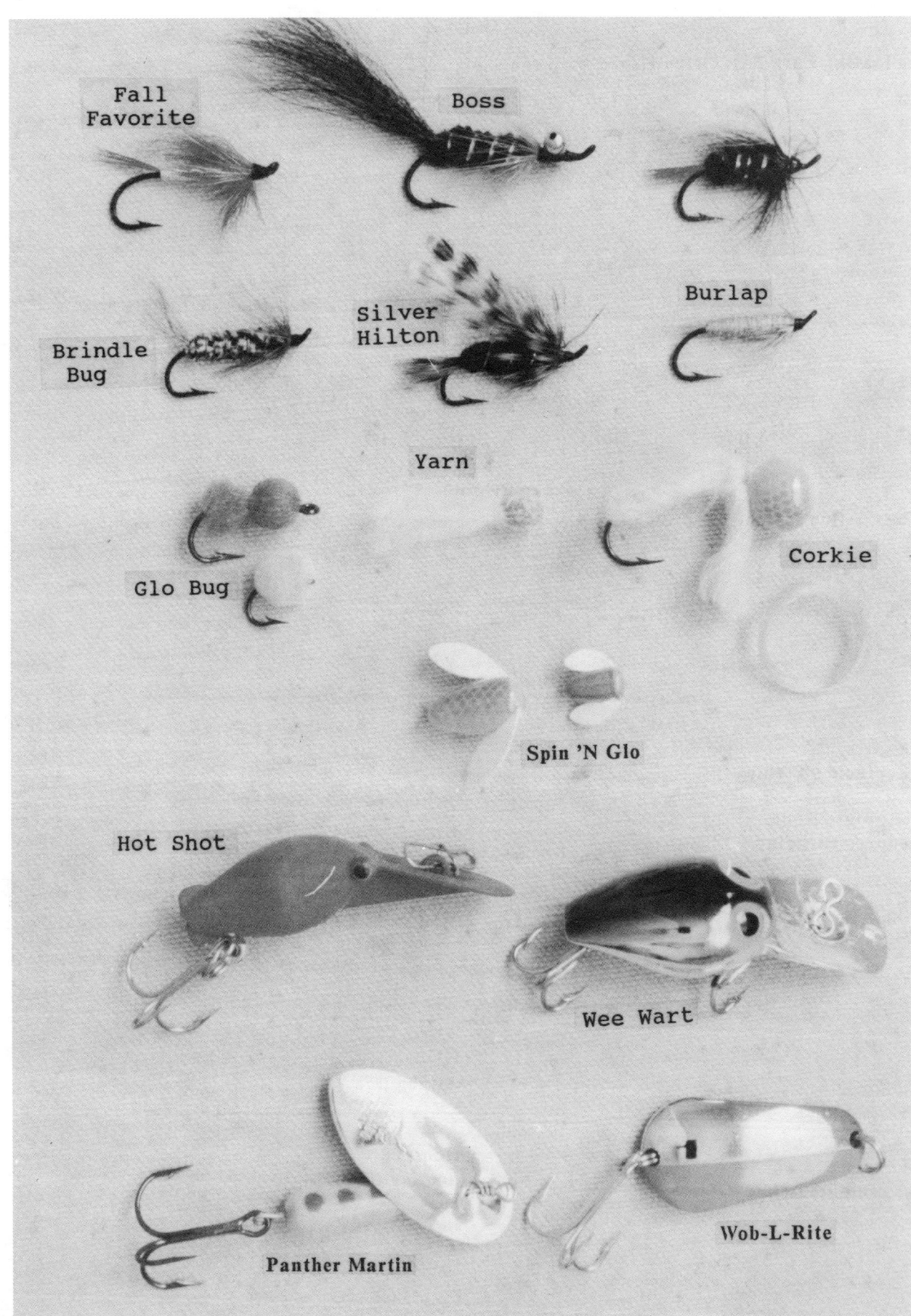

**Rod/Reel:** Because of the "feel" required to detect a Steelhead pickup, rods with flexible tips, especially graphite rods are preferred.

Conventional: Fenwick: EC85 - 8 1/2 foot
                            EC83 - 8 1/4 foot

   Reel: Ambassadeur 5000 or 6000 type reel with capacity for 200 yards of 12 lb. test mono.

Spinning: Light to medium weight reel with capacity for 100 to 150 yards of 8# to 15# mono.

   Fenwick: GFS83 - 8 1/4 foot graphite

Fly Fishing: 8 1/2 to 10 foot, 8 - 11 weight graphite.
   Fenwick: FF 85
   Sage: Graphite II, Model 990 RP
   G. Loomis:
Fly reel with capacity for 150 yds. of dacron backing + 70 yds. of 20# mono + a 30' shooting head, Hi-speed, Hi-D, fly line.
For early season half-pounders on the Klamath use a lighter, 4-6 wt. rod, floating or sinking tip fly line and a 6# tippet.

**Technique:** Steelhead fishing is a challenge. Here is why:

1. There is a large amount of fishing area. The Klamath is over 190 miles long. Every mile of it will hold fish during some time(s) in the season. Other major rivers, the Eel and Russian are also quite long.

2. Winter storms can make streams or stream sections unfishable for up to 3 weeks.

3. Steelhead move upstream in groups. Areas separating these migrating schools hold little or no fish. Schools may move upstream 4-6 miles in one day. Most traveling is done at night.

4. Winter run Steelhead do not feed during their upstream voyage. This reluctance to strike forces precise lure placement for success.

5. Even if the Steelhead are currently known to be in a particular stretch of the river, they still will only be found in very limited holding areas (see Where: Structure). Unless you are very familiar with a section of the river or are very experienced at reading Steelhead water, there is a good chance you will be fishing dead areas.

STEELHEAD 248
Technique

6. Steelhead bites can be hard to detect. Especially when fishing bait, a Steelhead pickup can be very hard to recognize. Experience and close attention are needed.

7. Because of the necessity for placing the lure/bait near the stream bottom, snags and lost tackle are common.

So how do we deal with this challenge?

Steelhead Strategy:

1. Get current reliable information by calling information numbers - **See Steelhead Information and Stream Clearing Speeds**.

    A. Where are the fish? - Steelhead move up the river in clusters.

    B. What are the water conditions? - look for clearing water with 2 to 3 foot visibility. **See River Clearing Map**

    Some stream areas clear considerably faster than others. It can vary from 1 - 2 days to 3 weeks. **See Stream Clearing Map**.

    The upper sections of rivers clear quicker than the lower sections.

    Smaller feeder streams and their junction with the major rivers are fishable earlier.

    C. What's the weather report? - if its raining hard now or expected soon, don't go.

2. If you are new to Steelheading, I very highly recommend hiring a guide. Learn as much as you can during this guiding trip. This could save you man-years of effort.

3. In an area with recently reported fish and good water condition;

    A: Fish known Steelhead areas - **See Steelhead Hotspots Maps**, See Structure.

    B: Limit your time fishing unproductive waters. Consistently good anglers stay on the move until fish concentrations are found.

    If fishing lures, if no action, move on after covering the area with casts.

If fishing bait, which is a slower process, if no action move on in 30 to 45 minutes.

Keep moving until successful.

4. It is helpful to intimately learn a certain stretch of water. If you have fished a known Steelhead area before and have gained knowledge of its fish holding structure, and the reports say fish are in the area and the water is right - fish it again, learn more, catch more Steelhead!

Steelhead Tactics:

1. Backtrolling (boat fishing) with Hot Shot, Wee Wart, Flatfish.

   This technique is very similar to backtrolling for Salmon. The major difference is the use of double ender drift boats. This technique requires a full time boat handler.

   Work the structure area slowly and thoroughly covering the width of the suspected holding area, and very slowly slipping downstream. It can take an 8 hour day to properly fish a 5 mile stretch of water.

2. Bait/Floating Lure Drifting.

   This technique can be used from the bank, wading, or from an anchored boat.

   If the current is strong enough to move a drift rig
      and the bottom is relatively smooth
      and free of sunken timber and other snags
      use a drift fishing rig.

   Work the near water first.

   Make a quartering cast upstream of the structure/holding area.

   Maintain enough line tension during the drift so that;

   a. You can feel the occasional tapping when the weight hits the bottom.

   b. You don't interfere with the downstream drift of the lure/bait.

If a slower current area causes the lure to stop, reel in slowly only until the current again picks up the rig.

Use "tailing" when necessary to extend a drift to downstream holding areas. Tailing is a controlled release of line. With a spinning reel this is done by reeling backwards slowly. With a conventional casting reel, freespool and thumb control does the job.

Some runs will require systematic coverage (nearest water first). This is especially true if there are no obvious holding structures and this is new water to you.

Be careful when retrieving your rig not to disturb unfished holding areas (fish closer areas first).

3. Sinking Lure Drifting with Bear Valley Spinner, Gold Panther Martin, Wob-L-Rite Spoon.

   If Holding water is not deep,
      or the current is to slow for a drift rig,
      or the area would cause too much snagging with a drift rig,
Use a spinner, spoon, or wobbler.

This technique can be used from the bank, wading, or from an anchored boat.

DON'T cast and retrieve.

Drift these lures, allowing the current to move them through the same critical fish-holding structures. Maintain a slight line tension on the lure during the drift to enhance correct lure action and reduce snagging.

They must be just off the bottom. Vary lure weight and style to keep it on the bottom or use the pencil lead drift-fishing rig.

Use a swivel to minimize line twisting.

4. Fly Fishing

Fly fishing can be a very effective technique. Clearer waters are required for flies to be visible. Most fly fishing is done during the fall for half pounders.

|              | |
|---|---|
|              | Note that fly fishing tackle is also used for backtrolling. No casting is required. The rig is simply let out behind the boat the same as with conventional rigs. |
| **The Law:** | Special restrictions and closures are common. Consult current DFG regulations. Steelhead are included within the "Trout" regulations. |
| **Records:** | State: 27 lbs. 4 oz.; Smith River; Dec. 1976<br>IGFA: 42 lbs. 2 oz., Alaska, 1970 |
| **Info:**    | **See Info Map** |
| **Access:**  | Guides: A list of guides can be obtained by calling; |

        North Coast River Guides Association
        707-539-9534

        or the information sources shown on the Info Map can recommend good local guides.

        Bank Access and Launching:

        See Streamtime Maps for the Russian, Eel, Klamath, and Smith rivers. These maps accurately describe river access areas and drift boat launch/take-out spots.

        More Detail: For a complete description of major north coast rivers fishing access, see;

        "California Steelhead" by Jim Freeman

**See Also:**     Salmon, Rainbow Trout

STEELHEAD 252

# STEELHEAD INFORMATION NUMBERS

These sources will also recommended good local guides.
Cities indicated have suitable lodging.

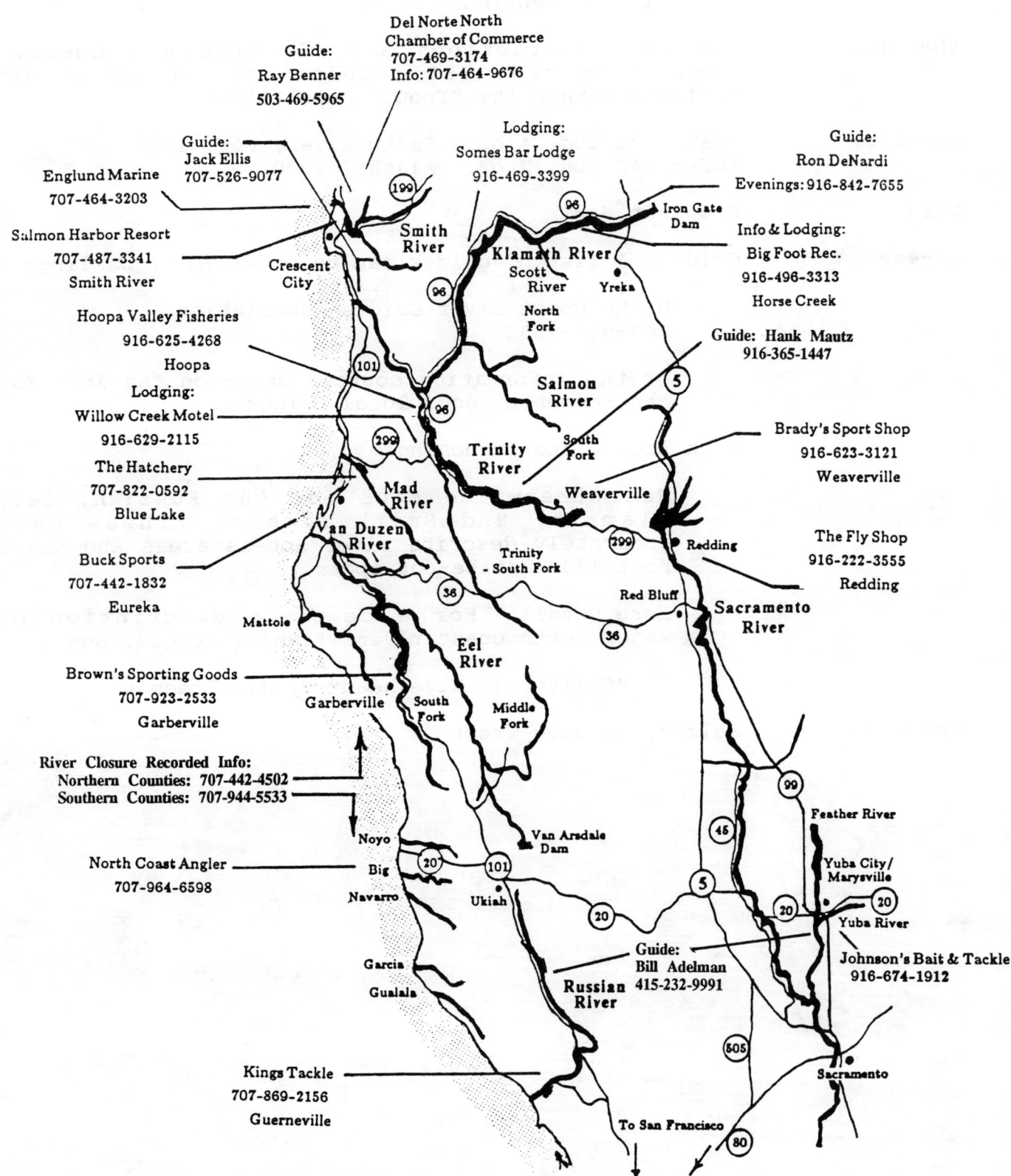

**Guide Jack Ellis holding a bright Steelhead**

## STURGEON:

**Where/When:** SAN FRANCISCO BAY

**SEE MAPS:**

Structure:

Sturgeon feed on the bottom.

Shallow dropoffs in 15 to 20 foot deep water

Areas where water slows in moving to deeper water at the shoulders of deeper water channels

Along rip lines - one side is still and flat, the other side is moving and choppy. Fish the moving water side of the rip.

Sturgeon are sensitive to fishing pressure. Fish in the proven spots but stay a distance from partyboats and masses of private boats.

November to December: Especially San Pablo Bay
December: Especially Middle Bay with shrimp until herring run in late December. Also west side of bay from California City to Golden Gate Bridge. From the San Rafael/Richmond Bridge between #19 & # 23 pillars and down towards Paradise Cay.
Late December and January: Northern part of South Bay during herring runs using roe.
February to March: Especially in Sacramento/San Joaquin Delta soon after rains have muddied the bay. Also can be good in South Bay area.
March - probably the best sturgeon fishing time in San Pablo Bay.
April: San Pablo Bay.
April to June: Sacramento River: Between Colusa & Princeton on Ghost Scrimp at NIGHT.

**When:** When Bay is flushed by medium-to-heavy winter rains.
During big (winter) tidal swings with 5 or more feet difference between the high and low tides.
Early morning and late afternoon minus tides greater than 5 feet. The last 2 hours of an incoming tide to high tide. The last half hour of an outgoing tide.

Sturgeon are sensitive to fishing pressure. Anglers seem to have more success during weekdays and other uncrowded periods.

**Bait/Lures:** Grass Shrimp, Mudshrimp, or Ghost Shrimp - put 4 to 6 on the hook at once. Thread on the hook, tail first, with the point coming out slightly from the head.
Mudsucker - not as good as shrimp.

**Bait/Lures continued:**

Herring Roe - during the herring spawns, only herring roe will work. Herring season starts late December.

**Rig:** Rod: 6' to 7', with light tip
Reel: Open-faced, capacity of 200+ yards of 30# to 40# test mono such as Penn 500M, Daiwa 50H, 300H, etc.

### Sturgeon Rig

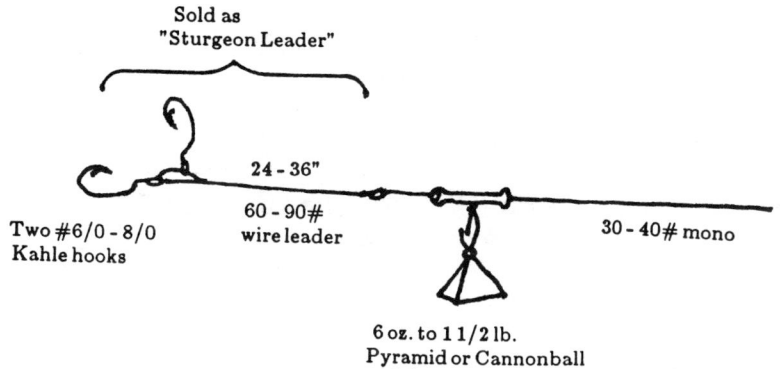

**Technique:** Cast out 15 yards from the boat.
Leave weight on the bottom - it must be flat on the bottom. Use pyramid or cannonball sinkers, flat sinkers tend to plane off the bottom during strong tidal flows.
Set the rod down and watch the tip, the bite is a pumping action.
Set the hook when the rod tip is down.

Sturgeon will drop a bait as soon as they feel any resistance. Therefore a device called a balance bar can be used to improve success. The bar is notched and lays across the boat stern. After casting out, the rod is balanced on the bar such that the slightest tug on the bait will move the balanced rod down. The alert angler must then quickly pick up the rod at the same time moving the tip in the direction of the pulling fish. When the fish pulls on the bait again - set the hook.

Look for jumping Sturgeon. Anchor downstream of the jumps. Sturgeon swim with a current - down current.

**The Law:** One per angler.
From March1, 1999 to Feb. 28, 1991 the legal size range is from 42" to 72".
From March 1, 1991 to Feb. 29, 1992 the legal size range is from 44" to 72".
There are special closures on the Klamath River.

**Records:** State: 468 lbs., July 1981, Carquinez Straits
IGFA:      "            "              "
Commercial: 1800 lbs., Fraser River, B.C., Canada.

STURGEON 256

**Info:**       For San Pablo Bay, etc.:

        Loch Lomond Marina
        (415) 456-0321

        Bill's Bait
        Martinez
        (415) 229-3150

        Emeryville Sportfishing
        415-654-6696 recording

        Port Sonoma Bait & Tackle
        707-763-9296

For South Bay:

        Sun Valley Bait & Tackle
        415-343-4690 recording

        Coyote Bait & Tackle
        415-463-0711

**Access:**     Guides: Jay Sorensen
        209-478-6645

        Barry Canevaro
        916-777-6498

        Jack Findleton
        916-487-3392

Launching Ramps - See Appendix A: Salt Water Launching Sites

Partyboats:

    For San Pablo Bay area:

        Loch Lomond Marina
        (415) 456-0321

        Emeryville Sportfishing
        415-654-6696 recording

For Sacramento River- Carquinez Strait, Suisan Bay, etc:

        Crockett Marina - multiple boats
        415-787-1048

        Martinez Marina
        415-757-2946 Nobilis

**See Also:**   Striped Bass, Sevengill Shark, Soupfin Shark, Leopard Shark

STURGEON 257

# STURGEON FISHING SPOTS
## San Pablo and Middle Bay

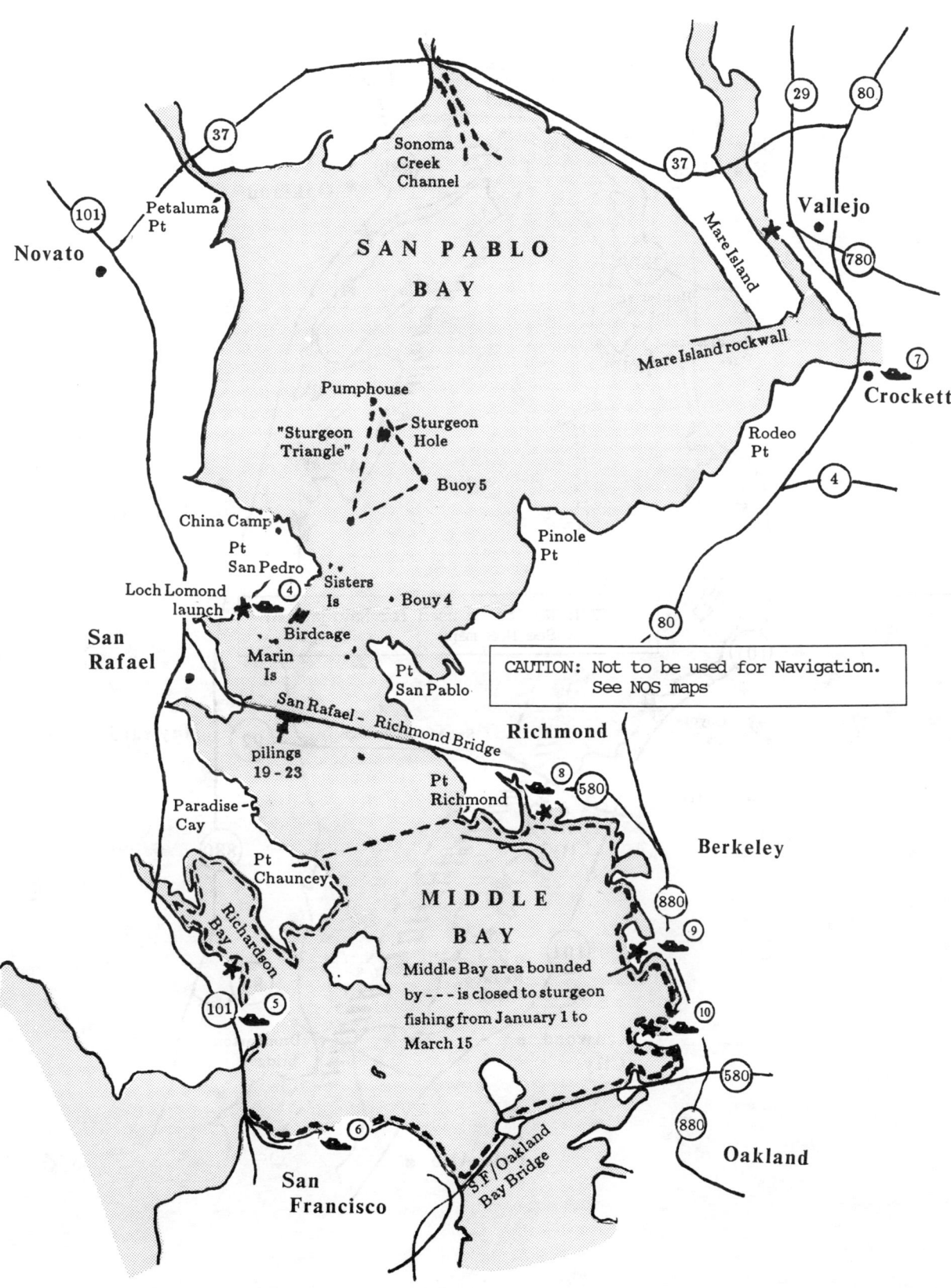

# STURGEON FISHING SPOTS
## South Bay

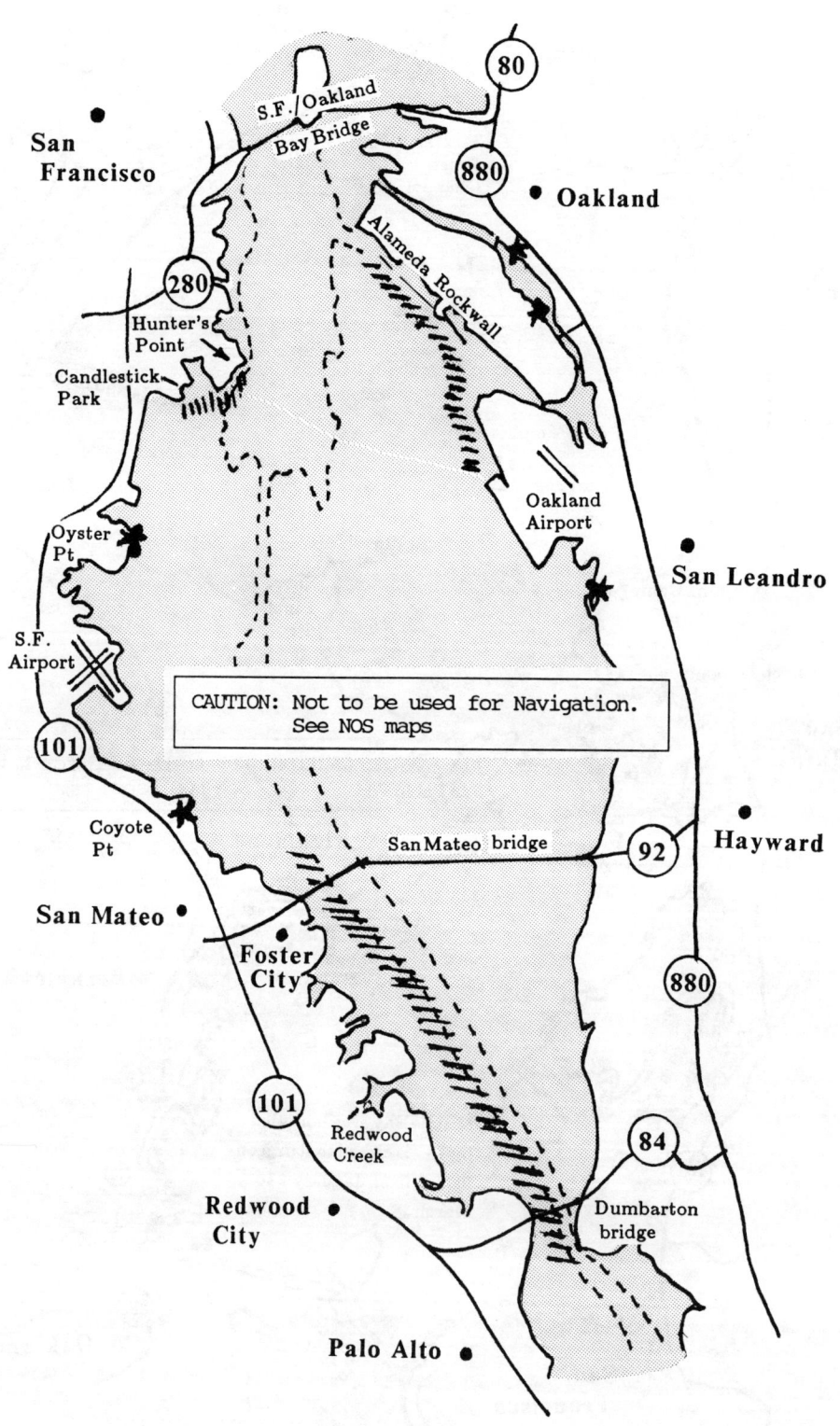

# STURGEON FISHING SPOTS
## Delta Area

CAUTION: Not to be used for Navigation. See NOS maps

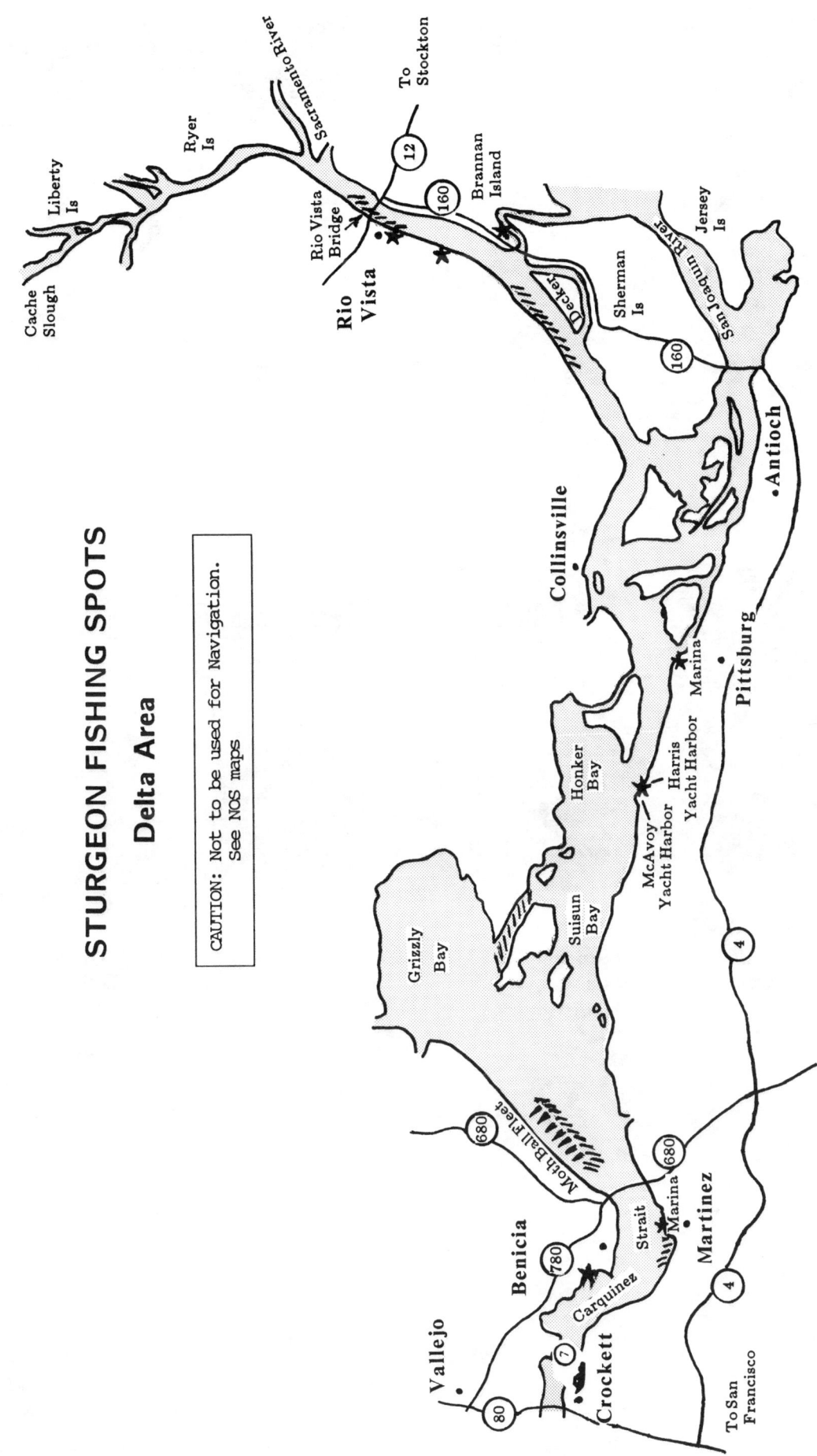

**A 362 lb. White Sturgeon. Current regulations require releasing a fish this long**

**A nice size Striper and Sturgeon caught with Guide Jay Sorensen**

**BROOK TROUT:**

| | |
|---|---|
| **Where:** | Mountain streams and lakes at 7000 foot elevation and higher |

Lake Kirman, near Bridgeport, **See map in Rainbow Trout section**
Higher lakes of the Mammoth Lake chain
Parker Creek - north of June Lake Loop
Walker Creek -    "              "
Creeks emptying into Saddlebag Lake
Lundy Creek above Lundy Lake
Lake Sabrina - out of Bishop, near inlet in spring

**When:** The fall season is best for Lake Kirman.
    About a 3 mile walk to the lake
      Best if can fish weedline - need a float tube

Brook Trout spawn in the fall and are more active and hungry. They do not require running water to spawn, so often are located in clear, quiet pools.

**Bait/Lures:** Yellow Panther Martin
Red worm on small bronze hook

**Rig:** Ultra-light to light spinning or flyfishing tackle.
Use light 2-4# mono

**The Law:** Generally 5 fish, no size limit (1990-91)
See regulations for exceptions.
Lake Kirman special regs (1990-91): Season - last Saturday in April through Oct. 31, Minimum Size - 16" total length.

**Records:** State: 9 lbs. 12 oz.; Silver Lake; September 1932
IGFA: 14 lbs. 8 oz., Canada, 1916

**BROWN TROUT:**

**Where:**  **SEE MAPS**

    Lakes:  Eastern Sierra Region:
            Twin Lakes, Bridgeport
            Pleasant Valley Reservoir - near Bishop. Night fishing allowed.
             Grant Lake - June Lake Loop
             Silver Lake - June Lake Loop
             Crowley Lake

            Other Areas:
             Frenchman Lake - near Davis Lake
             Stampede - north of Lake Tahoe

    Streams - Eastern Sierra Area:
        Robinson & Buckeye Creek - (near Bridgeport and Twin Lakes)
        Rush Creek (near Grant Lake)
        Owens River
        East Walker River (below Bridgeport Reservoir)
        Convict Creek (near Crowley)

Structure:

    Lakes: In 50 - 60 degree water. Inlet stream areas are cool water areas - prime fall season spots. Fish the dark side of rocks, shady banks, shorelines and shoreline points. Almost all big Browns are caught in water less than 15 feet deep.

    Streams: Fish pockets in white water rapids, during low-water conditions, that would be difficult to reach at higher stream levels. In the fall, Browns will begin their spawn by heading into the streams entering into the lake.

    If you see someone wearing a cap that says "Sierra Brownbaggers" you are in the right place. This is an exclusive club requiring the owner to have caught 2 Brown Trout over 10 lbs.

**When:**  The opening and closing seasons - early April, Mid-September through October
Note that Pleasant Valley Reservoir is open all year - best season is from December through March
At night where allowed: Inyo County
                     NOT Mono County
First and last hour of daylight
Bad weather;
  - windy, broken surface conditions and wave-washed shorelines.
  - cloudy, low light conditions

# TROUT, BROWN

**Bait/Lures:** The type and size of lure varies considerably depending on weather you are seeking a small, stream Brown versus a giant Twin Lakes Brown Trout.

- Bait: Live minnows drifted under bubbles (not legal in some areas)
  Soft-shelled crayfish
  Red worms
  Nightcrawlers

- Flies: Muddler Minnows
  Streamer Flies
  Hornburg Special

- Lures for smaller fish:
  small Scroungers
  Finger Jigs
  small Kastmasters (chrome or gold)
  small Roostertails
  Mister Twister black/chartreuse Crappie jig

**Rig:** Depends on technique and area, from light flyfishing to medium weight trolling gear.

**Big Fish Techniques:**

Casting Shad Raps:
- cast out and work by reeling in a few feet to pull lure beneath the surface 2+ feet
- let lure suspend temporarily
- twitch or reel in a short distance
- repeat

Trolling for big Browns:
- Troll with lure well back of the boat - 40 to 50+ yards. Big Browns are easily spooked.
- Use 6 - 8# test quality mono.
- Troll slowly with lure 5 feet off the bottom in water 10 to 20 feet deep.
- Vary the trolling pattern and speed.
- First hour of daylight - use floating Rapala, after that user Magnum (sinking, countdown)
- #13 to #18 Sinking Rapalas in rainbow or silver & black patterns.
- 6" Plugs - Rebels - rainbow trout pattern
- Storm's ThinFin - shad pattern in shad lakes

**The Law:** Generally 5 in Lakes but many exceptions. See current DFG regulations under "Trout & Salmon".

**Records:** State Record: 26 1/2 lbs., Upper Twin Lake, 1987
IGFA: 35 lbs. 15 oz., Argentina, 1952

**Info:** For Twin Lakes, Bridgeport; Ken's Sporting Goods, 619-932-7707; Mono Village Campsite, 619-932-7071
For Crowley Lake & Pleasant Valley Reservoir, Culver's Sporting Goods, Bishop; 619-934-8474

TROUT, BROWN   264

**Access:** Rental boats and motors are available at both Twin Lakes, Bridgeport. See Mono Village Resort at the end of Upper Lake. There are also good launch ramps at both lakes.

Pleasant Valley Reservoir has bank fishing only. Public parking lots are located at the end of Pleasant Valley Dam Road (about 7 miles north of Bishop) and at Gorge Rd. (about 13 miles north of Bishop).

Rental boats are available at Crowley Lake. There is also a good launch ramp near the store and rental boat area. Boat Rentals: 213-485-4853 (That's right, the Los Angeles Dept. of Water & Power controls this!)

**See Also:** Rainbow Trout

Jim Niemiec

# BROWN TROUT FISHING AREAS
## Eastern Sierra Region

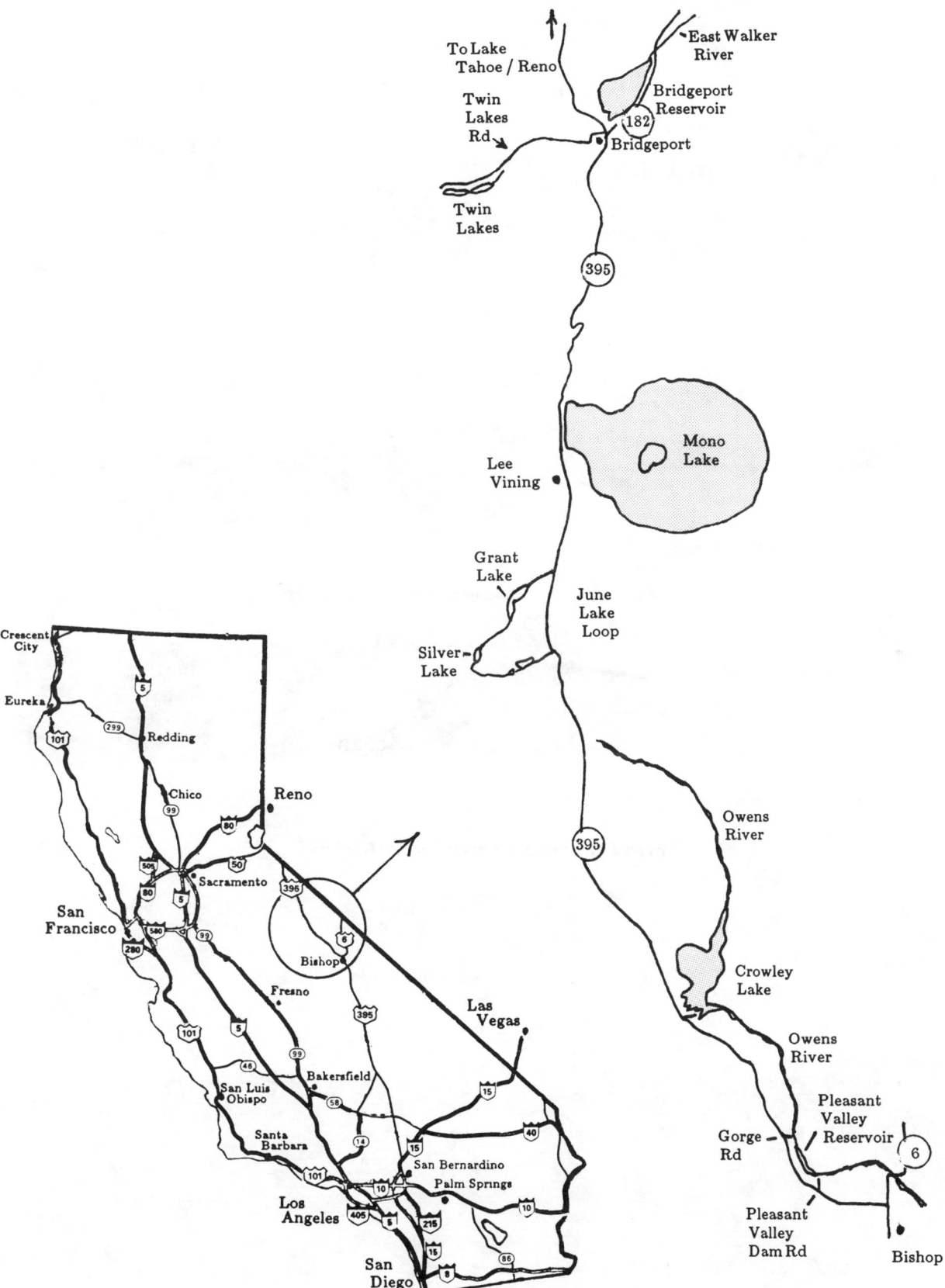

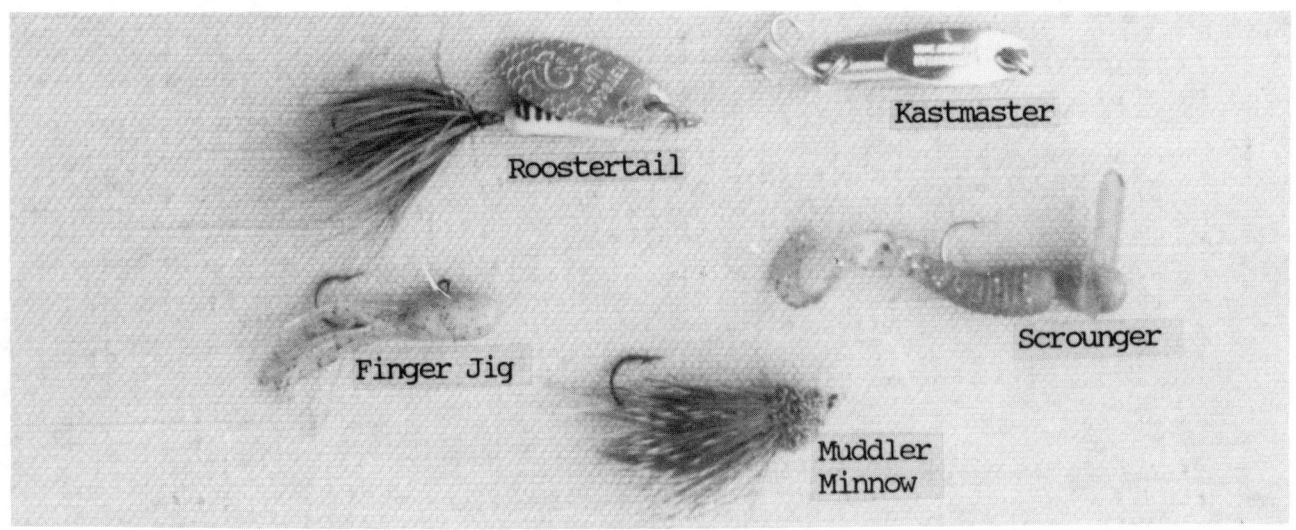

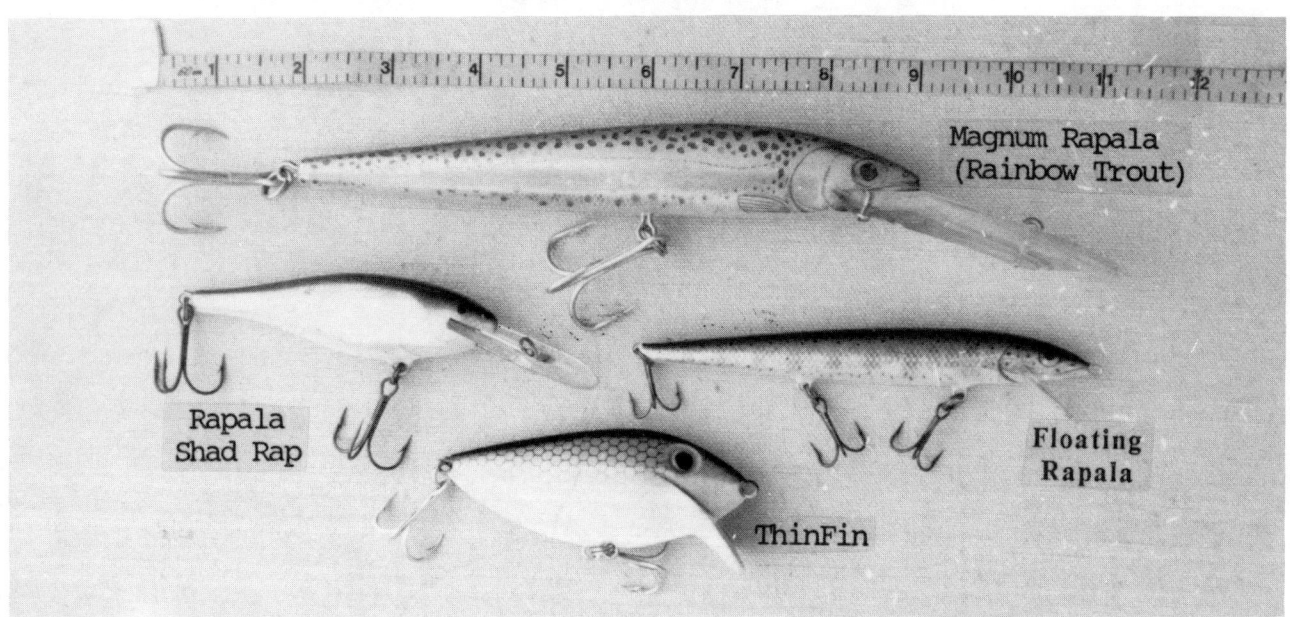

**Lures for Trophy-Sized Brown Trout**

## CUTTHROAT TROUT:

**Where:**
Walker Lake - Nevada
   10 miles north of Hawthorne
   1 hour drive from Lee Vining
   1 1/2 hours from Bishop

Pyramid Lake - Nevada

Topaz Lake - Calif. & Nevada

**When:**
Late November through early March
Early spring when Cutthroats move into shallow water.
Storm fronts turn of fishing action for 2+ days.

**Bait/Lures:**
Powerbait
K8 & K10 Kwikfish, V20 Flatfish & larger
Tor-P-Do Wobblers (1/2 - 3/4 oz.)
Colors: Green & black, green & white, frog pattern, red & white

**Rig:** Lightweight rigs, 4 - 6# line.

**Technique:**
Very slow trolling with lures.
Downriggers are used to troll at deeper levels.
Fly fishing with dark Wooly Worms.

**The Law:**
Non-Resident License: $40 annual (1989)
   10 day license - $25
   3 day - $17

**Records:**
Walker Lake Record: 19 lbs, 1968
IGFA: 41 lbs., Pyramid Lake, Nev., 1925

**Info:**
Walker Lake:
   Gun and Tackle Shop
   Hawthorne
   702-945-3266

Mineral County Chamber of Commerce
702-945-5896

Pyramid Lake
   702-673-3667

**Access:** There are launch ramps at Sportsman's Beach and the State Park. At times, especially in the later spring season when the fish come into the shallows to spawn, shore fishing can be as good as trolling.

# CUTTHROAT TROUT
## Walker Lake, Nevada

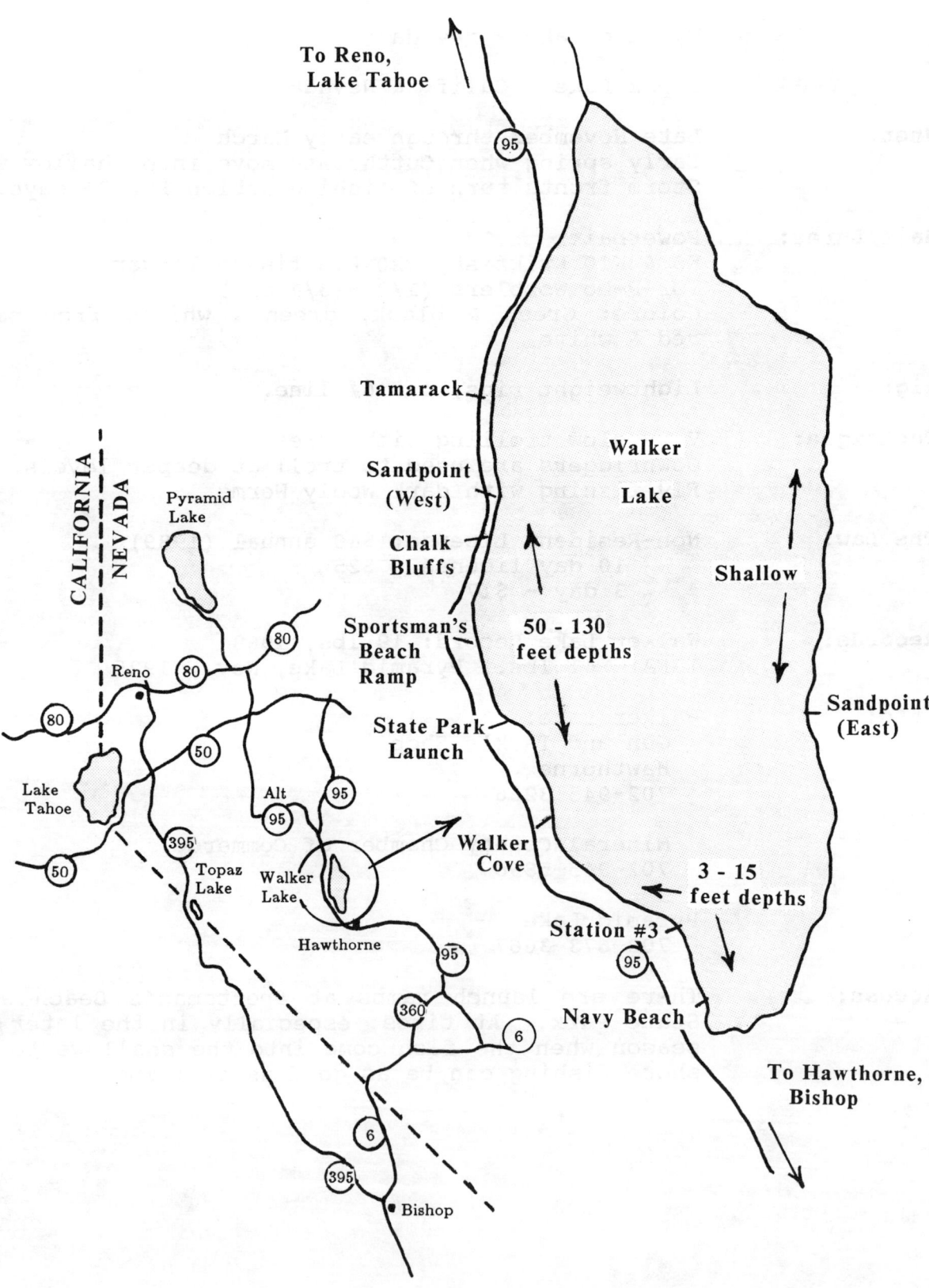

# GOLDEN TROUT:

**Where:** SEE MAP

**When:** See open season under "The Law"

**Bait/Lures:** No. 14 or 16 dry flies:

| | |
|---|---|
| Sierra Bright Dot | Mosquito |
| Damsel Fly patterns | Elk Hair Caddis |
| Doc's Twin Lake Special | Hare's Ear Nymph |
| Brown Leech | Pheasant Tail |
| Charlie Crockett | Scud |

Small (1/16 - 1/8 oz.) Gold/Yellow lures:

| | |
|---|---|
| Super Duper | Dardevle |
| Met-l fly | Panther Martin |
| Mepps | Kastmaster |

**Rig:** Fly Fishing rig or ultra-light spinning

**Technique:** The best technique is to use a fly and bubble rig, with the fly on a 6 foot length of 2 - 4# mono leader. Generally the best times to fish are early evening and very early morning hours when the lake surface comes alive with the dimples of trout feeding. Simply cast out the fly-and-bubble rig and retrieve very slowly. Carry a good floatant for applying to the fly, since at times the fish will only hit a fly that is riding high on the surface.

**The Law:** Cottonwood Creek area (1990-91):
Season: July 1 to October 31. Limit: 5, artificial flies only single barbless hooks. Cottonwood Lakes 1,2,3 and 4 and tributaries are always closed.

Golden Trout (John Muir) Wilderness (1990-91)
Season: Last Sat. in April through Nov. 15. Limit: 5, artificial flies only single barbless hooks

A hiking/camping permit is required for the Golden Trout Wilderness and Cottonwood Creek areas. For a permit, write:

Mount Whitney District Forest Station
P.O. Box 8
Lone Pine, California   93545

The Pack Train services listed on the area maps provide permits for their customers.

**Records:** State: 9 lbs. 14 oz.; Virgina Lake; August 1952
IGFA: 11 lbs., Wyoming, 1948.

# GOLDEN TROUT LAKES - 1
## Cottonwood Lakes Area

Access: Cottonwood Pack Station
(619) 878-2015

Note: Cottonwood Lakes 1, 2, 3, and 4 and their tributaries and the north fork of Cottonwood Creek and its tributaries are closed to all fishing.

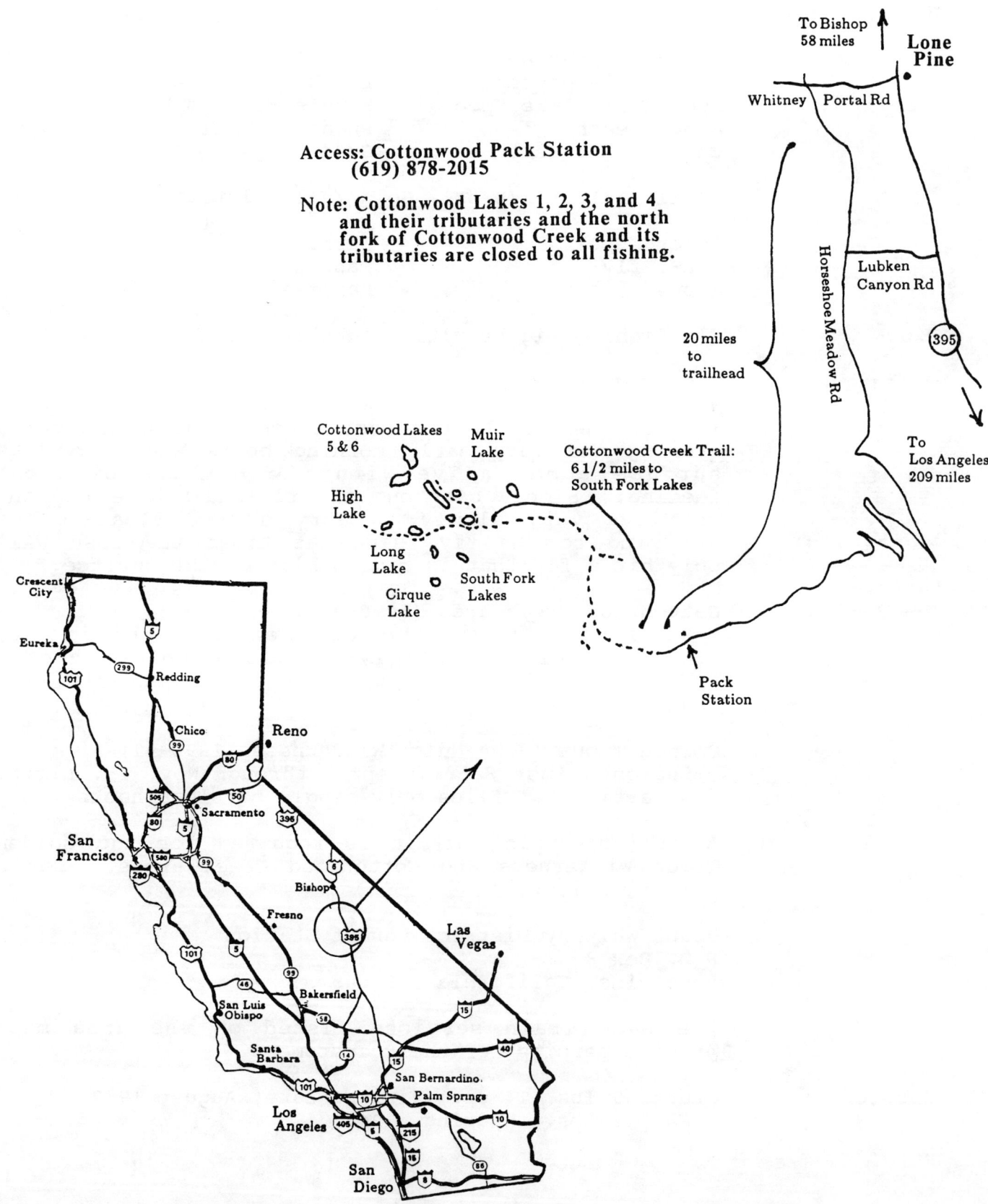

# GOLDEN TROUT LAKES - 2
## Golden Trout Wilderness

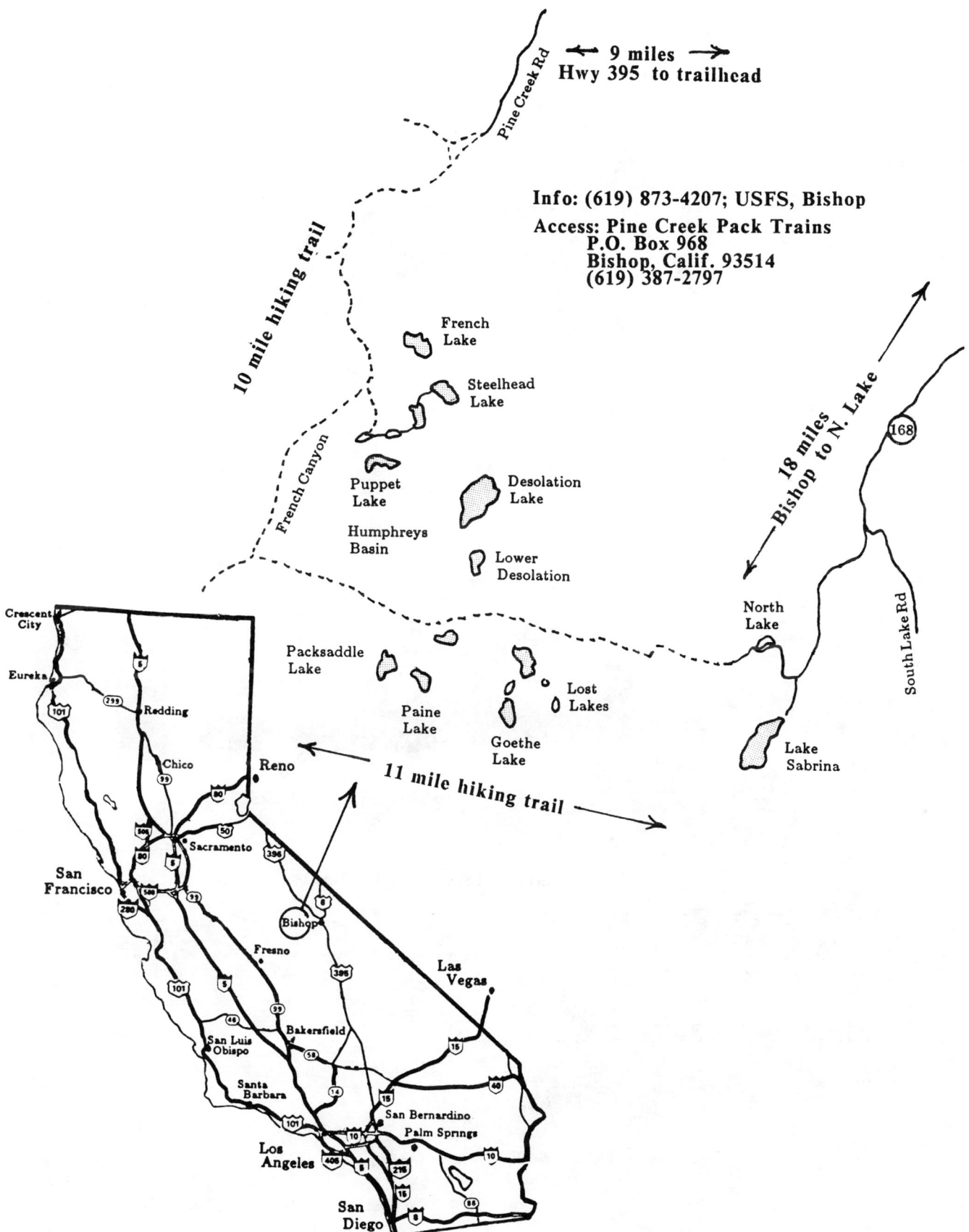

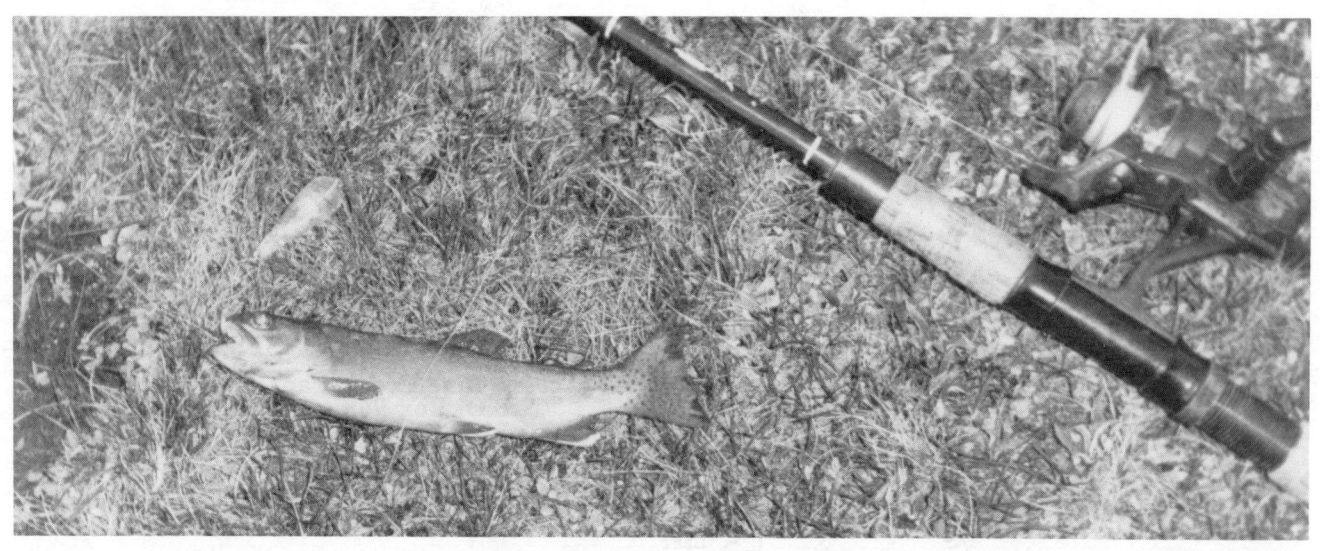

**Puppet Lake   John Muir Wilderness**

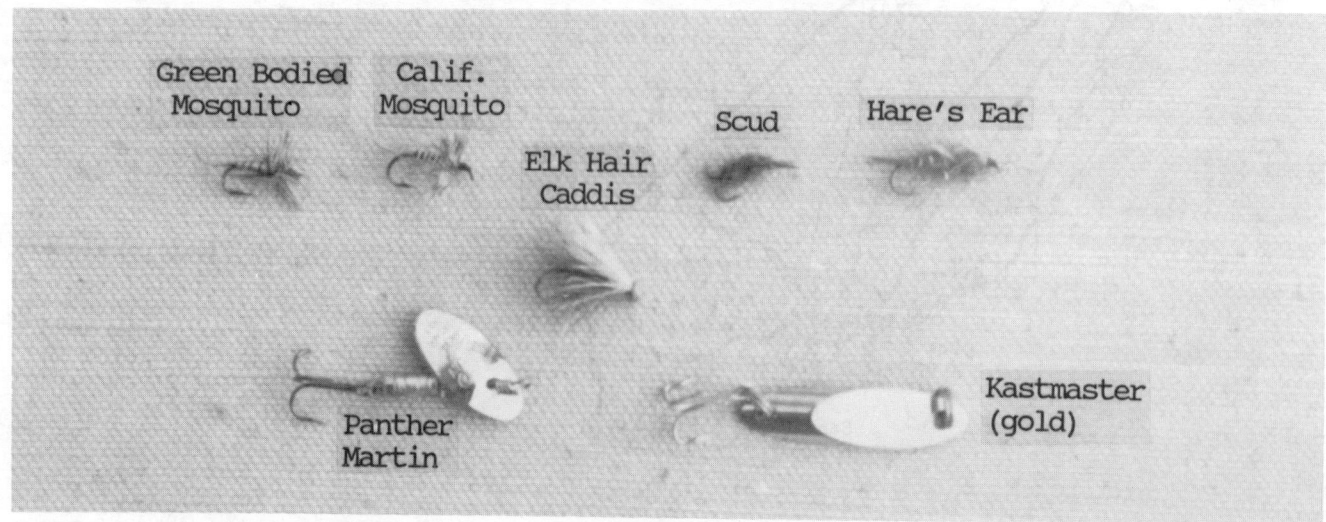

**MAKINAW TROUT (LAKE TROUT):**

**Where:** Hot Spots: Lake Tahoe, Fallen Leaf Lake, Donner Lake

**See Map**

Structure:

Deep water, usually holding just off the bottom near cliffs, rocky ledges, points, large boulders.

Mackinaw prefer water temperature from the upper 40s to the lower 50s.

Larger fish are most often found at depths from 100 to 200 or 300 feet. The preferred depth will vary with the season & water temperature.

Smaller fish will frequent shallower water.

Larger fish tend to be loners most of the year but will mix with the smaller fish and become more vulnerable to the hook in the fall (September & October). Trolled plugs can catch these larger fish.

**When:** Lake Tahoe: Best - winter months through April and early May. Good in September & October

Donner Lake - This lake is best in February and March near north shore near old highway and around "the islands" off the south shore.

Early morning hours - first light to about 9 or 10 AM are most productive. Late evening hours, 5 PM+, can also be good.

**Bait/Lures:** Redsides, Shiners, Paiute Sculpins, Tahoe Suckers, Tui Chubs. All these minnows are native to Lake Tahoe minnows. Mackinaw prefer Paiute Sculpins.

**Rig:** Depends on Technique. **See Diagram.**

**Technique:** SLOW TROLLING - along edge of dropoffs

A good depth finder that reads to 300 feet is a <u>must</u>. If you get a strike, or fish, retroll the area.

Note that Makinaw are great followers. You need to alter the action of the trolled lure to motivate them to strike. Try pumping the rod, temporarily changing the trolling speed or direction, raise or lower the downrigger weight a short distance.

**TROUT, MAKINAW**

**Technique continued:**

Bait/Lures: Minnows, J-plugs, T55 Flatfish, Rebel or Rapala plugs, Shakey Pete, or rubber minnows. Colors: Blue & Chrome, Chrome, Green.

Tackle:

<u>Wire Line Trolling</u>:

- Use a stout rod with a roller tip
- Saltwater reel - 300 yards of 30-50# mono
- Wire line - Braided wire kinks less, single strand sinks best
- mark wire with fingernail polish or paint
- make trial runs at fixed rpm over known depth
- set marks at 100, 150, 200, 250 feet

<u>Downrigger Trolling</u>:

- Use a medium wt. trolling rod
- levelwind reel - 200 yards, 20# mono

JIGGING:

Limited to less than 150' depths
Reel: Medium wt. 200 yards of 12 - 20# mono
Lures: 3 to 4 oz. spoons. Examples: Krocodile, Kastmaster, Hopkins, Buzz Bomb, Apex, Bomber slab spoon with or without bucktail. Colors: White, yellow, chrome.

**The Law:** (1990-91) Lake Tahoe, 5 trout with no more than 2 being Makinaw Trout. Note that a Calif. license is honored on the Nevada side of the lake. Fallen Leaf and Donner Lake, 5 Makinaw trout. Note however that Makinaw trout are included in the "Trout" regulations along with salmon and trout of all species in determining daily bag limits. Also see regs. for special seasons.

**Records:** State: 37 lbs. 6 oz.; Lake Tahoe; January 1974
IGFA: 65 lbs., Canada, 1970

**Access:** Guides - North Lake Tahoe:

Mickey Daniels, "Big Mack" Charters
Tahoe City
800-877-1462

**Access:** Guides - North Lake Tahoe continued

> Larry & Pam Schuelke, "Kingfish"
> Tahoe City
> 916-525-5360

Guides - South Lake Tahoe:

> Bruce Hernandez
> 916-577-2246
> Specializes in light tackle jigging
>
> Rick Muller, Outdoorsman Store
> 916-544-4358
>
> Jeff Vogl, First String Guide
> 916-577-5065

**See Also:** Kokanee Salmon, Rainbow Trout, Brown Trout

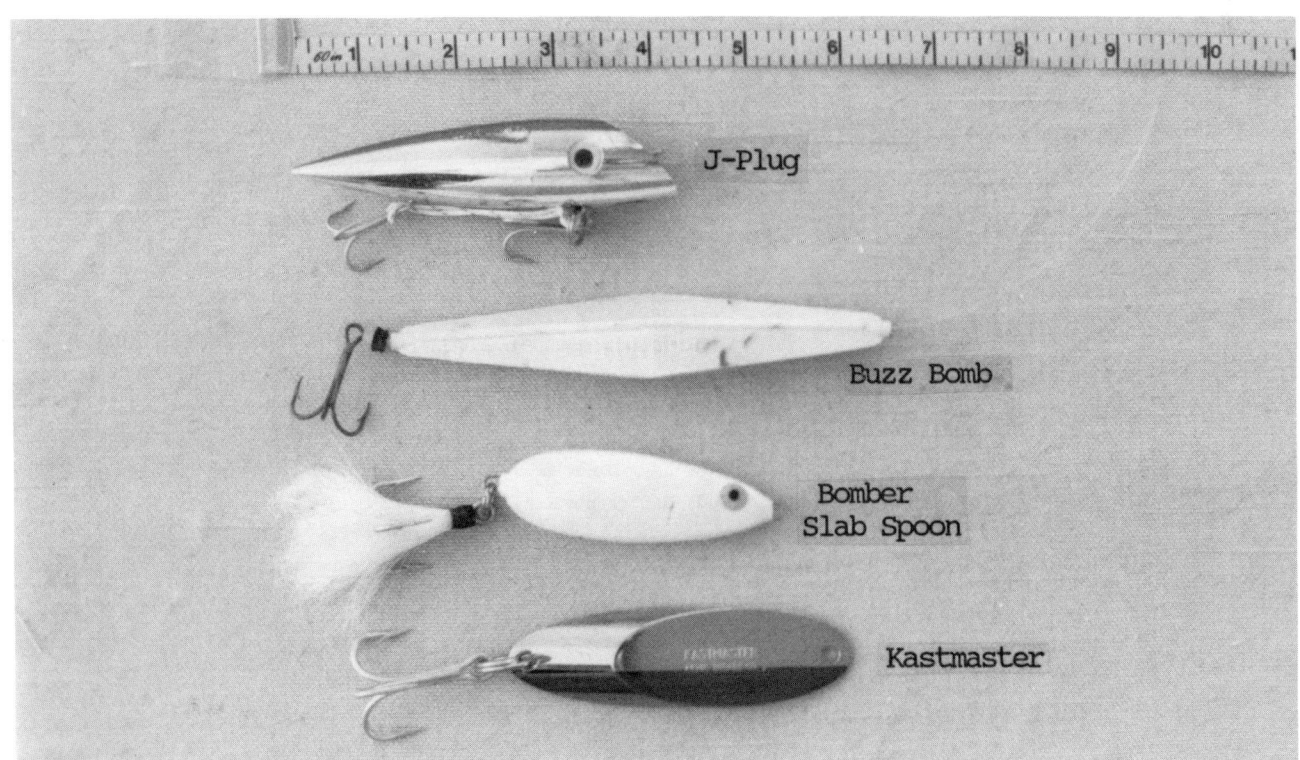

# MAKINAW TROUT RIGS

### Jigging

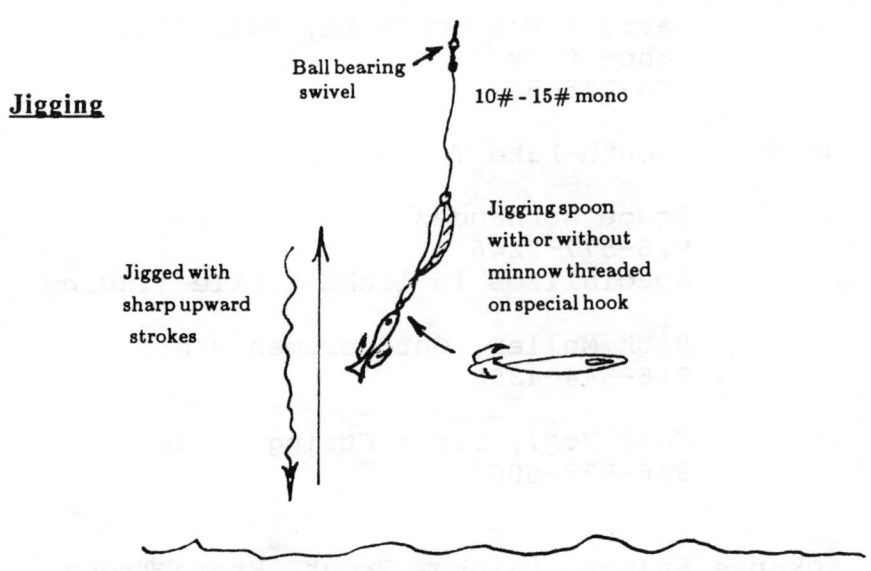

### Slow Trolling, Downriggers

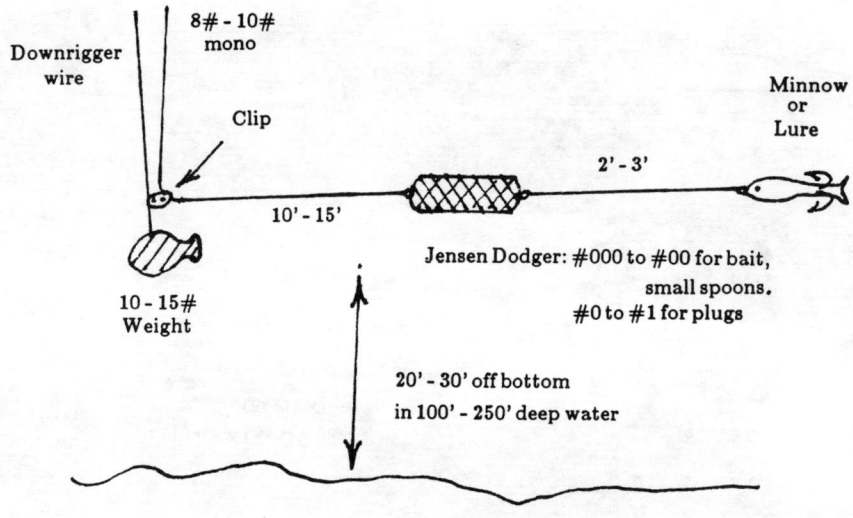

### Live Bait Drifting

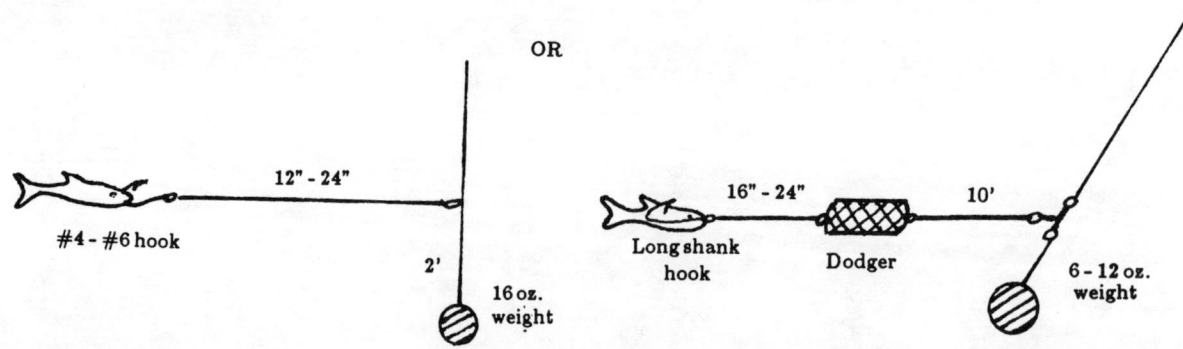

# MAKINAW TROUT
## Lake Tahoe Area

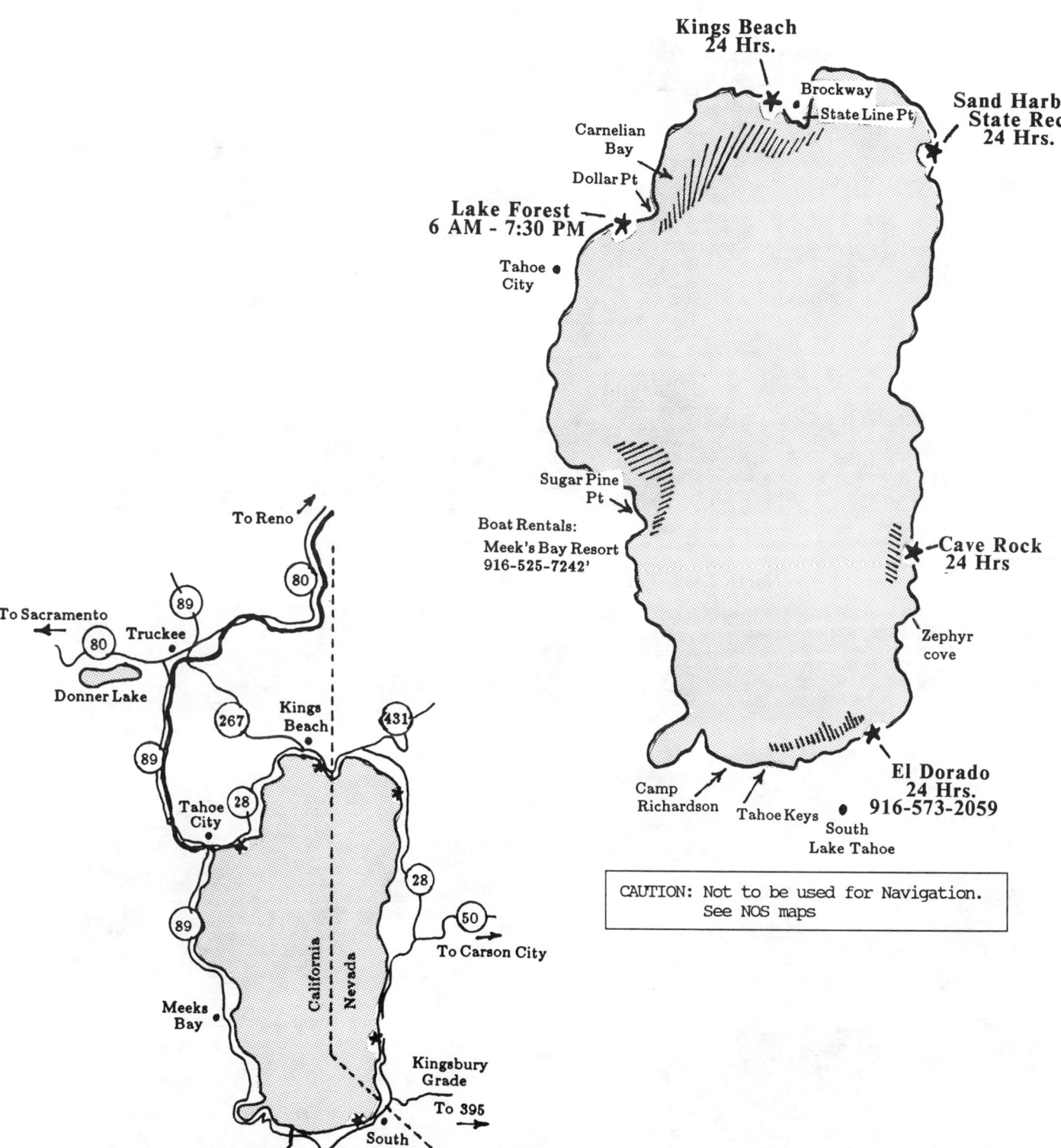

TROUT, MAKINAW 278

**North Lake Tahoe Guide Mickey Daniels**

**South Lake Tahoe Guide Bruce Hernandez**

# TROUT, RAINBOW

**RAINBOW TROUT:**

**Gen. Info:** Rainbow trout are stocked in thousands of lakes and streams throughout California. The maps I have included in this guide are for a select few lakes and streams which I feel offer the best trout fishing in that area.

There are countless ways of fishing for trout. The following recommended techniques may not be the best technique for a particular lake, or time. However, these are proven, consistent ways of catching trout. I would suggest that you become familiar and adept at these recommended techniques before inventing your own.

**Where/When:** The Rainbow Trout fishing information is organized in the following order:

1. Lake Fishing:

   Cool weather months (late Oct.
     or early Nov. through early May) .... Page 280
   Lake Structure Diagram ................ Page 283
   Warm weather months (June
     through Sept. or early Nov.) ........ Page 285
   Rigs .................................. Page 287

2. Stream Fishing ........................... Page 289

   Stream Structure Diagram .............. Page 290

3. Select Lake & Stream Maps:

   Calif. Trout Area Index ............... Page 292
     San Francisco Area .................. Page 293
     Overview Northeast Calif ............ Page 294
       a. Upper Sacramento
          & McCloud Rivers ............... Page 295
       b. Pit & Fall Rivers, Hat Creek ... Page 296
       c. Lake Almanor Area .............. Page 297
       d. Davis Lake Area ................ Page 298
       e. Truckee River /
          Martis Lake .................... Page 299
     Eastern Sierra, Bridgeport - Bishop Area:
       i. Bridgeport Area ................ Page 300
       j. Rivers & Lakes ................. Page 301
       k. Planted Creeks ................. Page 302
       l. Crowley Lake ................... Page 303
     Mother Lode Lakes ................... Page 304
     Southern California Lakes ........... Page 305

**The Law:** Generally 5 in lakes but trout restrictions and limits vary considerably by area. See current Dept. of Fish & Game "Trout & Salmon" regulations.

TROUT, RAINBOW

**More Info:** "Trout Fishing in California" by Jim Freeman Covers northern California lakes and streams.

## RAINBOW TROUT, Lakes

### When - Cool Weather Months:

**Where/When:** In Southern California good cool-water trout action usually starts in late October or early November and lasts through early May. In northern California, the cool weather trout season is May through mid-June, mid-to-late September through early November.

Structure: **See Diagram**

1. Around stream inlets - early season and late season, and mid-season during early morning hours and the last hours of dusk.

2. Shoreline points and off weedlines - morning hours.

3. Deeper waters of lake off dropoffs - mid-day hours. Depth will vary with light intensity and water temperatures.

**Bait/Lures:** Generally listed in order of preference/success but popularity varies considerably by area:

Bait: Floating Cheese / Power Bait
 Nightcrawlers
 Salmon Eggs
 Marshmallows
 Crickets

Lures: See Trout Lure Pictures following

TROUT, RAINBOW 281

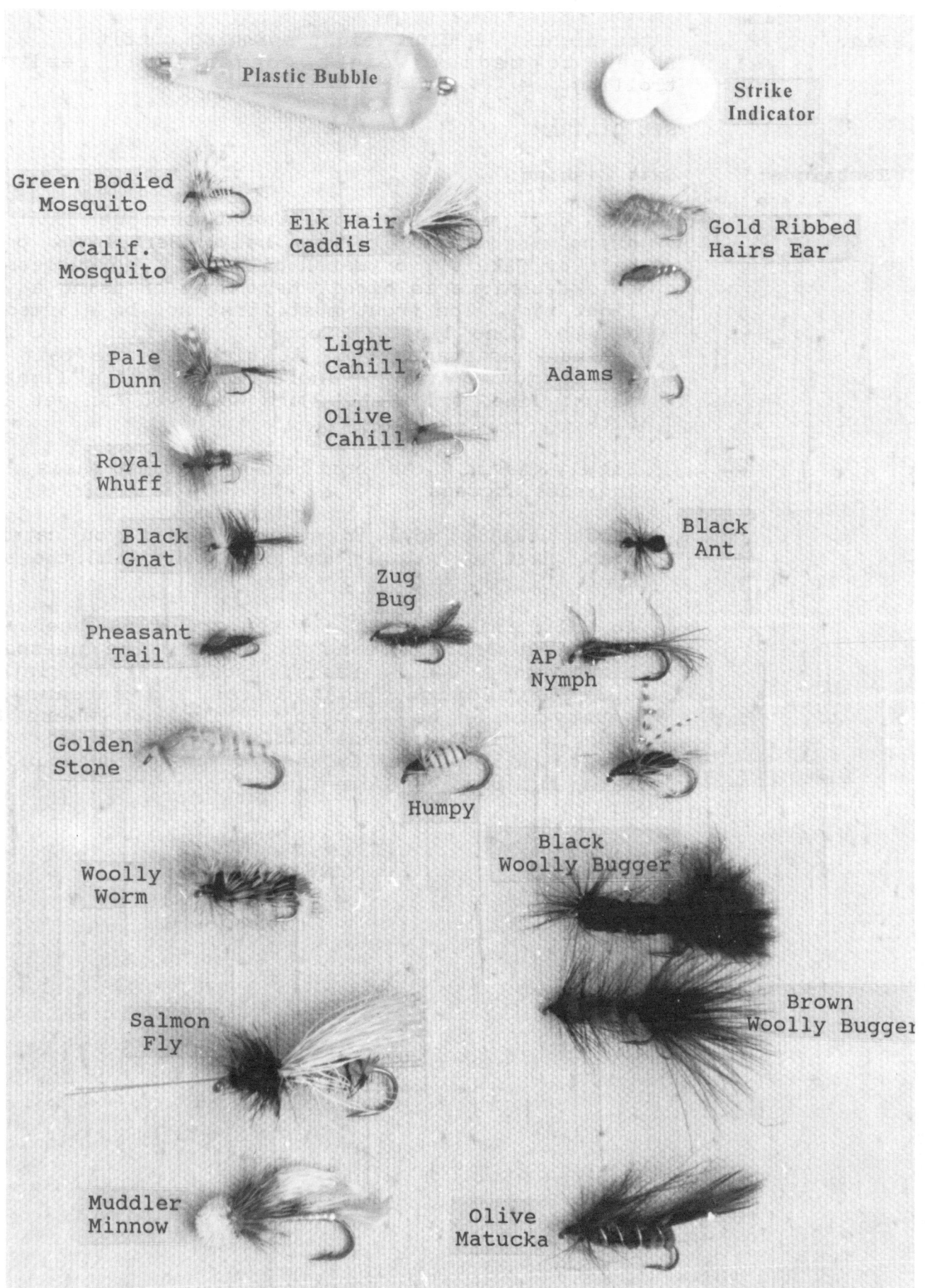

TROUT, RAINBOW 282
Lakes - Cool Weather Months

**Rig:** Ultra-light to Medium weight spinning outfit
Light to medium weight conventional reel for trolling.

**SEE DIAGRAM**

**Technique:** Bait Fishing:

The most popular shoreline technique involves using a floating cheese bait (Berkeley's power bait or Zeke's), or marshmallows. The success of this technique is highly dependent on using a very light rig. The trout must first not be alarmed by a heavy mono line. Secondly the fish must feel minimum resistance when it picks up the bait and starts moving away. Therefore, use the lightest weight line, split-shot, and hook you can get away with.

Slowly moving the bait on a regular basis, can increase success.

Trout usually move in schools so if you catch a fish, bait up quickly and cast back into the same spot.

In California, almost all the trout out there are from the DFG stocking program. The newspaper lists, on a weekly basis, usually Friday in the sport's section, what lakes and streams, by county, will be stocked. Find out where the stocking truck unloads and fish that area. The trout will eventually spread out throughout the lake, but it takes some time.

# TROUT LAKE STRUCTURE

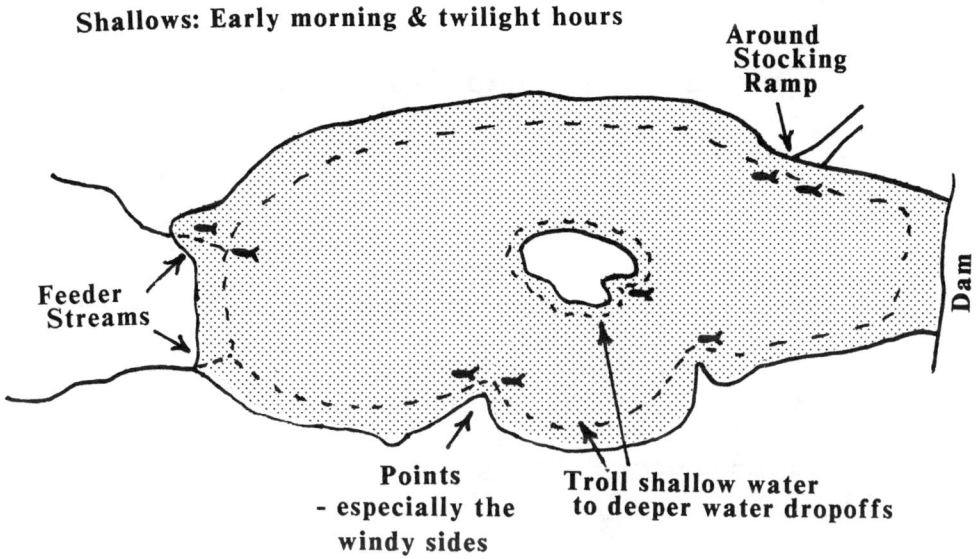

Shallows: Early morning & twilight hours

- Around Stocking Ramp
- Feeder Streams
- Points - especially the windy sides
- Troll shallow water to deeper water dropoffs
- Dam

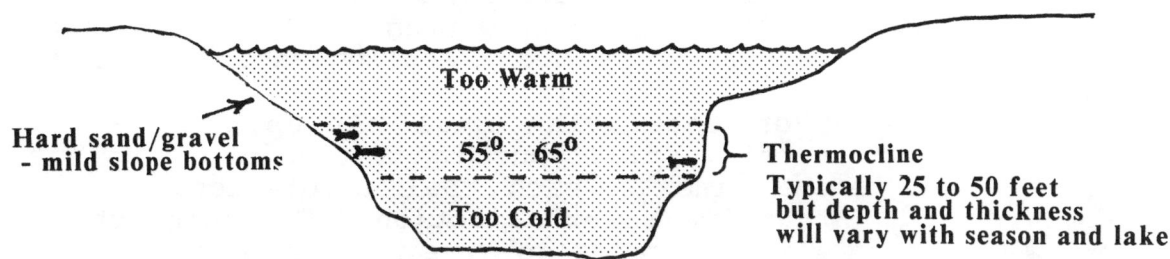

Warm Season Months: July through early September

- Too Warm
- Hard sand/gravel - mild slope bottoms
- 55° - 65°
- Too Cold
- Thermocline Typically 25 to 50 feet but depth and thickness will vary with season and lake

TROUT, RAINBOW
Lakes - Cool Weather Months

Trolling:

For surface and shallow depths during early morning hours, deeper waters during mid-day.
Lures: Kastmasters - gold/silver, Roostertails, Super Dupers, #7 Floating Rapalas, Needlefish

- Troll SLOWLY off structure, see Diagram.
- Set trolling speed by holding your lure over the side and varying the motor speed until the natural lure action is maximized. Spinners should spin regularly and constantly, spoons should wobble, NOT spin.
- Vary the speed of the troll.
- Troll in "S" pattern, gently weaving the boat back and forth.
- Occasionally pull on the rods to give the lure more action.
- Troll at different depths - use a "troll-eze" device, Lake Troll, or adjustable weights rig.
- Electric-motor-trolled fly or finger jig - especially during evening, surface bite.

Shoreline Lure Fishing in Lakes, early morning hours and dusk:,

Lures: Roostertail; Finger Jig - smoke, smoke sparkle, smoke rainbow, rainbow sparkle; Small Scrounger - white or smoke colors

- Keep moving to find fish and,
    look for dark, shady spots
    look for dropoffs
    fish on the windy side of points
    fish near water/creek inlets
    fish different depths
- Generally avoid days following full moon nights
- Keep the bait/lure moving
- When retrieving small lures with a spinning outfit, stick your index finger out to intercept the line on each reel revolution. This gives the lure an extra action. Twitching the rod tip slightly can also give desired lure action.

Bubble & Fly Fishing:

- Works best in the early morning and late dusk periods. It may be important to keep the fly on the surface by applying floatant.
- Try to get in a position with the wind at your back. The wind blows the insect hatch off the land points and over the water. The fish will migrate toward these shore areas at sunset.
- Retrieve the fly VERY SLOWLY to minimize the bubble wake. Twitch the rod tip irregularly to give action to the fly.
- Strike as soon as the fish takes the fly.

**RAINBOW TROUT, Lakes:**

**When - Warm Weather Months:**

Generally from mid-May through early September.

**Where:** Structure - **See Diagram**

How to find the Thermocline:

1. Better fish finders will locate the thermocline as a hazy gray line at constant depth, usually between 25 and 60 feet, when the instrument sensitivity is turned up OR,

2. Find a deeper part of the lake and lower a temperature probe to detect where the temperature drops rapidly in a short range OR,

3. Use fish finder to locate consistent holding depth of metered fish suspended off the bottom usually between 25 to 60 feet down. Shallower readings will probably be bait fish, near bottom readings at greater depths will probably be rough fish OR,

4. Locate the right depth by altering either the length of line out, with lead core, or the weight used until a fish is caught, then switch other rigs to the right setup.

**Bait/Lures:** See listing under Cool Weather Months

**Rig** **See Diagrams**

**Technique:** General Warm Weather Strategy:

a. During the first and last 2 hours of daylight, feeder stream areas can be productive.

b. After the first 2 hours, move to intermediated depth areas off points and weedlines.

c. During mid-day hours, confine efforts to deeper water trolling techniques. It is vital to locate the fish holding depth, normally the thermocline, and carefully locate lure or bait trolling at that depth. See "Structure: How to locate the thermocline".

TROUT, RAINBOW
Lakes - Warm Weather Months

### Trolling:

#### Lead Core Line:

Lead core line is marked with different line colors every 10 yards. Fishing reports often indicate the number of "colors" to troll. For every color of line out, the lure depth increases by about 5 feet. Use a 30 foot leader of 8# mono tied to the leadcore with a nail knot. Recommended leadcore - Gladdings 18 lbs. test Mark V. Determine the proper trolling speed by holding the lure at a shallow depth and increasing speed until the action is right. Lead core lines and heavy rigs take most of the fight and fun out of trout catching - see Downriggers.

#### Downriggers:

Downriggers with depth counters combined with a good fish finder are the ideal rig for fishing deep. They allow the use of a light rig which makes the catching fun. Note that a downrigger will slow the boat some so for the ideal lure action run the boat a little fast before dropping the lure.

#### Adjustable Weight Rig:

The Luhr-Jensen Troll-eze can be used with various weights when searching for the right trolling depth. Start a search pattern by letting out a known length of line by reeling backwards "x" counts on the reel handle - try 30 to 40 turns first. Depths can be tested by letting out more line or by adding weight.

#### Deep-Water Bait Fishing:

Summer trout will be holding in upper 50's and lower 60's water temperature, normally found on the bottom in water depths of 25 to 60 feet. To be successful you need to pinpoint the correct depth by taking thermometer readings.

#### Deep-Water Bait Fishing:

Once the correct depth is determined, preferred fishing areas are any areas where a current may exist - areas where the wind keeps the water moving, aerators, reservoir inlets where fresh water is flowing. Look for gravel or hard bottom areas on gently sloping banks. Rigging: **SEE DIAGRAM**

TROUT, RAINBOW 287

# TROUT RIGS
## Ultra-light to Light Spinning Tackle

**Still Fishing:**

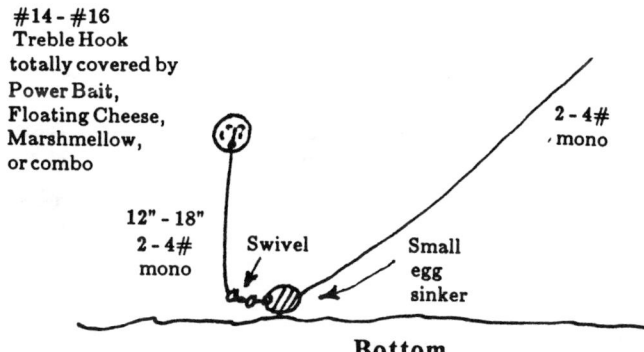

#14 - #16 Treble Hook totally covered by Power Bait, Floating Cheese, Marshmellow, or combo

12" - 18" 2 - 4# mono

Swivel

Small egg sinker

2 - 4# mono

**Bottom**

**Nightcrawler Rig:**

baitholder hook   small split-shot

Break off worm and thread over hook & split-shot

**Lake Surface - Slow Troll or Stream Drift**

For Lake Trolling - Troll Slowly (Electric) at 100+ feet behind the boat

Add nightcrawler, cricket or live minnow (where allowed)

#10 to #6 hook    3'    small split-shot    4 - 6# mono

**Lake Surface - Bubble & Fly**

Troll slowly with an electric motor with bubble 40 - 50 yards behind the boat. This technique is especially effective during twilight insect hatches.

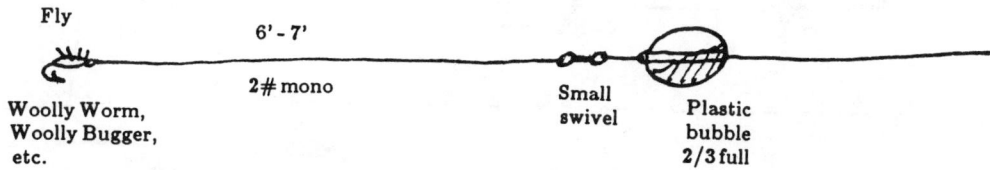

Fly

Woolly Worm, Woolly Bugger, etc.

6' - 7'
2# mono

Small swivel

Plastic bubble 2/3 full

# TROUT RIGS
## Ultra-light to Light Spinning Tackle

**Lake - Near Surface:**

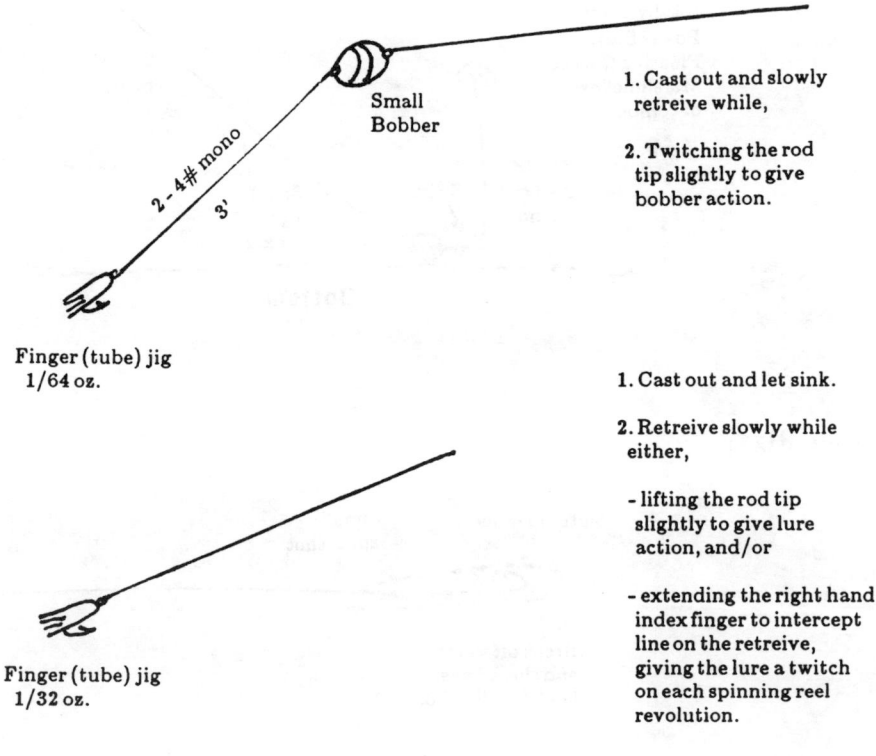

**Lake Below Surface Trolling:**

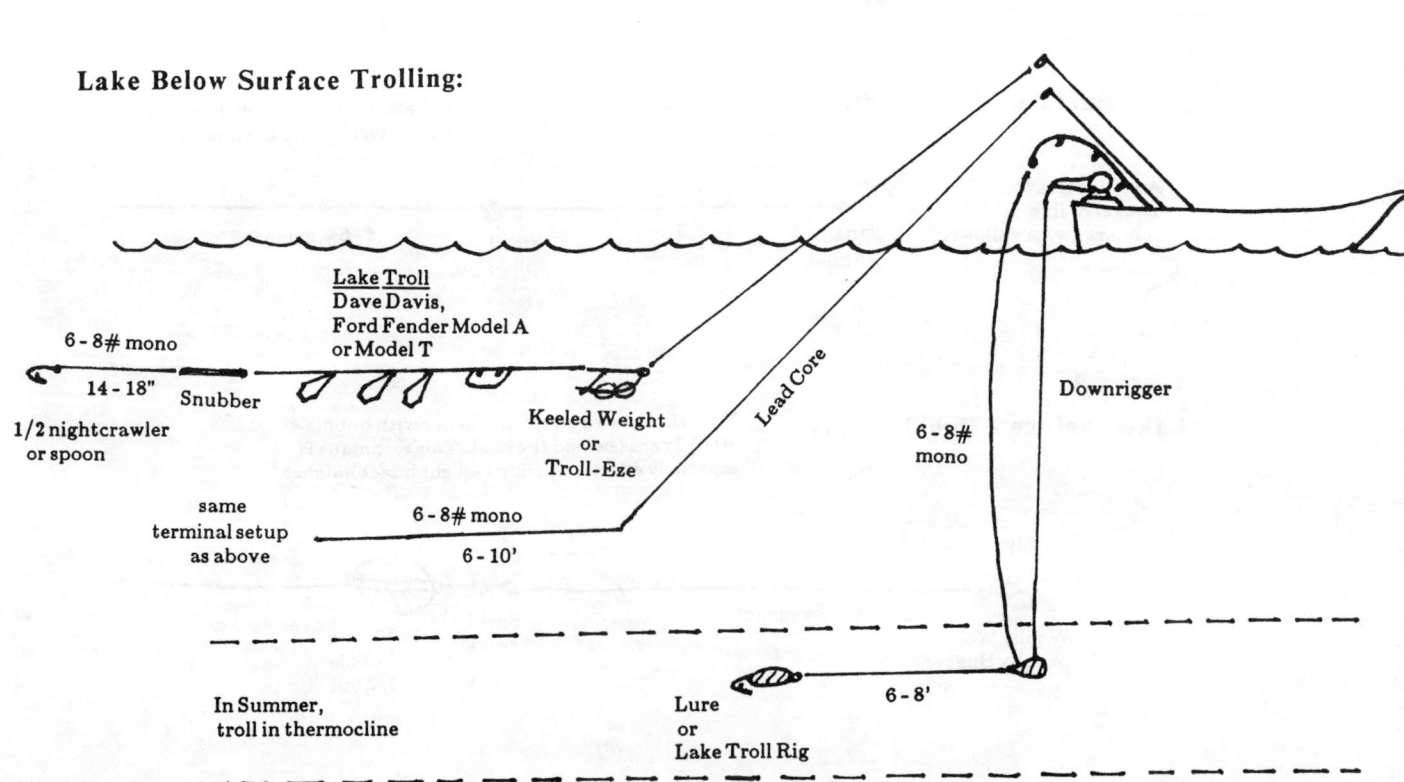

**RAINBOW TROUT, Streams:**

**Where:** Studies have shown that stream trout do 90% of their feeding on or near the bottom of the stream. Therefore, I recommend that unless you see the fish actively feeding off the surface, fish the bottom of the stream with lures, bait, or weighted flies.

Trout prefer cool water temperatures around 55 - 65 degrees. During the cold weather periods, they will seek out the warmest stream waters. During the warm mid-summer months, they will seek the coolest waters. Use the following guidelines for selecting likely stream sections to try.

1. Streams that drain open slopes - warm faster
2. Streams that drain slopes facing south - warm faster.
3. Low altitude streams - warm faster
4. Wide canyon streams - warm faster than deep and narrow canyon streams.

**See Diagram**

**When:** Early morning and twilight hours are usually the best time to fish a trout stream. Fish are generally active and feeding during these times. Some of the best insect "hatches" occur in the early evening.

In cold winter areas, trout tend to be less wary and more aggressively hungry in the early spring. This feeding aggression picks up again in the fall as the fish start to prepare for the coming winter.

In general Rainbow trout spawn in the early spring. This spawning puts mature, large trout in sections of streams close to where they empty into lakes.

Brown trout spawn in streams in the fall. Fish for them in stream sections near where the streams empty into lakes.

**Baits/Lures:** **See Lure Pictures in Lakes Section**

**Technique:** IF FISHING BAITS - walk upstream, cast the bait upstream and allow it to drift into the prime trout holding areas. Pools immediately upstream from fast moving water are trout rest areas - fish these pools and the riffles at the end of the pool.

Avoid making noise - do not stomp along the river bank.

IF FISHING LURES - walk downstream. Cast directly across stream and allow to drift, keeping the slack out of the line. When the lure drifts directly

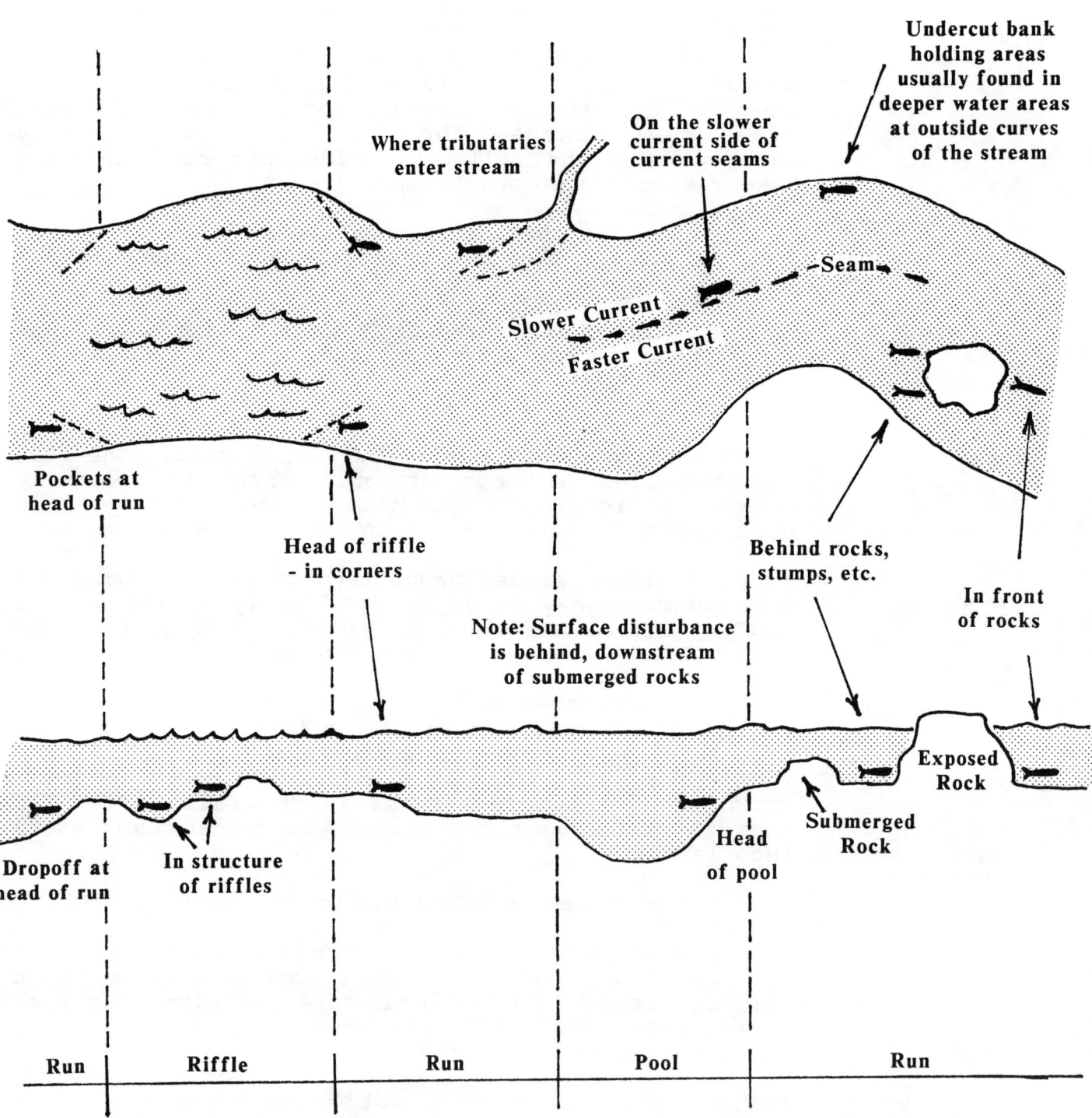

**Technique continued:**

behind you in the stream, slowly retrieve the lure with the occasional darting movements of a frightened minnow.

Put a split-shot against the head of a fly, for example a 2" Muddler Minnow fly and fish above technique.

Also use this method for fishing Finger Jigs.

**Info:** Southern Calif. Weekly Stocking: 213-590-5020

**Access:** Guides:

    Burney Basin - Pit, Fall & Hat streams
      The Fly Shop, Redding
      916-222-3555

    Upper Sacramento & McCloud Rivers
      Ted Fay Fly Shop, Dunsmuir
      916-235-2969

    High Eastern Sierra Packers Assoc., Bishop
      619-873-8405

    Clearwater Trout Tours
      274 Star Route
      Muir Beach, CA 94965
      415-381-1173
      Guided trips to Upper Sacramento, McCloud, Burney Basin, Tahoe/Truckee area, and Eastern Sierra region.

**See Also:** Brown Trout

## CALIFORNIA TROUT AREA INDEX MAP
### See following detailed maps for areas circled below

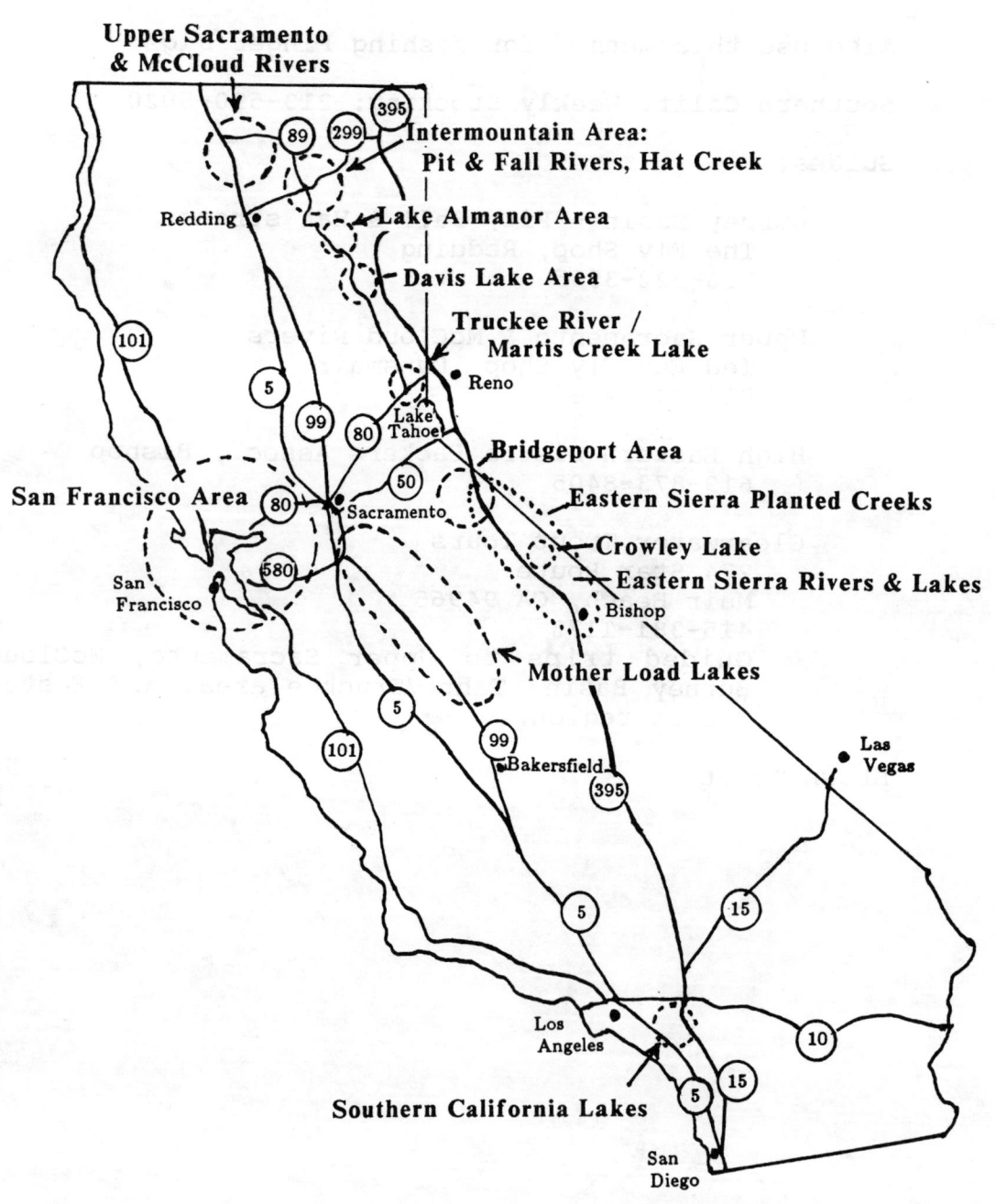

# TROUT LAKES
## San Francisco Area

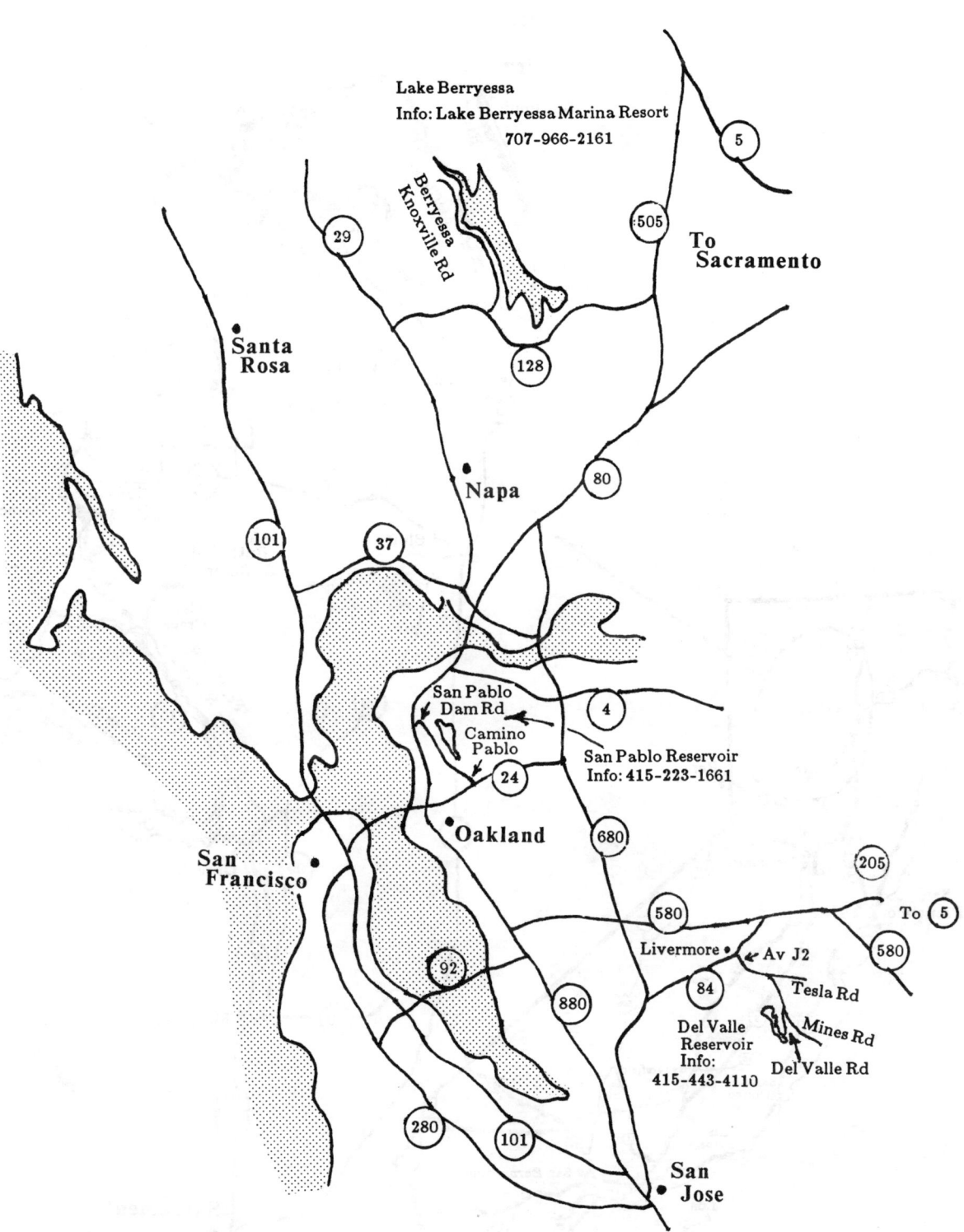

TROUT, RAINBOW 294

# TROUT LAKES AND STREAMS
## Overview – Northeast California

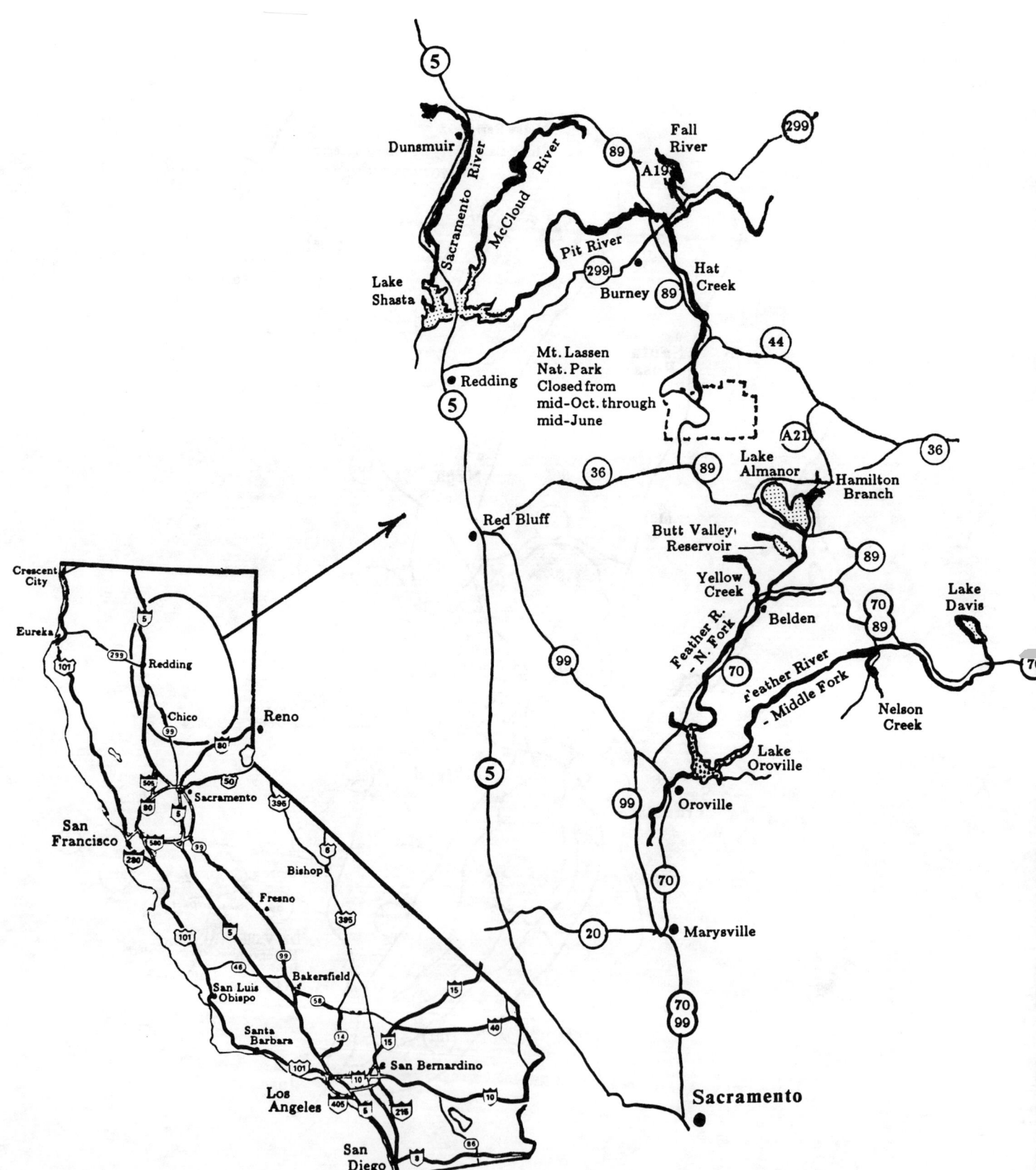

# TROUT LAKES AND STREAMS
## Upper Sacramento & McCloud Rivers

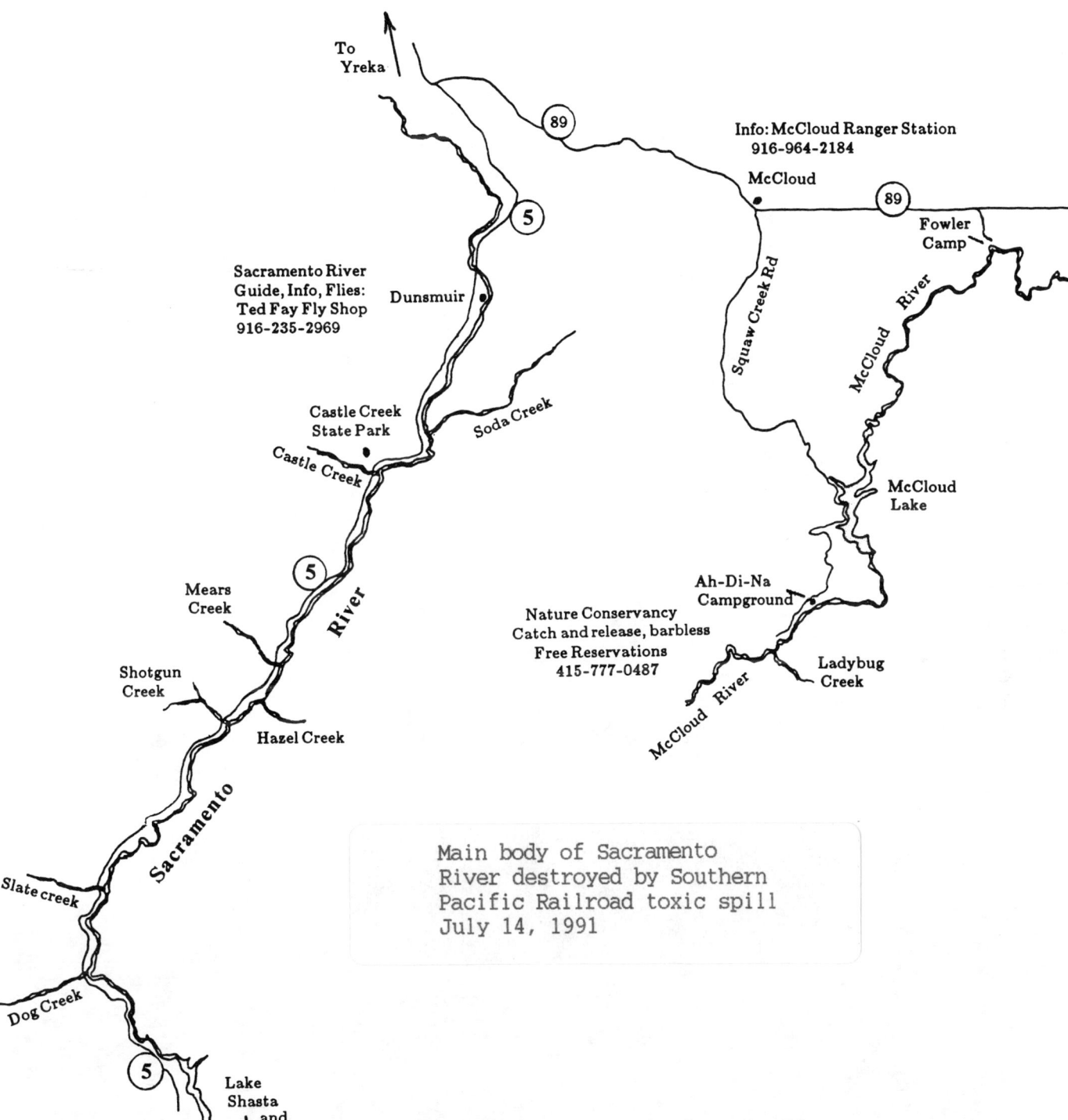

TROUT, RAINBOW 296

# TROUT LAKES AND STREAMS
## Intermountain Area: Pit & Fall Rivers, Hat Creek

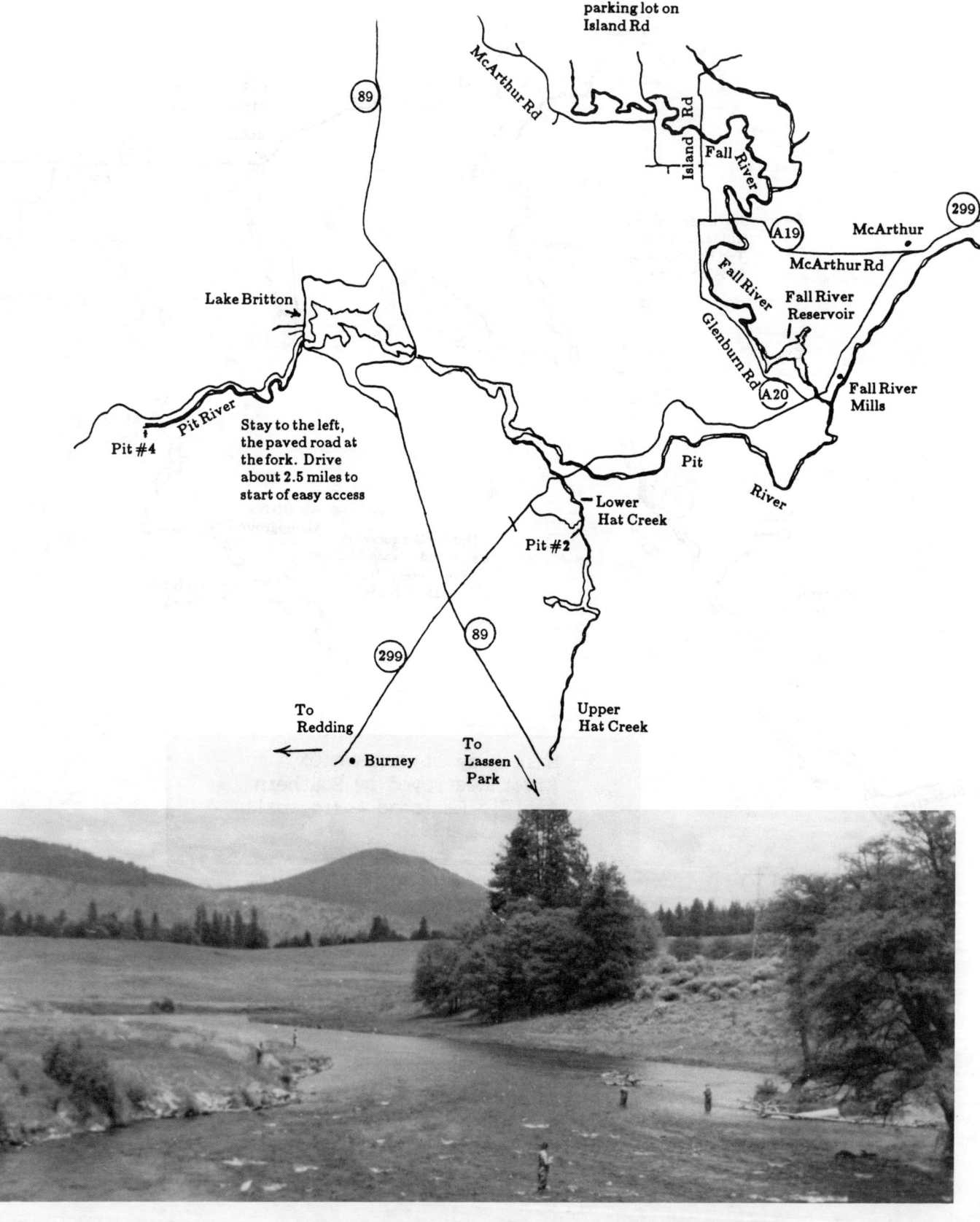

**Flyfishing for native Rainbows on the Hat Creek riffles below Pit #2**

# TROUT LAKES AND STREAMS
## Lake Almanor Area

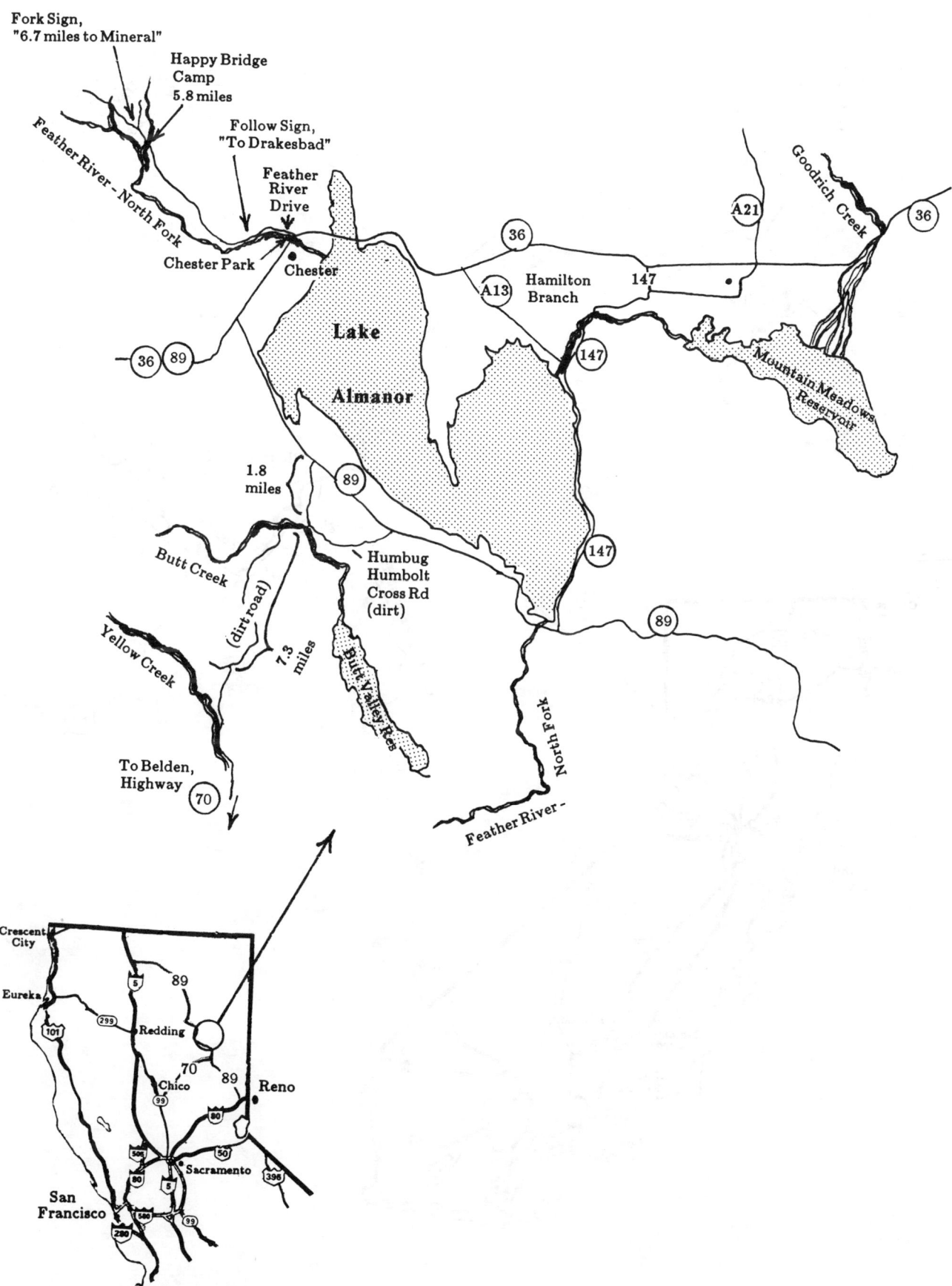

## TROUT LAKES AND STREAMS
### Davis Lake Area

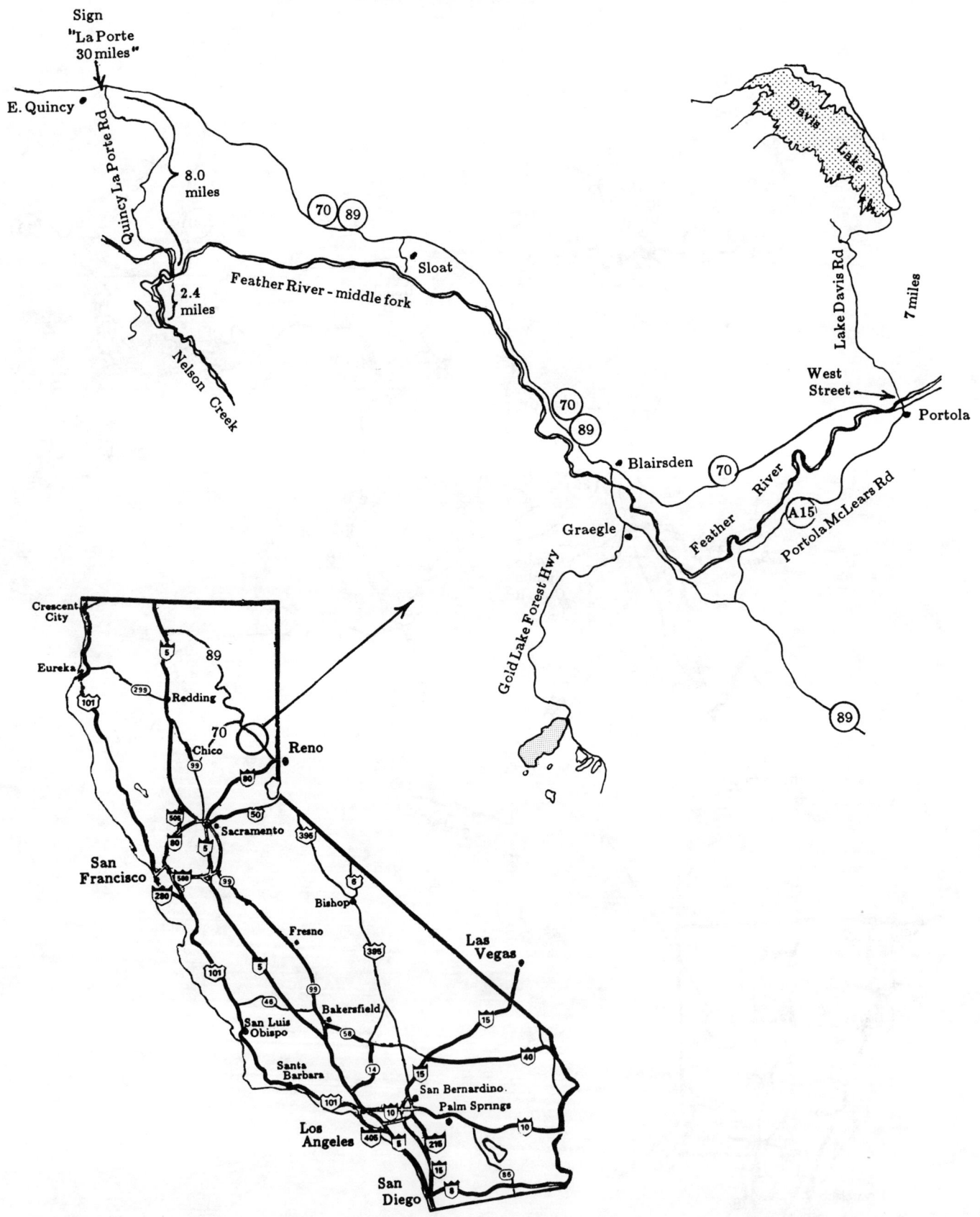

# TROUT LAKES AND STREAMS
## Truckee River / Martis Creek Lake

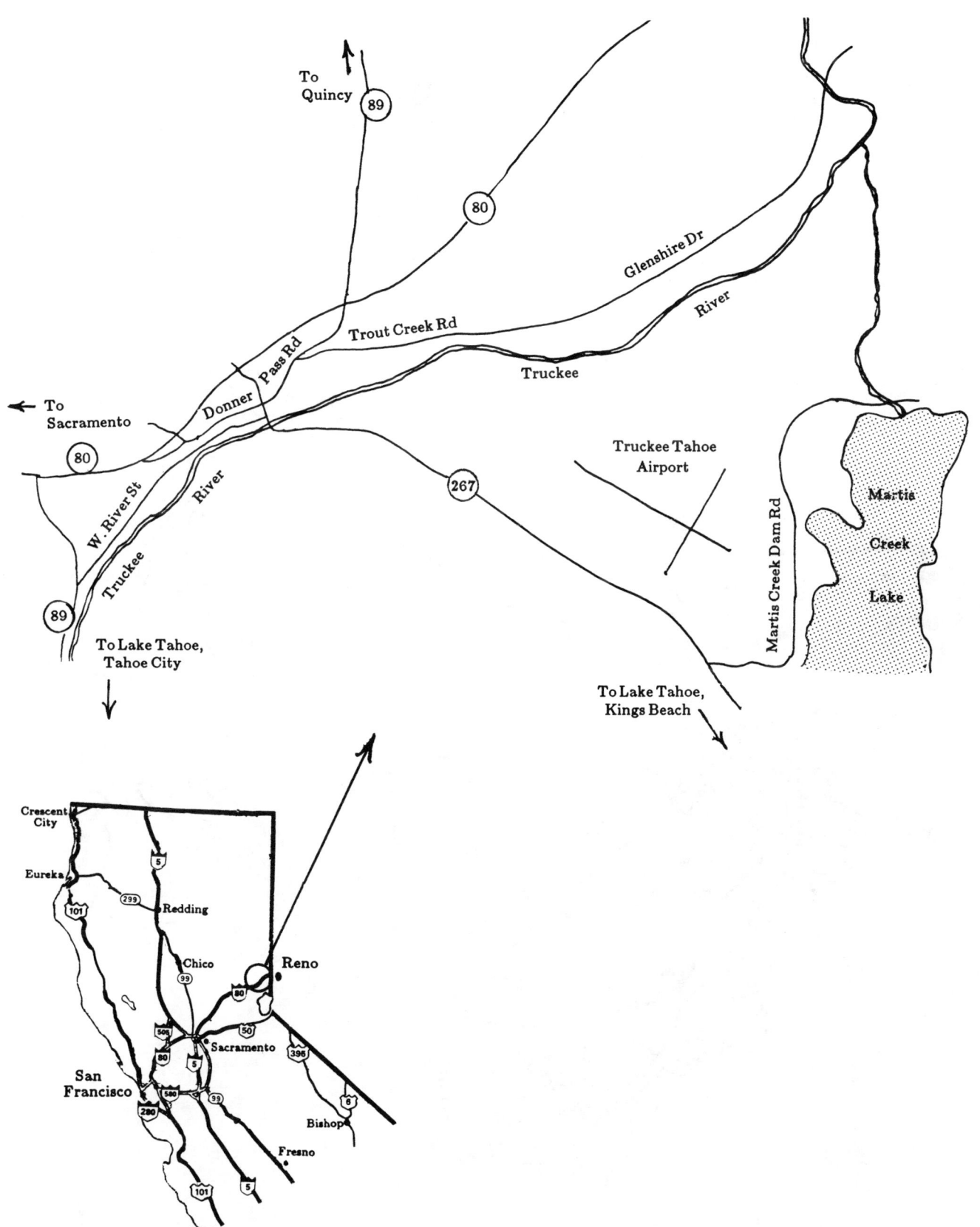

# TROUT LAKES AND STREAMS
## Bridgeport Area

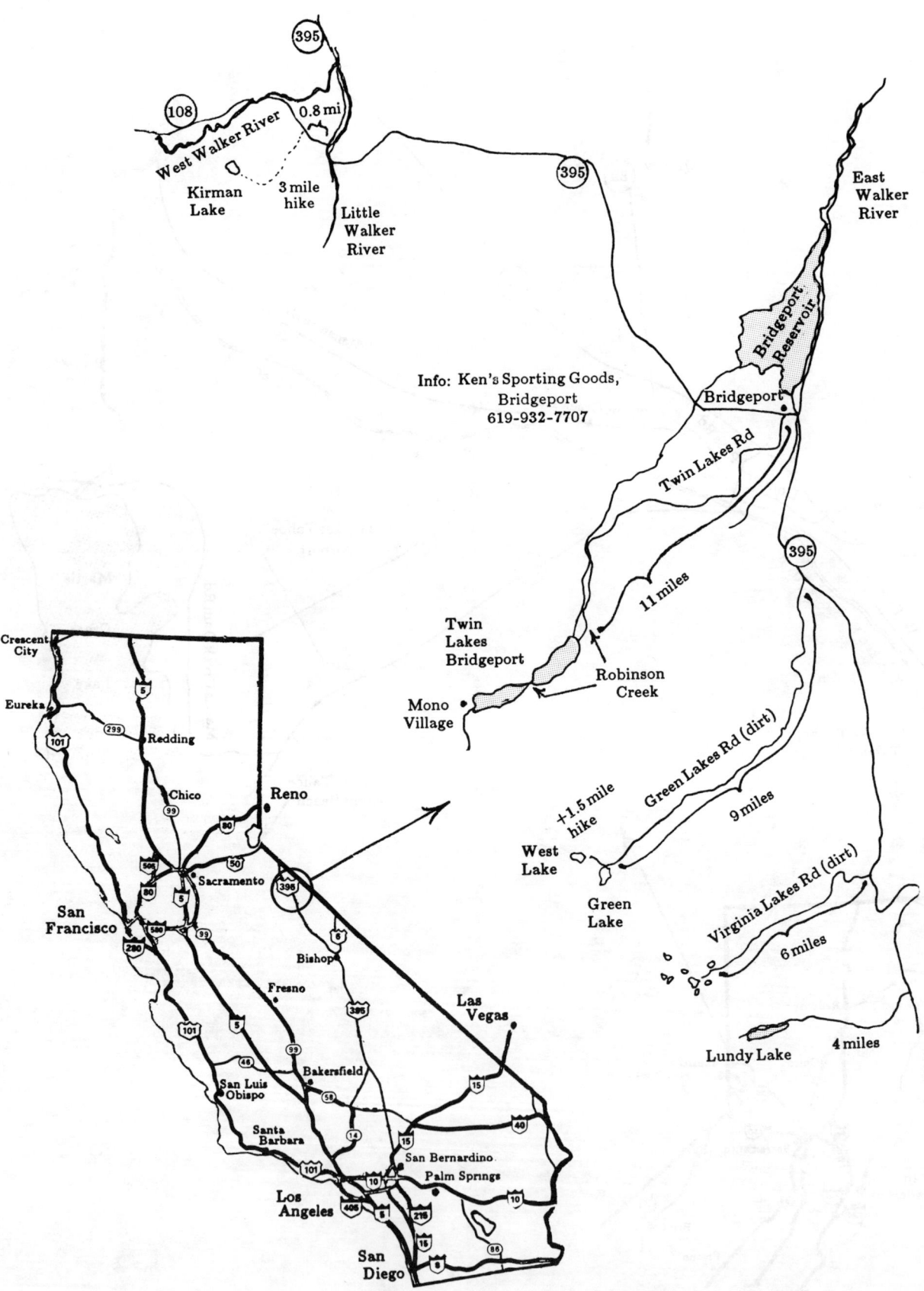

# TROUT LAKES AND STREAMS
## Eastern Sierra Rivers & Lakes

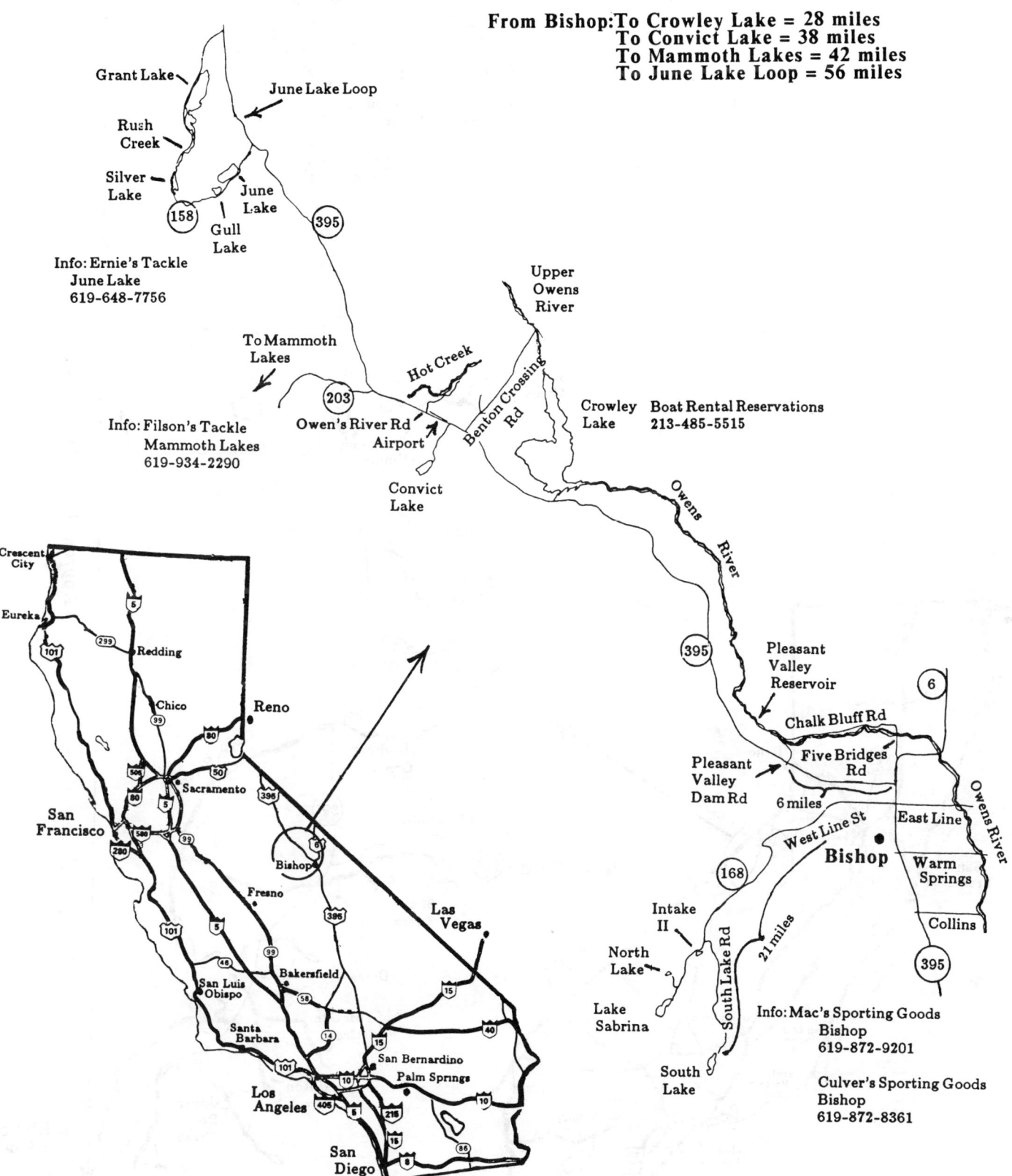

# TROUT LAKES AND STREAMS
## Eastern Sierra Planted Creeks

# TROUT LAKES AND STREAMS
## Lake Crowley

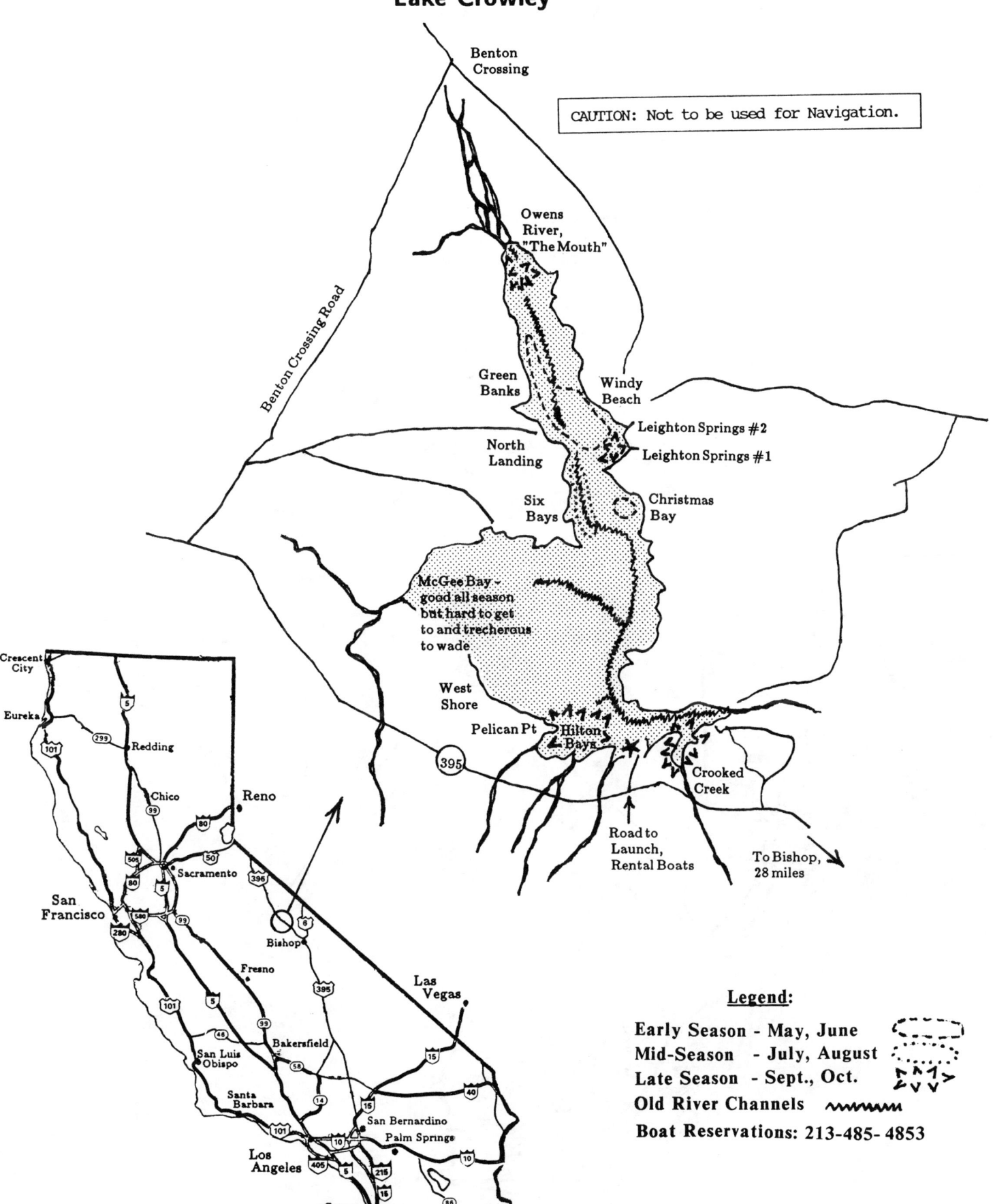

# TROUT & BASS LAKES
## Mother Lode Lakes

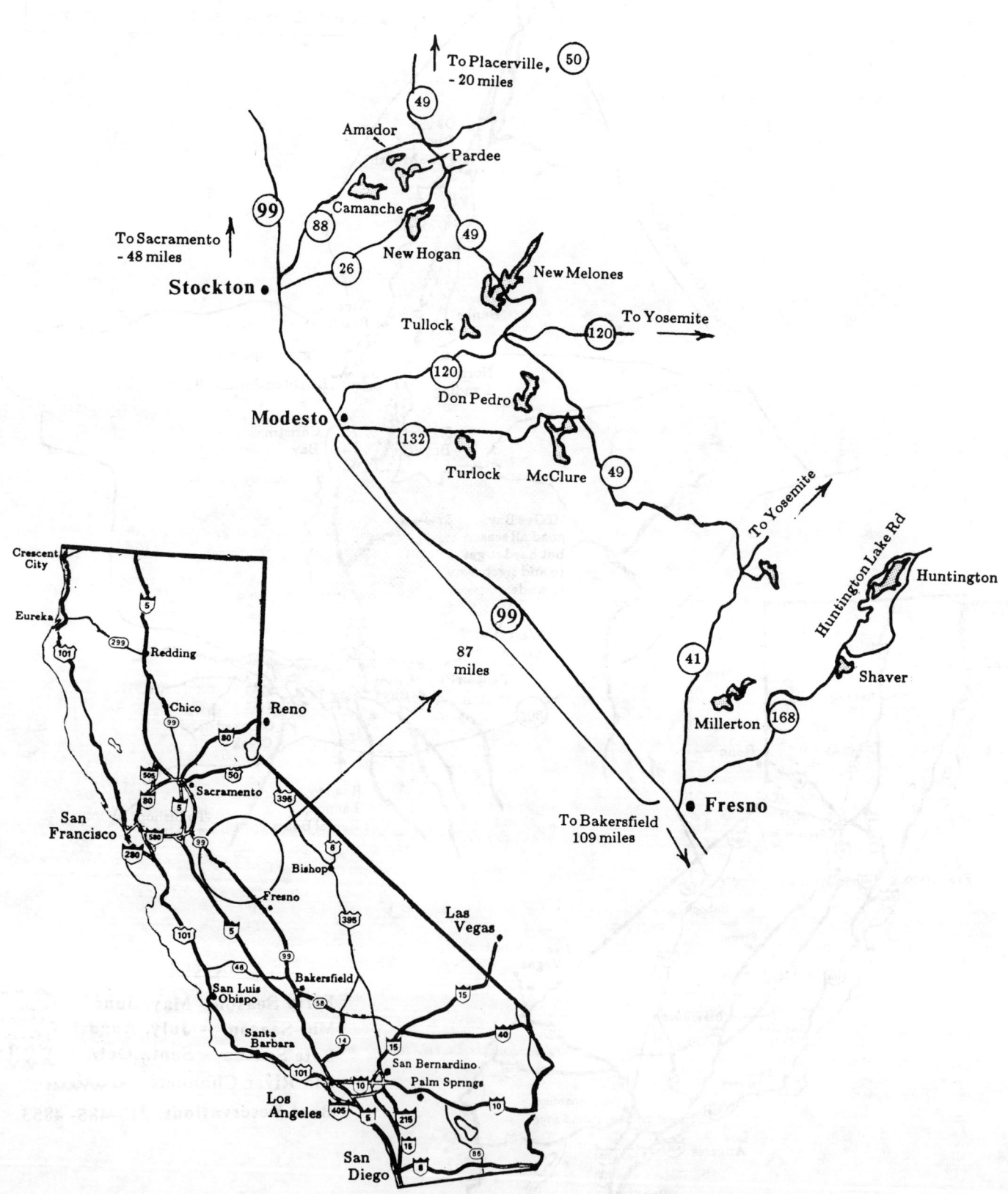

# TROUT LAKES AND STREAMS
## Southern California Lakes

No License Required
Entrance Fee Assessed
Heavily Stocked
Late October to early May
Boat Rentals

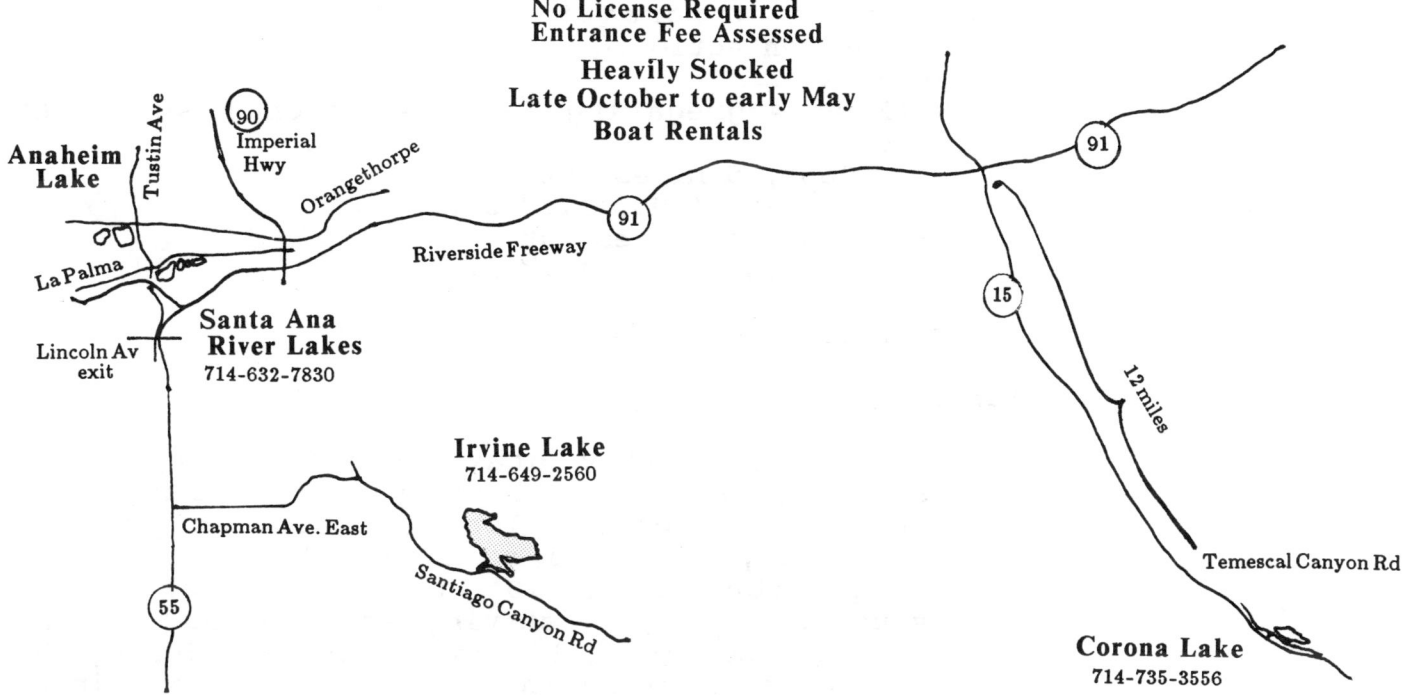

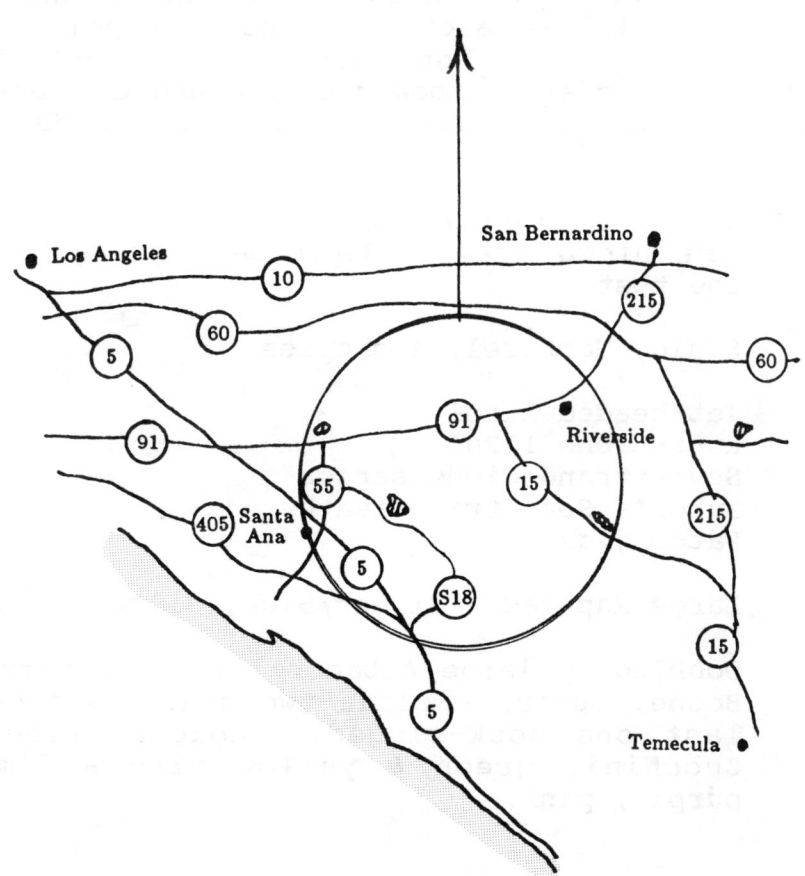

## BIGEYE TUNA:

**Where:** Albacore grounds off of San Diego
Prefers 64° to 70° water
Get current information and fish areas showing recent, proven action.
9 Mile Bank
FADS (Fish Aggregating Devices) from Mission Bay entrance;
- A - 266°, 5 miles out
  32° 46.5' N., 117° 21.3' W.
- B - 266°, 15 miles out
  32° 48.3' N., 117° 32.8' W.

See sources under **Info**.

Structure:

Bigeye generally stay significantly below surface, only occasionally moving toward the surface. Japanese longline studies put the Bigeye's preferences at 100+ fathoms and water temperatures of 50° to 59°. Other FAD studies show them staying at 200+ feet during the day and rising toward the surface during the evening and dark morning hours, still remaining well below the surface at depths around 60 feet.

When the Bigeye come toward the surface, they will be around the bait schools. Look for life - birds, dolphins, bait schools on the fish finder. Look for temperature breaks in waters 62-72°. Troll on the warm side of these break lines.

**When:** August through October
San Diego area - September through October usually the best

**Bait/Lures** Squid, Mackerel, Anchovies

Jet-headed lures
Kona-Clone 1220C
Sevenstrand Clone series
Zuker's Sea Strike feathers
Patco jigs

Large Rapalas - Silver/Blue, Silver/Black colors

Doubled-up large Albacore type feathers (Sevenstrand, Boone, Zuker) - slide two feathers together with the last one hook-rigged. Colors: Bleeding mackerel, Zucchini, green & yellow with a lime green head, purple, pink.

**Rig:** Penn 6/0 (114H), International 30, Shimano TLD25 size or larger reels
Short, fast taper rods, 5 to 6 feet long. Example: Sabre 655H
1/0 to 3/0 live-bait hook for anchovies, 6/0 for mackerel
50# - 80# Mono
Rod belt and harness

**Technique:** Trolling:

Best trolling times are at first and last daylight

Lures:
Troll jigs at 7 - 9 knots about 75 feet behind the boat. Don't let lure skip - if necessary use a large egg sinker to keep it down.
Long troll a magnum Rapala (CD18) about 125 feet back. Keep Rapala rod tips low to keep the lure deep.

Bait: Troll slow at 1 to 1 1/2 knots. **See Live Bait Bridle Rig Diagram in Marlin section.**
If using downriggers troll bait at depth of metered bait schools, else troll at thermocline where temperature break occurs.

If hit on the troll and you have bait, stop the boat, chum with anchovies, and cast a mackerel to the chum line. If you don't have bait, continue to troll.

Try dropping weighted, live bait down to school bait depth. Do this only in areas of very recent Bigeye action.

If fish are surface feeding, cast large Krocodiles or Scampis into the boils.

In Hawaii, they are caught at night using squid on downriggers, trolled near dropoffs. Try setting up a chum line at night. Set lines at various depths - one set at 50 feet. With any kind of current or wind condition, weight will be required to get the rigs down.

**The Law:** Limit 10, No size minimum. (1989)

**Records:** State: 208 lbs., San Clemente Is., November 1986
IGFA : 435 lbs., Peru, 1957

TUNA, BIGEYE   308

**Info:**  San Diego Angling Club
619-222-2502

See also Phone Fishing Info numbers in "More Detail" section.

Detailed Ocean Temperature Charts:
Ocean Imaging, 1289 1/2 Cave Street, La Jolla, CA 92037, 619-454-1993
This service will provide updated temperature maps twice a week, on Mondays and Thursdays via FAX transmission or mail for $233 (1990).

**Access:**  Guides:

Ron Costa, "Happy Kanake"
619-225-1770

San Diego 6-Pack charters:
  Call Fisherman's Landing
  619-222-0391
  Call H&M Landing
  619-226-1051 or 619-222-1144
  Call Pt. Loma 6-packs
  619-223-1627

**See Also:**  Yellowfin Tuna, Albacore

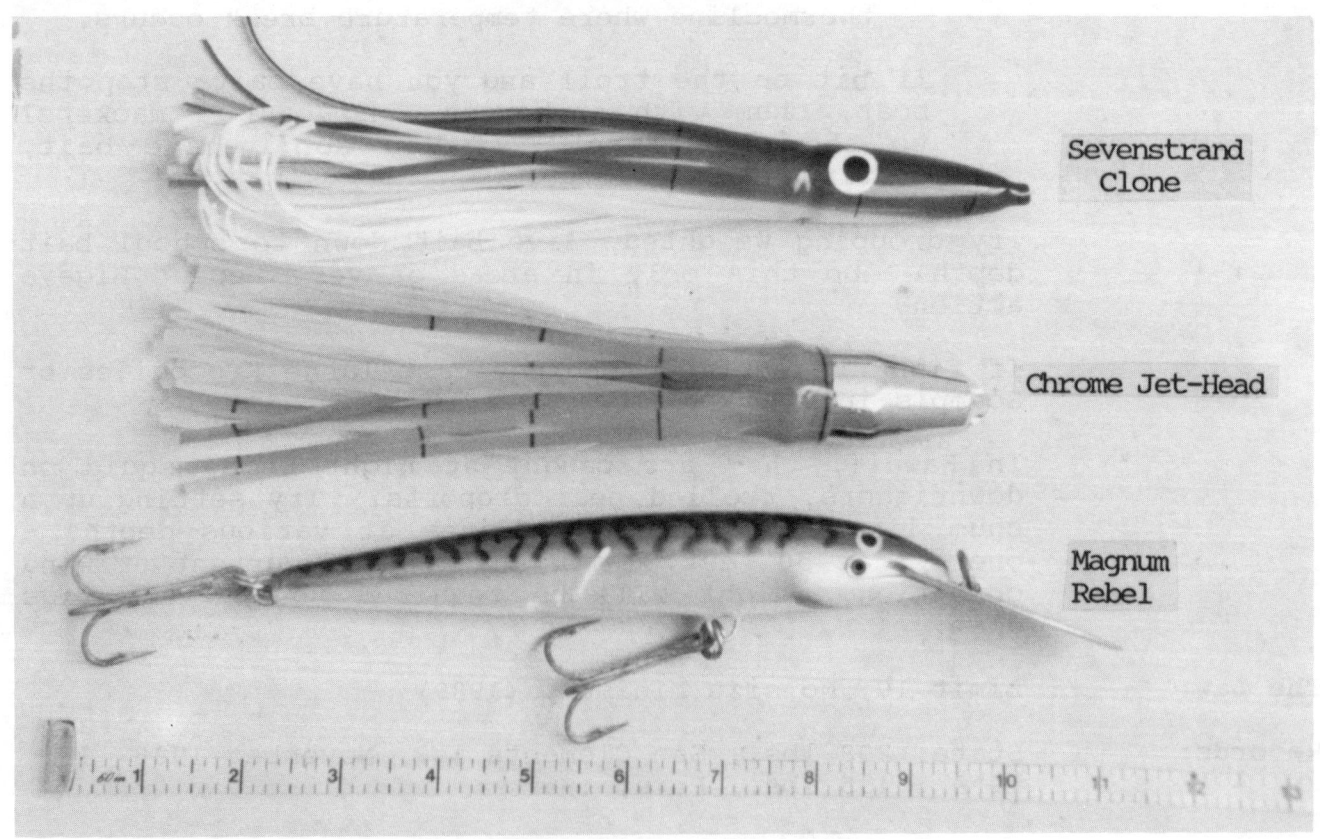

# BIGEYE TUNA RIGS

### Trolling Jigs:

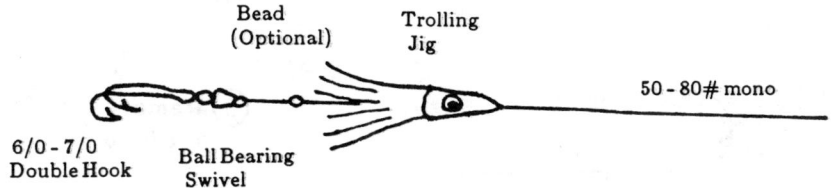

### Live Bait Slow Troll:
(optional off downrigger)

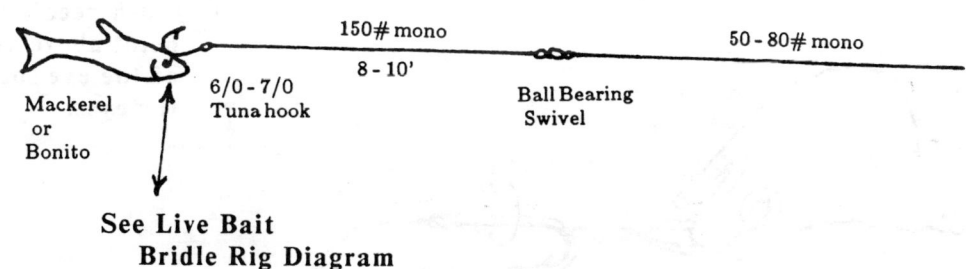

TUNA, BIGEYE 310

# TROLLING - LIVE BAIT BRIDLE RIG
## Troll Mackeral or Bonito at slow, idle speeds

① Turn the bait upside down to calm it, and hold in lap with a wet towel.

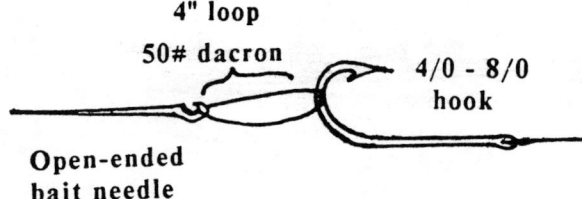
4" loop
50# dacron
4/0 - 8/0 hook
Open-ended bait needle

③ Remove line from bait needle and put loop over hook.

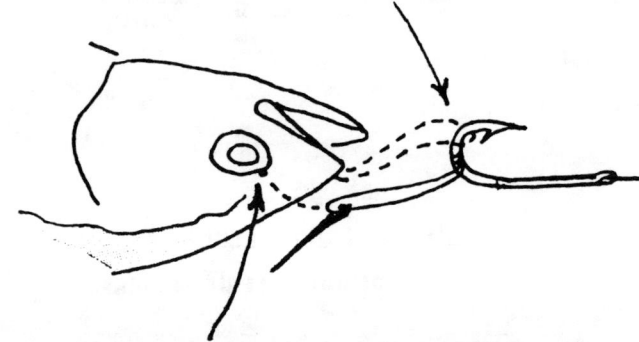

② Push needle through bait at point above and slightly forward of the eye socket. Do not puncture the eyes.

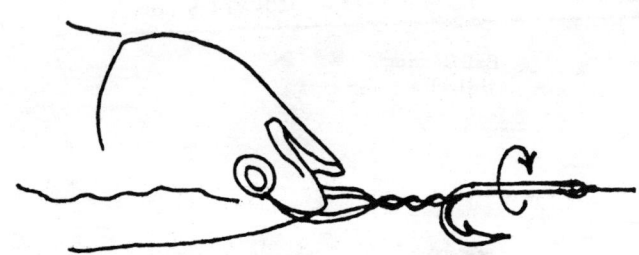

④ Twist hook until line tight.

**Alternative double hook rig for tail biters - Mako & Wahoo**

Lightly hooked or use rubber band

Multi-strand wire leader

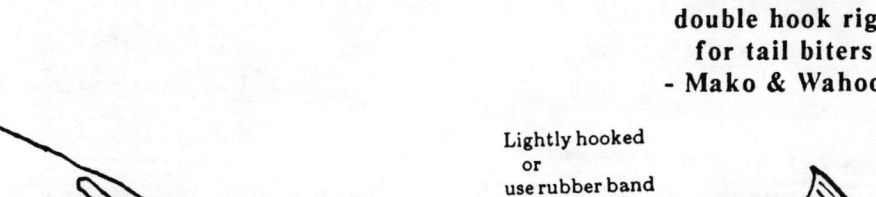

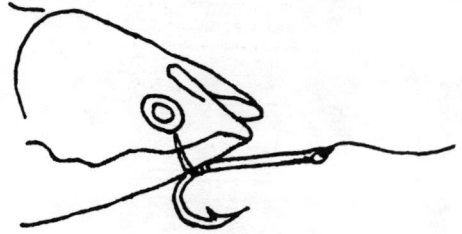

⑤ Insert hook point under the twisted loop at the bait's head to secure and prevent the bridle from unwinding.

TUNA, BIGEYE 311

**Charter Guide Ron Costa and a magnum-sized San Diego Bigeye**

TUNA, BLUEFIN   312

**BLUEFIN TUNA:**

**Where:** Outer islands and outer banks,
San Clemente and Catalina
Cortes Bank & Tanner Bank

Sometimes caught with the Yellowtail runs at Catalina island and the Coronados islands.

Consistently caught at Guadalupe Is, Baja - See Long Range Section.

**When:** August - November
Especially late September to early November at Cortes and Tanner Banks.
Other years into November at San Diego outer banks.

**Bait/Lures:** Live anchovies or mackerel.

**Rig:** Depends on fish size:

1. School size fish in 15 - 25# range

    - use extra light line, 10 - 15# mono
    - #4 - #2 bait hooks
    - the liveliest anchovy you can find

2. Larger fish (40+ lbs.)

    - Use at least 30# mono, 40 lb. mono will give you considerable more "breathing room" without scaring away too many more line-shy fish. Middle weight, conventional reels such as Penn 505H, Daiwa 30SLH, Shimano TLD 15, Newell 445 work well.
    - 9/0 hooks for green mackerel, 3/0 to 5/0 for smaller Spanish mackerel or sardines, #2 to 1/0 hooks for anchovies.

**Technique:** These fish can be very boat and line shy. Baits must be placed away from the boat - 50 to 75+ yards.

A plastic casting bubble can be rigged to keep the bait fairly near the surface even when bait is some distance from the boat.

**The Law:** No limit or size restrictions. (1990-91)

**Records:** State: 140 lbs., Oct. 1986, Cortes Bank

**Info:** See following landings

**Access:** Check for scheduled 1 1/2 to 2 day, late fall Cortes Bank trips out of Long Beach Sportfishing; 22nd St. Sportfishing, San Pedro; and Helgrens, Oceanside.

**See Also:** Yellowtail

A 50 lb-class, fall run, Cortes Bank Bluefin

The jackpot weigh-off can be tough on the deckhand

## YELLOWTAIL: (JUREL)

**Where:** SEE MAP

Off inshore kelp paddies, under offshore drifting kelp paddies, and near offshore islands either near the surface or hugging close to the bottom in $67°+$ waters.

Offshore Islands:  Catalina
Coronados
Santa Barbara

Kelp paddies:  Horseshoe Kelp
La Jolla Kelp

The 150 spot - the double oil rigs
Rocky Point
Point Dume
Pt. Vicente

Also Yellowtail fishing can be excellent at Baja offshore islands on shorter 3-day trips to San Benites to mid-range trips as far as Alijos Rocks. See Baja - Long Range section.

Also in the Sea of Cortez, especially in an area from Loreto up to Bahia de Los Angeles. See Baja - Sea of Cortez section.

**When:** May through mid-November
Generally better in early morning hours.

May, early-June

May and June can be a good time to look for Yellowtail in the kelp paddies 5+ miles off Dana Pt. and in the channel between Catalina and the mainland.

June, July, early August at the Coronados

This is usually the best run of the year. Early to mid-July usually the prime time. Catalina Is. can also be good at this time.

August - September

Catalina - 100 yards off the rocky shore next to the sandy isthmus. Also the 150 Spot, the Long Beach offshore oil rigs, and Horseshoe Kelp can see action during these months.

# SOUTHERN CALIFORNIA – PRIME OCEAN FISHING AREAS

CAUTION: Not to be used for Navigation.
See NOS maps

## SOUTHERN CALIFORNIA – PRIME OCEAN FISHING AREAS

| | Latitude/Longitude | Course/Distance |
|---|---|---|
| 1. 60 Mile Bank | 32° 04.0'/118° 13.0' | From Pt. Loma<br>220° / 60.0 NM |
| 2. 150 Kelp<br>Double Oil Platform<br>called "Elly & Ellen" | 33° 07.5'/118° 35.0' | From Alamitos Bay<br>170° / 9.5 NM |
| 3. Anacapa Is. | 34° 02.4'/119° 21.5' | From Oxnard, Pt. Hueneme<br>203° / 10.3 NM<br>From Ventura Marina<br>180° / 13.6 NM |
| 4. Barn Kelp | 33° 18.6'/117° 29.1' | From Oceanside Harbor<br>315° / 9.6 NM |
| 5. Big Kelp Reef (BKR) | 34° 02.0'/118° 45.3' | From Marina del Rey<br>270° / 14.2 NM |
| 6. Catalina Is. | .................... | From Alamitos Bay<br>215° / 23.8 NM to<br>Ship Rock, 2 Harbors |
| 7. Clemente Is. | 33° 2.1'/118° 36.8' | Castle Rock - NW end |
| 8. Coronado Is. | 32° 26.5'/117° 25.0' | From Pt. Loma<br>170° / 12.5 NM |
| 9. Cortes Bank | 32° 26.5'/119° 07.5' | From Marina del Rey<br>186° / 97 NM<br>From Pt. Loma<br>250° / 95 NM |
| 10. Deep Hole | 34° 01.5'/118° 57.5' | From Marina del Rey<br>277° / 24.2 NM |
| 11. Horseshoe Kelp | 33° 40.0'/118° 13.5' | From Alamitos Bay, out<br>from Federal Breakwater<br>212° / 4.8 NM |
| 12. La Jolla Kelp | 32° 50.0'/117° 17.5' | From Mission Bay<br>310° / about 3 NM |
| 13. Point Dume | 33° 49.0'/119° 00.0' | From Marina del Rey<br>262° / 17.0 NM |
| 14. Pt. Loma Kelp | 32° 42.5'/118° 16.3' | From Mission Bay<br>just south of entrance<br>to Pt. Loma |
| 15. Pt. Vicente | 33° 45.2'/118° 24.6' | From Marina del Rey<br>155° / 13.2 NM |
| 16. Rincon Reef | 34° 19.4'/119° 27.0' | From Santa Barbara<br>170° / 10 NM |
| 17. Rocky Point | 33° 47.8'/118° 24.4' | From Marina del Rey<br>151° / 10.3 NM |
| 18. Santa Barbara Is. | 33° 29.2'/119° 01.8' | From Marina del Rey<br>211° / 41.0 NM<br>From Newport<br>250° / 41.0 NM |
| 19. Santa Cruz Is.<br>West Point | 34° 04.6'/119° 55.1' | From Santa Barbara<br>198° / 24.2 NM |
| San Pedro Pt. | 34° 02.0'/119° 31.2' | From Oxnard, Pt. Hueneme<br>235° / 17.4 NM |
| 20. Tanner Bank | 32° 42.0'/119° 08.0' | From Marina del Rey<br>190° / 83.1 NM |
| 21. Topanga Bubbles | 34° 01.5'/118° 34.2' | From Marina del Rey |

YELLOWTAIL 317

**When continued:**

September - early November, especially if squid available.

Cortes and Tanner Banks. This is your best bet for large fish north of Baja.

Catalina and Clemente Islands

**Bait/Lures:** Live squid
Live anchovies
Live mackerel, sardines

Jigs - Salas 6X, Salas 6X Jr, Salas YoYo 4, Also similar jigs from Sea Strike, Tady.
Colors: Blue & White, Green & Yellow, Chrome

**Rig:** Bottom Bait Rig: Penn 4/0 with Newell "Yellowtail" conversion or equivalent reel. 5 1/2 to 6 foot medium to medium-heavy action rod. Example: Sabre 655.

Bottom Jigging: Replace above reel with higher speed reel, 4:1 ratio or better.

Surface Jigging: Replace above rod with 7 to 10' foot medium weight rod. Example: Fenwick 1870, Sabre 870.

**SEE DIAGRAM**

**Technique:** Bottom Jigging

If you are in "shallow" water, let the jig sink to the bottom. Yo-yo off the bottom by repeatedly lifting the rod sharply and then lowering it to let the jig flutter back to the bottom. Watch for hits on the drop.

Another effective yo-yo technique is to drop the jig to the bottom while being alert for hits on the fall. Let the jig lie briefly on the bottom, then reel it toward the surface as fast as possible. High speed reels sporting 4:1 or greater gear ratios are helpful here. Stop about half way up to the surface and repeat.

Anchovies, Mackerel, Squid, or Sardines on the surface.

Yellowtail can be wary and boat shy. You must get your bait/lure away from the boat, at least 30 to 40 yards. The best place to have your bait is in the chum line 40 - 50 yards behind the boat. If possible, anchor the boat. A drifting boat can spook a school of Yellowtail.

**Technique continued:**

Hook mackerel in the nose area, through the membrane just forward of the eyes or hook lightly behind the anus so you can jerk free when you want to change bait. Anus hooking can force a mackerel to swim deeper.

Squid:

Fish squid just off the bottom near the islands. Use 20-40# line with a 3/0 short-shanked hook. Use a sliding sinker rig with a 2-3 oz. sliding sinker

If the fish are near the surface, cast out, freespool to get away from the boat and work slowly back toward the boat. Keep working the squid at a distance (40 - 50 yards) from the boat.

Double hook the squid - once through the tail and back.

Try mackerel fillet: mackerel rig with 1-2 oz. egg sinker

1. Let sink slowly to the bottom
2. Jig slowly back to the boat

Kelp Paddies:

Approach at slow speed from the downwind side. Live bait - flyline first, then use a 1 - 2 oz. rubbercore weight to take the bait off the surface.
Lures - vary the rate of retrieve.
Misc. - If using dead anchovies, hook them through the jaw. Use the rod tip to give the anchovy movement.

**Records:** State: 62 lbs.; La Jolla; 1953
IFGA: 78 lbs.; Alijos Rocks, Baja; 1987

**The Law:** Limit: 10
No size restrictions

**See Also:** White Sea Bass, Bluefin Tuna under kelp paddies

# YELLOWTAIL BOTTOM FISHING RIGS

**Sliding Sinker Rig:**

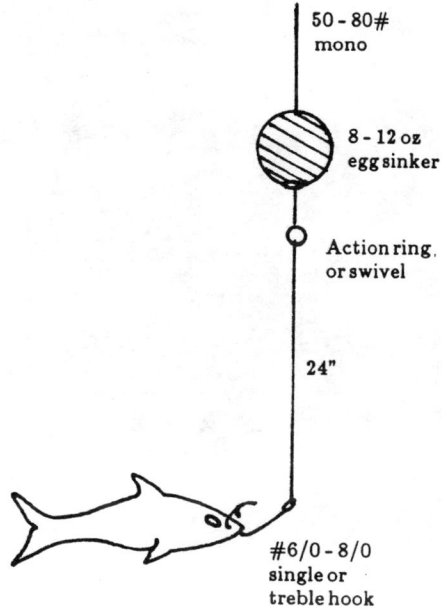

**Dropper Loop Rig:**

See Knots Section for how to tie

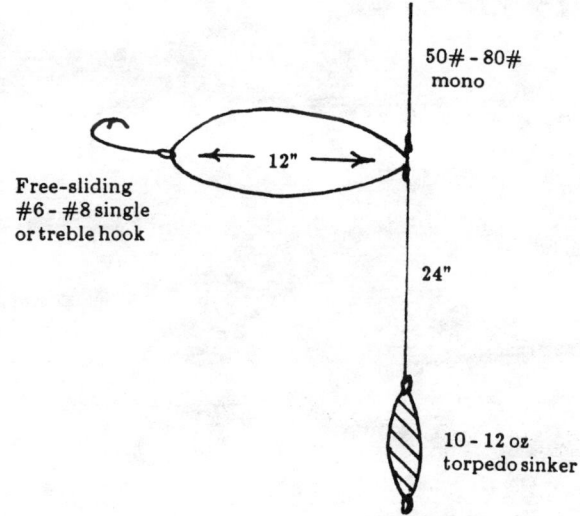

Typical Yellowtails caught in June at the Coronados Islands

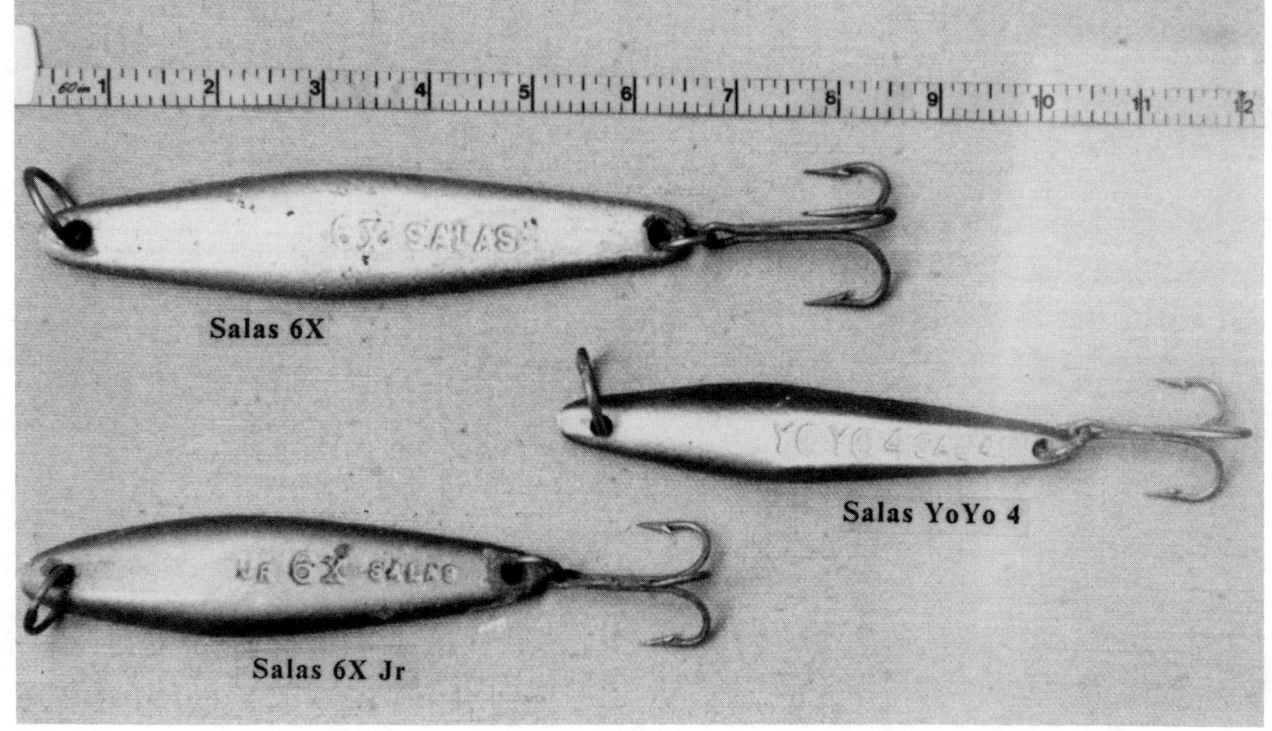

Salas 6X

Salas YoYo 4

Salas 6X Jr

**Bay/Harbor Fishing:**

Contents:
    San Francisco Bay ............... page 323
    Long Beach ...................... page 325
    Newport ......................... page 327
    Mission ......................... page 329
    San Diego ....................... page 329

**IN GENERAL:**

**Where:** Structure:

    Around Docks, pilings, seawalls, bridge abutments, buoy lines - especially in the shade.
    Any underwater structure such as around ledges, dropoffs, and holes.
    Clam beds - old or new.
    Rocky, gravel bed areas.

**When:** During large tidal water movement.

**Bait/Lures:** Bloodworms, Innkeeper worms, frozen squid, frozen/salted anchovies, ghost shrimp

Small, 1/4 to 3/8 oz., 2 inch, leadhead type lures:

    Scampis, Scroungers, Worm Kings, Shakin Shad
    Haddock's Split Tail Grubs
    Small plastic grubs - esp. chartreuse, shrimp, and clear colors

Bomber model "A" - chrome or chrome with black back for slow trolling

**Rig:** Lightweight spinning or casting, 4-6# mono. Example: Ambassadeur 5500C reel + 5 1/2 ft. graphite rod

**Technique:** Always work the bait or lure with the tide movement - cast up-current and allow the offering to move with the current.

Keep the lure/bait near or on the bottom.

Work the lure/bait with the rod tip by repeatedly, slowly moving the rod from about the 9 o'clock position (horizontal) to the 12 o'clock position (vertical), and reeling down the slack.

DON'T expect a strike. Watch for slight hesitations in the movement, drift of the line. Set the hook on all these hesitations.

Also, slow troll with deep diving plugs just off the bottom on light 6-8# mono. Use 1/4 to 3/8 oz. rubbercore sinker to reach depths of 15 to 25 feet. Troll breaklines at these depths.

Bay/Harbor Fishing 322

**Guide Mike Gardner holding a Spotfin Croaker**

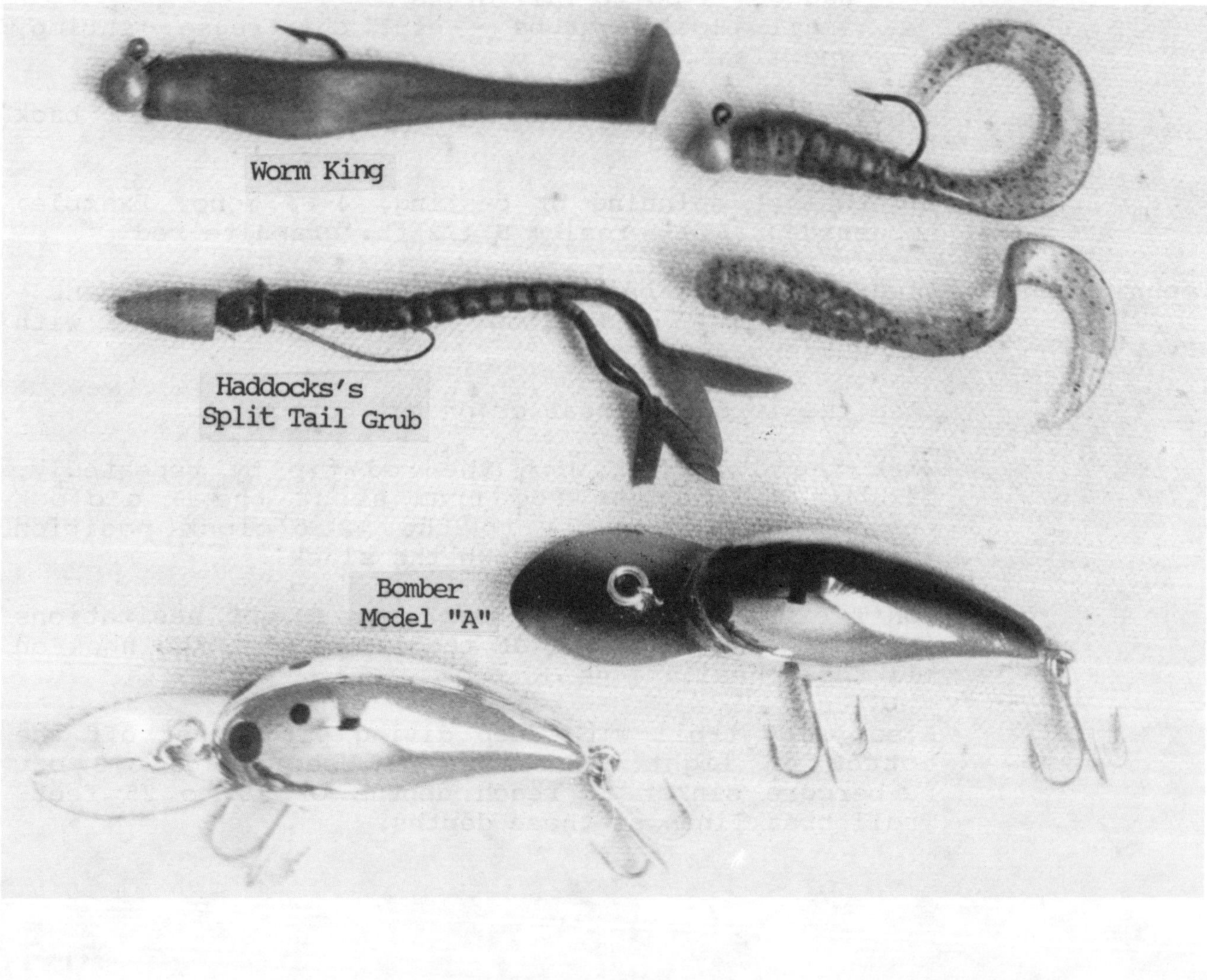

Worm King

Haddocks's Split Tail Grub

Bomber Model "A"

## SAN FRANCISCO BAY:

Note that San Francisco Bay differs from the other bays listed in having potential for large game fish such as Striped Bass, Salmon and Sturgeon and large Sharks.

**When/What:**

SUMMER Months - Potluck fishing

> Stripers - South Tower of Golden Gate Bridge. Best months are July through September. See Striped Bass section for details.
> Halibut - See Halibut section for details. Best months are June and July.
> Rockfish - Cabezon, Lingcod, China & Blue rockfish.

FALL months - Salmon

> August and September are best months for salmon, east and northeast of Tiburon in an area called "California City". See Salmon section for more detail.

WINTER Months - Shark and Sturgeon.

> See Sturgeon section for specifics.
> See Shark section for specifics.
>
> Horse Smelt (Jacksmelt):
>   When: January through March
>   Where: 1. South Bay - Fisherman's Park in Anza Industrial Park (Burlingame).
>   2. Oyster Point Marina - S. San Francisco.
>   3. Candlestick Pt. State Park

WINTER and early SPRING - Perch

> Around docks and pilings
> Technique: From a boat, anchor upstream/current of the structure and let bait (cut mussels/clams drift down-current to fish holding area.

# SAN FRANCISCO BAY
## Shore/Pier Fishing Access

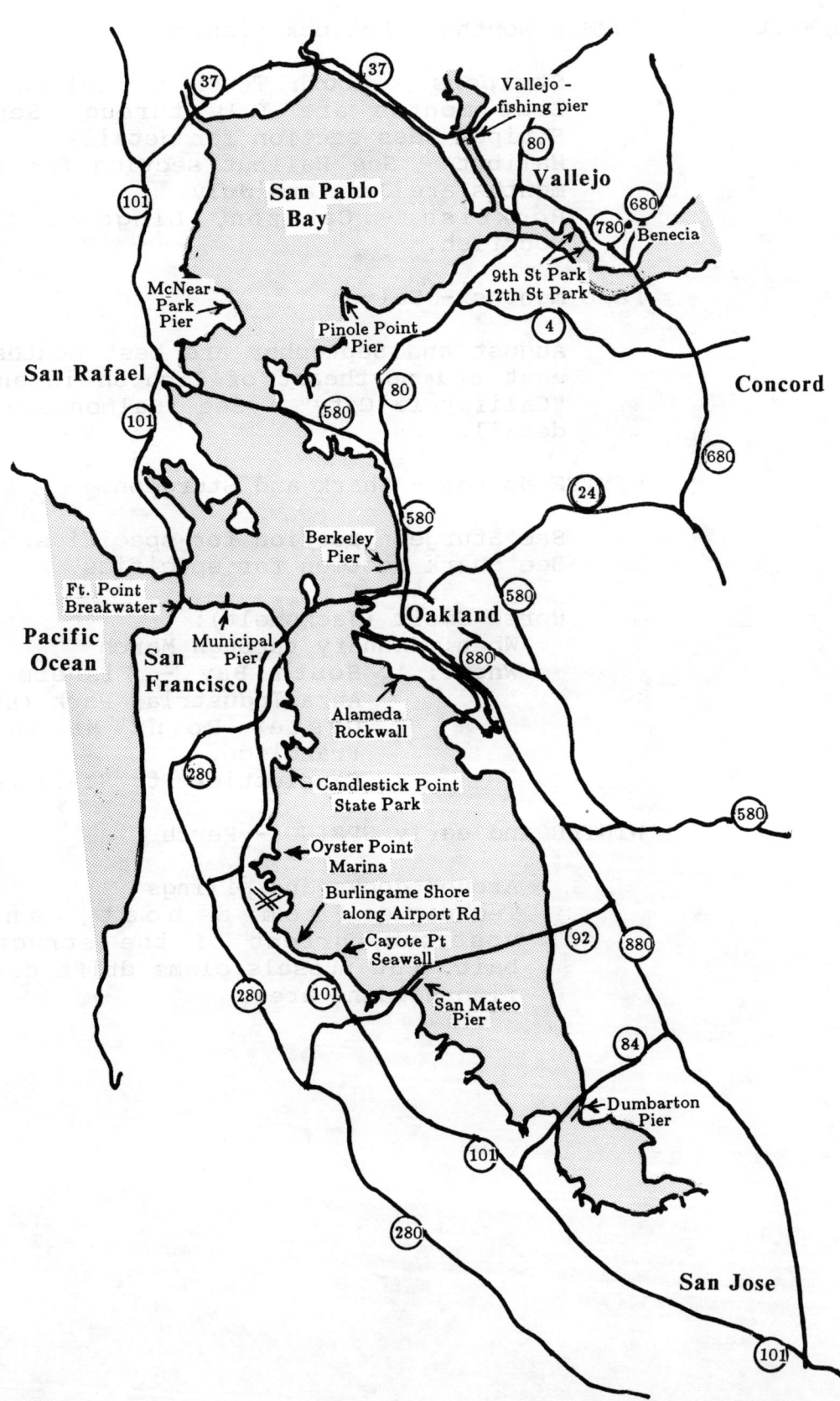

# LONG BEACH HARBOR:

**Where:**     **SEE MAP**

**When:**     Summer - various species/areas - **SEE MAP**. Winter - the breakwater for Calicos.

Evening hours for the Federal Breakwater - incoming, large tidal flows. Mild sea conditions.

**Fish Types:**     Sand Bass, Spotted Bay Bass, Calico Bass, Halibut, Croaker

**Bait/Lures:**     Early, low-light hours - pink colored baits with skirts

Daylight hours - Lime green grubs or crawlers on leadhead jigs. Other colors - shrimp, white, melon.

Western Plastic's Shaking Shad or a Worm King in chartreuse, gold colors. Use with leadhead.

The Federal Breakwater -
  Scampi or Mojo
  Size: 1/4 to 1/2 oz. leadheads
  Add small piece of squid as sweetener

**Rig:**     For breakwater fishing use a 5 1/2' graphite rod + a lightweight Ambassadeur 5500C type reel, elsewhere use lightweight gear, conventional or spinning.

15 - 20# mono for Calicos off the breakwater, lighter 4 to 6# line elsewhere.

**Technique:**     A trolling motor is very helpful.

Work the bait by lifting the rod tip.
Work the rod tip repeatedly from about the 9 o'clock position to the 12 o'clock position.
If action is slow, try a lighter rig and fish further away from the islands, on the beach side.
Cast sideways to the current flow.
Let the current move the lure.
Constantly reel in the slack line.
Watch for changes in the action of the bait. These changes indicate a pickup.
If there is a pickup, keep the rod tip down and reel in as you set the hook.

**Access:**     Guide:
  Mike Gardner
  (714) 993-2328

Boat Rental:
  Club Nautico, 213-431-4899

Bay/Harbor Fishing 326

# LONG BEACH HARBOR

CAUTION: Not to be used for Navigation.

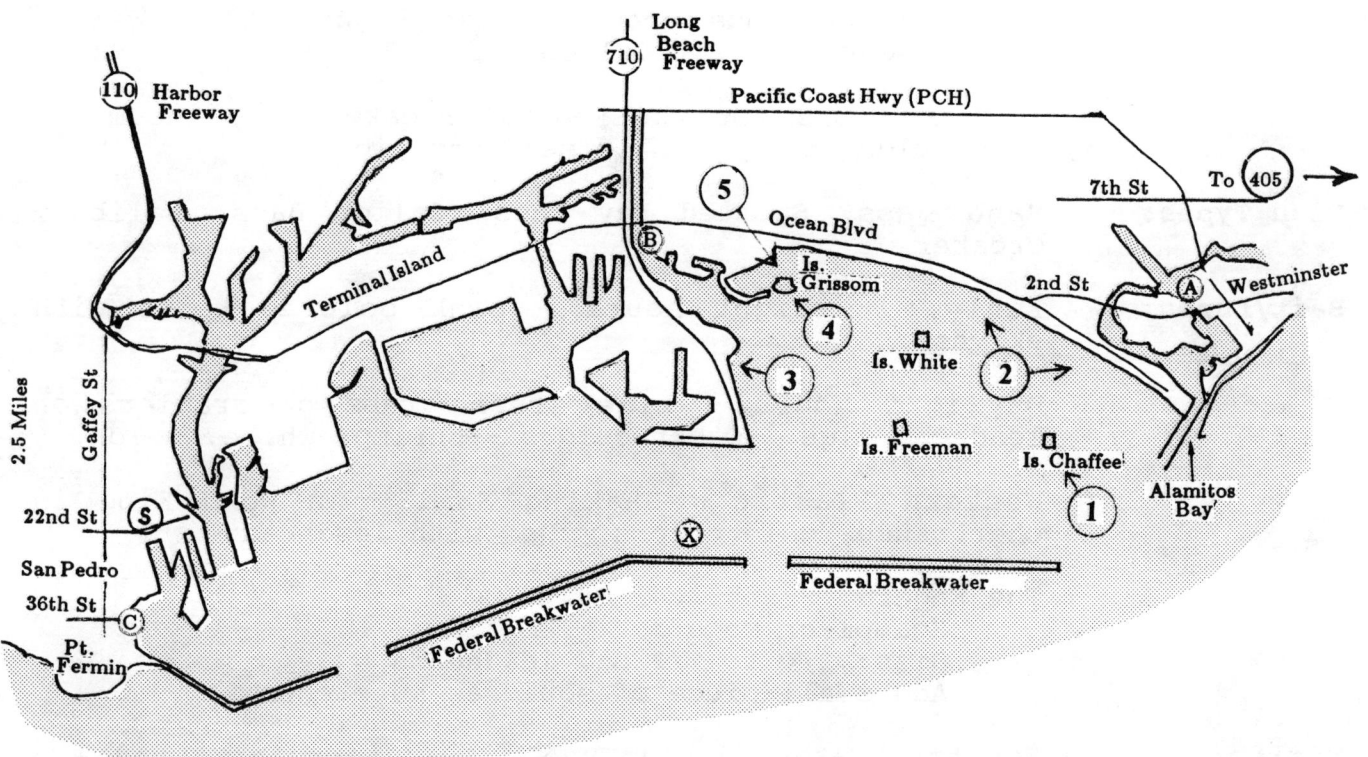

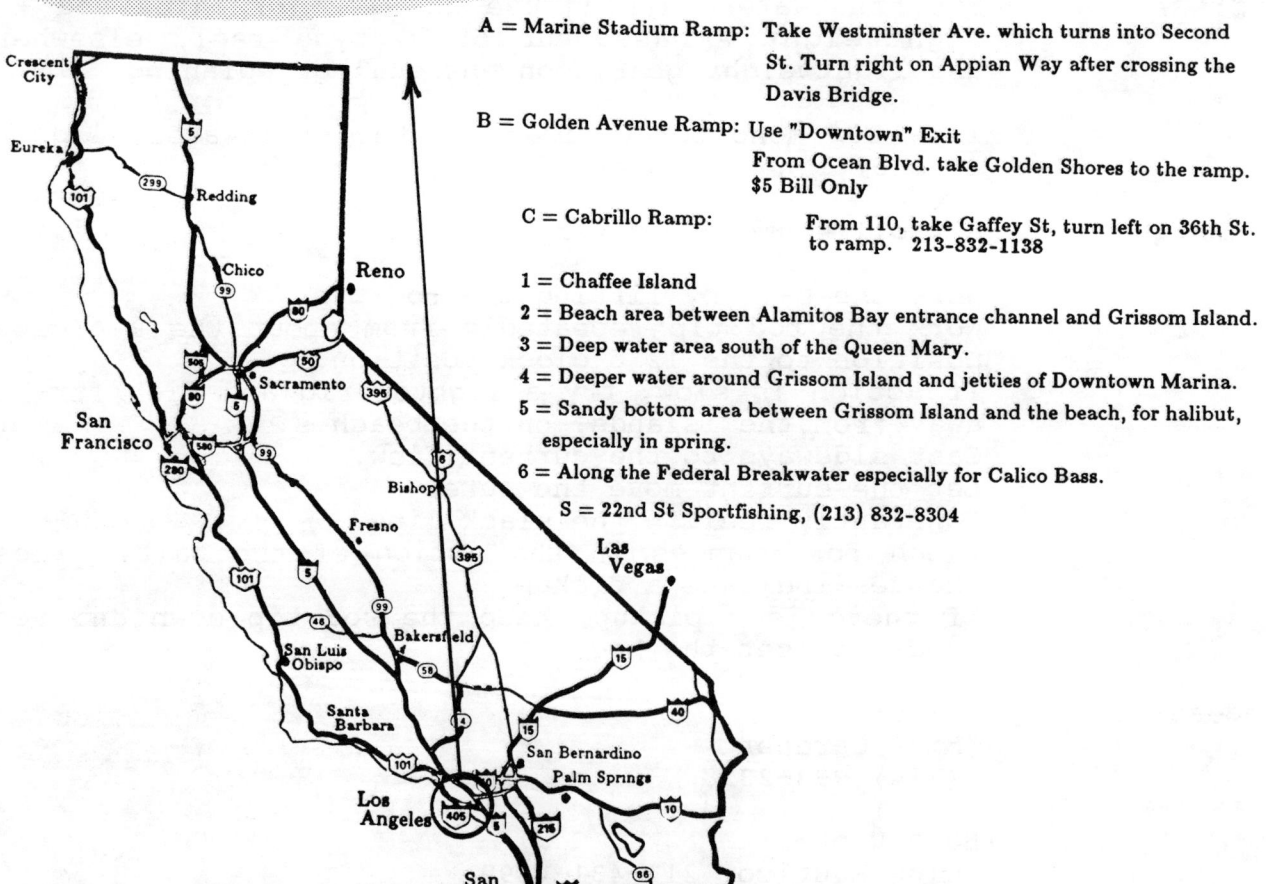

A = Marine Stadium Ramp: Take Westminster Ave. which turns into Second St. Turn right on Appian Way after crossing the Davis Bridge.

B = Golden Avenue Ramp: Use "Downtown" Exit. From Ocean Blvd. take Golden Shores to the ramp. $5 Bill Only

C = Cabrillo Ramp: From 110, take Gaffey St, turn left on 36th St. to ramp. 213-832-1138

1 = Chaffee Island

2 = Beach area between Alamitos Bay entrance channel and Grissom Island.

3 = Deep water area south of the Queen Mary.

4 = Deeper water around Grissom Island and jetties of Downtown Marina.

5 = Sandy bottom area between Grissom Island and the beach, for halibut, especially in spring.

6 = Along the Federal Breakwater especially for Calico Bass.

S = 22nd St Sportfishing, (213) 832-8304

**NEWPORT:**

**Where:** SEE MAP
Structure:

    Shady areas - under docks, along seawalls, etc.
    Ledges & dropoffs
    Around Buoy lines

**When:** During large incoming tides

**Fish Types:** Sand Bass, Spotted Bay Bass, Calico Bass, Halibut, Croaker, Bat Rays, Striped Bass.

**Bait/Lures:** Corbina: Innkeeper worms, Ghost Shrimp
Bass:   Small leadhead jigs, Scampis, Scroungers, Lunker Lures, Haddock's Split Tail Grubs, Worm King or Shakin Shad
     Colors: Gray, Silver Flake, Rootbeer, Motor Oil, Anchovy pattern. Worm Kings in X-rated, anchovy, or brown bait colors.
     Plastic Grubs - 1/4 oz., 2 1/2 to 3", Colors: Melon, Motor oil, Chartreuse

Croaker: Innkeeper worms or bloodworms

In rocky/gravel areas in 10 to 20' deep water - use deep diving plugs.

**Technique:** Always work the bait with the tide/current.

Sandbass will be in open area, over sandy bottoms.

For Spotted Bay Bass, you must be on the bottom, near structure - near pilings, in the shadows below docks, isolated rockbeds, etc.

For Croaker: use bait holder hooks with either bloodworms or Innkeeper worms. Croaker will play with bait before taking. Must wait until weight is on the line. Look for muddy/sandy bottom holes, channels.

Jacksmelt are in the bay in January and February. They can be found throughout the bay but concentrate near the bait tank at the Pavilion. Fish near the surface with live or dead anchovies, or bloodworms. Larger bait will catch larger fish.

**Access:** Rental boats are available with bait (anchovies) at Davey's Locker - 714-673-1434 or you can fish off their dock at the Pavilion plus use live anchovies from their bait receivers for a moderate charge.

Guide: Mike Gardner - 714-993-2328

# NEWPORT BAY

Bay/Harbor Fishing 328

CAUTION: Not to be used for Navigation.

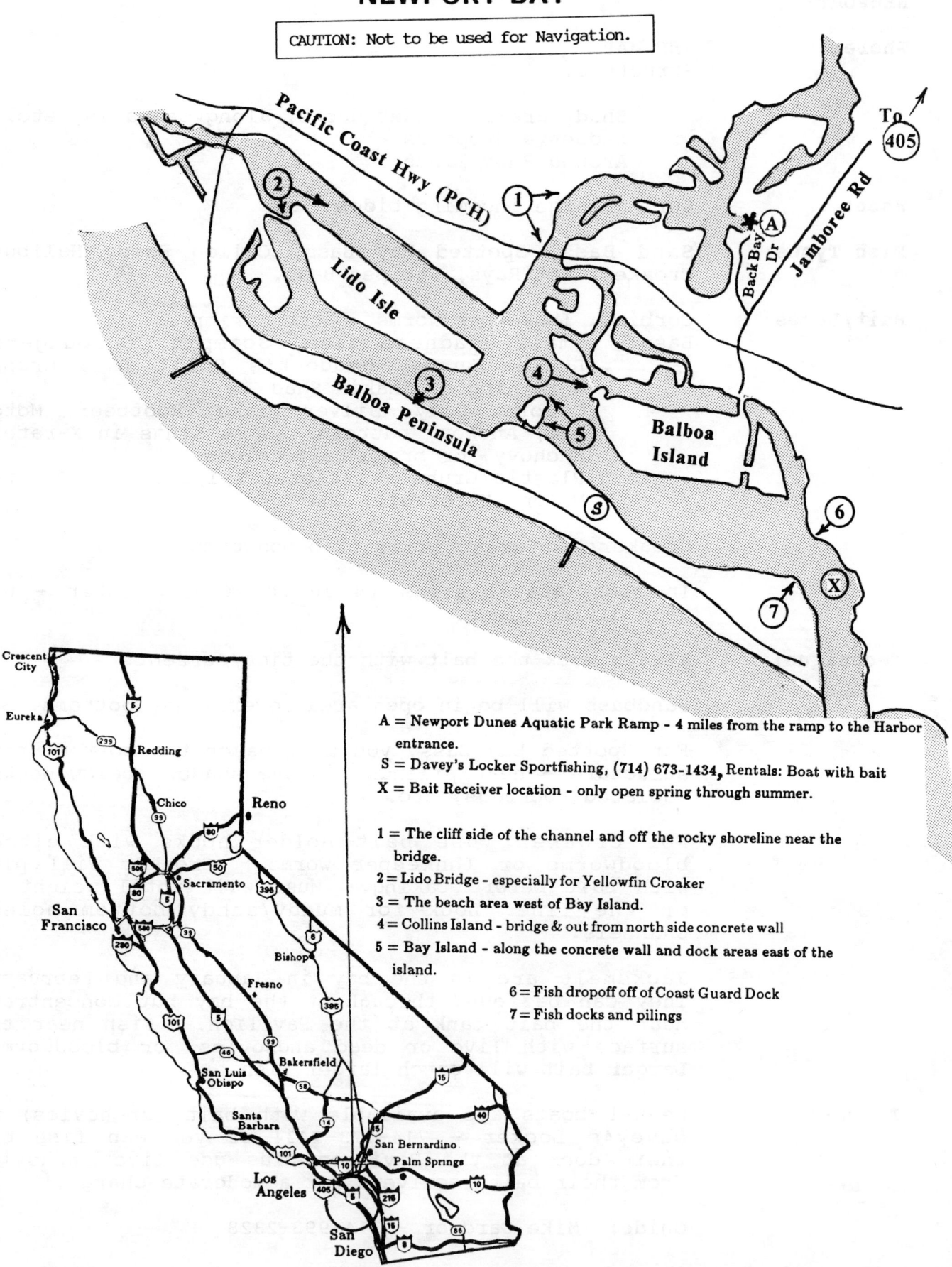

A = Newport Dunes Aquatic Park Ramp - 4 miles from the ramp to the Harbor entrance.
S = Davey's Locker Sportfishing, (714) 673-1434, Rentals: Boat with bait
X = Bait Receiver location - only open spring through summer.

1 = The cliff side of the channel and off the rocky shoreline near the bridge.
2 = Lido Bridge - especially for Yellowfin Croaker
3 = The beach area west of Bay Island.
4 = Collins Island - bridge & out from north side concrete wall
5 = Bay Island - along the concrete wall and dock areas east of the island.
6 = Fish dropoff off of Coast Guard Dock
7 = Fish docks and pilings

## MISSION BAY:

**Where:** SEE MAP

**Fish Types:** Sand Bass, Spotted Bay Bass, Calico Bass, Halibut, Croaker, Bat Rays, Leopard Sharks.

**Bait/Lures:** Halibut - drifted live anchovies, Worm King or Shakin' Shad. Colors: Shad or minnow imitations, Scroungers - silver
Spotted Bay Bass - Grub plastics, Paddle tail plastics. Color: pink
Croaker - Bloodworms, Ghost shrimp, Innkeeper worms, clams, Plastic grubs - chartreuse
Leopard Sharks and Rays - Cut mackerel, frozen squid, salted anchovies

**Technique:** Plastic lures - slow down and bump it along the bottom. Let it drift with the tide, along the bottom.

**Info:** Dana Bait & Tackle, 619-225-0440

**Access:** Guide: Jim Murphy
619-566-0868

Rental boats: Dana Basin Ramp, 619-226-1066

---

## SAN DIEGO BAY:

**Where:** SEE MAP

The bait barge - sharks at night
   sand bass
Zuniga Jetty - south boundary of San Diego bay. It juts out from North Island and is submerged for most of its length.

**When:** During large tidal flows

**Fish Types:** Sand Bass, Spotted Bay Bass, Calico Bass, Halibut, Croaker, Opaleye, Smoothhound (Sand) Sharks.

**Info:** Hook, Line & Sinker - 619-224-1336

**Access:** Guide: Jim Murphy
619-566-0868

Boat Rental: Club Nautico, near H&M landing, 619-222-3013

Bay/Harbor Fishing  330

# MISSION BAY

CAUTION: Not to be used for Navigation.

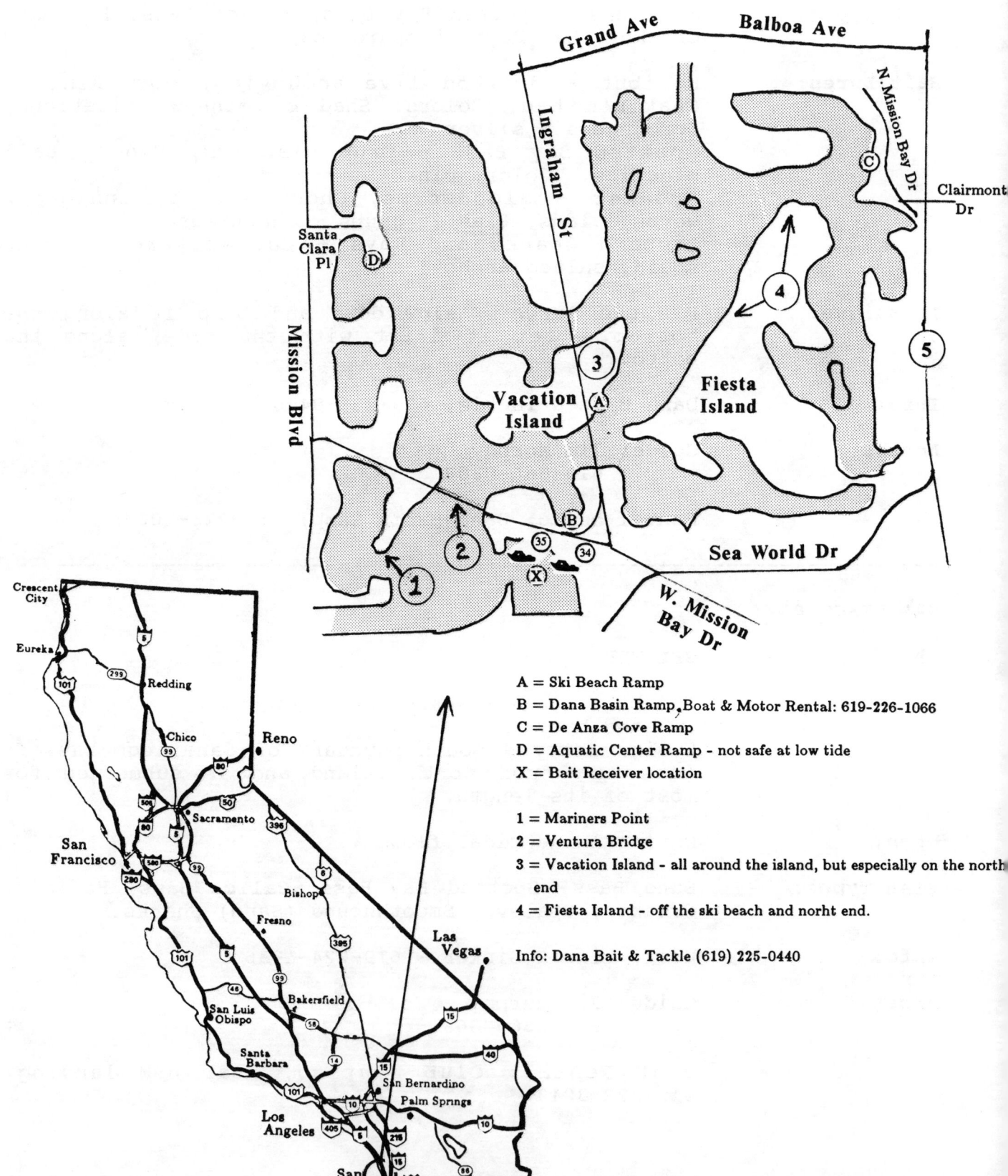

A = Ski Beach Ramp
B = Dana Basin Ramp, Boat & Motor Rental: 619-226-1066
C = De Anza Cove Ramp
D = Aquatic Center Ramp - not safe at low tide
X = Bait Receiver location

1 = Mariners Point
2 = Ventura Bridge
3 = Vacation Island - all around the island, but especially on the north end
4 = Fiesta Island - off the ski beach and norht end.

Info: Dana Bait & Tackle (619) 225-0440

# SAN DIEGO BAY

Bay/Harbor Fishing 331

CAUTION: Not to be used for Navigation.

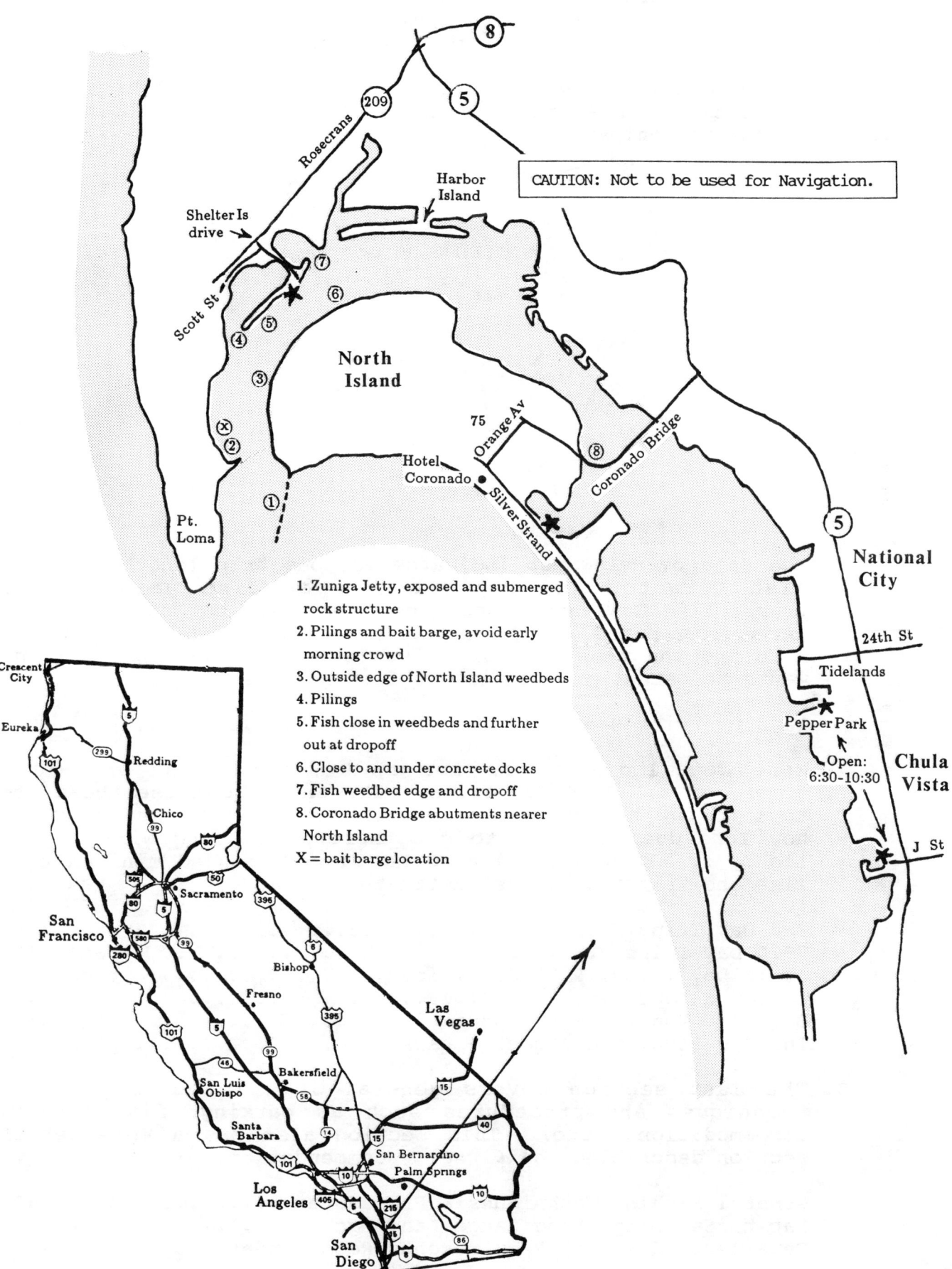

1. Zuniga Jetty, exposed and submerged rock structure
2. Pilings and bait barge, avoid early morning crowd
3. Outside edge of North Island weedbeds
4. Pilings
5. Fish close in weedbeds and further out at dropoff
6. Close to and under concrete docks
7. Fish weedbed edge and dropoff
8. Coronado Bridge abutments nearer North Island

X = bait barge location

## BAJA LONG RANGE TRIPS:

The Baja long range fishing information is organized as follows;

This section outlines basic travel and fishing information for San Diego based, Long Range trips to areas on the Pacific Ocean side of the Baja, Mexico peninsula.

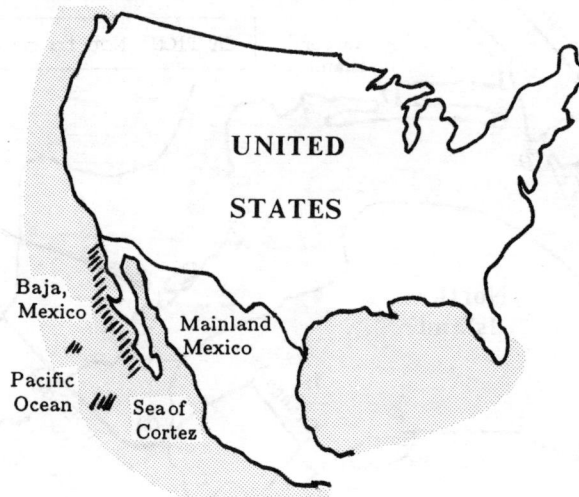

= area described in this section

1. The Baja overview map indicates various trip lengths, types of fish targeted and typical jackpot fish weights. The prospective Baja angler can use this chart to generally decide on a trip based on the number of days he wants/has time to fish and the time of year he wants to go, the type of fish he wants to catch, or the size of fish he is seeking.

    Baja Overview Map .................................. page 334

2. More detailed sections for a) 3-5 day trips, b) 7-10 day trips, or c) 13-16 day trips. The angler can use these areas to find out the general trip itinerary - where are we going?, how long does it take to get there?, how long will I get to fish?,... Each section also has a recommended minimum tackle list and trip/tackle cost estimate.

    3-5 Day Trips ...................................... page 335
    7-10 Day Trips ..................................... page 340
    13-16 Day Trips, & 23 day Trips .................... page 346
    Leader Setups ...................................... page 351
    Big Game Monofilament Connections .................. page 352
    The Big Fish, techniques & tackle .................. page 353

3. The last section covers general long range trip fishing techniques and procedures such as parking, fish handling, accommodations, etc. This section also has a more detailed section describing rod & reel recommendation.

    General Fishing Techniques & Procedures............ page 357
    Map to San Diego Long Range Landings .............. page 360
    Detailed Rod & Reel Requirements/Recommendations .. page 361

BAJA LONG RANGE TRIPS 333

Yellowfin Tuna

Jim Niemiec

Yellowtail

Alijos Rocks Wahoo

# BAJA LONG RANGE TRIPS
## Baja Overview Diagram

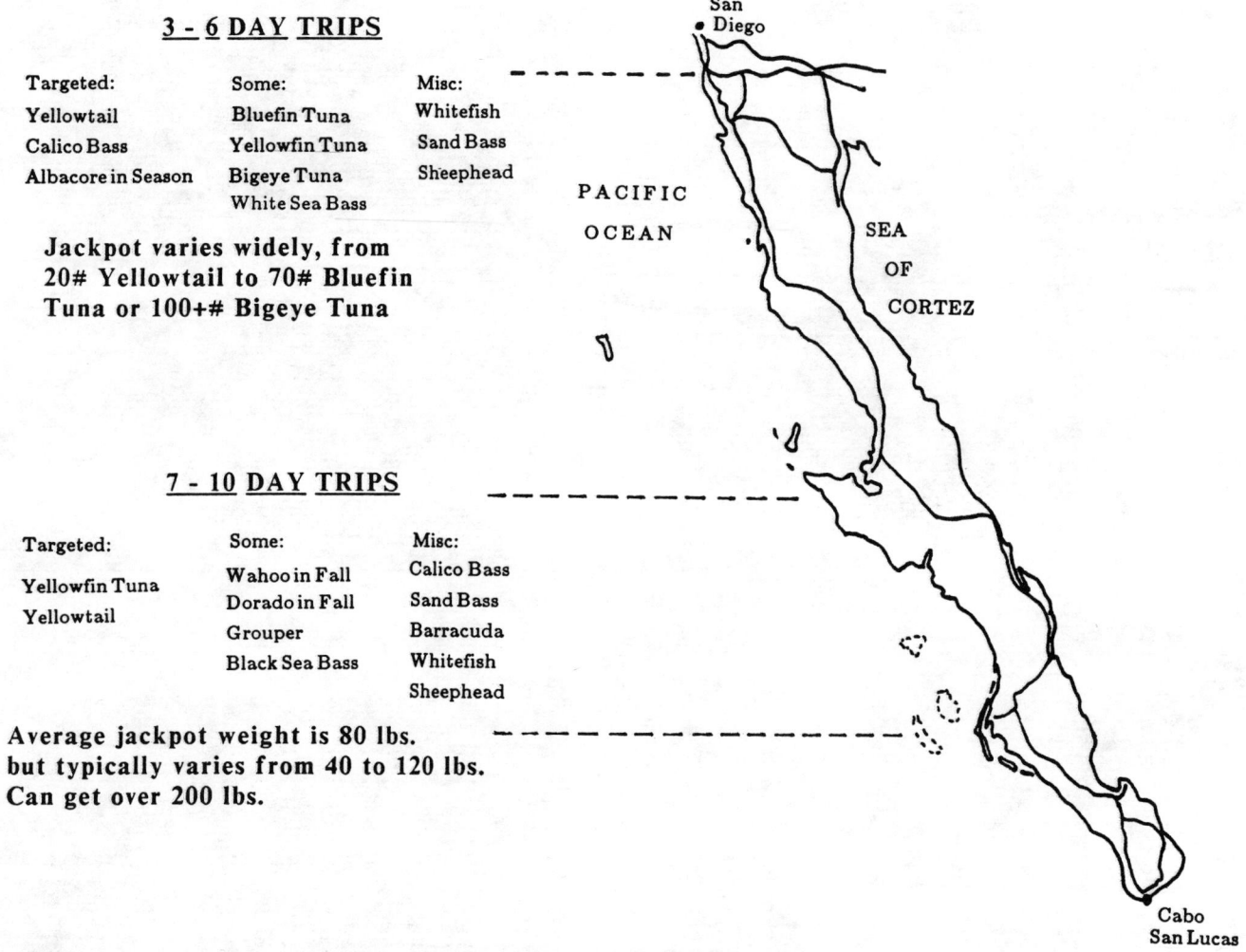

### 3 - 6 DAY TRIPS

| Targeted: | Some: | Misc: |
|---|---|---|
| Yellowtail | Bluefin Tuna | Whitefish |
| Calico Bass | Yellowfin Tuna | Sand Bass |
| Albacore in Season | Bigeye Tuna | Sheephead |
| | White Sea Bass | |

**Jackpot varies widely, from 20# Yellowtail to 70# Bluefin Tuna or 100+# Bigeye Tuna**

### 7 - 10 DAY TRIPS

| Targeted: | Some: | Misc: |
|---|---|---|
| Yellowfin Tuna | Wahoo in Fall | Calico Bass |
| Yellowtail | Dorado in Fall | Sand Bass |
| | Grouper | Barracuda |
| | Black Sea Bass | Whitefish |
| | | Sheephead |

Average jackpot weight is 80 lbs. but typically varies from 40 to 120 lbs. Can get over 200 lbs.

### 13 - 18 DAY TRIPS to Revillagigedo Islands

(These are really 16 - 18 day trips with an option to fly home from Cabo eliminating the 3 day boat ride home)

| Targeted: | Some: |
|---|---|
| Yellowfin Tuna | Grouper |
| Wahoo | Amberjack |
| | Rainbow Runner |
| | Pargo |

Average jackpot weight is 220 lbs. but typically varries from 130 to 260 lbs. Can get over 300 lbs.

### 20 - 23 DAY TRIPS
to Clipperton Is.

# BAJA LONG RANGE
## Typical 3 to 5 Day Trips
### Trips Scheduled Primarily in Summer, Early Fall

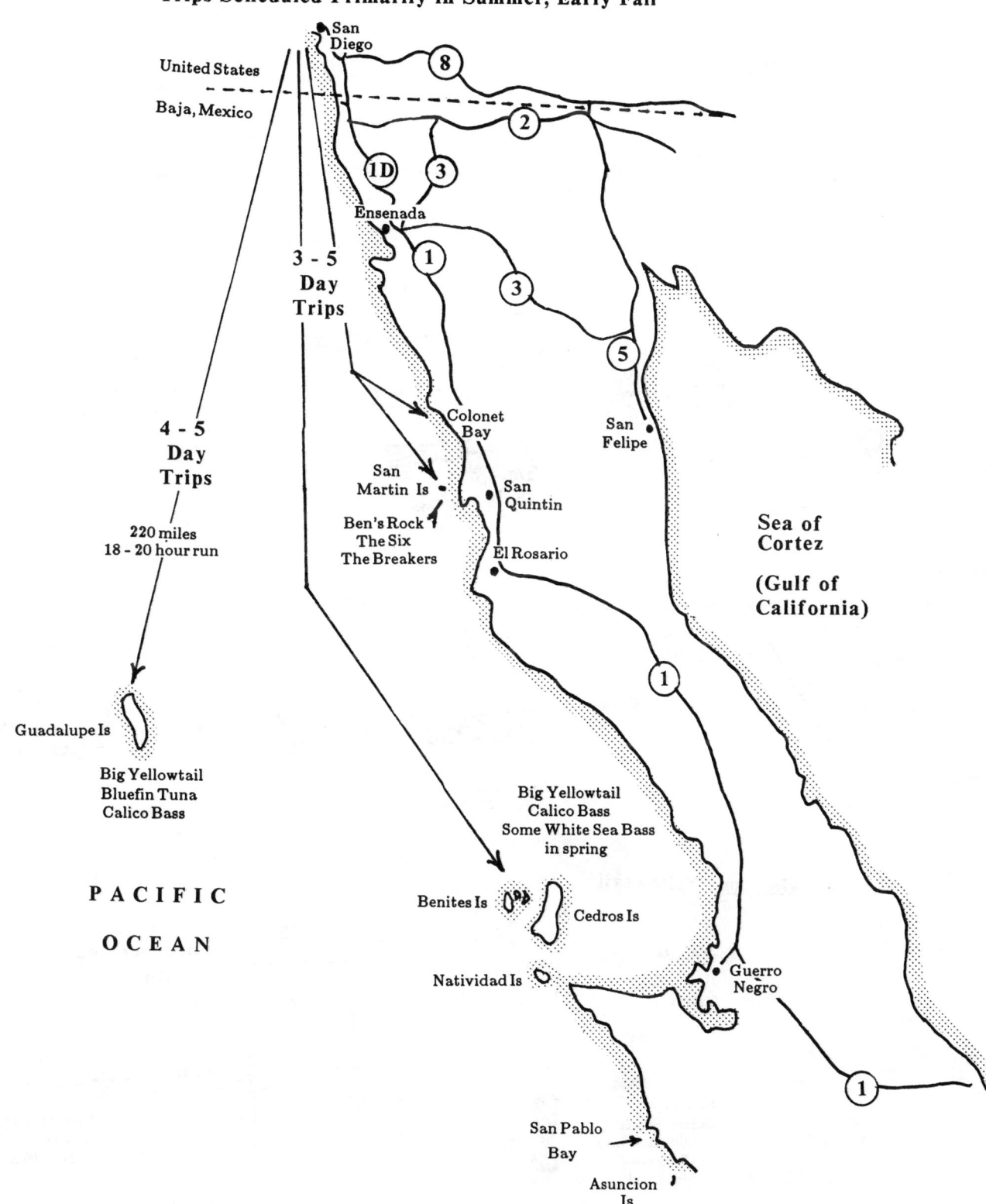

# BAJA LONG RANGE TRIPS
## 3-5 Day Tackle / Techniques Diagram

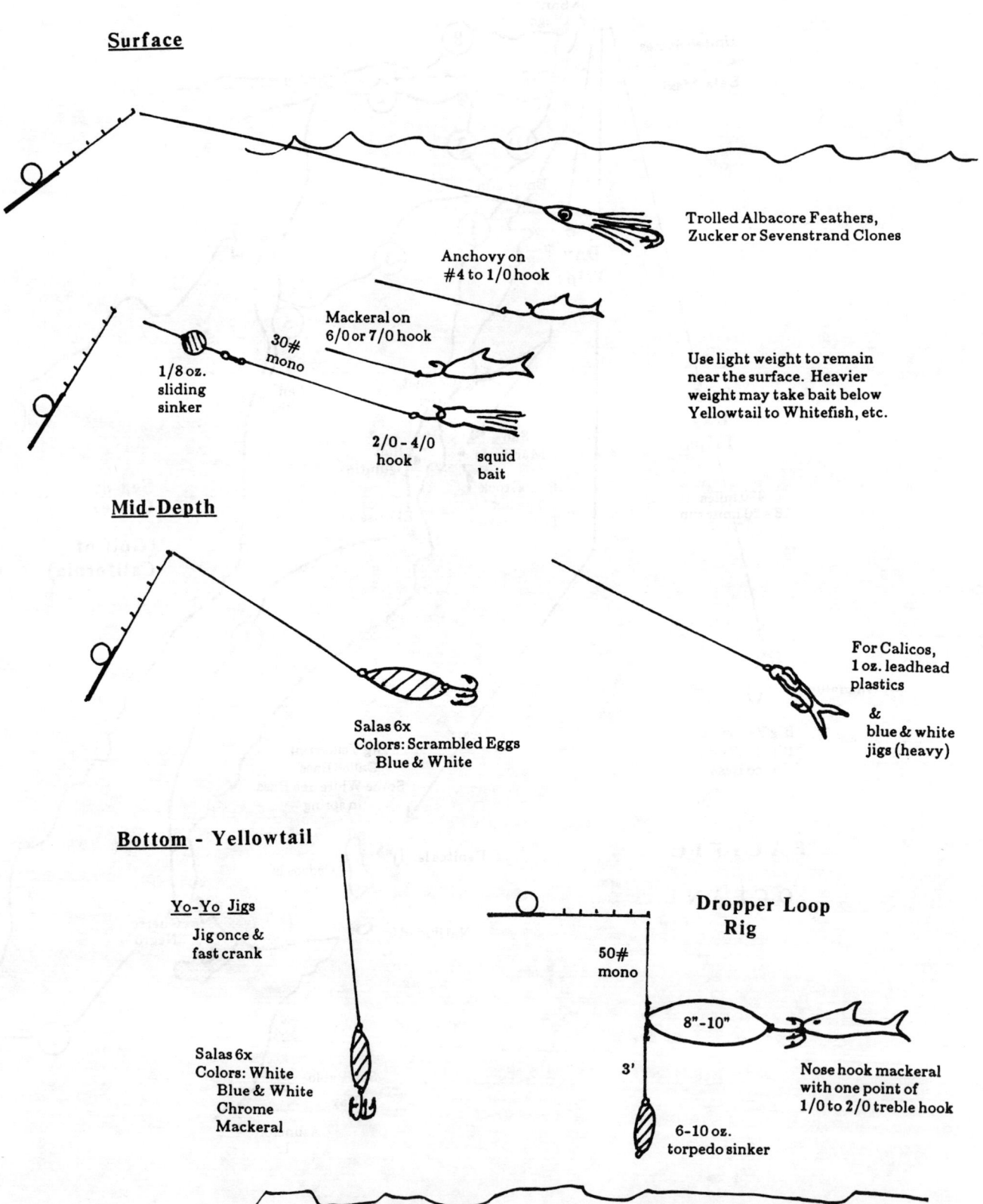

## WHAT DO I NEED? - HOW MUCH DOES IT COST?
### A 5 Day Trip

Boat Costs:   Boat   -   $600 - $800 depending on number of anglers

           Tip   -   30 - 50
           Mex. Lic.   20 ($4/day)
           Jackpot   15
           Soda/Beer   15
           ---------------
           Boat Subtotal:   $680 - $900

Terminal Tackle - Minimum Requirements:

   Jigs/Lures:
       3 each color for Tuna & Yellowtail

           Sea Strike LR Jr - Heavy @ $5.60/each = 16.80
               Green or blue mackerel pattern
           Salas 6x Jr or Sea Strike LR Jr - Heavy
               Scramble Eggs - @ $4.80/each   = 14.40
                   (brown, yellow, white)
               Blue & White   - @ $4.80/each   = 14.40
               Green & Yellow - @ $4.80/each   = 14.40

   Leadhead plastics for Calicos - 3 to 4 dozen plastic tails with 2 to 3 dozen leadheads approx. $30.00:

       Scampi, Worm King, Mojo on 1/4 to 1 oz. leadhead jigs. Colors: Chartreuse, smoke, smoke sparkle, silver sparkle, motor oil, rootbeer, etc.

   Trolling Lures: 3 Albacore feather type lures (Zuker) with large double hooks (7/0). Colors: Zucchini, Bleeding Mackerel, Mexican Flag @ $4.50 each = $13.50.

                                   ---------------
           Terminal Tackle Subtotal:     $103

Miscellaneous Gear:

   Hooks: #4, 2, 2/0 - 25 to 50 each; 25 each of 7/0 & 8/0 ($13)
   Rubbercore sinker: 1/4, 1/2, 1, & 1 1/2 oz, 6-12 of each ($7)
   Weights: 8 - 12 oz. torpedo or 10, 8 oz. egg sinkers for bottom fishing. ($10)
   Extra spools of Mono: 1 lb. - 50# or 60# ($22); 1/2 lb. - 40#, ($12); 1/2 lb. - 30# ($12), 1/2 lb. of 20 or 25# mono ($20).
   More Misc. gear - Yozuri bait catching rigs (4 @ 2.99 = $11.96), Shorty Boots ($22.75), Gloves ($2.95), Dikes and Dike holders ($6.50 + $3.39), Leather Rod belt ($12), Hook sharpener ($5).

                                   ---------------
           Misc. Gear Subtotal:     $160

BAJA LONG RANGE TRIPS  338

## WHAT DO I NEED? - HOW MUCH DOES IT COST?
### A 5 Day Trip

<u>Rods & Reels</u> - <u>Minimum</u> Requirements:
(For alternative rods/reels - see "Detailed Rod & Reel Requirements/Recommendations")

1. A surface bait 20# to 40# mono rig. Reel with excellent freespool. Recommended: Penn 500M with 25# mono plus 30# and 40# mono Newell replacement spools. A rod rated for 15 to 40# mono, 6 1/2 feet or longer, with flexible tip for lobbing anchovies. Recommended: Fenwick 1270C. Rental: Rod and Penn 500 reel with 25# mono - $20.

2. For surface to mid-depth jig casting or bait fishing: A surface iron rig rated for 30 to 50# mono. Reel: A medium to high speed reel. Recommended: Penn 505HS. Rod: a 7 to 10 foot rod rated for 1 - 6+ oz. jigs. Recommended: Sabre 670 or Fenwick 1670. This outfit can also serve as a bottom jig yo-yo rig or a bottom, medium-heavy bait rig, using live mackerel for Yellowtail. Rental: Penn 500 reel with 40# mono - $25.

3. Yo-yo jig fishing outfit for fishing jigs off the bottom. Reel: A medium to high speed reel with capacity for about 200 yards of 60# mono. Recommended: Penn 113HL. Rod: A medium-heavy to heavy, 5 1/2 to 6 foot rod. Recommended: Fenwick 1655XH. Rental: Penn 113H reel with 60# mono - $30.

4. A medium heavy 60 - 80# bottom dropper-loop bait fishing rig. Reel: Medium speed reel. Recommended: Penn 114HL Rod: A 5 1/2 to 6 medium-stiff to stiff rod. Recommended: Sabre 655XH or Fenwick 1655XH. Rental: Penn 114H with 80# mono - $32.

5. A trolling outfit loaded with 80# mono. Reel: Heavy duty reel with capacity for 475 yards of 50# mono. Recommended: Penn 114HL. Rod: A medium-heavy to heavy, 5 1/2 to 6 1/2 foot rod with at least a stripper and terminal roller guide. Recommended: Fenwick 1665H or Sabre 665H rod. Rental: Penn 114H with 80# mono - $32.

```
                                                        ---------------
                    Rod & Reel Rental Subtotal:              $139

Plus:       Parking @ $2/day     -    $10
            Blown Ice - 200#     -     20
            Fish Cleaning ??
                                                        ---------------
                             Plus Subtotal:               $ 30+
                                                        ===============
                    Total Estimated Cost:   $1112 to $1332
```

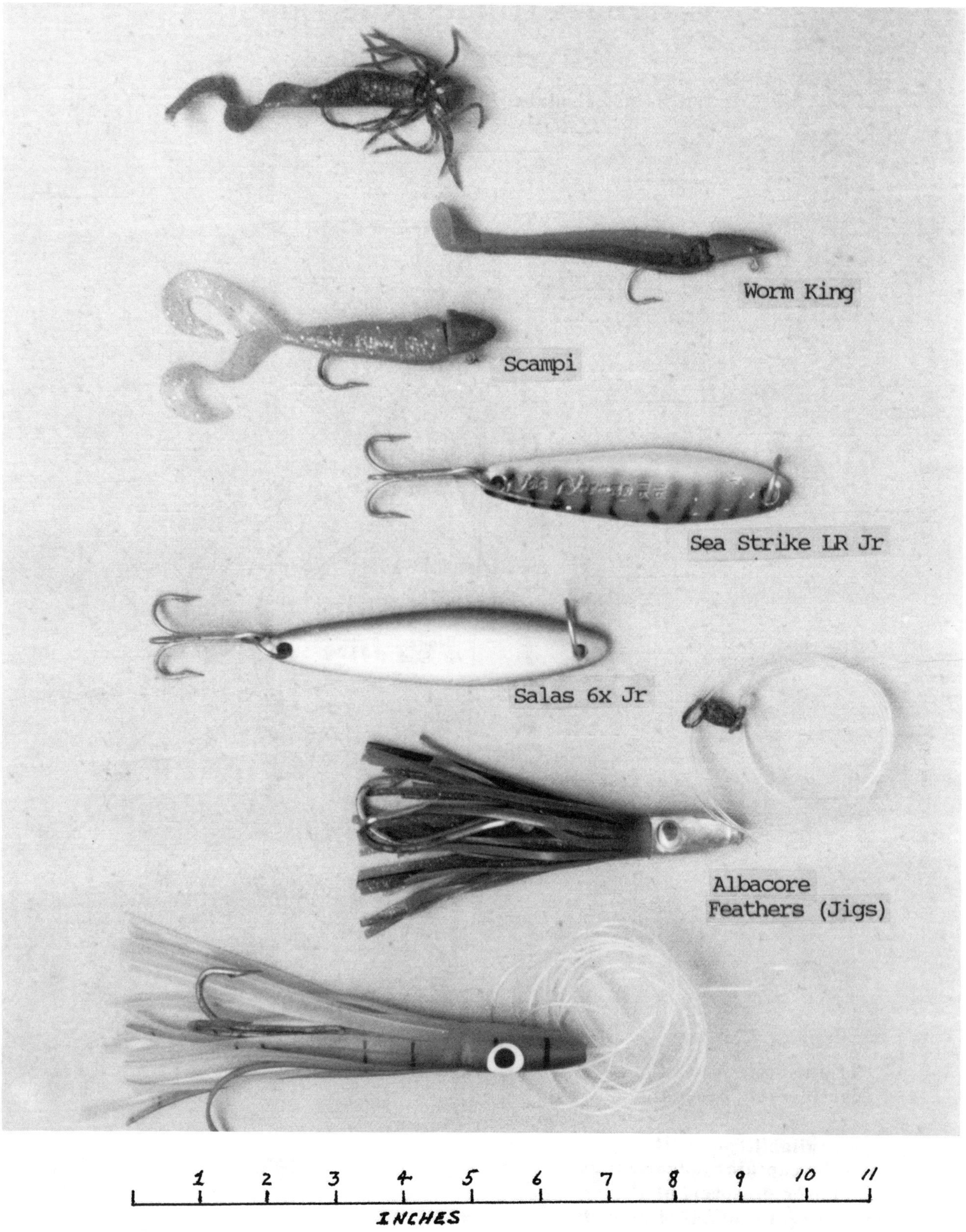

BAJA LONG RANGE TRIPS    339

Worm King

Scampi

Sea Strike LR Jr

Salas 6x Jr

Albacore
Feathers (Jigs)

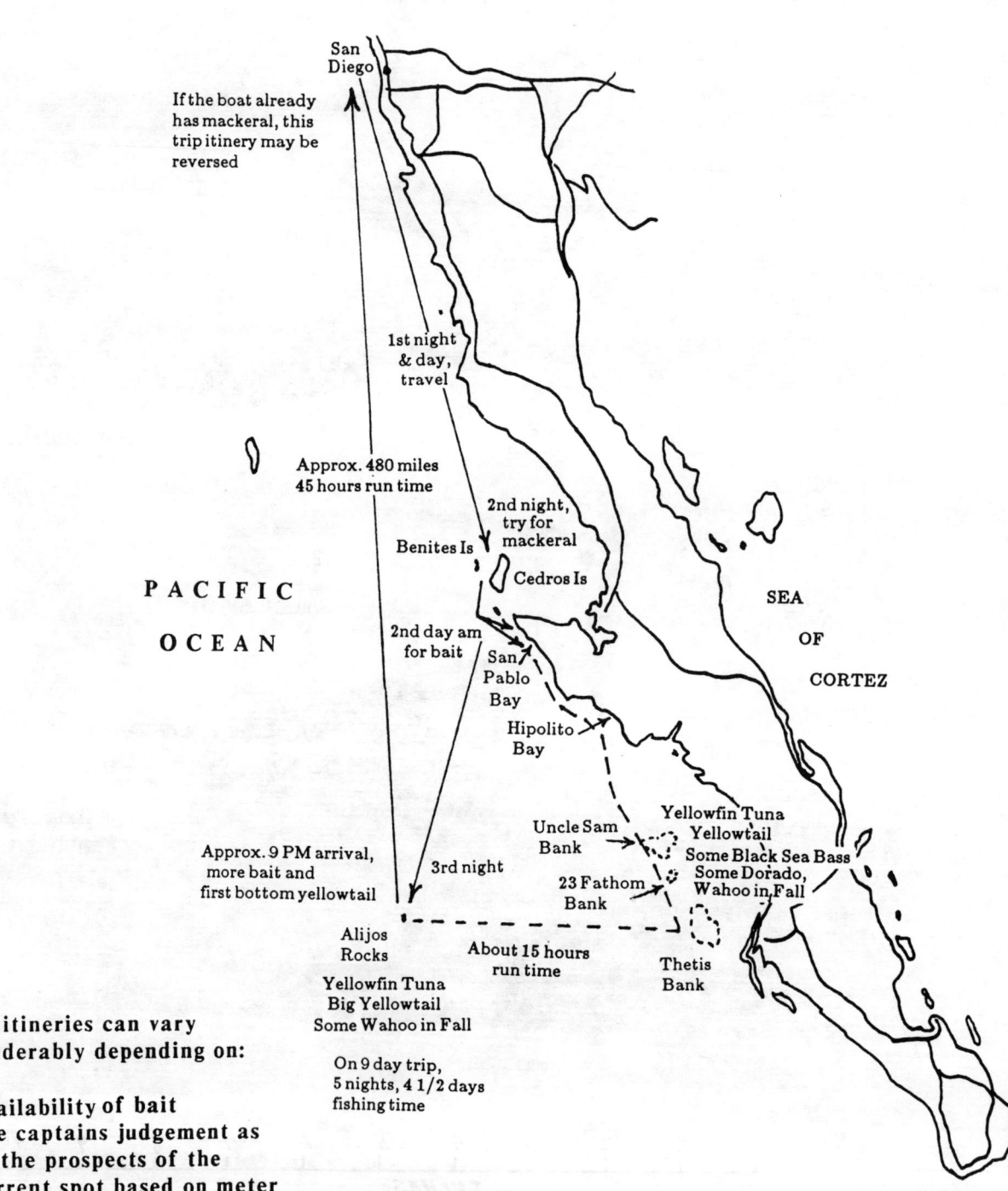

# BAJA LONG RANGE TRIPS
## 7-10 Day Tackle / Techniques Diagram

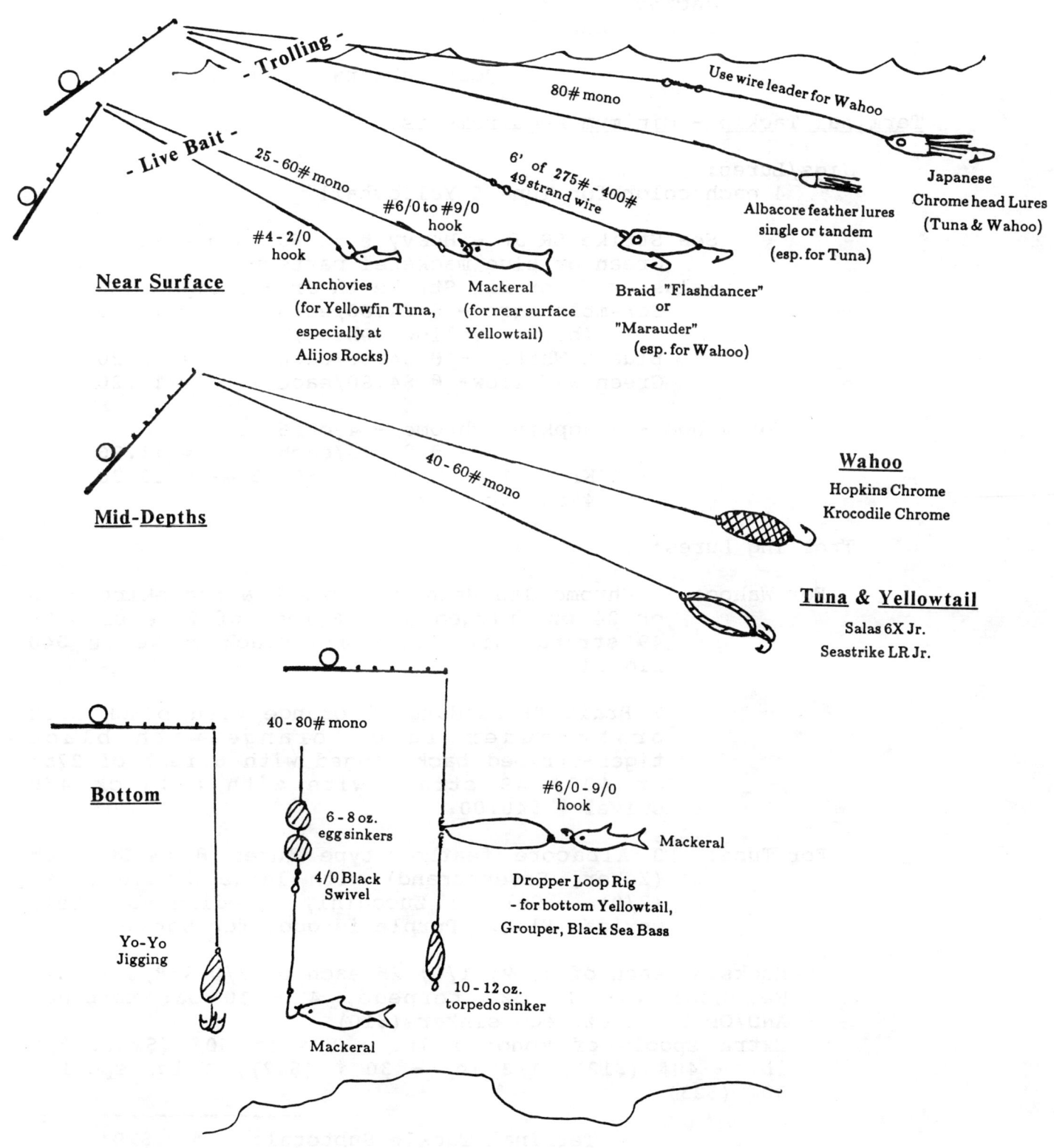

## WHAT DO I NEED? - HOW MUCH DOES IT COST?
### A 9 Day Trip

<u>Boat Costs</u>:  Boat - $1200 - 1600 depending on number of anglers
Tip  -    75 - 100
Mex. Lic.   36
Jackpot     30
Soda & Beer 20

Boat Subtotal: $1361 to 1786

<u>Terminal Tackle</u> - <u>Minimum</u> Requirements:

Jigs/Lures:
4 each color for Tuna & Yellowtail

Sea Strike LR Jr - Heavy @ $5.60/each = 22.40
Green or blue mackerel pattern
Salas 6x Jr or Sea Strike LR Jr - Heavy
Scramble Eggs - @ $4.80/each = 19.20
(brown, yellow, white)
Blue & White - @ $4.80/each = 19.20
Green & Yellow- @ $4.80/each = 19.20

For Wahoo - 2 Hopkins chrome - 4 or 6 oz.
- @ $5.98/each = 11.96
- 2 Krocodile chrome @ $6.65/ea = 13.30
4 oz. or 6 oz.

Trolling Lures:

For Wahoo: 1 Chrome Jap Head with black & red skirt - 16 or 24 oz. rigged with 6 feet of 275# or 400# 49 strand wire and a 4/0 black swivel @ $40 rigged.

1 Braid "Flashdancer" orange with black back or Marauder lure, orange with black tiger-striped back rigged with 6 feet of 275# or 400# 49 strand wire with a black 4/0 swivel @ $40.00.

For Tuna: 3 Albacore feather type lures @ $4.50 each (Zuker, Sevenstrand) with large double hooks (7/0). Colors: Zucchini, Bleeding Mackerel, Mexican Flag. Purple is good for Dorado.

Hooks: 50 each of 4, 2, 1/0; 25 each of 7/0 & 8/0 ($13)
Weights: 4 - 12 oz. torpedo, 4 - 10 oz. torpedo, AND/OR 8 - 8 oz. egg sinkers ($10)
Extra spools of Mono: 1 lb. - 50# or 60# ($22), 1/2 lb. - 40# ($12), 1/2 lb. - 30 # ($12), 1 lb. spool - 80# ($23)

Terminal Tackle Subtotal: $291

## WHAT DO I NEED? - HOW MUCH DOES IT COST?
### A 9 Day Trip

<u>Miscellaneous Gear</u>:

Yozuri bait catching rigs (4 @ $3 = $12), Shorty Boots ($23), Gloves ($3), Dikes and Dike holders ($6.50 + $4), Leather Rod belt($12), Big game rod belt (Braid or Taniguchi) rents a $1/day = $9, and Kidney harness rents at $2/day = $18, Hook sharpener - $5, Trolling Strap - $5.

----------
Misc. Gear Subtotal:      $98

<u>Rods & Reels</u> - <u>Minimum</u> Requirements:
(For alternative rods/reels - see "Detailed Rod & Reel Requirements/Recommendations")

1. For surface to mid-depth jig casting or bait fishing: A surface iron rig rated for 30 to 50# mono. Reel: A medium to high speed reel. Recommended: Penn 505HS. Rod: a 7 to 10 foot rod rated for 1 - 6+ oz. jigs. Recommended: Sabre 670 or Fenwick 1670. Rental: Penn 500 reel with 40# mono - $30. This outfit can also serve as a bottom jig yo-yo rig or a bottom, medium-heavy bait rig, using live mackerel for Yellowtail

2. Yo-yo jig fishing outfit for fishing jigs off the bottom. Reel: A medium to high speed reel with capacity for about 200 yards of 60# mono. Recommended: Penn 113HL. Rod: A medium-heavy to heavy, 5 1/2 to 6 foot rod. Recommended : Fenwick 1655XH.

3. For Bottom Bait Fishing - Yellowtail, Grouper, Pargo, Black Sea Bass:
A medium heavy 60 - 80# bottom dropper-loop bait fishing rig. Reel: Medium speed reel. Recommended: Penn 114HL Rod: A 5 1/2 to 6 medium-stiff to stiff rod. Recommended: Sabre 655XH or Fenwick 1655XH. Rental: Penn 114H with 80# mono - $38.

4. Trolling for Tuna or Wahoo or for big surface Tuna bait fishing. Reel: Heavy duty reel with capacity for 800 yards of 50# mono, loaded with 80# mono. Recommended: Penn Encl. 50SW (2-speed). Rod: Short 5 1/2 to 6 foot, moderate taper rod rated for 40 - 100# mono. Recommended: Sabre 655 XXH or Fenwick 1655 XXH. Rental: 50SW Reel & Sabre 6455XX1H rod - $105. This rig can also double as a bottom fishing outfit for giant sea bass or grouper.

5. Lightweight for mackerel bait catching with Lucky Joe or Yozuri rigs. Reel: Lightweight reel with capacity for 300 yards of 30#. Recommended: Penn 500. Rod: 6 to 7 foot medium weight rod. Recommended: Fenwick 1270 or Sabre 270 Rod. Rental: Penn 500 reel with 25# mono - $30.

## WHAT DO I NEED? - HOW MUCH DOES IT COST?
### A 9 Day Trip

<u>Rods & Reels</u> - <u>Minimum</u> Requirements continued:

    6. Optional: For Dorado & small surface Tuna:
       Heavy Saltwater Spinning Reel and Fenwick 1670, 7' rod.
       No Rental Available.

                      Rod & Reel Rental Subtotal:      $139

<u>Plus</u>:       Parking @ $2/day  -  $10
               Blown Ice - 200#  -   20
               Fish Cleaning ??

                              Plus Subtotal:       $30+

                   Total Estimated Cost:    $1,919 to $2,344

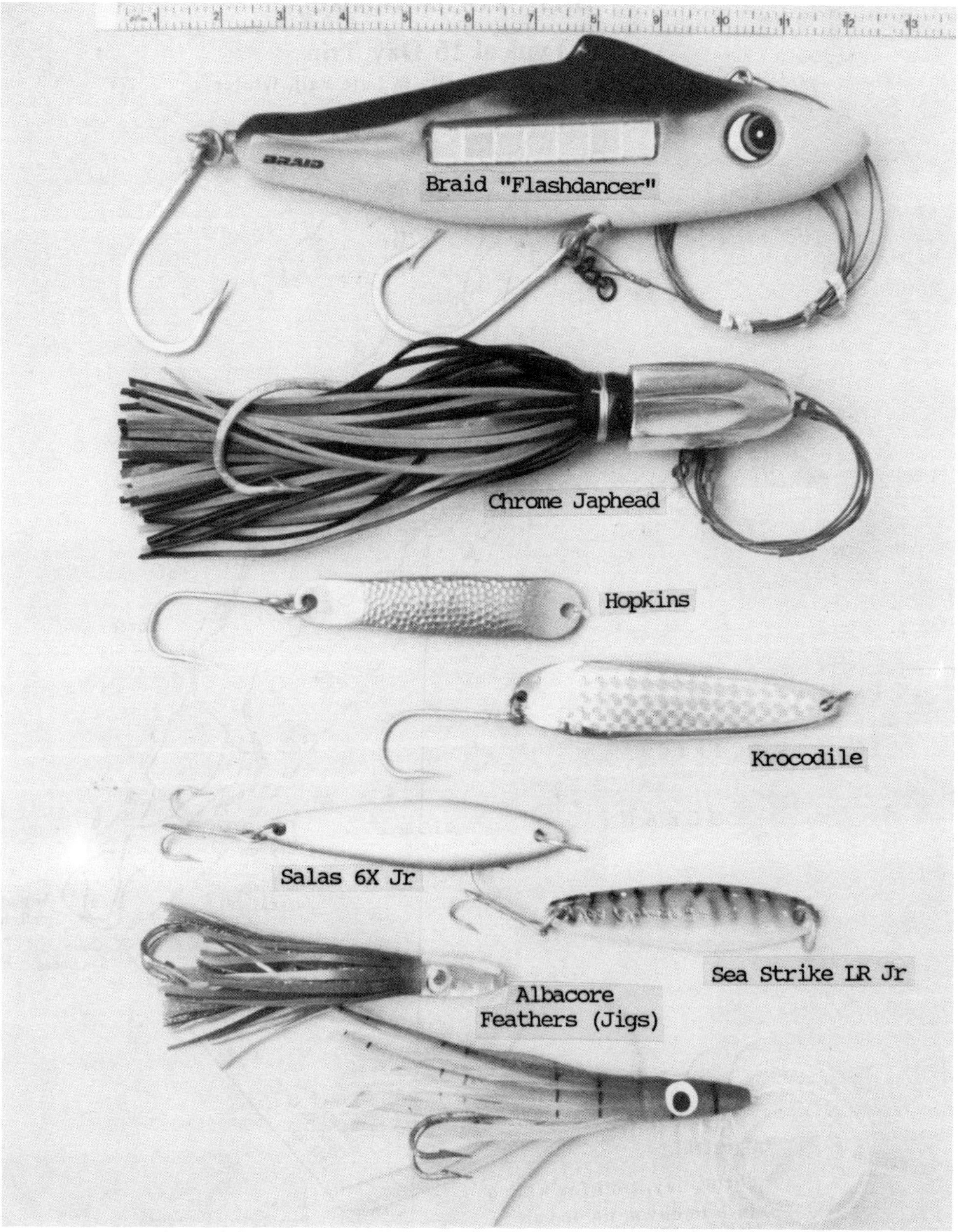

# BAJA LONG RANGE TRIPS

Braid "Flashdancer"

Chrome Japhead

Hopkins

Krocodile

Salas 6X Jr

Sea Strike LR Jr

Albacore Feathers (Jigs)

# BAJA LONG RANGE
## A Typical 16 Day Trip
### Trips Scheduled Primarily in Late Fall, Winter

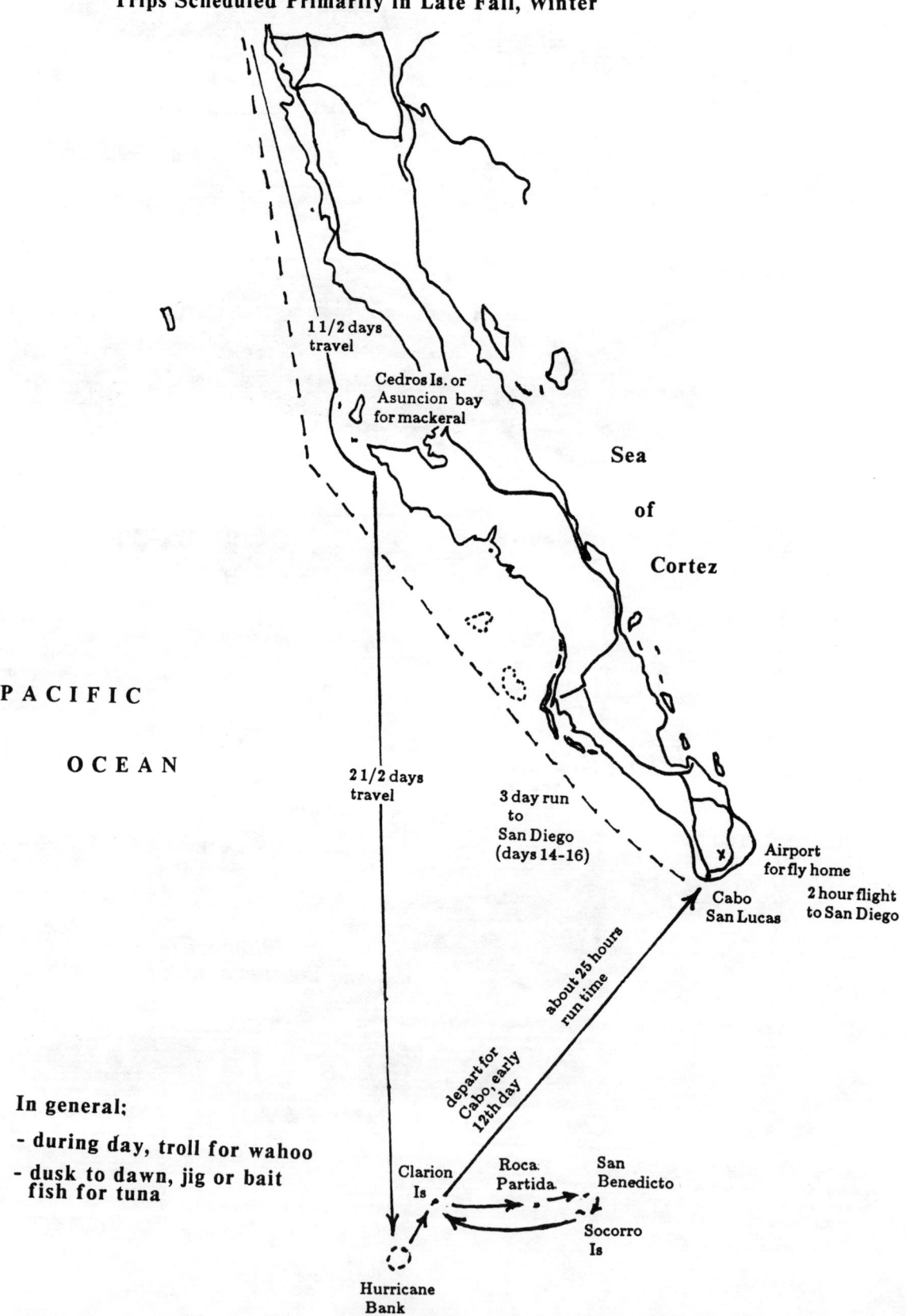

# BAJA LONG RANGE TRIPS
## 16 - 18 Day Tackle / Techniques Diagram

### Surface

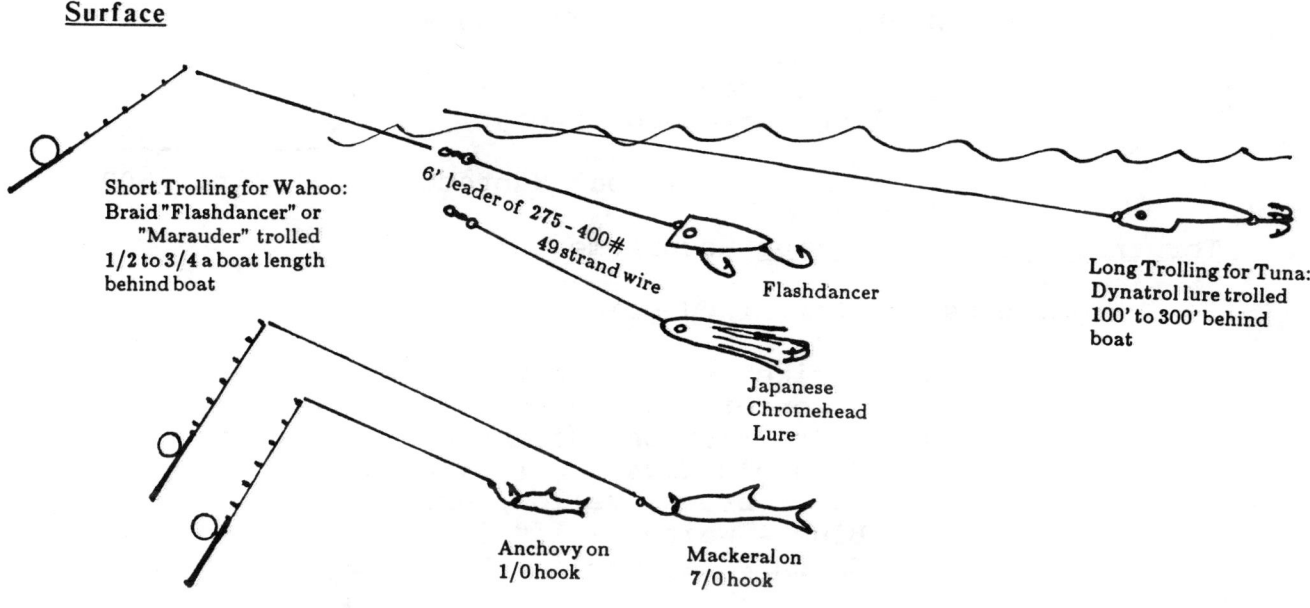

### Mid-Depth

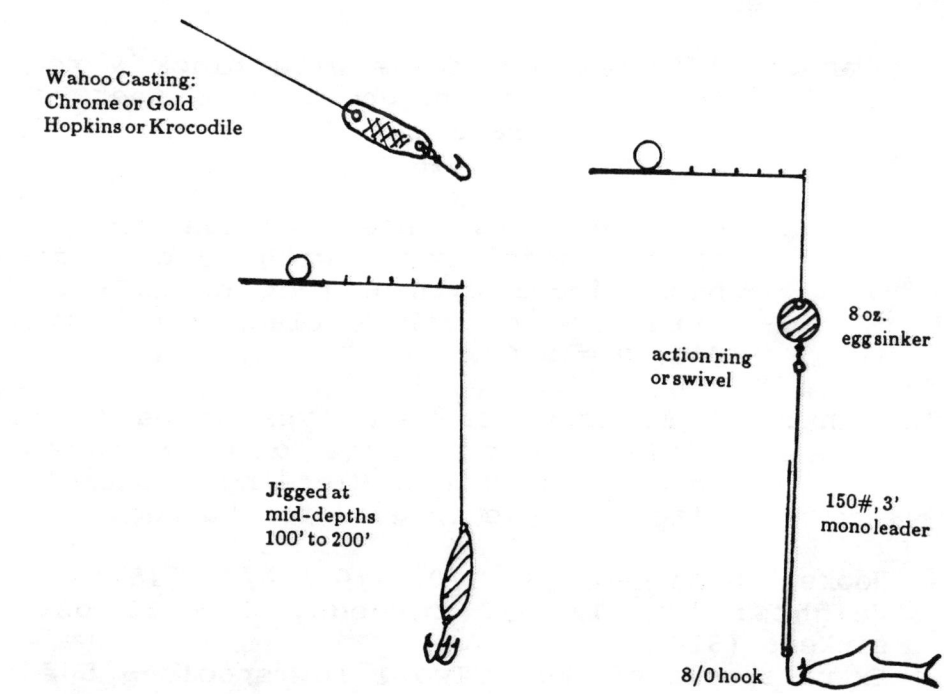

BAJA LONG RANGE TRIPS    348

**WHAT DO I NEED? - HOW MUCH DOES IT COST?**
A 16 Day Trip (13 days with fly home)

<u>Boat Costs:</u>

| | | |
|---|---|---|
| Boat | $2400 - 2700 | depending on number of anglers |
| Tip | $120 - 240 | |
| Mex. Lic. | 64 | |
| Jackpot | 50 - 75 | |
| Soda & Beer | 40 | |
| Fly Home from Cabo | 120 (LAX) | |
| (flight arranged by boat) | | |

Boat Subtotal: $2,794 to $3094

<u>Terminal Tackle</u> - <u>Minimum</u> Requirements:

Jigs/Lures - a few mixed colors:

Sea Strike LR Jr - Heavy, 2 @ $5.60/each = 11.20
  Green or blue mackerel pattern
Salas 6x Jr or Sea Strike LR Jr - Heavy
  Scramble Eggs - 2 @ $4.80/each        = 9.60
    (brown, yellow, white)
  Blue & White  - 1 @ $4.80/each        = 4.80
  Green & Yellow- 1 @ $4.80/each        = 4.80

For Wahoo - 8 Hopkins chrome or gold - 4 or 6 oz.
            - @ $5.98/each         = 11.96
          - 2 Krocodile chrome  @ $6.65/ea = 13.30
            4 oz. or 6 oz.

Trolling Lures:

For Wahoo: 2 Chrome Jap heads with black & red skirt - 16 or 24 oz. rigged with 6 feet of 275# or 400# 49 strand wire and a 4/0 black swivel, 2 @ $24.00 = $48

4 Braid "Flashdancer" orange with black back or Marauder orange with black tiger-striped back rigged with 6 feet of 275# or 400# 49 strand wire with a black 4/0 swivel, 4 @ $40.00 = $160.

For Tuna: 3 Albacore feather type lures @ $4.50 each (Zuker) with large double hooks (7/0). Colors: Zucchini, Bleeding Mackerel, Mexican Flag. Purple is good for Dorado.

Hooks: 50 each of #1, 1/0, 7/0 & 8/0 ($15)
Weights: 4 - 12 oz. torpedo, 4 - 10 oz. torpedo sinkers ($10)
Extra spools of Mono: Two 1 lb. spools - 50# or 60# @ $22 = $44 , Two 1 lb. spools - 80# @ $22 = $44

Terminal Tackle Subtotal:        $390

## WHAT DO I NEED? - HOW MUCH DOES IT COST?
### A 16 Day Trip

<u>Miscellaneous Gear</u>:

Yozuri bait catching rigs (4 @ 2.99 = $11.96), Shorty Boots ($22.75), Gloves ($2.95), Dikes and Dike holders ($6.50 + $3.39), Leather Rod belt ($12), Big game rod belt (Braid or Taniguchi) rents at $1/day = $16, Kidney harness at $2/day rental = $32, Hook Sharpener - $5, Trolling Strap - $5, Wire leader spools - 27# for Wahoo anchovies, 40# for Wahoo mackerel, Crimpers, Sleeves, Action Rings, Swivels ($30)

                                   Misc. Gear Subtotal:      $148

<u>Rods & Reels</u> - <u>Minimum</u> Requirements:
(For alternative rods/reels - see "Detailed Rod & Reel Requirements/Recommendations")

1. For surface to mid-depth jig casting or bait fishing: A surface iron rig rated for 30 to 50# mono. Reel: A medium to high speed reel. Recommended: Penn 505HS. Rod: a 7 to 10 foot rod rated for 1 - 6+ oz. jigs. Recommended: Sabre 670 or Fenwick 1670. Rental: Penn 500 rod/reel with 40# mono - $35 or Penn 4/0 (114H) reel and rod with 60# mono for $38. This outfit can also serve as a bottom jig yo-yo rig or a bottom, medium-heavy bait rig, using live mackerel for Yellowtail

2. Trolling for Tuna or Wahoo or for big surface Tuna bait fishing:
A Penn Encl. 50 sized reel like below will suffice for Wahoo trolling, however a lighter rig will do the job with less effort, more action for the angler. Rental: Penn 6/0 (114H) at $45, or Penn 50SW reel and Sabre 6455XXH rod at $105.

3. Big Tuna Bait Fishing:
For 50# - 150# Tuna: Use a Penn International 50, 50W, or 50SW, Shimano TLD 20 or 25. Rental: Penn 50SW and Sabre 6455XXH rod at $105.
For 150# and bigger Tuna: Use a Penn International 50SW (2 speed), an 80, or 80SW. Note that the 80 size Penns are considerably heavier than the 50 series and considerably more difficult to handle. Rental: Penn 50SW and Sabre 6455XXH rod at $105.

4. Optional: Tuna Long Trolling: Use a Penn Encl. 50W, or 80 with 80 - 100 # mono with Sabre 655 XXH rod or Fenwick PacificStik 1655 XXH rod. Rental: Use one of the above 50SW outfits.
Plus backup rod(s) and reel(s).

                Rod & Reel Rental Subtotal:    $290 to $353 +
                                                               backups

BAJA LONG RANGE TRIPS  350

## WHAT DO I NEED? - HOW MUCH DOES IT COST?
A 16 Day Trip

Plus:   Parking @ $2/day   -   $32
          Blown Ice - 200#    -    20
          Fish Cleaning ??

                                        Plus Subtotal:      $52

                  Total Estimated Cost: $3,674 to $4,037+

# BAJA LONG RANGE TRIPS
## Leader Setups

### Wahoo Bait

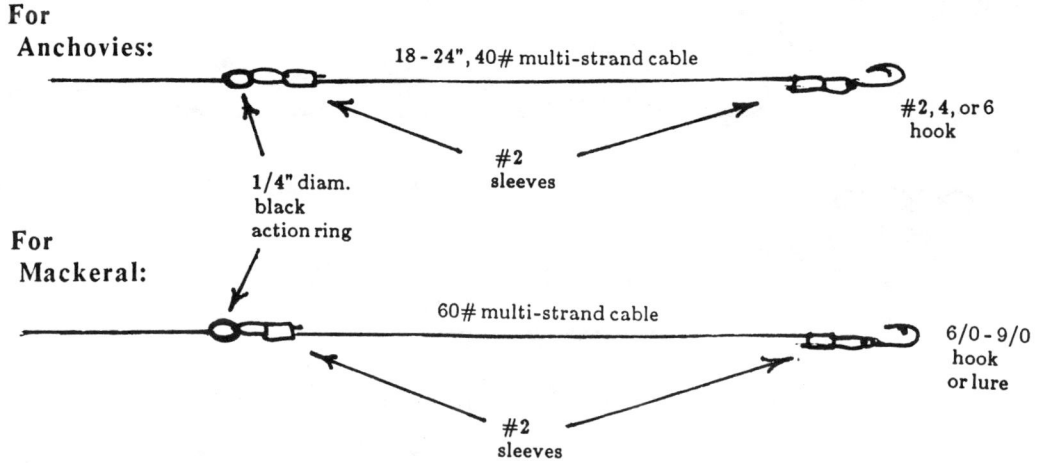

### Wahoo Trolling

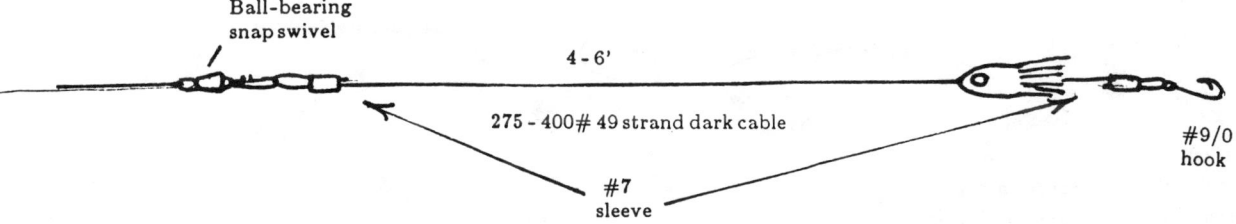

### Tuna Bait

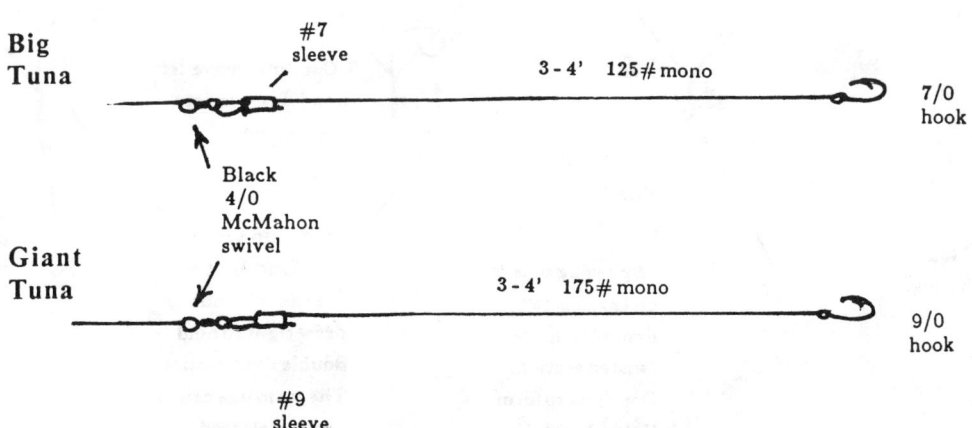

# BIG GAME MONOFILAMENT CONNECTIONS

### UNI-KNOT

**Easy to tie with either single or double line, heavy mono**

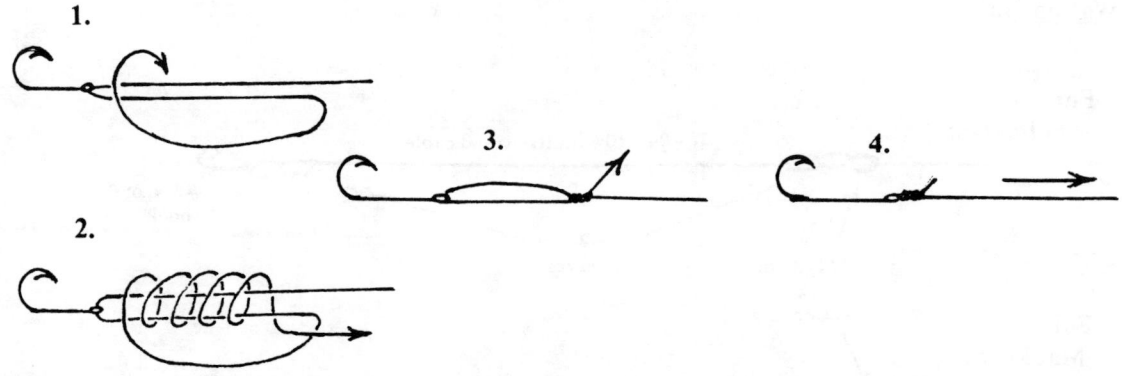

### BIMINI KNOT

**Double lines greater than 5' require a second person**

1. Pull about 15 feet of line out from the rod/reel and make 20 twists in a doubled line.

2. Step both feet through loop and extend loop around knees.

3. Outward pressure of knees in loop causes twisted section to be tight.

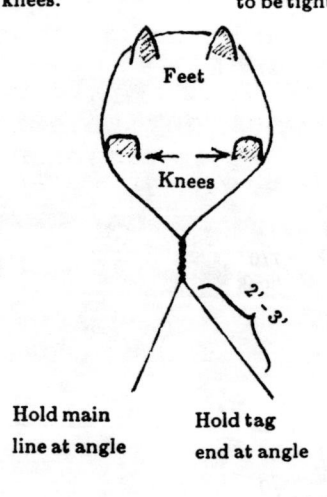

Hold main line at angle    Hold tag end at angle

Hold main line

4. Move tag end to almost a right angle to twisted section.

5. By easing tension on tag line, tag line will roll over twisted section. Continue to form tight, double thick section until get to open loop.

6. Carefully move left hand down to hold double line while

7. Forming a simple overhand knot with the tag end and draw tight to hold double twist section. The main line can now be released.

8. Take tag end and twist around loop line, moving back toward double knot. Pull tight and trim to finish knot.

**THE BIG FISH:**
300+ Lb. Yellowfin Tuna

**Where:** Almost all of the big tuna have been caught on 14 to 16 day trips to the Revillagigedo Islands chain - San Benedicto, Roca Partida, Socorro, and Clarion. Big fish are also found at Hurricane Bank and on the 23 day trips to Clipperton Island.

**When:** The big fish have been caught in the winter from December through March. At the Revillagigedo islands, the great majority of tuna are caught at night or daybreak hours. The hours between 11 PM and 4 AM are best for the big fish.

**Rig:** Reels:

Penn International 50SW 2-speed reels loaded with 80 to 100# mono. Shimano Beastmaster 50/80, 2-speed reels. Some anglers opt for the larger Penn 80 or 80W reels and comparable Shimano reels but these reels are considerably heavier and harder to handle.

Rods:

5 to 5 1/2 foot stiff-action rods with all roller guides. Roller guides should be AFTCO or Fuji. Rod blanks should be Sabre 6455 XXH or 655 XXH, Fenwick 1655 XH; Calstar Baja Boomer Series or TSS (Two Speed Stick).

Other:

Rod belt with gimbal and Kidney harness. Braid and Taniguchi are quality manufacturers. The rod belt gimbal reduces the left-to-right torquing that makes a larger reel difficult to handle.

Use a round shanked hook. Use an 8/0 or 9/0 for caballito baits. Use an 6/0 or 7/0 hook for salami mackerel. Use a 2 to 3 foot leader between the main line and the hook such as a double line Bimini twist or a 150# mono leader.

It is critical to wind the mono quite tight on the reel. With the high drag settings necessary to stop big tuna, a loosely wound line will dig into the spooled line, snag and either rip the hook loose or snap apart.

**Technique:** Mackerel & Caballito Fishing

By far the most big tuna are caught on live bait. It is critical to get the bait away from the boat. A skilled angler can lob cast a mackerel 50 feet with a

BAJA LONG RANGE TRIPS  354
The Big Fish

**Technique continued:**

Penn 50 reel. The rest of us may resort to stripping off some free line and hand pitching the mackerel. If a mackerel feels pressure he will resist it by swimming the other way. You can encourage a mackerel to swim away from the boat by tightening the line either by lifting the rod or by thumbing the freespool backwards until there is line pressure on the bait.

Lone big tuna will hold beneath a anchored boat at night. They will be 100 to 200 feet below the boat. Use a 4 to 6 oz. sliding sinker above your terminal leader or double-line Bimini twist. Go to the bow and lob the mackerel out. Once the mackerel is at depth, follow it toward the stern as it drifts back with the current and repeat. It may be hours between bites with this technique but it can produce quality fish.

At night or early dusk, flyline a mackerel or caballito at a distance from the boat, up to 150 yards.

A relatively small number of big tuna have been caught long trolling up to 150 to 300 feet behind the boat, especially with Dynatrol and Salas TNT lures.

**How to Fight a Big Tuna:**

- Preset the strike drag on your reel to about 25% of your line test. For example if you have 80# mono, set the drag at 20 to 25#.

- When a big tuna first picks up your bait while free-spooling, lower the rod tip to point at the running fish, keep a light finger on the spool to prevent overrun, and wait for a mental count of 5 or 6 seconds. Flip the drag into the "strike" position and when the line draws tight, set the hook hard twice.

- Get into your padded rod belt and kidney harness as quickly as possible. The deck hand will assist you.

**How to Fight a Big Tuna:**

- As the fish makes its initial long run, and for the few long runs that follow, JUST HOLD ON in the most comfortable position possible. This means bending the knees, and leaning back to offset the forward pull of the heavy, preset drag. To minimize the strain on the rod arm, it should be extended, not bent, reaching high on the hyphalon foregrip.

- Once the fish has paused in its run, start a steady pumping action with the hips, reeling line in when the

**Technique continued:**

rod tip lowers. Done properly there should be very little or no bending of the back or the arm holding the rod. The optimum pumping action will move the rod tip repeatedly between approximately 30° and 60°. Try to start reeling before dropping the rod tip and continuing reeling through the length of the lowering rod tip. Try to keep the action smooth and steady to minimize tearing a hook hole in the tuna's mouth. Do not take a rest, the fish will recover faster than you will.

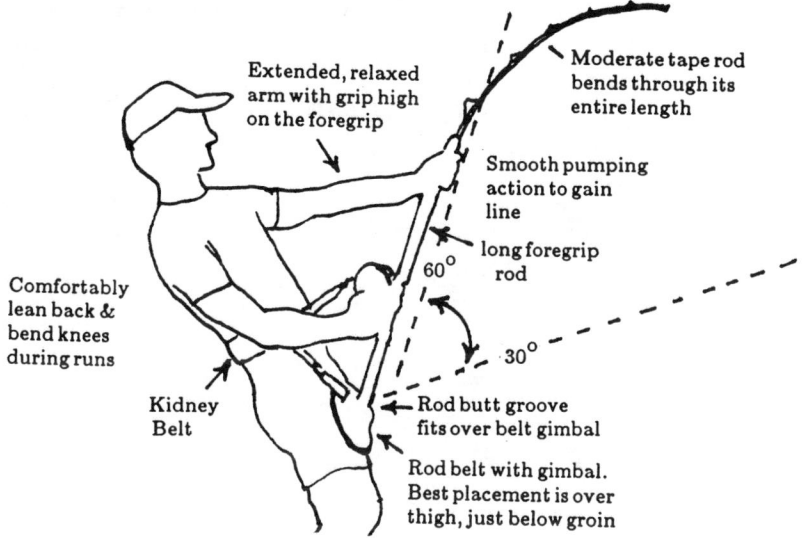

- When the fish is close to the boat and almost straight down from the rail, you will need to lower the rod tip and reach out from the rail to avoid having the line abrade on the hull or hull attachments. To do this it will probably be necessary to unbuckle the reel from the kidney harness. This is an especially critical period of the fight as you are tired, the fish is dangerously near the hull and its abrasive connections, and there is less give in the short length of mono to correct any errors in your stroking technique.

- When the fish is straight up-and-down and tired, it will turn on its side showing color and start swimming in a tight circle. If you are fortunate enough to have a 2-speed reel, now is the time to use that low gear. But first you must get the fish headed upward. Reel down on the fish so the rod tip is lowered. Now strongly pump the fish up. Near the top of the swing, push the 2-speed button to put you in low gear and start cranking. Maintain strong lift on the fish as you slowly lower the rod tip to a more comfortable position while still cranking hard on the low speed. The purpose here is to keep that fish headed upward. Continue cranking the fish up to the gaff - do not pump and retrieve. If you don't have a 2-speed the best technique is to short stroke the fish toward the surface or, if you have the nerve, to pin the mono on

## The Big Fish

**Techniques:** the foregrip with your thumb on the upward pumping motion. Short stroking is a shorter, quicker version of the pump-and-retrieve action with the rod moving up and down only 4 or 5 inches. Again the purpose is to keep the tuna's head up and moving toward the surface.

**Records:** All Tackle Record, 80# test, 388#, San Benedicto Is., 1977
On 50# mono, 361#, Socorro Is., 1981
On 130# test, 357#, Clarion Is., 1987

**Access:** See Diagram

## GENERAL TECHNIQUES & PROCEDURES - Fishing:

During daylight hours fish searching techniques are used to locate actively feeding schools of gamefish. Fish searching techniques include;

- trolling near-surface lures
- metering fish schools on sonar
- sighting feeding surface fish or floating kelp paddies

TROLLING:

During the day, trolling is most frequently used to locate fish. Trolling teams of 4 or 5 fishermen are set up and take turns at the stern, rotating either when a fish is caught or after a reasonable length of time (30 minutes).

The best type of trolling lure varies by the type of fish sought. Albacore feathers work well on tuna in the standard Zucchini, Mexican Flag, and Bleeding Mackerel colors. These are best trolled approximately 3 to 4+ wakes behind the boat. The same feathers with a purple skirt and trolled off an outside corner will increase your chances of catching a Dorado. The best lures for Wahoo are Japanese Chromehead lures, Braid "Flashdancer", or Marauder. Wahoo lures are best trolled very close to the boat, typically 1/2 to 2/3rds the boat's length off the stern. See section describing individual fish species for more details.

HOOKUP:

If a fish is hooked on the troll, someone yells out "hookup" loud enough for the captain to hear and cut the engines bringing the boat to a "sliding" stop. The trollers not hooked up are expected to retrieve and rack their rigs quickly to make way for the bait and jig fishermen. However, an effective trolling technique when another troller gets a hit is to put your reel in freespool, let line stream out for 2 or 3 seconds, and then rapidly reel in your lure. This will often get hits from nearby fish.

JIG CASTING:

Jig casters very quickly cast out their iron jigs while the boat is still sliding to a stop. The casts are made vertically to the boat direction and the boats forward movement brings the lures behind the boat. Timing is sensitive on these firsts casts as the "best" cast depends on several factors such as, 1) the first cast in usually has the best chance of a strike, 2) if you cast while the boat is still rapidly moving forward you may end up with too much line out when the boat finally stops, 3) some skippers will not let you cast until they give the OK.

The best general technique is to freespool and let your jig sink until it is about a 45 angle down from the surface. Retrieving

## JIG CASTING continued

fast from this angle is effective for either Wahoo or Yellowfin Tuna. While free-spooling, pay close attention to the action of the line/lure as jigs are often hit on the fall. Another effective action, is to stop mid-way on the retrieve, let the lure sink, than return to the rapid retrieve.

Once the boat has stopped, the angler can either continue to cast jigs or go to bait. Stick to jig casting until it is obvious that the fish school has been drawn close enough to the boat for the bait fishermen to start getting hookups.

## BAIT:

Schooled game fish will often follow a troll-hooked fish up to the boat. This often happens with both Albacore and Dorado. Both species are typically not boat shy and bait that is only a short 10 to 20 yards from the boat can be picked up. Large Dorado schools will often follow a troll-hooked fish up the a boat and simply stay there within feet of the boat while hundreds of them are caught on anchovies and mono to 30 or 40 lb. test. Yellowfin Tuna and Yellowtail are often more cautious and hold more distant from a boat. Often the biggest obstacle to success is getting the anchovy far enough away from the boat. Unsophisticated methods such as coiling out some free line and pitching the anchovy out with an overhand toss can be the difference between success and failure. Big Tuna at the Alijos Rocks and at nearer shore hotspots such as Uncle Sam Bank, Thetis Bank, etc. are very partial to anchovies, and wont take a mackerel.

While trolling, if the captain meters a big school of fish below the surface, he will stop the boat over the school and get the deck hands to lay out a chum line. The deck hand starts to regularly toss live anchovies over the stern. Often the below surface school will follow this chum line to the surface and to the boat. This is when live bait fishing really turns on.

Mackerel are easier to fish than anchovies since they can carry a decent size hook and their weight makes distance casting easy. The Tuna at the the Revillegegiddo Islands will take mackerel and in other more northern spots, mackerel are the preferred bait for Yellowtail. Mackerel typically are in limited supply and as such are doled out by the crew only when the signs indicate a good bite in the making. The single most important point in mackerel fishing is to let the fish take time to swallow the bait.

Fishing with mackerel can be easier since the mackerels weight makes distance casting much easier.

## PERSONAL ITEMS:

Bring all of your own toiletries. Don't forget to bring towels

## GENERAL PROCEDURES - Housekeeping, etc.

- they are NOT supplied. Don't forget to bring plenty of sunscreen. Be careful about any pills that you bring. They need to be specifically identified as legal items. Long Range fishing boats are boarded by Mexican and American Coast Guard boats looking for illegal drugs.

FISH CARE:

Fish are put in a below deck hold shortly after being caught where a cooled, concentrated, brine solution is continually sprayed over, and pumped through them keeping the temperature at a chilly $14^{\circ}$. As the boat nears the landing, the deckhands pile the fish in the stern. At the landing beer and pop fees and the tip are collected and the fishermen take their gear off the boat. The crew than loads the fish into push carts, which pairs of passengers push up the docks. The fish are again unloaded in a pile on the concrete at the foot of the docks and other anglers wearing gloves or using hay hooks, sort the fish into individual piles matching the tag on the gill plate to number plates affixed to the concrete walkway. Once the fish are sorted, the call for the jackpot, 2nd place, and 3rd place fish is made. Troll caught fish are NOT eligible for the jackpot. The jackpot money is split 50% to the largest fish, 25% to 2nd place, and 25% to 3rd place. The anglers are now on their own to handle their fish. Right next to where the fish are unloaded will be workers for a canning company that will offer the following services;

1. Trade you 1 can (6 1/2 oz.) of tuna for 2 lbs. of only Yellowfin Tuna, Bluefin Tuna, or Albacore.

2. Charge for cleaning, packing, and shipping (if desired) of part or all of your catch.

For those fish you decide to clean yourself, you will somehow need to get them home in reasonable condition. The solutions, of course, vary depending on the number of fish. For the large quantities caught on many trips, a shell covered, pickup truck is needed. Line the bed with a heavy plastic sheet. There is an ice vendor within steps of where the fish are unloaded. 200# to 400# of blown ice will usually suffice to cover your catch. Fold the heavy plastic cover over the fish and ice to retain the cold and you are on your way. I hope you have someone back home to help you clean/fillet those fish!

# BAJA LONG RANGE SPORTFISHING LANDINGS
## San Diego, California

| Fisherman's Landing | H & M Landing | Point Loma Sportfishing | Lee Palm's Sportfishing |
|---|---|---|---|
| (619) 222-0391 | (619) 222-1144 | (619) 223-1627 | (619) 224-3857 |
| Rentals: (619) 226-8030 | | | |
| Polaris Supreme | Spirit of Adventure | American Angler | Red Rooster III |
| Royal Star | Deluxe | Point Loma | |
| Searcher | | Vagabond | |
| Qualifier 105 | | | |
| Qualifier 120 Excel | | | |

A small parking lot fronts the landings. It costs $2/day when validated by a long range boat. The lot is almost always full. Arrive early to secure parking.

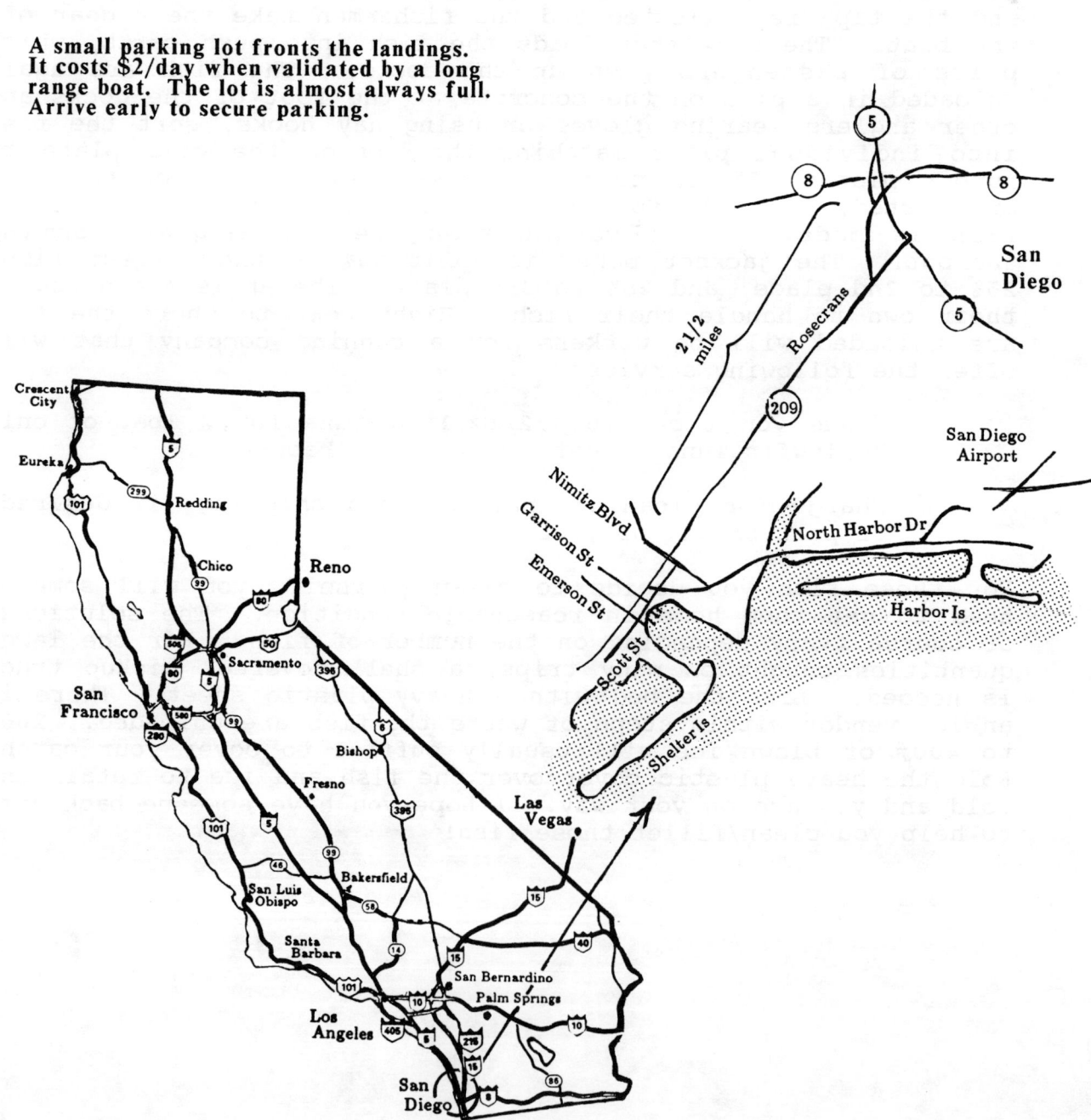

## Rod & Reel Requirements

**All Long Range Trips**

Reel: In General: Ideal trolling rods differ by the area fished. Adequate reels range from 6/0 size to very large Penn International 80W reels. The easiest way might be to use the biggest reels recommended, however these heavier reels are more expensive, difficult to handle, and less sporting on the smaller fish. In general, these trolling rigs may also be used for bait fishing with mackerel, sardines, or cabalitto for the bigger fish. See below for recommendations and alternatives.

For 3 - 5 day trips, you need to be equipped for Big Eye Tuna to 120 lbs., a 6/0 Penn Senator II 114HL or 114HLW reel will suffice.
Alternatives: Daiwa 600H, 900H

For a 7-10 day trip to Alijos, etc.; you need to be equipped for Yellowfin Tuna to 150+ lbs. A Penn International 50 or 50S size reel will suffice.
Alternatives: Shimano TBM 30/50, TTS 50, TTS 50W

For a 14 - 16, or 23 day trip for normal trolling activity you need to be equipped for Wahoo to 100# and an occasional Tuna rarely to 250+ lbs. A Penn International 50W or 50SW will suffice.
Alternatives: Shimano TTS 50W, TBM 50/80, FinNor 6/0 Wide

For a 14 - 16, or 23 day trip a Penn International 80, 80S, 80W, or 80SW is recommended for tuna long trolling.
Alternatives: FinNor 9/0; Shimano 80/130

Rod: In General: A medium-heavy to heavy action rod, 5 1/2' to 6' long, with roller stripper guide and roller-tip guide, rated for approximately 80 to 130 lb. line.
Recommended: Sabre 655XXH
Alternatives: Sabre 665XH, 6455XXH, Fenwick 1655XH, 1655XXH; Custom rods made with Sabre blanks 6450XXH, 6455XXH, 6460XH, 6460XXH, 655XH, 655XXH, 660XH; Calstar - Baja Boomer series or TSS (Two Speed Stick) series. Both Penn and Shimano have heavy duty rods in this category.

BAJA LONG RANGE TRIPS
Rod & Reel Requirements

## GIANT (> 150#) TUNA BAIT FISHING:
14, 16, & 23 Day Trips

This rig is for the really big fish caught on 14 - 16 day and 23 day trips. The majority of these fish are caught at night, with the boat at anchor.

Reel: In General: A heavy duty reel with capacity of approximately 600 yards of 80# mono (800 yards of 50#). The reel must have a proven, very heavy duty drag system to withstand blistering runs of giant tuna under heavy drag conditions - 25# - 40# settings. A 2-speed reel is highly recommended. These reels come with a higher speed gear ratio in the 3/1 to 4.1/1 range and a low speed, power gear at 1.2/1 to 1.4/1.
Recommended: Penn International 50SW (2-speed) or 50W
Alternatives: Penn 80, 80W, FinNor, Shimano TBS 50/80, TBS 80/130.

Rod: In General: A one piece, moderate taper rod, with a large diameter butt measuring 5' to 5 1/2' long. Should have all roller guides and an extend (14" - 18") foregrip above the reel seat to facilitate an extended arm grip (see diagram). Should be rated for approximately 80 to 130# line.
Recommended: Sabre 6455 XXH
Alternatives: Sabre 655XXH, 6450XXH, 6455XXH; Fenwick 1655 XXH; custom rods made with CalStar blanks - Baja Boomer or TSS (Two Speed Sticks) series. Both Penn and Shimano also have heavy duty rods in this category. Also comparable Calstar and Kunnan rods.

## BIG (50# TO 150#) TUNA BAIT FISHING:
All Long Range Trips

The prepared (lucky) long range angler will want to ALWAYS have a big tuna bait outfit already rigged and close at hand. On the mid-range, 7-10 day trips it will have a large anchovy hook (1/0 - 2/0) tied on ready for Yellowfin Tuna. On the 3-5 day, or 14-16 day trips it will have a mackerel sized hook (6/0 - 9/0) ready for Bigeye Tuna or Yellowfin Tuna. This rig can also be used as a nighttime setup for catching the larger scad (salami) mackerel on 16 - 18 day trips.

Reel: In General: A reel with approx. 400 yds. of 50# mono or greater and with a single moderate gear speed reel is sufficient.
Recommended: Penn Intl. 50 or 50S with 60# mono, Penn Intl. 50W or 50SW with 80# mono.
Alternatives: Daiwa 600H; Penn 114HL, Penn International 30W.

**BIG (50# TO 150#) TUNA BAIT FISHING continued:**

- Rod: In General: A one piece, moderate taper rod, 5 1/2 to 6 1/2 feet long, with line class rated in the 40# to 80# range. Stripper and roller guides are not a necessity. Note that the heavier rods recommended for giant tuna can also be used for these smaller fish.
Recommended: Sabre 655XH
Alternatives: 655XH, Sabre blanks 660XH, 6455XH, 655XH; Fenwick 1655XH; Comparable Calstar and Kunnan rods.

**JIG CASTING - WAHOO, SMALLER TUNA, YELLOWTAIL**
All Long Range Trips

- Reel: In General: A medium weight, high speed retrieve reel, with a light casting action for maximum distance. The gear ratio should be approximately 4:1 or more. Acceptable reel capacity varies from 300 yards of 30# (TLD 15) to 400+ yds. of 40# mono. Note that his rig can alternate as a nighttime bait catching rig.
Recommended: Penn Master Mariner 349H
Alternatives: Newell G338F, G440F, G447F; Penn 505HS, 113HL with Newell "Yellowtail Special" conversion; Shimano TLD 15; Daiwa 400H, 350H.
- Rod: In General: A 7' or longer rod with an action tip and stiff backbone for casting distance, rated for 1 to 6 oz. jigs, and with the beef to bring in 70#+ fish. The line class should be in the 20 to 50# range. The longer rods (8'to 10') can cast longer but are more difficult to handle.
Recommended: Fenwick 1670C or Sabre CA 6670C
Alternatives: Fenwick 1670C, 1665HC; Sabre 670C, Sabre blanks 610, 6465; Longer Rods (> 7') Sabre 670-8, 670-9; Calstar T90 (9') blanks and comparable Kunnan rods.

**SURFACE BAIT FOR < 60# FISH (TUNA, YELLOWTAIL, WAHOO, DORADO):**
All Long Range Trips

This rig is for fishing anchovies and small mackerel on or near the surface.
- Reel: In General: Must have excellent freespool that allows an anchovy to take line out freely. Will need an aluminum or graphite spool with a capacity of 300 yds. of 40# mono or greater.
Recommended: Shimano TLD 20
Alternatives: Newell G334F; Penn Intl. 30W, 113HL with Newell "Yellowtail Special" conversion, Penn 112H converted to a Newell "Tuna Special" reel.

BAJA LONG RANGE TRIPS
Rod & Reel Requirements

SURFACE BAIT FOR < 60# FISH (TUNA, YELLOWTAIL, WAHOO, DORADO) continued:

- Rod: In General: Should have light sensitive tip for anchovy lobbing and control, and should have a moderate stiff base for handling 60# fish. Generally 6 1/2 to 7 feet long. Rated for 20# to 50# mono.
  Recommended: Fenwick 1865
  Alternatives: Sabre 865, 865XH; Fenwick 789, 1870; Comparable Calstar and Kunnan rods.

Note that a large, saltwater spinning outfit is excellent for catching school Dorados on bait. Dorado are especially prevalent on fall 7-10 Day trips.

BOTTOM JIG FISHING - ESPECIALLY YELLOWTAIL:
Especially for 3-5 Day & 7-10 Day Trips
(Also some Pargo, Amberjack on longer trips)

A middle-of-the-line rod and reel will suit both bottom jigging and surface jig casting. A 6 1/2 or 7 foot rod with a flexible tip and rated for up to 50 or 60# mono will cast well but still be short enough and have the backbone to move Yellowtail off the bottom however a shorter 5 1/2 to 6 foot rod will make the work much easier. A moderately high speed reel with 40# to 60# mono can work for both casting and bottom jigging.

- Reel: In General: Same type of reel as Jig casting with a high speed gear ratio but requiring less line capacity. Typical capacity 370 yards of 30# mono but load with 40# or greater test mono.
  Recommended: Daiwa 350H
  Alternatives: Penn 113HL with Newell "Yellowtail Special" conversion, 505HS; Newell P440F; Daiwa 400H

- Rod: In General: You want a stiffer rod than casting for moving the bottom brutes on up. Rated for 30 to 80# mono, 2 - 8 oz. lures.
  Recommended: Fenwick 1665XHC
  Alternatives: Sabre blanks 655XH, 655H, 665XH, 660XH; Comparable Calstar and Kunnan rods.

## BOTTOM BAIT - YELLOWTAIL, GROUPER, BLACK SEA BASS, ETC.
Especially for 3-5 Day & 7-10 Day Trips

Usually a trolling rig will suffice for bottom fishing also. The trolling rod has the stiffness required, and the trolling reel is usually loaded with around 80# mono which works well fishing bottom baits. Between being anchored for bottom fishing and your turn to troll there is plenty of time to change terminal rigging.

Reel: In General: Doesn't require large capacities, but needs to be sturdy and have a low gear ratio for handling heavy terminal weights, and cranking in heavy, stubborn bottom dwellers.
Recommended: Penn 114HL (6/0)
Alternatives: 113HL

Rod: In General: You want a shorter, stiffer rod than with bait or jig casting for some of these hefty fish.
Recommended: Fenwick 1655XHC
Alternatives: Fenwick 1655XHC, Sabre blanks 655XH, 655; Comparable Calstar and Kunnan rods.


## BAIT CATCHING, LIGHT SPORT (Optional):
All Long Range Trips

Reel: In General: A reel with capacity for about 300 yards of 30# mono and a good freespool.
Recommended: Penn 500M
Alternatives: Penn 500SL, 500M (Newell Replacement Reels 30# &40#), Squidder 140L; Newell G229F; Daiwa 30H

Rod: In General: A light-weight, medium-length (6 1/2 to 7 1/2') rod rated for 15 to 40 lb. mono.
Recommended: Fenwick 1270
Alternatives: Fenwick 1865, 1870; Sabre 270, 865, 870

BAJA SEA OF CORTEZ FISHING

**BAJA SEA OF CORTEZ FISHING:**

The Baja long range fishing information is organized as follows;

This section outlines basic travel and fishing information for the eastern shore, Sea of Cortez side of the Mexican Baja Peninsula.

= area described in this section

1. Basic Requirements for Baja Travel &
   Inshore Fishing ................................. Pg 367

2. Travel Planning Map ........................... Pg 373
   - travel distances, weather, best fishing seasons.

3. Access Map ..................................... Pg 374
   - ramps, pangas, major hotels, etc.

4. Major Game Fish listing ....................... Pg 376

   Fishing Guide:

   The Baja Catch
   An Inshore Fishing Manual for Baja Calif.
   by Neil Kelly & Gene Kira
   Apples & Oranges
   Valley Center, Calif.

**TRAVEL GUIDE:**

   The Magnificant Peninsula
   by Jack Williams
   P.O. Box 203
   Sausalito, CA 94966

**Basic Requirements for Baja Travel:**

PAPERWORK:

The following documentation is required, but for the motorist enforcement is very lax;

Proof of Citizenship:

If you are arriving in Mexico from other than the U.S. or Canada, you will need a valid Passport for identification. If you are arriving from the U.S. or Canada, your birth certificate or a certified copy will suffice.

Tourist Card

If you intend to stay over 72 hours or travel below Ensenada, you will need a Tourist Card. This is a 2-part form available from the following listed Mexico travel clubs, AAA, the airlines serving Baja, and from many travel agencies.

Complete this form and be prepared to submit 1 copy when entering Mexico and 1 copy when leaving. If driving south on Mex 1, there is a checkpoint about 10 miles south of Ensenada at Maneadero. If <u>open</u>, stop at this small building just off Mex 1 on the way down and on the way up. In reality, the checkpoint is irregularly open and very few tourists stop on the way back to turn in their pink copy.

Insurance

Motor Vehicle insurance is available from shops at the border, at San Ysidro or from one of the listed Mexico travel clubs at a discount. Insurance is available by the day, week, year, etc. If you plan on traveling in Baja for more than 15 days over a 12 month period, an annual policy will cost less.

You also need insurance for your trailer
    AND
your boat while its on the trailer or on your vehicle
    AND
your boat when its in the water.

Agencies specializing in Mexican Auto/Trailer/Boat Insurance:
(Note that significant discounts are possible by joining one of the Baja Travel Clubs listed below)

## Basic Requirements

**PAPERWORK** continued:

    Instant Mexico Auto Insurance
    (Auto, Boat, Fishing Lic., Boat Lic.)
    223 Via de San Ysidro
    San Ysidro, CA 92073
    Calif: 800-345-4701
    Other: 800-638-0999
    619-428-4714

    Lewis & Lewis Ins. Agency (Auto & Boat)
    8929 Wilshire Blvd
    Suite 220
    Beverly Hills, CA 90211
    213-657-1112
    213-655-6830

    International Gateway (Auto, Boat, Boat Lic., Fishing Lic.)
    3450 Bonita Rd., #103
    Chula Vista, CA
    Calif: 800-423-2646
    619-422-3022

    Government of Mexico, Dept. of Fisheries
    1138 India Ave., Suite 125
    San Diego, CA 92101-3516
    619-233-6956 or 619-233-4324

Only in-the-water hull insurance can be covered by United States insurance. U.S. insurance for your vehicle and trailer is not honored in Mexico. You must purchase Mexican insurance.

Insurance for a $10,000 Kelly Blue Book valued vehicle for 7 days at $6.73/day + $2 document fee + 15% Tax = $56.48 (1990). There are large discounts for longer term policies - 70% for an annual policy.

Car Permits are NOT required in Baja. However, if you plan on taking your car across the gulf on a ferry, you will need a permit. They are available from Mexican insurance companies or the Mexican Department of Tourism.

Fishing licenses are required for anglers 12 years or older. Boating permits are required for any boat even remotely tied to fishing. Both can be obtained from the Mexican Department of Fisheries, San Diego, Calif., 619-233-6956 or 619-233-4324 and also from the Instant Mexican Auto Insurance address listed above. Selected Southern California and Arizona tackle shops also have these forms - ask the person at the above number for the store nearest you. Many hotel charter boats include licenses in their package price.

## Basic Requirements

PAPERWORK continued:

Minors:

If you are traveling with minor(s) and both parents are not in attendance, you need a notarized "Permission for a minor child to travel in Mexico" form available from the Mexican Department of Tourism located in major cities - L.A., San Diego, San Francisco.

Pets (dogs & cats) are usually no problem but a current rabies certificate may be helpful and the cautious traveler will want to obtain a certificate of health from the Mexican Consulate.

TRAVEL & LODGING:

Almost any vehicle is appropriate for travel to Baja. However you will be restricted from traveling certain areas and roads depending on what you are driving. From most limited to unlimited, at the bottom is the large RV that is restricted to the limited paved roads and RV parks to the heavy duty 4-wheel drive vehicles that can reach remote beaches. Generally a sturdy pickup truck will suffice for almost all areas.

Fuel supply can be irregular, especially the availability of unleaded "NOVA" gas. Don't let your fuel supply drop below the half full level. The most reliable locations for gas supplies are Ensenada, San Quintin, Guerro Negro, Santa Rosalia, Loreto and La Paz. Be prepared for the long, 220 mile stretch between El Rosario and Guerro Negro.

For superior (Baja standards) lodging alternatives see the Baja Access map.

Maps: Excellent Baja California road maps are produced by the Automobile Club of Southern California (AAA) and USA Maps in La Verne, Calif at 213-593-3601

FOOD & DRINK:

Stay with bottled liquids (water, soda, or beer). Avoid fresh fruits and uncooked vegetables. Some people have no problem, most are susceptible to Montezuma's revenge.

LANGUAGE:

English is understood at all major hotels and by many Mexicans in the major cities. Elsewhere take along and use;

Easy Spanish by Shirley Herd
S. Deal & Associates
1629 Guizot St.; San Diego, CA 92107

BAJA SEA OF CORTEZ FISHING
Basic Requirements

FISHING:

Rigs:

The following is a minimum tackle recommendation for mid-sized inshore fish species of the Sea of Cortez.

1. Spinning Outfit:

   - 7 to 8 foot medium to light-heavy weight spinning rod with a saltwater spinning rod with capacity for 150+ yards of 25# mono. Reel examples: Penn 550 SS, Shimano 4500, Daiwa ST7070.

2. Conventional Casting Outfit:

   - 6 1/2 to 7 1/2 foot rot rated for 12-30# mono and able to cast 3/8 oz. to 3/4 oz. lures. Example: Sabre 2710

   - Conventional reel with capacity for 300-400 yards of 20-30# mono. Example: Penn 500, Jigmaster; Daiwa 50H, etc.

Lures: Trolling: 4 1/2 to 6" jointed Rebel and Rapala plugs. Bring replacement treble hooks and split rings for these plugs. Troll and cast these plugs off a 6-12" wire leader.

Casting: Leadhead plastics - Scampi, Worm King, Shakin Shad, Scrounger. Colors: Chartreuse, Rootbeer, Red-Flaked. Spoons, 1-3 oz size. Krocodile, Kastmaster, Hopkins.

Jigging: Salas 6X Jr, Salas 6X. Colors: Blue & White, Yellow & Green, Scrambled Eggs. Sea Strike LR Jr. Colors: Green Mackerel, Blue Mackerel.

Technique:

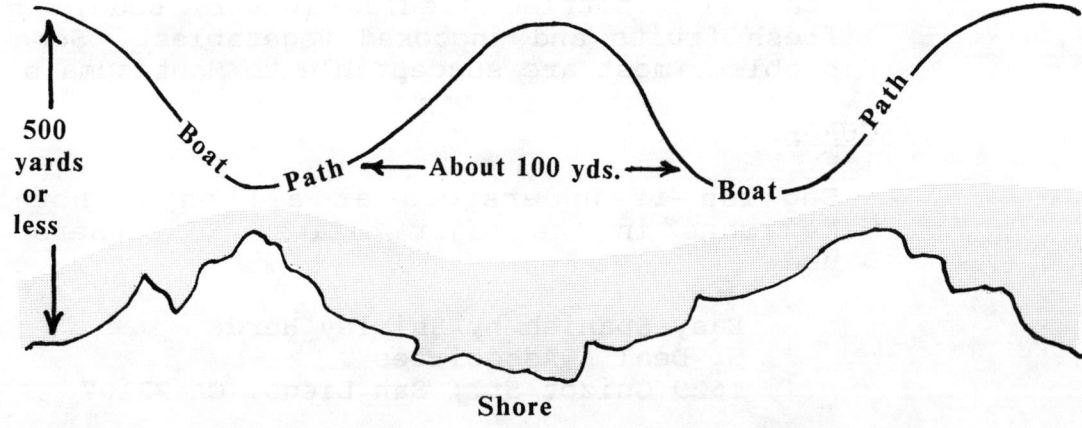

## Basic Requirements

The number 1 method of fishing access is beach launching. It is very commonly used in Baja using lightweight aluminum or inflatable boats. The surf conditions along most of the Sea of Cortez coast is not a deterrent to easy launching and landing.

Larger trailered boats can be launched at the few developed launch ramps. See Access Map for launch ramps.

Many of the popular fishing areas have panga fleets that are available with guide for a reasonable charge. Cruisers are available through major hotels - see separate recommended lodging list.

MISC: Polarized Glasses, Sun Screen, Head Cover, Drinking Water, an air compressor that works out of the cigarette lighter, 1 or more spare tires, Bug repellant, enough cash (not all 20 dollar bills) to pay for pangas, bait, beer, etc. Major hotels take credit cards.

## TRAVEL CLUBS:

Vagabundos del Mar
P.O. Box 824
Isleton, Calif. 95641
707-374-5511

Mexico West Travel Club
3450 Bonita Road
Suite 107
Chula Vista, CA
619-585-3033

Baja Fun Club
223 Via de San Ysidro
San Ysidro, CA 92073
(Instant Mexico Insurance Office Bldg.)
619-690-1505
800-638-0999 (outside Calif.)
800-345-4701 (Calif.)

## TRAVEL AGENCIES SPECIALIZING IN BAJA TRAVEL:

Fishing International
P.O. Box 2132
Santa Rosa, CA 90211
800-950-4242

BAJA SEA OF CORTEZ FISHING  372
Basic Requirements

Travel Agencies Specializing in Baja Travel continued:

>Big Game Fishing
>77 Jack London Square
>Oakland, CA 94607
>Calif. 415-834-2555
>800-458-2879

>Baja Safari
>P.O. Box 1827
>Monterey, CA 93942
>800-248-9900 or 408-375-2252

>Baja Fishing Adventures
>2221 Palo Verde Ave., Suite D
>Long Beach, CA 90815
>213-594-9441
>800-451-6997 (CA only), 800-458-3688 (USA)

>Squidco Sportfishing International
>San Diego
>800-227-4387 or 619-233-5201

# BAJA - SEA OF CORTEZ
## Fishing and Weather Calendar

Mileages and hours are accumulated totals starting from the U.S. border south on Highway 1. Mileages in parentheses () indicate mileages and hours between major points. Mileages indicated as "side trips" are for roads connecting with Highway 1. Do NOT drive at night.

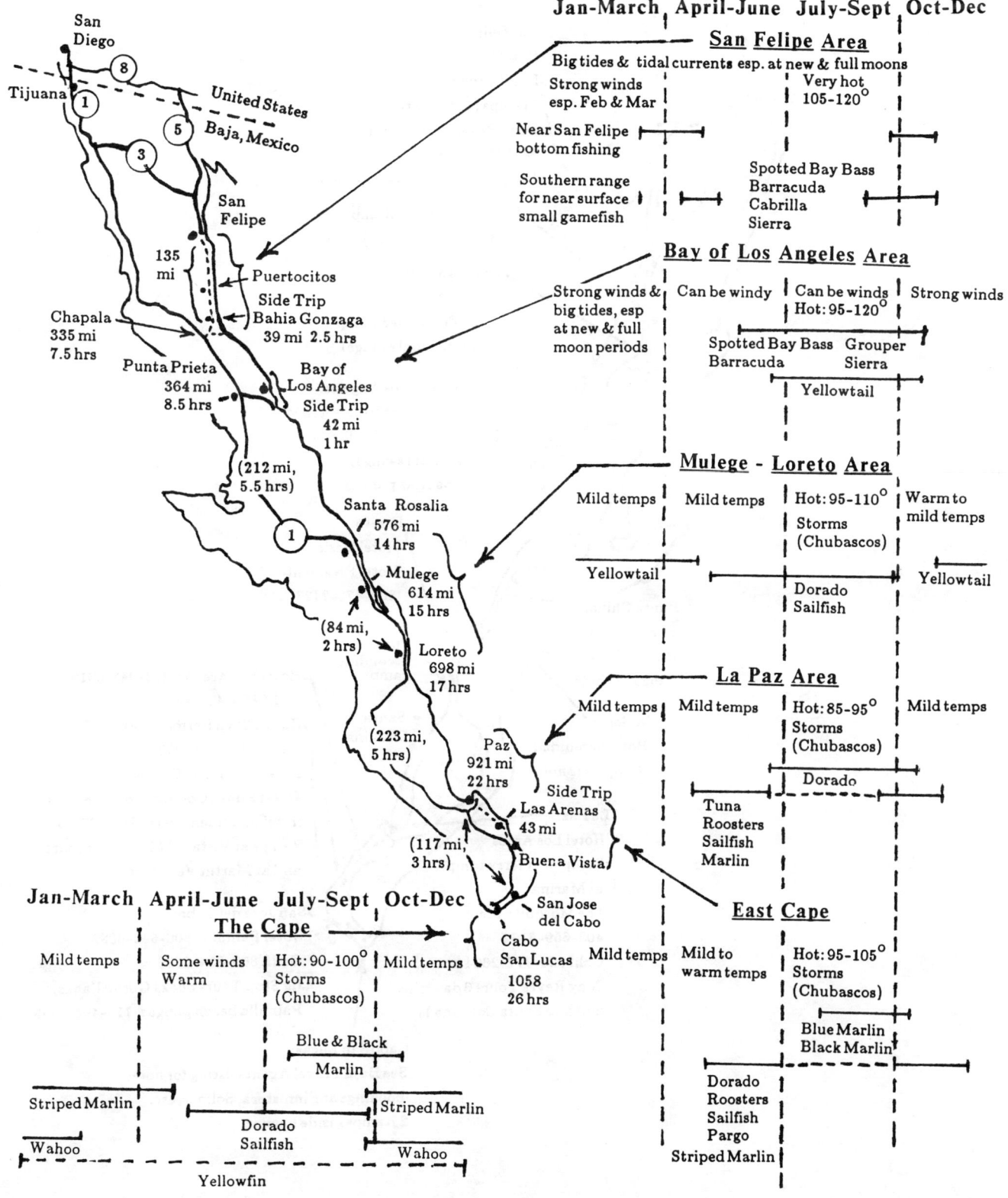

## SEA OF CORTEZ ACCESS

**Note that the limited access provided by the following semi-civilized launch ramps and commercial interests can be greatly expanded by the use of a beach launched inflatable or small aluminum boat**

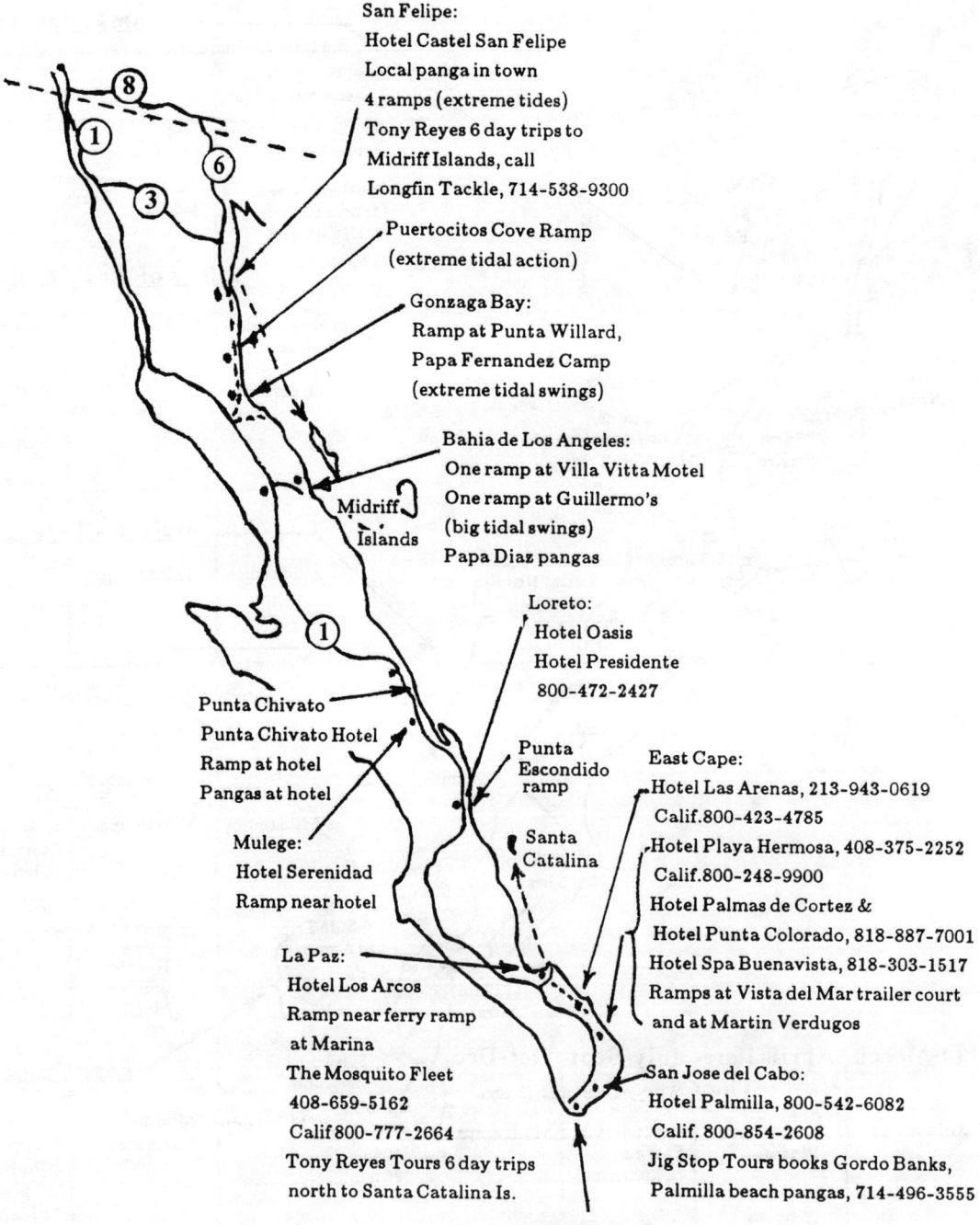

Mexicana Airlines: 800-531-7921
213-646-9500

Aero California: 800-258-3311

San Felipe:
Hotel Castel San Felipe
Local panga in town
4 ramps (extreme tides)
Tony Reyes 6 day trips to
Midriff Islands, call
Longfin Tackle, 714-538-9300

Puertocitos Cove Ramp
(extreme tidal action)

Gonzaga Bay:
Ramp at Punta Willard,
Papa Fernandez Camp
(extreme tidal swings)

Bahia de Los Angeles:
One ramp at Villa Vitta Motel
One ramp at Guillermo's
(big tidal swings)
Papa Diaz pangas

Loreto:
Hotel Oasis
Hotel Presidente
800-472-2427

Punta Chivato
Punta Chivato Hotel
Ramp at hotel
Pangas at hotel

Punta Escondido ramp

Santa Catalina

East Cape:
Hotel Las Arenas, 213-943-0619
Calif. 800-423-4785
Hotel Playa Hermosa, 408-375-2252
Calif. 800-248-9900
Hotel Palmas de Cortez &
Hotel Punta Colorado, 818-887-7001
Hotel Spa Buenavista, 818-303-1517
Ramps at Vista del Mar trailer court
and at Martin Verdugos

Mulege:
Hotel Serenidad
Ramp near hotel

La Paz:
Hotel Los Arcos
Ramp near ferry ramp
at Marina
The Mosquito Fleet
408-659-5162
Calif 800-777-2664
Tony Reyes Tours 6 day trips
north to Santa Catalina Is.

San Jose del Cabo:
Hotel Palmilla, 800-542-6082
Calif. 800-854-2608
Jig Stop Tours books Gordo Banks,
Palmilla beach pangas, 714-496-3555

Cabo San Lucas:
See Baja Travel Agents listing for hotel
bookings at Finnistera, Solmar, etc.
2 Ramps inside harbor

Clown Hawkfish

Needlefish

Jack Crevalle

Triggerfish

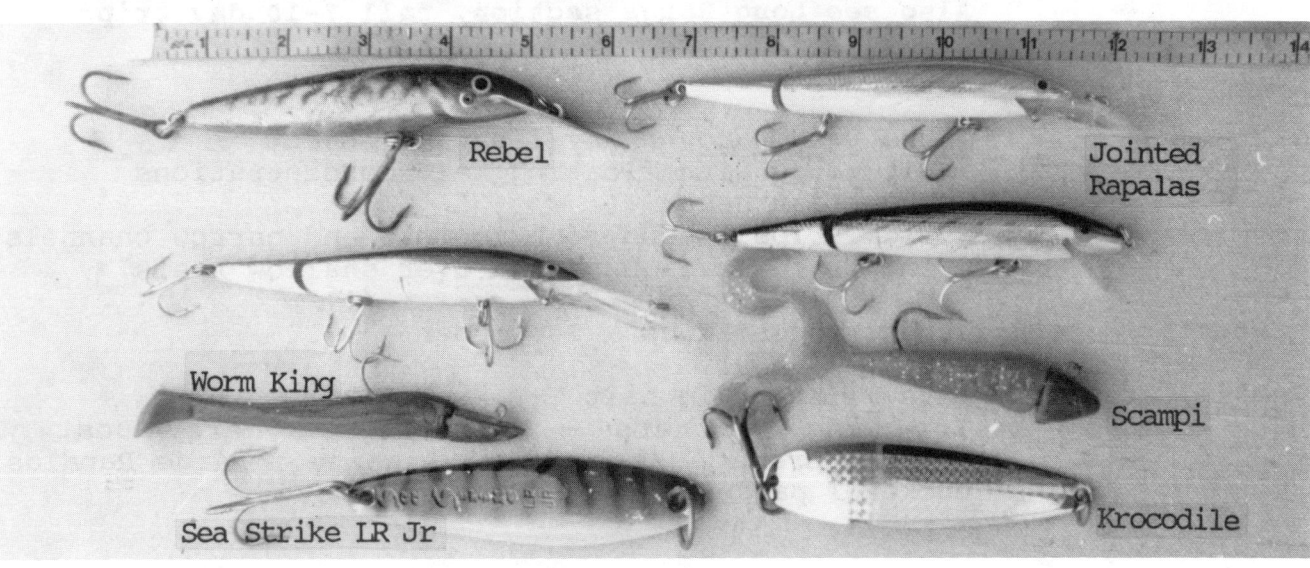
Rebel, Jointed Rapalas, Worm King, Scampi, Sea Strike LR Jr, Krocodile

## BLUE MARLIN, BLACK, STRIPED MARLIN:

**Note:** For Striped Marlin baits/lures, rigs, techniques - See Striped Marlin in alphabetical listing of gamefish. The following text, unless noted, is for Blue or Black Marlin.

**Where:** Prefer 75° to 82° water.
Cape Area - San Jose del Cabo, Gordo Banks
Cabo San Lucas

**When:** Striped Marlin:
November to March

Blue Marlin & Black Marlin:
Late July to early November
Note that the big females come in at the end of this range, around October & November.

**Bait/Lures:** Bait: Skipjack, small Dorado
Lures: Zuker - ZM7 or ZM6; Sevenstrand Pro Series PR8, etc.

**Rig:** Heavy duty reels in the 50, 50W to 80, 80W range. 80 to 130# mono with 15 - 20 foot long, 250 - 400# mono leaders and 9/0 to 12/0 hooks.

**Technique:** Techniques vary widely. In general lures are trolled. Outrigger lures are trolled at the 3rd and 4th wakes. Flat lines are trolled at the 2nd and 3rd wake. Flat lines are rigged to tagline clips off the transom to allow for a dropback.

**Records:** World: All Tackle - 1,376# Blue - Kona, Hawaii
80# Test - 915# Blue - Cabo San Lucas

---

## DORADO (other names: Mahi Mahi, Dolphin)

**Where** From Mulege south to lands end.
**Also see Long Range section, fall 7-10 day trips**

Structure:

Under and around any floating object
Rip lines with floating kelp concentrations
Near fish nets
Tidal rips around rocky points and narrow channels
Inlets to small bays and Over shallow reefs.

**When:** June through August, September

**Bait/Lures:** Live Bait, strip bait
Trolling Feathers - Albacore feathers. Best jig colors: Green & Yellow, Red & White.; Large Rapalas - mackerel pattern, large Rebels

## DORADO continued

**Rig:** Light to medium light conventional reel or large salt water spinning reel with 20 to 40# mono. Hook size ranges from #1 hook for anchovies up to 6/0 or 7/0 for mackerel or strip bait.

**Techniques:** Troll around structure areas listed under "Where".

Live bait or strip bait trolling - troll at 1 - 2 knots, with bait approximately 50 feet back and near the surface.

Once a fish is hooked and brought to the boat, its presence in the water will keep the school nearby. Continue to chum, and let other anglers get their baits into the water and even get hooked-up before boating your fish. This will keep the bite going.

**Records:** IGFA: 87 lbs., Costa Rica, 1976

---

## ROOSTERFISH (PAPAGALLO)

**Where:** Especially the East Cape area with good fishing extending north to La Paz

Structure: Shallows where rocky bottom areas meet sandy beaches

**When:** Late April to mid-July, Best May, June

**Bait/Lures:** Live bait is best. Mullet (Lisa), sardines, small Mackerel, Sabalo.

**Rig:** Light-medium to medium class conventional reels or saltwater spinning reels with 20 to 30# mono. Heavy lines are not necessary with Roosterfish since they are open water fighters.

**Technique:** Flyline live bait on a 1/0 to 3/0 hook.
Cast the bait in front of and to the outside, beach side of any visible fish. Try slow trolling with live baits about 70 feet behind the boat.

Cast a Kastmaster to the shore and retrieve fast.

The Roosterfish will often just lightly carry a bait in its mouth for up to a minute before getting serious. The Roosterfish prefers to stay in open water thus drastic attempts to keep him away from the rocks should not be made.

**Records:** IGFA: 114 lbs., La Paz, 1960

## TUNA, YELLOWFIN

**Where/When:** Prefers 72° to 80° waters.

    Cabo San Lucas, San Jose Del Cabo - all year
    Cerralvo Is., East Cape - April to December
    La Paz - May to November
    See Long Range Baja section.

    Larger fish are below smaller schools
    Larger fish under pods of feeding propose

**Bait/Lures:** Sardines, Caballitos, Mackerel - in front of porpoise school

Chrome Japheads with white feathers. Zuker tuna feathers or Sevenstrand Tuna Clones - purple, zucchini, or Mexican flag patterns.

Magnum Rapalas or Rebels.

**Rig:** Medium to light-heavy rigs loaded with 20 to 50 lb. mono will usually be sufficient. Most Yellowfin in the Cape area are football size, 40 lbs. and less.

**Technique:** Troll jigs at 8 - 10 knots, 100-120 feet back. Slow troll Rebels or Rapalas over 100 - 300' deep reefs (near Cerralvo Island and Las Arenas)

See also "Baja - Long Range Trips" section.

**Records:** IGFA: 388 lbs. 12 oz., Mexico, 1977

---

## WAHOO: (SIERRA GOLFINA)

**Where:** Baja Cape - Cabo San Lucas (Golden Gate and Jamie Banks) & San Jose del Cabo (Gordo Banks)
Some at East Cape (Cerralvo)
Shallower, 120 to 300 foot deep, water around islands and seamounts
Also see Baja Long Range Trips, 7 - 10 day and 16 - 18 day trips.

**When:** November through March, best in December and January
First hours of dawn.

**Bait/Lures:** Mackerel

Trolling Lures:

    Heavy leadhead feathers - i.e. Zuker models, larger and smaller tuna feathers. Chromed Kona Jet heads, Marauder, Flashdancer, Albacore feathers. Best colors: Red & black, black, purple & black, purple & red, red & white.

**Bait/Lures continued:**

    Large Rapalas. Colors: Gold & green, blue & white. When trolling Rapalas, make sure the rig swivel doesn't ride the surface.

    Hooks: 9/0 & 10/0 with one hook near head of lure.

Casting Jigs:

    Krocodile (5-7oz.) or Hopkins (4-6oz.); Salas 6x Jr.; Sea Strike LR Jr., 21, 22, or 23. Colors: Chrome, black & red, mackerel.

**Rig:** SEE DIAGRAM

**Also see - LONG RANGE BAJA section**

Use a 4/0 or 6/0 (Penn 113H or 114H) reel with 40 - 50# mono and black ball bearing swivels.

Troll jigs, Marauders, Flashdancers or Rapalas to locate fish.

Troll circular pattern around subsurface plateaus. Smaller peaks or humps on plateau surface are ideal.

**Technique:** Troll jigs at 6 - 10 knots and close to the boat, less than 75 yards back. Wahoo will often hit the shortest trolling lure.

When hit on trolled lures, drop back a large Scampi or cast a jig. Let jig sink while watching for a hit. Allow jig to drop until line into water forms about a 45 degree angle or the lure is from 50 to 100 feet deep. Retrieve fast - a high speed 4/1 or 5/1 ratio reel works well. On a hit, do NOT strike, but continue to reel in vigorously until Wahoo starts taking out the drag. Then set the hook hard without loosing the bend in the rod.

A Wahoo usually will hit a jig from the side, grabbing it in the middle. Its bite is so strong that the the hooks are not pulled into its jaw. If the Wahoo feels any slack in the line he will simply drop the lure.

On long-range boats, Wahoo are frequently sought by trolling a fathom mark - the contour of a single depth on the charts. When a Wahoo hits a trolled jig, chances are there are more Wahoo ahead on that same fathom mark. Jig casting off the bow can be just as fruitful as running to the stern.

**Records:** IGFA: 155.5 lbs., Bahamas, April 1990
A 137 lb. Wahoo was caught off Cabo in 1985

PARGO 380

**PARGO:** (Dog Snapper)

**Where:** Las Arenas at Punta Perico and west to Los Muertos (pangas leave from Arenas).
Cabo Pulmo (pangas leave from Spa Buena Vista and Rancho Buena Vista)
Structure: Shallow water rocky bottom reefs.

**When:** Late May through September.

**Bait/Lures:** Live Sardines, Mullet, Mackerel.
Cordel Spot - blue & silver, black & silver.
Magnum Rapala, deep diving - mackerel, blue mackerel.

**Rig:** Medium weight rig for 30 - 40# mono and/or a heavier weight 4/0 to 6/0 reel (Penn 113 or 114) with 80# mono for muscling the bigger fish of the rocks.

**Technique:** Troll plugs or slow troll live bait over shallow reefs (30 to 50 feet deep). Troll bait 50 to 75 feet back. With live bait thumb control freespool and give line on a pickup followed by a delayed strike.

**Records:** IGFA: 72 lbs. 12 oz., Panama

Skipjack

Pargo

1/2 Day Panga Catch off Gordo Banks

APPENDIX A 381

# SALTWATER LAUNCH RAMPS - NORTHERN CALIFORNIA

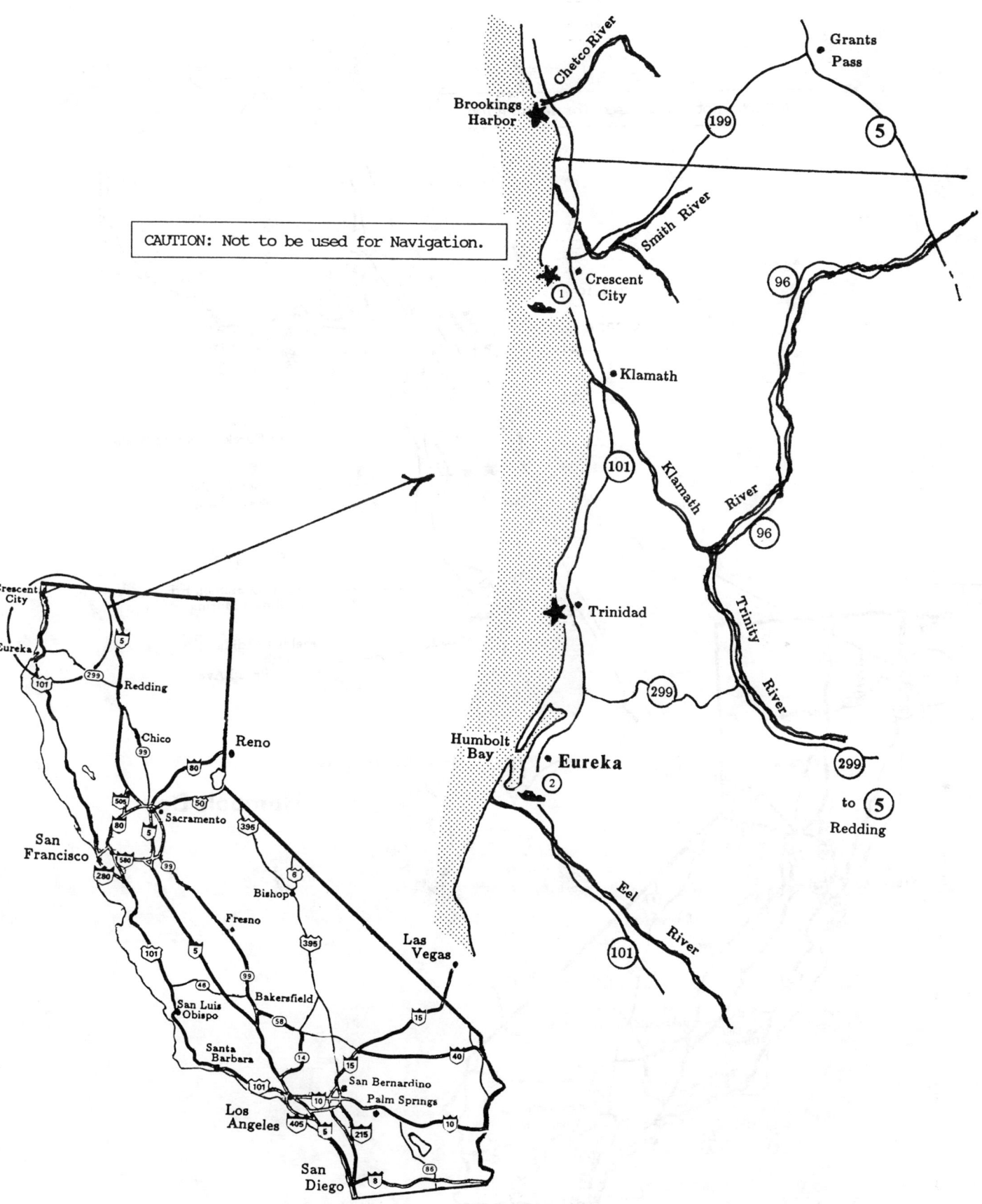

CAUTION: Not to be used for Navigation.

APPENDIX A 382

# SALTWATER LAUNCH RAMPS - NORTHERN CALIFORNIA

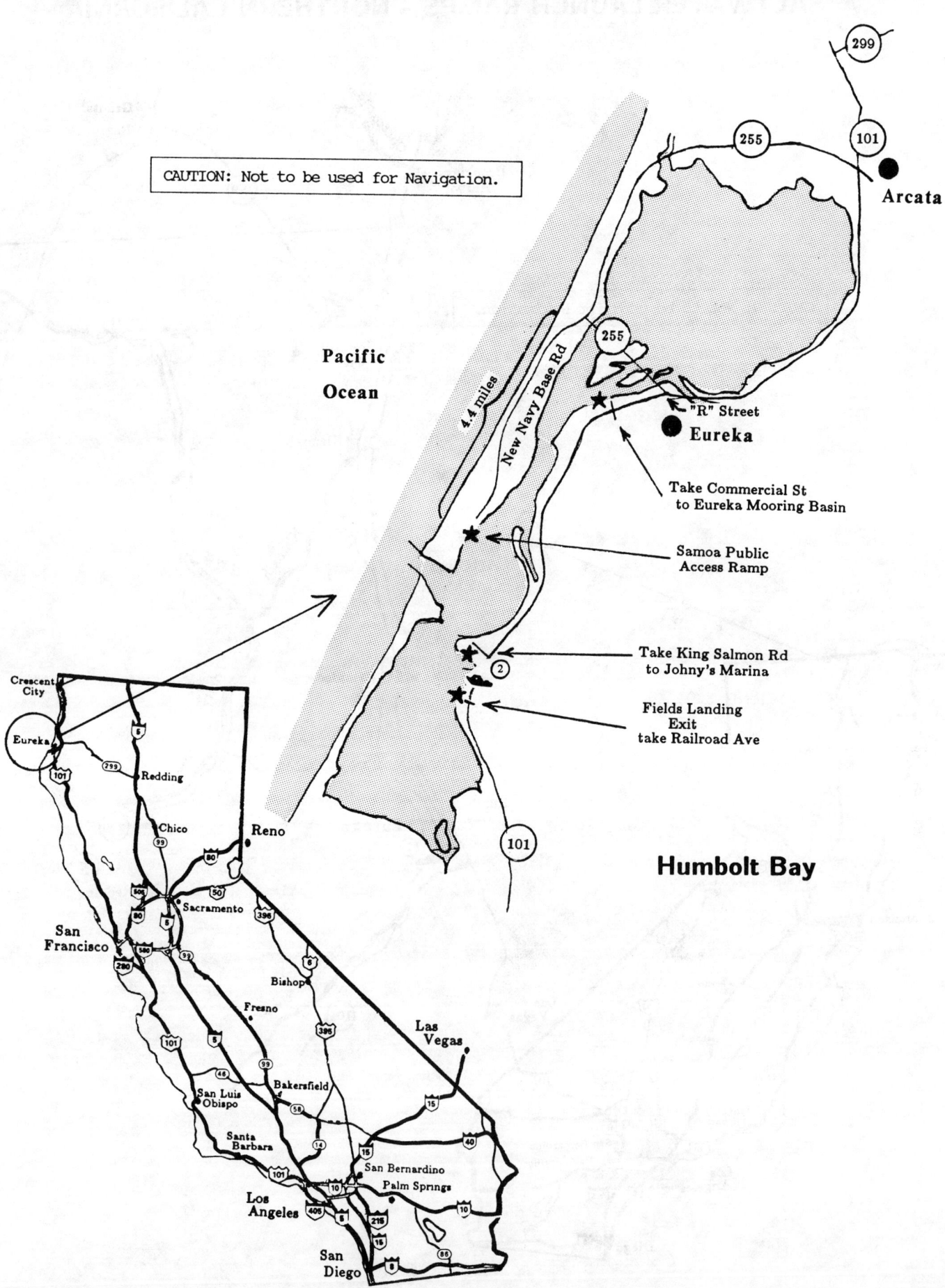

CAUTION: Not to be used for Navigation.

APPENDIX A 383

# SALT WATER LAUNCH RAMPS - NORTHERN CALIFORNIA

CAUTION: Not to be used for Navigation.

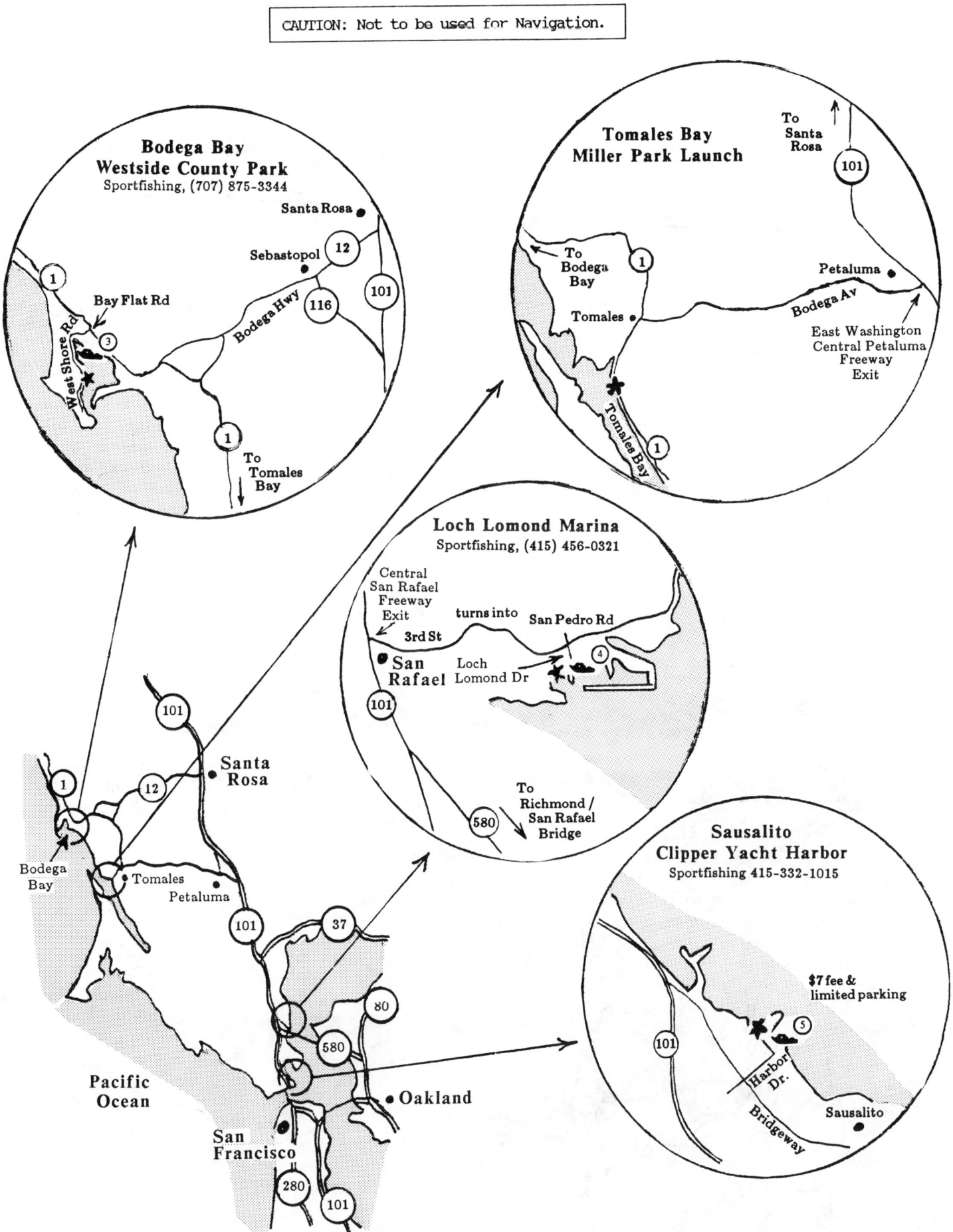

APPENDIX A 384

# SALT WATER LAUNCH RAMPS - NORTHERN CALIFORNIA
## San Francisco Bay

CAUTION: Not to be used for Navigation.

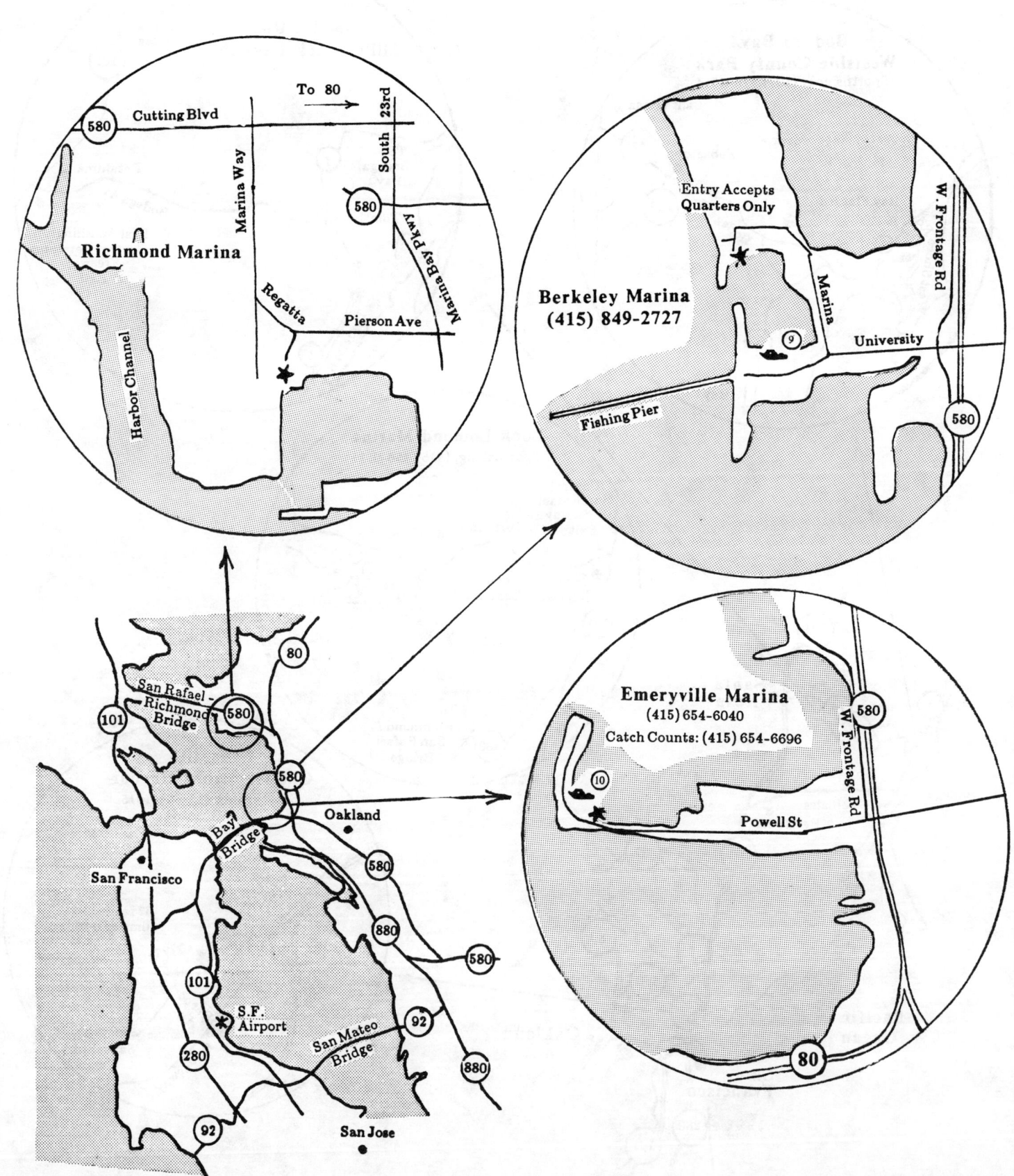

APPENDIX A 385

# SALT WATER LAUNCH RAMPS - NORTHERN CALIFORNIA
## San Francisco Bay

CAUTION: Not to be used for Navigation.

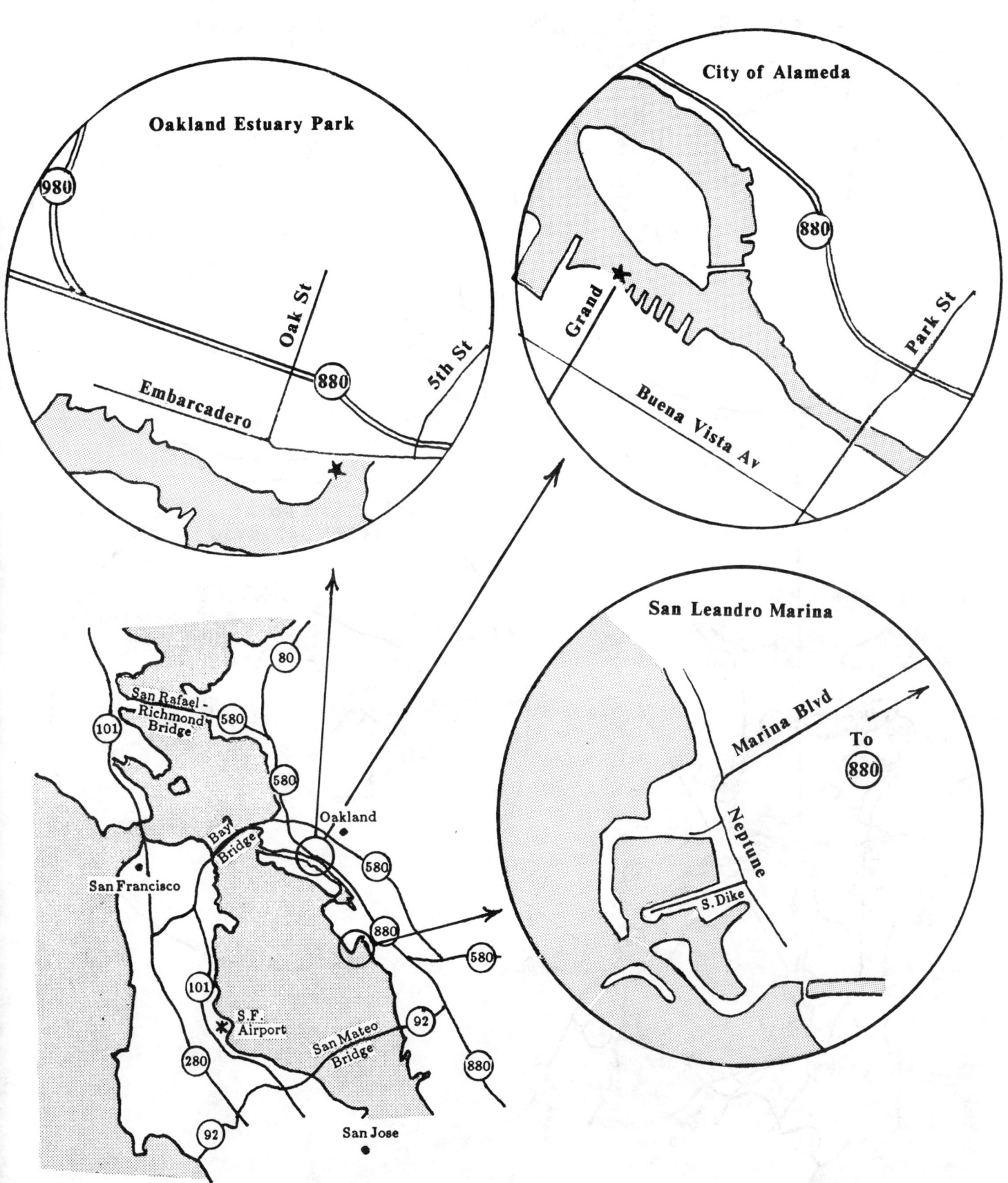

APPENDIX A  386

# SALT WATER LAUNCH RAMPS - NORTHERN CALIFORNIA
## San Francisco Bay

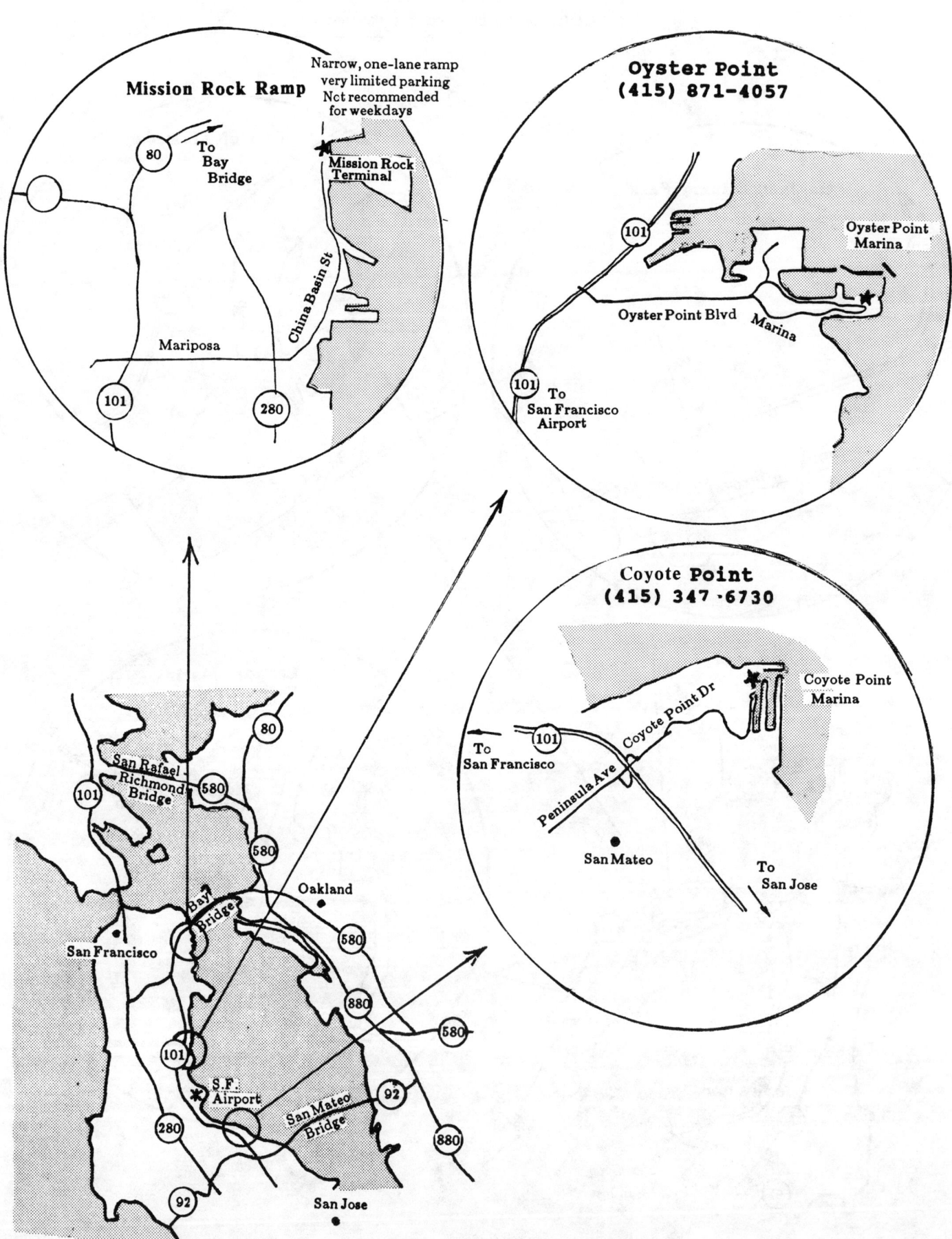

APPENDIX A 387

# SALT WATER LAUNCH RAMPS - NORTHERN CALIFORNIA

CAUTION: Not to be used for Navigation.

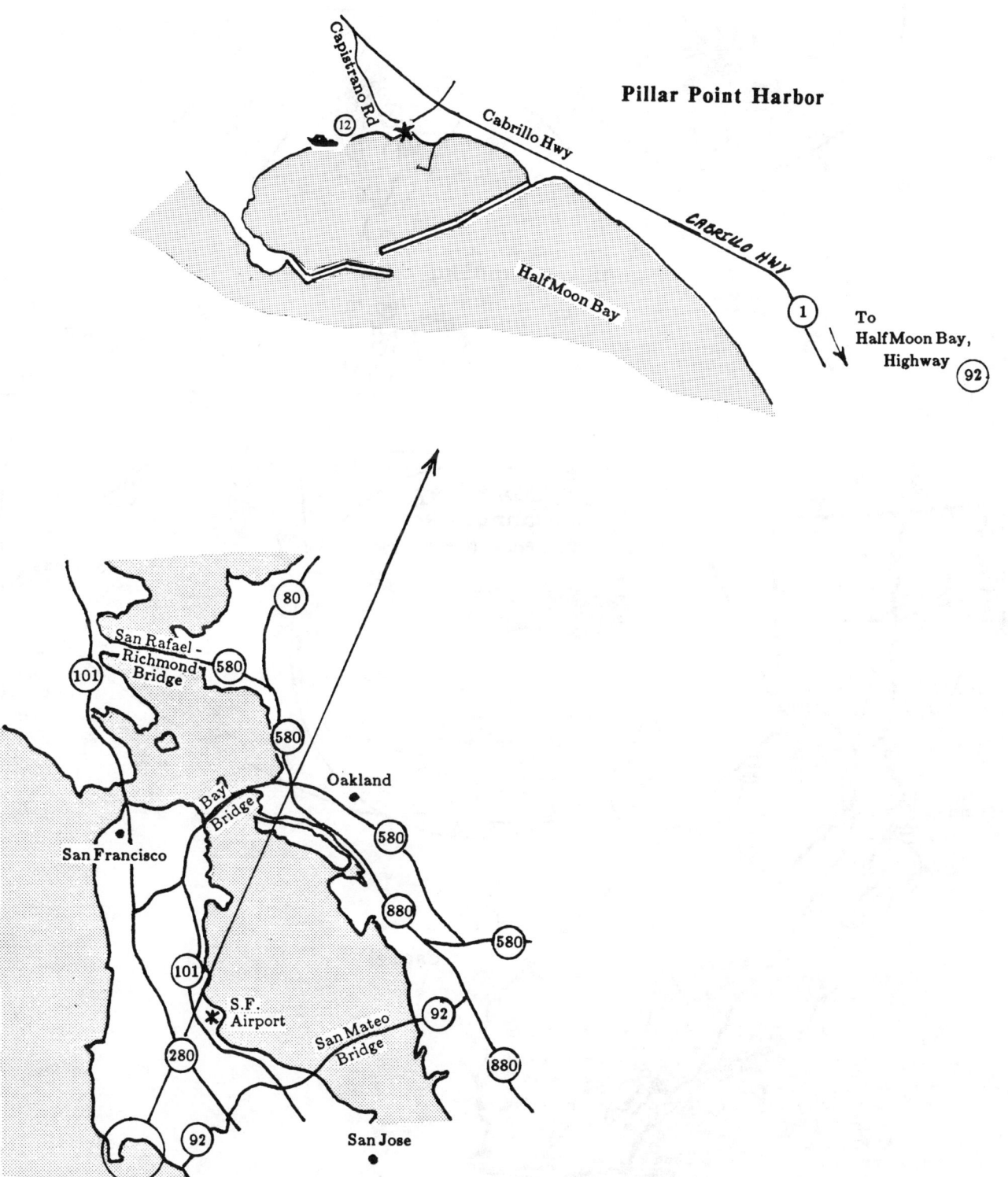

# APPENDIX A

## SALT WATER LAUNCH RAMPS - NORTHERN CALIFORNIA

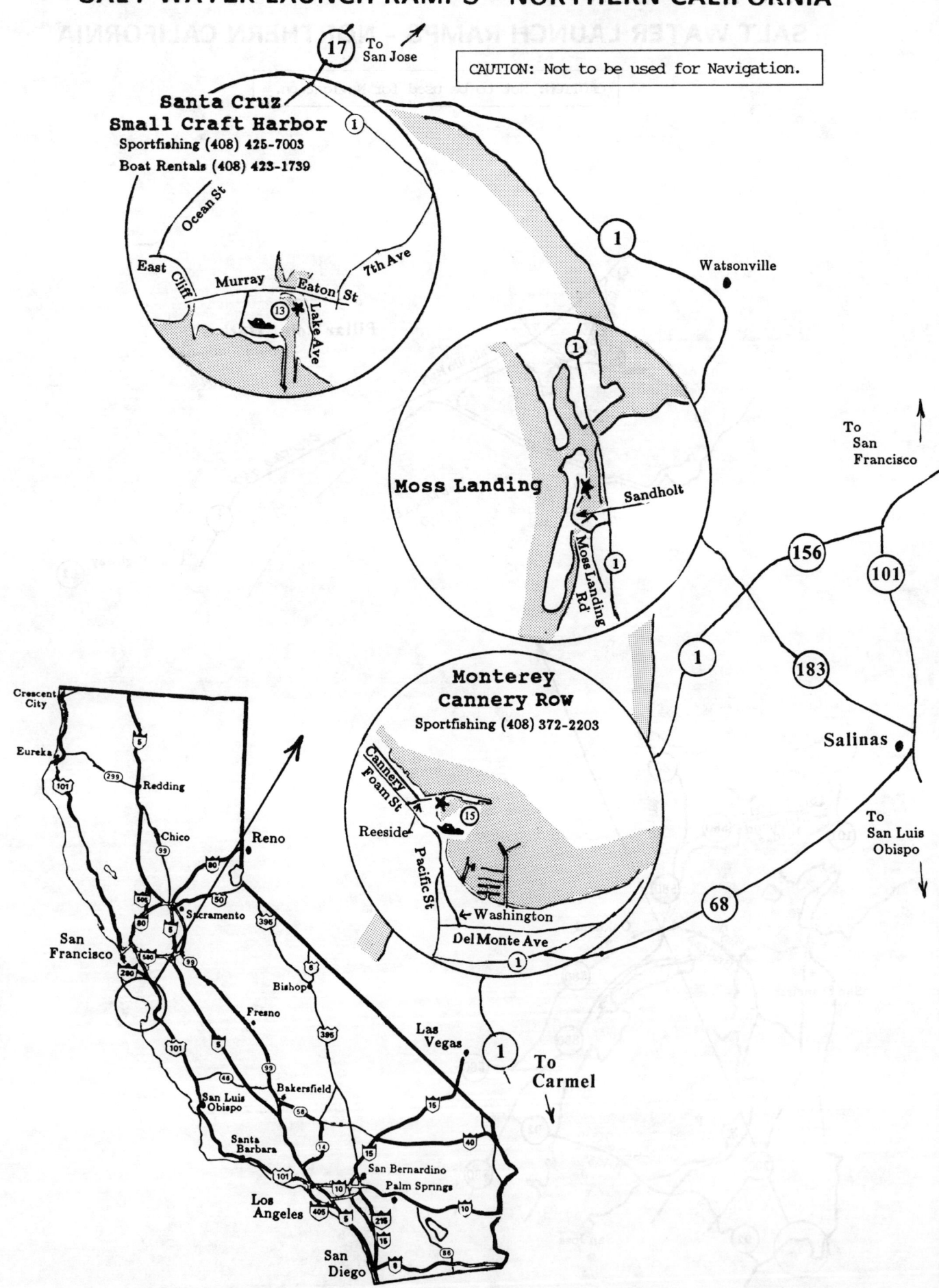

APPENDIX A 389

# SALT WATER LAUNCH RAMPS - SOUTHERN CALIFORNIA

CAUTION: Not to be used for Navigation.

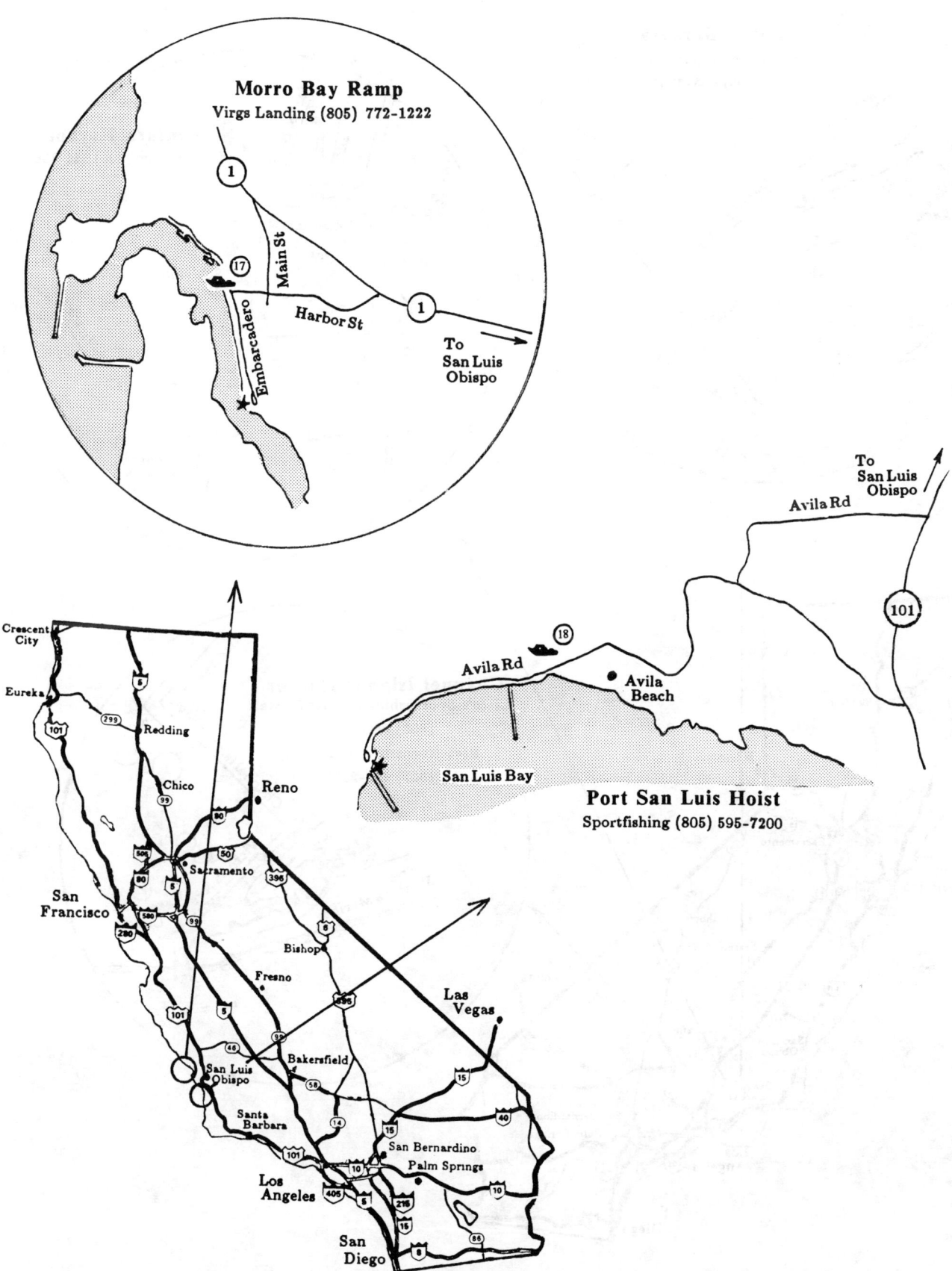

APPENDIX A 390
# SALT WATER LAUNCH RAMPS - SOUTHERN CALIFORNIA

CAUTION: Not to be used for Navigation.

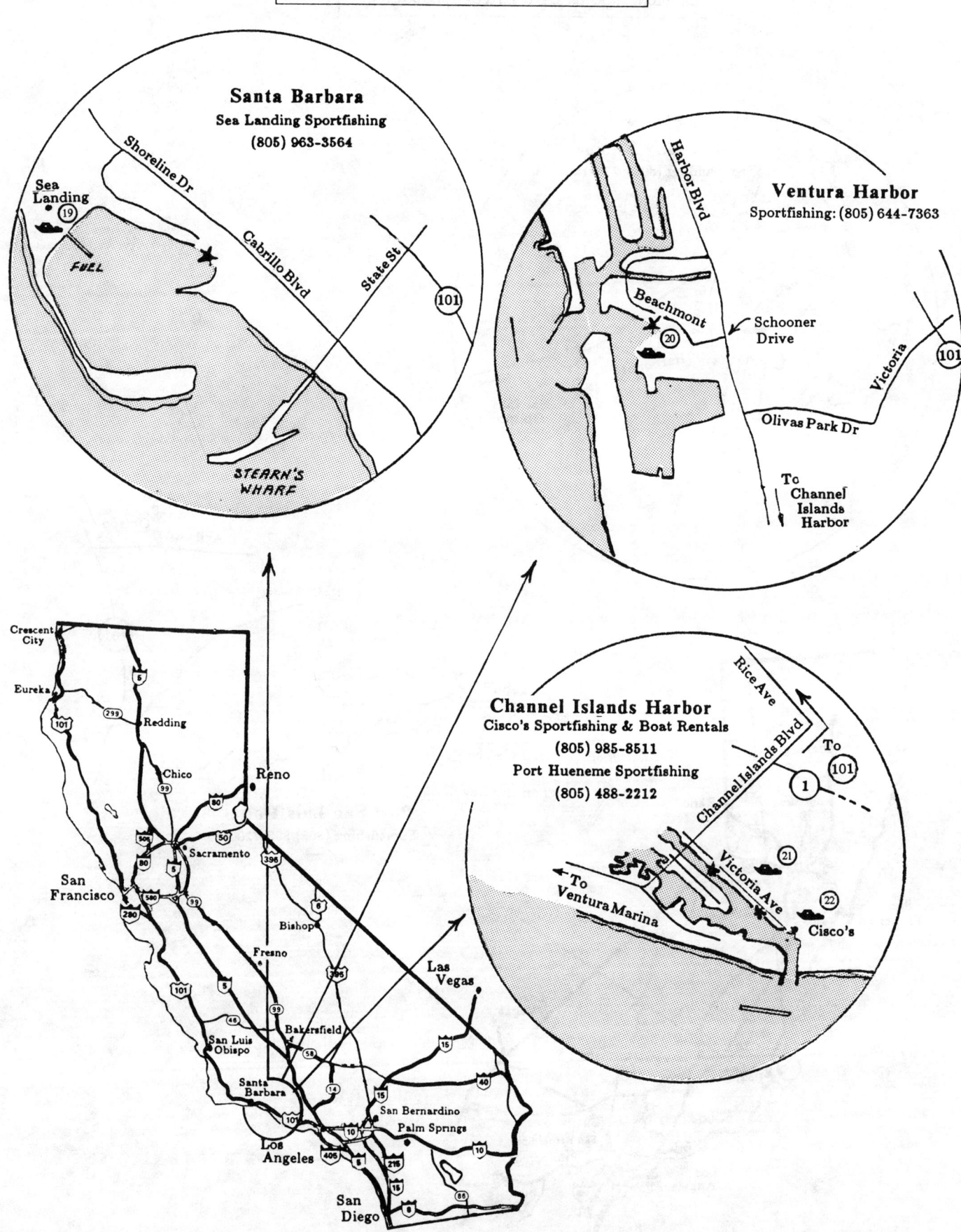

# SALT WATER LAUNCH RAMPS – SOUTHERN CALIFORNIA

CAUTION: Not to be used for Navigation.

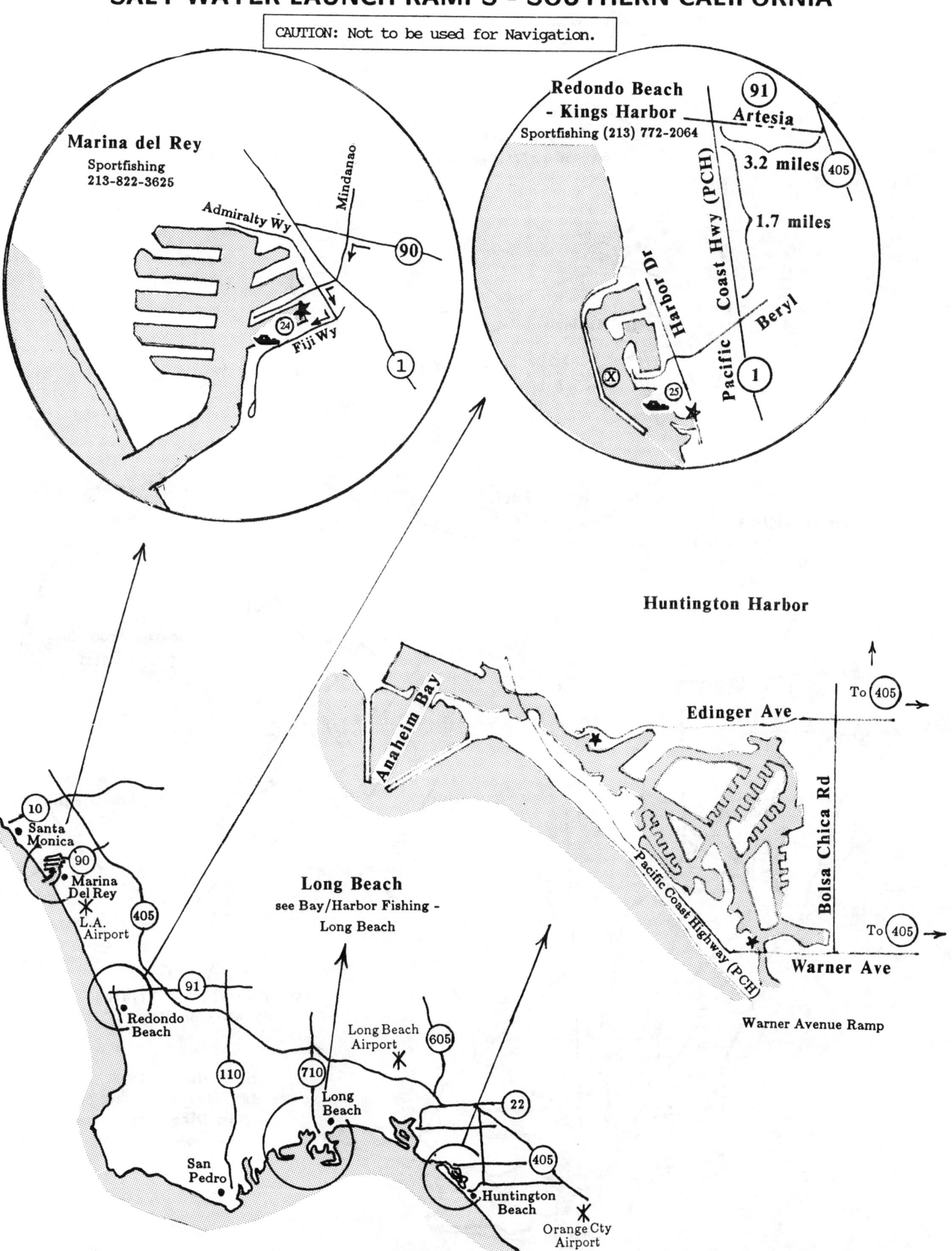

# SALT WATER LAUNCH RAMPS - SOUTHERN CALIFORNIA

CAUTION: Not to be used for Navigation.

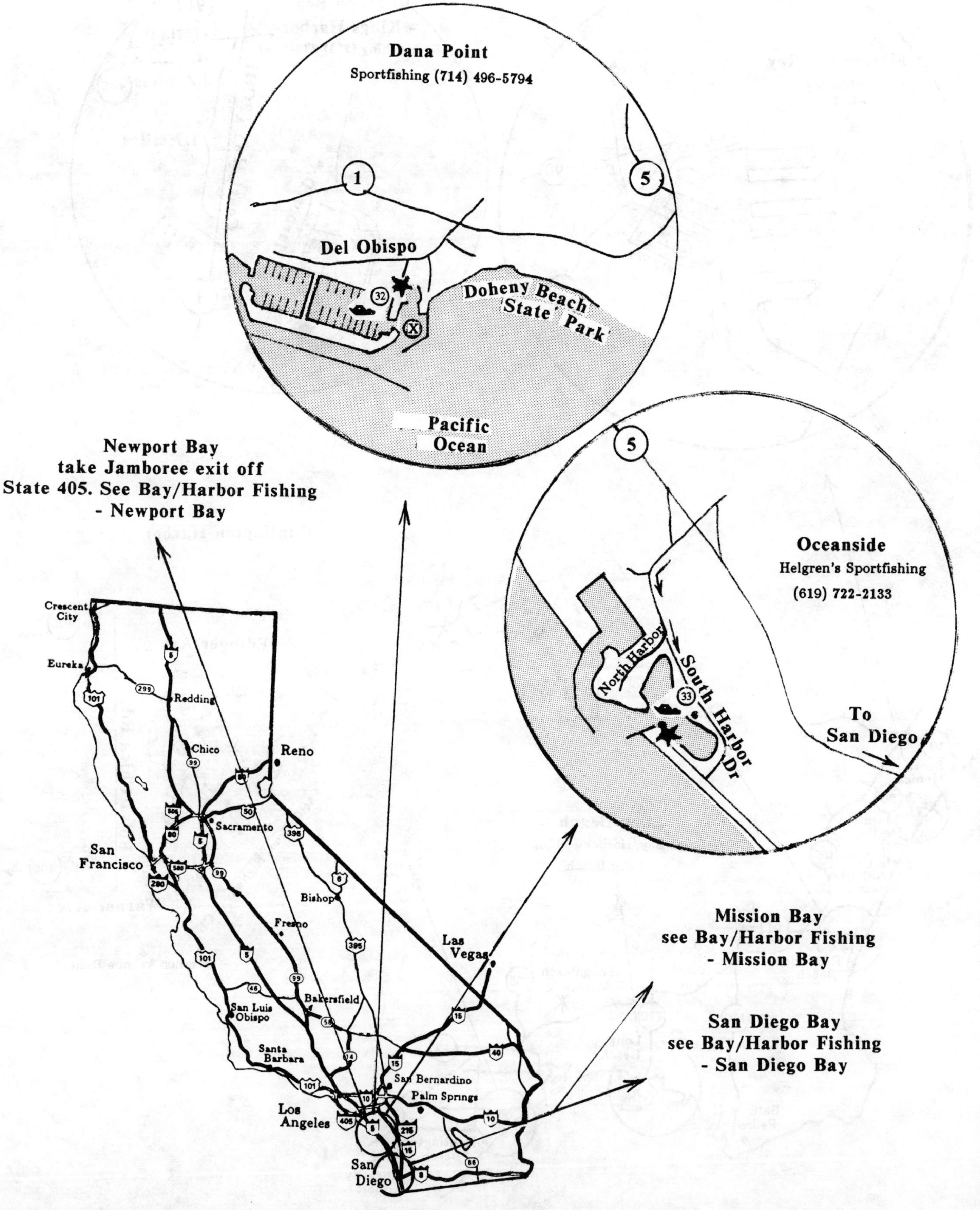
Dana Point
Sportfishing (714) 496-5794
1
5
Del Obispo
32
X
Doheny Beach State Park
Pacific Ocean
Newport Bay
take Jamboree exit off
State 405. See Bay/Harbor Fishing
- Newport Bay
5
Oceanside
Helgren's Sportfishing
(619) 722-2133
North Harbor
South Harbor Dr
33
To San Diego
Mission Bay
see Bay/Harbor Fishing
- Mission Bay
San Diego Bay
see Bay/Harbor Fishing
- San Diego Bay
Crescent City
Eureka
Redding
Chico
Reno
Sacramento
San Francisco
Bishop
Fresno
Las Vegas
Bakersfield
San Luis Obispo
Santa Barbara
San Bernardino
Palm Springs
Los Angeles
San Diego

APPENDIX B
SPORTFISHING LANDINGS / PARTYBOATS

Listing ordered from Northern landings to Southern landings

1. Crescent City, Lenbrooke Sportfishing, 707-464-7687
   Across from Englund Marine on Citizen's Dock Rd.
   or call Chamber of Commerce at 707-464-3174

2. Eureka, King Salmon Charters, 707-442-FISH (3474), May to Sept.
   3 miles south of Eureka on King Salmon Ave
   or call Chamber of Commerce at 707-442-3738

3. Bodega Bay Bait & Tackle - Bodega Bay, Porto Bodega Marina
   1 mile north of Tides, left off Hwy on Eastshore Dr.
   707-875-3344, See "Salt Water Launch Ramps" for map.

4. Loch Lomond Marina Bait Store - books for "Superfish"
   415-456-0321, See "Salt Water Launch Ramps" for map.

5. Caruso's- Sausalito, 415-332-1015, See Salt Water Launch Ramps map

6. Muny's Sportfishing - San Francisco, 415-673-9815
   Books for Fisherman's Wharf Boats

7. City Bait - Crockett, Crockett Marina, 415-787-1048

9. Berkeley Marina, University Ave. West off I-80, 415-849-2727
   See "Salt Water Launch Ramps" for map.

10. Emeryville Marina, 415-654-6040, See Salt Water Launch Ramps map.
    Recording: 415-654-6696

11. The Fury - Pt. San Pablo, Private Phone: 415-357-4390

12. Pillar Point / Half Moon Bay
    Huck Finn II, 415-726-7133
    Captain Johns Trips, 415-726-2913

13. Rain Song Sportfishing - Santa Cruz Harbor, 408-462-3553

14. Stagnaro-Santa Cruz, 408-425-7003, See Salt Water Launch Ramps map

15. Monterey Sportfishing-Monterey, 96 Fisherman's Wharf, 408-372-2203
    See "Salt Water Launch Ramps" for map.

16. San Simeon Landing, across Hwy 1 from Hearst Castle
    805-927-1777, 800-347-9717

17. Virg's - Morro Bay, 1215 Embarcadero, 805-772-1222
    See "Salt Water Launch Ramps" for map.

18. Paradise Sportfishing - Avila Beach, Port San Luis
    805-595-7200, See "Salt Water Launch Ramps" for map.

19. Sea Landing - Santa Barbara, Cabrillo St. at Bath
    805-963-3564, See "Salt Water Launch Ramps" for map.

APPENDIX B
SPORTFISHING LANDINGS / PARTYBOATS   394

20. Ventura Sportfishing - Ventura Harbor
    1500 Anchors Wy., 805-644-7363, See Salt Water Launch Ramps map.

21. Port Hueneme Sportfishing - Oxnard, Port Hueneme Harbor
    805-488-2212, 805-488-4715, See "Salt Water Launch Ramps "map

22. Channel Islands Sportfishing (Cisco's) - Oxnard,
    Port Hueneme Harbor, 4151 S. Victoria
    800-322-3474, 805-985-8511, See Salt Water Launch Ramps for map.

23. Malibu Pier Sportfishing, End of Malibu Pier, 213-456-8030

24. Marina del Rey Sportfishing, 13759 Fiji Way, 213-822-3625

25. Redondo Sportfishing - Redondo Beach, 233 N. Harbor Dr.
    213-372-2111, 213-772-2064, See Salt Water Launch Ramps map.

26. 22nd St. Landing - San Pedro, 141 W. 22nd St., 213-832-8304
    213-832-3918 (Ct), See Harbor Fishing - Long Beach Harbor map.

27. Ports of Call Sportfishing - San Pedro, 213-547-9916

28. Long Beach Sportfishing (Queens Wharf), 555 Pico Av, 213-432-8993

29. Belmont Pier - Long Beach, Ocean & Termino, 213-434-6781

30. Seal Beach Pier - Seal Beach, Ocean & Main, 213-598-8677

31. Davey's Locker Sportfishing - Balboa, 400 Main St.
    714-673-1434, See "Harbor Fishing - Newport Harbor" for map.
31. Newport Landing - Balboa, 309 Palm, 714-675-0550

32. Dana Point Sportfishing - Dana Point, 34675 Golden Lantern
    714-496-5794, See "Salt Water Launch Ramps" for map.

33. Helgren's Sportfishing - Oceanside, 315 Harbor Drive South
    619-722-2133, See "Salt Water Launch Ramps" for map.

34. Seaforth Landing Sportfishing - San Diego
    Mission Bay - Sea World Drive Exit, 1717 Quivira Rd, 619-224-3383

35. Islandia Sportfishing - San Diego, Mission Bay
    1551 W. Mission Bay Dr., 619-222-1164

36. H & M Landing - San Diego, 2803 Emerson St.
    619-224-2800 (Fish Ct), 619-222-1144

37. Fisherman's Landing - San Diego, 2838 Garrison St.
    213-930-1015 (Fish Ct), 619-224-1421 (Ct), 619-222-0391

38. Pt. Loma Sportfishing - San Diego, 1403 Scott St.
    619-223-1626 (Fish Ct), 619-223-1627

39. Lee Palm's Sportfishing-San Diego, 2801 Emerson, 619-224-3857

## Sources of Current Fishing Information

Northern Calif:   From Monterey Bay to San Francisco
                  Touchtone phone recording:
                  900-844-FISH (3474)

                  Emeryville Sportfishing Center
                  Info Recording: 415-654-6696

Southern Calif:   Touchtone phone recordings:
                  (213) 976-TUNA
                  (818)   "
                  (619)   "

                  Sportsmans Info Exchange
                  (213) 496-1455

Also see specific fish, for other info sources.

MAGAZINES & NEWSPAPERS:

1. The Fish Sniffer - bi-weekly newspaper format. Concentrates on mid-to-northern California. Also covers Oregon and Baja.
   Northern Calif. Angler Publications Inc., P.O. Box 994, Elk Grove, CA 95759, 800-748-6599 or 916-685-2245
2. Fishing & Hunting News - bi-weekly newspaper format. Is published in specific areas editions including So. Calif, Northern Calif, and the Sacramento - mid-state area.
   Outdoor Empire Publishing, 511 Eastlake Ave. E., Seattle, Washington 98109, 206-624-3845
3. Western Outdoor News (WON) - weekly newspaper format. Concentrates on So. Calif. Angling but covers entire state and Baja.
   Western Outdoor News, 3197-E Airport Loop Drive, Costa Mesa, CA 92626, 714-546-4370
4. California Angler Magazine - monthly. Covers saltwater and freshwater angling adventures ranging across the Pacific Rim. Most articles deal with areas in California or Baja.
   P.O. Box 15261, N. Hollywood, CA 91615, 818-760-8983
5. South Coast Sportfishing - monthly. Concentrates on saltwater fishing adventures in So. Calif. and Baja.
   P.O. Box 16417, N. Hollywood, CA 91615, 818-760-8983

# APPENDIX D
## HOOK SIZE CHART 396

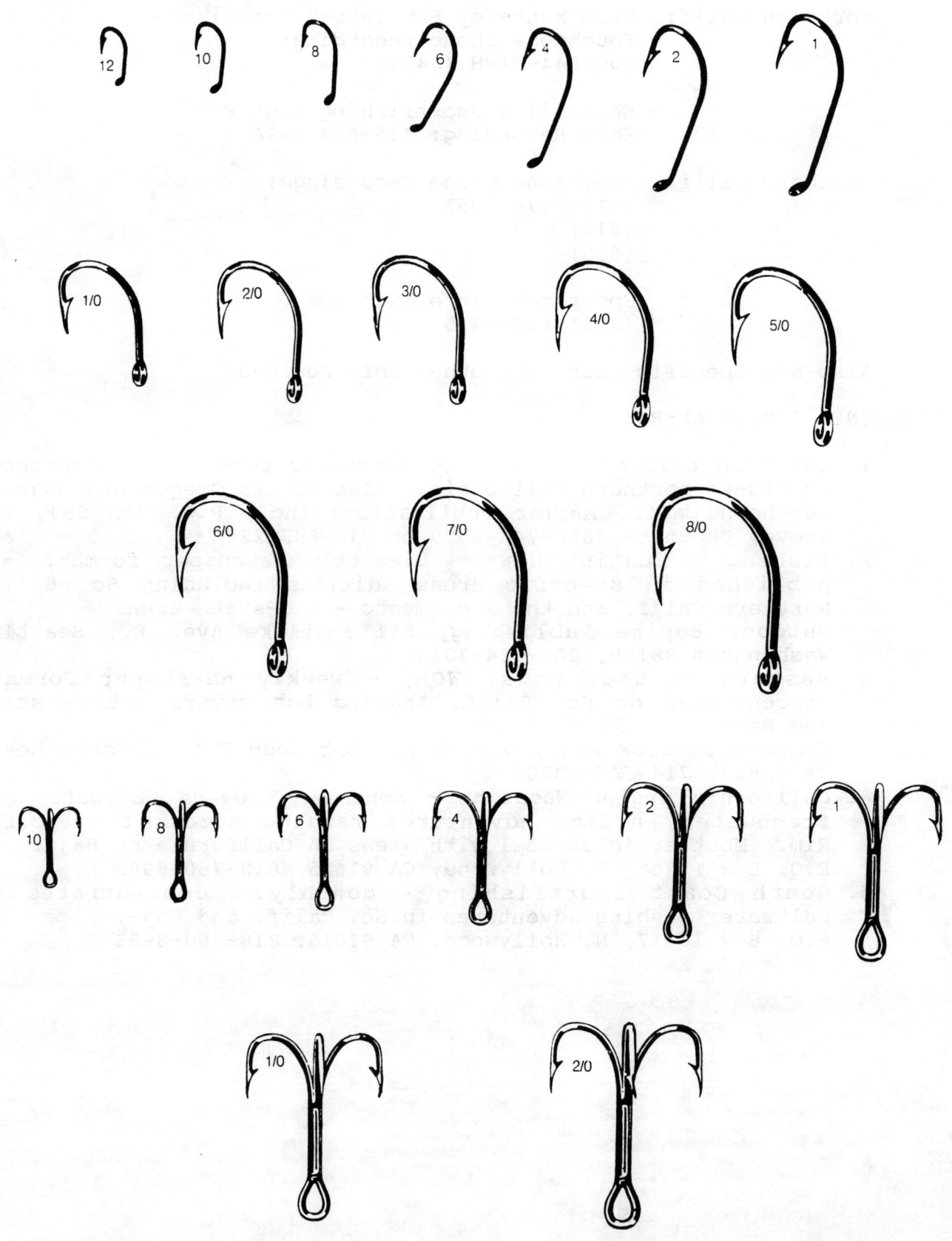

APPENDIX E
STANDARD FISHING RIGS

## SUGGESTED STANDARD FISHING RIGS

| CLASS | Ultra Light Weight | Light Weight | Light Middle Weight | Middle Weight | Heavy Middle Weight | Light Heavy Weight | Heavy to Ultra Heavy Weight |
|---|---|---|---|---|---|---|---|
| REEL TYPE | Spinning Fly Fishing | Spinning Casting Fly Fishing | Saltwater Spinning Casting Fly Fishing | Conventional | Conventional | Conventional | Conventional |
| CAPACITY | 100 Yds 6# mono | 200 Yds 10# mono | 300 Yds of 20# up to 300 Yds of 30# | 350 Yds of 30# up to 400 Yds of 50# | 400-500 Yds of 50# OR 600 Yds of 30# | 600 Yds of 50# up to 600 Yds of 80# | 700-1000+ Yds of 80# mono |
| EXAMPLES | — | — | Penn Squidder to Jigmaster Daiwa 30,50,300,350 Newell 200 to lower 300 series Shimano TLD 10 & 15 | Penn 113 Daiwa 600 Newell upper 400 series Shimano TLD 20 & 25 | International 30 size 4/0 to 6/0 size Penn 114 | 50-50W size 9/0 size | 80 to 80W size 10/0 to 12/0 size |
| ROD | 6 1/2 - 7 1/2' Spinning 7 1/2 - 9' Fly Fishing (Size: 3 to 5) Fibreglas or Graphite | 6 1/2 - 7 1/2' Spinning or Casting 7 1/2 - 9' Fly Fishing (Size: 5 - 7) Fibreglas or Graphite | 6 1/2 to 7 1/2 feet+ Conventional or Spin 7 1/2 - 9' Fly Fishing (Size: 7 - 9) Fibreglas or Graphite | 5 1/2 - 7' Fibreglas | 5 - 6 1/2' Fibreglas | 5 - 6' Fibreglas | 5 - 5 1/2' Fibreglas |
| LINE | 2 - 6# mono | 6 - 25# mono | 15 - 40# mono | 30 - 50# mono | 40 - 60# mono | 50 - 80# mono | 50 - 80+# mono |
| HOOK | #18 - #10 | #8 - #1 | #1 - 8/0 | #1 - 8/0 | 2/0 - 8/0 | 4/0+ | 6/0+ |
| USE FOR THESE SPORT FISH | Trout Crappie Panfish Surf for: Perch Corbina Bay Fishing Salton Sea for: Sargo Tilapia | Bass: Largemouth Sand Calico Barracuda Large Trout Small Striper Steelhead Rockfish Corvina | Salmon Sturgeon Striper Surface Yellowtail Albacore Small Yellowfin Dorado Roosterfish Shallow water Rockcod | Small Yellowfin Bottom Yellowtail Bluefin Pargo Sailfish | Striped Marlin Wahoo Shark Bigeye Medium size Yellowfin Large bottom fish: Grouper, Black Sea Bass Deep Water Rockcod | Large Yellowfin Very Large Shark | Giant Yellowfin Blue Marlin Black Marlin |

Normal use →
Light Tackle use ⇢

See also special rigs for: Long distance surf casting and Striper casting, deep water Rockcod, jig casting, Largemouth Bass flipping rig

# GLOSSARY

**3/0 Reel**  A reel with capacity for about 375 yards of 30 lb. test mono. Example: Penn 112HL.

**4/0 Reel**  A reel with capacity for about 600 yards of 30 lb. test mono or 300 to 375 yards (wide version) of 50 lb. monofilament. Examples: Penn 113HL, Penn 113HLW, Penn International 30.

**6/0 Reel**  A reel with capacity for 475 to 600 yards of 50 lb. mono. Examples: Penn 114HL, Daiwa 600H, Newell G454F.

**9/0 Reel**  A reel with capacity for about 750 yards of 80 lb. mono. Examples: Penn Intl. 80S.

A 9/0 Wide reel can hold about 950 to 1100 yards of 80 lb. mono. Examples: Penn Intl. 80TW, 80SW; Shimano TTS 80W; Daiwa Tournament 80W.

**12/0 Reel**  A reel with capacity for about 850 yards of 130 lb. mono or 1200 yards of 80 lb. mono. Examples: Fin-Nor 12/0; Shimano TBM 80/130.

## A

**Alvey Reel**  A reel that resembles a large diameter fly reel, but which can be rotated on its axis to cast like a spinning reel, then returned to its original orientation for line retrieval like a conventional reel.

## B

**Bird**  A hookless, surface-riding device used for marlin fishing. The bird is constructed to create a lot of surface turbulence.

**Blackmouth**  Slang name for King Salmon. Kings can be identified by their black inside mouths.

**Bleeding Mackerel**  A popular trolling jig color combination consisting of red & yellow.

**Bloodworm**  A marine worm, normally 3-4" long, commonly used for surf and harbor fishing.

**Blueback**  Slang for Silver, Coho Salmon

**Blue Water**  A subtle difference in the shade of water that usually indicates cleaner water. Inshore waters along the California coast normally tend to be some shade of greenish blue. Depending on multiple factors this greenish water fades into a blue tint anywhere from 2 to 10 miles offshore. Some species of fish avoid green water.

## C

**Bonito Shark**  Also called Mako Shark.

**Brown Bait**  Various small, bottom dwelling, inshore and harbor fishes such as Queenfish, Tomcod, Perch, etc. Good for halibut, Sand Bass, Calico Bass. Best size: 2 - 4" They are typically abundant near bait servers, on the bottom.

**Bullhead**  A small rockfish called a Staghorn Sculpin. Usually used as bait for Sturgeon in San Francisco Bay and the Sacramento Delta.

**Caballito**  A medium-sized bait fish found in Baja. The term means "little horse".

**California City**  A popular San Francisco Bay salmon fishing area located east and northeast of the Tiburon peninsula.

**Chum**  The action or the substance of a regular dispersion of live, dead, cut, or ground fish bait in order to attract and concentrate gamefish closer to the boat, dock, etc. and to work them into a feeding mood.

**Coho Salmon**  Same as Silver Salmon

**Color**  The first sight of the fish, as the angler brings it in from deeper water beneath the boat.

**Conventional Reel**  A reel where the spool shaft is perpendicular to the direction of the rod shaft.

**Cow Shark**  Alternate name for Sevengill or the rarer Sixgill shark.

## D

**Dodger**  A rectangular metal blade that is usually highly reflective and is used as part of the terminal rigging as a fish attractant. The Dodger is normally rigged within a couple of feet of the baited hook. Dodgers have a side-to-side swaying motion when trolled at optimum speed. (Also see Flasher)

**Drag**  Unnatural drift of a fly caused by the fly line crossing an area of varying current speeds. If the closer current is slower, an upstream belly will form in the line causing the fly to drift unnaturally slow. If the closer current is faster, a belly will form downstream causing an unnaturally fast drift. Drag will spook a trout. Drag is prevented by mending.

## E

**Ebb Tide**  Outgoing tide, period from high tide to low tide.

## F

**Feather** Slang term for a trolling jig that typically consists of a weighted head and a tail consisting of feathers, a plastic skirt, or a combination. These use to be made with just feathers - hence the name. See also **Jigs**.

**Firecracker** A small Yellowtail

**Flasher** A fish attracting metal blade, quite similar to a Dodger, that differs from a Dodger in that it rotates (spins) at a regular speed when trolled at optimum speed.

**Flood Tide** Incoming tide. Period from low tide to high tide.

**Flying Gaff** A gaff that has a removable hook with a rope attached. The fish is first gaffed similar to a fixed gaff, then the hook portion is released and the fish is controlled with the attached heavy rope.

**Freespool** A term used with conventional reels that means disengaging the drag so that the line-filled spool turns freely.

## G

**Gangion** A heavy-duty, multi-hook setup used for deepwater Rockcod angling. The hooks may be bare or dressed with yarn, mylar, etc to make a shrimpfly rig.

**Goat** Alternate name for a Sheephead.

**Gobey** (Goby) A small fish of shallow bay areas and sloughs. They are commonly used for bait. A mudsucker is a goby.

**Greenie or Greenback** A Pacific Mackerel.

**Grilse** A small, undersize King Salmon.

**Gulf of California** Pseudonym for Sea of Cortez, Vermillion Sea

## H

**Half Pounder** Smaller, 1/2 to 3 pound, steelhead that are prevalent in the fall runs.

**Handy Dandy** A brand of shrimpfly rig.

**Hay Hook** A very short hook gaff used for handling fish.

**Hookup!** Yelled when a fish hits a trolled lure, most often heard on Albacore charter boats. When the captain hears "Hookup" he stops trolling and starts chumming in an attempt to bring the Albacore school to the boat.

**Hoochie** (Hootchy) A plastic (rubber) squid/shrimp imitation lure that is either rigged alone or as a teaser up line from a jig lure. When rigged above a jig it imitates a small squid/baitfish being chased by another fish.

## I

**Iron**  Term used for metal jigs used in ocean fishing especially for Yellowtail, Calico Bass, Lingcod, Cowcod, etc.

## J

**Jack**  Also Jackspring. Small male salmon that re-enter streams a year or two earlier than normal. As a result they are quite small.

**Jig**  This term is used for widely differing lures from pure metal jigs like Yellowtail and Barracuda Jigs and Rockcod jigs, to much smaller leadhead jigs with plastic bodies and tails used for Bass fishing to trolling lures used for Albacore, Bigeye, and Marlin (see also Feather). It is also a verb which refers to the way a metal jig lure is fished.

## K

**Kahle Hook**  A type of hook with a wide throat and offset point.

**Kingfish**  Another name for a White croaker in San Francisco Bay.

## L

**Lake Troll**  A series of attractor blades on a mono line which is rigged on the line above the trolled lure or bait. The flashing blades are supposed to attract and bring fish in closer.

**Log**  A big Barracuda.

**Loran**  An electronic boating device, that works by receiving transmissions from government satellites. A loran can be very useful for accurately locating a specific longitude & latitude such as a known good fishing spot

**Lucky Joe**  A brand of baitfishing shrimpfly rig.

## M

**Mako Shark**  Also called Bonito Shark in California.

**Mexican Flag**  A popular trolling jig skirt color combination consisting of white & green & red

**Midshipman**  A bait fish used primarily for shark fishing in San Francisco Bay.

**Mojo**  A soft plastic and lead jig lure with a single tail that closely resembles the Scampi.

**Mudpuppy**  A salamander commonly used for bait.

**Mudsucker**  A small, shallow bay and slough fish, a goby, commonly used for bait.

## P

**Pinhead**  A very small anchovy.

**Pocket Water**  In very fast flowing rapids areas, the pockets are small, quieter water areas formed by large rocks or short, more level water stretches.

**Pusher**  A Marlin lure that has a flat head that pushes through the water, causing a lot of bubbles, surface turbulence.

**Plastics**  Any of a group of soft plastic lures, normally incorporated with a leadhead jig for weight.

**Potluck Boat**  Term commonly used in San Francisco Bay area to designate a boat that targets more than one species, such as stripers, halibut, salmon, shark, sturgeon, etc.

**Professional Overrun**  Facetious term used for a backlash tangle on a casting reel.

## R

**Red**  A red-colored rockcod, probably a Vermilion Rockcod.

**Riprap**  Streamside banks lined with rock.  These are man made and purposely provide bank erosion control and incidentally provide fish cover.

## S

**Salami**  A very large mackerel, (15" to 18+") commonly used for Tuna bait on long range boats fishing the Pacific side of Baja.

**Scampi**  A soft plastic and lead jig lure with twin horizontally placed tails that closely resembles Shabby Shrimp and Mojos.

**Sand Shark**  Alternate name for both Brown and Grey Smoothhound Sharks.

**Scad**  A very large mackerel, used for giant tuna bait in Baja waters.

**Sea of Cortez**  Pseudonym for Gulf of California, Vermillion Sea.

**Seam**  The border between 2 currents of water, one moving faster than the other.  This "line", usually oriented up-and-down stream, is a collecting spot for floating and subsurface insects.  Trout hold in the slower current side of seams.

**Shabby Shrimp**  A leadheaded, plastic jig closely resembling Scampi's and Mojos.

**Shaker**  An undersize Salmon (less than 22 inches)

**Shakin Shad**  A leadheaded, plastic jig that closely resembles the Worm King lures.

**Shrimpfly Rig**  Consists of multiple hook tied on a typical 3 to 5 foot length of mono. The hooks are dressed with yarn, feathers, colored fish skin, etc. This rig is used to catch bait such as mackerel. See also Gangion.

**Slammer**  A metal-lid covered bait tank usually reserved for holding live mackerel.

**Slime Stick**  Slang for barracuda because of their thick coating of skin slime

**Snubber**  A piece of elastic surgical tubing with a swivel at both ends which is rigged in line and is supposed to reduce strike breakoffs on light-line trolling rigs.

**Smolt**  A young, immature salmon.

**Slough**  Pronounced "Slew". Extensive shallow waterways that interlace the Sacramento Delta area.

**Sonar**  Normally refers to a fish finding device that uses sonar.

**Spiny Dogfish**  Same as stickleback shark. A common bottom shark in near shore areas and bays.

**Spooled**  A sad condition where a powerful fish has pulled off all the line on your reel and is still heading for the horizon.

**Staghorn Sculpin**  A saltwater sculpin commonly used for bait in the San Francisco Bay area. Also commonly called Bullhead.

**Standing End**  Longer line end of knot, etc. that leads to reel. Opposite of tag end.

**Stickleback Shark**  Common name used in the San Francisco Bay area for Spiny Dogfish.

**Strike Indicator**  Typically a brightly colored piece of yarn tied to a fly fishing leader at approximately twice the water depth up from the fly. The indicator is a visual aid in detecting trout hits. Commercial strike indicators take different forms.

**Swimmer**  A Marlin lure that has a back-and-forth swimming action.

### T

**Tag End**  Short end of knot, opposite of standing end which leads to the reel.

**Teaser**  A device used to excite a fish to strike. In Marlin fishing a large teaser (Bird) that puts up a lot of surface spray is used to lure the fish to the boat. See also Hoochie.

**Troll**  See Lake Troll

**Tules** Cattails

**Tyee** Slang name used to designate a big King Salmon.

## V

**Vermillion Sea** Pseudonym for Sea of Cortez, Gulf of California.

## W

**Worm King** A soft plastic and lead jig lure with a single tail that closely resembles the Shakin Shad.

## Y

**Yo-Yoing** A fishing technique used with metal jigs where the jig is given up-and-down movement by repeatedly sweeping the rod up and then letting it drop.

**Yozuri** A brand of baitfishing shrimpfly rig.

## Z

**Zucchini** A popular trolling jig skirt color combination consisting of orange & lime green.

**INDEX**

9 Mile Bank, 144, 306
14 Mile Bank, 144
23 Fathom Bank, 340
33 Fathom Bank, 340
43 Fathom Spot, 134, 135, 144, 154, 157
60 Mile Bank, 134, 135, 157
150 Kelp - see Oil Rigs
182 Spot, 144
209 Spot, 144
277 Spot, 144
279 Spot, 144

**A**

Ah-Di-Na Campground, 295
Alameda Launch, 385
Alameda Rockwall, 86, 233, 258
Alamitos Bay, 69
Albacore, 3, 4, **12-14**, 306, 308, 358, 359, 403, 404
Albacore Feathers - see Albacore Jigs
Albacore Jigs, 12, 13,
Alijos Rocks, 314, 340
Almanor Lake, 24, 279, map-297, 294
Amador Lake, 2, 3, 24, 101, 304
Amberjack, 364
American River, 174, 205, 207
Anacapa Island, 235
Anaheim Bay, 69
Anaheim Lake, 305
Anderson, 176
Asuncion Bay, 346
Asuncion Is., 335
Avalon Bank, 144
Avila Beach, 389

**B**

BKR see Big Kelp Reef,
Back Bouncing, 188
Backtrolling, 118, 170, 189, 249, 251
Bahia de Los Angeles - see Bay of L.A.
Baja Long Range Trips, 1, 314, **332-365**
    Baja Overview Map, 334
    3-5 Day Trips, 335
    7-10 Day Trips, 340
    13-16 & 23 Day Trips, 346
    Leader Setups, 351
    Monofilament Connections, 352
    Big Fish techniques, 353
Baja Long Range Trips continued,
    General Fishing Techniques & Procedures, 357
    Map to San Diego Long Range Landings, 360
    Detailed Rod & Reel Requirements, 361
Baja, Sea of Cortez, 1, 314, **365-380**
    Basic Requirements, 367-372
    Travel Planning Map, 373
    Access Map, 374
    Major Game Fish, 376-380
Bakersfield, 61, 292
Balls Ferry, 176
Barn Kelp, 66, map-68
Barracuda, **15-19**,
Basics, 6-9
Bass, Calico (Kelp), 4, **20-23**
Bass, Kentucky - see Bass, Spotted
Bass Lake, 193
Bass, Largemouth, **24-65**
    Buzz baits, 31, 35, 37, 44
    Calendar, 2, 4
    Carolina Rig, 42
    Chuggars, 52
    Crankbaits, 31, 33, 35, 37, 46-47
    Darter Heads, 50
    Deep Water Techniques, 56-57
    Do-Nothin, 42
    Doodle, Shake, Drag, 30, 35, 38, 41, 42
    Fall, 36-37
    Flipping, 54-55
    Jerking, 29, 37, 46-47
    Jig-N-Pigs, 48-49, 56
    Jigs, 30, 31, 48-49, 56
    Lake Maps, 54-64
    P-Heads, 50
    Plastic Worms, Grubs, 30, 31, 33, 34, 35, 37, 40-43
    Poppers, 52
    Post Spawn, 32-33
    Pre-spawn, 29-30
    Shallow Water Techniques, 40-55
    Spawn, 30-32
    Spinnerbaits, 30, 31, 35, 37, 44-45
    Splitshot Rig, 42
    Spoons, 30, 35, 36, 57
    Structure, 24-25

# INDEX

Bass, Largemouth continued,
  Summer, 33-36
  Surface Plugs, 52
  Texas Rig, 42
  Thermocline, 33
  Tube Baits, 50
  Twitching, 31,46
  Winter, 38
  Zara Spook, 51
Bass, Sand, 4, **66-68**
Bass, Smallmouth, 24,25,28
Bass, Spotted, 24,25,28
Bass, Spotted Bay, 69-70
Bass, Striped, 2,3,4,**71-95**
  Balanced Bar technique, 78
  Calendar, 73
  Colorado River, 90-92
  Cycle, 74
  Lake Maps, 81-82
  Rigs, 93
  Sacramento River, 83,87, map-89,
  San Francisco, 83-86,map-86
Bass, White, 4,**96-98**
Bay of L.A., 314,373,374
Bay / Harbor Fishing:
  General Information, 321-322
  Long Beach Harbor, 325-326
  Mission Bay, 329,330
  Newport Bay, 327-328
  San Francisco Bay, 323-324
  San Diego Bay, 329,331
Benedicto Is - see San Benedicto
Benites Is., 314,335,340
Berkeley Marina, 384
Berryessa Lake, 2,24,map-59,115, 293
Big Fish, 9,29
Big Kelp Reef (BKR), 200,201
Big River, 237
Bishop, 151,265,268,270,271,291, 292,301
Black Butte Lake, 115
Black Sea Bass, 365
Blythe, 104
Bodega Bay, 4,128,132,172,383
Bonito, 99-100
Breakwater Fishing, 21
Bridgeport, 265,300,302
Bridgeport Reservoir, 265,300
Brookings Harbor, 381,392
Buckeye Creek, 262
Bullard's Bar Reservoir, 193, 195,map-198
Bullet Jigs - see Finger Jigs

Burney Basin, 291,map-296
Butt Creek, 297
Butt Valley Reservoir, 3,297

## C

Cabo San Lucas, 346,369,373,374, 376,378
Cachuma, map-60,101
Calendar - See Fishing Calendar
California City, 177,178,254
Camanche Lake, 304
Carquinez Straits, 259
Casitas Lake, 24,map-60,101
Castaic Lake, 61
Catalina Island, 4,5,15,20,121, 134,135,143,157,200,201,235, 312,314,317
Catfish:
  Channel & Blue & White, 2,3, 4,**101-103**
  Flathead, 104-105
Cedros Is., 335,340,346
Channel Islands, 121
Channel Islands Harbor, 390
Chester, 297
Chico, 209,294
Chula Vista, 63
Chumming, 8,13,15,21,66,110, 201,213,218,219,230,307,317, 358,377
Clarion Is., 346,353
Clear Lake, 2,3,24,map-58,101, 115
Clemente Island - see San Clemente Is.
Clipperton Is., 334,353
Coho Salmon - see Salmon, Silver
Collinsville, 259
Colonet Bay, 335
Color-C-Collector, 27
Colorado River, 1,72,101,104
Colusa, 89,74,209
Convict Lake, 262,301
Cordell Banks, 2,3,128,map-132
Corona Lake, 101,305
Coronados Islands, 4,15,17-18, 126,200,312,314
Cortes Bank, 4,5,134,135,157, 200,312,317
Cortez - see Sea of Cortez
Corvina, 4,**106-114**
Cottonwood, 176
Cottonwood Creek, 269
Cottonwood Lakes, 269,map-270
Cowcod, 155-158

# INDEX

Coyote Point, 258,386
Crappie, 115-120
Crappie Jig lure, 96,117,151,263
Crescent City, 172,381
Croaker, 113
Crockett, 259
Crowley Lake, 151,262,264,265 map-393,301,map-303

### D

Dana Point, 20,143,314,392
Davis Dam, 76
Davis Lake, 262,map-298
Decker Is., 88
Deep Hole, 20,200,201
Del Mar Kelp, 235
Del Valle Reservoir, 293
Descanso Bay, 128
Dolphin - see Dorado
Don Pedro Lake, 304
Donner Lake, 193,273,277
Dorado, 363,364,376
Double Rig - see Oil Rigs
Downrigger, 143,183,**184**,194, 267,273,274,286,307
Dumbarton Bridge, 258
Dunsmuir, 294,295

### E

East Cape, 369,373,374,377,378
East Walker River - see Walker River
Eastern Sierra - see Sierra, Eastern
Eel River, 169,map-237
El Cajon, 62
El Capitan Reservoir, 24,map-62, 115
El Rosario, 335
Emeryville Marina, 384
Ensenada, 121
Escondido, 64
Eureka, 172,381,382

### F

FAD, 306
Fall River, 2,map-296
Fallen Leaf Lake, 273,277
Fanny Shoals, 132
Farallon Is., 2,3,128,map-132
Farnsworth Bank, 121,144

Feather River, 101,173,174, 175-176,205,207,209,210, 237,294,297,298
Finger Jigs, 117,151,263,281, 284,291
Fish Finders, 6,27,139
Fisherman's Landing, 360
Fishing Calendars,
    General, 2-5
    Salmon, 164-166
    Steelhead, 241
    Striped Bass, 73
Flats (The Flats), 66, map-68
Fly Fishing, 7
Folsom Lake, 2,3,101
Franks Tract, 88
Freeport, 209,210
Frenchman Lake, 262
Fresno, 1,24,304

### G

Garcia River, 237
Glossary, 401-407
Gold Lakes, 298
Golden Trout Wilderness, 269, map-271
Gonzaga Bay, 374
Goodrich Creek, 297
Gordo Banks, 373,376
Grant Lake, 265,301
Green Lake, 300
Grizzly Bay, 259
Grouper, 365
Guadalupe Is., 312,335
Gualala River, 237
Guerro Negro, 335
Gull Lake, 301

### H

H&M Landing, 360
Half Moon Bay, 86,178,387
Halibut, 2,3,4,**121-127**
Hamilton Branch, 297
Harrison Reef, 134,135,157
Hat Creek, 2,map-296
Havasu Lake, 4,73,90,map-92
Henshaw Lake, 4,map-64,115
Hipolito Bay, 340
Hodges Lake, 24,36,map-64,115
Hook Size Chart, 399
Hooks, 8

# INDEX

Hopkins Lure, 30,56,57,75,77,90, 99,108,109,201,274,342,348, 371,379
Horseshoe Kelp, 4,15,17-18,200, 201,235,314
Horsesmelt - see Jacksmelt
Hot Creek, 301
Humbolt Bay, 215,232,381,382
Hunters Point, 258
Huntington Beach, 17,68
Huntington Flats, 66,map-68,200
Huntington Harbor, 69,143,391
Huntington Lake, 304
Hurricane Bank, 346

## I

Information Sources, 397-398
Intake II, 301
Iron Gate Dam, 242
Irvine Lake, 101,115,map-103,305
Isabella Lake, 24,map-61,115

## J

Jigging, 38,274,317,see also Yo-Yo
Jigs, 12, 15-16
John Muir Wilderness, 269
June Lake Loop, 265,301,302

## K

Kastmaster Lure, 30,36,56,57,75, 96,170,188,263,269,274,281, 284,371,277
Key, 10
Kings Harbor, 99,391
Kirman Lake, 261,300
Klamath River, 170,map-171,205 236,map-237,239,243,247,251 255
Knights Landing, 89
Kokanee - see Salmon
Krocodile Lure, 15,21,83,99,184, 188,274,307,342,348,371,379

## L

La Jolla Kelp, 17-18,200,314, 315
La Paz, 369,373,374,377
Las Arenas, 369
Launch Ramps - see Salt Water Launches

Lee Palm's Sportfishing, 360
Line, 7-8
Lingcod, 2,3,4,5,**128-136**
Loch Lomond Marina, 383
Lone Pine, 270
Long Beach, 17
Long Beach Harbor, 20,325-326
Long Range Baja Trips - see Baja, Long Range Trips
Loran, 6,138
Loreto, 314,369,373,374
Los Angeles, 1,4,61,79,81,121, 292
Los Molinos, 173,176,211
Lundy Creek, 261
Lundy Lake, 300

## M

Mad River, 237
Mahi Mahi - see Dorado
Malibu, 20
Mammoth Lakes, 261,302
Marina del Rey, 17,391
Marlin, Blue & Black, 376
Marlin, Striped, 4,5,**137-150** Baja-376
Martis Lake, map-299
Marysville, 209,210,294
Mattole River, 237
McCloud River, 2,294,map-295
McClure Lake, 304
McNears Point, 86
Mead Lake, 4,90
Micro Jigs, 117,151
Millerton Lake, 24,304
Miramar Lake, 62
Mission Bay, 329,map-330
Mission Rock Ramp, 386
Modesto, 1,304
Mohave Lake, 4,90
Montara Beach, 86,178
Monterey, 12,180,388
Monterey Bay, 2,3,4,121,160, map-168,179,map-180,215
Mooching, 186
Moon Phases, 6
Morena Lake, 24,map-63
Morro Bay, 4,12,128,map-133,389
Moss Landing, 180,388
Moth Ball Fleet, 259
Muir Beach, 178
Mulege, 369,373,374,376

# INDEX

## N

Nacimiento Lake, 4,96,map-97
Naples Reef, 20
Natividad Is., 335
Navarro River, 237
Nelson Creek, 298
New Hogan Lake, 304
New Melones Lake, 304
Newport Bay, 327-328
Newport Beach, 17,68,143
Nightcrawler worms, 26,110
Nimbus Basin, 210
North Lake, 301
Northeast Area, 1
Northwest Coast, 1,169
Northwest Rivers, 1,169
Noyo River, 237

## O

O'Neill Forebay, 72
Oakland, 385
Oceanside, 68,392
Oil Rigs, 15,134,135,157,314
Oroville Lake, 294
Osborne Bank, 134,135,144,157
Otay Reservoir, 24,map-63,101
Owens River, 262,265,301
Oxnard, 179,map-181
Oyster Point, 258,386

## P

Pacifica, 178
Pardee Lake, 193,304
Pargo, 364,380
Parker, 92
Parker Creek, 261
Partyboats - see Sportfishing Landings
Perch, Sacramento-see Sacramento Perch
Perris Lake, 24,101,map-103
PH-meter, 27
Pillar Point, 86,178,387
Pine Flat, 24
Piru Lake, 73,79,map-81
Pit River, 2,map-296,294
Pitching, 54
Pittsburg, 259
Pleasant Valley Reservoir, 262, 264,map-265,301
Plunking, 188
Point Buchon, 133

Point Conception, 168,201
Point Delgada, 200
Point Dume, 125,314
Point Estero, 133
Point Loma Kelp, 15,17-18
Point Loma Sportfishing, 360
Point Sal, 133
Point Vicente, 314
Port Hueneme, 179
Port San Luis, 389
Potatoe Banks, 154,157
Princeton, 74,89
Puertocitos, 374
Pumphouse, 86
Punta Chivato, 374
Punta Escondido, 374
Pyramid Lake (Calif), 72,73, 80,81
Pyramid Lake (Nev), 267

## R

Ramona, 62,64
Rapala Lure, 9,21,29,31,32,33, 35,37,46,52,75,121,216,263, 274,284,306,307,317,371,376, 378,379,380
Rebel Lure, 46,52,75,77,83, 85,87,263,274,371,376,378
Red Bluff, 176,209,211,294
Red Bluff Diversion Dam, 176
Redding, 173,176,292,294
Redondo Beach, 17,99,125,391
Reel Selection Guide, 400
Reno, 1,268,291,292
Revillagigedo Is., 353
Richmond Marina, 384
Rincon Point, 200
Rincon Reef, 134,135,157
Rippin, 52
Rio Vista, 88,259
Riverside, 103
Robinson Creek, 262,300
Roca Partida Is., 346,353
Rockcod, 2,3,4,5,**154-159**
Rockfish, 160-161
Rocky Point, 200,201,314
Rod Selection Guide, 400
Roosterfish, 377
Roostertail lure, 96,169,243, 263,281,284
Rush Creek, 262,301
Russian River, 169,205,map-237

# INDEX

## S

Sabrina Lake, 74,261,301
Sacramento City, 210
Sacramento Delta, 2,3,73, 74,87,map-88,101,254,map-259
Sacramento Perch, 151-153
Sacramento River, 1,2,3,73, 74,77,87,map-89,173,174, 175-176,205,206,207,map-209, 211,map-237,291,map-295
Saddlebag Lake, 261
Salmon:
   King (Chinook), 2,3, **162-192**
     Klamath River Mouth, 170
     Monterey Bay, 179
     North Coast Ocean, 172
     North Coast Rivers, 169
     Sacramento & Feather River, 173
     San Francisco Coast & Bay, 177
     Techniques
       Diagram, 182
       Ocean, 183
       River, 188
     Ventura, Oxnard area, 179
   Kokanee, 3,**193-199**
   Silver (Coho), 162
Salmon Grouper - see Bocaccio
Salmon River, 237
Salt Water Launches, 381-392
Salton Sea, 4,106-114
San Andreas Shoal, 88
San Antonio Reservoir, 3,4,73, 80,82,97
San Benedicto Is., 346,353
San Bernardino, 79,81
San Clemente Is., 5,12,20,134, 135,157,200,235,312,317
San Diego, 1,4,12,62-64,68,121, 143,306,312,332
San Diego Bay, 20,215,329, map-331
San Felipe, 373,374
San Francisco: 293
   Bay, 1,2,3,73,74,84-85, map-86,121,map-124,175,177, 215,232,233,254-256,map-257 258,shore/pier fishing - 323-324
   Ocean, 1,3,12,73,74,76,83-84 map-86,121,132,177,map-178
San Joaquin River, 88

San Joaquin Valley Lakes, 304
San Jose del Cabo, 369,373,374, 376,378
San Leandro Launch, 385
San Luis Obispo, 12,133
San Luis Reservoir, 2,72,73,80, 82
San Martin Is., 335
San Miguel Is., 128
San Nicolas Is., 158
San Pablo Bay (Calif), map-86, 254,255,256,map-257,see also San Francisco Bay
San Pablo Bay (Baja), 335,340
San Pablo Reservoir, 393
San Quintin, 335
San Quintin Flats, 86
San Simeon, 128,133
San Vicente Reservoir, 24,62,101
Santa Ana River Lakes, 101, map-103,305
Santa Barbara, 1,60,390
Santa Barbara Is., 134,135, 157,200,314
Santa Catalina Is. - see Catalina Is.
Santa Clara Shoal, 88
Santa Cruz, 121,160,map-161,388
Santa Cruz Is., 200
Santa Monica Bay, 15,121,map-125
Santee Lakes, 62
Sargo, 108,110,113
Sausalito, 383
Scampi lure, 20,21,22,66,128, 160,307,321,325,327,337, 371,379
Scott River, 242
Scrounger lure, 15,21,22,36,66, 160,263,281,284,321,326,329, 371
Sea of Cortez - see Baja, Sea of Cortez
Seabass - see White Seabass
Shad, 2,**205-212**
Shark:
   Blue, 213-234
   Leopard, 232
   Mako, 4,213-234
   Sand - see Smoothhound
   Sevengill, 2,215,**232**
   Smoothhound, 215
   Soupfin, 3,**232**
   Stickle Back, 215
   Thresher, 229
Shasta Lake, 24,294

# INDEX

Shaver Lake, 193,304
Sheephead, 235
Shrimpflies, 129,154
Sierra, Eastern, 2,3,262,301,302
Silver Lake, 262,265,301
Silverwood Reservoir, 4,72,73,
 79,115
Slide-see The Slide
Smith River, 169,236-237,251
Soap Banks, 2, 128
Socorro Is., 346,353
South Bay, map-86,map-233,254,
 255,256,map-258,see also San
 Francisco Bay
South Lake, 301
Southeast Bank, 134,135,157
Spiny Dogfish - see Shark,
 Stickle Back
Sportfishing Landings, 393-396
Stampede Reservoir, 193,262
Steelhead, 2,3,**236-253**,
 map-237
Stinson Beach, 178
Stockton, 1,74,304
Striper - see Bass, Striper
Stroking, 52
Sturgeon, 2,3,**254-260**,
 map-257
Suisan Bay, 259
Sutherland Reservoir, 24,map-64

## T

Tahoe Lake, 1,2,3,193,194,195,
 map-197,262,268,273-277,291,
 292
Tanner Bank, 4,5,134,135,154,
 157,312,317
Temecula, 64
Temperature Guage, 27,139
The Cape - see Cabo San Lucas
The Slide, 144
Thermocline, 27,33,143,193,194,
 285,307
Thetis Bank, 340
Thornton Beach, 86,178
Tides, 6
Tijuana, 126
Tilapia, 107,110,113
Tomales Bay, 215,383
Topanga Bubbles, 125,200
Topaz Lake, 267
Trinidad, 172,381
Trinity Lake, 24
Trinity River, 170,205,236,
 map-237,239

Trout:
 Brook, 261
 Brown, 2,3,**262-266**
 Cutthroat, 267-268
 Golden, 269-272
 Makinaw, 2,**273-278**
 Rainbow: 2,3,**279-305**
Truckee River, 291,map-299
Tullock Lake, 304
Tuna: 4
 Bigeye, **306-311**,362
 Blue-Fin, 4,**312-313**
 Yellowfin, 353-356,358,
 362-363,364,378
Turlock Lake, 304
Twin Lakes, Bridgeport 193,
 262,264,map-265,map-300

## U

Uncle Sam Bank, 340
Uvas Lake, 115

## V

Van Duzen River, 237,map-237
Ventura, 1,179,map-181,390
Verona, 89,210
Virginia Lakes, 300

## W

Wahoo, 357,363,378-379
Walker Creek, 261
Walker Lake, 267-268
Walker River, 262,265,300
Water Temperature Guage - see
 Temperature Guage
White Seabass, 200-204
Wohlford Lake, map-64,115
Worm King lure, 21,22,66,69,321,
 327,329,337,371

## Y

Yellow Creek, 297
Yellowfin - see Tuna, Yellowfin
Yellowtail, 4,**314-320**, 358,
 363,364,365
Yo-Yo, 317, see also Jigging
Yuba City, 210
Yuba River, 205,209,210,237
Yuma, 104

ORDER BLANK

For an additional copy of FISHING CALIFORNIA: A travel guide to proven spots & proven methods, send $19.95 + $3.15 for shipping and sales tax = a check for **$23.10** payable to:

Sabertooth Publishing
P.O. Box 2956
Laguna Hills, CA 92654

**Ship to:**

Name: _____

Address: _____
_____

City: _____ State: _____ ZIP: _____

Please pay by Check or Money Order.